Managing Usenet

Managing Usenet

Henry Spencer and David Lawrence

O'REILLY™

Cambridge · Köln · Paris · Sebastopol · Tokyo

Managing Usenet
by Henry Spencer and David Lawrence

Copyright © 1998 O'Reilly & Associates, Inc. All rights reserved.
Printed in the United States of America.

Editor: Paula Ferguson

Production Editor: Clairemarie Fisher O'Leary

Printing History:

       January 1998:   First Edition.

This book is printed on acid-free paper with 85% recycled content, 15% post-consumer waste. O'Reilly & Associates is committed to using paper with the highest recycled content available consistent with high quality.

ISBN: 1-56592-198-4

Table of Contents

Preface .... *ix*

1: Introduction *1*

   1.1 Netnews and Usenet *1*
   1.2 A Brief History *3*
   1.3 How It Works *5*
   1.4 What You Need *10*

2: Getting Ready *11*

   2.1 Getting a Feed *11*
   2.2 How Much News? *12*
   2.3 Propagation Issues *21*
   2.4 Hostnames *22*
   2.5 Local Newsgroups *23*
   2.6 Internal News Networks *23*
   2.7 Filesystem Layout *27*
   2.8 Choosing the Software *31*

3: News Operations *34*

   3.1 Managing the Flow *34*
   3.2 Control Messages *37*
   3.3 Newsgroup Changes *41*
   3.4 Expiry Policy *52*
   3.5 Archives and Backups *54*
   3.6 Unwanted Newsgroups *55*

   3.7   Security Considerations *56*

   3.8   Getting Help *59*

4:   ***Installing C News*** *62*

   4.1   The C News and NNTP Distributions *62*

   4.2   Preparing to Build C News: quiz *64*

   4.3   Building C News *76*

   4.4   Checking C News *78*

   4.5   Installing C News *78*

   4.6   Preparing to Build the NNTP Reference Implementation *80*

   4.7   Building the NNTP Reference Implementation *87*

   4.8   Installing the NNTP Reference Implementation *88*

5:   ***Configuring C News*** *89*

   5.1   C News Control Files *89*

   5.2   NNTP Reference Implementation Control Files *112*

   5.3   Verifying C News Installation *114*

   5.4   Loose Ends *114*

   5.5   Cleaning Up *117*

6:   ***Running C News*** *119*

   6.1   Testing a New Installation *119*

   6.2   Article Flow *127*

   6.3   Common Problems *132*

   6.4   Logs and Trouble Reports *134*

   6.5   Wrapping Up *137*

7:   ***Installing INN*** *138*

   7.1   The INN Distribution *138*

   7.2   Preparing to Build INN *143*

   7.3   Building INN *167*

   7.4   Installing INN *169*

8:   ***Configuring INN*** *177*

   8.1   How to Update Files *177*

   8.2   Control Files *179*

   8.3   Scripts *198*

9: Running INN *213*

    9.1   Starting INN *213*
    9.2   Testing the Installation *219*
    9.3   Normal Operation *230*
    9.4   Ongoing Maintenance *236*
    9.5   Log Files *240*
    9.6   Troubleshooting Common Problems *254*
    9.7   Wrapping Up *257*

10: Choosing and Installing Newsreaders *258*

    10.1 Installing Newsreaders *258*
    10.2 Operational Issues *260*
    10.3 Popular Newsreaders *260*
    10.4 More Information *269*

11: You're a Network Manager Now *272*

    11.1 Network Optimization *272*
    11.2 Managing People *274*
    11.3 Your Site and the Law *276*

12: Leaf Nodes *283*

    12.1 Plenty of Power *284*
    12.2 Maintaining the Active File *288*
    12.3 Dealing with Your Feed *289*
    12.4 Record Keeping *290*

13: Hub Nodes *291*

    13.1 Volume, Volume, Volume *292*
    13.2 Transmitters *299*
    13.3 Additional Automation *304*
    13.4 The Political View *312*

14: Gatewaying *318*

    14.1 Known Worldwide Gateways *318*
    14.2 Posting via Mail *319*
    14.3 Setting Up a Gateway *320*
    14.4 Programming a Gateway *339*

15: Moderating Newsgroups *343*

    15.1   Creating a Moderated Group *344*
    15.2   Getting Postings to the Moderator *345*
    15.3   Preparing Articles for Distribution *348*
    15.4   Putting the Articles in the Group *362*
    15.5   Moderators' Software Tools *362*
    15.6   The Political Side *363*

16: Newsgroups and Their Names *380*

    16.1   A Brief Survey *380*
    16.2   Namespace Theory *384*
    16.3   Changing the Namespace *394*

17: A Brief History of Usenet *406*

    17.1   Origins *406*
    17.2   Growing Pains *410*
    17.3   Namespace History *413*

18: Anatomy of a News Article *424*

    18.1   Basic Layout and Character Codes *425*
    18.2   Headers *427*
    18.3   Body *438*
    18.4   Control Messages *440*
    18.5   MIME *445*

19: Flow and Processing of Traffic *450*

    19.1   News Propagation *450*
    19.2   Article Storage and Indexing *454*
    19.3   Batching for Transmission *461*
    19.4   Transmission by UUCP *462*
    19.5   Transmission by NNTP *465*
    19.6   Last-Resort Transmission Methods *468*

Index *471*

Preface

This book is about administering Netnews servers. Netnews, a.k.a. Usenet, is a distributed bulletin-board system. Actually, the Netnews software can be used to build such systems for your own purposes or to tie into existing ones; Usenet is just the big worldwide system that everyone knows about. Netnews systems make information available to a large community at a low cost; they are much more efficient than mailing lists.

The users of such a system see a single "electronic community" and take little notice of the different computers and the distances between them. This electronic community can be a valuable source of information and assistance, in addition to entertainment and argument. Usenet is the quintessential example: A request for information or help can reach thousands of people, often including some of the world's top experts, and useful information and up-to-the-minute news reports are posted on a regular basis. Usenet is a worldwide network, reaching every continent and nearly every computer-using country. Hundreds of thousands of articles are posted to Usenet every day, and the traffic is doubling every year.

This book tells you how to set up the most common Netnews software, whether for participation in Usenet or for your own more local electronic communities, and how to manage it once it's set up. You probably already have some idea of what Netnews is like from the reader's perspective. If you don't, some hands-on time reading news would be useful. It's hard to imagine the perspective of a new user if you've never been one.

Between the two of us, we draw on a lot of Usenet and Netnews experience. We've tried to be quite specific with the advice we give in this book, in the hope that you might be able to avoid some of the problems we've encountered. Henry Spencer is the co-developer of C News, one of the news servers covered in this book, and has been running news systems since 1981 (when it only took a few minutes a day to read *all* the news). David Lawrence spent more years than he cares to remember as news administrator for UUNET Technologies, the first of the big, central news feed sites and still one of the largest. He's also been the moderator of *news.announce.newgroups* for nearly seven years.

What's in This Book

We've tried to include just about everything that you, as a news administrator, might ever want to know about Netnews and Usenet. This means you might not be very interested in some of the chapters, or, at least, not yet. The path you follow through this book may vary, depending on what kind of news system you are running and whether you've inherited an operational system or are charged with creating one. In the end, we expect you'll read most of the chapters here. But for now, you may want to decide which chapters to read carefully and which ones to skim, based on the following descriptions of who you are and what you are doing:

- *Everyone* should read Chapter 1, *Introduction*, for an introduction to news and Chapter 2, *Getting Ready*, for a look at the basic decisions involved in running a news system.

- *Creating a new news system.* Pay careful attention to the section at the end of Chapter 2 about which software package to use. Skim through Chapter 3, *News Operations*, to get an idea about what's involved with the day-to-day running of a news system. After you have decided whether to use C News or INN, read Chapters 4 through 6 (C News) or Chapters 7 through 9 (INN) for complete information on installing and setting up your server software. Finally, read Chapter 10, *Choosing and Installing Newsreaders*, to learn about setting up newsreader software.

- *Administering an operational news system.* Read Chapter 3 for details on the technical aspects of news administration and Chapter 11, *You're a Network Manager Now*, for coverage of the non-technical issues. The information in these two chapters is mostly independent of exactly what software you're running.

- *Running a small news system that isn't feeding other sites.* If your system fits this description, it is a *leaf node*. Read Chapter 12, *Leaf Nodes*, for notes on how to get news set up so that it will leave you alone most of the time.

- *Running a big news system that feeds many other sites.* If your system is (or hopes to be) a central one that feeds lots of other sites, it is a *hub node*. Read Chapter 13, *Hub Nodes*, for information on how to cope. It's not possible for the news software for a hub node to be completely hands-off, but you can make your life easier by preparing carefully.

- *Gatewaying between newsgroups and mailing lists.* Read Chapter 14, *Gatewaying*, for information on how to do it right. Doing it wrong is easy, but unwise.

- *Running a moderated newsgroup.* If you are in charge of a group where the news postings have to be approved by a moderator, read Chapter 15, *Moderating Newsgroups*, for information on how to be a technically and politically competent moderator.

- *Receiving the worldwide Usenet newsgroups.* If your news system is going to be receiving Usenet newsgroups, read Chapter 16, *Newsgroups and Their Names*, for a quick look at what's available and how Usenet is administered.

- *A history buff.* If you ever want to know more about how Netnews and Usenet came about, Chapter 17, *A Brief History of Usenet*, is for you.

- *A stickler for details.* If you ever need to know all the nitty-gritty details of the format of news articles, Chapter 18, *Anatomy of a News Article*, tells all (well, almost all, with pointers to where to look for the rest). If you need to know the technical details of how news is stored and moved around the network, Chapter 19, *Flow and Processing of Traffic* is a compendium of such specialized information.

Conventions Used in This Book

Italic is used for:

- Pathnames, filenames, and program names
- New terms where they are defined
- Newsgroup names and Internet addresses, such as domain names, URLs, and email addresses
- Comments to the reader in sample command lines

`Constant Width` is used for:

- Parameter names and values that are set in configuration files
- Environment variables
- Command-line options

`Constant Italic` is used for:

- Placeholders that indicate that an item is replaced by some actual value in your own configuration file
- Placeholders in command-line options

Constant Bold is used for:

- Command lines and options that should be typed verbatim on the screen. Note that the **%** character is used to represent the shell prompt in command lines.

Getting the Scripts

In a few places in the book, we provide scripts that may be useful in running your news system. There are also a few such scripts that we mention but do not show. All of our scripts are available at:

```
ftp://ftp.oreilly.com/pub/examples/nutshell/musenet
```

Request for Comments

Please help us to improve future editions of this book by reporting any errors, inaccuracies, bugs, misleading or confusing statements, and plain old typos that you find anywhere in this book. Email your bug reports and comments to us at: *bookquestions@ora.com*.

Please also let us know what we can do to make this book more useful to you. We take your comments seriously and will try to incorporate reasonable suggestions into future editions.

Acknowledgments

Many people have been very patient with us while we were writing this book. Henry thanks Ruth for being understanding about all the nights he stayed up late to finish a chapter, and the cats (especially Jodi and Toby) for keeping him company when Ruth gave up and went to bed without him. Dave thanks his wife, Diane, for her quiet understanding all of those times that he too had to work late into the night.

We both want to thank O'Reilly & Associates for not feeding us to the dogs when we went a very long time past the deadlines in our contract. Our editors, first Mike Loukides and then Paula Ferguson, must have taken a lot of flak over this. We're deeply grateful to them, for persistently maintaining that it would be worth the wait, and to the rest of O'Reilly, for believing them.

We thank James Brister, Dan Brockman, Geoff Collyer, Bruce Jones, Tom Limoncelli, and Rich Salz for their contributions as technical reviewers. They spotted quite a few things that needed fixing and provided a lot of useful advice. Henry also thanks Ruth for going over his chapters with a fine-tooth comb.

Chris Lewis provided information on software for combating egregiously multiply-posted articles. Tim Pierce and Ron Newman took some time to provide some information on the Good Netkeeping Seal of Approval for newsreader programs.

Steve Bellovin, Stephen Daniel, Jim Ellis, and Tom Truscott got us, and the world, into all this in the first place.* We're grateful, we think.

When Jerry Peek was an internal author for O'Reilly, he worked on the INN chapters and provided some valuable feedback on their contents.

At O'Reilly & Associates, we thank Clairemarie Fisher O'Leary for copyediting and managing the project, Claire Cloutier LeBlanc and Sheryl Avruch for providing quality assurance, Elissa Haney for providing production assistance, and Bruce Tracy for writing and Seth Maislin for implementing the index.

---

* See Chapter 17 for the awful details.

In this chapter:
- *Netnews and Usenet*
- *A Brief History*
- *How It Works*
- *What You Need*

1

Introduction

This chapter provides a quick introduction to Netnews and Usenet for people who don't know what it's all about. If you've administered a news system in the past, nothing in this chapter is likely to be new to you, although you might want to read it in case you haven't seen all the terminology. If you're coming into news administration completely fresh, this chapter covers the basics you need to understand before starting to install news software. Considerably more detail on many of the topics covered here can be found in Chapters 16 through 19.

In this chapter, we'll discuss what Netnews and Usenet are and how they came to be. The chapter also provides a brief sketch of how Netnews works, mostly to introduce the terms and concepts. And finally, we'll touch briefly on what you need to get a Netnews system started.

1.1 *Netnews and Usenet*

Netnews (often shortened to just "news") and Usenet are often used as synonyms, although technically that isn't quite right.

Netnews is a set of standards and a vast array of available software that are used to build distributed bulletin-board systems. An *article*—which can be anything from a short note to a huge program—that is *posted* on one of the computers participating in such a system quickly becomes available for reading on all the other systems. The participating computer systems, or *hosts*, do not have to trust each other (much), there is no need for central administration, and the connections between the hosts do not need to be continuously available or particularly reliable. The users see a single "electronic community" and take little notice of the different hosts and the distances between them.

Usenet was the first Netnews-based electronic community, and is still probably the largest. Usenet is composed of *newsgroups* (sometimes abbreviated to just "groups") that are arranged in various *hierarchies*, as you'll see later. Usenet is a "logical network," a set of cooperating hosts that exchange news articles using a wide variety of communications networks. (The oldest of these communications networks uses UUCP and was referred to as UUCPnet; this is sometimes confused with Usenet.) Usenet is a worldwide network, reaching every continent and nearly every computer-using country. More than 850,000 articles are posted to Usenet every day—a traffic volume of well over 8 gigabytes* per day—although it is common for small hosts to receive only a carefully chosen subset of the total traffic.

So, what is all this good for? Netnews systems make information available to a large community at low cost: unlike messages on a mailing list, only one copy of each news article is sent to and stored on each host. The electronic community that develops using Netnews can be a valuable source of information and assistance, in addition to entertainment and argument. Usenet is the ultimate example: a request for information or help can reach thousands of people, often including some of the world's foremost experts, and useful information and up-to-date news reports are posted on a regular basis.

1.1.1 Usenet Software

This book tells you how to set up the two most common Netnews software packages for Unix systems: C News and INN. We'll also tell you how to manage the software once you have it set up, whether for participation in Usenet or for your own more local electronic communities. The book describes how the Netnews software works, what sorts of problems you can expect, and how to cope with them. Usenet is our main example, but the same principles apply to other electronic communities as well. If your system doesn't run some flavor of Unix, a lot of the general discussion is still applicable, but you'll have to find Netnews software for your particular system.

In addition to C News and INN, which are free software packages, there are a number of commercial news servers available for a variety of platforms. Here is a list of some of the other servers, both commercial and freeware, that we know about, with URLs where you can get more information:

Cyclone
   http://www.highwind.com/

---

* This estimate is based on news traffic in October 1997.

D News

>   *http://www.netwinsite.com/*

Diablo

>   *http://www.backplane.com/diablo/*

Microsoft Exchange Server

>   *http://www.microsoft.com/exchange/*

Netscape Collabra Server

>   *http://home.netscape.com/comprod/server_central/*

1.2 A Brief History

It will help you to know a little bit about the history of Netnews and Usenet. For a longer treatment of Usenet history, you can read Chapter 17, *A Brief History of Usenet*. Right now we're just going to tell you enough to get you started. This discussion also introduces a number of terms you'll see throughout the book.

Electronic communities resembling those of Usenet existed before Netnews, in the form of mailing lists on the ARPAnet. Messages were mailed electronically to a central distribution mailbox, and software would then mail a copy of each message to each person on the list. However, relatively few people had access to the ARPAnet, and more importantly, the mailing-list technology became quite cumbersome when the number of participants in a mailing list got large.

Usenet and Netnews started at Duke University and the University of North Carolina, in 1979. The Netnews software developed there,* now known as A News, is what got Usenet started. The network's early growth was centered at Duke. The original authors and organizers were inspired by the example of the ARPAnet mailing lists, but they had no clear idea of how their network would develop: they thought that typical traffic would be a few articles a day!

They did, however, have the wisdom to see what was already becoming apparent on the ARPAnet: mailing lists are a poor way to broadcast to a large community. When the number of participants becomes large, it's much better to put messages in a public area where they can be read by everyone, rather than sending each participant a separate copy. Practical issues may require each system to have its own copy of the public area, but this area can be kept up-to-date by having each system pass new material along to its neighbors. (This may all sound obvious now, but in 1979 it was new and radical.) The A News software implemented a system that adhered to this decentralized design, and the rest is history.

---

* Written primarily by Stephen Daniel, with contributions from Steve Bellovin, Jim Ellis, and Tom Truscott.

Usenet traffic grew rapidly and it quickly became clear that A News wasn't up to handling it. In the early 1980s, Matt Glickman and Mark Horton largely rewrote the software to produce B News, which altered the format of articles and changed a number of other details. After some initial floundering, the software and the standards stabilized. B News is now completely obsolete, but the standards and practices it set up are still in use, and all modern news software is compatible with it in key areas.

Around this time, different implementations of Netnews software started to appear, and thus it became desirable to have a written definition of the article format and related items. Mark Horton did this in 1983 as an Internet Request For Comments (RFC) document: RFC 850. Later, small revisions by Rick Adams produced RFC 1036, which is getting rather dated but is still the current Netnews standard. Henry Spencer started work on a major revision, which got as far as a preliminary draft and then stalled; efforts are now underway to get this going again.*

Usenet traffic was originally carried mostly over UUCP, but interest in carrying it over the Internet (the successor to the ARPAnet) soon developed. In early 1986, Brian Kantor, Phil Lapsley, and Erik Fair developed and documented a news transmission protocol for the Internet, called Network News Transfer Protocol (NNTP). Although there are now several implementations of NNTP, the original implementation was often known as just NNTP, which can cause confusion. It is better to refer to the original implementation as the NNTP Reference Implementation; it is nearly obsolete now, although the NNTP protocol is not.

Usenet traffic continued to grow steadily, and the Netnews technology began to be used for other purposes as well. The growth in traffic eventually started to expose serious performance problems in B News, and a complete reimplementation, called C News, was done by Geoff Collyer and Henry Spencer at the University of Toronto. Work on C News started in 1985; the full release appeared in 1989. Over time, C News has been expanded and improved; it is one of the two major Netnews implementations now in use on Unix systems.

The other modern Unix implementation, INN, appeared in mid-1992. Although C News was a complete rewrite of B News, it followed the structure of B News fairly closely. Rich Salz made a clean break by implementing INN from scratch. His approach was designed for hosts with abundant resources and multiple continuously live connections to other hosts.

Both C News and INN are referred to as transport subsystems or news transports, although "transport" is also (confusingly) applied to the networks used to ship articles from host to host. It's more accurate to call C News or INN a *relayer*: the

---

* The draft can be found as */pub/news.txt.Z* or */pub/news.ps.Z* at *ftp.zoo.toronto.edu*. Information about the revived effort can be found at *http://www.landfield.com/usefor/*.

software is responsible for receiving news articles, storing the articles on its own system, and relaying the articles to other hosts.

B News established a de facto standard for how news articles are stored and indexed. This standard made it possible to write *newsreader* software to display the articles for human reading in a way that was independent of the relayer being used.* Somewhat later, NNTP provided another standard way for newsreaders to fetch articles. (Yes, NNTP lives a double life: as a relayer-to-relayer transport protocol and as a newsreader-access protocol.) There are now a wide variety of newsreaders available for many different systems. Some newsreaders look at the articles directly, most now use NNTP, and a few can go either way.

1.3 How It Works

There are two perspectives from which you can view what's going on in a Netnews system. From the user's perspective, a Netnews system is all about news articles: reading them, composing them, and replying to them. From the system's perspective, it's a fair bit more complicated, which is why you need this book. We'll examine things from the user's perspective first, in order to introduce some of the terminology you'll see throughout the book. Then we'll take a look behind the scenes at how the relayer software works and get you started down the path to administering your own Netnews system.

1.3.1 A User's View

As a Netnews user, you read, compose, and reply to news articles. Sometimes you compose an article from scratch; other times you compose it as a *followup* to another article. After being composed, a news article is *posted* to one or more newsgroups. Each newsgroup is a separate bulletin board, although you can *cross-post* an article so that it appears in more than one newsgroup. Newsgroups have multi-part names that indicate what they are about: for example, the newsgroup *comp.lang.pascal* is about the computer programming language Pascal.

Newsgroups are organized in hierarchies, based on common parts of their names. For example, *comp.lang.pascal* and *comp.lang.ada* are both within the *comp* hierarchy. They are also both within *comp.lang*, but the top-level hierarchy, such as *comp*, is usually the most important hierarchy that a newsgroup belongs to.

Historically speaking, after some early changes were made, Usenet consisted of seven hierarchies: *comp*, *sci*, *news*, *misc*, *rec*, *soc*, and *talk*. A number of other

---

* Note that some documents refer to newsreaders simply as "readers." In this book, we use "readers" to mean humans reading news. Elsewhere, you may see the same distinction made in a different way, with the humans again called readers, but the software packages called "reading agents."

hierarchies, such as *alt* and *bionet*, appeared later. Although these later additions didn't start out as part of Usenet, they're typically considered to be part of Usenet now, so we'll speak of them that way.* (For a more detailed discussion of all of this, see Chapter 16, *Newsgroups and Their Names*.) It's also common to have localized hierarchies that exist only within a geographic region or an organization, such as a company or university.

When you compose an article, you can also specify a *distribution*, which is intended to restrict its spread. For example, a notice of a Pascal users' group meeting in San Francisco might be posted to *comp.lang.pascal* with a distribution of *sf*, indicating that it should not be relayed outside the city. Unfortunately, distributions are poorly understood and often sloppily administered: a significant number of articles specify nonsensical distributions, and as a result, many relayers are configured to simply ignore distributions.

A news article is an ASCII text file that bears a close resemblance to an Internet electronic mail message. It contains some *headers*, an empty line that terminates the headers, and a *body*. Headers must follow a precisely specified format; the body is essentially any ASCII text. Figure 1–1 shows a sample article.

As you can see, each header begins with a name that indicates what it contains. Some of the headers, such as From, Subject, and Date, may be familiar to you from email. Others, like Path, Newsgroups, and Expires, are unique to Netnews. The order of the headers does not matter, but the contents of most of the headers have to follow strict rules. For example, there is only one correct way to write the contents of the Date header. Chapter 18, *Anatomy of a News Article*, discusses the rules in more detail; the RFCs should be consulted for the fussy fine points.

Many different headers may appear, but a news article must have one (and only one) of each of the following headers: From, Subject, Date, Message-ID, Path, and Newsgroups. Three of these headers are of special note for news: the Message-ID header gives every article its own unique identifier, different from that of any other article; the Newsgroups header specifies which newsgroups the article has been posted to; the Path header is a record of the hosts the article has passed through.

Fortunately, when you post an article, you normally do so via software that acts as a *posting agent*. Most newsreaders, in fact, function as posting agents. The posting agent makes life a lot simpler for you by supplying some of the headers, such as Message-ID, and fixing up others, like ensuring that the contents of the Date header are in a standard form. If there's something wrong with the article, the posting agent may reject it or suggest revisions. Once the posting agent approves

---

* When we need to refer to the "original" seven hierarchies, we'll be explicit about that.

```
From: eggman@kiwi.ora.com (R.I. Red)
Path: uunet!impala!kiwi.ora.com!eggman
Newsgroups: news.announce
Subject: Usenet Etiquette -- Please Read
Message-ID: <642@kiwi.ora.com>
Date: Fri, 22 Nov 1996 11:14:55 -0500 (EST)
Followup-To: news.misc
Expires: Sat, 4 Jan 1997 00:00:00 -0500 (EST)
Organization: O'Reilly & Associates, Sebastopol, CA

Politeness is a virtue even in person, but it is essential
on Usenet. When you are addressing many thousands of people,
which might include your friends, your current or future
employer, or even your mother, a little bit of courtesy goes a
long way.  This general principle has certain practical
implications which may not be obvious to newcomers.

. . .
```

Figure 1-1: A sample news article

of your article, it is sent to your host's relayer, much as if it had arrived from another host.

It's possible for a newsgroup to be *moderated*. A *moderator*—usually one or more people, but sometimes automated software—decides what can and cannot be posted to a moderated newsgroup. This normally provides higher-quality content, at the price of delays in posting and the possibility that a posting may be rejected inappropriately by the moderator. If you try to post an article to a moderated newsgroup, the posting agent mails the article to the moderator for consideration, rather than sending it to your host's relayer.

1.3.2 The Relayer Software

When the relayer software receives a posted article, it performs two tasks: it files the article in a *news database* that gives newsreaders access to the article, and it passes the article on to other hosts. The relayer's exact actions are usually governed by control files that indicate which newsgroups and distributions are passed on to which other hosts. (It is possible, and indeed fairly common, for a host to get only selected newsgroups instead of all of Usenet.) An article is only passed to another host if the article is being posted to a newsgroup that is to be sent to that host, if the article has a distribution that is to be sent to that host, and if the host's name does not appear in the article's Path header. (The Path rule prevents an article from traveling around in circles, and in particular, from being passed back to the host from which it arrived.)

In principle, the news database could be organized in any way that the relayer pleases. In practice, however, there is a standard organization that many newsreaders expect to find. The articles themselves are organized as files in an *article tree*, with each part of a newsgroup's name corresponding to a directory. For example, articles in *comp.lang.pascal* are filed in the directory *comp/lang/pascal*. The exact location of the article tree in the filesystem is a configurable option. Although */usr/spool/news* was the traditional location (and some newsreaders still expect to find it there), most hosts store news in a separate filesystem, as we'll discuss in Chapter 2, *Getting Ready*.

Within the directory for each newsgroup, there is a file for each article. The filenames are just numbers in sequence, so the fifty-seventh* article in *comp.lang.pascal* is *comp/lang/pascal/57* and the next article in that newsgroup is then *comp/lang/pascal/58* (both within */usr/spool/news* or wherever). When an article is crossposted, the file for it appears in each of its newsgroup directories; each entry is typically a link to a single file. For example, if articles A and B are posted to *comp.lang.pascal* only, article C is crossposted to *comp.lang.pascal* and *comp.lang.lisp*, and article D is posted to *comp.lang.lisp* only, the article tree might look like what is shown in Figure 1–2. Here A and B are articles 57 and 58 in *comp.lang.pascal*, C is both article 59 in *comp.lang.pascal* and article 1195 in *comp.lang.lisp*, and D is article 1196 in *comp.lang.lisp*.

The relayer also uses some index files to keep track of news articles. The *active file* lists each known newsgroup, the highest article number in it, and some additional control information. The *history file* lists all of the articles currently on the host. These files, and a number of other control files, are found in a directory of their own, traditionally */usr/lib/news*. Modern news systems also maintain pernewsgroup *overview files* that contain information about the contents of all of the articles for the benefit of newsreader programs.† The overview files are either located in the article tree (as a *.overview* file in each directory) or in a separate tree with the same structure as the article tree.

Obviously, most hosts cannot keep all Usenet articles on file forever; sooner or later their owners will get tired of buying more disk drives to hold all those articles. Most hosts that get all of Usenet find it impossible to keep more than the last few days' traffic. Sometimes selected newsgroups are *archived* by copying them to

---

* That is, the fifty-seventh article in the *comp.lang.pascal* newsgroup received by *this host*. The article will almost certainly have a different number on another host.

† These overview files, invented by Geoff Collyer, have largely replaced an assortment of older indexing databases that were specific to individual newsreaders.

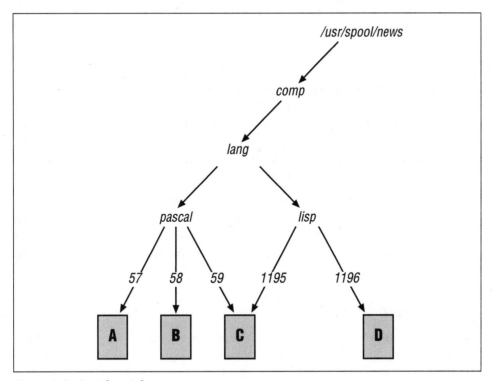

Figure 1–2: Sample article tree

magnetic tape or some other off-line storage medium. In any event, another job of the relayer software is to *expire* news articles when they are deemed to be too old: the articles are deleted from the tree and their entries removed from the history file. (In fact, expiry is the primary raison d'etre of the history file: it's the master list of articles, and the expiry software usually works from it.)

A relayer normally passes articles to other Netnews relayers. However, it is also possible for *gateway* software (which is essentially a special kind of relayer) to transform news articles into a non-Netnews form and pass them on by other means (or vice versa). In particular, it is common to have gateways between Netnews and mailing lists. The most common reason for this is to make Netnews services available to people on primitive networks that do not transmit news, only email. Chapter 14, *Gatewaying*, discusses gatewaying in more detail.

When an article arrives at a relayer, the article is typically filed and then passed along to other relayers. However, there are special articles called *control messages* that have other effects, subject to the approval of the relayer. The most common type of control message is a request that a previously posted article be *canceled*, or in other words, deleted from all hosts that still have it. Chapter 18 describes control messages in more detail, while Chapter 3, *News Operations*, talks about how they affect you.

Articles are passed between hosts by a number of *transports*. The most common transport nowadays is the transport half of NNTP, running over a TCP/IP network. This is an interactive protocol that lets one relayer ask another, "Do you have article XYZ?" and lets the other answer, "No, please send it to me," or, "Yes, don't bother." The original transport for Netnews was UUCP, a batch protocol that transfers files and accompanying commands using autodialing modems. UUCP is still in widespread use on the fringes of Usenet, since many smaller hosts do not have TCP/IP connections to the rest of the world.

While NNTP and UUCP are the most common news transports, news can actually be sent via almost anything that can carry data. It is possible to get news from relayer to relayer via email, which can be useful in restrictive networks that don't allow anything else. It's even possible to ship news on magnetic tape or CD-ROM, if you don't care too much about delays.

1.4 What You Need

The next chapter goes into considerable detail about what you should think about before setting up the Netnews software. Overall, though, to get Usenet traffic, you need three things:

- Another host that is willing to give you a *feed*, or, in other words, relay news articles to you

- A communications link to that host that is fast enough to carry the expected traffic and runs a suitable transport protocol

- Suitable Netnews software, typically C News or INN

You may have noticed that there's nothing in that list about getting permission or paying a fee. Some news hierarchies are sent only to hosts that meet certain qualifications or pay a regular fee, but the "original" Usenet newsgroups, as well as quite a few other hierarchies, are free (assuming you can arrange a feed and a communications link, both of which might cost money). There is no central Usenet administration to tell you that you can't join or to demand that you pay. This lack of central organization has its disadvantages, but it is also a major reason why Usenet has spread so far and so quickly.

In this chapter:
• *Getting a Feed*
• *How Much News?*
• *Propagation Issues*
• *Hostnames*
• *Local Newsgroups*
• *Internal News Networks*
• *Filesystem Layout*
• *Choosing the Software*

2

Getting Ready

This chapter discusses issues that you should think about before diving into the Netnews software. If you're going to be setting up a news system from scratch, taking some time to get things right at the start can spare you a lot of grief over having to change things later. If you've inherited an operational news system that you need to administer, this chapter will help you make sure that things are set up sensibly. Finally, if you've administered a news system in the past, you may be familiar with some of these issues, but it's still a good idea to at least skim this chapter.

In this chapter, we'll discuss obtaining a news feed and help you figure out how much news you can afford to get. We'll also describe how to choose hostnames and names for local newsgroups and how to organize your news handling, including multiple-server configurations and filesystem layout. The chapter ends with a section that helps you choose the appropriate relayer software.

2.1 Getting a Feed

If you want to set up a news system, the first thing you need to do is find a news feed. Essentially, you need to find someone who already has a news feed and is willing to pass it along to you. Since a major feed involves a considerable commitment of resources, this cannot be taken for granted. Even hosts that are willing to provide feeds to others often sharply limit the number of feeds they will provide.

If your host is part of a large organization, there may already be a group within it that is charged with supplying news feeds. Organizations that have substantial internal news networks usually find it best to invest some resources in organizing and monitoring the internal flow paths to improve efficiency, minimize resource use, and simplify the response to emergency situations.

Failing that, the traditional way to find a feed is to look around for local hosts that already have feeds and ask them for a feed or for a referral to one. Historically, universities have been major Usenet hubs, although most of them have been trying to scale back their roles in local news propagation as volume has grown. Local user groups or system administrator associations may be able to provide referrals.

Predictably enough, when sufficient demand for news feeds began to appear, commercial suppliers also appeared, willing to provide feeds to anyone for money. UUNET Communications Services, which later became UUNET Technologies, was the first of these, but there are now quite a few commercial news suppliers. Some of these companies are large national organizations, while others are regional or local companies.

Ultimately, who you get a feed from may be a matter of who you can communicate with, or more importantly, who you can communicate with efficiently or economically. If your feed is coming by modem, you'll want somebody within your local calling area if at all possible. If it is coming over an Internet connection, you'll want to avoid feed paths that traverse low-speed links or multiple gateways, whose owners might be annoyed by sudden heavy traffic. If you are planning a full feed, or even a major subset of one, you'll want to look very carefully at communications performance. Communications paths where you pay for bandwidth are generally better than ones where you pay by the byte.

Your choice of transport method is a related issue. If you're getting a substantial feed over a modem, you'll want to use UUCP so you can do batching and compression to minimize overhead and maximize throughput. Even over an Internet connection, it's possible to run UUCP, although it may take a special version of UUCP. This can be the best method if the link is intermittent, if the speed is low, or if the cost is high. If an Internet link is relatively fast, cheap, and continuously available, NNTP is probably a better solution, especially if you want to get more than one feed for the sake of reliability or speed.

2.2 How Much News?

Once you have a news feed, you need to think about how much news you can afford to get. A *full feed*, including the eight mainstream Usenet hierarchies (*comp, humanities, misc, news, rec, sci, soc,* and *talk*), the other major worldwide hierarchies (notably *alt*), and a typical scattering of regional and local newsgroups, greatly exceeds 8 gigabytes a day, spread over about 850,000 articles.*

It's possible to get only a *partial feed*, picking and choosing the material that you want. Obviously, how much news you get depends on what your interests are,

---

* This estimate is based on news traffic in October 1997.

whether you're feeding news to other hosts (and if so, what their interests are), and what resources you can afford to devote to news. Only the last of those considerations can really be addressed here.

There are four resources that news volume might strain: storage space, communications bandwidth, processing power, and your patience.

2.2.1   Storage Space

Storage space can be the biggest limitation on news volume. Disk technology has kept up with the growth in news volume pretty well; modern disk drives are large enough and cheap enough that storing a full feed for a reasonable length of time is not impossibly expensive. Problems usually arise when a fixed amount of disk space must be shared with other uses, or when there has been inadequate allowance for growth.

For most purposes, the measure of news volume that you care about is the data volume, in bytes (or more accurately, gigabytes). For some space estimates, however, you'll need to be able to convert between data volume and article count. There is a simple rule of thumb for this: a Usenet article averages about 3000 bytes. This has been surprisingly consistent for 15 years, despite traffic growth by many orders of magnitude.

Be warned, though, that this is an *average* over the traditional discussion-oriented Usenet newsgroups. Some atypical newsgroups, like the ones used to distribute program sources and binaries, have much higher average article sizes. Although the 3000-byte rule is a good conservative basis for planning, it's best to obtain actual data on the newsgroups you plan to receive.

2.2.1.1   Available space

Some caution is necessary when translating news volume to required disk space, as there are several complicating factors.* For one thing, news is stored one article per file. So there are lots of (usually) small files. This matters because most systems allocate space for files in fixed-size blocks. The size of a block is usually either 512 or 1024 bytes, but sometimes it can be as large as 4096 bytes.† The amount of space actually allocated to a file is an exact multiple of the block size. Since the space has to be big enough to hold the file, there is generally some wasted space at the end of a file. For example, on a system with 1024-byte blocks,

---

* Note also the discussion of filesystem layout in Section 2.7; not all of these things necessarily go on the same filesystem.

† For example, on the IBM RS/6000 systems the block size is 4096 bytes. On many BSD-derived systems, there is a "block size" that is typically 4096 or 8192 bytes, but the relevant number here is the "fragment size," which is usually 512 or 1024 bytes.

a 2500-byte article would have to be allocated 3072 bytes (three blocks). A reasonable rule of thumb is that the waste averages half a block per article. If you are dedicating a filesystem to news and you have a choice of block size, smaller is better.

Another issue of filesystem configuration, assuming your article tree is on a separate filesystem, is that BSD-derived filesystems have a "minimum free space" configuration parameter, *minfree*, which makes a certain amount of space unavailable to normal users. The normal threshold is ten percent of the total storage space on the filesystem, because various aspects of filesystem performance begin to deteriorate when a filesystem gets very close to full. For a news filesystem, however, you may be more worried about capacity than performance, and in that case, some reduction of the minimum free space threshold might be in order. A value of five percent seems to work acceptably well.

A news system consumes some overhead per article in the form of index information, in the *history* file and associated files. These files typically aren't large compared to the articles, but they aren't negligible either. The index information requires about 100 bytes per current article, and 50 bytes per recently expired article.* As of mid-1997, for a reasonably full feed, the space needed is perhaps 80 megabytes total. Note also that the expiry program rebuilds the index files; the temporary files that it uses in the rebuild process are as large as the index files themselves.

Overview files also consume significant overhead. The overview file for a newsgroup contains information about each article in the newsgroup, for the benefit of sophisticated newsreaders. An overhead file typically requires 250-300 bytes per article.

Unless your incoming news feed is very reliable, you have to be prepared to handle an occasional outage followed by a surge of news. This can add another couple of days' worth of news to your system temporarily. Limiting the incoming flow when space gets short can help, but you still need some margin for surges.†

Finally, when you are estimating required space, bear in mind that Usenet volume is growing steadily. For ten years, the growth doubled every 18 months with a remarkable coefficient of nearly 1.0. This curve was blown away starting in late

---

* See Section 3.4 for the reasons why information about recently expired articles is retained on the system. As a rule of thumb, if you're expiring articles in less than a week, you can figure that they'll be "recently expired" until they are a week old.

† Usenet volume used to show cyclic variation on several time scales. Traffic used to peak late in the work week and was noticeably lower on weekends. On a longer scale, traffic tended to be lower than usual during the (North American) summer, and to surge in September when (North American) students returned to school. There was also a sharp drop during the December holiday season, with other fluctuations that corresponded to lesser school holidays.

1995; we're not confident that there's any accurate data to plot growth these days. It's not enough to be prepared to handle today's traffic; if you don't want to be scrambling for disk space a few months from now, you have to allow room for expansion.

2.2.1.2 Inodes can run out too

A further complication is consumption of inodes, the data structures that Unix uses internally to describe files. Each file requires one inode. On most Unix systems, the number of inodes in a filesystem is fixed when the filesystem is set up, and running out of inodes has consequences similar to running out of space. To allow a reasonable safety margin, a good rule of thumb is that a filesystem used to store news articles should have one inode for every 2 Kbytes of space. Unfortunately, satisfying this rule of thumb can be difficult, depending on the type of filesystem you're using.

A BSD-derived filesystem is divided up into cylinder groups; there are usually 16 cylinders per group. Typically, a cylinder group can contain at most 2048 inodes. Bearing in mind that inodes and other overhead take up some of the space, a bit of arithmetic suggests that you're in trouble if your cylinders are larger than perhaps 500 Kbytes each, which is common on modern disks.

The BSD program for initializing a filesystem, *newfs*, usually tries to allocate one inode for every 2 Kbytes, and it can be told to allocate even more inodes. But if the allocation you ask for requires too many inodes per cylinder group, *newfs* quietly reduces your allocation request to fit within the limit of 2048 inodes per cylinder group. The only fix is to reduce the number of cylinders in the cylinder groups for the filesystem. This solution doesn't reduce the capacity of the filesystem, although if taken to extremes it might cause a slight performance degradation. Just how you reduce the size of cylinder groups varies, depending on your system, but it's normally done by supplying options to *newfs*. It should resemble the following:

```
% newfs -c 8 filesystemname          # only do this if necessary
```

This command puts only 8 cylinders in the cylinder groups for the specified filesystem.

Note that you can only adjust the number of cylinders in the cylinder groups when you are setting up a filesystem. It's not something you can change later, except by wiping out the entire contents of the filesystem and starting afresh. We advise that you check your article-tree filesystem after it is made but before you start filling it with news. Use *df* to find out how much free space there is (be careful about what units the space is being measured in) and *df* with -i to find out how many free inodes there are. Then do the division.

Very old System V filesystems don't have cylinder groups; modern ones do because they're BSD-derived. On very old systems, you may encounter a different problem: a limit of about 65,536 total inodes per filesystem, which is rather low for hundreds of megabytes of news. All you can do about this problem is to spread your news over several smaller filesystems. Older news software had trouble with crossposted articles in this case, especially if the system did not support symbolic links, but modern relayers cope properly, although they sometimes need minor adjustments for this case. (See the discussion of filesystem layout in Section 2.7).

2.2.1.3 How long to keep it?

Obviously, volume per day needs to be multiplied by the number of days that you keep news to determine an appropriate amount of storage space. And how long you keep news is largely your decision.

The relayer software's expiry program takes care of getting rid of old news. Expiring news more often than once or twice a day is awkward, since the expiry operation itself can take up to several hours. Exactly how long it takes is a function of how much news you get and how long you keep it. The more news you get, the more articles the expiry program has to dispose of. In addition, the more articles that are stored on your system at the moment, the more articles the expiry program has to consider disposing of. The load on your system at expiry time is also a factor. All of these factors mean that realistically you can only plan to run the expiry program once or twice a day—there's no use trying to be more precise than that.

You get to specify how long your news system keeps old news. Various considerations, such as what you are doing with news, play into this decision. For example, if your system is feeding news to other hosts, you have to retain news articles at least long enough to feed them out again, as most transport software works from the stored copies on your system.* This is rarely an issue if the outbound feeds are keeping up with the incoming flow, but if there is a backlog (e.g., because a host or a communications link is down temporarily), there can be a substantial delay between reception and retransmission. Even a well-run host can be down for a couple of days if it dies late Friday night and the maintenance crew doesn't come on duty until Monday morning (this once happened to one of the authors). You have to decide how much of a backlog you're willing to tolerate, but if you are going to do a good job of feeding other hosts, you should keep news for at least two or three days.

---

* A common question is "Can't I just feed out a copy of what I receive, without having to unpack it, store it as individual articles, and then bundle it up again?" The short answer is "No" because the articles you feed other systems are not exact copies of what you receive. See Chapter 19, *Flow and Processing of Traffic*, for the details.

Deciding how long to keep news for your own users to read is more difficult. In the early 1980s, when volume was low, it was common to keep everything for a month, so that people could catch up with news after a vacation. This usually isn't practical anymore unless you are very selective about which newsgroups you get. If you don't keep news for at least four days, however, people who go away for a long weekend will see gaps. You should probably try to keep newsgroups that are relevant to your work, or that are popular with your users, for at least a week. See the discussion of expiry policy in Section 3.4 for more information on the expiry process. (If you're running C News, it has a program, *expirebot*, that may be helpful in automatically adjusting expiry times; see Section 5.1.2.4.)

The upper limit on how long to keep news is mostly a question of available space. Nothing will break in the news software if you do try to keep everything for a month. About the only thing you really need to watch is how long expiry takes. As we mentioned above, the expiry processing has to at least consider each article as a candidate for expiry, so part of the time it takes is proportional to the number of articles you keep around.

It's quite possible, and indeed usually desirable, to keep different newsgroups for different lengths of time. This can help with storage space issues. Beware, though, of assuming that the interesting newsgroups are small, so that you can keep them around for a long time if you conserve space by getting rid of the "trash" more frequently. Unless you are very selective about what you consider "interesting," you may find that there is more interesting news than you think. Actual measurements are a much more reliable guide than intuition,

2.2.1.4 A rule of thumb

By now you may be feeling overwhelmed by the number of factors that determine just how much storage space you need for news. If so, just remember that the storage requirements depend mostly on volume; a quite modest amount of space will suffice if you only get a handful of newsgroups. The other important factor is what you are doing with news (i.e., feeding news to other sites or just providing for local readers).

A reasonable rule of thumb is that you need five days' worth of disk space at a minimum. This amount allows you to keep news for a bare minimum of three or four days (either for readers who want to catch up after a long weekend or for customer systems that might be down for a couple of days) and it still gives you some margin for error. You'll need to check the current Usenet volume (ask whoever's feeding you for current numbers) if you're going to have a full feed, or do some calculations on your own for a partial feed, and then perform the multiplication to estimate your disk space needs. Finally, remember that the volume will double in a year or so.

How Much Space?—A Checklist

Here's a checklist for the issues you need to think about when deciding how much space you need for a given volume of news:

- Are your volume estimates up-to-date and accurate?

- An average of a half a block of space is wasted per article.

- Ten percent of the storage space on a filesystem is unavailable unless *minfree* is reduced.

- The history file consumes 100 bytes per current article and 50 bytes per recently expired article.

- The overview files consume 250-300 bytes per article.

- When setting up a filesystem for news, be sure that you have one inode per 2 Kbytes. Reduce cylinder group size if necessary.

- How long are you going to keep news?

- Do you have a reasonable cushion of space for surges?

- Do you have a reasonable margin of space for growth, or when will you buy your next disk drive?

2.2.2 *Communications Bandwidth*

Nine gigabytes per day is more than 110,000 bytes per second or nearly 900,000 bits per second. Clearly, a full feed can be a considerable strain on communications resources as well as disk space. And remember that whether you get a full feed or a partial one, its volume will double in about a year, so you need to plan ahead.

With the best available modems and reasonably effective data compression, even a modest partial feed over a modem connection still requires several hours a day of connect time. Beware of fantastic modem data rates quoted in sales literature, which tend to assume that the modem's own data compression will be highly effective; it's hard to get much better than a factor of two in compressing news, and newsgroups carrying images or binaries often don't compress even that well. For news, it is often better to pre-compress the data in the host before transmission, which renders in-modem compression useless.

Clearly, if you want a substantial feed, it is much more practical to use dedicated lines, preferably high-speed ones. Even so, care is indicated, especially if the transmission is done using NNTP. Most Internet data paths do no data compression and NNTP has no provisions for compression either.

Another limitation is that the original version of NNTP is a "lockstep" protocol: about four times per article, one end must wait for the other end to respond, and there is no provision for pipelining operations to do setup for the next article while the current one is being sent.* If the end-to-end propagation delay is long or one of the hosts is heavily loaded, the throughput of an NNTP connection can be far below what you might expect on that line. For example, a completely clean link with a round-trip time of 500 milliseconds can support a theoretical maximum of 86,400 articles per day, which is nowhere near a full news feed.

It's hard to predict delay problems in advance. If there is reason for concern, you should start with a small news feed and enlarge it gradually while you watch how long it takes to bring across each day's news. If you do have trouble, it is possible to get multiple simultaneous NNTP feeds (which reduce the amount of time spent idle) or to get a compressed-batch UUCP feed (which reduces bandwidth requirements via compression, at the price of increasing the load on the upstream site).

Simply getting a news feed can place a substantial burden on communications facilities; the problem worsens considerably if you are supplying feeds to several other hosts. You need to pay careful attention to the volume of data transmitted, how it will grow (remember, it doubles every year or so), and what other demands there may be on your communications links. As a rule of thumb, if your predicted news traffic is more than half your available bandwidth, you'll need to make some changes or news will have a serious impact. But it's possible to get in trouble long before that on things like round-trip time. Our advice is to do the arithmetic carefully, allow for a large safety margin, and recheck the situation regularly.

2.2.3 *Processing Power*

As used here, *processing power* is some sort of vague combination of CPU speed, available memory, and sustained disk transfer rates, among other things. The details are very system-specific, but the issue is universal: will your chosen news load slow your system to a crawl?

When it comes to receiving news for your own use, the short answer is "probably not." Assuming you are running modern news software on hardware that is not hopelessly outdated, processing power should not be a major problem. You don't need the latest, greatest, and fastest CPU for news. You may want to consider fast disks, especially if you're going to support a lot of readers, but even they are not essential.

---

* There is a new "streaming" version of NNTP that fixes this problem (see Section 19.5.3), but it is nonstandard and not all software supports it yet.

The one borderline exception to this happy picture involves systems that are short of memory. INN is generally comparable to C News in terms of performance* (and sometimes it provides better performancs), but it is a memory hog by comparison. C News was originally developed on 16-bit machines and is still fairly miserly in its memory consumption, while INN assumes that you have some megabytes to spare. If you're trying to run INN on a machine that is short of memory (or is shared with memory-intensive users), you may have a problem. Mind you, C News too will run better with plenty of memory; it's just that its performance doesn't deteriorate so rapidly when memory is in short supply.

Feeding news to other hosts can be somewhat more of a problem. The actual transmission is not a serious consumer of processing power, unless the number of feeds gets large. (Chapter 13, *Hub Nodes*, discusses some of the special considerations of operating a major news "hub," with many outgoing feeds.) However, if you are using data compression to minimize the number of bits sent over slow or expensive communications links, the compression and decompression can have a major effect on your system load. If the feeds that use in-host compression are not overwhelmingly large or time-critical, sometimes you can cope by doing the compression outside "prime time" hours, so it gets done when the system is otherwise quiet.

In short, processing power should not be a serious resource limitation unless you have a very slow system, are trying to run INN on a memory-starved system, are feeding many other hosts, or are doing a lot of expensive data compression that cannot be postponed to quiet times.

2.2.4 Administrator Time

The good news is that modern news software on a stable system will pretty much run itself, placing no significant regular demands on your time. The bad news concerns the phrases "pretty much" and "significant regular."

If you're new to administering a news system, you're obviously going to need a certain amount of time to set up the software and the feeds and become familiar with the routine administrative tasks. This may take considerably longer if you make some mistakes along the way, or if your system is unstable enough to cause complications.

Small amounts of administrative time are needed on an ongoing basis. It is possible to leave a news system on autopilot, but it's not recommended. You need to

---

* Unless you are running a news hub, in which case C News suffers from not having a refined NNTP interface.

make minor administrative decisions now and then, and respond promptly if the software yells for help.

Finally, you'll need to budget occasional lumps of time to deal with growth: enlarging the system resources, reducing the news feed, or both. Even a system that is left on autopilot will eventually become unreliable or fail altogether, as growth overwhelms the available system resources.

All of these time commitments are at least slightly related to the volume of news you get, if only because anything that interferes with a gigabytes-per-day data flow tends to become a major crisis rather quickly.

2.3 Propagation Issues

At one time, in connection with attempts to replace the Internet's unwieldy and huge mailing lists with newsgroups, there arose a school of thought that put a high priority on extremely rapid propagation of news. A lightly loaded Internet site relaying email (e.g., from a mailing list to individual list members) can typically pass it on within seconds. The new school of thought suggested, loudly, that NNTP news transmission ought to show similarly short delays. Traditionalists, accustomed to the UUCP world view in which end-to-end propagation delays of days were considered normal, said, "C'mon, it's only news," and dubbed these upstarts "The Church of Instantaneous Propagation."

Older news software, notably C News and the NNTP Reference Implementation, is oriented toward occasional batch transmission and does not support instantaneous propagation very well. Rapid propagation requires a relayer like INN, where the relayer is active all the time and is ready to act on very short notice. There is a fundamental conflict between instantaneous propagation and efficient use of transmission links, since instantaneous propagation tends to require either continuously open connections or frequent setup and teardown of connections. It is also fundamentally difficult to combine instantaneous propagation with batching and data compression.

Trying to achieve instantaneous propagation also encourages sites to connect to a large number of other sites via NNTP, since this increases the probability that at least one of those sites will pass along a given article very quickly. This trend has been dubbed "The Church of Massive Redundancy."

Membership in either church is not for the faint of heart or the short of resources. There is a measurable cost, both in machine resources and in administrative complications, involved in trying to achieve instantaneous propagation. Remember, most news traffic *isn't* particularly time-critical.

2.4 Hostnames

For news purposes, your host may have more than one name. You probably already have a hostname for mail purposes, typically an Internet domain name like *kiwi.ora.com*. That's fine, and the news software needs to know about it, but you'll also need to pick a *news name* for your host. Your host's news name is the name by which neighboring news hosts—the ones that feed news to you or get feeds from you—know your host. The users of your news system never see this name; it is strictly for the internal purposes of the news software.

The news name doesn't have to be the same as the name used by whatever software actually transmits the news from one host to another. For example, a host that transmits news by both UUCP and NNTP is known by its UUCP name to UUCP software and by its Internet domain name to NNTP software. These two names are usually not the same because UUCP names are often limited to eight characters, while almost all Internet names are longer than that. Various control files make the connection between the news name and the transmission name. (However, if you're going to be doing only one kind of transmission, it can be convenient to use the transmission name as the news name.)

What *is* important, however, is that the news software on your host and the relayers on your neighboring hosts agree on your host's news name. Disagreements can cause various nasty problems. For instance, if the names do not agree, when you send some news to your neighbors, they will immediately send it back to you. Your news system will reject the looping articles as duplicates, but the effect on transmission bandwidth can be serious if volume is high. So when you choose a news name, you have to inform your neighbors about what it is. If you need to change your news name, the change must be coordinated very carefully with your neighbors.

So, what should your host's news name be? Nowadays, the best choice is usually its Internet hostname. Even if you are not connected to the Internet directly, this name is a unique name that everyone agrees on.

There is one little catch. Internet hostnames are case-insensitive: *kiwi.ora.com* is the same as *Kiwi.ORA.Com*. However, most news software considers news names to be case-sensitive, so capitalization matters. You must pick a standard capitalization style for your news name and make sure all your neighbors know what it is. The best choice is the all-lowercase form (i.e., *kiwi.ora.com*, not *Kiwi.ORA.Com*) as this is the most standard and least error-prone convention.

2.5   *Local Newsgroups*

As part of your news configuration work, you will want to create some local news-groups, specific to your host or at least to your organization. At the very least, you'll need a local newsgroup or two for testing the news software as you get it going. (It is a serious breach of etiquette to broadcast test messages to thousands of other hosts by using a worldwide newsgroup for testing.)

Originally, the standard convention was that a newsgroup with no dot in its name was local to a single host. For example, the traditional name for a general-discussion newsgroup was *general*, while the traditional name for a test-messages newsgroup was *test.*

The problem with this convention is that a lot of people use such names, which causes crosspostings to have interesting consequences. If someone on a faraway host crossposts an article to a worldwide newsgroup, say *comp.lang.c*, and also to his own local *general* newsgroup, that article goes out marked as being in news-groups "comp.lang.c,general". If your host gets *comp.lang.c*, this article will appear both in *comp.lang.c* and in your local *general* newsgroup, which tends to cause confusion and difficulties.

As a result, it is better to use some sort of organization-specific name for your local newsgroups. For example, if you're setting up Netnews at Fred's Widget House, it's better to name your general-discussion newsgroup *fwh.general* and your test newsgroup *fwh.test*. There is some small chance of crossposting confusion even with such names, but it is greatly reduced.

One final caveat is that you should try to choose a reasonably specific naming convention. If you're at Kiwi University, *kiwi.general* or *kiwiu.general* is better than *ku.general*, even if "KU" is the usual abbreviation. There are certainly other universities whose names start with K! Long ago, both the University of Toronto and the University of Texas originally chose *ut.general* for a general newsgroup, and the result was years of headaches.

2.6   *Internal News Networks*

If your organization has a number of systems connected by high-speed networks, you probably don't want to keep news databases on all of them. It's better to have one or two central servers maintaining news databases, with users on other hosts reading news via the network. Such a setup is shown in Figure 2–1.

The basic tradeoff here is between multiple transmissions and unnecessary trans-missions. If users read via the network and if ten users read a particular article, that article gets transmitted over the network ten times. Moreover, those transmis-sions have to be done when the users ask for the article, not at some other time

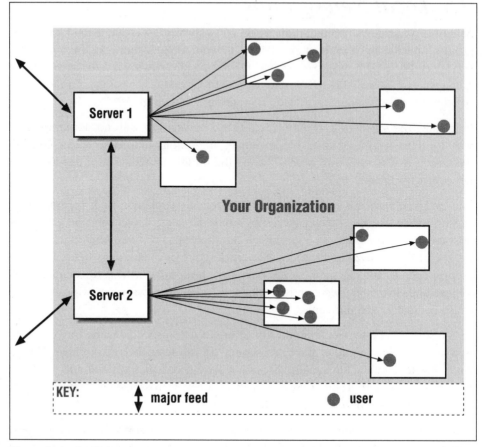

Figure 2-1: Central news servers

that might be more convenient. If each host has its own database, however, the article only gets transmitted once and the timing can be arranged to suit local needs. On the other hand, if users read via the network, only the articles that are actually read get transmitted. If each host has its own database, every article has to be transmitted, on speculation that somebody might read it.*

In general, it's best to have *official* news servers, with specific people responsible for maintaining them, even though this does mean some expenditure of resources on a service that might be considered frivolous. Think about it this way. If your organization's network is connected to the rest of the world in almost any way, it is seductively easy for people to set up unofficial news connections. Because such

---

* It would make sense to have some sort of intermediate solution, in which a central server would get everything, individual hosts would get only selected traffic, and newsreader software would know how to search for an article in several possible places. So far, support for this is very limited.

unofficial connections are uncoordinated, they will undoubtedly use a good deal more of your organization's resources than official ones. And because the connections are clandestine, it is difficult to contact their administrators quickly to deal with security problems. Thus, it's better to have a few official "gatekeeper" hosts that are responsible for maintaining the news connection between your organization and the outside world. It is also better to give those hosts competent administrators and open-minded policies, as this minimizes the incentive to create unofficial alternatives.

If you are planning a server-based arrangement, there are two key issues you need to think about: how to organize the servers and how to have newsreaders access the databases on those servers.

2.6.1 News Servers

Obviously, central news servers need adequate resources, including plenty of disk space, and they should be solid, reliable systems. It's best to plan on not doing much else on those systems. In addition, they should be well-placed on your network: the routes the incoming feeds take through your network should be direct and fast. It's also desirable for the newsreader-to-server connections to be relatively direct and fast, although the volume there is much lower than for the feeds themselves. If you have a central high-speed backbone network with other networks fanning out from it, putting the news servers directly on the backbone is a good idea.

Whether you should have just one server, or more than one, depends on your circumstances. If you have several clusters of systems with relatively slow inter-cluster links, a server in each cluster is clearly preferable. The servers should feed each other news so that they all have the same articles available, but having the articles go from server to server over a slow link once is better than having them go from server to newsreader over the same slow link repeatedly. If your network performance is fairly uniform, you might want to have a pair of servers for reliability, depending on how much you value news access. Otherwise, there's no particular reason you cannot use just one server, assuming it can handle the load.

If you have multiple servers, but want to make this fact largely invisible, you can use a technique called *mirroring*. This technique maintains a *slave* server's news database as an exact copy of that on a *master* server. See Section 13.1.2 for details.

2.6.2 Access to Servers

Newsreaders can access news servers in any number of ways, but there are two dominant methods: using the newsreader half of the NNTP protocol to fetch articles from a daemon on the server and reaching into the server's disks via network filesystems such as NFS. Some modern newsreaders can use either method. There are conflicting stories about which method is best, although both can be made to work well. (Mixed approaches can also be found; in particular, a server can let people read via NFS but require them to use NNTP for posting.)

Routing news access through an NNTP daemon gives you better access control, in theory, and often in practice. The daemon can enforce access limitations and do security checks; it provides a single access point where decisions can be made. An NNTP daemon can even implement normal-looking access to news that is stored in some form other than an orthodox article tree. Finally, NNTP newsreaders can be implemented on systems whose filesystems are too warped to ever support network filesystems.

Another security-related issue is that the NNTP daemon, if properly written, only provides access to the news database in a relatively limited way (i.e., mostly read-only). By contrast, network filesystems are notorious for being weak links in system security. A sloppily configured network filesystem can also react rather badly when a server goes down, even if the data involved is something relatively unimportant like news.

Speaking of importance, many network filesystem implementations give remote access a high priority that is difficult to adjust, so newsreaders may have priority over other, more important tasks. Ordinary programs, like NNTP daemons, are accorded less importance and can be customized to lower their priority even further, if needed. (A server that is dedicated entirely to news processing should nevertheless give processing of incoming news priority over reading, so that the news database stays up to date.)

However, there are some benefits to using a network filesystem for news access. For example, network filesystems are better optimized to handle many concurrent accesses to the same data. (In principle, NNTP daemons could do some clever caching based on knowledge of news reference patterns, but at the moment they generally do not.) A network filesystem needs fewer processes to handle heavy loads and it has fewer bottlenecks. Network filesystems are also more flexible: extra indexing information can be made available simply by placing it in the article tree as files, whereas doing this with NNTP requires defining extensions to the protocol and then implementing them in the daemon. Similarly, having access to the news database as ordinary files permits manipulations that are awkward or impossible to do through NNTP, although admittedly this is not a common requirement for most users.

If the news-reading load on your system is light, it probably doesn't matter much which approach you choose. If you are particularly concerned about security, NNTP gives you better control, although possibly at the cost of custom modifications to daemon code. If your load is particularly heavy, a network filesystem may perform better and give you more throughput from a given set of equipment. (Experiences do vary somewhat, however, so you may want to run systematic tests in your own environment.) Finally, if you have many people who want to use newsreaders that only talk NNTP, which is quite common nowadays, you don't really have a choice!

If there's nothing that pushes you strongly in either direction, choose NNTP. The world is clearly moving toward NNTP for news reading, and going along with that may save you future pain.

2.7   Filesystem Layout

There are several sets of files in a news system, and you need to decide where to put each of them. This can be a moderately complicated decision, depending on the disk space you have available and the layout of your filesystems. You might want to review the discussion of storage requirements in Section 2.2.1 before you proceed.

Much of your news software, including non-NNTP newsreaders, will have to be configured to know about the locations of these files.

2.7.1   Big Files

The bulk of any news system is the article tree itself; it can easily consume several gigabytes of space. It's best to put the article tree in a filesystem of its own, or at least in one that is used for a minimum of other activity. Some customization of the configuration parameters for the filesystem may well be desirable, as discussed earlier in Section 2.2.1.2. The article tree was traditionally stored in */usr/spool/news*, but since it's usually in its own filesystem these days, many systems just put it in */news*. That's the location we'll use throughout the rest of this book.

The article tree can be split across several filesystems, at some cost in awkwardness and administrative headaches, if your system supports symbolic links.* If possible, try to keep the symbolic links at the highest level of the article tree (e.g., give *alt* its own filesystem) because this tends to make administration easier and minimizes site-specific changes to software. (For example, C News utilities that traverse the entire article tree cope automatically with symbolic links at the top level, but need system-specific alterations to cope with symbolic links lower down.)

A better way to split the article tree across partitions, if your system supports it, is *striping*: combining two or more actual partitions into a single logical partition that

---

* Modern versions of C News cope pretty much automatically. INN needs some adjustments, as described in Section 9.3.2.

comprises a single filesystem. This avoids the annoyances of symbolic links and can enhance performance as well.

The overview files are the next largest space consumer in a news system. They are usually about ten percent of the size of the article tree, using 250-300 bytes per article. The overview files can be placed in the article tree itself, but it is usually better to put them in a separate tree, so a newsreader looking for an overview file doesn't have to search for it in a directory that contains hundreds of articles. A good place to put these files is in an *over.view* subdirectory of the top-level article tree directory.* In other words, we recommend that you put the overview files in */news/over.view*, and that's the location we'll use henceforth.

The control and index files for news were traditionally stored in */usr/lib/news*. Most of these files are fairly small, but there are two prominent exceptions: the *history* file and the log files. On modern systems, the usual convention for a collection of small control files is to put them in a subdirectory of */etc*. However, because the *history* file and the log files are so large, we recommend that you put the news control files in */var/news*, and that's the location we'll use throughout the book.

The single biggest news file is the *history* file, which contains one line per current or recently expired article. It is used both for indexing and as the master control file for expiry. It is accompanied by a pair of auxiliary files, *history.pag* and *history.dir*, that implement an index into *history* itself. Using the modern *dbz* indexing package, the auxiliary files are typically a fraction of the size of *history*. As of mid-1997, for a reasonably full feed, the space needed is perhaps 80 megabytes total. These files get rebuilt by the expiry program; the temporary files that are used in the rebuild process are as large as the files themselves. (Some expiry programs leave an old copy around until the next run, to "reserve" the space for the temporary files.)

If your system supports symbolic links, it's typically possible to relocate the *history* file and its associated files, although any software that renames them (as the expiry program typically does) has to know about it. Some people put the history files in the same filesystem as the article tree—since logically they are part of the article database, not control files for it—although this does hurt performance.

The news log files are the final big consumer of storage space, and some relayer programs put them in with the control files. The sizes of the log files vary somewhat depending on the relayer software you are running, but even one line of text per article gets large when hundreds of thousands of articles arrive every day.

---

* The dot in the directory name guarantees that the name will never conflict with part of the article tree itself.

Relayer software generally includes provisions for "rolling over" these log files—moving them to a new file once a day, and keeping only the last few days' files—so that the files do not just grow without limit. Here again, symbolic links make it easy to relocate the logs, as long as the roll-over software knows about it.

The relayer software itself typically lives in yet another location. The software isn't very large, especially compared to the article database. */usr/lib/newsbin* was the closest to being a traditional location, but there has always been more diversity in this particular choice. The usual policy now is that programs for major software subsystems go in subdirectories of */usr/libexec*, so we'll use */usr/libexec/news* as the location for the relayer software throughout the book.

2.7.2 Filesystems and Disk Drives

Although it might seem easier to put all the news files in a single filesystem, there are a couple of good reasons why you do not really want to do that.

The main reason to split the files between different filesystems is that you'll see a considerable performance improvement if the *history* file and the log files are on a separate disk drive from the article tree. Not just a different *partition*, mind you, but a different *disk drive*. This obviously isn't practical if your system has only one disk drive, but if it has two, splitting the load across them can help a lot. And if you've got three, putting the overview files on the third can help too.

Another reason for splitting things up is that some backup systems only operate on entire filesystems. In other words, you cannot control what gets backed up any more precisely than that. If this is the case on your system, you probably want to arrange the news files so that the files that should be backed up are on filesystems that get backed up, while the files that are not worth backing up are on filesystems that do not.

In general, it is desirable to back up the small news control files, especially the *active* file. Backing up the *history* file, however, is usually not worth the trouble. The file is large and the most important parts of it can be regenerated from the article tree if necessary. Backing up the log files is pretty useless as well, which makes a strong case for putting the history files and log files on a separate filesystem if you can. The existing software, alas, sometimes makes this difficult.

Backing up the article tree and the overview files is usually not worthwhile, unless you have internal newsgroups whose contents are of long-term importance. (In that case, you might want to put these groups on a different filesystem from the main article tree.) Backing up the article tree requires a huge amount of space, while losing a few days' news is usually no more than a nuisance. Some expiry programs support an "archiving" feature that provides an alternate way of saving specific newsgroups' traffic permanently, if you need to keep track of certain newsgroups.

Some systems offer optional filesystem optimizations that can be useful for news. These are worth serious consideration if you're planning a high-performance news system. The optimizations are normally applied only to the filesystem(s) that contain the article tree. Precisely how these optimizations are invoked is system-specific, although they often involve options to the *mount* command.

BSD-derived filesystems force the software to wait for completion of certain writes, to help guarantee filesystem integrity in the event of a crash. If you have reliable hardware, you may be more concerned about the performance of your article tree than its crashproofness, especially since occasionally losing a bit (or a lot) of news is no more than a nuisance. Some systems allow a filesystem to operate "asynchronously," which eliminates the forced waits. Be warned, however, that this optimization is a little risky; it is possible to lose the entire filesystem in a crash if you're unlucky.

A standard Unix filesystem updates the "access time" of a file every time the file is read. On a busy news server, these updates can involve a lot of overhead to maintain fairly uninteresting information. Some systems offer a way to specify that the access times on a filesystem should not be updated, which can make a busy article tree respond substantially faster. This optimization, unlike asynchronous operation, is not risky.*

2.7.3 Ownership

Most news administrators allocate a separate user ID, which we'll call the *news owner,* to own the news database. The news owner is typically *news.* Using a separate ID minimizes the possible damage from misbehaving programs, and otherwise simplifies news administration. Most of the news software should be run under that user ID. Depending on the exact software involved, however, some of it may have to run as *root.*

Most news software doesn't care about the exact permissions on files, but it does have to be able to make files and directories in the article tree and the control-files directories. Normally, those directories and everything within them are owned by the news owner, so everything functions smoothly.

For the most part, the news programs themselves do not have to be owned by anybody in particular. On general principle, they probably shouldn't be owned by the news owner, so that a misbehaving or overly trusting program cannot be

---

* Note, however, that the C News *expirebot* program (see Section 5.1.2.4) needs the access times, so this optimization is incompatible with use of *expirebot.*

tricked into damaging other programs. There are a few exceptions for programs that have to be set-UID, owned by the news owner or by *root*, so that they can run with special powers. We'll cover the details of program ownership in Chapters 4, *Installing C News*, and 7, *Installing INN*, when we actually talk about setting up the relayers.

2.7.4 NFS

In general, it is highly desirable to run the relayer software on the machine that owns the disk drives holding the news database. In particular, it is a serious mistake to make the relayer access any of its data over NFS. If you can possibly avoid that scenario, do so.

One reason is that NFS is a performance disaster, even with a fast network. It's good enough for a lot of purposes, but for bulk data handling, it is no substitute for local disks with a good local filesystem. If you get anything near a full news feed, you'll quickly regret any decision to put the news database on the other side of NFS from the relayer software.

The other reason is that NFS's imitation of genuine Unix filesystem semantics is pretty sloppy and this can cause problems. In particular, the locking protocols that are used by some relayer programs simply do not work reliably over NFS. If you must locate part of the news database remotely, make the article tree and overview files remote but leave the control and index files local. You won't like what this does to performance, but at least things should pretty much still work.

2.8 Choosing the Software

Finally, of course, before you start installing software, you have to choose which software to install. This breaks down into two reasonably independent issues: which newsreaders and which relayer. The interface between newsreader and relayer is standard enough that it's quite possible to mix and match. Indeed, it's fairly common to have more than one newsreader in use. Unless you've got a complex cluster of servers, however, you'll probably want to pick one, and only one, relayer.*

2.8.1 Which Newsreaders?

It's hard to say very much about the newsreaders. They are constantly evolving, and user preferences tend to be matters of personal taste and what people are accustomed to, so objective evaluation is difficult. In any case, this is not a

---

* See Chapter 13, and Section 13.1.3 in particular, for advice about situations in which hybrid systems may be appropriate.

decision that has to be made all at once. Adding a new newsreader is just a matter of compiling it and installing it. And when you install a new newsreader, the old ones can remain in use. So newsreader selection is mostly a matter of how many you want to document and support.

Chapter 10, *Choosing and Installing Newsreaders*, contains thumbnail sketches of a few of the major newsreaders. There are more than this book could possibly cover, but that chapter tries to get you started. Your users may already have specific preferences, in which case you should try to accommodate those.

2.8.2 Which Relayer?

Picking C News or INN as your news relayer is a bigger decision. Here there is basically no possibility of straddling the fence: you have to choose which package you'll use to maintain your news database. The two packages are distinctly different in style and approach, and their administrative procedures differ greatly as well.

Neither relayer is overwhelmingly superior to the other. Either of them can be made to work satisfactorily in almost any situation. At the moment, the best we can do is to cite some good and bad points of each relayer and let you decide which one to use:

- C News is older, better shaken down, and has been ported to a wider range of systems. INN, being newer, has been able to draw on the experience of C News and take different approaches in troublesome areas.

- C News runs well on systems with a small amount of memory. In fact, it was originally designed to work on 16-bit machines (although it no longer does that very well). For INN, you need several megabytes of memory to spare.

- C News is designed to stay out of the way of people doing other work on the same system. INN prefers to run on a dedicated news server.

- INN's NNTP handling is tightly integrated with its relaying, while C News relies on a separate NNTP package, which is a definite weak spot.

- INN integrates most of its functionality into one big server program, while C News splits functions into smaller programs. This makes INN more complex, with greater potential for obscure bugs and less room for customizing, but avoids some of the problems C News has with inconvenient boundaries between programs.

- INN generally has a more active user community now, with more people contributing proposed improvements, although C News has suffered less from changes in support arrangements and proliferation of unofficial versions.

If all of those good and bad points haven't helped you pick a relayer, here are a few situations in which use of either C News or INN is specifically recommended:

- If you have multiple incoming NNTP feeds, you should consider running INN. Its integrated NNTP handling deals with this situation much more gracefully.

- If you don't run NNTP at all, much of INN's complexity buys you nothing, so you may want to consider running C News.

- If you are running your news server on a system that is dedicated to news, INN may have an edge.

- If your news system has to get other work done as well, C News may have an edge.

- If you are short of physical memory, run C News, not INN.

- If you have a very odd or very old system, you'll probably find it easier to get C News running.

- If one or the other relayer package (but not both) comes with your system, life will probably be a bit simpler if you use that one.

- If none of the above considerations apply strongly, but you are familiar with one relayer and not the other, pick the one you know.

- If you're not familiar with either one, but your friends are, pick the one your friends know. This should make it easier to find help when you need it.

If you still can't decide which relayer to use, try reading the software-setup chapters (Chapters 4 through 6 for C News, and Chapters 7 through 9 for INN). Those chapters should help you decide which relayer is more appropriate for your particular system and needs.

3

News Operations

In this chapter:
- *Managing the Flow*
- *Control Messages*
- *Newsgroup Changes*
- *Expiry Policy*
- *Archives and Backups*
- *Unwanted Newsgroups*
- *Security Considerations*
- *Getting Help*

This chapter discusses the technical side of keeping a news system running. If you've inherited an operational news system, this chapter will tell you about all of the routine things you'll need to do to administer the system. The emphasis here is on normal operations, since the details of troubleshooting are software-specific (see Chapters 6, *Running C News*, and 9, *Running INN*).

If you don't have an operational news system, you need to read this chapter before you read the chapters on the relayer software you've chosen. The material here will help you understand the essentials of news server operation.

In this chapter, we'll look at how to manage your news flow and how to respond to news control messages. We'll also talk about how to keep your list of newsgroups current, give you some advice on deciding when to expire news, and discuss news archiving and backup. Finally, we'll give you some pointers on where to get help if you can't solve a news problem yourself.

We've postponed non-technical administrative issues until Chapter 11, *You're a Network Manager Now*. Here we are concerned with keeping the software working, rather than with what people do with it. This chapter also sticks to general issues, while Chapter 12, *Leaf Nodes*, talks about operating a news system in the quiet backwaters where it can be left more or less on autopilot, and Chapter 13, *Hub Nodes*, talks about operating a major news hub that needs careful attention.

3.1 Managing the Flow

As you may have gathered from Chapter 2, *Getting Ready*, the dominant problem you'll face in keeping news running properly is keeping the articles flowing smoothly into and out of your system. With volume greatly exceeding 8 gigabytes per day, the sheer volume of data quickly turns any disturbance in the flow into a major crisis.

3.1.1 Disk Space

There is no substitute for having ample disk space for news, both for your own article tree and for network flows. You need to keep ahead of the space situation, because the volume of news is growing inexorably. By the time it is obvious that you've got a problem, it will be too late to deal with it painlessly.

Any single measurement of free space is necessarily misleading because the volume of news fluctuates quite substantially, as we already mentioned in Chapter 2. A good time to check available space is just before the Thursday-night expiry run, since volume sometimes drops considerably over the weekend. (Don't do it on Friday night because that is part of the weekend; the weekly peak of disk usage tends to occur on Thursday night.)

You should always leave a substantial margin of free space, over and above your worst-case measurements, because of the unevenness of news flow. In particular, be aware of the long-term variations mentioned in Chapter 2. If the news areas of your disks are showing signs of inadequacy in late August, you will surely be in big trouble when the North American student population returns from summer vacation and starts posting news in September.

Remember, if you want your news software to run smoothly and not bother you, you need a large safety margin in disk space. The extra space is not wasted—it is the price you pay for peace of mind. The alternative is having to nurse your news system constantly, which can quickly become a terrible headache.

3.1.2 Surges

Apart from predictable variations in flow throughout the week and the year, there are sometimes surprises. If the host that feeds your system news is down for a while, or the link between your host and your system is down, you'll be in for a deluge when it comes back up. (This is one good reason for having multiple feeds.)

Even a few hours of down time can create a significant surge, still visible days later in disk usage and network traffic. If your feed is down for several days and you get anything approaching a complete Usenet feed, your news system is in for a traumatic experience. This is when you find out how well your news software copes with full disks. If the administrators at your feed host are on the ball, they may be able to slow things down somewhat to spread the surge out, but that only solves part of the problem.

It's a good idea to be alert for such outages, so you can prepare yourself to cope with the results. Even if you personally disdain news as a gross waste of time (and there is some justice in that view), it may be worth reading one or two newsgroups, simply so you'll notice a sudden ominous silence.

Then, of course, there's the possibility that it's your host that's been down for a while. This is, if anything, even worse: not only are you getting all the pent-up articles flooding in, but if your host has been down, it hasn't been expiring old news. In such a situation, one of the best actions is to do an immediate expiry run with considerably shorter expiry times than usual, to make room for the incoming deluge. In fact, it's worth doing this *before* you start accepting incoming news again, if that's practical.

If worst comes to worst, Geoff Collyer (the co-author of C News) had a relevant observation: "Hey, it's only Netnews." It can be better to throw incoming news away for a day than to try to accommodate it all when your resources plainly aren't adequate. Some newsgroups might be important to your users (or to hosts downstream of you), but it may be easier to make alternate arrangements to get copies of the articles in those newsgroups. If communications bandwidth or cost is a serious issue, you might even be able to get the administrators of your feed host to throw the news away without ever sending it to you.

If this seems too drastic, a more expensive but also more selective technique involves temporarily configuring your news system to discard less-important newsgroups or hierarchies.* A still more expensive variant is to tighten up expiry times severely and do repeated expiry runs in fast succession until the surge passes. These methods at least differentiate between important and unimportant newsgroups.

3.1.3 Lumps

If the communications link used for your news feed is slow, you may have problems when some dolt posts a single enormous news article. Unfortunately, this does happen occasionally. For example, on at least one occasion, the complete text of the Bible has been posted as a single article.

If the time required to send a huge article to you exceeds the mean time between failures (MTBF) of your communications link, and the communications software is unable to restart a failed transmission in the middle, your news feed may be essentially out of order until something is done. Huge articles can also overflow spool areas, cause malfunctions in inadequately robust communications software,

---

* With C News, this can be done for whole hierarchies using the ME line of the *sys* file; see Section 5.1.2.1. With INN, it has to be implemented by using *ctlinnd changegroup* to turn off individual newsgroups; see Section 9.4.

or delay more-urgent traffic by clogging up the link. Hosts that get very restricted news feeds and consequently don't normally need much space for news might even run out of disk space.

To try to avoid this situation, modern news software limits transmission size. However, this limitation typically has to be done at the sending end, not the receiving end, so you're at the mercy of the administrators of your feed host here. In the absence of help from them, the best you can do is to be alert to the possibility and try to deal with it when you see it happen. Just what you can do depends on software details; it may be possible to cause the transmission to fail in such a way that it will not be re-tried. If worse comes to worst, an emergency call to the administrators of your feed host may get action.

3.1.4 Outbound Feeds

So far, we've discussed what you can do about incoming traffic. But of course, your incoming traffic promptly becomes outgoing traffic to any hosts that you feed. What we've said above will be a fairly good guide to what your neighbors' administrators would like to see from you. Note, in particular, that they'd probably appreciate advance warning of likely problems, such as scheduled down time. It's important to know how to reach the administrators by non-computer means (for example, by having up-to-date phone numbers for them).

The counterpart to incoming surges is outgoing backlogs. When a host you feed is unresponsive, for whatever reason (e.g., down time, broken communications links, misconfigured software), news will pile up on your system waiting to go to them. This is a common problem, so news software generally limits the size of backlogs and reports them when they do happen.

Again, you really need to know how to contact the administrators of your news neighbors by non-computer means, so you can ask them what the problem is. What you do then is up to you, although you should give some weight to how they feel about it (for example, whether they expect to have enough disk space to deal with the surge when the flow starts again). It may be better to turn a feed off temporarily than to let it pile up a backlog that will be difficult to clear. You might also want to clear out some existing backlog, by deleting spooled files or paring down to-be-sent lists.

3.2 Control Messages

Your news system will occasionally notify you about things that need attention or that might warrant closer inspection. Some of these things are status reports or warnings of trouble, specific to the particular relayer software you are running. Some may concern impending or current shortages of disk space, a problem area that both C News and INN try to keep an eye on. Control messages are another kind of notification that you'll see from your news system.

As we discussed briefly in Section 1.3.2, control messages are requests for special action that are embedded in special news articles. Some are routine things that needn't come to your attention, but some are more serious. You'll hear from your news system, typically by email, if one of these becomes an issue.

3.2.1 Newsgroup Addition and Deletion

The control messages that you'll hear about most frequently are requests to add newsgroups (*newgroup*) and delete newsgroups (*rmgroup*). In the very beginning of Usenet, there was some hope that adding and removing groups could be done automatically, but that hope was quickly shattered. Automatically creating newsgroups when articles arrived for them was a total disaster—there are too many typos—and the scheme was quickly changed to one based on explicit requests in control messages. Even that wasn't a complete solution, however, because people could (and did) send out control messages at whim.

Modern news software permits some degree of automation of these functions by letting you configure it to act on some requests automatically and to refer other requests to the news administrator. The usual pattern is that some or all requests to add newsgroups are acted on automatically, with notification to you after the fact, while all or almost all requests to delete newsgroups are simply referred to you. Adding a spurious newsgroup is comparatively harmless, whereas deleting a genuine one can be very disruptive; hence the difference in approach.

There is no substitute for being familiar with the procedures followed in the different Usenet hierarchies and with the people who implement them. For example, as of mid-1997, all legitimate *newgroup* and *rmgroup* requests in the eight "mainstream" Usenet hierarchies* are issued by David Lawrence using the address *group-admin@isc.org*,† and current distributions of C News and INN are configured (by default) to know this. The *alt* hierarchy, by comparison, is near-total anarchy, with newsgroups created more or less at the whim of posters. The notion of a "legitimate" *newgroup* request is meaningless in *alt*. Finally, local and regional hierarchies often have relatively informal policies about newsgroup addition and deletion.

In general, it is unwise to configure your news system to carry out *rmgroup* messages automatically, except perhaps for well-controlled hierarchies internal to your organization. Dealing with *newgroup* messages automatically is more of a

---

* These are *comp, humanities, misc, news, rec, sci, soc,* and *talk.*

† Although Lawrence is no longer with UUNET, the control messages still also come from *tale@uunet.uu.net* because thousands of news systems have that address in their control files.

judgment call; policies range from wide open to fairly restrictive. There are some systems that accept essentially any *newgroup* request in *alt*, for example, and others that ignore any such *newgroup* request unless a user on that host has specifically asked for that newsgroup.

If you do have your software refer some *newgroup* messages to you for a decision, you should deal with them fairly promptly. It's annoying to lose the first few days of traffic in a new newsgroup because the news administrator didn't get around to creating it. (Some news systems do keep the articles around, but there's no good way to move them into the newsgroup retroactively.)

Decisions on *rmgroup* messages can safely be deferred, however. Some news administrators let them accumulate and deal with them once a month or so. Even when everyone agrees that a newsgroup should die, traffic in it usually tails off slowly rather than dying abruptly, so being a bit slow about killing the newsgroup may even be beneficial. Also, if a supposedly dead newsgroup continues to show vigorous activity, this is a hint that you should scrutinize that *rmgroup* message very carefully before acting on it.

3.2.2 Checkgroups

RFC 1036 vaguely describes a control message, *checkgroups*, that compares your *active* file against a list of groups that theoretically should exist on your system. The intent is to provide a semi-automated way of verifying that you really have all the "official" newsgroups in one or more hierarchies. Some hierarchies do still post *checkgroups* control messages periodically. Other hierarchies stopped doing this due to poor *checkgroups* support in early news software. However, these hierarchies do post the necessary data in ordinary news articles, so that a news administrator can feed it to a *checkgroups* utility if desired, as described in Section 3.3.2.1.

The mail you'll get from receiving a *checkgroups* message is pretty much the same as the output you get from running the *checkgroups* or *docheckgroups* utility described in Section 3.3.2.1. As such, the message should be handled in much the same way as the output. The one extra complication is that you need to decide whether or not you believe the *checkgroups* control message, as it is possible to forge them. The only advice we can offer here is to be suspicious of any message that calls for radical changes, especially the deletion of many newsgroups.

3.2.3 Cancel Messages

One type of control message that you don't hear much about, and don't want to hear about, is requests for cancellation of articles. The *cancel* control message was meant to let a user cancel an article she posted, for example if she discovered that it contained a mistake. The *cancel* message is also (mis)used for a number of other functions, including some attempts to limit abuses of the Net, such as advertising.

You might think you'd want to know about *cancel* messages, but you really don't: there are too many of them and it's impractical to give them any sort of useful scrutiny. Most current news software does not even try to notify you about them.

If you change your software to notify you about *cancel* messages, perhaps because you're using the messages for limited purposes in a well-controlled internal network, you'll have a decision to make when one appears. If you're being conscientious, you should examine the cancellation, which is supposed to include an explanation, and the original article to decide what should be done. Your choices are to delete the original or leave it alone. Ultimately it's a judgment call, and generally the heavens aren't going to fall if you get it wrong.

3.2.4 Sendsys and Its Relatives

In the very early days of Usenet, substantial efforts were devoted to network mapping. (There was a time when a complete map of Usenet, drawn with ASCII characters, would fit on a single 24 × 80 terminal screen.) Some aids to this were built into the news software in the form of control messages that requested any news host that received them to email information to a central point.

These control messages, *sendsys* and *version*,* have great potential for abuse, since they can make hundreds or thousands of hosts all send email to the same address. Unfortunately, such "sendsys bombing" was relatively commonplace, so modern news software tries to mediate the potential harm. Unless you're located within an organization that manages its news flows carefully and does organized mapping, most *sendsys* messages you receive are malicious mischief, rather than genuine attempts at network mapping. (There seems to be rather less abuse of *version*, probably because *sendsys* usually comes first in the documentation.) Even when there is no active malice involved, a *sendsys* message that is not restricted to a very small geographical area is almost certainly a mistake.

Modern news software tends to take various precautions against *sendsys* requests, such as delaying replies to these messages or requiring that certain restrictions be met (e.g., that the return address specified must be of a particular form). The delayed reply, in particular, makes it possible for local authorities to notice a mali-

---

* There is also a very obsolete third one: *senduuname.*

cious *sendsys* and issue a cancellation request for it, preempting most of the replies.* If you're running modern news software and using a normal configuration, you shouldn't need to take manual action on *sendsys* or *version* messages.

3.3 *Newsgroup Changes*

Making sure that your news system has a view of Usenet that is consistent with what the rest of the world sees is an important service, both to your own users and to users and administrators around the network. If your users post to a newsgroup that has been superseded by a renaming, or was never widely approved to begin with, that gives the group a false appearance of credibility. This can lead other administrators to create the group, in the belief that they missed something, which then leads other users to post to the group—a vicious circle that leads to duplication of topics and disrupted online communities. Keeping abreast of the commonly accepted changes to the newsgroup namespace is not terribly difficult, but it does require a little time. The natural evolution of the Usenet namespace sees the addition and removal of hundreds of newsgroups per year.†

You should also be aware that news software lets you have a newsgroup on your system whether or not it's included in your news feed. Your system (and your users) cannot tell if there really is no traffic for a group or if you just aren't receiving the traffic. This situation can be especially confusing if a few crossposted articles are trickling in to a group that you are not otherwise getting.

3.3.1 *Hearing About Changes*

There are several ways in which you might find out about changes to the newsgroup namespace, and some of them are more reliable than others.

3.3.1.1 *newgroup and rmgroup control messages*

The usual way for sites to be informed about changes to the namespace is by *newgroup* and *rmgroup* control messages. Modern news systems include provisions for flexible handling of these messages according to who sent them and what group they affect. The control of their handling is described in Section 5.1.2.2 for C News and Section 8.2.4.1 for INN. In addition, the sample control files supplied with the software distributions are set up to know about the accepted authorities for some of the major Usenet hierarchies, as described in Section 3.2.1.

---

* This is one situation where someone other than the author can legitimately issue a *cancel* for an article.

† A more detailed look at newsgroup namespace management can be found in Chapter 16, *Newsgroups and Their Names*.

The intent of *newgroup* and *rmgroup* control messages is that they propagate only to sites that are most likely to want them, as defined by the existing feeds for those sites. For example, if a new group is created in *comp*, the *newgroup* message should propagate to those sites that get *comp*. This mostly works, although configuration errors can cause incomplete propagation of *newgroup* messages. *rmgroup* messages should only arrive for groups that you are receiving. Be warned that an *rmgroup* message might be your only control-message notice of a reorganization for a group that you want, especially if there was hierarchal migration involved. For example, when *rec.skate* became several *rec.sport.skating.** groups, the *newgroup* messages for them did not go to sites that received *rec.skate* but not *rec.sport.**. Thus, the *rmgroup* message was the only way for those sites to find out about the reorganization.

Due to the vagaries of article propagation, we suggest that you do not rely solely on control messages to track namespace changes. If you suspect that you have missed a control message, you can check an archive of most of the widespread *newgroup* and *rmgroup* control messages that have been sent since early 1991: *ftp://ftp.isc.org/pub/usenet/control*. The messages are stored in mail-style folders arranged in subdirectories by top-level hierarchy. It contains all widely propagated messages since early 1991, except for a brief gap in August 1992.

3.3.1.2 news.announce.newgroups

The clearinghouse for changes to the "mainstream" Usenet hierarchies is *news.announce.newgroups*. People who want to add or remove groups from those hierarchies submit a Request for Discussion (RFD) to *news.announce.newsgroups*. The RFD is discussed for a few weeks to try to resolve any problems people have with the proposal. Unless there is significant opposition or apathy to the idea, the final proposal usually gets submitted in a Call for Votes (CFV) article, which is an interest survey that tries to gauge whether there is sufficient interest among readers at large. If the proposal succeeds, the moderator of the group, David Lawrence, issues the appropriate control message to implement it.

The control message to create a group includes the date the final results of the proposal were announced, the yes/no result of the vote, the *newsgroups* file description for the group, and the charter for the group. For a moderated group, the control message also contains the moderator's contact and submission addresses. If the new group supersedes another group, that information is also provided. C News and INN systems that are automatically honoring the message extract the description and add it to their *newsgroups* files; the other data is for information only and is not meant to be added to files on the system.

A *rmgroup* message from the *news.announce.newgroups* moderator similarly describes why the group is being removed.

A few status postings appear regularly in *news.announce.newgroups* to help people keep up with events in the namespace management process without having to examine each individual proposal. The "Current Status of Usenet Newsgroup Proposals" article is posted around the beginning of every week and lists all of the groups that have entered the formal discussion phase in the previous 30 days, as well as proposals that are in the voting stage. "New Usenet Groups" is posted at the same time, with a complete accounting of all pending namespace changes, as well as the changes that have occurred during the previous month. Finally, the "Bogus Usenet Groups" article is posted every two weeks. It lists groups that are considered to be invalid by a majority of administrators for such reasons as having been superseded by another group or not having ever had a formal proposal and successful vote. These articles can be useful for keeping track of changes in the mainstream hierarchies without having to rely on control message propagation.

Archives of *news.announce.newgroups* postings since late 1989 can be found in *ftp://ftp.isc.org/pub/usenet/news.announce.newgroups*.

3.3.1.3 *checkgroups control messages*

We've already discussed *checkgroups* control messages, but they are worth mentioning again here, as *checkgroups* messages and equivalent postings can help you keep track of the "official" newsgroups in various hierarchies. Section 3.3.2.1 describes how to use *checkgroups* messages with a *checkgroups* utility.

3.3.1.4 *Other sources*

A *checkgroups* utility can work from data obtained from a wide variety of sources; it doesn't have to come from a *checkgroups* control message or equivalent posting. It can also come from an announcement of a new hierarchy, a copy of the *newsgroups* file from a neighboring news system, or the lists of groups posted in *news.lists.misc*. Many sites on the Net regularly grab the ISC (Internet Software Consortium) *newsgroups* file from the archive at *ftp://ftp.isc.org/pub/ usenet/CONFIG/newsgroups*. Doing that occasionally is the ultimate way of verifying that you're up to date, at least for one view of the worldwide newsgroups.

3.3.2 *Making Changes*

Both C News and INN require a valid newsgroup to be listed in a control file named *active* in the control-files directory—if you use our suggested directory organization, the file is */var/news/active*. The formats of the *active* files for the two relayers are essentially the same, with four fields per line, separated by single spaces. The fields are: the group name, the maximum article number in the group, the minimum article number in the group, and a control flag for the group. The flag is usually either y for an unmoderated group or m for a moderated one. Here are three sample lines:

```
control 0001671903 0001530841 y
alt.config 0000064329 0000050548 y
news.announce.newgroups 0000006307 0000006117 m
```

The maximum and minimum fields are fixed length (now typically ten digits) and padded with zeros* because they are updated in place. They were historically only five digits wide, but the growth of Usenet has made that limit too small—observe the count of articles in the *control* pseudogroup above, taken directly from UUNET's active file in 1995.

There are a few associated files that are also of note. The *active.times* file records when newsgroups are added and by whom. The *newsgroups* file contains names and one-line descriptions of newsgroups, for the benefit of users and newsreader software.

The key to making changes is to get these files updated without corrupting them. C News' *relaynews* and INN's *innd* constantly modify these files, so you have to obtain a lock on the files to avoid trampling on the contents. The *newgroup* and *rmgroup* control messages take care of all this automatically when they make changes, but you need to know the manual procedures because typical configurations will refer doubtful cases to you.

3.3.2.1 checkgroups utilities

C News and INN both include utilities to compare your system's *active* file, which lists the newsgroups your system knows about, with a separate list of newsgroups. Named for the *checkgroups* control message, the scripts take a list of group names and descriptions, one per line, and try to validate the name and moderation status of every group in your *active* file. They do this in every top-level hierarchy that is common between *active* and the list, and report what groups they believe should be removed, what groups should be added, and what groups need their moderation status changed. The utilities output a shell script that can simply be run to make the necessary changes.

As discussed earlier, the list fed into the *checkgroups* utility can come from any of a number of sources. You can modify the list to exclude groups that you do not want and include groups that it does not list; alternatively, you can edit the *checkgroups* output to delete unwanted changes. Note that the utilities report only on top-level hierarchies that are mentioned in the input list. So, for example, if you

---

* C News actually manages the minimum field more flexibly. The maximum field remains zero-padded, although it is widened automatically if necessary.

feed in a list that contains only the *bionet* groups, the script only checks for missing or extra *bionet* groups.

Here's how to use the *checkgroups* utilities for both C News and INN:

```
% cnewsdo checkgroups <group-list >check.out                    # C News
% /usr/libexec/news/control/docheckgroups <group-list >check.out   # INN
```

Be sure to examine the output before implementing the changes. Remove any lines that mention group changes that you don't agree with. You should then have a ready-made script that you can feed directly to the shell to make the changes. With INN, use `sh -x check.out` so that each command is echoed as it is executed, as this can help you pinpoint a problem if something blows up. With C News, the changes are made en masse rather than one newsgroup at a time, so the output from `-x` isn't useful and you should just use `sh check.out`.

3.3.2.2 Single updates

If you are only adding a group or two at a time, both C News and INN provide simple interfaces for doing so. Let's add *comp.security.announce*, a moderated group, for each type of news system:

```
% cnewsdo addgroup comp.security.announce m              # C News
% ctlinnd newgroup comp.security.announce m              # INN
```

(Before using this method with C News, you may want to read the discussion of *addngs* later in this section, as it is a better method for adding groups.)

You can add an unmoderated group using the same commands; use the `y` flag instead of the `m` flag.

The INN command also takes an optional final argument that is the email address of the person who has asked for the group to be created. If this argument is not present, the address defaults to your own login name. C News just uses your login name. This information is recorded in the *active.times* file, although nearly no software makes use of it.

WARNING   Do not use the *makegroup* script that came with INN prior to version 1.5.1 to add local newsgroups. The script sends out a control message, asking that the group be made at other sites! The Net used to see more accidentally leaked control messages from this cause than from any other, wasting the time of administrators around the world. (It is not an accident that C News contains no such script.) In fact, it is recommended that you not use *makegroup* even if you do want to send a control message. (See Chapter 16 for more detail on sending control messages.)

Deleting a group is quite similar to adding a group. For example, here's how to to remove the superseded *news.admin* group:

```
% cnewsdo delgroup news.admin                    # C News
% ctlinnd rmgroup news.admin                     # INN
```

You can also alter the control flag for a newsgroup. For example, here's how to change *sci.aeronautics* to a moderated group:

```
% cnewsdo newsflag sci.aeronautics m             # C News
% ctlinnd changegroup sci.aeronautics m          # INN
```

(This group was revoted to be a moderated group, after it had already been formed as an unmoderated group.) More information on moderated groups, including how to configure the mailing of submissions to the moderator, can be found in Chapter 15, *Moderating Newsgroups*.

After making any changes, you should update the *newsgroups* file to reflect changes to the descriptions of newsgroups. C News does most of this automatically, while INN does not.

If you've added a newsgroup, you need to put a description for it into the *newsgroups* file. If you're using C News, the *addgroup* utility has already supplied a *newsgroups* line, albeit a not very informative one. To edit the file without stepping on the software's toes, do the following:

```
% cnewsdo locknews                    # might take a few minutes
news system locked by you
newslocked% vi newsgroups             # or use your favorite editor
newslocked% exit
news system unlocked now
```

An alternate method that is perhaps simpler is to supply the *newsgroups* description as an extra argument to *addgroup*:

```
% cnewsdo addgroup comp.security.announce m  "Security announcements"
```

The *addgroup* utility supplies the " (Moderated)" string automatically for a moderated newsgroup, so there's no need to put that in yourself.

A still better method, especially if you've already got a suitable *newsgroups* line from a Usenet posting, is to put the *newsgroups* line (including the " (Moderated)" string, if any) in a file (named, say, *descriptionfile*) and use the newer *addngs* utility instead of *addgroup*:

```
% cnewsdo addngs <descriptionfile
```

The *addngs* utility does all of the work, including adding the newsgroup and updating the *newsgroups* file, based on the *newsgroups*-style line supplied as input.

The Newsgroups File Format

The format of lines in *newsgroups* is a bit ill-defined, but the convention that the *news.announce.newgroups* moderator uses for generating the *news.lists.misc* postings is:

```
group.name              Description. [(Moderated)]
```

The group name starts at the beginning of the line. There should be one or more hard tabs (assume 8 column tabstops) to get to the start of the description at column 24. The description should start with a capital and end in a period and not be more than 56 characters (80 minus 24) long. If the group is moderated, it should contain the string " `(Moderated)`" after the description. (Note that there is a space after the period and before the open parenthesis.) In terms of length, the moderated string is not counted as part of the description.

If the group name uses more than 23 characters, just one tab is used. The goal is to keep the entire line under 80 columns, so if the group name is 25 characters long, you have 8 fewer description characters to work with for the description.

Overly long descriptions can sometimes be made to fit this format by dropping "puff" phrases like "Discussion of," which don't meaningfully contribute to the description. It's usually fairly easy to keep a description within the 80 column mark, except when a group name is very long. Hopefully, in such a case, the group name itself contains quite a bit of descriptive content.

C News requires one final step in adding a new group: you have to make sure that the **ME** pattern in your *sys* file matches the group. If it doesn't, C News rejects articles that you receive for the newsgroup with the log message "no subscribed groups." This isn't usually an issue when creating a new newsgroup in a hierarchy that you already receive, but it requires careful attention when a new hierarchy is involved.

To update the *newsgroups* file with INN, you must lock the file against *innd*'s control message headers. You can do this by pausing the server or by leaving the server running and using a wrapper script like the one shown in Example 3-1.

Example 3-1: A Locking Wrapper for Editing Newsgroups

```
#! /bin/sh
# "ving" --- like "vipw", but works on the newsgroups file

## configure path to innshellvars
##   =()<. @<_PATH_SHELLVARS>@>()=
```

Example 3-1: A Locking Wrapper for Editing Newsgroups (continued)

```
. /news/lib/innshellvars
LOCK=$LOCKS/LOCK.newsgroups

if shlock -p $$ -f $LOCK; then
  :
else
  echo "$0: could not lock newsgroups file; try later" >&2
  exit 1
fi

${VISUAL-${EDITOR-vi}} $NEWSGROUPS

rm $LOCK
```

3.3.2.3 Bulk updates

If you want to add or remove a lot of groups in the *active* file, the simple command-line interfaces are inefficient because they must run one or more processes and lock the news system each time they are run. The best way to accomplish a large *active* file modification depends on the software you are using.

In C News, bulk updates are relatively easy and bulk additions are particularly simple. The *addngs* utility described above is perfectly happy to accept more than one *newsgroups*-style line as input and efficiently add all of the newsgroups. *addngs* does, however, object to adding newsgroups that are already present, unless you give it the -q option:

> % **cnewsdo addngs -q** <*descriptionfile*

In this case, *addngs* ignores description lines for newsgroups that your system already knows about.

With C News, bulk changes of moderation status are almost as easy. Again, put together a file with *newsgroups*-style description lines, including the " (Moderated)" strings for moderated newsgroups. Then feed the file to the *setngs* utility:

> % **cnewsdo setngs** <*descriptionfile*

This utility adjusts the control flag of each newsgroup mentioned in `descriptionfile` to what the file calls for. The utility does complain if asked to adjust the status of a nonexistent newsgroup; as with *addngs*, the -q flag shuts it up.

For bulk deletions, put together a file of newsgroup names, one per line, and feed it to the *delngs* utility:

> % **cnewsdo delngs** <*descriptionfile*

(The input file can be a *newsgroups*-style description file, although here C News ignores the descriptions.) Once again, a nonexistent newsgroup does cause a complaint unless you use -q.

With INN, the procedures for bulk updates are less straightforward. Adding groups in bulk can be done by editing the *active* file directly. To avoid corruption of the database, the server must not be accepting any articles and it must have its in-memory copy of the *active* file flushed to disk. When you are done editing the *active* file, you must tell *innd* about the new file. The lines that you add have to be in the standard format: group name followed by a space followed by two fields of digits (ten zeros each for a new group) separated by a space, then finally another space and the flag for the group. Here is how you can manually add all of the groups created in the *rec.photo* reorganization:

```
% cd NEWSCTL
% ctlinnd pause 'adding new rec.photo groups'
% ctlinnd flush ''      # syncs the in-memory copy of active file to disk
% cat >>active <<EOF  # note well: appending to the file, not overwriting
rec.photo.advanced 0000000000 0000000000 y
rec.photo.darkroom 0000000000 0000000000 y
rec.photo.help 0000000000 0000000000 y
rec.photo.marketplace 0000000000 0000000000 y
rec.photo.misc 0000000000 0000000000 y
EOF
% ctlinnd reload active 'rec.photo reorg'
% ctlinnd go 'adding new rec.photo groups'
```

Removing groups in bulk is a process similar to adding them. Pause and flush the server, then get the updated *active* file into place. Reload the *active* file and start the server running again.

Another way to perform a large *active* file modification is to create a file that contains the modified entries, lock out *innd* and other utilities from making modifications to the *active* file, and then edit the file as needed.

Deleting an entire hierarchy is easy with a properly anchored regular expression in an editor, but picking groups out of hierarchies you are already getting, perhaps in response to the output of a *checkgroups* run, can be a little tricky. Here's one way to do it. Take the list of groups you want to remove and save them to a file. Preface each line with ^ and trail each line with [ ]. Then quote the regular expression metacharacters that can appear in group names, notably . and +. Run the whole thing through *egrep* and doublecheck that you removed as many lines as you wanted. Then move the new *active* file into place as with the bulk adding of groups, like so:

```
% # server paused and flushed
% wc -l < file-of-groups-to-remove 102
% wc -l < active
```

```
1102
% egrep -f -v file-of-groups-to-remove active > active.new
% wc -l < active.new
1000
% mv active.new active
% # reload active and unpause server
```

The same regular expression file can be used to prune the *newsgroups* file of the removed groups. Be sure to lock it first as described in Section 3.3.2.2.

Note that even with *innd* paused, both *ctlinnd newgroup* and *ctlinnd rmgroup* will try to update the *active* file. The server should not normally be running those commands if it is not accepting articles, because the *newgroup* and *rmgroup* control messages that trigger them won't be arriving. However, it is possible that such a message arrived before you paused the server and is still in the process of being executed. Be sure to do a *ps* to check for any active control message scripts, like *newgroup* or *rmgroup*, before proceeding with the *active* file update. Of course, you can be foiled if someone else comes along and either unpauses the server or tries to make updates without worrying about locking.

WARNING   A *ctlinnd rmgroup* command that is issued while the server is paused will result in your *active* file being corrupted. You can guard against this happening accidentally by adding the following two lines to the beginning of the CCrmgroup function in the source code to *innd/cc.c*:

```
if (Mode != OMrunning)
        return CCnotrunning;
```

A *ctlinnd newgroup* command done while the server is paused does not suffer the same problem.

Here's a command that generates a list of *active* file entries from a *newsgroups*-style list of groups and their descriptions. The list of groups can be passed on standard input; the *active* file entries are written to standard output. The output can then be appended to the *active* file directly while the news system is locked:

```
awk '{print $1, "0000000000 0000000001", /\(Moderated\)$/ ? "m" : "y"}'
```

Just adding lines to the *active* file in this way has a trap for the unwary. If you add a second line for a group that is already in the *active* file, INN will be very unhappy about it. For example, if you have an up-to-date list of the *comp* groups and want to add them to the existing *comp* groups you already carry, you can't just take the whole thing and run it through the command above. The *checkgroups* utility, described above, avoids this problem by preparing a list that contains only the necessary changes.

The output of INN's *checkgroups* should be examined before feeding it to *sh*. If the changes number more than about a dozen, you might want to do it using the bulk update method described earlier in this section. Building a list of groups for addition is straightforward, but removing them or changing them is a little more tricky. One approach to the problem is to post-process the output from the utility, but that's a waste of effort compared to modifying a copy of the utility itself. The *checkgroups* utility uses a nice flat list of groups, so you can modify it to write the list in a different output format that is more suited to efficient mass changes.

When you are all done adding and removing groups, under INN don't forget to update the *newsgroups* file as necessary.

3.3.2.4 *Other active file flags*

There are a few other values of the *active* file control flag that INN and C News support. These values can be useful in special situations.

When the control flag is set to **n**, the newgroup does not accept any locally generated postings. The only articles that appear in the group are those that come in from neighbor sites (or from your own site via a mechanism that looks like it is from a neighbor site, such as through *rnews*). This flag is useful when you know a group is in transition to being removed. You can change the control flag to **n** so that your site does not generate any more postings to the group. Using the **n** flag is basically an extra-nice gesture of good Net citizenship. It is not something that is really expected of you because currently there is no automatic way to set the flag via control messages.

Setting the control flag to **x** for a group causes any articles posted only to that group to be completely discarded. This is a useful tool when your neighbor is sending you something that you can't manage to make him stop, but that you don't want to waste any resources storing. Because C News forwards articles that it files in the *junk* pseudogroup (used for articles in unknown newsgroups), administrators at C News sites might want to add known bogus groups with the **x** flag set. Using this flag cuts off the propagation of those groups, which should lessen the appearance to others that they are widely accepted groups. However, any articles that are crossposted to both bogus groups and valid groups do still propagate.

INN's **j** flag allows *innd* to accept articles for groups that you don't want stored in the regular newsreader space, but do want to be able to propagate to neighbors. The articles are instead stored in the *junk* pseudogroup and propagated according to their Newsgroups headers.

Finally, the **=** flag can be used to file articles from one newsgroup in another group. The **=** flag is followed by a newsgroup name; it is reminiscent of B News' aliasing mechanism, but it is not the same. Unfortunately, newsreader programs have not figured out how to deal with this flag very well, so it seems to have very little utility in the real world.

WARNING   B News used to have an "alias" feature for newsgroups, but it did not behave the same as the modern = flag. The alias feature treated all references to the old name as being for the new name, all the way down to rewriting the headers while processing an incoming article. That, coupled with B News' policy of mailing unapproved moderated-newsgroup articles to the moderator even when the article was generated at another site, meant that aliasing an unmoderated group to a moderated group would cause a tremendous volume of mail to be sent to the moderator. For this reason, any sites still running B News are asked not to alias previously unmoderated groups to moderated ones.*

3.4 Expiry Policy

Your news software comes with a default expiry control file, but you'll probably want to alter it some. The details of the file depend on the software, but the underlying issues of expiry policy do not. We discussed this briefly in Section 2.2.1.3; now we'll take a closer look.

Ultimately, when you expire news is a compromise between keeping articles around so people can read them at their leisure and getting rid of them to save disk space. There was a time when most news hosts kept everything for a month, but that was long ago. The more disk space you have for news, the longer you can keep things. Longer is better, but eventually the overhead starts to grow and the law of diminishing returns sets in.

The theory behind keeping news for a month, back when that was practical, was that it kept articles around long enough so that people could go on vacation and catch up on news when they got back. Neither the keeping nor the catching up is really practical any more, but the basic principle is still relevant: think about how long you should keep news to cover typical interruptions in news reading.

If you can afford the space, keeping news around for a week is good. That lets people fall behind for a few days when they get busy; it also allows particularly busy people to keep up by reading news only on weekends.

An expiry time of about four days is the bare minimum for satisfactory reading. If you make it much shorter than that, people who go away over a long weekend

---

* In B News' defense, both design decisions—aggressive group aliasing and mailing unapproved articles—made some sense, especially at the time of the Great Renaming and the reimplementation of moderated groups. They just proved to be mistakes in the long run.

start missing news. It's very hard to follow an ongoing discussion when there's a gap in it once a week.

Of course, considerations like these apply mostly to newsgroups that your users actually read. If you're getting certain newsgroups only to pass them on to other hosts, not because your own user community is interested, you may be able to expire them more quickly. This does depend on having some idea of what your users read, and getting that information can, unfortunately, be rather difficult. (If you're going to be running C News, its *expirebot* program can be helpful here; see Section 5.1.2.4.)

How quickly you can expire news that is "just passing through" depends on how you transmit it and how responsive your neighbors are. Typically, the articles need to stick around long enough for the transmission software to pick them up, which happens only when it's ready to transmit them. If news flows quickly (say via NNTP) and backlogs are rare, keeping news for one day may suffice to get it out the door. If you have UUCP neighbors who connect only intermittently, or who run substantial backlogs for other reasons, you may need to keep news for several days to make sure that they get it. Whatever your policies on this are, you should make them clear to your neighbors, since they don't get any explicit warning that news is expiring before it has a chance to reach them.

These basic issues aside, you may want to consider the nature of individual newsgroups, or hierarchies, when setting expiry times. It's tempting, and arguably reasonable, to set short expiry times on newsgroups that contain many large articles (e.g., the "binaries" newsgroups). Moderated newsgroups have some tendency to be of higher quality than unmoderated ones, so you might want to keep the moderated ones longer. Newsgroups that are of special interest to your organization are good candidates for longer retention. However, newsgroups that exist mainly to distribute very large volumes of data might deserve fairly short expiry times.

Another issue that comes up regarding expiry policy is explicit expiry dates. Normally, when you set the expiry time for a newsgroup, you're only setting the time for articles that do not carry explicit expiry dates. In general, there's no harm in having articles expire early, but explicit expiry dates can also keep articles around longer than usual. There are some cases where it is reasonable to keep articles around for longer than usual, but you may want to set some limits.

As a precaution against the occasional pest who sets truly ridiculous expiry dates, you probably want to set an absolute upper bound on expiry. For example, the default C News expiry control file sets an absolute limit of 90 days, which is long enough to permit fairly long retention of articles that really deserve long lives, while still enforcing their eventual disappearance.

It is also a good idea to keep an eye on explicit expiry dates. Once in a while, someone will decide that his articles deserve to expire when he wants them to, not when you want them to. It can be particularly annoying when the moderator of a moderated newsgroup does this and all of the articles in that newsgroup suddenly start carrying explicit expiry dates. This behavior amounts to an abuse of the facility; for normal traffic, expiry times on your system should be *your* decision. It is possible to override such expiry dates on a newsgroup-by-newsgroup basis, once you're aware of such a problem.

Becoming aware of the problem is a bit harder. C News has a utility program, *bad-expiry*, that looks for newsgroups with suspicious expiry-date patterns. Not all such newsgroups are actually problem areas, however. There are a few newsgroups, like *news.announce.newusers*, that legitimately set long expiry times on articles. Even so, such cases do deserve a look to see if the long expiry times suit your particular needs.

One final issue in expiry policy involves the *history* file entries for articles. These entries should be retained for at least a week, even if the articles themselves expire sooner, so that the news software can detect duplicate copies of arriving articles. The details of setting the retention time for *history* entries depend on the software, but the key issue does not: an incoming article that is older than the *history* file's retention time is discarded, on the theory that it's almost certain to be a duplicate.

You want to keep as much history as you can, to avoid accidentally rejecting an article that was simply slow to reach you. (Article flow in most of Usenet is rapid these days, but out on the fringes of the network it can still take a while.) The tradeoff here is that the history file gets bigger too. You really shouldn't reduce retention time below about a week, though, because then slow articles really do start getting lost. As of mid-1997, a one-week retention time for a site getting a reasonably full feed of the mainstream Usenet newsgroups produces a *history* that is about 80 megabytes. That number can go considerably higher, however, if you get all of the specialized and regional hierarchies.

3.5 Archives and Backups

In many organizations, certain news articles are worth saving for future reference. Internal newsgroups are an obvious example. Usenet newsgroups that are professionally relevant in some way might be another. When sheer volume makes it impossible to keep the articles online forever, you have to do something else about archiving them or backing them up.

In general, you need to be selective about archives and backups. There was a time when some news hosts saved everything on tape, but that was long ago—the tape racks started to fill up too quickly. While it's not impossible to save everything, given high-capacity tape drives and plenty of tapes, it just isn't worth it. Saving only those articles that you're likely to want is much easier.

There are several ways of archiving. The simplest, and perhaps the best, is to have an extra outgoing news feed that feeds the news to an archiving program instead of to a neighboring host. This method archives the news promptly, lets you be reasonably selective, and can typically be done without requiring extra disk space.

Alternately, some expiry programs can be told to copy articles in certain news-groups to an archiving area instead of just deleting them. This technique requires a separate archiving area, which gets copied to tape when it fills up (or, preferably, before then).

Either way, it's possible to automate the housekeeping for archiving to the point where all you need to do is mount a tape occasionally. (People with robotic tape libraries or optical-disk jukeboxes don't even need to do that.)

In any case, if you're doing archiving, you should occasionally take a look at what's being archived, how bulky it is, and how often you actually need it. In these days of widespread Internet access and numerous archive sites, keeping your own archives is less important than it once was.

Of course, if the filesystem where your article tree resides gets backed up as part of your normal system backups, you don't need to worry about separate archiving schemes. However, backing up the article tree is a dreadful waste of tape. You may want to back up specific parts of the article tree, such as those containing internal newsgroups, but few hosts consider general Usenet news important enough to be worth backing up. If the news gets lost in a crash, there'll be a fresh lot along in a few days anyway.

3.6 Unwanted Newsgroups

The day may come when your system is receiving a newsgroup that you don't want, or that you want to restrict access to. There are limits on what can be done about unwanted groups, but let's take a quick look at what is possible.

If you don't want to get the newsgroup at all, you have several options. Obvi-ously, you can ask your feed site to stop sending it to you. If that isn't practical (or just isn't quick enough), you can arrange for the newsgroup to be discarded on arrival, at the cost of the resources necessary to get it to you.

If you're running C News, you can alter the ME line in the *sys* file (see Section 5.1.2.1) to exclude the newsgroup from your subscription list, which causes it to be discarded on arrival. The advantage of this method is that you can block whole sub-hierarchies (e.g., all the *alt.binaries.** newsgroups) with a single change; the disadvantage is that it can get a bit clumsy if you want to block a bunch of unrelated individual newsgroups.

The other way to cause a newsgroup to be discarded on arrival is to set its control flag in the *active* file to **x**. Here's how:

```
% cnewsdo newsflag newsgroup x                   # C News
% ctlinnd changegroup newsgroup x                # INN
```

This method has the same effect as altering the *sys* file, although it has to be done separately for each newsgroup. (Also, if there's any possibility that you might want to reinstate the newsgroup, you have to keep track of whether it's moderated or not, so you can set the flag back to the right value, **m** or **y**.)

If you're willing to get the newsgroup but don't want to pass it on to other sites that you feed, you have to alter your *sys* file for C News (see Section 5.1.3) or *newsfeeds* file for INN (see Section 8.2.2.1) to specify that the newsgroup should not be sent to the other sites.

If you're willing to get the newsgroup and pass it on to other sites, but don't want your own users reading it, that gets tricky. It's not possible to pass the group on to other sites without having it present, at least briefly, on your own system. If your users read news via local (non-NNTP) newsreaders, you can set the permissions on that part of the article tree to exclude everybody but the news owner. If you've got newsreaders that use NNTP, you'll have to dig into the configuration details of the NNTP daemon software, which may have ways of restricting what people can read. (The reader daemon usually runs as the news owner, which makes permission changes unhelpful.)

3.7 Security Considerations

Netnews does not generally pose any major security threats, except for one notable case. The software itself may need careful configuration, but the opportunities for exploiting it to cause damage are limited. The security problems with news arise mostly from the software performing its legitimate function.

3.7.1 Vulnerabilities via Mail

The only major security problem ever found in news was the result of some systems using the UCB *Mail* program, intended as a mail-user interface for humans, in an unintended role. Originally, the *mail* program (note, no capital M) was a separate and much simpler program. Programs that wanted to send mail generally invoked *mail*; in particular, both C News and INN invoke *mail* to send mail in response to control messages. As a result of licensing issues, many modern systems have simply replaced the old *mail* program with *Mail*. That created two security holes in news systems because two features of *Mail*, meant for interactive use, remain active even when *Mail* is invoked non-interactively.

First, *Mail* provides some command escapes, like the reading-in of arbitrary files, triggered by starting an input line with a tilde (~). Second, and even worse, *Mail* can be made to execute arbitrary commands on the system if you can get a string surrounded by backquotes (`) passed to it as a destination address. News systems can be steered into encountering either of these bugs by sending them suitably crafted control messages. The improper actions are done with the permissions of the news owner, who fortunately is not *root* on most systems, but that still presents many opportunities for mischief.

INN versions prior to 1.7 and copies of the C News Cleanup Release not including patch CR.K are vulnerable to one or both of these problems. If you have a vulnerable version, you should upgrade at once.

INN prior to version 1.5.1 also had a vulnerability in its control message handling: it inadequately guarded against shell metacharacters in an *eval* command. This again resulted in the possibility that a control message could cause arbitrary commands to be executed (as the news owner) on your system.

3.7.2 Attacks from Outside

Aside from the above, there is not a lot that an outsider can do, via news, in an attempt to sabotage your internal operations. Obviously, she can try to overwhelm your system with sheer news volume, but Usenet does that anyway. She could try sending extremely large news articles (see the discussion of "lumps" in Section 3.1.3) in hopes of causing something to break, but good news software won't fail due to this type of attack.

3.7.3 Leakage

The Usenet newsgroups are not a security issue, except insofar as their tendency to overflow disk drives might be considered a denial-of-service attack. More serious problems can arise when the same technology is used for newsgroups internal to your organization. It's relatively natural to use such newsgroups for work functions, such as coordinating activities in large groups of people. News is more efficient than a mailing list for this purpose. However, if anything discussed on such newsgroups is confidential, you suddenly need to pay attention to where those newsgroups do and don't go. The "flooding" algorithm used to transmit news (see Chapter 19, *Flow and Processing of Traffic*) is extremely good at finding any path by which articles can leak out of a supposedly closed network.

If you do plan to use Netnews for such purposes, you need some central news administration to supervise news propagation. If there is also Usenet news traffic involved, you should have one or more official gatekeeper hosts to forward news in and out of the organization, as discussed in Section 2.6. The alternative to official connections is unofficial ones, and it is much easier to run security audits when you know where the gatekeepers are and who operates them. An organized approach to Netnews can also have other benefits, such as having a central authority that can rearrange news flow paths to minimize load on communications links.

A different form of leakage occurs when knowledgeable insiders misunderstand how far a news article will travel and inadvertently post confidential material to newsgroups that go outside the organization. The only real solution to this problem is user education, but some administrative restrictions might help. In particular, it may be useful to have your news software forbid crossposting a single article to both internal and external newsgroups.

Such a limit on crossposting, if enforced by your gatekeepers, can also help in another area. It's quite possible for an outsider to post an article to both a Usenet newsgroup and one of your internal newsgroups, if he knows the name of the internal newsgroup. While this in itself isn't harmful—apart from potential nuisance value and confusion—it could mislead your own users into posting followup articles that also go to both newsgroups.

There is one other potential information leak that you should plug. Both the NNTP protocol, and the old *ihave/sendme* control-message protocol (see Section 18.4), allow an outsider to ask for any article by its message ID. This capability is not as useful as it once was because message IDs these days are not very predictable, but if you have confidential material in some newsgroups, precautions should be taken. Your news software probably should have *ihave/sendme* disabled entirely, since such control messages can be piggybacked on legitimate news articles.

A firewall can prevent NNTP connections to your internal hosts, but gatekeeper hosts may legitimately need to talk NNTP to outsiders. Such gatekeepers should be very careful about who they talk to. A gatekeeper can be configured to reject requests by message ID using the NNTP *ARTICLE* command and some related commands. You may also decide that your gatekeeper should not carry confidential newsgroups at all. It may be tempting to make a gatekeeper host double as your main internal news server, but that's not necessarily wise. For more information about NNTP and firewalls, see *Building Internet Firewalls*, by D. Brent Chapman and Elizabeth D. Zwicky, from O'Reilly & Associates.

3.7.4 Letterbombs and the Like

Newsreader software needs to be a bit careful about what comes in the news. In particular, it's a mistake for a newsreader program to just pump an article's text out to the user's screen, since many terminals and terminal emulators support special magic "escape sequences" that can have harmful effects. Modern newsreader software generally is fairly careful in this area.

You need to educate your users about dealing with things that come in the news. Obviously, programs can contain "Trojan horse" attacks. This is a serious issue even for programs posted in source form, and the problem is truly acute when binaries are involved. Such problems are no different from the classic computer-virus problems of passing floppy disks around, but users may not be familiar with them in this context.

Subtle forms of such problems appear when email software, or the hardware it uses, tries to be clever about interpreting the contents of articles. For example, a PostScript document is a program, and it can cause damage to a carelessly configured printer.*

3.8 Getting Help

If you just cannot sort out some problem with Netnews, where do you turn? There are a variety of resources available, but the general rule is: start local and work up.

First and foremost, read the documentation that came with your software. Often it's not very well written, but it usually does contain a lot of answers. This book should also be of help.

Remember that you are part of a network. When you've got a problem, the first people to ask are your news neighbors, and especially the administrators at your news feed. They may have seen the problem before; it may even be partly their problem. They've probably gone through much the same experiences you have, and quite possibly not that long ago. On the other hand, they may be busy people, and they don't necessarily have an obligation to help you sort out your own problems. If you do decide to talk to them, and you're a relatively inexperienced news administrator, Section 12.3 offers some hints on how to do this effectively.

Local user groups offer the next possible source of help. When people have common problems, getting together to talk about them and help each other solve them is fairly natural. Get acquainted with any local groups in your area. Networking is all the rage nowadays; many people are grappling with the same problems you

---

* An amazing number of computer installations are very careful about making their users choose nonobvious passwords, but leave the passwords in their PostScript printers set to the default "0".

have and maybe together you can sort them out. If there's no suitable local group, you might even consider starting one.

If you're really getting desperate, there is always the possibility of paying someone to help. You need to develop some in-house expertise to keep things running, but if you've got problems that should need solving only once (possibly including training your in-house people), hiring a consultant to sort them out could be a reasonable thing to do. It's going to cost more than doing it yourself. However, the work will probably be finished sooner, and with fewer lurking boobytraps to surprise you later. You have to decide what you can spare more: money or effort. Finding a good consultant can be a little tricky; the best advice we can give is to ask around locally.

If your news system is more or less working, or if you have access to a working news system on another host (perhaps the one that is going to feed you news), one way to get help is to use news itself. There are several newsgroups devoted to news software, and most major news-software authors read them at least intermittently. The three that are probably most relevant are:

news.software.b
> News transmission software in general and C News in particular. (The name of the newsgroup is a historical accident, dating to the days when B News was operational.)

news.software.nntp
> NNTP software in general and INN in particular.

news.software.readers
> Newsreader software and user interfaces for news in general.

It's best to read a newsgroup for a little while before posting questions to it, unless you've got a major emergency. In particular, you should always seek out and read the newsgroup's Frequently Asked Questions (FAQ) list before posting a query, because the FAQ list covers many common new-user problems. Newsgroup readers tend to be heartily sick of being asked the same old questions by people who can't bother to do their own reading first. You'll likely get more help, more rapidly, if it's clear that you have made an effort.

The FAQ lists for these newsgroups, as well as most other mainstream Usenet groups, are stored in various archives around the Internet. One such archive is at *ftp://rtfm.mit.edu/pub/usenet/*. As a general rule, FAQ lists for all mainstream groups are posted to the group *news.answers*, which means that if you search through *ftp://rtfm.mit.edu/pub/usenet/news.answers/index*, you should be able to find the location of just about any newsgroup's FAQ. When we talk about FAQ lists and other periodic postings related to news in this book, we'll try to point you to the archived file for the posting.

Finally, in a pinch you can always send email to the author(s) of the software. Do bear in mind that these people typically do not get paid to maintain news software or to help new users. Asking them should be a last resort, not the first thing you think of. Remember also that they're busy people and can't always answer their mail right away. If you've got a real emergency on your hands, it's better to seek local help.

Why is posting to a worldwide newsgroup read by thousands of people preferable to sending email to a smaller group or individual? Because you're more likely to reach other people who have experienced the same problem; they may either have an answer or be able to help you debug the problem. Also, asking a question in a newsgroup helps keep some of the load off the handful of people who actually do the work to keep the software going. Asking them only as a last resort is one way of showing your appreciation for all the free software they produce.

4

Installing C News

In this chapter:
- *The C News and NNTP Distributions*
- *Preparing to Build C News: quiz*
- *Building C News*
- *Checking C News*
- *Installing C News*
- *Preparing to Build the NNTP Reference Implementation*
- *Building the NNTP Reference Implementation*
- *Installing the NNTP Reference Implementation*

This chapter discusses how to get C News, build it, and install it. (For similar information on INN, see Chapter 7, *Installing INN.*) A discussion of the setup and configuration of C News is deferred to Chapter 5, *Configuring C News*, and testing, troubleshooting, and operations are covered in Chapter 6, *Running C News.*

This chapter assumes that you have read Chapter 2, *Getting Ready*, which discusses decisions you have to make before setting up your news software. The material from that chapter is not repeated here.

In this chapter, we'll look first at getting the software you need. Then we'll cover configuring, building, checking, and installing C News itself. Finally, we'll discuss configuring, building, and installing the NNTP Reference Implementation, if you need it.

4.1 The C News and NNTP Distributions

C News is available from most major FTP archive servers, such as *ftp.uu.net*. The current "home base" FTP site for C News is *ftp.zoo.toronto.edu*, where it is available for anonymous FTP in *pub/cnews.tar.Z*. You can also gain access to C News from its previous home base, *ftp.cs.toronto.edu*, as *pub/c-news/c-news.tar.Z*. Please avoid using either of these servers between 8:00 A.M. and 6:00 P.M. Eastern time (zone −0500).

There have been various releases of C News in the past, all of which were made obsolete by the Cleanup Release, which is what this book discusses. The Cleanup Release itself is updated by patches from time to time; the patches are designated CR.A, CR.B, etc. This book corresponds to the Cleanup Release with all patches up to and including CR.L. The home base sites always have the current version; the major archive servers sometimes lag behind. The patches themselves appear in the newsgroup *news.software.b*. These days, it's better to fetch the current version than to try to apply the patches.

The C News distribution is about 700 Kbytes as a compressed *tar* archive, and perhaps triple that, say 2 megabytes, when uncompressed and split into individual files. You'll need another 2 megabytes or more, depending on your system, to compile everything. The installed copy of the software uses perhaps 1.5 megabytes, again depending on your system.

To unpack the distribution, make a directory, which we'll call the *source area*, and change to that directory. We recommend that you put your copy of the distribution in the source area. If the distribution file is called *cnews.tar.Z*, you can unpack it as follows:

```
% uncompress cnews.tar
% tar xf cnews.tar
```

To see the list of files as they're unpacked, use **-xvf** instead of **-xf**. Since there are over 700 files, you probably won't find the listing to be very informative.

Now you have a whole bunch of files spread out in a number of subdirectories. There is one subdirectory for each major subsystem of C News, plus several for shared utilities and support tools. The *README.roadmap* file contains a brief guide to the structure of the subdirectories, if you need to know the details.

At present, if you want NNTP support in C News, you need to get a separate package to provide it. This package is sometimes called the NNTP Reference Implementation, and sometimes just NNTP: it was the first NNTP implementation. It too can be found on most major archive sites. Its home base site is currently *ftp.academ.com*. In the *pub/nntp/server* directory, you'll find the distribution in a file with a name like *nntp.1.5.12.2.tar.Z*. (If there is more than one such file, get the one with the highest number; version 1.5.12.2 is current as of late 1997.) The distribution is about 200 Kbytes compressed, and depending on your system you'll need another megabyte or so to compile the package. The installed copy of the software uses around 400 Kbytes, again depending on your system.

We suggest putting the NNTP Reference Implementation, which we'll henceforth refer to as the NRI, in an *nntp* subdirectory of your C News source area. Make that subdirectory, put your copy of the distribution in it, and unpack it as follows:

```
% uncompress nntp.1.5.12.2.tar
% tar xf nntp.1.5.12.2.tar
```

If you want to see the list of files as they're unpacked, use −xvf instead of −xf.

Again, unpacking the distribution gives you a whole bunch of files spread out in a number of subdirectories. The *README* file gives a brief description of the layout, if you need to know the details.

4.2 Preparing to Build C News: quiz

C News ships with a program that takes care of most of the pre-build configuration work for the software. The program used to be called *build*, but that was confusing because it didn't actually build the software. The modern incarnation is *quiz*, and it's located in the top-level directory of the source area. The first step in building C News is running *quiz* and answering its questions. Most of the questions are accompanied by brief explanations, to save you from having to refer constantly to C News documentation. You'll need your system manuals handy, though, and also pencil and paper to make some notes.

Almost every question in *quiz* has a default answer, which is the answer that is used if you just press RETURN in response to the question. The default answer to a question is shown in brackets ([]) after the question. For example:

```
How are you [fine] ?
```

If you just press RETURN at this point, the answer to the question "How are you?" is taken to be "fine." Don't assume that these default answers are always right for your system, however.

If you answer a *quiz* question with a line starting with an exclamation point (!), the rest of your answer is run as a shell command and the question is asked again. (There is one exception, as described in the next paragraph.) This feature lets you consult online documentation, even if you don't have multiple windows or job control.

If you have already run *quiz* in this particular source area, the program first asks you if you want to use the answers from last time as default answers. Also, if you answer any question with ! − this means "use the default answers for all remaining questions." These features are convenient if you only want to change one or two answers.

When *quiz* asks a yes-or-no question, you can reply with "y" or "n." The responses are taken as "yes" or "no," respectively.

4.2.1 Questions and Answers with quiz

We should caution you about one thing at this point: the details discussed in this section are for the version of *quiz* that comes with the Cleanup Release and are current as of late 1997. Things may change between the time this book is being written and the time you read it. They probably won't change much, but don't be surprised if an extra question appears, or the order or wording of the questions isn't quite as described here. Just do your best to understand and answer the questions; this section is intended as a general guide rather than an exact description.

After a brief introductory explanation, the first real information *quiz* asks for is the user name of the news owner:

```
C News wants to keep most of its files under a uid which preferably
should be all its own.  Its programs, however, can and probably should
be owned by another user, typically the same one who owns most of the
rest of the system.  (Note that on a system running NFS, any system
program not owned by "root" is a gaping security hole.)
What user should own news files [news]?
```

The default answer is usually correct here, since most news hosts have a user name *news* intended specifically for the news owner. Now *quiz* asks about the group name:

```
What group should own news files [news]?
```

Typically, the *news* user is put in its own group, also called *news*.

Next, *quiz* asks you to decide where to put the various components of the news system. First, it explains briefly:

```
You have to decide the locations, in the file system, of four major
parts of C News:  the article tree, the overview files (which may be
in the article tree, or may be elsewhere), the control files, and the
programs.  These locations are known, within much of the software, by
the names of the environment variables used to hold them.  There are
some traditional choices, not always the most reasonable in retrospect,
that some newsreader software may depend on.

purpose         variable    traditional location    reasonable location
-------         --------    --------------------    --------------------
article tree    NEWSARTS    /usr/spool/news         /news
overview files  NEWSOV      /usr/spool/news         /news/over.view
control files   NEWSCTL     /usr/lib/news           /var/news
programs        NEWSBIN     /usr/lib/newsbin        /usr/libexec/news
```

The "reasonable" locations listed above are those that fit best with the theory discussed in Section 2.7. There's no reason why you have to use those locations, however. You can put the various parts in other locations just by telling *quiz* your chosen locations. If you want different locations, but for some reason don't want to change the software's ideas of where things are, you can use *quiz*'s defaults and then make symbolic links from these locations to the real ones. This reduces performance slightly but does not otherwise bother C News.

Speaking of symbolic links, you may want to make symbolic links from the traditional locations to the real ones. This can make life a bit easier if you're dealing with old or badly written newsreader software that depends on the files being in the traditional locations.

quiz then asks about each location, with the reasonable locations as default answers:

```
Where should the article tree go [/news]?
Where should overview files go [/news/over.view]?
Where should control files go [/var/news]?
Where should programs go [/usr/libexec/news]?
```

Now *quiz* wants to know about the search path needed to find the usual Unix utility programs on your system. The appropriate answer can be relatively difficult to determine, since it's often not well documented, but looking at your own PATH environment variable might be helpful:

```
% echo "$PATH"
```

Typically, your path includes */bin* and */usr/bin*, and some directories of your own, but it might also include system directories like */usr/ucb* or */usr/contrib/bin*. Note that *quiz* is asking about the search path for the purpose of running the C News programs; getting the search path set up appropriately for compiling the software is a different issue and remains your problem.

If you've run *quiz* before in this source area, it asks if the search path from last time is still correct. If you answer "no," or if this is the first time you've run *quiz* here, the program starts from scratch, beginning with an explanation:

```
C News by default assumes that all normal Unix programs can be
found in /bin or /usr/bin.  Modern systems mostly have messed
this up, sometimes pretty badly, and other directories like
/usr/ucb or /usr/contrib/bin often must be searched to find
programs which one would think would be standard.
```

quiz then asks whether you want to add another directory to the search:

```
Is there any other directory which should be searched
to find standard programs on your system [no]?
```

If you answer "no," *quiz* goes on to the next issue: the *umask* (see below). If you answer "yes," however, *quiz* asks you to specify the directory:

```
What is the full name of the directory [/urk]?
```

There is no sensible default for this question; */urk* is just a meaningless placeholder. Once you type in a directory name (such as */usr/ucb*), *quiz* asks:

```
Should it go after (as opposed to before) the others [yes]?
```

A "yes" answer puts the directory at the end of the search path; a "no" answer puts it at the beginning. You should put directories at the end of the search path, unless you have a specific reason to do otherwise. Finally, *quiz* goes back and asks the "Is there any other directory . . . " question again, so you can add as many directories as you need.

After you finish adding directories and answer that question "no," *quiz* asks about the *umask*, which determines the permissions on newly created files:

```
C News normally uses a umask of 022, turning off only the others-write
and group-write bits in the permissions of files used.  (The
correspondence between bits and number is:  rwx = 421, so turning off
group-write bits and all others-access bits would be a mask of 027, for
example.)  Usually a umask of 002 or 022 is appropriate.
What umask should C News use [022]?
```

The *umask* specifies the permissions bits that are turned off when a new file is created. The value for *umask* contains three digits that correspond to the three sets of **rwx** permissions bits shown by *ls*: owner, group, and other permissions. The value for each digit is the sum of the numeric codes for the permissions (4 for **r**, 2 for **w**, and 1 for **x**) that should be turned off in that set. 022 is usually the best choice, as it turns the group and other write bits off, so that only the news owner can change news files and directories, but anyone else can use them. 002 is also reasonable to allow people in the *news* group to modify files. Note again that *quiz* is asking about the *umask* for the purpose of running the C News programs; getting the *umask* set up appropriately for compiling and installing the software is a different issue and remains your problem.

The shell files used by C News need to pick up their configuration information from a central configuration file. Normally this file is located in the *bin* subdirectory of the control area, but it is vaguely conceivable that you might want to move it, so *quiz* asks:

```
The shell files that are everywhere in C News want to pick up their
configuration parameters (mostly, the last few questions you have
answered) from a file at a known location; this is very hard to avoid
unless you play tricks with environment variables (see documentation).
What should the full pathname of the shell configuration file
be [/var/news/bin/config]?
```

The default answer *quiz* gives here is actually in *your* control area, as determined by your earlier answers. If you did indeed put the control area in */var/news*, *quiz* suggests the default answer shown above. Use the default answer for this question unless you really know what you're doing. Note that *quiz* is asking for the actual name of the file, not for the name of a directory to put it in.

Now *quiz* asks where it should report problems:

```
C News wants to mail some kinds of trouble and status reports. These are
divided into urgent reports (something went badly wrong) and non-urgent
reports (routine status info).  The mailing addresses for these should
probably be system mailboxes, rather than those of specific people, so
you won't have to change the software when you get a new administrator.
Where should C News mail urgent reports [newscrisis]?
Where should C News mail non-urgent reports [newsmaster]?
```

You can use whatever names you like for the two reporting addresses, but we suggest using the default answers if you don't have any specific reason to do otherwise. The non-urgent address can just be a mailbox that gets looked at from time to time. The urgent address, however, should be an alias that delivers the mail immediately to your system administrator(s), so that an urgent problem will be brought to their attention at once.

C News got started on 16-bit machines. The software has generally outgrown them now, but it still makes a stab at minimizing its memory use if you ask it to:

```
C News has libraries for "small" address spaces (16 bits) and "big"
ones (preferably 32 bits, but anything rather bigger than 16).
Which best describes your system [big]?
```

On almost any modern system, you should use the default answer: "big." Using "small" only reduces memory usage a little bit, but it slows things down significantly.

Now we get to one of the more tedious parts of *quiz*: determining what useful system calls and subroutines are missing on your system. Here's where you'll need your manuals. *quiz* starts out with a brief explanation:

```
Systems vary in whether certain library functions and system calls
are present.  C News contains reasonably portable versions of the
possibly missing library functions, and fake versions of the
possibly missing system calls, but it needs to know which are missing.
```

Then it asks, one by one, about a long list of things (although the list isn't as long as it used to be):

```
Does your system have    fcntl() [yes]?
Does your system have    fgetline() [no]?
Does your system have    getopt() [yes]?
Does your system have    gettimeofday() [yes]?
Does your system have    memcpy() [yes]?
Does your system have    mkdir() [yes]?
Does your system have    putenv() [yes]?
Does your system have    remove() [yes]?
Does your system have    rename() [yes]?
Does your system have    strchr() [yes]?
Does your system have    strerror() [yes]?
Does your system have    strspn() [yes]?
```

```
Does your system have    symlink() [yes]?
```

For most modern systems, you can answer "yes" to all of these, except for the one about `fgetline()`.*

There are a few more such questions that require more detailed explanations. For example, C News contains a fake `fsync()` routine that basically does nothing. The fake routine is considerably faster than the real `fsync()`, and just about as good, *if* you're running the news processing software (e.g., relayer, expiry program) on the host where the files reside. So *quiz* now asks, essentially, whether it is safe to use the fake `fsync()`:

```
We strongly, repeat STRONGLY, recommend that all news processing
(as opposed to reading) be done on the machine that has the disks.
NFS's imitation of the Unix filesystem semantics is too sloppy for
reliable processing.  Keeping processing local also speeds it up,
and permits C News to take some shortcuts.
Will processing be done over NFS [no]?
```

If you answer "no," the fake `fsync()` is used. That's the right answer if there isn't going to be a network between the relayer's host and the files.

C News uses an indexing package to maintain an index into its *history* file. Originally, this was the old *dbm* package found in Unix Version 7 (which appeared in 1979). These days, the *dbz* package, which is specialized for news and runs much faster, with much smaller files, is normally used instead of *dbm*. All of the pieces of the software that use the news database have to be compiled with the same package, as they are generally not file-compatible. At this point in *quiz*, C News used to ask what indexing package to use. Since *dbz* is the only sensible answer nowadays, *quiz* no longer asks about the indexing package.†

quiz continues on to some other library issues. In particular, some of the standard I/O routines in old Unix libraries were pretty inefficient, and substituting special speeded-up versions improved C News performance quite a bit. These substitutions were somewhat tricky, however, because the new routines had to fit in with a lot of undocumented details of the other I/O routines. So use of the substitute routines was made optional. After all, C News still worked with the system-supplied ones. These days, the system-supplied routines on modern systems are typically quite fast, and the undocumented details have changed enough that the substitute routines often don't work. For the benefit of old systems, though, C News still provides the option:

---

* The `fgetline()` routine was found in an early release of BSD 4.4, but not in the final release, and there are some name-conflict problems that need to be sorted out before C News can use the routine that replaced it.

† *dbz* is much better for this job than any general-purpose indexing package.

```
Some old systems have implementations of the Standard I/O library _
("stdio") in which fgets, fputs, fread, and fwrite are quite slow.  We
supply versions of these functions which are faster; they are compatible
with most old AT&T-derived stdios.  (They tend not to work on modern
systems, but modern stdio implementations are usually respectably fast.)
They can be a major performance win for C News.  There is a fairly
thorough compatibility check run before a commitment is made to use our
speedups; as far as we know, if the test works, the functions do.
Do you want to use our stdio speedups [no]?
```

It is always safe to answer "no" to this question, and if you run into difficulties in getting C News working, that's the first thing to do. If you do answer "yes," C News tries to determine whether the substitute routines actually work before using them, so all a "yes" answer really means here is "give it a try." In any case, you should probably answer "no" unless your system is more than five years old.

If you told *quiz* that your system has a `strchr()` function (which almost all systems now do), *quiz* asks about a fine point:

```
The strchr() function is usually slower than in-line C code
when small strings are involved, unless your compiler is very
clever and can generate in-line code for strchr().  Is your
compiler that good (okay to guess) [no]?
```

The only difference your answer makes here is in terms of efficiency, hence the "okay to guess" comment. Relatively few compilers are smart enough to generate in-line code for `strchr()`, although the number is growing.* If you're not sure, "no" is probably the best answer.

Header files are used by C programs to get the calling details for libraries. There are a few headers that C News has to be prepared to supply if your system does not, so *quiz* asks:

```
Some systems have header files that others lack, and C News
is prepared to fake missing ones.
Does your system have an ANSI-C-conforming <string.h> [yes]?
Does your system have an ANSI-C-conforming <stdlib.h> [yes]?
Does your system have an ANSI-C-conforming <stddef.h> [yes]?
```

Any system with an ANSI C (or ISO C) compiler has these header files. The first of these header files requires particular care, however, because the *string.h* header file exists on a number of old systems in an incomplete form. Header files are usually found in */usr/include*. If *string.h* does not include declarations for some functions with names that start with "mem", it is *not* ANSI-C-conforming. The other two header files have less historical confusion behind them, and if they are there on your system at all, they're probably ANSI-C-conforming.

---

* As of mid-1997, *gcc* does not seem to be smart enough, except perhaps with machine-specific help.

One of the first parts of C News to get built is the C News library, *libcnews.a. quiz*
addresses a fine point of building libraries:

```
Very old Unix systems needed the order of object modules in a library
chosen very carefully.  V7 introduced "ranlib" which removes the need
for this.  Many modern systems have the same facility built into "ar"
(look for the "symdef" or "symbol table" feature in the "ar" manual
page) so ranlib is not needed.  (Caution:  some SCO systems reportedly
have a ranlib, but use it only for cross-compiling, not for native
programs.) C News can cope with either (if you have neither, you're in
trouble).
Does your system use ranlib [no]?
```

Look at the manual page for your *ar* to answer this one.

The *make* program is next on the agenda. First, there are sometimes different versions of *make* around:

```
Usually "make" is named just "make", but sometimes there is more than
one version on a system.
What is the name of the make to be used [make]?
```

If you tell *quiz* to use something else, it may comment that one or two other
things need changing to match the program you are using. In general, C News
does not depend on unusual features of *make*, so you shouldn't need to use a
non-standard *make*.

However, the Cleanup Release's configuration system does need to use a feature
that is not completely standardized among implementations of *make*:

```
C News relies heavily on being able to put an "include" command in
a makefile, so that the contents of another file are automatically
inserted there when make runs.  The syntax for this varies.  The
possibilities for including a file named "../include/config.make" are:

svr4)   include ../include/config.make
bsd)    .include "../include/config.make"
other)  something else
noway)  make has no such feature

Sun systems use the svr4 syntax, as does GNU make.
Which one is appropriate [bsd]?
```

You'll have to read your *make* manual page carefully to sort this one out. If you
answer "other" or "noway," *quiz* comments on what you're going to have to do to
cope.

In the "other" case, you'll have to fix the file *conf/makeinc* after you're finished
running *quiz*, to tell C News how to do the inclusion. The file looks like this:

```
# makefile substitutions file
# how to include ../include/config.make
INCLUDE          include ../include/config.make
```

The last line contains the magic word `INCLUDE`, followed by a tab or two and the incantation that gets *make* to do the inclusion. As you can see, *quiz* gives you the "svr4" incantation as a starting point. Just change it appropriately.

In the "noway" case, *quiz* points you to the file *conf/maker*, which you can run as if it were *make*. When you do, it copies the *makefile* into a temporary file, edits the temporary file to do the inclusion, and then feeds the result to *make*. With any luck, this should do the job.

The next thing *quiz* asks about is the C compiler:

```
Historically the C compiler is named "cc", but this is not true on
some systems, and on others there are several different C compilers.
"Make" usually has a default C compiler, but you may want another.
Do you want to use a compiler other than make's default [no]?
```

In most cases, you should say "no," since C News does not need any special compiler features. If you say "yes," *quiz* asks for the name of the C compiler. Typically this is just something like "gcc"; you don't need to give a full pathname.

The options to C compilers are semi-standard, and normally –O, which requests a reasonable amount of optimization, is the only one needed (apart from some that C News supplies automatically). In case something else is required by an odd compiler, *quiz* asks:

```
Historically the only normal compilation option needed for most
programs is -O, but again compilers, especially newer ones, differ.
(NOTE:  some 386/486 compilers miscompile dbz if -O is used!)
What options should be given to the compiler [-O]?
```

The troublesome 386/486 compilers include those supplied by some major software companies, but not the GNU C compiler (*gcc*). Many systems now use *gcc* as their main C compiler, and in fact *cc* often invokes *gcc*, but the only way to be sure of this is to check your system documentation.

C News may also need to use special options when linking the various parts of a program together; this is typically done using the C compiler:

```
The final linking ("ld") step of compiling might need an option,
such as -n or -i, to produce the preferred form of executable file.
On most modern systems the default is right.  What options, if any,
should be given for linking []?
```

Nothing at all is usually the right answer here.

Finally, it's possible that system-specific libraries may be needed:

```
On unusual systems it may be necessary to link C News programs with
libraries other than the usual C library.  These can be specified as
either full pathnames or -l... options.  What libraries, in addition
to the one(s) picked up automatically by the compiler, should be used
when linking C News []?
```

Again, nothing at all is usually the right answer.

At this point, *quiz* addresses some miscellaneous configuration issues. First of all:

```
C News tries to limit the backlog of news batches spooled up for
transmission to a site, to control use of disk space.  To do this,
it needs to be able to determine the length of the queue of news
batches for a particular site.  This is UUCP-version-dependent.
There is a good chance that you will have to customize the "queuelen"
program.  C News knows about several versions:
     svr4     System V Release 4 uucp
     hdb      Honey DanBer, aka Basic Networking Utilities
     tay      Taylor UUCP, native mode
     sub      old uucp with subdirectories (e.g. /usr/spool/uucp/C.)
     vo       very old uucp, no subdirectories
     pre      prehistoric uucp, no subdirectories, no -g option on uux
     null     don't run uucp or don't care about queue lengths
Which one is most appropriate [hdb]?
```

Answering this question can be a little tricky, partly because there are a lot of new variations that are not covered in the list, and partly because it's hard to tell exactly which version you've got. "hdb" is the best bet except on SVR4-based systems, but it may not be quite right. If you're feeling unsure, or if you don't plan to have outbound feeds using UUCP, just answer "null" and worry about it later.

Here's another tricky one:

```
C News often wants to ask how much disk space is available.  The
format of output from the "df" command unfortunately varies a lot,
as does the availability of a system call to get the same information.
C News knows about several different versions (the first four are
preferred):
     statfs   system with standard statfs() (4.4BSD, some System Vs)
     ultrix   DEC Ultrix with DEC's own bizarre statfs()
     statvfs  system with statvfs() (many modern System Vs)
     ustat    system with ustat() (most System Vs)
     bsd      4.2/4.3BSD
     sysv     old System Vs
     xenix    some (all?) Xenixes; some System Vs, e.g. Microport, HP?
     sgi      Silicon Graphics Iris systems
     v7       plain old style:  no headers or fluff, just name and number
     null     don't know or don't care how much space is available
Which one is most appropriate [statfs]?
```

The first four answers allow the use of C code to invoke the appropriate system call, which generally works better than trying to understand output from *df.* Most modern systems fit one of these four choices. If you've got System V with both *statvfs* and *ustat*, *statvfs* is better. Again, you can always resort to answering "null" and worrying about it later, but you do want to answer this question eventually. News will fill your disks at some point, and it's much more pleasant to have the news system complain about it beforehand than to have it run the disk out of space.

In some cases, *quiz* warns you of potential problems with choices that are known to be troublesome. If you didn't specify one of the first four answers, and you didn't specify "null," *quiz* then asks:

```
Some "df" commands, especially on old systems, must be given
the name of a device.  Modern ones can be given any directory
name and the system handles the details of figuring out what
device is meant.  A few will take a directory only if it is
the "top" of a filesystem.  Will "df" accept any directory
name as an argument [yes]?
```

If your answer is "no," *quiz* tells you that you'll have to do some tinkering.

Next come a couple of queries related to disk space:

```
Are you planning to use expire to archive news on disk [no]?
```

The answer to this question isn't very important. If you say "yes," *quiz* tells you that you probably want to tinker with the *spacefor* program to let it know where your archiving area is and how much free space you want left there. (This really should be handled by having *quiz* ask you about the details. Someday it will be done that way.) Next:

```
Are you particularly short of disk space [no]?
```

Again, the answer is not very important. Either way, *quiz* suggests that you check the *spacefor* program's disk-space margins to see if they suit you. The answer to the question only affects the wording of the suggestion.

Now *quiz* needs to know whether you're going to be running C News on one machine that is part of a cluster:

```
Are you running C News on a group of machines hooked together with NFS,
run essentially as a single system with a single administration,
with articles filed on one "server" machine [no]?
```

If you answer "yes," *quiz* then asks you to identify the server:

```
Does your system have a "hostname" command [yes]?
```

This command is pretty universal now on networked systems, but if you don't have it, *quiz* wants to warn you that you'll need to tinker manually. Assuming you do have it, the next question is the obvious one:

```
What is the "hostname" name of the server [newsie]?
```

The default here is pretty useless; it is just a placeholder. *quiz* needs to know the name of the host on which certain operations should be performed.

Now *quiz* needs to know where to put a few things. First, it asks about the *rnews* and *cunbatch* programs:

```
The "rnews" and "cunbatch" commands (which are identical, the latter
being purely for backward compatibility with seriously old systems)
have to be installed somewhere where uucp can find them to execute
them.  It is not normally necessary for users to be able to run
them, so they need not go in the directories searched for normal
commands... although uucp often searches only those directories.
Where should "rnews" and "cunbatch" be put [/usr/libexec/news/input]?
```

The answer to this question is not important if you're not using UUCP for news feeds. If you are, you need to consult your UUCP manual, and perhaps adjust your UUCP configuration so that it matches what you tell *quiz*. The default is the *input* subdirectory of your program area. This is a good place if you aren't using UUCP at all or if your UUCP configuration is flexible enough to specify the location of individual commands, rather than just directories of commands. You probably want to allow UUCP to run things other than the news commands—notably, the *rmail* command that handles incoming mail—so if your UUCP configuration can't specify the locations of individual commands, you should put *rnews* and *cunbatch* somewhere like */usr/bin* or */usr/local/bin* and point UUCP there.

Next *quiz* wants to know where to put some user-interface programs:

```
The inews command, and also readnews+postnews+checknews if you're
going to use them, should go in one of the directories searched for
normal commands, so users can run them without special arrangements.
What directory should these commands go in [/usr/bin]?
```

The appropriate answer depends on how you've organized your system and where you put locally added commands. */usr/bin* is a reasonable choice, but some system administrators avoid modifying that directory, and put locally added things in */usr/local/bin* (or some such place) instead. The main issue here is to put the commands in a directory that's in your normal user search path, so that users don't have to fiddle with their search path just to access news.

Finally, *quiz* is done asking questions. The program saves your answers, so it can use them as the defaults if you need to run *quiz* again. The answers are saved in *conf/quiz.def.* Don't try to hand-edit that file; the answers are somewhat interdependent, and *quiz* may become confused if you change one answer but not the related ones that are also affected.

Now *quiz* builds three configuration files:

```
conf/makeinc
conf/substitutions
include/config.make
```

These files encapsulate *quiz*'s knowledge for use by the rest of the software. *conf/makeinc* is used to adjust each *makefile* to match the "include" syntax of your local version of *make*. *conf/substitutions* is used to adjust a number of files, so that they know about various locations you have specified. In particular, every shell file needs to know where the central configuration file is. *include/config.make* is the header file that every *makefile* uses.

When *quiz* says "done," it's done. Congratulations on having survived the interrogation. Now you get to build the software.

4.3 Building C News

Before you can build C News, you need to have run *quiz* successfully. Then you need to deal with any pressing issues that *quiz* told you about. In particular, make any necessary changes to the top-level directory's *makefile*. To actually build C News, type the following in the top-level directory of the source area:

```
% make
```

(Or use the preferred *make* command for your system.) The *makefile* in the top-level directory just coordinates the build process by invoking *makefile*s in the various subdirectories to do most of the work.

You can direct the output of the *make* command to a file, if you want to be able to peruse it after the build is done. However, if you told *quiz* to try to use the C News *stdio* speedups, it is important that you run *make* with its output directed to a terminal, not to a file. Some of the *stdio* speedup tests depend on the output going to a terminal.

The top-level *makefile* performs the following tasks:

1. It uses the *subst* command (located in the *conf* directory) to modify the *makefiles* in all of the subdirectories so that they know how the "include" feature works for your *make* program. For each file it's told to work on, *subst* reports whether it updated the file or not. Don't worry about the details; *make* stops with an error message if anything actually goes wrong.

2. It uses *subst* again to alter many other files to point to the various locations you specified while running *quiz*. Most of the affected files are shell files that need to know where to find the central configuration file. Again, the output of *subst* is a bit tedious and quite uninteresting. *make* stops automatically if something actually goes wrong.

3. It makes some auxiliary programs (shell files) executable.

4. It sets up the list of subdirectories to be used to build the C News subroutine library. The contents of the list depend slightly on whether the system has a small or big address space and whether you asked for the *stdio* speedups. If you did ask for the *stdio* speedups, the *makefile* tries to determine whether those speedups actually work on your system. Precisely what sort of output is generated here is unimportant. The attempt to build and run the speedup test program may well fail, perhaps messily with a number of error messages. If this happens, don't get upset, as the *makefile* copes properly (and displays a "don't panic" message on your screen for a few seconds to reassure you).

5. It invokes the appropriate *makefile* to build the C News subroutine library. This may take a little while. Again, if anything significant goes wrong, *make* stops, so it's not necessary to watch the output carefully. If you ever need to rebuild this library, or need to restart a library build after dealing with problems, here's the preferred command:

```
% make freshlib
```

This command removes the old library and then rebuilds it from the pieces, to make sure that things that aren't supposed to be in there any more don't get left in by mistake.

6. Finally, it invokes a whole bunch of *makefile* in the various subdirectories to actually build the software. This does take a while.

If the process ends with an "everything built successfully" message, the software is ready. If it fails and stops somewhere along the way, you'll have to cope. It's hard to give specific instructions for that because there are so many possibilities. One common problem is that all of the pieces of a program compile properly, but the attempt to put them together into a final program fails with a message about "undefined symbols," "unresolved references," or something like that. This probably means you made a mistake when *quiz* was asking you about missing functions and system calls—specifically, you told *quiz* that your system has something that it doesn't have. If you examine the error message for the failure carefully, you may be able to figure out which function is the problem.

4.4 Checking C News

At this point, you've built the software but you haven't installed it. You may be wondering whether or not it's going to work. The good news is that, to some degree, you can check whether the software is going to work. C News has built-in regression tests that check out many, although not all, aspects of the software's operation before installation. Running these tests is officially optional, but strongly recommended.

To run the regression tests, type the following in the top-level directory of the source area:

```
% make r
```

This command runs the regression tests in all of the subdirectories, so it takes a while. Note that among other tests, it attempts to send a couple of email messages to you, to partly check out the trouble-reporting system. If the process ends with an "all tests successful" message, almost everything in C News works as it should. Any other sort of termination message indicates that something is wrong.

Again, it is difficult to give specific instructions for coping with a failure because there are so many possibilities. One thing that is frequently a problem on non-commercial systems is the shell (*/bin/sh*). C News uses shell scripts very extensively, and relies heavily on a correct implementation of the shell. The behavior of the standard shell turns out to be fairly complex, and certain details are poorly documented. As a result, many of the attempts to reimplement the shell have had serious difficulties. Recent versions of most of them are workable; older versions often are not. There is no good fix for this except to upgrade to a more modern version of the shell.

The one thing you should not do about a failure in the regression tests is to ignore it. Any failure in the regression tests means that something is seriously wrong.

4.5 Installing C News

Once upon a time, C News tried to generate shell scripts to do the entire installation itself. Nowadays, sadder but wiser, C News leaves a few tasks up to you because there is just too much diversity in how they are done. The *makefiles* still do most of the detail work, though. Here are the steps for installing C News:

1. The first installation step you get to do yourself. You have to create the *NEWSARTS, NEWSOV, NEWSBIN,* and *NEWSCTL* directories and set their ownerships correctly. *NEWSBIN* can be owned by most anyone; it's often convenient to have it owned by the same user who owns the source area, so programs can be modified without having to change ownership all the time.

The rest of the directories should be owned by the news owner. All of these directories should at least be writable by their owners. You don't have to make any subdirectories under them; the *makefiles* look after that. (They don't create the topmost directories because that often requires special powers, especially to set the ownerships correctly, and the details tend to be system-specific.)

2. As the *NEWSBIN* owner, with a suitable *umask* (such as 022 and 002), type:

    ```
    % make install
    ```

    This command installs all of the C News programs, creating subdirectories under *NEWSBIN* as necessary. The *NEWSBIN* owner does not need to have write permission in the source area to run this command. However, you do need to have write permission wherever you want *rnews* and *cunbatch* to go.

3. As the news owner, again with a suitable *umask* (e.g., 022 or 002), type:

    ```
    % make setup
    ```

    This command installs all of the control files (and related files) in *NEWSCTL*, and sets up the rudiments of the news database. This process is done fairly carefully; if there are already files there—for example, if you are upgrading an existing system rather than setting up a new one—they are not overwritten. (Actually there are one or two exceptions, where control files must match the software release, but the files are ones you shouldn't have to customize.) Again, the news owner does not need to have write permission in the source area to run this command.

4. Running as the owner of */usr/bin* (or wherever you've decided to put the user-interface commands) and once again minding the *umask* setting, type:

    ```
    % make ui
    ```

    This command installs the user-interface commands, notably *inews* and *cnewsdo*. The */usr/bin* owner does not need to have write permission in the source area to run this command.

5. Now you have to make a decision: do you want to install the C News versions of *readnews*, *postnews*, and *checknews?* Together, they provide a simple user interface for reading and posting news. Sophisticated users won't have much use for these programs. However, we recommend installing them unless you've got a specific reason not to, such as having existing, fancier programs by those names. The programs are useful for testing, if nothing else, since they're so stupid that not much can go wrong with them. (In later chapters, we'll assume that you have installed them.) If you want to install these programs, now's the time. Running as the owner of */usr/bin* (or wherever you've decided to put the user-interface commands), with a suitable *umask*, type:

```
% make readpostcheck
```

As before, the */usr/bin* owner does not need to have write permission in the source area to run this command.

6. Next is another manual job, where system-specific programs are often needed. Change *NEWSBIN/input/newsspool* to be owned, both user and group, by the news owner. Then set its permissions to:

```
rwsr-sr-x
```

This can usually be done with the command

```
chmod ugts NEWSBIN/input/newsspool
```

but check your *chmod* documentation if that doesn't work for you. Actually, most of these permissions can be customized to suit you, but the **s** for user and group and the **x** for other are mandatory. The *newsspool* program is used to put user postings into the news system's incoming-articles directory, so it needs the power to create files in that directory. Hence its special status. This program is the only part of C News that needs special powers (and indeed, the only part that is prepared to use them wisely). Don't turn the **s** bits on for any other programs!

C News is now almost fully installed. You need to do some setup and configuration work before you can try it out. There are also a few final bits of installation work that need to be postponed until configuration is done (if you want to look ahead, see Section 5.4 for the details). Chapter 5, *Configuring C News*, covers setup and configuration. If you're not using NNTP, you can skip the rest of this chapter and proceed directly there.

4.6 Preparing to Build the NNTP Reference Implementation

Doing the pre-build configuration for the NNTP Reference Implementation (NRI) is a bit harder than doing so for C News because there is no *quiz* program to walk you through the details. There is documentation, notably in *README* and *README-conf.h*, but the process can be a bit of a challenge for a newcomer. (If you do plan to go through the documentation, one essential piece of information is that you are trying to set up the "server" software.) We'll try to guide you through the common configuration tasks so that you do not have to consult the documentation.

While there are a variety of things that may have to be done on an odd system, it's usually enough to edit the *conf.h* and *Makefile* files in the top-level directory of the NRI distribution. The distribution expects you to edit *conf.h*, so it supplies *conf.h.dist* and instructs you to copy this file to *conf.h* and then to edit the copy. (That way, you can always start over if necessary.) In the same vein, we suggest that you also copy *Makefile* to *Makefile.dist* before working on it and never alter *Makefile.dist*. So we start with:

```
% cp conf.h.dist conf.h
% cp Makefile Makefile.dist
```

Now you have to fire up your favorite text editor and edit *conf.h* and *Makefile*.

4.6.1   conf.h

The *conf.h* file contains many options, quite a few of which are obsolete. For a modern system, you should only have to alter a few options. We'll work through the file, more or less in order.

The NRI NNTP daemon refuses connections if your system load is above a certain threshold (assuming that the necessary information about load is available from your system). This is perhaps a reasonable idea, but the threshold is set far too low. A "load average" of 5 was a heavy load in the old days, but it's barely noticeable on a modern system, even a small one. Find the following line:

```
#define LOAD 5        /* Loadav above which server refuses connections */
```

Change 5 to something considerably higher. We suggest effectively disabling this check by setting LOAD to a very large number (e.g., 1000) for starters. If you do have a heavily loaded system, you can go back later, when you've got some idea of where you want the threshold to be, and change the setting.

You need to tell the NRI which indexing package you are using. As discussed earlier, *dbz* is the only realistic choice nowadays. To tell NRI that you are using *dbz*, find the following line:

```
#define NDBM          /* Use new-style (4.3) ndbm(3x) libraries */
```

Change #define to #undef and then find this line:

```
#undef  DBZ           /* True if we want to use dbz libraries */
```

Now change #undef to #define. Ignore the "IF YOU DEFINE THIS" comments that accompany the second line; we'll tell you what to do about them later.

You also need to tell the NRI that it should generate output for a modern C News system. Find the following lines:

```
#undef CNEWS            /* define this if you are running C News */
#undef CNEWS_CLEARTEXT  /* define this if you have a modern C News that
                           handles input files ending in ".t" as
                           cleartext */
```

```
#undef BATCHED_INPUT      /* define if you want to support C News style
                             batched input (not supported by B-NEWS)   */
```

Change each #undef to #define.

Originally, the NRI didn't handle multiple simultaneous incoming news feeds very well, and to some extent it still doesn't. As discussed earlier in Chapter 2, you might want to consider INN instead of C News for such situations. If you do want to run multiple incoming NNTP feeds with C News, however, there is a supplementary daemon, *msgidd*, that helps the NRI to cope with message IDs in this scenario. To request that *msgidd* be included as part of the NRI, find these lines:

```
#undef MSGID            /* define this if you want to run msgidd to keep
                           track of recent msgids via daemon */
```

Change #undef to #define. There are a few additional changes needed for *msgidd*; we'll discuss them a bit later in Section 4.6.3.

The NRI needs to know how to read directories on your system. (C News itself dodges this issue by invoking the *ls* command instead.) Most modern systems come with routines to read directories in their C libraries, so you should use them. To request use of these, find the following line:

```
#undef DIRENT                   /* If you have <dirent.h> define this */
```

As before, change #undef to #define.

Some systems have a mysterious and badly designed system call named vfork() that can give small efficiency improvements in some situations. If your system doesn't have it, you need to find the following line:

```
/* #define     vfork fork */
```

Delete the C comment symbols (the "/*" and any white space after it and the "*/" and any white space before it) around it to bypass the use of vfork().

The NRI, like C News, makes some attempt to avoid filling your file systems. You may want to look at the lines that define the symbols MINFREE and POSTBUFFER to decide if you want larger safety margins. We suggest that you enlarge the numbers somewhat; the default choices (4000 and 1000, respectively) were set when disks were much smaller and system administrators preferred to run closer to the edge than is usual now. Ten times those values would be a good start.

In addition to watching for exhaustion of disk space, the NRI is also capable of watching for shortages of inodes (see Section 2.2.1.2). For some reason, the NRI doesn't do this by default, so we suggest that you enable this feature. To do so, find this line:

```
/*#define MINFILES  MINFREE/4*/
```

Delete the C comment symbols to define the **MINFILES** symbol.

The NRI wants to create its output files (which are the input to C News) with wide-open permissions, so that they are readable and writable by anyone. We strongly recommend changing this "feature." Find the following line:

```
/* #define UMASK 022 */
```

Delete the C comment symbols so that the **UMASK** symbol is defined as 022. Change 022 to 002 if you want to retain the ability of people in the *news* group to modify the files.

You have to decide how the NRI maintains its logs. By default, it is set up to use the *syslog* logging facility. An alternative, arguably more consistent with the rest of C News, is to have the NRI use a log file.* To do that, find this line:

```
/*#define FAKESYSLOG    "/usr/lib/news/nntplog"*/
```

Delete the C comment symbols so that the **FAKESYSLOG** symbol is defined. The specified filename is that of the log file; we'll talk a bit later about where that file should be.

When a user is using the NRI to read news (remember that NNTP provides both news transport and news reading facilities), the NRI only allows the user's connection to sit idle for a limited time before shutting it down and letting the system reclaim the resources it uses. The NRI sets this timeout at two hours, which seems awfully generous. We suggest changing the timeout to half an hour or less, but this is a judgment call. If you want to change the timeout, find the following line:

```
#define TIMEOUT (2 * 3600)
```

Now change (2 * 3600) to something like 1800.

The NRI needs to know where various files are located. We'll talk more about this in a moment, but one particular issue needs to be handled in *conf.h*. By default, the NRI assumes that *NEWSOV* is the same as *NEWSARTS*, or in other words, that the overview files are stored within the article tree. This is not usually a big concern with the current C News since it automatically makes symbolic links from *NEWSARTS* into *NEWSOV*. However, if your system doesn't have symbolic links, you need to find the following line:

```
/*#define OVERVIEW_DIR "/usr/spool/overviews"   /* base directory */
```

Delete the C comment symbol at the beginning of the line (but not the one at the end) and change */usr/spool/overviews* to your *NEWSOV*. Ignore the stuff that

---

* Possibly C News ought to have the option of using *syslog* instead of log files. It doesn't yet.

follows, about "reference overviews," which relates to an experimental feature that nobody uses.

The NRI's NNTP daemon is vaguely under the impression that it should run as *root*, which is a bad idea. However, it does know that files fed to C News should not be owned by *root*, and that it should identify itself as someone other than *root* when running certain programs. You need to tell the NRI what user ID to use for these purposes; normally this should be the news owner. NRI thinks the news owner is *usenet*, but that is usually wrong. Find this line:

```
#define POSTER          "usenet"
```

Change *usenet* to *news* (or whoever your news owner is).

The NRI offers a number of ways to feed articles it has received to the news software. It has some odd ideas about how it should handle this task for C News, so we strongly recommend you change these. The simplest and least painful approach is to treat NNTP incoming news the same as news arriving from any other source: a file of news gets dropped into *NEWSARTS/in.coming* and C News deals with the file later. Any attempt to force processing to happen immediately creates more problems than it solves, and interferes with the smooth and rapid flow of news from system to system by making the NNTP connection wait while local processing is done.

However, the NRI wants to run something after it delivers a file, so C News provides an *incoming* command for it to run. At the moment, this command does nothing. Find the following line:

```
#define NEWSRUN                      "/usr/lib/newsbin/input/newsrun"
```

Change *newsrun* (not **NEWSRUN**) to *incoming*. (*/usr/lib/newsbin* may not be the right directory name either, as described in the next few paragraphs.)

Finally, *conf.h* contains full pathnames for a number of files and directories. A lot of these are probably wrong for your system. A simple rule of thumb is that any *conf.h* line that contains the string usr needs changing, unless it's just a comment. This rule covers a few lines we've already talked about.

All occurrences of */usr/lib/news* should be changed to your *NEWSCTL*. The following lines are scattered through the file—make sure you get them all. (The first line may have been uncommented earlier.)

```
/*#define FAKESYSLOG          "/usr/lib/news/nntplog"*/
#define OVER_FMT_FILE          "/usr/lib/news/overview.fmt"
#define ACCESS_FILE            "/usr/lib/news/nntp_access"
#define ACTIVE_TIMES_FILE      "/usr/lib/news/active.times"
#define ACTIVE_FILE            "/usr/lib/news/active"
#define DISTRIBUTIONS_FILE     "/usr/lib/news/distributions"
```

```
#define SUBSCRIPTIONS_FILE      "/usr/lib/news/subscriptions"
#define NEWSGROUPS_FILE         "/usr/lib/news/newsgroups"
#define HISTORY_FILE            "/usr/lib/news/history"
```

All occurrences of */usr/spool/news* should be changed to your *NEWSARTS*. Again, the following lines are not all in one place:

```
#define XINDEX_DIR  "/usr/spool/news/.index"
#define SPOOLDIR    "/usr/spool/news"
#define INDIR       "/usr/spool/news/in.coming"
#define BATCH_FILE  "/usr/spool/news/in.coming/nntp.XXXXXX"
```

(The first line is actually a historical relic, but you might as well fix it too.) You need to change the following lines to make them refer to the proper subdirectories of your *NEWSBIN*. Again, these lines are scattered throughout the file:

```
#define INEWS       "/usr/lib/news/inews"
#define RNEWS       "/usr/bin/rnews"                  /* Link to inews? */
#define NEWSRUN     "/usr/lib/newsbin/input/incoming"
```

For example, if your *NEWSBIN* is */usr/libexec/news*, those lines should become:

```
#define INEWS       "/usr/libexec/news/inject/inews"
#define RNEWS       "/usr/libexec/news/input/rnews"  /* Link to inews? */
#define NEWSRUN     "/usr/libexec/news/input/incoming"
```

Any other occurrence of `usr` that is not in a comment should be inspected closely, to see if it needs to be changed.

Congratulations! That completes the changes to *conf.h*.

4.6.2 Makefile

Fortunately, the changes to *Makefile* are less numerous. The file contains a few directory names that may need to be altered, and the file needs to be modified to use the C News header files and library.

First, find the following line:

```
CFLAGS= -O
```

You need to modify **CFLAGS** to make the compiler look in the C News *include* directory for header files. This has to be done with a full pathname. If your source area is */usr/src/local/cnews*, that line needs to become:

```
CFLAGS= -O -I/usr/src/local/cnews/include
```

You may also want to add any special options needed by your compiler.

Now find this line:

```
#DBLIBS = /usr/local/lib/dbz.o #/usr/local/lib/dbzdbm.o
```

This line needs to be uncommented, and furthermore, it needs to refer to the C News library, since that library contains the *dbz* routines. Do not try to do as the line suggests and pick out individual *.o* files from the C News library. You need more than one and it's easy to get it wrong. It's best to simply use the whole library:

```
DBLIBS  = /usr/src/local/cnews/libcnews.a
```

(Again, we have assumed that your source area is */usr/src/local/cnews*, for purposes of example.)

The *Makefile* also needs to be modified to specify where the programs are going to be installed. We recommend that you put them in an *nntp* subdirectory of *NEWSBIN*, to keep all the news software in one place. Find the following lines:

```
ETCDIR = /etc
# Where nntpxmit and nntpxfer is going to live
BINDIR = /usr/local/bin
```

Assuming that you want to follow our suggestion, and that your *NEWSBIN* is */usr/libexec/news*, change the lines to:

```
ETCDIR = /usr/libexec/news/nntp
# Where nntpxmit and nntpxfer is going to live
BINDIR = /usr/libexec/news/nntp
```

Finally, the *Makefile* as supplied tries to install the NRI manual pages onto your system. Systems now vary so enormously in how and where manual pages are stored that the *Makefile* almost certainly has the details wrong. Unless you are confident that it does the right thing, we recommend that you comment out the manual-page installation attempt and do it manually. To do this, find this line:

```
cd doc; $(MAKE) $(MFLAGS) $(SUBMAKEFLAGS) install
```

Make sure you get exactly this line, as there are several lines that are similar. Change the line to:

```
# cd doc; $(MAKE) $(MFLAGS) $(SUBMAKEFLAGS) install
```

4.6.3 Touchup Work for msgidd

As discussed earlier, you need to use the message-ID daemon, *msgidd*, if you've got multiple incoming NNTP feeds. *msgidd* is not as well integrated with the rest of the NRI as it might be, and running it requires some minor changes above and beyond the ones we've already covered in *conf.h*.

The *msgidd* software has a couple of pathnames compiled into it, in the *server/msgid.h* file.* Edit the file and find the following two lines (they're together at the top):

```
#define SOCKNAME        "/usr/lib/news/nntp_msgid"
#define PIDFILE         "/usr/lib/news/msgidd.pid"
```

Change both instances of */usr/lib/news* to your *NEWSCTL*.

The file *server/Makefile* must also be edited so that it knows it should install *msgidd*. Find the following line:

```
install: nntpd
```

Change it to:

```
install: nntpd install_msgidd
```

That's all you need to do to set things up for *msgidd*.

4.7 *Building the NNTP Reference Implementation*

To actually build the NRI, type the following in the top-level source directory for the NRI:

```
% make
```

(Or use the preferred *make* command for your system.) This command compiles the NRI software.

If the compilation fails and stops somewhere along the way, you'll have to cope. It's hard to give specific instructions for that because there are so many possibilities. One common problem is that all of the pieces of a program compile properly, but the attempt to put them together into a final program fails with a message about undefined symbols," "unresolved references," or something like that. This probably means that some necessary function or system call doesn't exist on your system. If you examine the error message for the failure carefully, you may be able to figure out which function is the problem.

There are a number of options in *conf.h* that are used to cope with strange systems. If you have trouble, you might need to invoke some of these options. The documentation in *README-conf.h* may help you to figure out which options you should use.

---

* Note that there is no consistency in filenames as to whether *msgidd* is spelled with one "d" or two.

4.8 Installing the NNTP Reference Implementation

Before you can install the NRI, you need to create the *NEWSBIN/nntp* directory and set it to be owned by the *NEWSBIN* owner. Now, running as the *NEWSBIN* owner, with a suitable *umask* (022 or 002 is suitable), type:

```
% make install
```

This command installs all of the programs. The *NEWSBIN* owner should not need to have write permission in the source area to run this command.

Now you need to copy the *overview.fmt* file from the top level of the NRI source tree to *newsctl*. As the news owner, again with a suitable *umask* (e.g., 022), type:

```
% cp overview.fmt /var/news
```

(Assuming that your *NEWSCTL* is */var/news.*)

The NRI is now almost fully installed. You need to do some setup and configuration work before you can try it out. That is the topic of Chapter 5.

In this chapter:
- *C News Control Files*
- *NNTP Reference Implementation Control Files*
- *Verifying C News Installation*
- *Loose Ends*
- *Cleaning Up*

5

Configuring C News

This chapter describes how to configure C News and arrange for the various pieces of it to be run in suitable ways, after it has been compiled and installed. (For similar information on INN, see Chapter 8, *Configuring INN*.) A discussion of testing, troubleshooting, and operations is deferred to Chapter 6, *Running C News*.

This chapter assumes that you have read Chapter 2, *Getting Ready*, which discusses decisions you have to make before setting up your news software. The material from that chapter is not repeated here. This chapter also assumes that you have gone through the procedures described in Chapter 4, *Installing C News*.

In this chapter, we'll go systematically through the control files for C News. C News uses control files to identify your system, to control the news you receive and how long you keep it, to handle the news that is sent to other systems and how it is sent, and to configure various user interfaces and the NNTP Reference Implementation. Once you have set up the control files, we'll look briefly at how to verify that you've installed C News correctly. Finally, we'll take care of a few loose ends that need to be tied up, and we'll clean up the mess we made when building C News.

5.1 C News Control Files

After you run *make setup* during the C News installation process, you have a preliminary set of C News control files installed in *NEWSCTL*. Now you need to edit some of the files. A few of them are probably right, but might need changes. Several others are supplied as examples only, and definitely need editing. We'll go through the control files one by one. They are all ASCII text files, so they can be edited with any text editor. (Beware, however, that some of the control files allow white space and comments beginning with #, while others do not.)

5.1.1 *Identifying Your System*

You have to identify your host to C News by telling it the host's name. C News can't easily acquire this information automatically because there are too many different ways of asking a system about it, and they often yield different results on the same system. In addition, you may not want to use the system name for certain purposes.

The *whoami* file contains your host's news name. The *mailname* file tells C News how to build a mailing address for your host, so that it can insert email addresses in news headers. The *organization* file specifies the contents of the Organization header, which identifies the origin of an article to its readers.

5.1.1.1 *whoami*

The *whoami* file contains a single line that lists the news name of your host (see Section 2.4). This name is used in Path headers, and is also sometimes known as the *relayer name*. The *whoami* file supplied by the installation process is:

```
nosuchsite
```

You *must* change this file so that it lists your news name. See Section 2.4 for a discussion of what the name should be, and who needs to know this information.

5.1.1.2 *mailname*

The *mailname* file also contains a single line. In this case, the file contains the name to be used in email addresses for this host. C News uses this information to fill in the From headers of news articles, to indicate the authors of articles. The *mailname* file should contain a full Internet domain name. For example:

```
kiwi.ora.com
```

The user's name and an @ are prepended to the mail name to form an email address. For example:

```
ruth@kiwi.ora.com
```

More complex forms are not supported, with one exception: if the *mailname* file contains an @, the prepended punctuation character changes to %. Thus, if the *mailname* file contains:

```
feathers@kiwi.ora.com
```

then the email address might be:

```
ruth%feathers@kiwi.ora.com
```

This feature provides limited support for hosts that do not have their own Internet domain names, but are attached to hosts that do. Using this feature is discouraged, however. Your host can, and should, have a domain name even if it's not directly on the Internet.

The *mailname* file supplied by the installation process is:

```
no.such.domain
```

Again, you *must* change this file so that it lists a valid domain name. The news posting software refuses to work if *mailname* is unchanged.

5.1.1.3 organization

The *organization* file specifies the default contents of the Organization header in posted articles. This information is for the edification of people at other hosts; it doesn't need to be in any special format. Again, the file contains one line of text. The installed file contains the following:

```
Sirius Cybernetics, Sirius City branch
```

You'll definitely want to change this information. As the supplied example suggests, you should include the geographical location of your organization, unless it's obvious from the name. Some examples:

```
University of Toronto
O'Reilly & Associates, Sebastopol, Calif.
Dept of Exobiology, Miskatonic Univ., Arkham MA
```

Try to keep the information brief, however. In particular, don't bother with a full mailing address.

5.1.2 Incoming News

The next set of control files that needs attention relates to receiving news, processing it, and keeping it on your system. The *sys* file is the central control file for your news system, but with respect to incoming news, all that matters is the first line of the *sys* file. This first line controls the newsgroups that C News is allowed to process. (This is related to, but not quite the same as, the list of newsgroups your system knows about; see Section 5.1.5 for more information.) The *controlperm* file specifies how control messages are processed on your host. The *explist* file controls how long news is retained on your host.

5.1.2.1 sys

The *sys* file is the central control file for the entire news system, so you need to be careful with it. It controls what newsgroups your system processes, and determines which newsgroups you send to other hosts, and how that's done. You *will* need to modify this file; the contents of the sample file are just intended to give you some illustrative examples.

We'll discuss the send-to-other-hosts function and other general aspects of the *sys* file in Section 5.1.3. Right now, all you need to know is that the *sys* file contains one line per host. The fields in each line are separated by colons (:). Empty lines and lines starting with # (comment lines) are ignored. However, white space within lines generally is *not* ignored. If you need to continue a long line onto a second line, you can use a backslash (\ ) followed immediately by the end of the line. The end of the line, and any white space that follows it, are ignored.

The first line in the *sys* file is usually a special line for this host. While it can be written using the host's news name, it is usually done with the special name ME, which means "this host." The sample *sys* file supplied during the installation process contains the following ME line:

```
ME:comp,news,sci,rec,misc,soc,talk,humanities,alt,can,ont,tor,ut,to
```

This ME line is required; it is the only line in *sys* that is required. The ME line normally has only two fields: ME itself and a *subscription list* for this host. The subscription list specifies which newsgroups this host processes. The subscription list is a list of newsgroup patterns that can be quite complicated; the *newssys* manual page supplied with C News goes into the details, if you need them.

If the newsgroup of an incoming article is not covered by the subscription list, the article is discarded. That means that it never appears on your system and it is not passed along to other hosts. If the newsgroup of an article is not in the *active* file (which means the group is not known to this host), but it is covered by the subscription list, the article gets filed in the *junk* pseudogroup and it is passed on to other hosts. If the newsgroup of an article is in the *active* file and it is covered by the subscription list, the article is filed in the appropriate newsgroup.

You need to alter the ME line to include the names of your own regional and local hierarchies. The sample ME line lists the mainstream Usenet hierarchies, *alt*, some sample regional and local hierarchies, and the special-purpose *to* newsgroups. The regional and local hierarchies are just examples: *can* (the Canada-wide newsgroups), *ont* (the newsgroups for the province of Ontario), *tor* (the newsgroups for the city of Toronto), and *ut* (the newsgroups for the University of Toronto). You should change these to your own regional and local hierarchies. You might have more or fewer of them, depending on what's being done in your region and within your organization.

WARNING   As mentioned above, white space generally is *not* ignored within lines in a *sys* file. In particular, do not put spaces after the commas in the subscription list.

5.1.2.2 controlperm

The *controlperm* file controls your news system's response to most control messages. A line in the *controlperm* file looks as follows:

```
comp,sci,misc,news,rec,soc,talk,humanities  group-admin@isc.org  n yv
```

Each line contains four fields separated by white space. Empty lines and lines starting with # (comment lines) are ignored. The four fields specify:

- A list of newsgroup hierarchies (again, be careful not to put spaces after commas).

- The email address of the author of the control message (or at least, the address of the "claimed" author of the control message).

- The control messages that the line applies to. This field is comprised of one or more letters from the set shown in Table 5-1.

Table 5-1: Control Message Types in controlperm

Letter	Control message
n	*newgroup*
r	*rmgroup*
c	*checkgroups*
s	*sendsys*
v	*version*

- How to handle messages that match this line. This field contains some combination of the letters shown in Table 5-2.

Table 5-2: Handling Control Messages in controlperm

Letter	Meaning
y	Yes; process the control message
n	No; don't process the control message
q	Quiet; don't report on the control message
v	Verbose; report on the control message in full detail

If neither q nor v is present, the default behavior is to report tersely. The difference between terse and verbose reporting is that verbose reporting includes the full text of the control message, while terse reporting just lists the requested operation.

When your news system processes a control message, it tries to match the message to one of the lines in the *controlperm* file. A particular control message can match multiple lines in the *controlperm* file, so the message is handled by the *first* line in the file that matches it. In the case of *newgroup* and *rmgroup* messages, the newsgroups field is matched against the name of the group to be created or deleted. For *checkgroups*, the newsgroups field is checked against the newsgroups of the control message itself, and one of them must match. *sendsys* and *version* messages can have only one newsgroup—such messages are ignored if cross-posted—and it must match.

The sample *controlperm* file is quite reasonable, so you may not need to modify it at all. If you've got some sort of organized management for newsgroups within your geographic area or your organization, you may want to add some *controlperm* lines to let the responsible authorities create and delete the appropriate newsgroups.

The first three lines of the sample file control newsgroup creation and deletion in the mainstream Usenet hierarchies:

```
comp,sci,misc,news,rec,soc,talk,humanities   group-admin@isc.org   n yv
comp,sci,misc,news,rec,soc,talk,humanities   group-admin@isc.org   r nv
comp,sci,misc,news,rec,soc,talk,humanities   any                     nr nq
```

David C. Lawrence, *group-admin@isc.org,*[*] issues the legitimate *newgroup* messages for the mainstream Usenet hierarchies, so we let the system process the *newgroup* messages from him. He also issues the legitimate *rmgroup* messages, but *rmgroup* is a more destructive operation (and his name can be forged), so we don't process *rmgroup* messages, but we do report them. Finally, a *newgroup* or *rmgroup* message for one of these newsgroups from anyone else (any in the second field means "any name") is ignored completely. In other words, it is neither performed nor reported.

The sample file contains similar lines for other well-controlled hierarchies, like *bit*, *bionet*, and *clari*, where the same person always issues the control messages.

Now we have to do something about *alt*, where the situation is more chaotic. The sample file offers a reasonable compromise:

```
alt                        any                    nr      nv
```

Newsgroup creation and deletion messages for *alt* are not processed, but they are reported verbosely, so that the news administrator can decide what to do about them. If you're sufficiently disgusted with the chaos in *alt*, just change nv to nq and you won't ever hear about *alt* groups.

Newsgroup names of the form *to.xyz* are used for special purposes. As such, these newsgroups should not be created or removed by control messages at all:

---

* Lawrence used to post these control messages as *tale@uunet.uu.net*, and he still posts duplicate messages using that address because of all the sites that still have that address in their control files.

```
to                        any                       nr   nq
```

Finally, any other newsgroup creation/deletion requests should probably be referred to the administrator for a decision:

```
all                       any                       nr   nv
```

The magic word `all` means all newsgroups. If you want to add extra lines to control *newgroup* and *rmgroup* messages for some local or regional newsgroups, you need to add them *before* this line.

So far, the sample file has only handled *newgroup* and *rmgroup* messages. Now we need to consider *checkgroups* messages. These control messages are fairly harmless because all they do is send mail to you. Furthermore, they do their own mailing, so they don't even need to be reported:

```
all                       any                       c    yq
```

Finally, we have to deal with the abuse-prone *sendsys* and *version* messages. These messages are still potentially useful for network mapping in local areas or within organizations. However, any such messages sent worldwide are surely malicious, so the sample file causes them to be ignored:

```
comp,sci,misc,news,rec,soc,talk any                 sv   nq
humanities,alt,bit,bionet     any                   sv   nq
```

ClariNet actually uses these messages operationally, so the sample file allows the system to process them:

```
clari                     clarinet@clarinet.com  sv   y
```

(This is only relevant if you get the ClariNet newsgroups, but it's harmless if you do not.)

We hope that all remaining hierarchies are fairly local, so *sendsys* and *version* should be legitimate within them:

```
all                       any                       sv   yv
```

In any case, the system imposes other restrictions on *sendsys* and *version* messages, and *controlperm* cannot override those. In particular, responses to such messages are delayed, to give administrators a chance to send out *cancel* messages for spurious ones. And the "local part" of the reply address must be *newsmap* or the message is completely ignored.

5.1.2.3 explist

The *explist* file controls when articles expire. The sample file provided during the installation process will probably need a bit of editing. If you haven't read Section 3.4 on expiry policy, you should read it now, as we won't repeat what was discussed there. (If you're finding it difficult to set an expiry policy, you might want to look at Section 5.1.2.4 for automated help.)

During expiry, the system uses the *explist* file to match the newsgroup of an article with an expiry policy. The expiry policy for a newsgroup is controlled by the *first* line in *explist* that matches the newsgroup. That means that you cannot control the expiry policy for a newsgroup by simply appending a line for that newsgroup to *explist*. The line must be inserted in the right place, before any other lines that match the newsgroup.

A line in the *explist* file looks as follows:

```
sci.space.shuttle,rec.aviation  x       7       -
```

Each line contains four fields separated by white space (so it is an error to put spaces after commas in the first field). Empty lines and lines starting with # (comment lines) are ignored. The four fields specify:

- A list of newsgroups

- A flag that controls whether moderated and unmoderated newsgroups are treated differently: u limits the line to matching only unmoderated newsgroups, m limits it to the moderated ones, and x matches both

- The number of days the articles in the matching newsgroups last

- The location where articles in the matching newsgroups are archived when they expire, where – means nowhere

The sample *explist* file begins with a couple of special lines. The first line specifies how long the news system should remember articles that have expired, so it can reject them if they show up again. By virtue of how the system works, this line also specifies how old an incoming article can be before it is rejected as too old. The sample file causes the system to keep track of expired articles for 14 days:

```
/expired/                       x       14      -
```

Two weeks is a reasonably generous limit; a larger value will result in a larger *history* file. It is unwise to reduce this setting below 7 days, however. This line only affects incoming articles and *history* entries for articles that have expired; it doesn't affect when an accepted article expires.

The second special line specifies some absolute bounds on expiry times:

```
/bounds/                        x       0-1-90  -
```

An article can specify its own expiry date. However, you don't want to let people specify expiry dates that are years from now just because they feel like it—it's *your* disk space their articles are occupying. This line specifies that the minimum time an article can spend on your host is 0 days and the maximum is 90 days (the

1 in the middle is just a placeholder, with no actual meaning). These are reasonable numbers and there shouldn't be any need to change them. The maximumtime setting does not stop you from specifying a longer expiry time for specific newsgroups.

The sample file contains some lines that cover local newsgroups, just as examples. You'll want to change these, at least to correct the names, and possibly to change the expiry times as well:

```
sirius.trivia              x       7        -
sirius.announce            x       never    -
sirius                     x       30       -
```

Note the use of **never** as the expiry time for a newsgroup that you want to keep permanently.

The following line provides an example of overriding the default expiry policy (specified later) for some newsgroups of special interest:

```
sci.space.shuttle,rec.birds     x       14       -
```

Of course, the newsgroups you consider to be of special interest will certainly be different, and you may want to specify a different expiry time too. You can add any number of such lines; this is usually more convenient than trying to cram everything into one line.

The sample file also contains some lines that throw trash away quickly:

```
news.groups                x       2        -
junk,tor.news.stats        x       1.5      -
```

Trash is in the eye of the beholder, of course. You might not find *news.groups* quite as boring as we do. The *junk* pseudogroup gets all the articles that aren't in any locally known newsgroup, so there's no need to keep it around once it has been passed to other hosts. *tor.news.stats* is included as an example of the fairly common practice of having a regional newsgroup in which hosts post newssystem status reports once a day. This is very useful for debugging network problems, but is only of short-term interest. Note that expiry times don't need to be exact numbers of days, although fractional days may not be too useful if you only run *expire* once a day.

Next we have a rather special case. The moderator of a moderated newsgroup can supply expiry dates for the articles he posts. Some moderators do this sensibly, putting long expiry dates only on articles of special significance, like Frequently Asked Questions lists. Some, alas, abuse the power, by deciding that everything they post should be kept for a long time, because it's great stuff and they know you'll want to clutter up your disk with it. In the summer of 1994, the moderator of *comp.binaries.ms-windows* was doing this. So we have this sample *explist* line:

```
comp.binaries.ms-windows        x        4-4       -
```

This line illustrates another form of the third field: two expiry times separated by a dash. The first time is the normal one that is applied to articles that don't supply their own expiry date. The second time is an absolute bound like the one in the */bounds/* line, but for this newsgroup only. The articles in this newsgroup expire in four days, regardless of any expiry dates they specify.

Finally, the last line of the sample *explist* covers all of the newsgroups that have not otherwise been covered:

```
all                             x        7         -
```

There should always be an `all` line at the end of your *explist*, regardless of whatever else you do. It is a serious error for there to be a newsgroup that isn't covered by some line in *explist*.

On the other hand, having an *explist* line that doesn't actually cover any newsgroups is not disastrous, but it does hint that somebody's misunderstood something. This situation typically occurs when an *explist* line tries to cover newsgroups that have been covered by an earlier line (e.g., a more-specific line is placed after the `all` line). The expiry software complains about this situation, to aid in catching such errors.

5.1.2.4 expirebot

If you receive news mostly for the benefit of your own users, you probably want to be fairly selective about expiry. Ideally, articles in newsgroups that your users read should be kept for a while, while groups that they don't read should be expired quickly to free up space. The problem with this approach is that it's difficult to track user reading patterns, especially since they change constantly. The *expirebot* program offers help with this problem.

expirebot helps by automatically preparing a more detailed *explist* file for you, based on the newsgroups your users are reading. When a newsgroup is being read regularly, *expirebot* boosts its expiry time, up to a specified maximum. When nobody is reading a newsgroup, *expirebot* reduces its expiry time, down to a specified minimum. Boosts are done quickly, while reductions are done slowly. There is some built-in inertia, so that a newsgroup's expiry time doesn't drop sharply if it's unread for a short period of time, like over a long weekend. There are also provisions for overriding *expirebot*'s decisions.

The original test system for *expirebot* knew about 3200-odd newsgroups and had a substantial user community. Once *expirebot* had been running for a little while and had a chance to assess user reading patterns, over 2800 of those newsgroups were reduced to the minimum expiry time. About 250 were read regularly enough to get boosted to the maximum expiry time. The remainder wandered up and down with occasional reading. Keeping track of all this by hand would have been utterly impossible.

There are a few prerequisites for using *expirebot*. First, you can't be feeding news to other sites, or at least not very much news to other sites. *expirebot* can't tell the difference between an outbound feed and your own readers, so anything that gets fed to another site looks like it's being read. Also, you can't be using the optimization described in Section 2.7.2 that suppresses the updating of access times on files. Access-time updates are the price you pay for using *expirebot*. You may also find that you have problems with particularly ill-behaved newsreaders that do extensive prefetching of articles.

On the positive side, *expirebot* doesn't care whether your users read news locally, via NFS, or via NNTP. It requires no modifications to newsreader software. And most importantly, it does not require invading your users' privacy by tracking exactly who's reading what.

To run *expirebot*, all you need to do is to make a minor modification to the news owner's *crontab* file, which runs various C News programs at regular times. We'll talk about installing the *crontab* file in Section 5.4. For now, all you need to know is that it's found in the *conf* subdirectory of the source area. In that file, you'll find the following lines (disregarding some comments that are also included in the file):

```
59 0   1-31 *  * /usr/libexec/news/expire/doexpire
#01 23 1-31 *  * /usr/libexec/news/expire/expirebot 0.1 5.0 2.0
#59 0  1-31 *  * /usr/libexec/news/expire/doexpire /var/news/expbotlist
```

The actual paths in your *crontab* file will be based on your *NEWSBIN* and *NEWSCTL*. This example assumes that your *NEWSBIN* is */usr/libexec/news* and your *NEWSCTL* is */var/news*, as we suggested earlier. To use *expirebot*, just comment out the first *doexpire* line and uncomment the other two, so the file looks as follows:

```
#59 0   1-31 *  * /usr/libexec/news/expire/doexpire
01 23 1-31 *  * /usr/libexec/news/expire/expirebot 0.1 5.0 2.0
59 0  1-31 *  * /usr/libexec/news/expire/doexpire /var/news/expbotlist
```

The three arguments to *expirebot* are the minimum expiry time, the maximum expiry time, and the initial expiry time for a new newsgroup. *expirebot* creates its new *explist* file under the name *expbotlist* in *NEWSCTL*. You can inspect the file if you're curious about what's happening. Note that *expirebot* "learns" your users' reading patterns, so the file will change steadily for the first week or two until a stable pattern emerges.

Using *expirebot* with the settings shown above causes articles in unread groups to expire very quickly, which means that at any given time only a sampling of recent articles are available in an unread group. This makes it hard for users to follow a discussion because some articles will expire before the users can read them. However, if people start reading the newsgroup every day, *expirebot* notices and starts cranking up the expiry time, so soon it is possible to follow discussions. Thus, you might want to pass along the same advice that the staff of the *expirebot* test system offered their users: "Every newsgroup has a sampling of articles. If you want to see everything in a newsgroup, just start reading it regularly."

expirebot still takes into account the expiry times you've set in your *explist* file. *expirebot* uses every line in *explist* that doesn't start with `all` as an override, so that you can force certain groups to expire quickly or slowly, regardless of readership. If you're using *expirebot*, we do recommend putting at least one override entry in *explist*:

```
misc.jobs,biz.jobs                x      0.1-0.1      -
```

This entry forces postings in those two sub-hierarchies to expire very quickly. You need to do this because *expirebot* cannot tell which newsgroup a crossposted article was read in. A sprinkling of job-related articles are crossposted to these sub-hierarchies, so when people read those articles in other newsgroups, *expirebot* thinks these sub-hierarchies are being read. Consequently, it boosts their expiry times. This is serious because they get a lot of traffic. *expirebot* does know which articles are crossposted and it reduces their importance in its decisions, but it can still be fooled.

It's worth keeping an eye on *expirebot* for a while when you first start running it, so you can spot these kinds of problems. In addition to looking at *expbotlist*, you may want to run *du* on your article tree, so that you can see which newsgroups are occupying a lot of space.

5.1.3 Outbound News: The sys File

Sending news to other hosts—including sending out articles posted at your host— is controlled by several control files. The *sys* file is the big one. Its main job is to control outbound news: what gets sent and to whom. Most of the details of exactly how outbound news gets sent are delegated to other files, which are discussed in Section 5.1.4.

5.1.3.1 Overview

Repeating what we said in Section 5.1.2.1, the *sys* file is the central control file for the entire news system, so you need to be careful with it. It controls which newsgroups your system accepts and which newsgroups you send to other hosts. You *will* need to modify this file; the contents of the sample file are just intended to give you some illustrative examples.

Here are a couple of sample *sys* file entries:

```
rocky/bullwinkle:comp,news/all:F:fred/togo
boris:comp,news,sci,rec,misc,soc,talk,humanities/all:f:
```

Each line in the *sys* file can contain up to four fields. The fields are separated by colons (:). In general, the news software reacts badly to white space within the fields, so don't put spaces after commas. As usual, empty lines and lines starting with # (comment lines), are ignored. If you need to continue a long line onto a second line, you can use a backslash (\) followed immediately by the end of the line. The end of the line, and any white space that follows it, are ignored. Thus, the following line has the same effect as the corresponding line in the above example:

```
rocky/bullwinkle:comp,\
        news/all:F:fred/togo
```

WARNING   White space before the backslash is *not* ignored. Don't put it in unless you want it to be part of the line. Also, don't put empty lines or comment lines in the middle of a continued line.

The four fields in a *sys* file entry specify: the host that the line refers to, the news-groups and distributions sent to that host, various transmission control flags, and the details of how news is sent to that host. The first and second fields can be divided into subfields by a slash (/). The third field typically contains one or two letters, each with independent meanings. The contents of the fourth field depend on the flags; in some cases, the fourth field can have white space within it.

The first line in the *sys* file is usually a special line for this host. While it can be written using the host's news name, it is usually done with the special name **ME**, which means "this host." The **ME** line is required; it is the only line in *sys* that is required. The **ME** line normally has only two fields, **ME** itself and a list of news-groups. If the third and fourth field are present, they are ignored, as are any sub-fields within the first and second fields. See the earlier discussion in Section 5.1.2.1 for the details.

If you want to keep things simple, the **ME** line is the only one you really need for initial testing, and you can comment out the rest of the lines (by putting # at the beginning of each one). However, you'll eventually want to send news to other hosts, if only so that your own postings to Net-wide newsgroups get sent out. Nothing gets sent out unless the *sys* file specifies it. In other words, the fact that news is coming in from another host does not mean that your news system automatically sends your own postings out to that host. If you want news sent out anywhere, you must say so in the *sys* file.

There are numerous ways to do things in the *sys* file. In this chapter, we're going to stick to the simplest and most important techniques. At this point, you have to know what transport software you'll be using to send news out. The details of transmission are handled in the *batchparms* file (see Section 5.1.4.1), but the *sys* file has to be set up properly first.

5.1.3.2 The basics

The easiest way to send news is to specify the newsgroups and distributions and put a Unix command in the fourth field.* This technique is so simple that it's useful only in special situations. Here's an example from the sample *sys* file:

```
daisy:soc.women,soc.couples/all::mail daisy@duck
```

This entry says that host *daisy* should get the newsgroups *soc.women* and *soc.couples*, with any distribution, and that each article should be sent by supplying it as standard input to the command *mail daisy@duck*. Note that the third field is empty; it does not specify any flags.

You'll see the `/all` in the second field of most of the example *sys* lines. You use this subfield value to tell the news software to ignore the distribution in the article. You usually want to ignore the distribution because of the uncontrolled nature of what goes into the Distribution header in news articles.

Note that you cannot just leave the `/all` out altogether, as that has a very different meaning. If there is a slash in the second field, it separates the newsgroup list from the distribution list. If there is no slash, the newsgroup list is also used as the distribution list. An article is only sent out if at least one of its newsgroups is in the newsgroup list and at least one of its distributions is in the distribution list. (An article that has no Distribution header is deemed to have the distribution *world*.) Since nobody's likely to put *soc.women* or *soc.couples* into the Distribution header, leaving out any mention of distributions in a *sys* line causes nothing to be sent for this *sys* line.

WARNING   There should be only *one* slash in the second field: it separates the two lists. Something like `comp/all,sci/ut,news/xyz` may look correct, but it's not allowed. The slash splits up the entire field, not just the part up to the next comma.

---

* The command should not use the `%` character, as it has special meaning (see the reference documentation for details).

5.1.3.3 Batching

The UNIX-command form of a *sys* file line is fine for sending occasional articles, but firing up a command for each article is ruinously inefficient for bulk transmission. Bulk transmission is done using *batching*: the *sys* file puts the filenames of the articles into a *to-go file* and then a separate part of C News (the *batcher*) handles sending the articles in large batches. Batching can take one of several forms, depending on the transmission details. Here's a simple example:

```
gladstone:comp.protocols.tcp-ip,comp.arch/all:f:
```

This line sends the newsgroup *comp.protocols.tcp-ip* and all the *comp.arch* newsgroups* (with any distribution) to host *gladstone*. The f flag is the usual one for UUCP transmission: it specifies putting the name and size of each article into a to-go file.

When you use the f flag, the fourth field specifies the name of the to-go file. Of course, in this case, there isn't anything in the fourth field. In this situation, the news software uses the default name for the file, which is *NEWSARTS/out.going/gladstone/togo* for the host *gladstone*.

WARNING   The relayer creates the to-go file if it doesn't already exist, but it does not create the directory to hold it. The standard installation procedure creates *NEWSARTS/out.going*, but creating directories within it is up to you. The *newswatch* anomaly-detection program (Section 6.4), which is normally run twice an hour, does try to report missing directories.

Here's an example of UUCP batching that uses a more typical line for a major news feed:

```
dewey:comp,news,sci,rec,misc,soc,talk,can,ont,tor,ut,to.dewey/all\
     :f:dewey/togo
```

This entry sends a wide variety of newsgroups, including some regional and local ones, with any distribution, to host *dewey* using UUCP-style batching. Here we've specified a to-go filename (although it is unnecessary because it's identical to the default filename for this host). If the filename doesn't start with a slash, it is taken to be relative to *NEWSARTS/out.going*. However, if it does start with a slash, the filename is used without any alterations.

---

* If you want to send *comp.arch* but not any of its subgroups, you can do that by saying `comp.arch,!comp.arch.all`.

Here's a case that is slightly more complex:

```
donald/donald.angry.duck:comp,news,sci,rec,misc,soc,talk,\
    to.donald/all,!ut:f:
```

We've used the default to-go filename again, but there are two new elements: exclusion of the *ut* distribution and the second subfield in the first field. The one real use for distributions is in a situation where you exercise tight control over when a distribution gets used, perhaps through your organization's administration. In this case, it can be useful to tell the news system not to send out articles with that distribution. Here, articles with the *ut* distribution are not sent to host *donald*, regardless of what newsgroups they're in.

5.1.3.4 The mysterious second subfield

Normally, a news article is never sent to a host that it has already visited, as determined by its Path header. Each host puts its news name in the Path header when it receives the article; the article is not sent to a host already named in the Path header. By default, the relayer tries to match the value of the first field against names in the Path header. However, the name specified in the first field is meant to be used primarily by the transmission software. What happens if the name you need to give the transmission software is not a news name that your host puts into the Path header?

This is where the second subfield of the first field comes in. A first field like don-ald/donald.angry.duck says to send articles to host *donald*, but not to send any article that contains the name *donald.angry.duck* in its Path header. You can even put multiple names in the second subfield if necessary: don-ald/a.b.c,d.e.f does not send an article if the Path header contains the name *a.b.c* or the name *d.e.f*. In addition, any article whose Path header contains the name *donald* is not sent in either case.

If you want to ensure that *only* the subfield is used to exclude against the Path header, put an exclamation point (!) in the first field and supply the name of the to-go file, like so:

```
don!ald/donald.angry.duck:comp,news,sci,rec,misc,soc,talk,\
    to.donald/all,!ut:f:donald/togo
```

A name with an exclamation point cannot be found in the Path header because the exclamation point is the delimiter there. We suggest supplying the name of the to-go file here just for tidiness, to avoid having the exclamation point included in the file name.

The second subfield is most commonly used when a host uses its full Internet domain name as its news name, but uses a shorter name for news transmission.

5.1.3.5   Local articles only

Here is another variation on a *sys* file line that you should know about:

```
scrooge:comp,news,sci,rec,misc,soc,talk,to.scrooge/all:LF:
```

This entry looks familiar, except for the L and F flags. (Incidentally, the transmission flags started out all being capital letters long ago, but are now a hopelessly confused mixture. Be careful; f and F are not the same.)

The F flag is simple. It's like the f flag, but it doesn't put the length of the article into the to-go file, just the filename. This is a bad idea for UUCP batching, which can do a better job if it knows how long the articles are, but it can be useful for more specialized situations. We use it here only as an example, not because it's necessary for the L flag.

The L flag is more complex. All by itself, it restricts transmission to only those articles that originated on this host. In other words, it only sends out local articles. This flag can be useful if you want to send your own postings out by some fast route, but you don't want to send everything that comes in from outside to that host. You may want to consider this option if you get your incoming news by a roundabout path, but also have a direct link to some fairly central news host.

The L flag can be followed by a number. In this case, it restricts transmission to articles that originated within that many hosts of your host. This feature is of rather limited use; you should read the *newssys* manual page carefully before using it.

5.1.3.6   Batching NNTP

NNTP is the one other major type of transmission link that is used frequently. While there are a variety of ways to interface NNTP software to C News, the method C News is really set up for just treats NNTP as another type of batching. The *batchparms* file needs to be set up appropriately for NNTP, but the *sys* file entry looks like a UUCP-batching entry with one small exception:

```
louie:comp,news,sci,rec,misc,soc,talk,to.louie/all:n:
```

The exception, of course, is the n flag, which tells the relayer to put the article's filename and message ID into the to-go file. NNTP software usually doesn't need the article length, but it runs more efficiently if it's provided with the message ID.

5.1.3.7   ihave/sendme

The *ihave/sendme* protocol (which is unrelated to NNTP, despite some similar terminology) lets one host tell another host about the articles it has available (*ihave*) and then allows the other host to ask for the articles it wants (*sendme*). See Section 19.4.3 for more details. The *ihave/sendme* protocol is largely obsolete because

NNTP handles this type of transmission much better, but just in case, here's an example of a *sys* line for an *ihave/sendme* news feed:

```
louie.wehave/louie:comp,news,sci,rec,misc,soc,talk,!to/all:I:
```

This line sends *ihave* messages to host *louie*, in collaboration with the batcher (which we'll discuss shortly). Note the I flag, the exclusion of the *to* newsgroups, and the rather odd form of the first field.

WARNING   We recommend very strongly that for setting up an *ihave/sendme* feed, you copy the supplied example and change names and newsgroups as appropriate, rather than trying to make up your own *sys* line from scratch. The *ihave/sendme* protocol and its implementation are complicated, and getting the details right can be difficult.

The one real complication of *ihave/sendme* is that the messages that the two hosts exchange are themselves sent as news articles. This is a bit odd—it would be more sensible to send them as mail—but in the early days, when mail software was often very primitive, it was easier if the news system handled its own communication. So the messages are sent as special articles in special newsgroups. By convention, such articles destined for host *louie* are posted to the newsgroup *to.louie*. Therefore, the *sys* file must arrange to send that newsgroup to that host:

```
louie:to.louie/all:f:
```

You cannot change this newsgroup naming convention without changing parts of the software. (For example, the batcher software knows it.)

If you are sending news to a host via *ihave/sendme*, bear in mind that it's a bit slow because the control messages must be exchanged before news can flow. You might want to also send them your local articles directly, without waiting:

```
louie:comp,news,sci,rec,misc,soc,talk,!to/all:Lf:
```

5.1.3.8 Asymmetric feeds

It's quite possible to have your incoming and outgoing news follow different transmission paths. In some cases (e.g., cheap, fast transmission channels that only work in one direction), it's even desirable. Remember that you only need *sys* lines for the outgoing paths. The only real complication is that you probably need to use the second subfield of the first *sys* field, as discussed above, to make sure that the incoming news from another site doesn't get sent to its outgoing path.

5.1.4   Outbound News: Transmission

The *sys* file, discussed in Section 5.1.3, determines what news articles get sent and to which hosts. Most of the details about exactly how outbound news gets sent are usually delegated to the *batchparms* file, however. In the case of moderated newsgroups, where locally posted articles are mailed to the moderator rather than sent out as news, the *mailpaths* file specifies how that's done.

5.1.4.1   batchparms

The *batchparms* file controls how batched transmission to other hosts is done. The *sendbatches* program reads the file to determine which hosts to do batching for and how. An entry in the *batchparms* file looks as follows:

```
goofy          u      500000  20       batcher | compcun | viauux
```

Each entry consists of five fields, separated by white space. The last field is a command that typically contains more white space. Empty lines and lines starting with # (comment lines) are ignored. The five fields specify:

- The news name of the host.

- The class of the host, which can be used to invoke batching only for specific sets of hosts. By convention, u signifies a host using UUCP batching and n signifies a host using NNTP batching.

- The nominal size of batches, before any data compression is done.

- The maximum number of batches allowed to be queued for the host at any one time (as counted by the *queuelen* program that *quiz* alluded to).

- The command used to send batches to the host.

sendbatches works by dividing the to-go file into batches estimated to contain articles up to the specified size, determining how many batches can be processed without exceeding the queue-length limit (or the limits of available disk space), and then processing each batch using the specified command. The command receives the relevant portion of the to-go file as its standard input. The command is also given two environment variables that may be of use: NEWSSITE, which is the news name of the host, and NEWSSITEDIR, which is the full pathname of the host's directory under *NEWSARTS/out.going*. (Historically, the terms "host" and "site" tend to be used interchangeably, although we've tried to be consistent and use "host" in our descriptions.) The command is run with *NEWSARTS* as the current directory. Any output from the command, whether on standard output or standard error, is considered an indication that something went badly wrong.

The sample *batchparms* file starts with a special line that defines a default set of limits and a default command:

```
/default/       u       500000  20      batcher | compcun | viauux
```

The magic hostname `/default/` marks this line as supplying defaults. If there is no such line, batching is only done for the hosts named in the *batchparms* file. If there is a `/default/` line, however, every directory in *NEWSARTS/out.going* is considered for batching and the settings from the `/default/` line are used for any hosts that don't have their own *batchparms* lines.

This `/default/` line probably doesn't need to be changed, provided that you want UUCP transmission to be the default mode of operation. 500 Kbytes is a reasonable pre-compression batch size for fast modems. Compression should squeeze it down to 250K or so, which will take a minute or two for transmission. You want batches to be large enough so that per-batch transmission overhead is spread over many articles, but not so large that a line failure in mid-transmission ends up wasting a lot of time retransmitting the portion already sent. A batch size should be equal to a few minutes' transmission. 20 batches, which is equal to a few megabytes of queued news for any one host, is a reasonable queue length.

The default command demonstrates the basic method for UUCP transmission with C News. The to-go file is run through *batcher*, which gets the articles and formats them into a batch. The output of *batcher* is then run through *compcun*, which compresses the batch and prepends a silly header that some news systems (but not C News) require. Finally, that output is sent to *viauux*, which hands the batch to the *uux* program (the relevant part of UUCP) with appropriate options.

Next we have an example suitable for slower lines:

```
pluto           u       100000  10      batcher | compress | viauux
```

This entry uses a smaller batch size for the slower line. The queue length is also smaller, because a smaller amount of news keeps the slower line busy for a while. (Alternatively, you could increase the queue size to keep the same amount of news queued up.) Finally, this host is known to be a C News host, so the command uses *compress*, which is more efficient than *compcun* and does not prepend a header.

Now here's a host that has a few complications:

```
dewey           u       500000  20      batcher | compcun -b12 | viauux -gn
```

Here *compcun* is being invoked with the `-b12` option, which it passes to *compress* to indicate that *compress* should limit itself to 12-bit compression. This level of compression is about the most that can be decompressed on a 16-bit machine without running out of memory. Also, *viauux* is being asked to tell *uux* to queue this traffic up with grade n. UUCP's grades specify transmission priorities. The normal priority for news is c, which is a fairly low priority. The grade n gives news an even lower priority.

The following host has a slightly different set of complications:

```
huey    u    500000-750000    20    batcher | gzip -9 | viauux -d gunzip
```

The nominal batch size remains the same (500 Kbytes), but here an absolute upper limit of 750 Kbytes has been set. The default upper limit is three times the nominal size. The command is using *gzip* rather than *compress* and is telling *gzip* to be extremely aggressive (which is expensive in CPU time, but does improve compression). The command is also asking *viauux* to pass the word to the other host that *gunzip* should be used to decompress the batch.

WARNING   The convention for communicating what decompression program to use is relatively new. Be sure that the host on the other end understands it before you try to use it. The question to ask is: "Does your *rnews* command support the C News -d option?" Unfortunately, as of mid-1997, INN's *rnews* command does not.

Now here's an example of how to set up an NNTP transmission link:

```
donald          n    40000    -          usenntpxmit donald.cia.gov
```

The batch length for NNTP is not the length of the articles themselves, but instead the length of the to-go file for an NNTP session. The to-go file contains one line per article, so a relatively small batch size is appropriate; 40 Kbytes is perhaps 500-1000 articles in a single NNTP session. The - in the fourth field tells *send-batches* not to bother with queue limits, which is appropriate because the NNTP software sends batches immediately, rather than queuing things up. The *usenntpxmit* command performs the transmission using the NRI's *nntpxmit* program. The argument supplied to it is the full Internet name of the host; if you don't supply an argument, it uses the name from the first field, which in this case is *donald*.

Finally, *ihave/sendme* feeds require some trickery. As mentioned earlier in the discussion of the *sys* file, the machinery here is complicated and subtle. You are better off copying an existing example, rather than trying to create the entries from scratch. The *batchparms* lines for an *ihave/sendme* feed to host *louie* are:

```
louie.wehave    u    40000    -          batchih | viainews
louie.ihave     u    40000    -          batchsm | viainews
louie.sendme    u    40000    -          batchra
```

The first line bundles the information from the *louie.wehave* line in the *sys* file into *ihave* messages and arranges to post them as articles. The second line, in collaboration with the relayer software, handles incoming *ihave* messages by preparing *sendme* messages that ask for any articles that your host does not already have. The third line, again in collaboration with the relayer software, handles incoming *sendme* messages as if the requested articles had been specified by a *sys* line containing the F flag. In all three cases, the software knows that the hostname is obtained by stripping off the last component of the given name (so it is *louie* in all three lines). As with NNTP, the batch length is just the length of the to-go file file for a session, so a relatively small batch size is appropriate; 40 Kbytes is perhaps 500-1000 articles per message.

In addition to those "magic" lines, you need an ordinary *batchparms* line (or a /default/ line) that tells the batcher how to actually get stuff to *louie*.

5.1.4.2 mailpaths

The *mailpaths* file specifies how to reach the moderators of moderated newsgroups.* The sample file supplied by the installation process contains the following:

```
sirius   %s@no.such.domain
all      %s@moderators.isc.org
```

When C News needs to find the moderator address for a moderated newsgroup, it searches in this file from top to bottom, looking for a line whose first field matches the newsgroup name. Then it uses the second field as the moderator address. If the second field contains %s, that is replaced by the name of the newsgroup with all dots changed to dashes. For example, if *biz.ora.eggbooks* were a moderated newsgroup, the first line of the sample *mailpaths* wouldn't match, but the second line would (all is a magic word). Therefore, the moderator address would be *biz-ora-eggbooks@moderators.isc.org*.

Newsgroup matching is a bit complex, but usually only the simple cases are of interest. In particular, all matches any newsgroup, and a name that is identical to the first parts of a newsgroup name matches the whole name. For example, the sirius line in the sample *mailpaths* matches newsgroups like *sirius.announce*. The other important rule is that a newsgroup's moderator address is specified by the first line it matches (not the line it matches best). These rules are about all you need to know to set up *mailpaths*.

The second field does not have to be an Internet-style address. It can be any address that your *mail* command accepts. Note also that it doesn't have to contain %s; that's normally used for matching multiple groups and sending them to a site that has the appropriate aliases.

---

* There are one or two other obscure features of *mailpaths* that are seldom needed these days. See the C News manual pages if you need details.

In most cases, all you need to do is to edit the first line of the sample *mailpaths* file to specify your local newsgroup names and a suitable address. You might want more than one such line. The `all` line of the sample file is already suitable for Usenet's moderated newsgroups. So if your local newsgroups have names of the form *ora.general*, your *mailpaths* file might look something like this:

```
ora.announce    root
ora.fred        fred@eggs.kiwi.ora.com
ora             %s
all             %s@moderators.isc.org
```

This file sends *ora.announce* postings to *root* on this host and *ora.fred* postings to *fred* on another host. Postings in other moderated *ora* newsgroups are sent to suitable mail aliases on this host (e.g., a posting to *ora.bicycles* goes to *ora-bicycles*). Everything else is sent to the standard mail aliases on *moderators.isc.org*.

The Internet hostname *moderators.isc.org* is actually an alias for a number of different hosts that have committed themselves to maintaining suitable mail aliases for all moderated Usenet newsgroups. So, for example, when a posting is sent to the *comp.risks* moderated newsgroup, the posting is actually passed along to *comp-risks@moderators.isc.org*, where it is redirected to any of a number of machines that has an alias for the actual moderator of the *comp.risks* group.

Note that *mailpaths* doesn't specify whether a newsgroup is moderated or not. That decision is made by the *active* file. The *mailpaths* file is only consulted when a newsgroup is already known to be moderated. As a result, putting the name of an unmoderated newsgroup in *mailpaths* has no effect.

5.1.5 Newsgroups

There are two control files that specify what newsgroups exist on your host, and that contain other information used by much of the news software. The *active* file is the final authority on what newsgroups exist on your system. Unfortunately, its format was originally defined somewhat inflexibly, so *active.times* was added later to contain some supplementary information.

These files don't need to be, and probably shouldn't be, edited manually. They do need changing, but the details of that are discussed in Section 3.3.2 and in Section 6.1.2.

5.1.6 User Interface

If you are using the C News *readnews* and *postnews* commands, you need to know about three small control files for them. The *readnews.ctl* file controls a few details of how *readnews* works, *postdefltgroup* specifies the default newsgroup for *postnews*, and the optional *postdefltdist* file specifies a default distribution for *postnews.* If you didn't install *readnews, postnews,* and *checknews,* you can ignore these files (or even remove them if you like, but they're tiny and harmless).

5.1.6.1 readnews.ctl

The sample *readnews.ctl* looks like:

```
defsub  sirius.announce,sirius.general
mustsub sirius.announce
```

The `defsub` line specifies the default subscription list: the newsgroups a user is shown if she doesn't make her own choices. The `mustsub` line specifies one newsgroup (and only one—it's not a subscription list) that the user is always shown, even if she tries to unsubscribe from it. You need to adjust these two lines to reflect the names you choose for your local newsgroups. We suggest that `mustsub` specify a newsgroup used only for important announcements, while `defsub` could specify that group plus one or two local newsgroups of more general interest. Non-local newsgroups can also be specified, although local groups are usually preferable.

There are one or two other things that can be done with *readnews.ctl,* but they are rather specialized and it's unlikely that you'll need them; see the *readnews* manual page for the details.

5.1.6.2 postdefltgroup

The *postdefltgroup* file contains a single line that names the newsgroup that is presented as the default when *postnews* asks the user for newsgroup name(s). The sample file contains:

```
sirius.general
```

Again, this should be changed to reflect your local newsgroup names. It should probably specify a general-interest local newsgroup that anyone can to post to.

5.1.6.3 postdefltdist

It's also possible to specify a default distribution for *postnews.* This is rarely useful and we recommend not doing it. If you really must, create a *postdefltdist* file in *NEWSCTL* and insert a single line that lists the default distribution.

5.2 NNTP Reference Implementation Control Files

The only control file for the NRI is the *nntp_access* file. This file controls which other hosts are allowed to communicate with your NNTP server. The *overview.fmt* file might look like a control file, but in fact it contains information that is internal to the software and should not be changed.

5.2.1   nntp_access

You have to create the *nntp_access* file in your *NEWSCTL* directory. The NRI installation process doesn't install a sample file, though there are samples given in some of the documentation. We'll give a quick overview here, omitting some fine points.

Each line in the *nntp_access* file contains three fields separated by white space. (There is an optional fourth field that can be used to limit access to specific newsgroups.) A line starting with # is a comment and is ignored, as are empty lines. Here's a sample file:

```
default          xfer    no
impala.ora.com   both    post
*.kiwi.ora.com   read    post
lemur.ora.com    no      no
```

The first field specifies a host, or a set of hosts. There are several forms allowed, but usually you use either a hostname (all in lowercase), or a portion of a domain name (all in lowercase) preceded by "`*.`". The special name `default` refers to any host; if there is a `default` line, it must be first. Any given host's access is controlled by the "most specific" line that applies to it, not the first line that applies to it. A line without an asterisk (`*`) is more specific than one with an asterisk, which in turn is more specific than a `default` line.

The second field indicates what the specified host(s) are allowed to do. Remember, the NNTP protocol lives a dual life, as a news transport protocol and a newsreader access protocol. The second field specifies whether a host is allowed to use the transport portion of the protocol and/or the newsreader portion. Table 5–3 lists the values that can be used for the second field.

Table 5–3:   Access Values for nntp_access

Value	Meaning
read	Host(s) can read news
xfer	Host(s) can transfer news to and from another relayer
both	Host(s) can both read and transfer news
no	Host(s) cannot read or transfer news

Our sample file allows any host that is not listed explicitly to transfer news, which is probably not a good idea, actually. It lets *impala* read and transfer news, while allowing hosts in the *kiwi* domain to read news. It also denies *lemur* either form of access.

The third field determines whether the specified host(s) are allowed to post news (`post`) or not (`no`). Note that transferring news to and from another relayer does not require `post` permission.

The best way to set up *nntp_access* is something like the following:

```
# readers
*.kiwi.ora.com          read    post
fred.kiwi.ora.com       no      no
# news feeds
impala.ora.com          xfer    no
walrus.ora.com          xfer    no
```

This file clearly distinguishes between the hosts that use the news-transport portion of the NNTP protocol and those that use the newsreader-access portion of the protocol. In terms of newsreader access, all of the hosts in the *kiwi.ora.com* domain are granted read and post access, except for *fred.kiwi.ora.com*, which is denied any access at all (maybe Fred is late with his current book). The hosts that feed news to and from this host are given transfer permission and nothing else.

5.3 Verifying C News Installation

Now that you have sorted out the control files to your satisfaction, it's time to move on to a verification step. Change directory back to the source area, and type the following:

```
% make cmp
```

This command performs a comparison between the files that have been installed and the files in the source area. It also runs some simple checks on file formats and such. If the command finishes with a "no worrisome differences" message, it looks like everything is installed properly, and there's at least a fighting chance that your control files are set up correctly too. You can disregard any complaints that don't cause *make* to stop. For example, the *makefiles* are aware that your *batchparms* file won't be the same as the sample one, so they may comment on this but won't treat it as a fatal error.

However, if you haven't at least changed the *mailname* and *whoami* file, you will find out now, because *make cmp* treats it as a fatal error.

There is, alas, no equivalent checking procedure for the NRI installation. (An inspection of the NRI *Makefile* might suggest *make check*, but in fact that does something quite different. It's meant to be used by the maintainers, for interacting with the source code control system. Don't do it.)

5.4 Loose Ends

Before you can move on to running C News, you need to take care of a few small chores to complete the installation process. These chores include creating mail aliases, setting up a *crontab* file, and configuring your system to start the news software during the boot process.

The first chore is to make any mail aliases necessary for trouble reporting. In particular, if you accepted *quiz*'s defaults for the trouble-reporting addresses, you need to set up the *newsmaster* and *newscrisis* aliases. Remember that the non-urgent address can send mail to a mailbox that only gets looked at occasionally, while the urgent address should go to human beings immediately.

You should also arrange that mail to likely looking addresses such as *news, usenet, newsmaster* (if it's not one of the trouble-reporting addresses), and the news owner (if it's not one of the above) goes to a suitable mailbox. People elsewhere on Usenet may send mail to one of these addresses if they need to get in touch with the news administrator on your system.

There are a few control messages, notably *sendsys* and *version*, that request that a reply be sent to the poster of the article. This is valuable for network mapping, but has also sometimes been used for half-witted practical jokes. To try to cut down on this problem, C News now refuses to cooperate unless the "local part" of the reply address is *newsmap*. Unless your site is engaged in network mapping, we suggest that mail arriving for *newsmap* be discarded: not returned, not forwarded, but discarded, silently and completely.

The next chore involves setting up a *crontab* file for C News, as much of the internal machinery of C News gets run at regular intervals by *cron*. The file *conf/crontab* in the source area is a suitable *cron* file. You need to give this file to *cron* as the news owner's *crontab*. The details of doing this are unfortunately system-specific, but two possible ways (after becoming the news owner) are:

```
% crontab <conf/crontab                    # SVR4
% crontab -r conf/crontab                   # BSD4.4
```

Read the manual pages on your system to be sure you are using the correct technique. If your system's *cron* is relatively old, you may have to incorporate a modified version of the file into a central system *crontab* file instead. In this case, you need to alter the commands in the file to arrange that they be run as the news owner; usually this requires wrapping them in an invocation of the *su* command. For example:

```
su news -c "command"
```

If you are using NNTP, you need to instruct your system's Internet daemon, usually called *inetd*, to activate the NRI NNTP server when another host attempts to connect to it. This can be moderately complicated, and it depends somewhat on how up-to-date your system's version of *inetd* is. On a modern system, you should find a line like the following in the */etc/inetd.cont* file:

```
#nntp    stream  tcp     nowait  usenet  /usr/libexec/nntpd       nntpd
```

In this case, you must delete the initial # that comments out the line. Then adjust the pathname and news-owner name (shown here as *usenet*, which probably isn't right) to suit your configuration. If you've used our suggested layout, you should change the pathname to */usr/libexec/news/nntp/nntpd*. Finally, you need to tell *inetd* to re-read the configuration file (either by rebooting or using *kill −HUP*).

If your system crashes and comes back up, C News' files may get left in an inconsistent state. C News includes a command that tidies up leftover junk: *newsboot*. You need to arrange to have */usr/libexec/news/maint/newsboot* run (as the news owner) when your system boots. Precisely how to do this is system-specific. One way is to add something like the following to the */etc/rc* boot-up command file (or to */etc/rc.local*, which is where some systems put local startup operations):

```
su news -c /usr/libexec/news/maint/newsboot
```

Here we have assumed that *NEWSBIN* is */usr/libexec/news*.

Interfacing to Transport Mechanisms

If you're using some unusual method of getting news from place to place, you may not be able to use C News' built-in setup for talking to the transport mechanisms. (You can ignore this information if you are using UUCP or NNTP; this material is for unusual situations.)

For incoming news, the basic goal is to get the news into a file in the *NEWSARTS/in.coming* directory. You can put temporary files in that same directory, as long as you make sure the filenames do not start with digits. You should also fix *newsboot* so it knows The preferred way to do the renaming is with the *mkinperm* routine in the C News library. You want a final name that is a sequence of digits (normally derived from the time of day) followed by a suffix that indicates the type of file. The only type that you should use is *.t*, which means that the file is plain text, not compressed or otherwise encoded.

For outgoing news, the most practical method is to get the filenames into a to-go file using the F flag in *sys*, and then write some suitable commands for use by a *batchparms* entry.

If you are running *msgidd* to help the NRI cope with multiple incoming NNTP feeds (see Sections 4.6.1 and 4.6.3), you need to arrange for *msgidd* to get started at boot time. If you followed our suggestion of putting the NRI software in an *nntp* subdirectory of *NEWSBIN*, *newsboot* notices this and starts *msgidd* for you.

If you did indeed build the NRI to use *msgidd*, the NNTP software may not function properly unless *msgidd* is already running. While *newsboot* handles this for you when the system is rebooted, you've now just finished installing the software and *msgidd* is not yet running. The simplest way to start it is just to run *newsboot* manually (as the news owner) before testing the NNTP software.

Finally, you may want to install the manual pages that are in the *man* subdirectory of the source area into your system's manual-page area. Once upon a time the organization of manual pages was simple and standardized, but that's not the case anymore, so it's difficult to give specific advice that would be right for your system. The manual pages (like the rest of the C News documentation) are supplied as *troff* source; if your system doesn't have a *troff*-compatible text formatter, see the *README* file in the *man* subdirectory of the sources for suggestions on how to proceed.

5.5 *Cleaning Up*

Cleanup is probably best postponed until after testing, which is the subject of the next chapter, but it fits in with building and configuring the software, so we're going to cover it now. If you've got plenty of disk space, you might want to go on to the next chapter and come back here when you have your system up and running. However, if you are short of disk space, you might want to do the cleanup now.

If you've still got the original *cnews.tar* file around, you can get rid of that now (unless you're hanging onto it in case you want to start over).

The best way to clean up in the source area is to use:

```
% make tidy
```

This command removes most of the files created by compilation, but it leaves the C News library around in case you need to use it for recompiling parts of C News or compiling other software. If you want to get rid of the library too, use the following instead:

```
% make clean
```

This is about as far as you really need to go for normal cleanup. The remaining leftovers from the build process are small, and starting over without them is tedious.

However, if you really want to start over from scratch, there are three methods of doing this. We present those methods here from the least drastic to the most. The least drastic option is to use:

```
% make veryclean
```

This command eliminates everything that the original *make* did, except that files changed by *subst* are still changed. However, the fact that they were changed has been forgotten, so the *subst* runs will get done again if you start from this point.

A more drastic option is to use:

```
% make spotless
```

After you use this command, you have to run *quiz* again, because the configuration files that *quiz* built are gone, and so most of the *makefiles* will refuse to work. The one thing that's left is your previous *quiz* answers, to be used as defaults for the next run of *quiz.*

If you want to get rid of your *quiz* answers, and thus get as close to a virginal copy of C News as can be had, you can type:

```
% make sterile
```

Again, this command does not produce a perfectly clean copy because the files changed by *subst* are still changed (but the fact that they were changed has been forgotten). After you run this command, you really have to start from scratch if you want to build C News again.

Of course, the ultimate way to get a clean copy is to start from *cnews.tar* again. In particular, that's the only way you can undo the *subst* changes.

For the NRI, the situation is much simpler. Just type the following in the NRI source directory:

```
% make clean
```

This command performs all the useful cleanup.

In this chapter:
- *Testing a New Installation*
- *Article Flow*
- *Common Problems*
- *Logs and Trouble Reports*
- *Wrapping Up*

6

Running C News

This chapter describes the operation of C News. It covers testing C News once it has been installed and troubleshooting it then and thereafter. The chapter also discusses a number of software-specific operational issues. (For similar information on INN, see Chapter 9, *Running INN.*)

This chapter assumes that you have read Chapter 2, *Getting Ready*, which discusses decisions you have to make before setting up your news software. The material from that chapter is not repeated here. This chapter also assumes that you have gone through the procedures described in Chapters 4, *Installing C News*, and 5, *Configuring C News*. Finally, if you haven't yet read Chapter 3, *News Operations*, which covers news operations in general, you should probably at least skim it before reading this chapter.

Although much of this chapter is applicable to old releases of C News, it is written to cover the Cleanup Release in particular. As a result, not all of the details are correct for older releases.

In this chapter, we'll talk about how to test C News and discuss how news flows through the various pieces of the relayer. Then we'll look at dealing with some common problems that can arise when running a C News system. We'll finish with a discussion of the logs and automatic trouble reports provided by C News.

6.1 Testing a New Installation

If you have the slightest doubt about whether C News will work on your system, you should have already run the regression tests as part of the installation process (see Section 4.4). If you didn't run the regression tests then, we suggest you go back and do it now if you have any doubts. The regression tests are not perfect, but if they work, most of C News works. More importantly, if they don't work, C News almost certainly won't work.

The rest of this section discusses some tests that should give you further confidence that the software works.

6.1.1 Posting Tests

Further testing requires posting articles, and that means posting them to some newsgroup. It's rude, at the very least, to send your internal tests out over the network to other hosts, so you should use a local newsgroup for testing.

As discussed in Section 2.5, you need to pick a top-level name for your local newsgroups. Furthermore, you shouldn't pick something that other people are likely to pick too, like *local*. For purposes of example, say that your organization is O'Reilly & Associates. You might pick *ora* as the top-level name for your local newsgroups. If you haven't already created some local newsgroups, now is the time to do so. For example:

```
% cnewsdo addgroup ora.general y "general news within ORA"
```

This command must be run as the news owner, or as the superuser; *cnewsdo* refuses to cooperate otherwise (and rightly so, because the command creates files and directories that should be owned by the news owner). The command should create the following entry in the *active* file:

```
ora.general 0000000000 00001 y
```

It should also create the directory *NEWSARTS/ora/general*. If you made *NEWSOV* the same as *NEWSARTS*, there should be an empty *.overview* file within the new directory. Otherwise, there should now be a new *NEWSOV/ora/general* directory with an empty *.overview* file in it. If any of this doesn't happen, or if *cnewsdo* or *addgroup* complains that something is very wrong—perhaps your file permissions are incorrect—and you need to investigate that now.

Assuming that you successfully created a newsgroup, the next step is to try to post an article to it. For that, you need posting software. The discussion here assumes that you installed C News' *postnews*. To use *postnews* to post a test article, start as follows:

```
% postnews ora.general
```

postnews begins by prompting you for a subject for the article:

```
Subject:
```

Your reply should be something like "test article."

Having obtained the subject, *postnews* now constructs a skeletal article and starts up a text editor so you can edit it. The choice of editor depends on whether you've set the `VISUAL` or `EDITOR` environment variables (see your system administrator or your system manuals if you need to know the details of this). If you haven't set either of these variables, you get *ed* as the editor. The skeletal article looks like this:

```
Newsgroups: ora.general
Subject: test article

REPLACE THIS LINE WITH YOUR TEXT (leave the preceding blank line alone)
```

At this point, just follow the helpfully provided instructions: replace the "REPLACE THIS" line with some sample text. For example, you might produce something like this:

```
Newsgroups: ora.general
Subject: test article

This is our first test article.
```

Now tell the editor to write out the new text and exit the editor. If you forget to write your new text out, *postnews* notices this, complains about it, and asks you whether you want to abandon the posting. If you answer "no" (or just "n"), it starts up the text editor again. If you didn't forget, *postnews* announces:

```
Posting...
```

A moment later it should terminate. If there are any nasty error messages along the way, something is wrong with *inews* or one of the programs it invokes.

If there aren't any complaints from *postnews*, go to the directory *NEWSARTS/in.coming* and look at the files there. There should be a directory named *bad* and a file named *headers*, which you can ignore for the moment. More importantly, there should be a file with a name something like *0.1215346940.t* that is owned by the news owner. That file should contain your article, dressed up with some more headers. It should look something like the following:

```
Newsgroups: ora.general
Path: eggman
From: eggman@kiwi.ora.com (R.I. Red)
Subject: test article
Organization: O'Reilly & Associates
Date: Fri, 11 Jul 1997 20:38:12 GMT
Message-ID: <Cywzzp.2C0@kiwi.ora.com>

This is our first test article.
```

The date, names, and organization will, of course, differ, and the gibberish before the @ in the Message-ID header won't be the same, but otherwise your article should be similar. Write down the contents of the Message-ID header. The date is expressed in Greenwich Mean Time (GMT); check that it's right for your time zone. (For example, the test article we used here was posted at 16:38:12 in North America's Eastern Daylight Time, so 20:38:12 GMT is right.)

This file should remain in the *in.coming* directory for only a few minutes. The next time *newsrun* is invoked by *cron*, the file is picked up and processed. The standard *crontab* supplied with C News runs *newsrun* every 15 minutes, at :00, :15, :30, and :45. Wait for it. (If you didn't find a file in *in.coming*, perhaps the file got there just before *newsrun* ran and you got there just after. In that case, the simplest thing to do is to post another test article.)

When *newsrun* runs, the article file should vanish from *in.coming*. Now go to *NEWSCTL*; several files there should have changed. First off, the *errlog* file should be empty. If it's not, examine its contents for an indication of what went wrong. In most such cases, the article itself can now be found in the *in.coming/bad* directory, so you can inspect it further.

Assuming *errlog* is indeed empty, look at *log*. It should contain a single line like the following:

```
Jul 11 16:45:02.608 (local) + <Cywzzp.2C0@kiwi.ora.com>
```

The date will, of course, be different. The stuff between the < and > will also be different, but it should be the same as in the Message-ID header of the article, so you should compare it to what you wrote down.

The *history*, *history.dir*, and *history.pag* files should all have changed as well. Don't bother inspecting the *history.dir* and *history.pag* files; *history.dir* is uninformative and *history.pag* is not readable text at all. (The *history.pag* file may suddenly appear to be very large; don't worry about that.) The *history* file should contain one line that looks something like:

```
<Cywzzp.2C0@kiwi.ora.com>    784241102~-~306    ora.general/1
```

The numbers in the middle will be different; that's harmless. The stuff between the < and > should again match the Message-ID header of the article. The last part of the *history* line indicates where the article was filed.

The line in the *active* file for the newsgroup should now look like this:

```
ora.general 0000000001 00001 y
```

Notice that the first number is now 1.

Back in *NEWSARTS/in.coming*, the *headers* file should also have changed, as indicated by its date, but it should be empty.

Now proceed to the directory in the article tree where the article has been filed; in our example, it's *NEWSARTS/ora/general*. (Note that the directory is *ora/general* even though the *history* file said *ora.general*; the dots turn into slashes when you're talking about the article tree.) In that directory, there should be a file named *1* and its contents should be the same as the now-vanished file in *in.coming*.

Next go to the overview directory, which is *NEWSOV/ora/general* in our example. (This may be the same as *NEWSARTS/ora/general*, depending on how you have set things up.) The *.overview* file in that directory should contain one line that looks something like the following (the long line is split into two lines here so you can read it, but it should be all one line in the file):

```
1      test article      eggman@kiwi.ora.com (R.I. Red)
       Fri, 11 Jul 1997 20:38:12 GMT     <Cywzzp.2C0@kiwi.ora.com>    306
```

Again, the dates and names will be different. The stuff between the < and > should again be the article's Message-ID, and the small number on the end should be the size of the article file in bytes.

Finally, check the *newscrisis* and *newsmaster* trouble-reporting mail addresses (or rather, wherever the mail to them ultimately goes) to make sure that there haven't been any reports of difficulties.

If all of the checks we've walked you through look okay, the article has been posted properly. Now it's time to try to read it. Become an ordinary user and give the following command:

```
% readnews -n ora.general
```

(Here again, we've assumed that you have installed C News' *readnews*.)

readnews should present you with something like:

```
--------------------
Newsgroup ora.general
--------------------

Article 1 of 1 (ora.general) Fri Jul 11 16:38:12 1997
From: eggman@kiwi.ora.com (R.I. Red)
Subject: test article
```

readnews then prompts you with a ? so that you can tell it what to do. Notice that the date and time have been translated back into your local time zone. If you hit RETURN in response to the prompt, you should get something like:

```
This is our first test article.
```

At the ? prompt, press RETURN again to see:

```
No more articles (press RETURN again to quit).
```

Another RETURN at the ? should make *readnews* go away.

If all of these tests worked, the article was posted properly and your C News system is working.

6.1.2 Setting Up for a Test Feed

Now it's time to start thinking about getting a news feed from another site. Apart from arranging with the other site for that to happen and setting up communications for it, you need to prepare your own news system for the feed. You should probably arrange to start with a small test feed of just a few newsgroups, so that you can check out the software and communications path under a light load. Once you are sure that the software is working properly, you can have your neighbor increase the feed to the full range of newsgroups that you want to receive.

The most important thing you need to do to prepare for the test feed is to find out what newsgroups your neighbor is going to feed to you. You need this information so that you can create the groups on your system. Newsgroups are *not* created automatically as articles arrive for them. Although you are starting with a small test feed, you can do the newsgroup creation for all of the groups you plan on getting in your full feed. That way you won't have to go back and create more groups when you are ready to turn on the full feed.

The best way to create the newsgroups on your system is to get a copy of your neighbor's *newsgroups* file and then edit it to remove newsgroups you're never going to get. You don't want to replace your own *newsgroups* file with your neighbor's file, however, because your file lists your own local newsgroups and you don't want to wipe those out. C News provides the *addngs* command for dealing with this situation. Suppose the copy of your neighbor's *newsgroups* file is in the file */tmp/ng*, and you've finished editing out any unwanted newsgroups. Become the news owner or the superuser and type the following:

```
% cnewsdo addngs </tmp/ng
```

This command looks after all of the details of adding the specified newsgroups to your system. In particular, it installs new *active* and *active.times* files and leaves the old ones in *active.old* and *active.times.o*, just in case.

You should also check the ME line in your *sys* file before you start your test feed, to make sure it permits all the newsgroups you want to receive.

WARNING   The *active* file is central to the operation of your news system, and
it's difficult to rebuild if it gets mangled. C News is very cautious
about modifying the *active* file and it tries to always leave a backup
copy when changes are made. You should do the same if you ever
modify the file by hand. The *checkactive* program can also be helpful in verifying that you got things right.

6.1.3   A Test Feed

When you are sure you're ready, have your neighbor start feeding you a few
newsgroups. If you're eventually planning to get a full feed of the "mainstream"
Usenet newsgroups, one good test is to get the *news* hierarchy. This hierarchy has
enough volume to make a good test, but not enough to be a serious problem if
something goes wrong. The test feed should also include whatever regional newsgroups exist in your neighborhood, for reasons that will become clear shortly.

Once the feed has been started, you should begin seeing news traffic coming over
whatever communications software you're using. News files should start showing
up in *NEWSARTS/in.coming*, *newsrun* should start processing them, and corresponding changes should start appearing in *active*, *history*, and *log*. The *errlog* file
should stay more or less empty; it may collect one or two complaints per day due
to incorrectly formatted control messages, but anything more than that suggests
trouble. There should be no messages to the *newscrisis* and *newsmaster* aliases,
except for a daily status report to *newsmaster*.

After you are happy that everything is running smoothly, the next step is to set up
a matching feed back to your neighbor, so that articles you post make it out to the
world. This requires a suitable line in *sys*, and probably one in *batchparms* too. Be
sure to create a subdirectory in *NEWSARTS/out.going* for your neighbor.

Be careful not to feed articles arriving from your neighbor right back to that host.
If your neighbor's news name (see Section 2.4) differs from the name you need to
use in *sys*,* use the *name/newsname* format for the first field of the *sys* entry. That
way, your news system knows that articles that came through *newsname*
shouldn't be sent back to *name*. (See Section 5.1.3 for more information about the
sys file.)

Once you think the matching feed is set up properly, find a regional newsgroup
that is used for test messages. Such newsgroups typically have names ending in
.test (e.g., *nyc.test* for New York City). If you have a choice, pick the group that

---

* This typically occurs when the transport software doesn't allow you to use the full news name for
some reason.

covers the smallest region. Right now, all you want to do is find out whether articles can get to the next host.

Now post a small test article to that regional newsgroup. It should be processed just like your earlier test postings, with one exception. The *log* line for the article should look something like this:

```
Jul 11 16:45:02.608 (local) + <Cywzzp.2C0@kiwi.ora.com> rooster
```

(This example assumes that your neighbor's *sys* file name is *rooster.*) This line is just like earlier *log* lines, except that now the name of your neighbor appears on the end, which means that the news system decided that this article should be sent to the neighbor.

The next step is to go to *NEWSARTS/out.going/rooster.* That directory should now contain a file named *togo.* Depending on how the news is to be sent, the *togo* file should list the filename of the news article and either the article length or its message ID.

The next time that *sendbatches* runs, the article should get sent, which means it should vanish from the *togo* file. The standard *crontab* supplied with C News runs *sendbatches* once an hour, at 40 minutes past the hour. If you know the details of the communications software, you can track the article's progress as far as its transmission to your neighbor. Once again, check that no complaints have gone to the *newscrisis* or *newsmaster* aliases.

To find out whether the article has been received and processed successfully on the neighboring host, you'll have to ask your contact there to check. It can be useful to have a "courtesy account" on that host, so you can check such things yourself, but that's rarely possible except when both hosts are within the same organization.

6.1.4 A Full Feed

Once you're sure that your test feed is working both ways, it's time to check that you've got plenty of disk space and to ask your neighbor to turn on a full feed (or as full a feed as you want, anyway).

At this point, you might want to watch the first little bit of traffic to see that nothing goes terribly wrong, but if the test feed worked, the full feed should too. Apart from the possibility of running out of disk space, the size of your feed doesn't really play a role in any problems you might have.

6.2   Article Flow

C News consists of many individual programs. When you are trying to track down a problem, you need to figure out which program is responsible. This can usually be done by tracking an article step-by-step as it is processed by the news system. Where the processing deviates from the normal course of events is where the problem lies. In this section, we'll describe all of the programs that take an article through the C News system, so that you can track down problems when they come up. Figure 6-1 shows the paths that an article can take through C News.

6.2.1   Incoming Articles

An article that is posted locally goes through *inews* and an assortment of subsidiary programs that hide behind it. The *inews* program itself just does some option handling and backward-compatibility tinkering. The article then goes to *injnews*, which invokes *pnews* to do the actual work of getting the article ready.* Then *injnews* decides whether the article should be mailed to a moderator or placed in *in.coming* for local processing.

The article is put into *in.coming* by *newsspool*, which first copies the article into a temporary file and then immediately renames it for processing, using the naming scheme described below. (The file is present under a temporary name so briefly that it's hard to notice, even if you are watching for it.) Only *newsspool* and some of the auxiliary programs invoked by *pnews* are C programs; the rest are shell scripts, for easier customizing.†

Articles that arrive via UUCP are handled by the *rnews* shell script. *rnews* checks the available disk space and possibly does some decompression before it invokes *newsspool* to place the articles in *in.coming*.

An article that arrives from outside via NNTP starts out as a temporary file in *in.coming* with a name like *nntp.12345*. When the complete file has been transferred, the NNTP daemon renames it for processing.

Files in *in.coming* that are ready to be processed have names of the form *0.1215346940.t* and are owned by the news owner. That's the most elaborate form of the name—either the prefix (*0.*) or the suffix (*.t*) can be omitted. The middle part of the name is simply an encoded form of the time, used to generate unique filenames. The prefix, if present, indicates a priority, with 0 being the first priority, 1 being next, and so forth; files without prefixes come last. Local postings have priority 0; there are no other predefined priority values. News articles

---

* Note that this *pnews* is unrelated to the *Pnews* program found in the *rn/trn* newsreader software.

† Although the complexity of some of the scripts admittedly hampers customization just a bit.

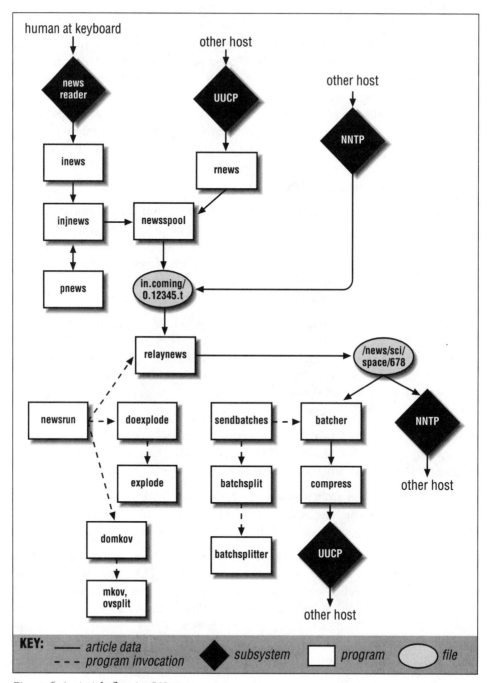

Figure 6-1: Article flow in C News

coming in from other systems do not normally have prefixes. The suffix, if present, indicates the type of the file: *.t* or *.T* means plain text, *.Z* means text compressed by the *compress* program, and no suffix means that the form of the contents is not known.

Aside from the question of whether it is compressed or not, a file contains either a single news article (as in the examples earlier) or a *batch*. A batch is comprised of one or more news articles, each preceded by a header line of the form:

```
#! rnews 627
```

Of course, the numbers will vary. The details of this process are described in Section 19.3.

6.2.2 *Processing by newsrun*

Articles and batches in *in.coming* are processed by the *newsrun* shell script.* As we mentioned earlier, the standard *crontab* supplied with C News runs *newsrun* every 15 minutes, at :00, :15, :30, and :45. When *newsrun* is invoked, it gathers up a *bunch*† of articles, decompresses any that need decompressing, and supplies their names to *relaynews*, which does most of the actual processing. If there's plenty of disk space and many files waiting to be processed, a bunch is 50 files. The bunch size is reduced if space is short, though, to avoid requiring too much temporary space.

The *relaynews* program is the heart of C News. It pulls batches apart into articles, checks the articles to see that they are valid and have not been seen on this host before, files them, logs them, and makes *history* entries for them. Originally, *relaynews* also placed filenames and article sizes into the *togo* files, but these days it does this indirectly; we'll come to that in a moment. For control messages that call for actions other than filing to be done, *relaynews* may invoke shell scripts located in *NEWSBIN/ctl* to perform the special actions.

If the *sys* file specifies feeds to other hosts, *relaynews* creates one or more *exploder* files in *NEWSARTS/out.master*, under names like *0*. The exploder files specify the names of the *togo* files and what is to go in them. Once *relaynews* is finished, *newsrun* runs the *doexplode* shell script, which in turn invokes the *explode* program. *explode* reads the exploder files and builds *togo* files. This two-step arrangement for building the *togo* files avoids problems with many *togo* files on an old system—old systems often severely limit the number of files one process may have open at a time. It's still possible to have difficulties with this,

---

* There are several options and facilities in *newsrun* that can be used to restrict processing based on priorities or suffixes; see the manual page for details.

† "Batch" is a better word, but it already has another meaning here.

actually, but only if you are feeding an enormous number of other hosts.* You don't need to worry about the details of how the exploder works; it's entirely automatic and is a part of *relaynews* for all practical purposes.

relaynews also creates the file *headers* in *NEWSARTS/in.coming*, which contains summaries of the headers of the articles it has processed. After the exploder files are processed, *newsrun* invokes the *domkov* shell script, which invokes the *mkov* and *ovsplit* programs. Between them, these two programs add the new articles to the appropriate overview files and the *headers* file is cleared out in the process. Again, this is all automatic and is part of *relaynews* for all practical purposes; we mention it only because knowing roughly how this process works might be useful for troubleshooting in certain situations.

When *relaynews* runs, it deletes all of the files that it successfully processes. If it encounters difficulties with a file, that file is left around. As its last act in processing a bunch of files, *newsrun* moves any survivors into the *bad* subdirectory of *in.coming*, making them available for human inspection. Usually, such files have been processed as thoroughly as they can be, so there is no point in moving them back up to *in.coming*. The files are only saved for inspection purposes as part of troubleshooting. (Bad files are most commonly caused by batches that don't follow the batch format properly, often because they've gotten mangled in transit.)

6.2.3 Batching

Once an article's filename (or message ID) has been placed in a *togo* file, further processing for transmission is handled by the *sendbatches* shell script and its auxiliaries. *sendbatches* is run by *cron*; the standard *crontab* file supplied with C News runs *sendbatches* once an hour, at 40 minutes past the hour. By default, *sendbatches* considers all hosts that have subdirectories in *NEWSARTS/out.going.*†

Before actually sending articles to a host, *sendbatches* considers whether there is enough disk space to send the articles, and also whether there is already too much outgoing news queued up for that host. How much is "too much" is determined by the entry for that host in in the *batchparms* control file. If there seems to be room to send some articles, *sendbatches* invokes the auxiliary program *batchsplit* (which in turn invokes *batchsplitter*) to divide the *togo* file up into *batch files*.

Batch files have names like *togo.3*. Each file represents one batch of articles to be sent to a host. Files named *togo.more* and *togo.next* are used to hold *togo* contents whose processing has been postponed. Each batch file is fed to the command

---

* If you are, you need to increase the value of NOPENBFS in *include/trbatch.h* in the C News source area, run make clean, and rebuild and reinstall C News.

† *sendbatches* has options that can be used to control which hosts it considers sending articles to; see the manual page for details.

specified in the *batchparms* line for the host. For UUCP transmission, the command typically uses the batch file to put a batch together (using the *batcher* program), possibly compresses it or encodes it for transmission, and then sends it out using the *viauux* program (which invokes the *uux* interface of the UUCP software). For NNTP transmission, the command typically does the whole job itself, invoking NNTP software to send the articles named in the batch file.

sendbatches keeps a record of current backlogs of outgoing news in the *batchlog* file in *NEWSCTL.*

6.2.4 *Expiry*

Articles are removed from the article tree when they reach the ages specified in the *explist* control file. This removal is administered by the *doexpire* shell script run by *cron.* The standard *crontab* supplied with C News runs *doexpire* once a night, at 00:59 local time.*

doexpire invokes the *expire* program to do most of the work. *expire* reads *explist* and acts accordingly, removing articles and rebuilding the *history* files. *doexpire* attempts to cope intelligently with some kinds of disk-space shortages, invoking *expire* with various options in hopes of getting at least some work done. In such cases, *doexpire* also reports the problem to the *newscrisis* alias.

After running *expire, doexpire* invokes two auxiliary programs to do secondary jobs. The *upact* program (a shell script, although a complex and subtle one) updates the third field of the *active* file to reflect the new minimum article number for each newsgroup. The *expov* shell script invokes the *expovguts* program to remove lines for expired articles from the overview files.

6.2.5 *Notes on Auxiliary Programs*

The *NEWSBIN* directory itself (as opposed to its subdirectories) contains a number of general utility programs that are used in many places in C News. A few of these are worth mentioning here:

- The *ctime* and *getabsdate* programs convert dates from decimal-second counts (used within programs and also for some filenames) to human-readable dates, and vice versa.

- The *spacefor* shell script (and in some of its variants, a *dospacefor* auxiliary program) determines how much disk space is free, less safety margins. At the moment, the safety margins can be set only by editing *spacefor.* C News tries

---

* This time has been chosen to avoid problems with Daylight Savings Time transitions, which typically happen at 02:00 and can affect times for an hour on either side. For example, in most of North America there is one night in October when the clock reads 01:00 twice.

to provide versions of *spacefor* to cover most current systems, but unfortunately the ways of getting access to this information are not well standardized.

- The *queuelen* shell script determ.XX "UUCP (Unix to Unix Copy)" "spool directories" ines how many news files have been queued up for transmission by UUCP to a given host. Here too there is sometimes a problem with a lack of standardization. Because there is no standard interface for this information, *queuelen* has to dig around in the UUCP spool directories and count files, and this is difficult to do portably. Several versions of *queuelen* are provided, but programmers with too much time on their hands keep inventing new and bizarre UUCP spool-directory layouts, so it's possible that none of them are quite right for your system.

- The *report* shell script handles all trouble reporting. If your host's mail system is strange, you may need to modify *report* to talk to it properly.

6.3 Common Problems

There are quite a few things that can go wrong with a software package as complex as C News. As a result, it's just not possible to provide recipes for dealing with all of them. However, there are some problems that are common enough that some specific advice is indicated.

6.3.1 News Processing Is Not Done

If articles or batches go into *in.coming* just fine, but then they just sit there and nothing happens, *newsrun* is not getting run properly. You probably didn't install the C News *crontab* file properly for *cron*, or there is something wrong with the *crontab* file you did install. It's hard to diagnose this problem in detail because the *cron* facility differs among systems.

6.3.2 All Articles Go into junk

It is absolutely necessary to set up your *active* file with the newsgroups you wish to receive. This is not done automatically as articles arrive. If the newsgroup of an incoming article looks okay according to your host's subscription list (the ME line in *sys*) but it is not in your *active* file, the article is filed in the *junk* pseudogroup instead. See Section 6.1.2 for information on how to set up your *active* file.

6.3.3 Newsgroups Exist but Articles Are Not Being Filed

If you're adding new newsgroups, there are *two* places you have to make changes: the newsgroups must be listed in the *active* file and they must be permitted by the subscription list in the *sys* file. If the subscription list for the ME line does not allow a particular newsgroup, then incoming articles in that newsgroup are discarded even if the newsgroup itself exists on your system. See Section 5.1.2.1 for a discussion of the ME line.

6.3.4   Local Postings Are Not Forwarded

If your local postings to regional or global newsgroups are not going out to your neighbor(s), you need to establish whether C News thinks they should be going out. Post an article to a regional test group and wait for *newsrun* to process it. Then examine the *log* entry for the article. Is the *sys*-file name of your neighbor mentioned there?

If the name is mentioned, then *relaynews* thought the article should go to that host, and at least tried to arrange it. You need to check the exploder, *sendbatches*, the programs mentioned in *batchparms*, and your communications software to find out where the article is getting lost.

If the name is not mentioned, then the article wasn't sent out because your *sys* file doesn't say it should be. In this case, the software is just doing what it's told, and the problem is in how you've configured it. You need to figure out what's wrong with your *sys* file; see Section 5.1.3 for information on setting up your *sys* file for outgoing news.

6.3.5   Incoming Articles Are Looping Back

If every incoming article you get from your neighbor is being sent back to that neighbor, there is some kind of confusion about the neighbor's name. The *sys* file name for the neighbor must match the neighbor's news name (the one it puts in Path headers) or C News simply doesn't know that those articles have already visited that host. A common scenario is that your neighbor is putting a full domain name in Path headers while you're using a short version in your *sys* file, or vice versa. The best fix is to agree on names.

A useful workaround, however, is to alter the *sys* line for that neighbor so that it uses the exclusion feature. Say your neighbor is putting *abc.def.ghi* in Path headers, while your *sys* file knows the host only as *abc*. If there is some reason you can't just agree on the name, start the *sys* line with `abc/abc.def.ghi:` rather than just `abc:`. This tells the news system to send only those articles that have not passed through *abc.def.ghi* to *abc*.

6.3.6 *Articles Are Not Expiring*

If articles come in just fine but don't expire when they should, there are several things you need to check.

First, are you sure those articles really should be expiring? Examine your *explist* file carefully, bearing in mind that a newsgroup's expiry is controlled by the first relevant line in that file, not by the most specific line. In other words, you need to read the *explist* file from top to bottom, rather than looking for the most obvious line.

Second, do those articles have explicit expiry dates, specified in Expires headers? If so, those dates control when the articles expire. The *explist* file can override those dates, but only if you specifically set it up that way. *explist* normally controls expiry times for articles that do not carry their own expiry dates.

Third, are those articles in the *history* file? If an article's message ID is <Cywzzp.2C0@kiwi.ora.com>, you can inquiry whether it's in *history* as follows:

```
% cnewsdo newshist '<Cywzzp.2C0@kiwi.ora.com>'
```

This command locates and shows the *history* line for that message ID, if any. If an article isn't in *history*, then *expire* simply isn't aware of its existence. Normally this happens only if the article was being processed at a time when the system crashed. Such "lost" articles can be recovered using the *addmissing* program.

expire program

Finally, if the articles are in *history*, are you sure that *expire* is being run? Check whether *doexpire* and *expire* are actually being accessed when they should be:

```
% ls -lu NEWSBIN/expire/doexpire NEWSBIN/expire/expire
```

(You need to fill in the actual name of *NEWSBIN*, of course.) If the dates shown by this command aren't around the time when *cron* should have run *doexpire* last night, there's probably something wrong with the news owner's *crontab* file.

6.4 *Logs and Trouble Reports*

In general, it's only necessary to consult C News' log files when you're actually doing troubleshooting. The *newsdaily* and *newswatch* scripts handle routine monitoring of the log files and send reports to the same aliases used for trouble reports.

6.4.1 Urgent Trouble Reports

Any message that is sent to the *newscrisis* alias (assuming you are using the suggested name) indicates something that needs immediate attention. Such messages are normally sent because *newswatch* has noticed something strange. There are a number of possibilities and it's difficult to give any general advice.

Disk-space shortages are the most common source of urgent reports. Any such complaint indicates that you are running too close to the edge. The only good fix is to find more space, either by expiring news more quickly or by freeing up space somewhere else. The reliable operation of a news system that is constantly short of disk space requires expert knowledge and constant attention; you should avoid this problem rather than try to solve it.

You may also see a complaint that a program (typically *expire*) ran short of memory. The usual problem here is that your system, as normally configured, does not let a single process use as much memory as it wants. Often there are per-process limits on data size. *expire* tries to bring a large amount of data into memory to speed things up; if that data doesn't fit within the per-process limit, performance suffers badly. The superuser can raise these limits, and in some cases remove them, but the details of this can be awkward and system-specific. It may be necessary to comment out the *doexpire* line in the news owner's *crontab* and invoke *doexpire* somewhat indirectly, with the superuser's *crontab* invoking a shell script along these lines:

```
#! /bin/sh
unlimit datasize
su news -c "/usr/libexec/news/expire/doexpire $*"
```

(The $* is so arguments can be supplied to this script and passed on to *doexpire*.)

6.4.2 Non-Urgent Trouble Reports

Messages sent to the *newsmaster* alias (again assuming you are using the suggested name) are for your information only and don't require rapid action.

Some such messages just indicate situations that are a bit odd, but that were handled satisfactorily by the software. For example, at most one *doexpire* should be running at a time, and *doexpire* does locking to be sure of this. If *doexpire* is started up and finds that another is already running, it reports the fact to the non-urgent alias and terminates. Such a report may indicate that you're trying to run *doexpire* too often, or that it's taking longer than expected for some reason.

One non-urgent message of note is the daily report from *newsdaily*. This message can contain various reports of odd situations and hints of trouble, such as old files lying around in *in.coming* or indications that disk-space shortages are persistently stalling batching of news to other hosts. If anything has been put into *errlog* since the last *newsdaily* run, *newsdaily* includes that in its report too.

One issue that *newsdaily* often reports on is unknown newsgroups: articles that showed up for some newsgroup(s) that your system doesn't know about. Sometimes this means your system is genuinely missing some newsgroups; other times it just means that somebody else is misinformed. See Section 3.3 for details on how to cope with such issues.

6.4.3 errlog

Anything that shows up in the *errlog* file is an indication of some kind of trouble. The messages in this file unfortunately come from a variety of sources, and they aren't very uniform or systematic (or even, unfortunately, time-stamped).

On a host that's getting a full Usenet feed, the most common sort of complaint in *errlog* is any of several indications that somebody botched the format of a control message. A mistake in the details of a control message is caught by the handler for that type of message; the different handlers report mistakes in various ways. However, if the message was so botched that *relaynews* couldn't make sense of it, didn't think it was safe to hand to a handler shell script, or couldn't find any handler for it, the problem shows up in *errlog*. In general, control-message problems can be disregarded; it's not uncommon to see several botched control messages a week.

6.4.4 log

When you are doing active troubleshooting, you may need to examine the contents of the *log* file. A typical *log* line looks like this:

```
Jul 11 16:45:02.608 (local) + <Cywzzp.2C0@kiwi.ora.com> rooster
```

A *log* line contains the following information from left to right:.

- *A date and time.* The time is given to the millisecond, although if your system clock is not that precise, the last digit or two (or even three) may be largely fictitious.

- *The name of the host that sent you the article in question.* Note that this is not the host the article originated from, but one of your neighbors that sent you the article. (`local`) means either that the article originated on your own host, or that this *log* line was generated by internal activity that doesn't relate to a specific neighbor. (For example, if you get a *cancel* control message, the control message is logged and then a (`local`) *log* line that refers to the article being canceled is generated.)

- *A classification code*, which is a single character that indicates the nature of the *log* line. Although there are a number of rarely seen special cases (consult the C News documentation for details), the overwhelming bulk of all *log* lines have classification codes of + or -. These codes mean "article accepted and filed" and "article rejected," respectively.

- *The message ID of the article*. Given this, the *newshist* command can supply the *history* line for the article, which tells you where the article has been filed so you can inspect it.

- *Supplementary information that depends on the classification code*. For +, it is a list of the other hosts this article was sent to. For -, it is the reason the article was rejected.

6.5 Wrapping Up

We hope you now have an operational C News system. If you didn't clean up the remains of the software build at the end of Chapter 5, you may want to go back to Section 5.5 and do that now. Chapters 3 and 11 contain a more complete discussion of day-to-day operations of a news system. Good luck!

7

In this chapter:
• The INN Distribution
• Preparing to Build
  INN
• Building INN
• Installing INN

Installing INN

So you've decided to use InterNetNews (INN), written by Rich Salz and now maintained by the Internet Software Consortium, as your relayer. This chapter helps you build and install INN in preparation for its service. If you aren't familiar with INN, you should budget about four hours to install the software from scratch.

This chapter assumes that you have read Chapter 2, *Getting Ready*. If you haven't, go back and do it now, as that chapter discusses decisions you have to make before setting up your news software.

In this chapter, we'll look first at getting the INN distribution and other software that you need. Then we'll cover configuring, building, and installing INN. As part of the installation process, you'll have to do some minimal configuration of INN, so that is covered here; Chapter 8, *Configuring INN*, discusses the full details of system configuration. Testing, troubleshooting, and normal operations are described in Chapter 9, *Running INN*.

Now, without any further ado, let's get on with setting up INN.

7.1 The INN Distribution

Before you can build INN, you have to get the sources. But before you get the sources, you should make sure that your system has the tools that it needs to make INN work.

7.1.1 Basic System Requirements

There are some minimal features that your system must have for the installation to be anything less than an arduous task. Chapter 2 covered general resource issues, from disk space to network bandwidth. Now here are some other considerations specifically for INN.

You should be running some form of UNIX on a machine without segmented memory, which basically means that as long as your CPU isn't a 286, you're probably fine. Your system should support basic Berkeley networking (i.e., `socket()` and family) and the `select()` system call. You also need a C development environment, complete with compiler, system include files, and libraries, to build the distribution. You might want to install a few other UNIX utilities, as described in the next section.

INN expects that real, continuous memory is plentiful. Having several free megabytes available helps to minimize paging by the master daemon, which is always running. A running size of over 40 megabytes is not unusual on a news server getting a full feed. Expect to use up to an additional megabyte for each NNTP client newsreader process that is simultaneously connected and an additional third of a megabyte for each outgoing feed.

You do not strictly need to have superuser access to install and run INN, and in fact you probably should do very little as superuser even if you do have that access. The only time you need root permission is when you associate the server with the normal port for network news connections (port 119). You can run INN on another port, however, as we will discuss later in this chapter.

INN's log file scanning program depends on certain features of *egrep* and *awk*. If your *egrep* program cannot handle a regular expression of about 100 characters, the log file scanning program will not work. You can test for this case by trying to *egrep* 100 "a" characters from */dev/null*. An error message such as "regular expression too long" means you need to install another version of *egrep*. Similarly, if *awk* has a problem with long lines or a lot of fields, you need to get a new *awk*. In particular, *awk* (or *nawk*) should be able to handle at least as many fields as sites you will be feeding.

You should have the *patch* program, which updates files based on a list of differences as produced by the *diff* utility. It isn't strictly needed for INN, however, we think you'll find that *patch* is quite useful for handling INN and other software that you get from the Net, so you'll be happy you installed it.

You should also have Perl on your system. Perl is a programming language that handles files and processes efficiently; it fills a gap between what can be done with the shell and with C. The essential parts of the news system do not yet rely on Perl, but this is likely to change in future releases of INN. INN's log file reporting script has been converted to Perl as a harbinger of future Perl use. More importantly, several user-contributed add-ons in the INN distribution use Perl and helpful community support often comes in the form of Perl programs. Perl, *patch*, and the perennial newsreader *rn* were all written by Larry Wall and they are all freely available on the Net.

Most of INN's beta testers use the GNU versions of *grep*, *awk*, and *sed*, so it is not always known whether the standard versions of these tools work with INN on a particular system. You may want to install these utilities, just to avoid any potential problems. If you already have *patch* and Perl on your system, the only reason you should need to get a new version is if the installed version is hopelessly out-of-date. The next section contains information on where to get these programs.

7.1.2 Retrieving the Sources

The Internet Software Consortium (ISC) archive is the primary distribution point for INN; see *http://www.isc.org/inn.html*. The ISC archive is accessible by FTP at *ftp.isc.org*. Look in */isc/inn* for:

inn-1.7.tar.gz

> This file contains the most recent release of INN as of late 1997.

inn.usenix.ps.Z

> This file is a PostScript version of the paper on INN that Rich Salz presented at the Summer 1992 USENIX conference.

patches

> This directory contains the official patches for various versions of INN.

The Free Software Foundation archives at *ftp.gnu.ai.mit.edu* contains versions of the UNIX utilities mentioned in the previous section. Look in *pub/gnu* for the following files. (Note that the filenames include version information. These versions are current as of late 1997; updates since that time will appear in files with similar names but higher version numbers.)

gzip-1.2.4.tar

> An uncompressed archive of the *gzip* file compression utility. You need this utility to uncompress the INN distribution and the rest of the archives listed here.

gawk-3.0.3.tar.gz

> A robust implementation of the *awk* programming language that does not limit line length or the number of fields.

grep-2.1.tar.gz

> A fast regular expression matcher that does not limit the size of regular expressions.

patch-2.5.tar.gz

> An updated version of Larry Wall's original program that can handle "unified" difference lists, a space-saving form of the regular context diff.

perl-5.004-04.tar.gz

> The latest version of the Perl programming language—a favorite of system administrators around the world.

sed-2.05.tar.gz

> A freely available implementation of the *sed* stream editor. Be warned that versions of GNU *sed* prior to version 1.13, as well as version 2.02, have bugs that make them useless with INN. If you already have GNU *sed*, make sure it isn't an afflicted version.

7.1.3 Unpacking the Sources

The INN distribution is about 1.2 megabytes, and about three times that, say 3.9 megabytes, when uncompressed and split into individual files. You'll need at least another 15 megabytes, depending on your system, to compile everything. The size of the installed news system is very system-dependent, but you can expect it to use several megabytes just for the software.

The INN distribution comes in a compressed *tar* archive that unpacks into a subdirectory. In other words, rather than creating several files and directories in *tar*'s working directory, the archive creates a subdirectory into which all of the distribution files are placed. The name of the subdirectory is the same as the name of the original *tar* file, with *.tar* stripped off.

To unpack the distribution, change to a suitable directory for holding source code that didn't come with your system, such as */usr/local/src*. After you have retrieved *inn-1.7.tar.gz* from the ISC archive server, put it in this directory. Then you can unpack INN as follows:

```
% gunzip -c inn-1.7.tar.gz | tar xf -
```

Once you have unpacked the archive, you can remove *inn-1.7.tar.gz*.

7.1.4 Making the Manual

INN comes with a manual that describes how to configure and build INN, *Installing InterNetNews*. Although this chapter can be used on its own to build the system, it is useful to have the distribution manual on hand as an additional reference. You'll find the manual in the top-level INN directory in the source area.

The manual is split into two separate files to accommodate shipping via multipart shell archives. The files can be rejoined with the following *make* command:

```
% make Install.ms
cat Install.ms.1 Install.ms.2 >Install.ms
chmod 444 Install.ms
```

The manual should be formatted with *nroff* or *troff*, using the *ms* macro package. For example:

```
% nroff -ms Install.ms | col > Install.txt
```

7.1.5 Source Directory Roadmap

Installing InterNetNews contains a brief overview of the contents of the distribution. The *MANIFEST* file in the top-level directory also provides a half-line description of each file and directory in the distribution. Here is another look at how the sources are organized:

inn-1.7

This top-level directory contains some programs used to build and install INN. It also holds INN's *COPYRIGHT* statement and distribution terms. While INN is freely available, it is not really public domain. There are a few liberal restrictions on its distribution that basically require credit to be given where credit is due. The *BUILD* file in this directory should be ignored; neither the installation manual nor this chapter suggests that it be used to build INN.

innd

This subdirectory contains the source for the master news server, which receives articles and determines how they are supposed to be handled. The news server is a constantly running daemon.

expire

This subdirectory holds the programs that are responsible for removing old articles from the system. It also contains a few programs that are useful for recovering news data files that have been corrupted or lost, which might happen if your system crashes.

frontends

Programs that are responsible for getting articles into the local news system are in the *frontends* subdirectory. *inews* posts a new article to the news system; it is usually called from programs that provide a better user interface.

rnews accepts fully formed articles, generally in batches from UUCP neighbors. *sys2nf* is useful if you need to convert your B News or C News style *sys* file to INN's *newsfeeds* file format.

backends

Programs in the *backends* subdirectory handle the post-processing of articles that *innd* has accepted. These programs include *innxmit* and *batcher*, which are used when sending articles via NNTP and UUCP, respectively. The *overchan* program caches article header information for newsreader programs.

nnrpd

> This subdirectory contains the source for the daemon that services newsreaders that use NNTP to read articles. INN forks an *nnrpd* process for each client newsreader.

config

> The configuration program and data files in *config* are used to configure INN to build on your system.

samples

> This subdirectory holds the shell scripts and data files that INN uses to run the news system.

site

> You need to customize many of the files in *samples*; the customized files should be placed in the *site* subdirectory. This makes it easier to track your changes when you update your system to a new release of INN.

7.2 Preparing to Build INN

The pre-build configuration work for INN takes two steps. First, you edit a file that contains all of the configurable options for the news system, setting the options as appropriate for your system. These values are then substituted into the source files that need them.

INN stores its configuration parameters in the *config.dist* master file in the *config* directory. To preserve the pristine state of *config.dist* so you can more easily apply official patches to it, copy this file to *config.data* before you edit it:

```
% cd config
% cp config.dist config.data
% chmod 644 config.data
```

The *config.dist* master file is set up to build INN on a system running BSD/OS 2.1. If you are trying to build INN for another operating system, you should check to see whether your operating system is represented in the *sample-configs* subdirectory of the top-level directory. If so, you could start with that sample configuration file by copying it, instead of *config.dist*, to *config.data*. For a Solaris 2.4 system, for example:

```
% cp sample-configs/config.data-solaris2.3-4 config/config.data
% cd config
% chmod 644 config.data
```

Be aware that the sample configurations often contain changes that are not strictly necessary for the operating system. Hopefully, these site policy differences, such as installation directories, will be eliminated (or at least greatly reduced) in an upcoming release.

The *config.data* file is divided into numerous sections, grouping related options that make it easier for you to navigate through the file. *config.data* also contains lots of comments to guide you through the configuration process. Here are some sample lines from *config.data*:

```
##
##  3.   OWNERSHIPS AND FILE MODES
##   Owner of articles and directories and _PATH_INNDDIR
#### =()<NEWSUSER                      @<NEWSUSER>@>()=
NEWSUSER                    news
```

Empty lines and lines starting with # (comment lines) are ignored.* Each data line consists of a keyword and a value, separated by one or more tab characters. The sample data line above shows the NEWSUSER option being set to the *news* user name. Many of the parameters in *config.data* take boolean values; these parameters should be set to DO or DONT (or DUNNO if not knowing the answer is a valid option).

WARNING   The format of each data line in *config.data* is very strict. A data line should start with a keyword, contain one or more tabs, and then list the value to be used. If there is no value, the tabs are still required. If there is a value, any trailing white space is also significant—and usually wrong.

Don't be daunted by the size of *config.data*. There are a lot of values in it that do not need to be changed for the vast majority of systems. We address all of the important options that you are likely to change, in the order in which they appear in *config.data*. You can refer to *Installing InterNetNews* for information about other options, if you think they really might be meaningful to you.

Let's tackle the hefty configuration file in two stages. First, we'll set the options that are largely independent of whatever hardware and operation system platform you are using. After that is done, we'll discuss any system-specific values you need to set.

---

* In case you are wondering, the ## comment lines are meant to provide useful comments, while the #### lines are there to support upgrading the file with *subst*. You should ignore the #### lines.

7.2.1 *System-Independent Options*

The following discussion is organized according to the headings you'll see in *config.data*. Within each section, we discuss the options in the order in which they appear in the file. Options that you shouldn't usually bother with are not described here. We also cover a few parameters here that are operating-system dependent because some more general, cross-system discussion of their significance is warranted.

7.2.1.1 *Make config parameters*

If your system fully supports the BSD `mmap()` system call, you should add `-DMMAP` to the end of the `DBZCFLAGS` value so that the *dbz.c* library module is compiled to use `mmap()`. The advantage of *mmap* is reduced filesystem I/O and increased resource sharing ability that can lower the overall memory requirements for your system. Several systems include broken implementations of `mmap()` that should not be used. These include Ultrix, Linux prior to version 1.3.57, and RS/6000 AIX (although this can be fixed with IBM's U413090 PTF patch). Systems that are known to work fine with `mmap()` include Digital UNIX 4.0, Irix 5.2, SunOS 4, and Solaris 2. If you are unsure, your best bet is to not use `mmap()`, run your system for a couple of weeks, and then reconfigure, recompile, and reinstall INN with `-DMMAP` to compare.

If you are using SCO Xenix/386 2.3 or are running System V on an Intel 386 CPU, do not enable the optimizer flag, `-O`, in `DBZCFLAGS` or *dbz.c* will be miscompiled. If `-O` is defined in `CFLAGS`, you need to delete `$(CFLAGS)` from `DBZCFLAGS`.

You may want to change the values of the options about manual pages, depending on how you want manual pages installed. `MANPAGESTYLE` is usually set to `SOURCE`, but you can change it to `NROFF-PACK` to only store the formatted manual pages in packed format on System V machines or `NROFF-PACK-SCO` for SCO's particular twist on the System V method. If you really don't want any manual pages installed, set `MANPAGESTYLE` to `NONE`.

The `MANX` parameters specify the location of the manual pages for INN programs and file formats. Modern systems have varying ideas about where to put these, so you may need to change the values here. If you want to point the `MANX` variables to your system manual page directories (which is only reasonable if you install few other packages on your system), then you should set all of the parameters to */usr/man/manl*, or whatever the local manual page directory is on your system.

A decision item that is common to all platforms is whether to compile programs with debugging information, so that you can use a symbolic debugger on them. While the distributed *config.dist* is set up to do so, you might not be able to compile with debugging if you also want your compiler to try to optimize the machine code it generates. If you want debugging information, we trust that you're well versed with your C compiler and can set `CFLAGS` and `LDFLAGS` appropriately. Most people should just change the `-g` switch to `-O` in each value.

7.2.1.2 Logging levels

You should change the value of `L_NOTICE` to be `LOG_NOTICE`, instead of `LOG_WARNING`, to head off some confusion between *syslog* priorities and the names of files. You should not have to change any of the other values, unless you are using an older *syslog* without the `LOG_NEWS` facility. Your *syslog* manual page should indicate whether you can use `LOG_NEWS`. If you cannot, you need to set `LOG_INN_SERVER` and `LOG_INN_PROG` to `LOG_LOCALN`, where *N* is a level that does not conflict with any others being used by the system-wide *syslog.conf* file.

7.2.1.3 Ownerships and file modes

The default values in this section are all quite reasonable. `NEWSUSER` should be set to the user ID for the news owner; we recommend using *news*, which is the default setting. You need to set up an account for the news owner in the system *passwd* file. The default group for the news owner should be set to `NEWSGROUP`, which is also *news* by default. You also need to create an entry for that group ID in the system *group* file.

You might want to change `NEWSMASTER` to have the value *newsmaster*. You should create mail aliases for both *usenet* and *newsmaster*, as people from other sites will expect either address to work to contact you should there be a need. These aliases should send messages to the people who are responsible for your news system.

We recommend that you set `GROUPDIR_MODE` to `02775`. This setting ensures that files and directories get the group ownership of their parent directory, no matter what the effective group ID of the process that creates them.

7.2.1.4 C library differences

The bulk of this section of *config.data* contains machine-specific options, which are covered in Section 7.2.2. There are, however, a few parameters that we need to discuss here.

Installing InterNetNews recommends that `LOCK_STYLE` be set to `NONE` because INN doesn't really lock any files using system lock functions. But the manual is wrong. Not only should you have `LOCK_STYLE` enabled in case you ever want to use *innxmit* without the provided scripts, but you also really must enable it if you intend to use the news overview database for the benefit of newsreader programs.

The recommended locking style is FLOCK, as it does not involve the overhead (and sometimes buggy nature) of the network lock daemon, *lockd*. If you are locking news system files across the network (and we recommend you avoid this if at all possible), you must choose a method that uses *lockd*. Both LOCKF and FCNTL support using *lockd*; you need to check the *lockf* and *fcntl* manual pages on your system to see which one you should specify.

You must set the CLX_STYLE parameter to the system call that properly sets the close-on-exec flag for a file descriptor. For most System V-derived systems, the value should be FCNTL. If you fail to set this option properly, it may not keep INN from compiling, but it will result in a lot of news processes hanging around long after they are useful.

WARNING   You might expect that the news system would not fully compile if you set one of these values incorrectly. Unfortunately, more than one system has been known to compile cleanly with an incorrect value for LOCK_STYLE or CLX_STYLE and then fail to perform locking or close-on-exec operations correctly. Be extra careful with these parameters.

The HAVE_UNIX_DOMAIN option specifies whether or not your system supports UNIX domain sockets. You need to determine if your socket() system call supports sockets that use internal Unix protocols. The best way to do this is to look at the socket() manual page for the accepted values for its first argument. The phrases "AF_LOCAL," "system internal protocols," or "Unix domain" are all tip offs that you can set this to DO. If it isn't obviously there, you must set HAVE_UNIX_DOMAIN to DONT.

7.2.1.5 C library omissions

Section 7.2.2 covers whether or not you need to list any .c and .o files in MISSING_SRC and MISSING_OBJ, as this information is system-specific. The one piece of system-independent advice we have is: do not set MISSING_MAN to anything unless you intend to install the objects from MISSING_OBJ in publicly available libraries. If you set MISSING_MAN and the objects are not made part of the standard system library, you should edit the relevant manual pages in the *doc* subdirectory of the top-level directory. In that case, the manual pages need references to the libraries that need to be linked in order to use the functions they describe, and their "See Also" sections should point only to other functions that are available on the system.

7.2.1.6 Miscellaneous config data

If your system has mmap() (and is not one of the systems with a broken implementation listed in Section 7.2.1.1), set ACT_STYLE to MMAP. One additional caveat is that on some SVR4 systems the last modification time of the *active* file is not updated when INN adds articles; see the System V information in Section 7.2.2.10.

The value you use for REM_STYLE is a matter of convenience. This option tells *inews* and new NNTP newsreaders that are compiled with the INN client library whether to look in INN's *inn.conf* file or in a *server* file used by the NNTP reference implementation for the name of the NNTP server to connect to. You have to install *inn.conf* for *inews* for other reasons anyway, so you might as well leave this option set to INND.

The RNEWS_SAVE_BAD option controls whether *rnews* saves articles that the server rejects. If you have any UUCP neighbors, you should set RNEWS_SAVE_BAD to DO if you want to be able to inform them about problems with their articles that stopped the articles from going any farther than your host. (There is currently no automated support for doing this; you might find notifying them to be too much trouble.) *rnews* is also used for any locally generated articles that *nnrpd* or *inews* spool when *innd* is unavailable, so you might want to turn RNEWS_SAVE_BAD on to see if your users are having any problems with posting.

The RNEWS_LOG_DUPS parameter is not important if you don't have any UUCP neighbors. However, if you have multiple UUCP feeds, you should set it to SYS-LOG if you want to determine how you can reduce the amount of redundant traffic over the links. This setting causes INN to log the duplicates using *syslog*.

The CHECK_INCLUDED_TEXT variable is controversial. Think about how you would handle being confronted by a user who wants to know why his posting was rejected because it included more text than it added. If you are inclined to answer, "I'm sorry, but that's because etiquette on the Net is to edit cited information to the most relevant context," leave the option set to DO. If your reaction is "How dare this fascist software dictate the style of articles!" or "Net etiquette is a good thing, but this attempt to enforce it is poorly thought out and does not have the desired results," keep your blood pressure down by changing the setting to DONT.

Set INEWS_PATH to DONT. This setting prevents the system from putting hosts in the *inews* Path header. This information is redundant with the NNTP-Posting-Host header that is also added to news postings.

The fifth field of the system password file is one of the most aesthetically abused items on many systems. The MUNGE_GECOS parameter specifies whether *inews* can try to deduce the user's name from the typical cruft found in the field. Leave this option set to DO and let it try.

If your system is tight on memory and you expect to keep a full feed of news around for at least a couple of weeks, set `INND_DBZINCORE` to 0. This setting prevents *innd* from keeping all of the *history* database pointers, which are a few megabytes, in memory. Although this setting will slow your news system down, the performance tradeoff could well be a win if it keeps your system from thrashing. If you disable `INND_DBZINCORE`, you should also set `NNRP_DBZINCORE_DELAY` to -1.

The `VERIFY_CANCELS` option controls whether the system verifies that the person sending a *cancel* message is indeed the person who posted the article being canceled. The problem with this kind of verification is that there are a lot of distributed environments in which a *cancel* message that a user posted for her own article appears to the system as if it didn't come from the same place as the original article. Setting this parameter to DO means that your readers will occasionally see articles that the original poster legitimately tried to cancel. More significantly, it also means that when a concerned news administrator tries to cancel a deluge of articles from a program that has gone wild, the *cancel* message will not be honored on your system. Setting the option to DONT simply means that an occasional miscreant will succeed in removing someone else's article.

Many people were unhappy about the introduction of the `LIKE_PULLERS` option in INN version 1.5. When this parameter is set to DONT, the system is supposed to guard against people pulling whole news feeds off of your server. Its implementation still needs a little work, however, because regular readers are experiencing undesirable delays after they read 100 articles in a session. Until a better implementation comes along (which is expected in the next version), you should set `LIKE_PULLERS` to DO.

If you are not using `mmap()`, INN brings the *active* and *history* files on disk up to date with the copies that it keeps in memory for every `ICD_SYNC_COUNT` articles it receives. If you get a very limited feed, or you are very concerned about losing information in the event of *innd* or the system crashing, lower this value to 1. The price you pay for the improved accuracy is slightly degraded performance from increased disk activity when many articles are coming in. If you want to improve throughput at the risk of some loss of data in the event of a crash, raise the value to 200 or even 500.

The `NNTPLINK_LOG` parameter is designed to support one of the operational modes of the *nntplink* transmission program, as described in Section 13.2.1. However, the filename information stored in the log when this option is set is also quite useful in researching problems not related to *nntplink*. If you can afford roughly 25 bytes per article on the logging disk partition, which is about 20 megabytes for an indiscriminately full feed (850,000 per day) or often under a megabyte for a more restrained feed, you should set the option to DO.

Enabling `IPADDR_LOG` causes INN to log by the hostname or the IP address of the system that sent each article it receives, rather than the hostname in the Path header that is traditionally used by news software. The hostname or address is much harder to spoof than the Path header, so enabling this option provides more secure auditing. Because of the better auditing, we recommended that you keep `IPADDR_LOG` set to DO.

Keep `LOCAL_MAX_ARTSIZE` set at `1000000L`, one million bytes, which is the default value for `MAX_ART_SIZE`. There's no reason to let your users post something so big that it will just be rejected on the many other news systems that are using the default value.

You can ignore the `HAVE_UUSTAT` variable if you are not sending news via UUCP. If you are going to be using UUCP, however, set `HAVE_UUSTAT` to DO to specify that *uustat* be used by *send-uucp* to discern how many news jobs are already queued for a site. If you don't have *uustat* on your system, set the option to DONT. In this case, a less accurate job counting method using *uuq* is used instead.

7.2.1.7 Paths to common programs

The next few sections of *config.data*, from "Paths to Common Programs" to "Log and Config Files," define a number of `_PATH` parameters. These parameters specify the locations of various pieces of the news system, including programs, the article tree, control files, and log files. You may want to change the values of some of these parameters to put pieces of the news system where you want them. As discussed in Section 2.7, you may want to change the locations of the various parts of the news system. To illustrate how this is done, we are going to assume you want to change to the locations used in Section 2.7: the article tree in */news*, overview files in */news/overview*, control files in */var/news*, and software in */var/libexec/news*. The easiest way to do that is to use the search-and-replace function of your editor to replace the default pathnames with the ones that you want to use.

As shipped, the *config.data* file organizes the various pieces of INN in the following locations:

/usr/news/bin

> This directory contains the INN daemons and other news programs. The more traditional locations were */usr/bin* or */usr/lib/newsbin*. As discussed in Section 2.7, however, we recommend using */usr/libexec/news* instead. We'll use the symbolic name *NEWSBIN* to refer to this directory from now on.

/var/news/spool

> This directory holds the article tree, as well as lists of what articles are to be sent to news neighbors. The traditional location was */usr/spool/news*, but we recommend using */news* instead, especially if your article tree is stored on its own filesystem. We'll use the symbolic name *NEWSARTS* to refer to this directory henceforth.

/var/news/etc

> This directory contains the news server control files. These were traditionally put in */usr/lib/news*, but we recommend using just */var/news* now. We'll use the symbolic name *NEWSCTL* for this directory.

/var/news/run

> This directory stores process ID files and filesystem sockets; it is fine as is.

/var/news/locks

> This directory contains the lock files for managing resources used by multiple programs; it is fine as is.

/var/log/news

> This directory holds copious statistical information about the operation of the news system. If your system puts other log files in */var/log*, as many now do, this is a good location.

After you have used search-and-replace to change any of the general paths that you are inclined to change, you may need to reconsider particular _PATH parameters. We'll go through these parameters in the order in which they appear in *config.data*, starting in the "Paths to Common Programs" section.

If you want to use *gzip* instead of *compress* for storing aged news logs, point _PATH_COMPRESS at the location of *gzip* and change _PATH_COMPRESSEXT to *.gz*. A side effect of this change is that you can unpack batches from your UUCP neighbors without needing to know whether they were compressed with *compress*, *gzip*, or *pack*.

_PATH_EGREP, _PATH_AWK, and _PATH_SED have to point at the utilities that work as described in Section 7.1.1. Be careful with relative pathnames here. By default, the PATH variable in *samples/innshellvars* (the shell script sourced by all other INN shell scripts) inherits PATH from its parent environment. You are safer using a full pathname for these programs.

If you have newsreaders already running on your system, they may expect to find *inews* in one or more locations. You either have to recompile the programs that use *inews* to point to the new location, or replace the other *inews* programs with symbolic links to actual copies of INN's *inews*, which is installed in

_PATH_INEWS. You cannot use C News' *inews* as is with INN, if you already have that version of *inews* on your system.

The UUCP system needs to know where to find *rnews* if you have incoming UUCP feeds. If you can't provide a path to UUCP, you need a symbolic link from */bin/rnews* to _PATH_RNEWS. If you don't have symbolic links, you should copy *rnews* instead. C News' *rnews* does not work with INN.

The first parameter to consider in the "Paths Related to the Spool Directory" section of *config.data* is _PATH_OVERVIEWDIR. If you have a separate disk that you can devote to the overview files, set _PATH_OVERVIEWDIR to the directory where the disk will be mounted to increase disk performance. If you mount it as a subdirectory of _PATH_SPOOL, include a period in the name (e.g., "*over.view*") so that it cannot ever conflict with a hierarchy name. From now on, we'll use the symbolic name *NEWSOV* to refer to the overview directory. Overview data takes up about ten percent of the size of the article tree, so plan partition sizes accordingly. If you do change _PATH_OVERVIEWDIR, you probably don't need to bother with making _PATH_OVERVIEW a hidden file, so you can remove the leading dot (.).

If you have globally replaced the directories named at the beginning of this section, or if you have left them alone, you should not need to make changes in the "Execution Paths for innd and rnews," "Sockets Created by innd or Clients," and "Log and Config Files" sections of *config.data*. The only exception is that, logically, both *innshellvars* and *parsecontrol* should be in *NEWSBIN*, not *NEWSCTL*, so you may want to adjust the _PATH_SHELLVARS and _PATH_PARSECTL parameters accordingly.

7.2.1.8 innwatch configuration

The *innwatch* program monitors your system resources to keep INN from consuming all of them. You can run your server a lot closer to the edge of total resource consumption than the default values in this section allow, especially if you are installing INN on a system (or at least some disk partitions) that is primarily dedicated to news.

innwatch can stop incoming news based on system load. You may want to disable that feature, however, because incoming news with INN is usually responsible for a very small fraction of whatever is driving the load up. If you are running INN on a machine that is dedicated to news, you should certainly disable this feature. You can raise the *LOAD parameters to something unlikely to ever be attained. Changing the values to 20,000 or more should be sufficiently ludicrous to effectively stop *innwatch* from ever shutting off incoming news.

Available disk space is a more meaningful concern. The default value of
INNWATCH_SPOOLSPACE is 8000; this can reasonably be lowered to 2000 if news
is the only thing fighting for space on the spool disk. The default value of 25,000
for INNWATCH_LIBSPACE seems high, but it is set that high to leave room for
INN to rebuild the *history* file. This file can *easily* be as large as 25 megabytes on a
system getting a full feed and keeping news for two weeks and is more like 250
megabytes in late 1997. Nevertheless, 25,000 leads INN to stop itself more than it
should. The problem is that *newswatch* doesn't take into account that the space
might be temporarily consumed by the very *expire* process for which it is trying to
reserve space. You can lower it to around 2000 also, as long as you take into
account anything else on the system that might want space in that partition.

Three parameters in *config.data* control how *innwatch.ctl* is configured to get free
space information: these parameters are INNWATCH_DF, INNWATCH_INODES, and
INNWATCH_BLOCKS. Set INNWATCH_DF to point to the *df* program on your system. Then use that program to find out which fields specify the number of free
blocks and free inodes (the latter shows up with the -i option) and set
INNWATCH_INODES and INNWATCH_BLOCKS accordingly. Now confirm the settings with the same *awk* command into which *innwatch* substitutes the field values. For example, in the following listing the free inodes show up in column
three, so set INNWATCH_INODES to 3 and use $3 as the field to print in a test
awk command:

```
% /bin/df -i /news
Filesystem   iused    ifree   %iused   Mounted on
/dev/sd2c      988   482850      0%    /var/news/spool
% /bin/df -i /news | awk 'NR == 2 {print $3}'
482850
```

It may seem pointless to actually confirm how well you counted by performing
the *awk* test, but this is one of the frequently misconfigured areas of INN. Dou-
blechecking that you got it right is a good exercise.

7.2.1.9 Tcl configuration

As of INN version 1.5, *innd* can be built with embedded support for Tcl, Perl,
both, or neither. If support for either of the languages is compiled in, the server
can then run each incoming article through a script written in the appropriate language. Such a script could be used to collect real-time information about articles
the server sees, or could even decide whether to have the server accept an article
at all. *innd* has built-in filtering mechanisms, but they are somewhat limited. A Tcl
or Perl script can filter articles based on criteria that cannot be expressed with the
built-in filtering mechanisms.

Compiling in such language support does make the server a little larger and more
complex, so if you're not going to use it, it is best to leave it out. If you want

support for an embedded scripting language, we recommend that you go with Perl because most scripts contributed to the news administration community are written in Perl. Embedded Perl scripts can also do something that Tcl scripts cannot— they can be executed on every article served to a newsreader client.

However, if you decide you really want to include Tcl support, you need to set `TCL_SUPPORT` to DO and then set the other parameters appropriately. `TCL_INC` should specify the *include* directory that contains the file *tcl.h*. On systems like BSD/OS that ship with Tcl, this is probably */usr/include*.

If you build INN with Tcl support, sample Tcl scripts are installed in `_PATH_TCL_STARTUP` and `_PATH_TCL_FILTER`. These scripts are very low impact and non-intrusive—they don't soak up CPU cycles doing unusual things— but you should know that they're there nonetheless. The files must exist if you compile with Tcl support, but they can be zero length.

The *README.tcl_hook* file in the top-level INN source directory contains additional information on using Tcl to filter news traffic. If your system does not come with Tcl, you'll need to get it. It is available at *http://sunscript.sun.com/TclTkCore/*.

7.2.1.10 PGP configuration

INN can authenticate changes to the newsgroup namespace by using the PGP authentication system, as described in Section 8.2.4.1. There is no good reason to set `WANT_PGPVERIFY` to DONT because even if you don't want to use PGP, you can just say so in your *control.ctl* file. Leaving `WANT_PGPVERIFY` set to DO simply says that you want the option to authenticate control messages with PGP; it does not place any burden on the system.

If you are going to use PGP authentication (and we certainly recommend it) but you don't yet have PGP, you can get information about both commercial and freeware versions at *ftp://ftp.csn.net/mpj/getpgp.asc*. You can worry about building PGP after you have INN installed. Just set `_PATH_PGP` to the directory in which you plan to install the *pgp* executable.

7.2.1.11 Local configuration

This short section (really short) contains the `_PATH_NEWSHOME` parameter, which INN 1.5.1 uses to set the `HOME` environment variable in *inndstart*. Set it to the home directory of the news owner (i.e., the `NEWSUSER` parameter you defined back in Section 7.2.1.3.) If you ever change the home directory of the news owner in the system's password file, try to remember that you also have to change it here.

7.2.1.12   actsync configuration

The *actsync* and *actsyncd* programs can be used to keep the newsgroup list (*active* file) on your INN server up to date with the newsgroup list at another site, perhaps your upstream site or a site like the Internet Software Consortium. (The *news.uu.net* site mentioned in the manual page is itself synchronized on *ftp://ftp.isc.org/pub/usenet/CONFIG/active*.) The variables set in this section are used to generate the *actsyncd.cfg* file, which uses the information to call *actsync*.

The ACTSYNC_HOST parameter is supposed to be set to the name of an authoritative host (like *news.uu.net*) to which your site can connect to do an NNTP *LIST ACTIVE* command. It can also be the name of a file in *active* file format, like the previously mentioned *active* file at *ftp.isc.org*. However, we recommend using a local temporary filename, such as */var/tmp/master.active*, as described in Section 8.2.4.2. You can then use any of several different methods to create the file before you process it.

All of the flags in ACTSYNC_FLAGS are described in the *actsync* manual page. For the initial configuration and build of INN, they are all reasonable enough, but you may want to make a few changes now to save yourself time later. We suggest that you change -g 7 to -g 0 and -s 79 to -s 0. These changes disable checks on the depth of hierarchies and the length of newsgroup names. Some non-joke newsgroups already have eight name elements, and a couple dozen more have seven elements—just one more spinoff away from being excluded with the -g 7 flag. If this all sounds like gibberish at the moment, don't worry about it yet. It really isn't that important to getting INN going.

7.2.1.13   Perl configuration

As we mentioned in Section 7.2.1.9, you can build *innd* so that it can use Perl scripts to process all of the news traffic coming into your server in real time. You need to have Perl version 5.003 or greater for this to work.

If you want to include support for Perl, set PERL_SUPPORT to DO. Then set up the PERL_LIB and PERL_INC variables by commenting out the blank lines and uncommenting the lines that contain actual settings. These values are for Perl5 built locally on a BSD/OS box, so you need to change the paths to the Perl5 *CORE* directory as appropriate for your system.

If you build INN with Perl support, sample Perl scripts are installed in the three locations specified in *config.data*. Like the sample Tcl scripts, these scripts don't really do anything, but they must be present if Perl support is compiled in. They can be zero length, but the samples do contain a lot of commented out code that can be instructive to review. The *README.perl_hook* file in the top-level INN source directory contains additional information on using Perl to filter news traffic.

7.2.2 Operating-System-Dependent Values

As shipped, *config.dist* is set up for a BSD/OS 2.1 system. If that is the type of machine you are using for your news system, you shouldn't have to change any of the values for the machine-dependent parameters. This section describes the parameters that need to be changed for other types of systems.

We've tried to cover a representative sample of different UNIX operating systems here, as we obviously cannot cover them all. We've covered some, but not all, of the systems for which there are user-contributed *config.data* files in *sample-configs;* we've also covered a few systems that do not have sample files.

For each system, there is a table that lists the parameters that need to be changed, as well as the values that should be used. The parameters in each table are arranged in the order in which they appear in *config.data.* These tables are derived mainly from differences between the sample files in *sample-configs* and the master *config.dist* file. So, if you are using your system's sample file, you don't actually need to change the parameters listed in the table. You may, however, want to examine the list to ensure that the settings make sense for your system.

The information on a particular system may also include some notes that do not correspond directly to *config.data* parameters. This information is provided here to keep all of the system-specific information in one place.

If you experience any problems with the suggested configuration, you can find the most up-to-date lore on specific machines in the INN Frequently Asked Questions (FAQ) list. The FAQ is posted weekly to *news.software.nntp* and is also available at *ftp://ftp.xlink.net/pub/news/docs/.* Parts 2 and 9 of the FAQ contain system-specific information.

If you are using a system that we don't cover here, but there is a sample *config.data* file for it, you can examine the differences between the sample file and the master *config.dist* file using *diff.* You should also consult Parts 2 and 9 of the INN FAQ, to see if there is any specific configuration advice for your platform.

7.2.2.1 AIX

Table 7-1 lists the configuration values for AIX 4.1.4. If you are using AIX 3.1, you need to set `MISSING_OBJ` to *syslog.o* and `MISSING_SRC` to *syslog.c*. You also need to replace *syslogd* as discussed in Section 7.2.3.2.

Table 7-1: INN Configuration Values for AIX 4.1.4

Parameter	Value
CC	cc
USE_CHAR_CONST	DO
CFLAGS	$(DEFS) -O2 -qarch=ppc -qtune=604
PROF	
LIBS	
LINTFLAGS	-b -h -wkD $(DEFS)
LINTFILTER	| sed -n -f ../sedf.aix
MANPAGESTYLE	BSD4.4
VAR_STYLE	VARARGS
LOCK_STYLE	FCNTL
HAVE_SETPROCTITLE	DONT
HAVE_TM_GMTOFF	DONT
FORK	fork
FDCOUNT_STYLE	SYSCONF
NEED_TIME	DO
CTYPE	isXXXXX((c))
MMAP_PTR	void *
_PATH_SH	/usr/bin/sh
_PATH_GZIP	
INNWATCH_DF	"/bin/df -v"
INNWATCH_BLOCKS	3

`mmap()` on RS/6000 machines can cause major system problems. Be sure you have the PTF U413090 patch applied if you want to use `mmap()`.

You should expect to waste a lot of space in the spool directories on RS/6000 machines. News articles tend to average around 2 Kbytes. The minimum block and fragment sizes you can get with an RS/6000 filesystem leave a lot of disk space unusable when tens of thousands of files of this size are stored.

7.2.2.2 BSD/OS

For BSD/OS 2.0, 3.0, and 3.1, you've already set the operating-system specific information. In versions of BSD/OS prior to version 2.0, you need to change a few *Makefile* variables for the build and installation processes to work properly. In the *Makefile* in each of the *config* and *site* directories, change SHELL to */usr/contrib/bin/bash*. In the *Makefile* in *lib*, delete the *./llib-linn.ln* dependency from the *install* target.

The modules *lib/remopen.c* and *innd/rc.c* do not compile on BSDI 1.1 because of conflicting types for *ntohs*. Find the following line in *lib/remopen.c*:

```
#if    !defined(ntohs) && !defined(NETSWAP)
```

Change it to:

```
#if    !defined(ntohs) && !defined(NETSWAP) && !defined(__bsdi__)
```

Now add similar `!defined(__bsdi__)` conditions in *innd/rc.c* around the
`htons` and `ntohl` definitions.

Even further back in the BSD/OS lineage, with BSDI version 0.9.4.1, you need to
install the GNU *sed* program. (See Section 7.1.2 for information on retrieving this
program.) The version of *sed* shipped with BSDI 0.9.4.1 silently runs into an infi-
nite loop while trying to process newsgroup control messages.

7.2.2.3 Digital UNIX

Table 7-2 lists the *config.data* parameters and values for Digital UNIX 4.0.

Table 7-2: INN Configuration Values for Digital UNIX 4.0

Parameter	Value
CC	cc
DBZFLAGS	$(CFLAGS) -DMMAP
LIBS	
VAR_STYLE	VARARGS
FORK	fork
RES_STYLE	TIMES
FDCOUNT_STYLE	SYSCONF
MMAP_PTR	void *
_PATH_COMPRESS	/usr/bin/gzip
_PATH_COMPRESSEXT	.gz
_PATH_GZIP	/usr/bin/gzip
INNWATCH_DF	/usr/bin/df

7.2.2.4 FreeBSD

Table 7-3 lists the *config.data* parameters and values for FreeBSD 2.0.

Table 7-3: INN Configuration Values for FreeBSD 2.0

Parameter	Value
DEFS	-I../include -pipe
CC	cc
USE_CHAR_CONST	DO
LIBS	-lgnumalloc
SIGVAR	int
HAVE_VFORK	DO

Table 7–3: INN Configuration Values for FreeBSD 2.0 (continued)

Parameter	Value
NBIO_STYLE	IOCTL
FDCOUNT_STYLE	SYSCONF

You should be cautious about using mmap() with FreeBSD. Certain releases of
FreeBSD have serious problems with mmap(), but performance without it is still
quite good. Version 2.2.1 of FreeBSD does not seem to have any problems with
mmap().

7.2.2.5 HP-UX

INN 1.7 has a sample configuration for HP-UX 9.05. Additionally, Part 9 of the INN
FAQ contains some example configuration settings for HP-UX 10, so we've based
the configuration table on that information. Be warned that the table in *Installing
InterNetNews* is relative to the old default configuration, which was for a SunOS
4.1 system. Table 7–4 lists the configuration values for HP-UX 10.20.

Table 7–4: INN Configuration Values for HP-UX 10.20

Parameter	Value
CC	cc
CFLAGS	$(DEFS) -g -Ae
DBZCFLAGS	$(CFLAGS) -Ae
LIBS	
LINTFLAGS	-b -h $(DEFS)
LINTFILTER	| cat
LOCK_STYLE	LOCKF
HAVE_SETPROCTITLE	DONT
HAVE_TM_GMTOFF	DONT
HAVE_VFORK	DO
_PATH_MAILCMD	/usr/bin/mailx
INNWATCH_DF	/bin/bdf

These settings use the unbundled ANSI C compiler. If you haven't bought the
unbundled compiler, you should be able to use *gcc* and *bison* for *cc* and *yacc*,
respectively. If you use *gcc*, remove **-Ae** from the various flags lines.

For other versions of HP-UX, you need to use the *bdf* command in place of *df* for
INNWATCH_DF. You may also need to set HAVE_SETSID to DO so *innd* starts
properly when the machine reboots.

See what happens with your HP-UX when you type the following:

```
% /bin/sh
% case foo; in '[') ;; esac
```

If */bin/sh* cannot handle this command without generating an error, you need to get a fix for SR #5003-009811 from HP.

HP system patch PHCO_5056 fixes a memory leak in HP-UX 9.01 that affects INN.

7.2.2.6 IRIX

Table 7–5 lists the configuration values for IRIX 5.2. The INN FAQ mentions that some unnamed people have had trouble trying to run INN on IRIX 5.1, but that IRIX 5.2 and 5.3 are much better.

Table 7–5: INN Configuration Values for IRIX 5.2

Parameter	Value
CC	cc
USE_CHAR_CONST	DO
DBZCFLAGS	$(CFLAGS) -DMMAP
LIBS	-lelf
LINTFLAGS	$(DEFS)
LINTFILTER	| sed -n -f ../sedf.sysv
RANLIB	echo
OFFSET_T	off_t
U_INT32_T	__uint32_t
INT32_T	__int32_t
LOCK_STYLE	FCNTL
HAVE_SETPROCTITLE	DONT
HAVE_TM_GMTOFF	DONT
FORK	fork
CLX_STYLE	FCNTL
MMAP_PTR	void *
_PATH_SENDMAIL	/usr/lib/sendmail -t
_PATH_COMPRESS	/usr/bsd/compress
_PATH_GZIP	/usr/sbin/gzip

The INN FAQ also contains some IRIX recommendations from Robert Keller. He recommends that you set `lbsize` to `4096` in */etc/fstab* for *efs* filesystems. This setting offers improved performance over the default setting of 32K that is normally used for pre-allocating space for new files. Keller says it is even better to use an *xfs* filesystem for news articles, no doubt in part because of the improved file creation and removal time in large directories, but be sure to increase the fundamental block size from 512 bytes to 2048 bytes when you create it. He has some more useful tips at *http://reality.sgi.com/rck/software/inn.html.*

7.2.2.7 *Linux*

Table 7–6 lists the configuration values for Linux 2.0.18. Part 2 of the FAQ contains a number of tips for other versions of Linux.

Table 7–6: INN Configuration Values for Linux 2.0.18

Parameter	Value
USE_CHAR_CONST	DO
PROF	-p
LIBS	
LINTFLAGS	
LINTFILTER	
HAVE_SETPROCTITLE	DONT
HAVE_TM_GMTOFF	DONT
FORK	fork
BIND_USE_SIZEOF	DONT
CLX_STYLE	FCNTL
NBIO_STYLE	IOCTL
FDCOUNT_STYLE	SYSCONF
CTYPE	isXXXXX((c))
_PATH_AWK	/bin/awk
_PATH_SED	/bin/sed
_PATH_GZIP	/bin/gzip
INNWATCH_INODES	4

7.2.2.8 *Solaris*

Table 7–7 lists the *config.data* parameters and values for Solaris 2.3 and Solaris 2.4. INN 1.7 now also includes a sample configuration for Solaris 2.5.

Table 7–7: INN Configuration Values for Solaris 2.3 and 2.4

Parameter	Value
DEFS	-I../include -DSUNOS5 -DPOLL_BUG
USE_CHAR_CONST	DO
CFLAGS	$(DEFS) -O
LDFLAGS	-g
LIBS	-lnsl -lsocket -lelf -lresolv
LINTFLAGS	-b -h $(DEFS)
LINTFILTER	| sed -n -f ../sedf.sysv
RANLIB	echo

Table 7-7: INN Configuration Values for Solaris 2.3 and 2.4 (continued)

Parameter	Value
ALIGNPTR	long
SIGVAR	int
LOCK_STYLE	LOCKF
HAVE_SETPROCTITLE	DONT
HAVE_TM_GMTOFF	DONT
CLX_STYLE	FCNTL
RES_STYLE	TIMES
FDCOUNT_STYLE	SYSCONF
ALARMVAL	unsigned
SLEEPVAL	unsigned
_PATH_SENDMAIL	/usr/lib/sendmail -t
_PATH_COMPRESS	/bin/compress
_PATH_AWK	/usr/bin/awk
_PATH_SED	/usr/bin/sed

Solaris is an SVR4-based system, so be sure that you set CLX_STYLE to FCNTL. Otherwise you'll be wondering why you have so many old new processes hanging around on your system.

As reported in the FAQ, TCP throughput can drop well below what it should be on Solaris 2.5 machines if Sun fixes 103169-05 and 103447-03 are not applied. For Solaris 2.5.1, fixes 103582-01 and 103630-01 address the same problems.

The FAQ also reports that while INN does work with Solaris 2.0 through Solaris 2.3, it may take a bit of effort to get it working. The problem is that there are a number of Solaris patches for these versions. Depending on which Solaris patches you have installed, you have to install certain INN patches. There are too many combinations of Solaris patches and INN patches for us to tell you exactly what you need to do for Solaris versions prior to version 2.5. The FAQ, however, does contain more detailed information if you are trying to build INN on such a system.

7.2.2.9 SunOS

Table 7-8 lists the configuration values for SunOS 4.1.

Table 7–8: INN Configuration Values for SunOS 4.1

Parameter	Value
LIBS	-lresolv
LINTFLAGS	-b -h $(DEFS)
POINTER	char
SIGVAR	int
HAVE_SETPROCTITLE	DONT
FORK	fork
NOFILE_LIMIT	126
ABORTVAL	int
QSORTVAL	int
FREEVAL	int
MISSING_SRC	strerror.c mktemp.c memmove.c
MISSING_OBJ	strerror.o mktemp.o memmove.o
ACT_STYLE	MMAP
_PATH_SENDMAIL	/usr/lib/sendmail -t
_PATH_AWK	/usr/bin/nawk

If you use NIS rather than DNS and your hosts do not return fully qualified domain names when they are looked up (as via *hostname*), you need to define *domainname* in the *inn.conf* file to specify the domain.

There is a bug with the **write()** system call under SunOS 4.1.1. You can repair the bug with Sun path 100622-01; this patch supersedes the 100293-01 patch mentioned in *Installing InterNetNews*. Get the patch and apply it.

Sun's *stdio* package has a lot of problems with file descriptors over 127, even though it can open more files than that. It is best to avoid the problem by keeping the number of open files needed by any INN process under 127. In particular, this means that if you have a lot of incoming peer transfer sessions to *innd*, or many outgoing channels—a combination of which often approaches 127—you should use *buffchan* to conserve open outgoing file descriptors. You can also set **NOFILE_LIMIT** to **126**, as indicated in Table 7-8 to constrain the number of open files, but this is not very efficient.

If you use the unbundled compiler, *acc*, you must also use the unbundled assembler. If you use *gcc* version 1, add *inet_ntoa.o* and *inet_ntoa.c* to **MISSING_OBJ** and **MISSING_SRC**, respectively, or add the switch **-fpcc-struct-return** to **DEFS**.

7.2.2.10 System V Release 4

As with HP-UX, there is no sample configuration file for System V Release 4. The table in *Installing InterNetNews* compares against the old default configuration, which was for a SunOS 4.1 system. So this section just discusses some known issues with SVR4 systems.

Sony and Dell machines must have `HAVE_UNIX_DOMAIN` set to `DONT`. Some System V machines need to have the *resolv* and *elf* libraries included with a `LIBS` value of `"-lresolv -lnsl -lsocket -L/usr/ccs/lib -lelf"`. Do not expect lint to be useful on System V machines; set `LINTLIBSTYLE` to `NONE`.

Many System V machines do not update the last modification time for the *active* file when you use `mmap()` to update the file. This isn't much of a problem except for looking anomalous. One program that does care and which you might be running if you are upgrading an old installation is *nnmaster*. This program is an obsolete database maintainer that comes with the *nn* newsreader. If you still run *nnmaster*, or have some other program that cares about the *active* file modification time, you can set up a *cron* job to *touch* the *active* file frequently to accommodate it.

7.2.2.11 Ultrix

Table 7–9 lists the *config.data* parameters and values for Ultrix 4.3.

Table 7–9: INN Configuration Values for Ultrix 4.3

Parameter	Value
CFLAGS	$(DEFS) -O
PROF	-p
LIBS	-lresolv -l44bsd
LINTFLAGS	-b -u -x $(DEFS)
LINTFILTER	| sed -n -f ../sedf.sysv
SIZE_T	unsigned int
UID_T	int
GID_T	int
PID_T	int
SIGVAR	int
HAVE_UNISTD	DONT
HAVE_SETSID	DONT
HAVE_WAITPID	DONT
USE_UNION_WAIT	DO
HAVE_VFORK	DO
FDCOUNT_STYLE	GETDTAB
ABORTVAL	int

Table 7-9: INN Configuration Values for Ultrix 4.3 (continued)

Parameter	Value
GETPIDVAL	int
_PATH_SENDMAIL	/usr/lib/sendmail -t
_PATH_COMPRESS	/usr/ucb/compress
_PATH_EGREP	/usr/local/bin/egrep
_PATH_AWK	awk
_PATH_SED	sed

Although Ultrix has an mmap() system call, it is not usable with INN.

While the *syslog* program that comes with INN does work on Ultrix, it may cause problems with other system programs trying to use it. You should either install it as an alternate *syslog* facility as described in Section 7.2.3.2, or get */pub/DEC/jtkohl-syslog-complete.tar.Z* from *gatekeeper.dec.com* and install it in place of the system *syslogd*.

You should use GNU *egrep* with Ultrix; point **_PATH_EGREP** to the appropriate location.

The *find* command on Ultrix does not support the -follow option to follow symbolic links. This is only used in *makeactive*, so you should never have a need for it. If ever you do, and you have divided your news spool with symbolic links, then you should use GNU *find*. Otherwise, you can simply edit out the -follow option from the *makeactive* source code and recompile.

7.2.3 Other Configuration Tasks

Before we can move on and talk about building INN, there are a few things not covered by *config.data* that you need to take care of.

7.2.3.1 Non-root operation

If you do not want or cannot get* superuser access for the system that will be running *innd*, edit *configdata.h* in the *include* subdirectory (of the top-level *inn* directory). Change **NNTP_PORT** to be a port number above 5000, which is typically the value of **IPPORT_USERRESERVED** in */usr/include/netinet/in.h*.

---

* If you cannot get superuser access for the installation, should you really be running news on the machine?

7.2.3.2 Using an alternate syslogd

If you need to use INN's *syslog* on your system, but you don't want to replace your system's *syslog*, you need to configure INN to use the appropriate one. Go to the *syslog* subdirectory of the top-level *inn* directory, so that you can edit the source files: *syslog.c* and *syslogd.c*.

If you are going to replace the system *syslogd*, you only need to delete the `#undef _PATH_KLOG` line from *syslogd.c*. You can ignore the rest of this section.

If you are not replacing the system *syslogd*, set the `_PATH` macros in both source files to something that does not conflict with the existing syslog.

If your system does not have UNIX domain sockets, `_PATH_LOGFILE` is irrelevant so you can comment it out. You need to uncomment `INET_SYSLOG` at the start of *syslog.c* and change `DO_INET_SOCKET` in *syslogd.c* from `undef` to `define`. You also have to judiciously rip out all of the code in *syslogd.c* that refers to the `AF_UNIX` sockets.

If you are not running *syslogd* as *root* and are not using UNIX domain sockets, you need to change port value `514` in *syslog.c* to a port above 5000. Then, in *syslogd.c*, delete the lines that look up the *syslog* service and replace the `sp->s_port` reference with whatever port you picked to replace `514` in *syslog.c*.

7.2.3.3 Using writev

If your system does not have the `writev()` call in its system library, INN has to fake it, at the cost of some efficiency. Add *writev.c* and *writev.o* to `MISSING_SRC` and `MISSING_OBJ`, respectively, in *config.data*. Then change to INN's *include* directory and do the following:

```
% mkdir sys
% ln uio.h sys/uio.h
```

7.2.3.4 Applying the DBZ patch

As of INN version 1.5, it is no longer necessary to patch *dbz/dbz.c* with *lib/dbz.pch* because it comes prepatched. If you try to apply the patch, *patch* reports, "Reversed (or previously applied) patch detected," confirming that you don't need to apply it. This section remains for anyone who has to deal with an earlier version of INN.

Normally the DBZ patch is applied during the build stage, but it seems to be missed often enough to warrant manually ensuring it happens. To do this, go to INN's *lib* directory and type the following (this requires having *patch* in your search path):

```
% make dbz.c
cat ../dbz/dbz.c >dbz.c
patch -s -p0 <dbz.pch
rm -f dbz.c.orig
```

If you said to use –DMMAP in DBZCFLAGS, or defined FORK as vfork, you must apply the DBZ patch. If you don't have the *patch* program, you should do it manually. If you don't even do this, you must add *dbzalt.o* and *dbzalt.c* to the MISS-ING_OBJ and MISSING_SRC parameters, respectively, in *config.data* and you cannot use –DMMAP or vfork.

7.2.4 *Making the Substitutions*

When you have finished the pre-build configuration work, change to the *config* directory and run *make*. The *subst* program is compiled and then used to update all of the files that need to be told about the parameters you've defined. (The *Installing InterNetNews* document says that you should run make sedtest first, to see if your *sed* is up to the task of doing the substitutions, but by default INN uses the C version of *subst* so the test is really not needed.) Here's what you should see:

```
% cd source-area/inn/config
% make
chmod u+w,g+w `grep -v '^;' <files.list`
make c || make sh || rm -f subst
cc -o subst subst.c
```

This step should not fail. If it does, you'll have to figure out how to fix it. We'd offer more helpful advice, but it really shouldn't fail.

7.3 *Building INN*

The hard part of getting INN installed should be behind you now. Provided that everything has been configured correctly for your system, the next two steps should go quickly and smoothly.

Do not bother with the *BUILD* script in the top-level directory of the INN source tree. Although it may give some people warm fuzzies to answer prompts, the script isn't doing anything complex and you'll have a better understanding of your system if you do the necessary steps yourself.

7.3.1 *Checking the Configuration*

INN does not provide a verification suite for your configuration, so as long as the substitutions happened without *make* exiting with an error, the easiest thing to do is go on to Section 7.3.2. If you're really ambitious, however, and your system has *lint*, you can read through the *lint* output to see whether there are any remarkable complaints. In the *lib* directory of the INN sources, do the following to check all of INN's library modules:

```
% make lint
cc -I../include -g  -target sun4 -c  strerror.c
cc -I../include -g  -target sun4 -c  checkart.c
  ... more compilations ...
lint -u -b -h -z -I../include
   five lines of source file arguments appear here
  | sed -n -f ../sedf.sun >lint.all
grep -v yaccpar <lint.all >lint
% cat lint
dbz.c(1390): warning: possible pointer alignment problem
dbz.c(1396): warning: possible pointer alignment problem
malloc, arg. 1 used inconsistently    llib-lc(441)  ::  dbz.c(808)
malloc, arg. 1 used inconsistently    llib-lc(441)  ::  dbz.c(1376)
free, arg. 1 used inconsistently      llib-lc(275)  ::  parsedate.y(193)
free, arg. 1 used inconsistently      llib-lc(275)  ::  parsedate.y(193)
free, arg. 1 used inconsistently      llib-lc(275)  ::  parsedate.y(212)
free, arg. 1 used inconsistently      llib-lc(275)  ::  parsedate.y(212)
free, arg. 1 used inconsistently      llib-lc(275)  ::  parsedate.y(218)
free, arg. 1 used inconsistently      llib-lc(275)  ::  parsedate.y(218)
wait3, arg. 1 used inconsistently     llib-lc(777)  ::  waitnb.c(33)
```

The sample output above was generated against INN version 1.4sec on a SPARC 10 running SunOS 4.1.3. Checking the *dbz.c* source file at the indicated lines indicates that the "possible pointer alignment problem" warning is expected, and that the argument being passed to `malloc()` is a `size_t`, which is fine on a Sun. The *parsedate.y* warnings are caused by code generated by Sun's *yacc*, and finally, the *waitnb.c* warning occurs because Sun's *lint* library wants to see `wait3()` take a union as its first argument, despite the fact that this is deprecated in the system documentation.

On another type of system, you should see a similar short list of harmless warnings. If you get many more, it is likely that there was a problem with something you specified in *config.data*. Try to find the source of the problem and fix *config.data*. Then rerun *make all* in the *config* directory before retrying the *lint* phase.

7.3.2 Building the Programs

To build the news system, go to the top-level directory of the INN sources and run *make*:

```
% cd source-area/inn-1.7
% make
```

This command double checks that the configured substitutions have been made, then builds the INN library, and finally goes to each subdirectory and builds the executables there. It should run without any problems, providing that the configuration for your system is correct.

7.3.3 Checking the Build

Unfortunately, INN does not provide a mechanism to automatically test the system like C News does, and it is especially hard to test it at all without the system installed.

To test INN without going live, which you might want to do if you are replacing an existing news system, you will have to devise your own tests. The best thing to do would be to specify pathnames that do not conflict with the installed system, redefine `NNTP_PORT` in *include/configdata.h* to an out-of-the-way port, and then install and test it as you like. When you're done testing, reset the pathnames and port and then rebuild and install.

The *nnrpd* newsreader server can be tested from the command line by making sure `stdin:RP:::*` is in the *nnrp.access* file, and *nnrp.access* is installed where the daemon expects to find it. *nnrpd* still needs to be able to talk to a running *innd* for posting to work, however.

7.4 Installing INN

There are two different ways to install INN: one that involves no superuser access at all, and another that uses a little superuser encouragement. Before you actually install the news system, however, you need to configure a few files for your site. These files have been copied from the *samples* directory to the *site* directory by the *make* run that built the system. The rest of this section directs you to the most important files that need to be initialized. We'll take a more thorough look at all of the control files and programs in *site* in Chapter 8.

7.4.1 Configuring Site Data Files

Go to the *site* directory to edit the following files. Any time you want to update one of these files, you should edit it in this directory, not where it is finally installed. After you are done editing, you can use *make install* here to update the installed version.

expire.ctl

This file should be changed to reflect your expected expiration policies. The example lines for groups that stay forever should be deleted. Here are some reasonable settings that could replace the default `*:A:1:10:never` line:

```
## This removes all articles from groups that no longer
## have an active file entry.  The U and M lines later get
## used for real groups.
*:A:0:0:0
## These keep articles for at least 1 day and up to 14 days
## Unmoderated groups (U) won't honor longer Expires headers
```

```
## Moderated groups (M) allow Expires headers up to 90 days
*:U:1:14:14
*:M:1:14:90
```

Adjust the 14-day expiry period for most articles to what you expect to be appropriate for your site (see Section 2.2.1.3). Be careful not to put any white space on non-comment lines, or things may not work the way you want.

hosts.nntp

You need to put the names (or addresses) of the machines that will feed you news in this file. If you do not have UNIX domain sockets, you need to include your server, as *nnrpd* needs to open an Internet socket to give *innd* any articles posted by your users. Do not enable passwords unless you have already worked them out with your feeds. If a peer server has multiple IP addresses, the hostname should resolve to an A record for all of them or you should list the IP addresses explicitly. If you leave localhost in this file, all NNTP newsreaders running on the machine itself need to know how to do a *MODE READER* NNTP command (see Section 9.2.2).

inn.conf

You should set organization to the name you want to be put in the Organization header of articles posted from your site. If your organization is mostly in one part of the world, it is nice to specify where, e.g., "Internet Software Consortium, La Honda, CA." Set server to the full hostname of the machine on which you are running *innd*. Finally, set *pathhost* to your UUCP name if you have one registered with the UUCP Mapping Project, or use the value of *server* otherwise.

newsfeeds

This is potentially the most complex file INN uses. There is a manual page for it in the *doc* directory. If you have an existing *sys* file for B News or C News, you can use *sys2nf* to help convert it, as described in Section 7.4.2. If you are bringing up a new site, a workable skeleton is as follows:

```
ME:!*/!local::
TESTING:!*::
```

To support the overview database for improved newsreader performance, add:

```
OVERVIEW!:*:Tc,WO:/usr/news/bin/overchan
```

Here we've assumed that you are using */usr/news/bin*, INN's default, for *NEWSBIN*; be sure to use the appropriate path to *overchan* on your system.

nnrp.access

Remove the *foo.com* line and comment and replace them with one or more lines that identify those hosts you want to be able to read news from your server. Normally, just wildcarding your organizational domain is sufficient.

nntpsend.ctl

This file can also get complex. A good initial configuration is to delete the non-comment lines in the file and replace them with your normal outgoing NNTP feeds, as described in the *newsfeeds* file. Do this after you configure your outgoing feeds in *newsfeeds*, as described in Section 9.3.1. For each feed, set the *site* field to the batchlist name as it appears in the *newsfeeds* file, set the *fqdn* field to the name of the host to which you send news, and leave the *size* and *args* fields empty.

send-nntp and *send-uucp*

Both of these files contain lines that set the variable `LIST` if no hostnames are passed on the command line. Note that *send-uucp* special-cases two such lines based on the time of day. If you intend to use these programs instead of *nntpsend* and *sendbatch*, respectively, you should update these `LIST` lines with the names of your own neighbors.

overview.fmt

The file should have its `Xref:` line enabled, but without the `full` keyword. The `full` keyword appears in the sample file because when the *trn* news-reader was first taught to use overview files, it needed the header name in the file. It and other overview-aware readers no longer need the header name present, so you can remove `full` and get back six bytes per article in the *over.view* files.

passwd.nntp

Delete the *news.foo.com* line from this file. If you are sending news to any sites that require that your server identify itself with a password, this is the file in which to identify them.

7.4.2 Replacing an Old News System

If you are replacing an existing news system on your server, you can only use a few of the files from it, other than the articles themselves. If the *active*, *active.times*, *newsgroups*, and *history* files exist on your system, you should keep them. Put all of these files in *NEWSCTL* and make sure that they are owned by the news owner.

INN provides a utility to help you convert an existing B News or C News *sys* file to INN's *newsfeeds* format. You can build it in the *frontends* directory with *make sys2nf*. Then use *sys2nf* with the `-a` and `-s` flags to point at your *active* file and *sys* files, respectively. The utility breaks each feed into an individual file in the sub-directory *feeds*; you can rejoin these files to make a *newsfeeds* file. Edit that *news-feeds* file to fix all occurrences of `HELP`. All you typically need to do is specify how to create batchlists that are appropriate for NNTP or UUCP transfer. In INN's format, this information is specified as `Tf,Wnm` and `Tf,Wnb`, respectively. If you had a `distributions` subfield specified in the *sys* file, you should also check them and remove any extraneous `.*` patterns that *sys2nf* may have added because distributions are simple keywords, not patterns.

If any of the newsreader programs on your system have installed files, such as their own libraries, you should retain those files.

We are assuming that you are leaving the article tree in the same location. If you need to move it and you are keeping it on the same partition, use *mv*. If you are moving it to a different partition, you need to use something like *tar* or *dump*.

Now make a backup of your old news system. Once that is done, you can remove everything else.

Make sure that any *cron* jobs for your old news system are disabled. Check your system startup files and remove anything that attempts to start the old news server.

If you are replacing a C News system that didn't use *dbz*, the existing article history database might need to be rebuilt. If the second field of the *history* file has a tilde (~) in each line, you can use it, but you must rebuild the associated database files as follows:

```
% cd NEWSCTL
% source-area/inn-1.7/expire/makehistory -or
```

If the second field in *history* does not contain tildes, as with B News systems prior to version 2.11.19, you should rebuild the history database entirely by scanning all of the articles in the news spool:

```
% cd NEWSCTL
% source-area/inn-1.7/expire/makehistory -o
```

Depending on how many articles you have online, scanning the entire spool to build a *history* file can take a very long time—easily a dozen or more hours if you have a few gigabytes of news stored.

7.4.3 Installing with Root Access

With the exception of filesystem permission issues, superuser access is only strictly necessary for one part of the INN system: binding its Internet socket to the privileged NNTP port. Doing the installation as the superuser can be convenient, though, for ensuring that the proper directories are all created and that everything has the correct ownership.

The *makedirs.sh* script in the top-level *inn* directory controls the directory creation process. If the required directory exists, nothing about it is changed. If the script needs to make the directory, it does so and then changes the user and group ownership to those specified in *config.data*. It is the change of user ownership via *chown* that requires superuser permission.

Directory permissions are hardcoded in *makedirs.sh*, not inherited from the GROUPDIR_MODE parameter in *config.data*. You might want to change 0775 to 2775 (near the end of the script) to enable set group ID on directories. This ensures that group ownership is inherited by new files and directories. Having set group ID enabled is only meaningful for some operating systems, but on most of those where it is meaningless it is no problem to have it turned on.

If you have installed the manual page directories in a standard system location like */usr/share/man* or */usr/local/man* instead of the default */usr/news/man*, those directories are not considered to be part of the news system. If *makedirs.sh* has to create a standard system directory that will eventually be shared by other, non-news manual pages, you should reset the ownership of the directory to a different user ID, like *root*, after it has been created.

The program that binds *innd*'s privileged port, *inndstart*, is installed by an obvious line in *innd/Makefile*. *inndstart* is the only file that does not have its ownership changed. It is installed with the permissions 4550 to make it setuid root. This allows anyone in the *news* group to start *innd* without having to become the superuser first. If the program is not installed by *root*, the installation process informs you that it needs to be installed by setuid root.

Now it's time to become *root* and change directories to the top of the INN source tree. When you are ready, type the following:

```
% make install
```

This command runs *makedirs.sh* and then installs all of the programs, manual pages, and control files into the appropriate directories.

7.4.4 *Installing Without Root Access*

If you don't want to or cannot do the program installation as the superuser, you need to make sure that the directories created by *makedirs.sh* all exist with the correct ownership and modes prior to installing INN. You can actually use *makedirs.sh* to do this, provided you comment out the ${CHOWN} ${NEWSUSER} ${DESTDIR}${F} line and run the script as the news owner.

Now you need to edit *installit.sh* (in the top-level *inn* directory) to do the *chgrp* regardless of whether it is being run by *root*. Look for the X-G case in the file and then delete the ${ROOT} && part of the ${ROOT} && CHGROUPIT=true line.

After ensuring that all of the required directories exist, change directories to the top of the INN source tree. Now you can run *make install*. You should do this as the news owner.

7.4.5　Final Installation Issues

If you are not replacing an old news system, you need to create the *active* and *history* files now. You can get an *active* file from your news neighbor or from an archive site, such as *ftp://ftp.isc.org/pub/usenet/CONFIG/active*. Call the file *active.old*; edit it to include only the groups that you want. You also need to reset the second and third fields for each group; these fields specify the maximum and minimum article numbers for the group. When you are done, install the file in *NEWSCTL*. The following shows a command you can use to reset the second and third fields and install the file:

```
% cd NEWSCTL
% awk '{print $1, "0000000000 0000000001", $4}' < active.old > active
```

You also need a *history* file. You can create an empty one as follows:

```
% cd NEWSCTL
% touch history
% /usr/libexec/news/makehistory -ir
% mv history.n.dir history.dir
% mv history.n.pag history.pag
```

After all of the programs and control files have been installed, there are a few last things you need to set up to complete the installation.

7.4.5.1　Boot-time startup

The *rc.news* script pointed to by _PATH_NEWSBOOT needs to be invoked when your system starts up. On most Berkeley-derived systems, you can accomplish this by running *rc.news* at the end of */etc/rc.local*. On System V style systems, you need to put a reference to the script in a directory like */etc/init.d*, where it is run when the system comes up. Do this by putting a file named *S99news* there. This file is a one-line executable shell script that invokes the real *rc.news* as follows:

```
#! /bin/sh
su news -c /usr/news/bin/rc.news >/dev/console
```

This example assumes the new owner is *news* and *NEWSCTL* is */usr/news/bin*; be sure to use the appropriate username and path for your system. And don't forget to make *S99news* executable.

Prior to version 1.5 of INN, *rc.news* had to be run as *root* because it had *su* commands in it. As of version 1.5, *rc.news* expects to be running as the news owner. If you are upgrading an older INN system, be sure to note this change in the appropriate startup script.

7.4.5.2 cron

You need to install a few *cron* entries on your system. The following is a reasonable start, as long as you substitute the appropriate pathnames for your system:

```
# Run daily maintenance in the wee hours of the morning.
# The first argument tells expire to not complain about
#    groups that have been removed, and generate a few
#    expiration statistics.
# delayrm speeds the history rebuild stage of expire, and
#    optimizes the actual article removal process
# expireover is to purge the newsreader data cache of old data.
# See the news.daily manual page for more.
02 2 * * * /usr/news/bin/news.daily flags=-qv1 delayrm expireover
# Flush any spooled articles (safety; shouldn't happen often)
08 * * * * /usr/news/bin/rnews -U
```

These entries should be put into the news owner's *crontab*. If you do not have
per-user *crontab* files on your system, you have to install them in the regular system *crontab* file and arrange to have them run as the news owner. This typically
involves wrapping the entries in invocations of the *su* command. For example:

```
su news -c "/usr/news/bin/rnews -U"
```

7.4.5.3 syslog

The *syslog* directory contains a sample *syslog.conf* file that is configured to use the
log paths you specified in *config.data*. If you are using your system's *syslogd*, use
this file as a guide in adding the appropriate entries to your own system *sys-
log.conf*. If you are using INN's *syslog* and did not replace your system *syslogd*,
you can use the file as is.

7.4.5.4 mail

As mentioned in Section 7.2.1.3, mail to **NEWSMASTER** and **NEWSUSER** (as in *con-
fig.data*) should be directed to a mailbox that is checked regularly. We recommend using mail aliases to direct the messages to the appropriate administrators,
rather than having them actually log into the news accounts. That way someone is
sure to at least be aware of any mail that is sent.

7.4.5.5 uucp

If you are using UUCP, you need to be sure that *rnews* is permitted to run on
incoming batches. If you have an *L.cmds* file (as comes with Version 2 UUCP systems), add *rnews* to that file. If you have a BNU *Permissions* file, be sure that the
COMMANDS option for each machine that needs to run *rnews* lists the program.
You also need to ensure that the UUCP system can find *rnews*; install it as suggested in 7.2.1.7.

7.4.6 *inncheck*

Now you should check your installation with the *inncheck* program in *NEWSBIN*. This program requires Perl to run. *inncheck* informs you if the file ownerships or permissions for any files are not what is expected. It also checks whether the contents of some of the control files are consistent with their prescribed formats. Simply run it without any options; any messages it produces should be self-explanatory.

At this point, you should have INN built and installed. Fully configuring, testing, and troubleshooting your news system comes next, after which you should be ready for production service. These topics are covered by Chapters 8 and 9.

8

Configuring INN

The INN system can't run without being told what it is expected to do. Like C News, many of the supporting functions for the actual transport software are provided as shell scripts that can be customized to suit individual news administrators. This chapter describes the control files used to describe the details of your site's setup and the customizable scripts.

Several of the files mentioned in this chapter (*expire.ctl*, *hosts.nntp*, *inn.conf*, *newsfeeds*, *nnrp.access nntpsend.ctl*, *overview.fmt*, and *passwd.nntp*) were minimally described at the end of Chapter 7, *Installing INN*, because they are important to have correct for your local operation right from the start. If you skipped Section 7.4.1, please take a moment to review it and ensure your system has a reasonable initial configuration.

8.1 *How to Update Files*

INN provides a handy mechanism for making local updates to the many scripts and control files in the news system without fear of losing those modifications when official patches are applied. Though it does mean you might have to occasionally apply an official patch manually to not lose a change, the benefits of keeping the original sources unmodified and having a *make* command detect changes to files you have modified is worth it.

The distributed versions of the scripts and the sample control files are based in INN's *samples* subdirectory. The installed versions of the files come from the *site* subdirectory. The scripts are mostly identical copies of their *samples* versions; you are usually going to be editing the control files. The procedure for editing either type of file is essentially the same: Do not edit the *samples* version of the file; change only the *site* version. Then run *make install* in the *site* directory.

Some changes to control files require asking *innd* to reload the information. You can either use the appropriate *ctlinnd reload* command, or run *make reload-install* to have *innd* reload all of the files it knows about, regardless of whether any of them changed. The specific files that may need to be reloaded after an update, and their *ctlinnd* commands, are as follows:

newsfeeds

```
% ctlinnd reload newsfeeds 'added/removed site to feed'
```

hosts.nntp

```
% ctlinnd reload hosts.nntp 'included/excluded site from peers'
```

overview.fmt

```
% ctlinnd reload overview.fmt 'added/removed header field'
```

Note that *innd* can't reload the `pathhost` parameter from *inn.conf*. If this value is changed, the server must be restarted.

WARNING   *make install* in the *site* directory should be done as the superuser, so that the *touch* command works on read-only files. Since all of the *site* files are normally owned by the news owner when installed, you can also do the install as the news owner as long as you edit the sole instance of the *touch* command in the *installit.sh* file (in the top-level INN source directory) to use the `-f` flag.

The *Makefile* contains several other targets to help you maintain your local changes. These can be used to indicate differences between the *samples* versions and installed versions of the files or to replace the *site* versions with fresh copies. *make* or *make all* copies any files missing in *site* from *samples*. If there is a newer version of a *site* file in *samples*, these commands squawk loudly about it, complaining that the file has changed, regardless of whether it really has. It is programmed this way on the assumption that you ran *make clean* after a previous install, even if you didn't. *make clean* removes any files that are identical to their *samples* directory counterparts.

The drawback of doing the *make clean* is that redoing *make* in the *site* directory results in having all of the *samples* files copied back and subsequently mentioned during *make install*, even if they are not re-installed. This is very noisy for the usual case of having only one file changed. The drawback of not doing the *make clean* is that any patches applied to the original files in the *samples* directory result in *make* complaining that each updated file "has changed; please update," even if you haven't made any local changes to the file in question. To have the best of both worlds, only do a *make clean* before applying patches to the *samples* files.

The *make diff* command helps identify the files that have really changed between the newer *samples* files and the *site* files. It displays all of the changes, including both the updated patch to the *samples* file and any local changes you may have made in *site*. If you have made changes, you'll have to reintegrate them with the new version in *samples*—but don't change that *samples* file. Copy it to *site* and edit in your change there.

After you have updated *site* files, *make diff-installed* tells you the differences between those files and any of the older installed files. This can be useful for seeing just what files are going to change with *make install*, so that the extra noise of *make install* can be more readily ignored.

8.2 *Control Files*

Making sure all of the control files have the correct information for your system is an important part of the setup of INN. The default values are, for the most part, not intended to be acceptable for your system. They are also potentially insulting or embarrassing; you really don't want postings coming out from your site if you have not edited *inn.conf.*

Most control files come with a reasonably instructive comment at the beginning that describes the format of the file, so that information is not repeated here. This section instead describes the purpose of each file and what should appear in it. The discussion of control files is organized by the primary function of the various files.

8.2.1 *General Operation*

This section describes *inn.conf,* which is the source of general system information for several INN programs, and *innwatch.ctl,* the configuration file for the program that helps keep an eye on the general state of the system.

8.2.1.1 *inn.conf*

Various client programs ,in the INN suite get information from the *inn.conf* file. This file needs to be available on every host that runs *inews* and *rnews*, as well as the server running *innd.* The values that can be configured are listed alphabetically, except for the first, because of its importance for in cooperation with your neighbors.

pathhost

> The pathhost variable states the one name by which all neighboring hosts identify your site. When a neighboring feed sees this name in a Path header, it knows not to send you that article, since you have already seen it. The value of pathhost is also used as the string that appears as the banner when a

connection is made to *innd* or *nnrpd* and as the first field of the Xref header. It defaults to your hostname as fully qualified by your domain name if it is not set in *inn.conf* (see also the `domain` parameter, next).

If you set `pathhost`, and we recommend that you do so explicitly rather than rely on the default, the name that you choose should also be qualified by your domain name so it does not conflict with other server names (imagine the propagation nightmares if 3000 sites all tried to claim they are the site named *news*). If you have a name registered with the UUCP Mapping Project, that can be used without a domain qualification, thereby saving a few bytes per article.

Unlike other *innd* configuration values, `pathhost` cannot be reloaded with a *ctlinnd* command. If you change it, you need to restart *innd* to use the new `pathhost` value.

domain

The `domain` parameter is used to generate a fully qualified domain name if the domain is not included in the hostname. INN assumes that the hostname has a domain if it has a `.` character in it; otherwise the value of `domain` is appended. The setting of this value affects the default values for `pathhost` and `fromhost`, and the hostname that appears in Message-ID headers of articles generated at your site, whenever *innd* can't automatically determine the domain from host lookups.

If you are trying to use `domain` to affect the default `pathhost` value, you need to restart the *innd* server when you change it.

fromhost

The value of `fromhost` is used by *inews* (but not *nnrpd*) to build the host part of From and Sender addresses in locally generated articles that need them. It is also used to generate the contact address listed in the output of NNRP's `HELP` command.

The default value of `fromhost` is the fully qualified domain name of the host, which might be affected by `domain`, mentioned above. If the environment variable `FROMHOST` is set for *inews* or *nnrpd*, its value overrides any *inn.conf* or default value.

moderatormailer

`moderatormailer` is a `printf`-style expression that is used to submit articles to the moderators of groups that are not listed in the *moderators* file (see Section 8.2.2.5). Since our recommendation is not to use the *moderators* file for anything except local groups, this is a very important variable if you want your users to be able to easily make contributions to moderated newsgroups.

This variable should be a template for email addresses. When *inews* or *nnrpd* is trying to make a submission, it takes the moderated group's name, changes every dot to a dash, and replaces the `%s` of the template with it. Thus, with a template of:

```
moderatormailer: %s@moderators.isc.org
```

rec.music.info becomes *rec-music-info@moderators.isc.org.*

We recommend using the above template. The host part should be set to one of the "mailpaths" sites, sites that have volunteered to keep up-to-date with the constantly changing submission addresses for moderated groups. More information on these sites can be found in Section 15.2.1.

organization

inews and *nnrpd* insert the value of `organization` as the Organization header of locally generated articles that do not already have an Organization header. This value is overridden by the environment variable `ORGANIZATION` if it exists.

You really want to make sure you change this from the default. If you don't, articles generated by your site will go out proclaiming that you run "A poorly-installed InterNetNews site." Its new and improved value should include the name of your organization and its geographic location (such as city, state, and country), all within 66 characters (so the entire header fits on one line). For example:

```
organization: University of Toronto, Ontario, Canada
organization: O'Reilly & Associates, Sebastopol CA, USA
organization: Dept of English, Oxford Univ, England
```

If you don't define `organization` and there isn't one in the article being submitted, none is added.

server

This variable specifies the NNTP server to which *inews* and *rnews* connect. This value is also used as the default value for various other minor client programs. As distributed, *inn.conf* defines it as `localhost`, which might well work at your site if the only programs using *inn.conf* are on the same machine as the server. If not, set `server` to the fully qualified name of your INN host.

If `NNTPSERVER` is set in the client's environment, that value is used instead of the *inn.conf* value. If `NNTPSERVER` is not in the environment and `server` is not defined in *inn.conf,* then *inews, rnews,* and other clients that need the name of the server will all fail to work. There is no built-in default value.

`mime-version, mime-contenttype, mime-encoding`

> If the `mime-version` value is set, MIME (Multipurpose Internet Mail Extensions) headers are added to any article your site originates that does not already have them (see Section 18.5 for more information on MIME). The value of `mime-version` becomes the value of the MIME-Version header and should usually be set to `1.0`.
>
> The `mime-contenttype` parameter is used as the value for the Content-Type header in articles that do not have one, but only if `mime-version` is set. It is not used otherwise. If `mime-version` is defined, but `mime-contenttype` is not, the Content-Type header is set to `text/plain; charset=US-ASCII`.
>
> The `mime-encoding` value is used for the Content-Transfer-Encoding header if `mime-version` is set and the article being posted does not have the header. It is not used otherwise. If `mime-version` is present but `mime-encoding` is not, `7bit` is used.
>
> If articles coming from your site are generally in 7-bit ASCII, we recommend that you not bother with the MIME options. Since the worldwide Usenet is by default 7-bit ASCII, these extra headers are just needless verbiage. They are also a little annoying in some newsreaders that can display special MIME messages because there is a little bit of a display skip that happens when it hits a MIME article than ends up just being a regular text message.

8.2.1.2 innwatch.ctl

The *innwatch.ctl* file controls the *innwatch* program that monitors your system resources to keep INN from consuming all of them. If you're fortunate, you'll never really have to touch the internals of the *innwatch.ctl* file because it's pretty darn gross in there. If you don't believe us, check it out. Then take a look at the *innwatch.ctl* manual page and think about how much time you'd like to spend writing such a control file.

There is essentially one common problem that you might have to edit *innwatch.ctl* to solve, and that's handling of the free space information. The problem is that the common, desirable task of finding out how much free space is available on a disk is probably the single most incompatible function across Unix variants. The widely varying output formats can make parsing a real pain. If *innwatch* is claiming your system doesn't have enough free space when it really does, the *df* command and its parsing should immediately be suspect. If you can't get *innwatch* to find the free space numbers by tweaking the `INNWATCH_DF`, `INNWATCH_INODES`, and `INNWATCH_BLOCKS` parameters in *config.data* as described in Section 7.2.1.8, you'll have to come up with a consistent way to get the correct free space numbers on your system and update *innwatch.ctl* appropriately.

If you are running your article spool on more than one filesystem partition, you need to duplicate all of the lines that monitor the space available in *NEWSARTS* and edit them appropriately to look at each of the other partitions.

8.2.2 News Flow

There are several files that are collectively responsible for directing the flow of news at your site. These files limit who can send you news, who you send news to, what articles you send, and how locally generated articles are processed. Collectively, these files are responsible for directing the flow of news at your site.

8.2.2.1 newsfeeds

The *newsfeeds* file's primary purpose is to select articles for redistribution to other sites. It can also be used to build lists of incoming articles for other purposes (like statistical analysis). Additionally, the file defines the Distribution header values your site accepts and can have your server reject articles that come from particular sites. As perusing the *newsfeeds* manual page might suggest, this can be a very complicated file. However, the majority of sites on the Net only need to have very simple entries to make batchlists of articles to feed their neighbors; sample entries for different types of transmission are described in Section 9.3.1.

As described in Section 7.4.1, the *newsfeeds* file that comes distributed with INN should be wholly replaced with one appropriate for your site. You can either install the example minimal *newsfeeds* file we presented in that section, or use *sys2nf* to convert your existing B News or C News *sys* file.

The basic form of a *newsfeeds* file entry is:

```
sitename[/exclude,exclude...]:\
        pattern,pattern...[/distrib,distrib...]:\
        flag,flag...:parameters
```

An entry consists of four main fields, separated by colons (:). Each of the first two fields can have subfields; the optional subfield is separated from the main information by a slash (/). A line can be continued anywhere with a backslash (\) immediately preceding the end of line; the backslash, newline, and white space starting the next line are stripped to internally make one long line. Any other white space is significant and almost certainly shouldn't be in the entry, except perhaps to separate program arguments in the parameters field.

The sitename field should be set to the neighboring site's news name, which is the name that it puts in the Path header of articles passing through it. The value of this field is case-sensitively checked against the Path headers of incoming articles to prevent retransmission to the neighboring site if it has already seen the article. As such, it is the primary guard keeping you from trying to feed all of the news that you get from a peer right back to it.

The exclude subfield of the sitename field describes other strings, separated by commas, to match against the Path header. If any match, the article is not sent to the site. This is primarily of benefit for special program feeds like mail gateways. It is also used between sites that share a common feed and that want to keep their own link from passing articles that they should get from the other feed.

The pattern field describes the patterns to match against the Newsgroups header of each article that has not been excluded by the tests of the first field. The patterns used are called *wildmat* patterns and are described in their manual page as being like Bourne shell file wildcards. Though the question mark (?) and bracket-enclosed character sets ([]) are special characters for wildcard matching, a newsgroup subscription pattern normally only makes use of the asterisk (*) to match zero or more occurrences of any character.

An exclamation mark (!) leading a group pattern means to exclude sending groups matching its pattern from the set of already matched groups. An at sign (@) leading a group pattern means the same thing, but it has special behavior in the presence of crossposting. More on these two types of negation and crossposting in a moment.

Patterns for hierarchies should be specified from the higher level of the hierarchy to the lower levels. This is because the last matching pattern is what determines whether the article is sent or not. A simplified description of the algorithm, using an example of one group name in the Newsgroups header, is that each element of the subscription is checked in turn and if the group name matches the pattern element, the article is selected to be sent. If there is a ! in front of the group name, it is deselected instead. Putting a more general pattern after a more specific one cause all articles matched by the specific pattern to have the intended disposition reversed by the more general pattern.

Group subscriptions are not hierarchically recursive as they are with some other news systems. Using `comp` in a B News or C News *sys* file feeds all of the *comp* hierarchy, but with INN it does not feed anything. `comp.*` should be used to get the entire hierarchy. To exclude the computer systems groups from such a feed, using the less-to-more-specific rule explained in the preceding paragraph, you can use `comp.*,!comp.sys.*`.

Wildcards are best specified on a newsgroup name element boundary, right after the dot in a group name. For example, use `rec.arts.*` rather than `rec.arts*` to feed all of *rec.arts*. Feeding a hierarchy that has a group as its root should be done with two patterns, like `comp.graphics,comp.graphics.*`. This bit of consistency helps make it especially clear what is intended and avoids the possible accident of having something like `comp.arch*` forwarding not only the hierarchy on computer architecture but also the one on computer archives.

Article matching is liberal with regard to crossposted articles in the presence of `!`-style negation. Thus, a feed that gets `rec.*,!rec.sport.*` has an article sent to it if it is posted to any *rec* group besides the *rec.sport* groups, even if the Newsgroups header includes some *rec.sport* groups, and regardless of what order those groups occur in the header. This is quite different from `@`-style negation, which ensures that the article is not sent no matter what groups it is crossposted to. Many people find such aggressive blocking of a group at their feed very useful for things like the *warez* and *binaries* groups, to keep that voluminous traffic entirely off of their servers. Contrary to the *newsfeeds* manual page's declaration, the location of an `@`-style negation does not seem to matter at all with regard to how it works (based on an inspection of the code). Depending on which way you think things are more clear, you might want to put them in the same higher-to-lower order as you would with `!`-style negation, or put all `@` negations at the start or end of the subscription list to highlight them.

The two pseudogroups of *control* and *junk* bear special mention. Unlike other systems that forward an article based on its Newsgroups header, INN sends articles based on where it has filed them. Generally speaking, you don't want to forward articles in the *control* and *junk* pseudogroups. Even if you have a very open feed to your neighbor, excluding *control* and *junk* explicitly is a good idea.* Say that you use the pattern `*,!alt.*` because your neighbor has gotten tired of the group creation scheme of the *alt* hierarchy and requested that you stop sending him *alt*. With this pattern, however, you're still forwarding all of the *newgroup* and *rmgroup* control messages for *alt*. Adding `,!control,!control.*` stops that.† Blocking the *junk* pseudogroup helps keep down the amount of confusion on the Net about whether a group is widely considered valid or not. Full feeds are thus best started with `*,!control,!control.*,!junk`.‡

The distributions subfield of the pattern field follows the group subscription patterns. It has no provisions for wildcarding, so each token is literal. These tokens are matched against the Distribution header to determine whether to send an article that has already matched the sitename and group pattern criteria. If there is no

---

* If you haven't configured WANT_TRASH as DO, you shouldn't be filing anything in *junk*, so you don't have to worry about a `!junk` exclusion. However, putting it in anyway helps you if you ever recompile *innd* with WANT_TRASH enabled.

† The `!control.*` is there in case you created subgroups to file control messages based on their specific type, such as *control.newgroup*. Always using `!control,!control.*` ensures that control messages get caught right from the start, no matter what changes you eventually make to control message filing.

‡ If you are using the somewhat dated *to.site* group system for specially directed control messages, `!to,!to.*` should also be added to that full feed.

distributions subfield, the selected article is sent. A group-selected article without a Distribution header is also always sent.* An article with a Distribution header has its distributions matched against the tokens in the distributions subfield. If any of them match, the article is sent; if none do, it is not.

Matching can be done in either an inclusive or exclusive manner. Inclusive tokens are those that describe specifically the distributions that are to be sent, like `na,usa,world` to send any articles that have any of those words in their Distribution headers. Exclusive tokens start with an exclamation mark (`!`) and describe the distributions not to send; all others are passed. Thus, `!local` forwards an article unless it has a "Distribution: local" header. If it had an anomalous "Distribution: local, world" header,† the article is still sent because the `world` token matches the implied "send everything else."

WARNING   Mixing inclusive and exclusive tokens in the distributions subfield is useless and potentially confusing. `/send-this,!but-not-this` behaves exactly like `/!but-not-this`, which means to send every distribution except *but-not-this*, regardless of whether it is *send-this* or something else entirely. Stick to specifying either the distributions to send or those to exclude. Remember, too, that the distributions are only text strings, not wildmat patterns.

The third field of the *newsfeeds* entry specifies various flags that either add further limits to the articles that are sent or describe how to interpret the fourth field. The full complement of flags is described in the *newsfeeds* manual page; most people never need most of them. For an NNTP feed, you'll generally only need to set Wnm, which tells *innd* to interpret the fourth field as the name of a file to which to write the path to the article and its message ID. The NNTP transmitter uses the message ID for *IHAVE* or *CHECK* negotiations, as described in Section 19.5.

Finally, the fourth field is used to specify any parameters needed by the flags set in the third field. In the case of Wnm, the fourth field names the output file for the article information. In this case, relative pathnames are interpreted relative to _PATH_BATCHDIR. If the field is empty, *innd* uses a file named the same as the sitename in the first field. For NNTP feeds controlled by *nntpsend*, this field can be left blank.

---

* There is a flag that can be sent in the third field, Ad, that requires a Distribution header for the article to be sent, but it is extremely uncommon to use it.

† Posting software is notoriously lame about checking the Distribution header and users have been seen posting with headers just like this one.

Here again is the minimal *newsfeeds* file you may have configured in Section 7.4.1:

```
ME:!*/!local::
TESTING:!*::
```

The `ME` line is special. There should only be one `ME` entry in a *newsfeeds* file; if it exists, it should be the first entry in the file. As with other lines, the second field is the pattern field and it can have an optional distributions subfield.

WARNING   The `ME` line in a *newsfeeds* file functions very differently than it does
             in a B News or C News *sys* file. In particular, rather than defining
             what groups your site takes (with INN, only the *active* file is used for
             that), the pattern field (second field) of the `ME` entry in a *newsfeeds*
             file is internally prepended to the pattern fields of the other feeds
             listed in the file. This "feature" generally only helps to obfuscate the
             intention of each subscription by detaching some very important
             information from the individual lines. Using `!*` as the pattern field
             of the `ME` entry means that each subscription is started with a clean
             slate of having no groups as part of its feed. Thus, the pattern listed
             for a feed completely describes the groups the site should get.

Although the `ME` distributions subfield does nothing for C News, for INN it defines what distributions your site is willing to accept. INN does not place any limitations on articles without a distribution header. If an article has a distribution header, INN matches the article against the `ME` line according to the same basic rules it uses for the other lines. If there are no negations, only the listed distributions match; if there are negations, anything that is not negated matches.

The flag field and the parameters field are completely ignored for the `ME` entry. You cannot use them to add requirements to articles you receive.

As far as statistics are concerned, you can play with the flags field of a feed definition to write various forms of data. For example, if you wanted to do an analysis of the Distribution headers you have received, you could make a *newsfeeds* entry like this:

```
dist!stats:*:Tf,Ad,WD:
```

This lists the distribution of every article that has a Distribution header in the file *NEWSARTS/out.going/dist!stats*.

8.2.2.2 *hosts.nntp*

The *hosts.nntp* file names the hosts that are allowed to transfer news to your site; it is one of the files that *innd* reads when it starts and needs to be reloaded with a *ctlinnd reload* command when it is updated. It also needs to be reloaded if one of your peers changes their host's DNS **A** records, which are the records that identify the IP addresses for machines, because *innd* caches the IP addresses for fast lookup and it does not expire them like a DNS server would.

The default file certainly needs to be changed from your site, unless you really managed to obtain a news feed from *news.foo.com* (a host that has valid DNS records but does not really run news). Just list the hostname of every machine that is supposed to send you news, one per line, with a colon following it. You can also use an IP address if for some reason you can't get reliable A record information for the site from hostname lookups.

If you require a password for a site to send news to you, the password that you both agreed on should be entered in clear text after the colon. The password cannot contain a colon because that would indicate the start of the optional third and last field. The password can be up to 240 characters—for you really wordy people, remember that it has to be able to fit into the NNTP command length limitation as part of an *AUTHINFO PASS* command.

The last field takes a *newsfeeds*-style group subscription pattern; it describes what groups the sending site is allowed to transmit articles for. This field can be used to keep articles from the outside world from appearing in your local groups. If the article is crossposted to other valid groups on your server and the sending host is allowed to transfer them, the article is still accepted for those other groups; if not, it is rejected. This field should not be used to reject articles for groups you just do not want; that's what your *active* file is for.

WARNING   If you don't remember to put the colon at the end of the line for a
              site that does not need a password to send you news and does not
              have restrictions on the groups it can transfer, *innd* refuses to run
              because of the syntactically incorrect line. This is a common error.

Most sites that you want to serve will fall into one of two groups: reader sites and peer feed sites. Any machine that is listed in *hosts.nntp* is considered to be a peer feed site, so when *innd* receives a connection from a machine that has the IP address of one of the machines listed in *hosts.nntp*, it sets up a transfer session. No reader services are available in this transfer session, so if the client machine really wants to read news and not transfer it, the client has to send a *MODE READER* NNTP command to become a reader client. (The reverse is not true; a reader cannot become a peer feed.)

Finally, in the unlikely event that you have chosen to run *innd* with the -a flag, which allows any host to transfer news to your site, the *hosts.nntp* file is not used for access control. It can, however, still be used to enable logging by hostname, rather than just IP address.

8.2.2.3   *nntpsend.ctl*

For a site with about half a dozen or fewer outgoing feeds,* *nntpsend.ctl* is a reasonable way to manage NNTP article transmission. The *nntpsend* script, which you should run periodically from *cron* (every 15 minutes is good), handles the execution of *innxmit* sessions based on what is configured in *nntpsend.ctl*. If you have a larger site, see Chapter 13, *Hub Nodes*, for better ways of handling numerous feeds.

The distributed file contains two example non-comment lines that should be removed. In their place, you should insert a line for each host you feed. Each line should start with the name for the site that you used in its *newsfeeds* entry and be followed by the Internet hostname or address for the site. The third and fourth fields, which are for size and flags, can be left empty if you desire, or set according to the *shrinkfile* (size field) or *innxmit* (flags field) manual pages. If these fields are empty, *nntpsend* does not need the colons delineating them as missing fields.

WARNING   *nntpsend* expects that the news name you used for the site as the first field in both its *newsfeeds* and *nntpsend.ctl* entries is also the name of the resulting batchlist for the site in *NEWSARTS/out.going*. There is no way to change this expectation (short of editing the actual *nntpsend* script), so you can't use the last field of the *newsfeeds* entry to name the batchlist file something else if you want it to work with *nntpsend*.

8.2.2.4   *passwd.nntp*

If another site requires your site to authenticate itself to transfer news, the user and password you have agreed on should appear in *passwd.nntp* if you are using the *innxmit* transmitter. The distributed version of this file has an example line that can be removed.

The hostname in the first field should be the same as the Internet hostname you are using to tell *innxmit* where to send its news, but character case doesn't matter. The user and password fields are in unencrypted text and can both take any character except NUL, NL, or colon—we recommend printable ASCII for readability— to a maximum total line length of 255 characters. The *nntp.access* documentation with INN says that the fourth field can contain the type of authentication to use, but *innxmit* only supports *authinfo*, which is the default if there is no fourth field, so putting anything here is pointless.

---

* This number is off the cuff and has little scientific support.

When sites running *innd* authenticate your connections for news transfer by using the *AUTHINFO* NNTP command, they only care about *AUTHINFO PASS* and ignore any *AUTHINFO USER* command. However, sites running the NNTP Reference Implementation, and perhaps others, require the user information, so it is a good practice to always have it defined too.

Because this file contains passwords, it should not be accessible to anyone but the news system. Be careful about having it on a filesystem that is exported to remote systems, where it is easier to compromise.

8.2.2.5 moderators

The *moderators* file allows you to define patterns for the handling of submissions to moderated newsgroups. It is used by *inews* and *nnrpd* before they try to use the `moderatormailer` value from *inn.conf*. Contrary to the numerous defaults in the distribution, we recommend that you use only one line to send all submissions through the sites that maintain global lists of aliases. In fact, you can make the file empty and depend on `moderatormailer` in *inn.conf*. This approach is preferable because the global aliases are kept up-to-date, while most other sites are not.

You might think it would be a good idea to maintain the submission addresses of all moderated groups that you get in this file, but honestly it is not. If you do, you will regret it because it is difficult to keep current on updates to submission addresses. Address changes are usually coordinated through *moderators-request@isc.org* and are only reflected in public postings about once a month. You are better off just leaving this job to the mailpaths sites (see Section 15.2.1).

The best utility for the *moderators* file is with groups of very limited distribution. For example, you might have moderated groups in your organization's own hierarchy that you want users to be able to post to like normal groups. By defining them, or a pattern for them, in your *moderators* file, you can have submissions directed appropriately.

If you do not have a need to define groups that aren't listed at the mailpaths sites, you don't even need the *moderators* file and you can just use `moderatormailer` in *inn.conf*. *moderators-request@isc.org* would be happy to hear of any widely distributed groups that are not listed or that have incorrect addresses at mailpaths sites.

8.2.2.6 distrib.pats

INN's *inews* and *nnrpd* insert a Distribution header into articles posted from your site if they do not already have one and if they are posted to a group that matches one of the group name patterns in *distrib.pats*. If the Newsgroups header of the article matches more than one line, the line with the largest value in its first field is used.

The distribution concept that was set forth in RFC 1036 was a noble idea but ultimately a grand failure. It has several problems that are not worth the effort of solving. In fact, they probably couldn't really be solved even if all the major sites got together and came up with a way to make things work as they were intended.

Some of the problems include: extremely poor user education about what distributions are for, poor posting interface support for ensuring that reasonable distributions are used, a lack of a meaningfully coordinated distribution namespace, and paths between two sites in the same distribution that reasonably pass out of the distribution before returning. For the last, imagine two sites in Texas who get their only feeds from UUNET, based in Virginia. UUNET carries all of the *tx* groups to serve such feeds, but if it could not get and pass distribution to *tx*, there would be a notable hole in its service. Beyond that, some sites specifically want all traffic, no matter its distribution.

Our personal recommendation is to just forget about using Distribution headers unless you rule the feeds on all of the sites that should get a particular distribution with an iron fist. Even then you might be surprised by a leak. It is best to control the targeting of your articles to appropriate audiences by posting in the most appropriate newsgroups. For topics of local interest, use a local hierarchy.

"Distribution: inet" is especially problematic because a lot of current administrators do not even know that there are some "special" groups in the main, worldwide namespace. (See Section 17.3.3 for more information on the INET distribution.) Even the ones who are trying to be responsible by restricting the distributions that they get end up with a slightly broken feed because they are not aware that certain groups are in the *inet* distribution.

As shipped in versions prior to 1.5, INN's *distrib.pats* tried to add "Distribution: inet" to any article posted to those groups that were part of the special INET/DDN distribution as of July 1992. There have been many changes since then, so if you have an older version of INN, you should be sure to modify the *distrib.pats* file. Simply remove the lines for the two *ddn* groups, *comp.emacs*, *comp.music*, *comp.org.eff.news*, *comp.org.eff.talk*, *comp.windows.x.announce*, *rec.mag.fsfnet*, and *news.software.nntp*.

For these reasons, it is probably best to ensure that the *distrib.pats* file is defining no forced distributions in your initial setup, and then only add local, regional, or other special entries when you are fully sure that it is the right thing to do. Also try to be sure that your specifications degrade gracefully in the face of a changing namespace, even if you were to do no further maintenance of the file. In other words, specify `100:my-hierarchy.*:local`, rather than individual groups in *my-hierarchy*, to cover all new groups and not leave behind stale references to old groups. Again, we recommend against using distributions at all unless the set of machines that the distribution is meaningful for is tightly controlled.

8.2.3 Expiry

The decisions involved in getting rid of old articles to make room for new ones are common to all news systems and are discussed in Section 3.4. This section helps you implement the decisions that you've made.

The *expire.ctl* file tells the *expire* program how to decide whether an article is too old to be kept around any more. It also defines how long your system should remember message IDs in the *history* file, so that *innd* can reject subsequent offerings of the same article correctly. *expire* reads the file when it starts.

The default *expire.ctl* file might be fine for your system, but it should really be tuned to suit your disk space and your available memory. The latter is relevant because the size of the index for the *history* file can dramatically hurt performance if it is too large to fit into memory.

There is a line in the default file that looks like:

```
*:A:1:10:never
```

The **never** in the last field says to keep all articles with Expires headers until whenever the header says the article should be removed. Since this header can be abused, you might want to cap the limit at something relatively large but still finite, like 90 days. Do this by replacing the word **never** with the maximum number of days of retention.

The most important thing to remember about *expire.ctl* is that the last line to match a given article is the one that is applied to make the decision about keeping it. This is especially important to keep in mind with crosspostings, as you have to decide which set of retention times is more important and order your file accordingly. Here's a commented, example *expire.ctl* that illustrates this:

```
# This is the default expiration time for an article --- remove it as
# soon as expire runs!  Isn't that a daft policy?  No, not really,
# because there are two lines following it which will cover most
# articles.  This line will only end up covering articles for groups
# which you have removed from your active file and hence don't want
# using space any more.
*:A:0:0:0
# These two lines cover articles for all groups in the active file.
# Both allow articles with Expires: headers to be around for as little
# as a day if they have short expiration times, and will keep articles
# without Expires: headers for a week.  Articles which have Expires
```

```
# headers in unmoderated groups are given a little leeway for longer
# retention, but not much.  Those in moderated groups can stay for
# nearly three months, as it is expected that the typical moderator has
# given better thought to a meaningful retention period.  The moderated
# group line comes after the unmoderated group line for those cases
# in which the moderator has crossposted to unmoderated groups.
*:U:1:7:10
*:M:1:7:90
# We want to keep the main worldwide hierarchies a little longer than
# the default for the regional/alternative hierarchies that we carry.
comp.*,humanities,misc.*,news.*,rec.*,sci.*,soc.*,talk.*:U:1:10:10
comp.*,humanities,misc.*,news.*,rec.*,sci.*,soc.*,talk.*:M:1:10:90
# Due to our interest in group creation politics, this can stay for
# two weeks just in case we get behind on it.
news.groups:A:1:14:90
# But note that articles from these two groups are often crossposted to
# news.groups, and we want to keep them longer.  So it comes after the
# news.groups line.
news.announce.newgroups,news.lists:A:1:30:90
# This one, though, we want to get rid of faster because it is higher
# volume and not readable prose (similar observations about the rest of
# Usenet notwithstanding).  Keep it long enough to propagate it to
# neighbors, but that's it.
comp.mail.maps:A:1:3:3
# We never want to expire the groups posted to our local hierarchy.
mysite.*:A:never:never:never
# Finally, this is the minimum amount of time we should hang on to
# message-ids in this history database, despite whatever time they
# expire.  The number should be the same as or greater than the -c
# parameter to innd and serves to keep the message-id around long
# enough to log a duplicate, just in case you are offered the article
# again after it has expired.
/remember/:14
```

As with other files that use wildmat-style patterns, it is recommended that you never use the asterisk (`*`) wildcard without preceding it with a dot (`.`) (i.e., `comp.arch,comp.arch.*` instead of `comp.arch*`). The existence of the *comp.archives* hierarchy shows how this can be a problem; there is no guarantee that something similar won't happen to some hierarchy with which you might want to take a `*` shortcut.

8.2.4 Control Messages

Control messages (not to be confused with control files) are special types of network news articles that usually come from off-site and request your system to perform some administrative task. The common tasks are pretty narrowly defined to be removing articles (*cancel*), creating or removing groups (*newgroup* and *rmgroup*), verifying the groups that should exist in a hierarchy (*checkgroups*), sending information about your system (*sendsys*, *senduuname*, and *version*), and implementing a special type of feed usually used by UUCP systems (*ihave* and *sendme*). They are described in detail in Section 18.4. Though there are many configurable scripts that handle the processing of control messages, there is only one control file that directs the show.

8.2.4.1 control.ctl

The *control.ctl* file tells INN how to handle control messages that arrive at your site. Nearly all control message types are handled by scripts forked by *innd* while it continues to receive articles. Only *cancel* is coded directly into the server daemon because it is very common and needs to be highly efficient. Because *cancel* is hardcoded, it cannot be affected by *control.ctl*, but all other functions can.

control.ctl matches the issuer of the control message (the address in the Sender header, or in From if there is no Sender header) with the group that it affects (for *newgroup* and *rmgroup*) and the requested function to determine its action. The order of lines is significant, as the last line that matches the group and sender is the one that is used. The possible actions are to process the message automatically (`doit`), to send a mail message to the news administrator requesting that it be done (`mail`), to log receipt of the request to a file (`log`), or to silently ignore the request (`drop`). When the `doit` action is specified, it can be supplemented by an additional action: `doit=mail` to process the message and send mail to the news administrator or `doit=`*logfile* to process the message and log it to the specified file. The `log` action can also specify a particular log file, using the form `log=`*logfile*.

A decision about whether to perform the desired action can be based on a more secure authentication method that uses PGP. If the fourth field of a line is `verify-`*keyword*, where *keyword* is the PGP user ID you are authorizing to make changes, the action is performed if all the other criteria match and the PGP signature is found and verified. If a PGP signature cannot be found and verified, INN treats the *control.ctl* line as though the action were `mail`.

The *control.ctl* file distributed with INN is adequate for most installations. By default, most standard control messages for which it does not find a more specific rule are logged by type in INN's standard log directory. The full control message is logged, with instructions about how to perform the requested function if you choose.

WARNING   In the default configuration, all *ihave/sendme* control messages are
            dropped without notice; this needs to be changed if you set up such
            a UUCP feed.

Several lines are provided for handling *newgroup* and *rmgroup* messages for hierarchies you might have in your feed. As shipped, INN allows *tale@uunet.uu.net*, the moderator of *news.announce.newgroups* since early 1991, to automatically add and remove groups in the mainstream Usenet hierarchies if you have PGP. If you still want to trust him, please change the address to *group-admin@isc.org*.

If you have PGP and want to use the more secure authentication system, you'll have to set up the PGP key rings. The best and easiest way to do this is to *su* to the news owner. If HOME is set in your environment, make sure that it is set to the home directory of the news owner. Also make sure that PGPPATH is not set. Then get the file *ftp://ftp.isc.org/pub/pgpcontrol/PGPKEYS* and put it in */tmp*. Finally, run the following:

```
% cd ~news
% mkdir .pgp
% pgp -ka /tmp/PGPKEYS
```

Each time you are asked "Do you want to certify any of these keys yourself (y/n)?" answer n. When you are done, there should be a file in the news owner's home directory named *pgp/.pubring.pgp*, and *pgp -kv* should list several PGP user IDs from the *PGPKEYS* file. Don't worry about having some in there for hierarchies that you don't want; it is purely *control.ctl* that determines whether a key user ID on the key ring is of any significance for honoring control messages.

WARNING   Configuring automatic *rmgroup* handling that is not limited to specific addresses and verified with *pgpverify* is a very bad idea, as it can corrupt the consistency of your *active* file and spool databases, especially if a *newgroup*/*rmgroup* war is being waged in *alt*.

Even if you do configure *rmgroup* in a hierarchy for just one possible address, but don't have the PGP signature verified, it is possible for a forgery to be sent in the name of one of the hierarchy maintainers that is not really from him. INN cannot tell that the message is a forgery and treats it as though it were sent by the real maintainer, so the group will vanish from your *active* file (although the articles still exist until they are expired).

You can get a copy of a *control.ctl* file that is kept more up-to-date on who is nominally in charge of hierarchies by fetching *ftp://ftp.isc.org/pub/usenet/CONFIG/control.ctl*. It uses PGP authentication where it can.

8.2.4.2 *actsync.cfg*

This is a good place to mention the *actsync* program and its simple wrapper, *actsyncd*. If you choose to maintain your *active* file with *actsyncd*, it should be called periodically from *cron* (four times a day is fine) with the full path to *actsync.cfg* as its argument. The information in *actsync.cfg* is used to create an *actsync* command to synchronize your *active* file with that of a remote site that you consider to be authoritative.

If you configure *actsync.cfg* to use a local filename instead of a hostname, as suggested in Section 7.2.1.12, you can call the script shown in Example 8–1 from *cron* instead of simply calling *actsyncd*. The script is just a simple skeleton that isn't automatically integrated with whatever you defined in *config.data*, so you'll have to adjust paths as necessary. You could add code that gets ISC's *newsgroups* file to update your own *newsgroups* file, or use some different method for retrieving or generating the list of valid groups.

Example 8–1: The sync-from-isc Script

```
#! /bin/sh -e
# sync-from-isc --- synchronize with the ISC active file

# directory to store the remote active file
WORKDIR=/var/tmp
# to lock against simultaneous runs of this program
LOCK=$WORKDIR/`basename $0`.lock

cd $WORKDIR

if ! shlock -p $$ -f $LOCK; then
  echo "$0: could not lock $LOCK; try later" >&2
  exit 1
fi

# retrieve ISC's active file with a non-interactive ftp session
# requires the freely available ncftp program by Mike Gleason
ncftp ftp://ftp.isc.org/pub/usenet/CONFIG/active.gz
# decompress it
gzip -df active
# move it to the name set as ACTSYNC_HOST in INN's config.data
mv active master.active

# run actsyncd to update the local active file
actsyncd /var/news/etc/actsync.cfg

# remove the lock & leave master.active for personal reference
rm -f $LOCK

exit 0
```

8.2.5 Newsreaders

Two control files from the *site* directory are directly related to newsreader operation. *nnrp.access* controls who is allowed to establish NNTP newsreader sessions, while *overview.fmt* defines the format of an auxiliary database that makes newsreaders more efficient.

8.2.5.1 nnrp.access

Client newsreader access via NNTP is controlled by the *nnrp.access* file. It describes, based on hostname, what groups may be read and who can post articles. The order of lines is significant, as the last line in the file that matches the hostname is the one that is applied. This means your defaults should come first.

Stripped of some of its (lengthy) comments, INN's *nnrp.access* as distributed is:

```
## Default is no access, no way to authentication, and no groups.
*:: -no- : -no- :!*
##  Foo, Incorporated, hosts have no password, can read anything.
*.foo.com:Read Post:::*
stdin:Read Post:::*
localhost:Read Post:::*
127.0.0.1:Read Post:::*
```

This has a very reasonable default of keeping your server blocked to everyone— well, almost everyone. If the people at the real domain *foo.com* ever want to read news from other servers, they'll probably find more than one server that will let them in. The *foo.com* line should be removed from your installation, unless you are *foo.com*, or a good friend.

The five colon-separated fields specify:

- A host pattern that must match for the rest of the fields to apply

- A permissions field that defines reading or posting permission

- A user field and a password field that are used together to permit only certain authorized users to post articles

- A newsgroups field that contains a *newsfeeds*-style subscription pattern that says what groups may be accessed

In the permissions field, *nnrpd* only looks for a capital R or a capital P to allow reading or posting, respectively.* It should go without saying, but probably can't, that if any password access is used in this file, the file should not be generally accessible. Of course, it does still need to be accessed by the news owner.

Here's an example of an *nnrp.access* file that uses all of its features:

```
# default: don't let the whole world read from us.
# The user, pass and groups fields are redundant
# but syntactically necessary.
*:: -no- : -no- :!*
# all the hosts from our corporate domain can, by default,
# read and post without restrictions
```

---

* In INN prior to Version 1.5, the user and password fields were used only to control posting permission. They did not have any effect on what groups could be read. Conversely, the newsgroups field only affected what groups could be read. It had no effect on what groups could be posted to.

```
*.ora.com:RP:::*
# kiwi is in our domain but isn't allowed to read or
# post to the New Zealand newsgroups
kiwi.ora.com:RP:::*,!nz.*
# one of our staff regularly accesses us from a public
# site; let him read anything after authenticatin himself
# as long as he doesn't get his password wrong (again!)
world.std.com:RP:mikey:SoMEpaSSword:*
```

8.2.5.2 overview.fmt

The *overview.fmt* file defines the format of the data that is written to the news overview database—the summary of articles that some newsreader programs can use to improve their performance. The news overview database is described in Section 19.2.5.

The distributed *overview.fmt* file is usable as is. The only line that bears mentioning is the **Xref:full** line, which benefits several newsreaders. The main advantage is greatly increased speed and accuracy in marking crossposts as read. When a user reads an article, a good newsreader not only remembers it as read in the newsgroup that was being used at the time, but also in any other newsgroup the user reads, so she does not have to see it again. Additionally, sometimes people want to automatically select or ignore articles based on the groups to which they might be crossposted, such as when an *alt.tasteless* thread manages to show up crossposted in *rec.pets.cats*. The presence of Xref allows both of these things to happen more efficiently.

You shouldn't change this file unless you want to reconfigure and possibly reprogram many newsreaders that use the overview database. While some programs think they should look at *overview.fmt* to find out what is available in overview files, others rely on the specification of the overview format, which says that the content and order of the first eight fields is standard, fixed, predetermined, and not user-configurable. If you feel you must change the file, you'll have to dive into the code of the newsreaders you support to find out how they will be affected, and even if you make sure they're fine, there could well be other newsreader clients accessing your server that will be negatively affected by changing the format.

Any time *overview.fmt* is changed, you should remove all of the old overview files and rebuild them with *expireover*.

8.3 Scripts

The INN distribution maintains its many auxiliary scripts the same way it keeps the control files, so they should be modified in the *site* directory the same way too, as described in Section 8.1. This section describes all of the installed scripts that come with INN and notes why they are needed and how they are generally used. They are */bin/sh* scripts unless otherwise noted. Since changing the scripts is very much a matter of personal taste, very few suggestions are made about how you might want to edit them. In general, you are better off not altering a script unless it exhibits some behavior you just can't stand.

If you do need to update a script, use the same *make install* procedure that you would for configuration files. You don't have to worry about trashing a running instance of an updated script because the installation procedure uses *mv* as the final step for putting the code in place. Thus, a running instance continues to use the image of the original program.

8.3.1 General Operation

INN has several scripts that are used regularly in all aspects of the system. Some of these can also be used to check to see that everything is operating normally. *inncheck*, *innshelvars*, *innstat*, *innwatch*, and *rc.news* are all described here. Though *news.daily* serves multiple operational functions, it is not covered here. It is mentioned briefly in Section 8.3.5, but because of its operational importance, it is covered more extensively in Section 9.5.6.

8.3.1.1 inncheck

inncheck is a standalone Perl script that you can run to sanity check the configuration of your INN system. Besides checking the existence, ownership, and permissions of INN's configuration files, *inncheck* tries to verify the data in several of them to ensure that it is consistent with what should appear in the file. *inncheck* complains about anything that doesn't seem quite right. If everything is in accord, there is no output.

If you want to be extra careful about catching subtle problems with your system soon after they appear, you might want to run *inncheck -pedantic* daily from the news system's *crontab* file. If there is output when it runs, *cron* sends the news owner a mail message with the discrepancies that it has found. See the *news.daily* manual page for other *inncheck* options.

8.3.1.2 innshellvars

The *innshellvars* file is meant to be sourced by all other INN shell scripts so that they can pick up the pathnames you have configured. It also sets the file creation permissions mask (*umask*) to the value that you have defined. In almost all cases, if you want a pathname available as a variable in a shell script and it is not defined in *innshellvars*, you should probably just set it separately in the script that requires it.

8.3.1.3 innstat

The *innstat* script is normally only called by *news.daily* to dump a current snap-shot of the system into the daily report (see Section 9.5.6), though it was probably designed to be used interactively too. The script first does a *ctlinnd mode* and then follows it with a *df* of some of the partitions on which dynamic news data is stored (it might miss some, like multiple article spool partitions or a separate news overview filesystem). It then shows the sizes of batchlists and log files, lists any active log files, and finally shows all the open *innd* channels printed by *ctlinnd name*.

All in all, this data is about as useful to have in the daily report as the *ps* output of all the machine's processes would be to have once a day. In most cases, it is just distracting noise, enough so that you get used to ignoring it. It probably won't grab your attention even when there really is something meaningful to notice. You can tell *news.daily* not to include *innstat* output by adding the `nostat` keyword to its command line.

8.3.1.4 innwatch

innwatch is a relatively large shell script that normally gets started from *rc.news* when `DOINNWATCH` is set to `true`. It runs continuously, sleeping most of the time but waking up periodically (every 10 minutes as shipped with INN; use `-t` to change that) to check on the current state of the news system. Its checks are controlled by *innwatch.ctl*, a very hairy configuration file described in Section 8.2.1.2. We're assuming here that you haven't tried to change it.

When *innwatch* wakes up, if it sees that *innd* is gone, it sends a message to news-master about it. *innwatch* then goes back to sleep, continuing on its sleep-awake-check cycle. When it next wakes up and sees that *innd* is running again, it sends another message.

If *innd* is running, as it should be, *innwatch* checks the load average on the machine and throttles *innd* if it is too high compared to the value you set for `INNWATCH_HILOAD` in *config.data*. Similarly, it unthrottles *innd* if it was previously throttled for a high load and the load has come down below `INNWATCH_LOLOAD`. Then it checks, in order, the free disk space on the article spool, batchlist, and control files partitions, and the free inodes in the article spool. It throttles *innd* if any of these fall below acceptable limits, but it does not try to unthrottle when they return to a tolerable level.

Finally, *innwatch* looks to see if the *news.crit* log file has changed. If it has, that probably means that *innd* throttled or shut down because of an error, so *innwatch* sends newsmaster the contents of the log file. The file that is watched for updates can be changed with the `-l` flag.

8.3.1.5 rc.news

The *rc.news* shell script is supposed to be called during your news server's boot procedures. As we said in Section 7.4.5.1, it should run as the news owner, which means it should be invoked via a *su* command in the startup procedure.

The first thing *rc.news* does is clean up old locks and other cruft left behind by processes that did not exit cleanly when the server went down. Then it tries to recover the *active* file if *active* vanished for some bizarre reason. *rc.news* then starts *innd*. If it appears *innd* did not exit cleanly (the old *innd.pid* process ID file still exists), *innd* is started with the -r flag so that the *active* file is immediately renumbered before any new articles are accepted. This is done because it is likely that there were unflushed updates pending for *active* when the old *innd* process stopped.

If you do not want to run *innwatch* on your system, find the following line in *rc.news*:

```
DOINNWATCH=true
```

Change it to:

```
DOINNWATCH=false
```

The value of DOINNWATCH is used in a shell && list, so it has to be a command that exits with a zero status when it is called.

The last task *rc.news* performs is to look for an existing *expire.rm* list of articles to remove. If such a list is on the system, it probably means that the system went down while *expire -z* was running. This could possibly have happened after the *history* file was completely rewritten, such that future *expire* runs will not encounter any record of the articles that were previously written to *expire.rm*. In this case, to be safe, *rc.news* runs *expirerm* on the *expire.rm* file. Though an attempt is made to prevent multiple runs from clashing with each other (and it succeeds most of the time), this isn't completely safe because of some subtle bugs with how the list files are named and moved around. Situations where any articles are left behind, however, are rare enough that you don't need to worry about this problem (but it will be fixed in a future release, of course).

8.3.2 News Flow

The scripts in this section are responsible for coordinating sending articles to your news neighbors. They do not directly transmit the articles, but rather get them to the programs that do. The articles that get transmitted are selected by *innd* based on the *newsfeeds* file, as described previously.

8.3.2.1 nntpsend

nntpsend is a wrapper script around *innxmit*, usually run from *cron* to push news to your neighbors. When *nntpsend* is run without arguments, it sends news to any site listed in *nntpsent.ctl* that has a non-empty batchlist. This normal operation is covered in detail in 9.2.4.

If you provide news name and Internet hostname pairs on *nntpsend*'s command line, only those sites are sent news. They do not need to be listed in *nntpsend.ctl*, but if they are, then any flags specified in *nntpsend.ctl* for the site are added to those specified on the command line. Command-line options override the same options specified in *nntpsend.ctl*. For example, take a *nntpsend.ctl* file that looks like this:

```
uunet:news.uu.net::-T3600 -r
```

Say this is used with an *nntpsend* command line that looks like this:

```
% nntpsend -T86400 uunet news.uu.net
```

This results in an *innxmit* command that looks something like this:

```
innxmit -T86400 -r -t180 news.uu.net /news/spool/out.going/uunet.nntp
```

The `-t180` is a default argument from *nntpsend* that can be overridden with an explicit `-t` option. It specifies how long, in seconds, *innxmit* should wait to make the initial connection with the remote site.

8.3.2.2 send-ihave

The *send-ihave* script is run periodically when you have established an *ihave/sendme* feed as described in Section 9.3.1.3. This script is responsible for generating *ihave* control messages full of message IDs you can offer to the other end of the feed. The messages are posted to your own server with *inews*, where a *newsfeeds* entry should match it for the site's batchlist. Each message then propagates to the other site like any other article.

8.3.2.3 send-nntp

Like *nntpsend*, *send-nntp* is an interface to calling *innxmit* to send news to your NNTP neighbors. It is effectively a redundant program in the distribution, and since it lacks the flexibility of *nntpsend* for specifying flags, it can safely be ignored. The only notable difference between it and *nntpsend* is that *send-nntp* runs every site in sequence in the foreground, rather than forking multiple *innxmit* processes in parallel in the background.

8.3.2.4 send-uucp

The *send-uucp* script can be used to queue batches for transmission to your UUCP feeds. For the most part, it does not have the flexibility of INN's *sendbatch* for managing queues and controlling how batches are written. The one thing it does have that *sendbatch* does not is a built-in notion of what sites it should be feeding and at what time of day it is acceptable to do so. If that would be useful to you, it isn't hard to lift the "Who are we sending to?" block of code from *send-uucp* and put it in *sendbatch*. If you do, put a `set` − `$LIST` after the grafted block and you should be good to go. Sites with more than a dozen or so UUCP feeds may find *newsxd*, described in Section 13.1.5, to be more convenient.

8.3.2.5 sendbatch

The *sendbatch* script is used to queue batches for transmission to UUCP feeds. Based on the B News program of the same name, it allows you to specify a size cap on how much can be queued for the site, how much can be queued by one invocation of *sendbatch*, how big individual batches can be, whether a special batch encoding should be used, whether the batches should be compressed or not, and some less frequently used options. The use of *sendbatch* for setting up a UUCP newsfeed is described in Section 9.2.4.

8.3.3 Expiry

The *expirerm* script that comes with INN can improve the time and resources used by your system for the removal of old articles. This script is called by *news.daily* if the `delayrm` option is used. It takes the output file that was generated by *expire* -z and sorted by *inn.daily* and removes all of the articles listed. As distributed, it calls *fastrm -eus* to do the removal. If the removal completes successfully, it renames its input file to *expire.list* (in the log directory). If it fails, a mail message is sent to the newsmaster observing that "Expire had problems removing articles."

You might need to modify *expirerm* if you cannot get *fastrm* to work on your system (which would be very unusual). You can comment out the `RMPROC` line that uses *fastrm* and uncomment the less efficient *xargs rm* line. Also, if you run your article spool on more than one partition, you have to remove the −u option to *fastrm*, so it does not try to change directories via a relative path. You don't have to remove the −u option, however, if your second partition is mounted where it logically belongs in the spool hierarchy (e.g., */news* and */news/alt/binaries*).

8.3.4 Control Messages

As described earlier, most of INN's handling of control messages is done through the calling of scripts whose general behavior is orchestrated by *control.ctl*. There is a specific script for each type of control message that can be received. In general, if the action specified by *control.ctl* for a control message is `doit`, the appropriate script takes care of automatically processing the control message. If the action is `mail` or `log`, the script mails the control message to the news administrator or logs it, respectively. The *writelog* script, discussed in Section 8.3.5, is used to write to logs.

8.3.4.1 parsecontrol

The *parsecontrol* script is sourced at the start of each of the scripts that are called by *innd* to handle control messages. Its mission is to set the `ACTION` variable in the control script to whatever behavior is specified in *control.ctl* for the type of control message, its sender, and possibly the group it is trying to affect.

8.3.4.2 pgpverify

If a control message has a sender and a group name that matches a line in *control.ctl* with a fourth field of the form `verify-keyword`, *pgpverify* uses PGP to ensure that the X-PGP-Sig header contains a valid signature. The X-PGP-Sig header lists the various headers that are to be verified with the signature, as well as the signature itself. The signature is compared against the headers named in X-PGP-Sig and the entire body; so much as one character being different causes the signature check to fail. Similarly, if there is no X-PGP-Sig header, the check fails. If the signature can be fully verified, *pgpverify* lets *parsecontrol* know that the effective action should be `doit`; otherwise the effective action becomes `mail`.

8.3.4.3 newgroup

The *newgroup* script is forked by *innd* when a *newgroup* control message is received. It runs the *parsecontrol* script to find the `newgroup` lines in *control.ctl* and to decide what to do, based on both the sender of the *newgroup* request and the group being created (or having its moderation status changed). If the action is `doit`, the group is added to your *active* file with *ctlinnd newgroup*. A confirmation message is then sent to the news administrator. If the body of the control message includes a "For your newsgroups file:" line followed by a line that starts with the group's name, the line is added to *newsgroups*. Other *control.ctl* actions are handled as with other control messages.

One change you might want to make to the *newgroup* script is to have it follow the *ctlinnd newgroup* `group.name` command with *ctlinnd renumber* `group.name`. That way, if a group that had been removed is recreated before all of the old articles have expired, the old article numbers won't cause any problems, such as *innd* trying to put a new article at the number of a file that already exists.

8.3.4.4 rmgroup

The *rmgroup* script is forked by *innd* when a *rmgroup* control message is received. It runs the *parsecontrol* script to find the `rmgroup` lines in *control.ctl* and to decide what to do. If the action is `doit`, the group is removed with *ctlinnd rmgroup* and a confirmation notice is mailed to the news administrator. If the group had an entry in *newsgroups*, it is removed. Other *control.ctl* actions are handled as with other control messages.

8.3.4.5 checkgroups

The *checkgroups* script is forked by *innd* when a *checkgroups* control message is received. It runs the *parsecontrol* script to find the `checkgroups` lines in *control.ctl* and to decide what to do. If the action is `doit`, the script calls *docheckgroups* with the body of the article to do that actual work, mailing the differences encountered to the news administrator. Other *control.ctl* actions are handled as with other control messages.

8.3.4.6 docheckgroups

The *docheckgroups* script is what gets called by *checkgroups* to process the body of a *checkgroups* control message. The script compares the body of the control message with the groups in the *active* file on your server.

It is also useful as a separate script because you can pass any list of newsgroups through it, without having to wrap the list in a formal control message. The script checks any top-level hierarchies mentioned in its input. Unfortunately, you can't use it just to check a subhierarchy, like *comp.sys* in *comp*, without having all of the groups in the top-level hierarchy that are outside of the subhierarchy being reported as incorrect. Moderated groups are identified by the string " (Moderated)" appearing at the end of the line; everything else is considered unmoderated.

The output of the script is a series of *ctlinnd* commands that can be fed to the shell for execution. Rather than piping the results directly from *docheckgroups* to the shell, we recommend that you save the output to a file, manually inspect that file to see whether it does only the changes that you think should be made, and then feed the possibly edited output to the shell.

The output might also include comment lines at the end that note changes you should make to the *newsgroups* file. Extracting this information from the *docheckgroups* output is a bit of a pain; it is much easier to edit the *newsgroups* file to remove all the previous lines of the affected hierarchies and replace them with the the input you originally passed to *docheckgroups*.

8.3.4.7 sendsys

The *sendsys* script is forked by *innd* when a *sendsys* control message is received. It runs the *parsecontrol* script to find the `sendsys` lines in *control.ctl* and to decide what to do. If the action is `doit`, the script sends your entire *newsfeeds* file to the requester, unless an argument is provided in the *sendsys* message. If an argument is present and it matches the name in the first field of one of your *newsfeeds* entries, just that entry is sent. If there is an argument but it doesn't match, nothing is sent. Other *control.ctl* actions are handled as with other control messages.

8.3.4.8 version

The *version* script is forked by *innd* when a *version* control message is received. It runs the *parsecontrol* script to find the `version` lines in *control.ctl* and to decide what to do. If the action is `doit`, the script sends to the requester the INN version information that is coded directly into the *version* script. Other *control.ctl* actions are handled as with other control messages.

8.3.4.9 ihave

The *ihave* script is forked by *innd* when an *ihave* control message is received. `ihave` control messages are used to implement a special type of news feed, generally over non-interactive communications sessions, and are not to be confused with the NNTP *IHAVE* command. The *ihave* script runs the *parsecontrol* script to find the `ihave` lines in *control.ctl* and to decide what to do. If the action is `doit`, the script calls *grephistory* with the body of the article to find the message IDs of the articles that your system does not have. The results are turned into the body of a *sendme* control message posted in the *to* group of the site that sent the *ihave*. This control message should propagate to the site as part of their normal feed (as long as *newsfeeds* was configured to send the required *to* group). Other *control.ctl* actions are handled as with other control messages.

8.3.4.10 sendme

The *sendme* script is forked by *innd* when a *sendme* control message is received. It runs the *parsecontrol* script to find the `sendme` lines in *control.ctl* and to decide what to do. If the action is `doit`, the script calls *grephistory -s* to generate a list of articles based on the message IDs in the body of the control message. This list is appended to the batchlist of the site that sent the *sendme*. Other *control.ctl* actions are handled as with other control messages.

One desirable improvement to this script would be to have it do proper locking of the batchfile when the list is appended to it. There is the chance for corruption from two concurrent *sendme* script executions (not as unlikely as you would think, since all the articles from your UUCP neighbor will probably arrive in bunches). There is also a window where the batchlist might be removed after *sendme* opened it and began appending. Since both of these could reasonably be described as bugs, a fix for the problem would be good to integrate into the distribution.

8.3.4.11 senduuname

The *senduuname* script is forked by *innd* when a *senduuname* control message is received. It runs the *parsecontrol* script to find the `senduuname` lines in *control.ctl* and to decide what to do. If the action is `doit`, the script mails the output of the *uuname* command to the requester. *uuname* doesn't exist on most systems any more, so this is a pretty useless control request. Other *control.ctl* actions are handled as with other control messages.

8.3.4.12 default

The *default* script is forked by *innd* when an article has a control message type that is not covered by another control message script. The *default* script runs the *parsecontrol* script to find the `default` lines in *control.ctl* and to decide what to do. If your default action is `mail`, an "Unknown control message" notice is sent to the newsmaster. Both `doit` and `log` actions result in an "Unknown control message" line being logged. No other work is done with the article.

8.3.4.13 makegroup

This script has not been included in INN since Version 1.5; this section is included as a warning in case it still exists on your system. Unlike the other scripts in this section, *makegroup* is not involved with the processing of existing control messages, but was rather intended as an aid for the creation of *newgroup* messages. To the extent that we can curse in this family book, we curse this program. More than any other single program, it has been responsible for many *newgroup* messages propagating beyond their intended bounds. In our exchanges with people who have used it to create groups, many do not even realize that they should have been using *ctlinnd newgroup* instead. The result is that group creation messages for groups that were never supposed to leave a very limited domain are littering the mailboxes of news administrators around the world.

Please do not use this program unless you are absolutely sure of what you are doing. Even then, you might not want to use it because people will tend to wonder whether you really do know what you are doing, since so many other people using *makegroup* don't. *newgroup* messages created by *makegroup* are readily identifiable by the pattern of their message IDs and bodies.

Chapter 16, *Newsgroups and Their Names*, has an in-depth discussion of both the technical and political issues associated with creating newsgroups. We beg of you, please read it before sending *newgroup* or *rmgroup* messages.

8.3.5 Log Processing

Several scripts are involved with log files. The *news.daily* script is central to many daily operations, including logging. The *writelog* script is used by other scripts to write logs and send mail. There are also some scripts that do post-processing on the data that is logged every day.

8.3.5.1 news.daily

The *news.daily* shell script is intended to be run periodically (daily is a good but not necessary choice) to handle article expiration and log rolling tasks. *news.daily* is covered extensively in Section 9.5.6.

8.3.5.2 innlog.pl

innlog.pl is a Perl script that should work fine with either Perl version 4 or version 5. It parses the information that various programs, notably *innd*, *nnrpd*, and *innxmit*, have logged via *syslogd*. It is called from *scanlogs* with the log file read from standard input. The reception, transmission, and readership summaries generated from *innlog.pl* appear in the daily report that is produced by a normal run of *news.daily*.

8.3.5.3 scanlogs

scanlogs is the script called by *news.daily* to rotate the log files and to report on their contents. The log file reports are covered in Section 9.5. *scanlogs* assumes that the statistical information on *innd*, *nnrpd*, and *innxmit*, logged at the L_NOTICE level you configured when you built INN, is in *news.notice*. *scanlogs* has to be edited if you put that log someplace else.

8.3.5.4 tally.control

If you log *newgroup* and *rmgroup* control messages to the files *newgroup.log* and *rmgroup.log*, *tally.control* updates *control.log* when *scanlogs* rotates those log files. The *control.log* file keeps a count of how many *newgroup* or *rmgroup* messages have been sent for a group. It doesn't distinguish between the two types of control messages, so "15 group.name" in *control.ctl* could mean 15 *newgroup* messages, 15 *rmgroup* messages, or anything in between. Nothing else uses *newgroup.log*, *rmgroup.log*, or *control.log*, at least not programmatically.

8.3.5.5 tally.unwanted

The *tally.unwanted* script is called by *scanlogs*, which in turn is run by *news.daily*, to update *unwanted.log* with the count of groups that your server has rejected for not being present in the *active* file. It gets this information from the *news* log and merges it with any existing counts in *unwanted.log*.

Please remember when you look at this log that a high group count is not necessarily indicative of a valid group that you should be carrying. For example, a berserk gateway once spewed thousands of messages from a mailing list into the newsgroup *comp.dcom.lans.novell*; the group was never discussed outside the site that was doing the gatewaying and was not approved by the normal procedures for creating a group in the *comp* hierarchy. Similarly, groups that once were valid but have been superseded often show up with high counts in *unwanted.log* until people migrate away from them, and creating the group would be counterproductive for that migration.

Chapter 16, contains a lot of information about how groups are created. Section 3.3 talks about how you can responsibly add valid groups to your *active* file. Please do not haphazardly create groups on your server just because they are mentioned in *unwanted.log*.

8.3.5.6 writelog

The *writelog* program is only used by control message scripts. Depending on the action that you selected in *control.ctl* for a particular control message, it either mails the entire article to the newsmaster or writes it to a log file. If the action is `doit` or `doit=mail`, *writelog* is called with an argument that says to mail the control message. If the action is `log=`*log-file* or `doit=`*log-file*, *writelog* writes the control message to the specified log file.

writelog uses the log file argument that is passed to it fairly blindly, so if it is a relative pathname, the log file is relative to whatever directory *writelog* is in when called. The control scripts that come with INN all avoid surprises by making sure the path is always absolute. If the path that you specified for *log-file* is not absolute, the *parsecontrol* script turns it into a pathname relative to the directory in which most of INN's logs are kept, with *.log* appended. For example, `doit=newgroup` as the action in *control.ctl* saves the article in *newgroup.log* in the log file directory named by `PATH_MOST_LOGS`.

8.3.6 Embedded Scripting Languages

If you compiled in support for Tcl (see Section 7.2.1.9) or Perl (see Section 7.2.1.13) to be called directly on each article your server receives (and, in Perl's case, each article posted by an NNRP client newsreader), several scripts from the *samples* directory come into play. Both language systems work essentially the same way, in terms of how they are initialized and used on individual articles.

8.3.6.1 startup.tcl, startup_innd.pl

When *innd* is started, it loads the startup file for the appropriate language. This file should define the functions `filter_before_reload` and `filter_after_reload`. Those functions are used to envelop every reading and parsing of the filtering script that handles each incoming article on the first load and on every subsequent load caused by *ctlinnd reload*. The functions are called with no arguments and do not have meaningful return values.

The startup file can also be used to initialize some global variables for the filtering script. The existing samples simply log the start and end of the reload event; for Perl to do this you have to uncomment four `print` statements. As you can see, they really don't need to do anything important; they're just hooks.

8.3.6.2 filter.tcl

The *filter.tcl* file should define the procedure `filter_news`. It can also define any additional procedures that you need to use to support whatever you are doing in `filter_news`. The `filter_news` procedure is called after the entire article is collected from the sender and its headers have been syntactically validated, but before valid newsgroups and distributions have been checked, and hence before the article has been fully accepted and filed into the news system. If you happen to be running the Perl filters also, the Tcl procedure is called after the Perl `filter_art` function.

`filter_news` takes no arguments and is expected to return a string. If the returned string is "accept", the article is accepted, pending the result of the newsgroups and distribution checks. If the returned string is not "accept", the article is rejected with the reason given in the string you return.

The headers of the article are available to the filter in the associative array `Headers`, indexed by the header name and having the value of the content of the header. For example, `$Headers(Newsgroups)` could have the value `sci.fractals`. Any header that *innd* does not know as a standard header is not available in `Headers`. The Xref header is also not available, and Lines might not be available, even though *innd* will be sure to generate an Xref header by the time the final article is written to disk.

The body of the message, which is everything that follows the empty line that ends the headers in the flat article, is available in the variable `Body`.

A predefine procedure named `checksum_article` is also available. This performs a 32-bit checksum on the body of the article (headers not included) and can be used to identify multiple copies of the same article. You can call it just like any other Tcl procedure; it takes no arguments and returns an integer value.

WARNING The message ID of an article rejected by a Tcl or Perl filter is only saved in the *history* if you configured REMEMBER_TRASH as DO. If you are not remembering trash, you could process the article again when another feed offers it to you. Be careful of this possibility if you are trying to count the number of postings of the same message body.

8.3.6.3 *filter_innd.pl*

The *filter_innd.pl* file should define the functions `filter_art` and `filter_mode`. It can also define any additional functions that you need to use to support the filtering you are doing. The `filter_art` function is called after the entire article is collected from the sender and its headers have been syntactically validated, but before valid newsgroups and distributions have been checked, and hence before the article has been fully accepted and filed into the news system. If you happen to be running the Tcl filters also, Perl's `filter_art` is called before the Tcl `filter_news` procedure.

filter_art takes no arguments and is expected to return a string value. The null string "" indicates that the filter accepts the article, which then still has to make it through any Tcl checks and the newsgroups and distributions checks before being fully accepted by the server. If `filter_art` returns a non-empty string, that string is used as a reason for rejection, to be returned to the sending site and logged locally.

The headers of the article are available to the filter in the associative array `%hdr`, indexed by the header name and having the value of the content of the header. For example, `$hdr{'Expires'}` could have the value "1 May 99 00:00:00 GMT." If a header does not exist, referencing it through the `%hdr` array results in the undefined value, not the null string. (This makes a difference if you have Perl warnings turned on by setting `$^W` to non-zero, as you should.)

Contrary to what *README.perl_hook* and the introductory comments to *filter_innd.pl* say, Bytes is not available to `%hdr` because it is generated only after the article has been fully accepted by the server, for the purposes of the WH flag in the *newsfeeds* file. The Xref header is also never available, and Lines might not be available, even though *innd* will be sure to generate an Xref header by the time the final article is written to disk. Any headers that are not known as standard to *innd* are not in `%hdr` either.

The body of the article is unfortunately not available to *filter_art* in the current implementation, but this is expected to change in the next release.

The `filter_mode` function is called every time that the server changes mode with the *ctlinnd* command. It is called with no arguments and is expected to return no meaningful value. The associative array passed to `filter_mode` has three keys, `Mode`, `NewMode`, and `reason`. The two mode keys can have a value of "running," "paused," or "throttled," with `Mode` representing the current operating state and `NewMode` the state about to be entered. The value of `reason` is a string of the reason given on the *ctlinnd* command line.

8.3.6.4 filter_nnrpd.pl

The *filter_nnrpd.pl* file should define the function `filter_post` to scan postings being made by newsreader clients before they enter the news system. It can also define any additional functions that you need. The file is loaded by *nnrpd* when it starts and cannot be reloaded by an existing *nnrpd* server, so updates to the script are only picked up by newly starting reader clients.

The `filter_post` function is called after the entire article is collected from the posting client, all its headers have been generated and parsed for syntactic correctness, and the article is ready to be offered to the server. `filter_post` takes no arguments and needs to return a string value. The null string "" indicates that the filter accepts the article, and it is then sent to the server (which does its own full set of checks on the article). If `filter_post` returns a non-empty string, it is used as a reason for rejection, to be returned to the posting client and logged locally.

The headers of the article are available to the filter in the associative array `%hdr`, indexed by the header name and having the value of the content of the header. For example, `$hdr{'NNTP-Posting-Host'}` could have the value "kiwi.ora.com". If a header does not exist, referencing it through the `%hdr` array results in the undefined value, not the null string. (This makes a difference if you have Perl warnings turned on by setting `$^W` to non-zero, as you should.) Only those headers that *nnrpd* explicitly knows about are in the `%hdr` array. In addition to those defined in RFC 1036, this includes NNTP-Posting-Host, Mime-Version, Content-Type, and Content-Transfer-Encoding.

The body of the article is unfortunately not available to available to `filter_post` in the current implementation.

In this chapter:
- *Starting INN*
- *Testing the Installation*
- *Normal Operation*
- *Ongoing Maintenance*
- *Log Files*
- *Troubleshooting Common Problems*
- *Wrapping Up*

9

Running INN

So you've configured, built, and installed INN as directed by Chapter 7, *Installing INN*, and now it sits quietly there, taking up some directory space but not actually doing anything useful. Now we'll cover what you need to do to get INN running. After you read this chapter, you'll have the sleeping beast awakened and ready to run on its news processing treadmill. We'll run INN through a basic fitness test before it embarks on its vigorous exercise program. We'll also cover the occasional care and feeding sessions it needs to keep it in peak form.

9.1 Starting INN

The obvious place to begin with testing your installation is by trying to start it up. Obvious, but a tad hasty. We'll be starting INN shortly, but first you need to make sure that INN's logging is working.

9.1.1 Verifying Syslogging

The article reception program (*innd*), the article sending program (*innxmit*), and the newsreader serving program (*nnrpd*) all use *syslog* to record statistics and errors. This logging is done via the *syslogd* program, which should always be running on your system. Because many of the problems you might encounter with the system are reported this way and not with an interactive error message, it is important to verify that this logging is working as expected. A more detailed look at *syslog*, beyond simple verification, appears later in this chapter in Section 9.5.

A quick way to check whether *syslog* is working as you want it to on your system is to use the *logger* program. If this Berkeley-derived program does not exist on your system, you can build it with a *make logger* command in the *syslog* subdirectory of the INN source tree. You can execute *logger* like this:

```
% logger -p news.crit testing syslog for news
```

If your *syslog.conf* file includes the proper news facility lines per the configuration you did in Section 7.4.5, this should have deposited a line with your message in the files *news.crit*, *news.err*, and *news.notice* in the log directory (_PATH_MOST_LOGS) you specified. If the message appeared in all three files, you're in business. If it didn't appear in all three files, you've got a problem.

The first thing to check is whether there are actually lines for the *news.crit*, *news.err*, and *news.notice* selectors in *syslog.conf*. If there are, make sure the files that they reference actually exist, because *syslog* ignores selectors that don't reference existing files. If they don't exist, create them in the log directory with the *touch* command.

Now make sure *syslogd* has reinitialized itself from *syslog.conf*. You can do this by sending a HUP signal to the *syslogd* process with the *kill* command.* Finally, try rerunning the *logger* example given above.

If it still doesn't work, but *syslog* is really running, there is one last thing you can check. Some *syslog* packages, like the one delivered with SunOS, have a static limit on the number of different selectors that can be used. Try starting *syslogd* with the –d flag. Now, when it initializes from *syslog.conf* it prints a cryptic matrix of what the various selectors are supposed to be for different message destinations. You need to be sure that your news facility destinations are all represented. If the problem is that you have too many selectors, try trimming out unused, useless entries.

If none of this has helped you find the problem, you could try installing the *syslogd* program from INN's *syslog/* directory (see the *README* file there). You really need to get this problem figured out before you move on.

9.1.2 Starting the News System

In an ideal world, all that should be necessary to start the INN server and have it run until the system goes down is to run the *rc.news* startup script. Unfortunately, things are never that simple, so this section covers startup issues that you need to know about.

---

* Some systems keep the process ID of the running *syslogd* process in a file named *syslog.pid*, either in the same directory as *syslog.conf* or in */var/run*. If your system doesn't, you'll have to determine its process ID by grepping the output of *ps*.

The *rc.news* script is only meant to be run at the time that the system reboots; it expects to run as the news owner. Since it is possible that the system went down unexpectedly, *rc.news* tries to determine whether *innd* was shut down cleanly and whether the very important *active* file still exists. It also tries to assess whether the downtime affected the *news.daily* maintenance run, clears out some lock files, and starts *innwatch* if you are using it.

WARNING   Because *rc.news* unconditionally removes lock files, as well as *innd*'s process ID file and control channel socket, it should never be run after the news system is up. A script that can be safely used for restarting *innd* is included below.

If you have any flags that you want to pass to the server, or if you want to run *innwatch*, edit the start of the *rc.news* script according to the procedure described in Section 8.1. Normally, you shouldn't have to set any flags, as *innd* runs fine without any of its options specified. There are two options you might consider using, however.

One is the −c switch, which needs a numeric argument to tell *innd* to reject articles older than that number of days. The default is 14, but if you do not have 14 days of /remember/ time in the *expire.ctl* file, you should use the −c switch to specify how many days you do have. If the *innd* cutoff age is older than the /remember/ value, you are susceptible to reaccepting old articles your server has already seen.

The other option that bears mentioning is the −L switch. This tells *innd* to only make the first link for a crossposted article and then determine where the other links should be without actually making them. It reduces the amount of time that *innd* has to wait for disk I/O. On a server that has no client newsreaders, but only outgoing feeds, you need do nothing else other than add the flag. On a machine that supports reader clients, you should also add the following to your *newsfeeds* file (with the appropriate path to the *crosspost* program, of course) to create the links that the newsreaders use to access the crossposted articles:

```
X!POST:*:Tc,Ap,WR:/usr/news/bin/crosspost
```

The *innd* server has several more options that are not described here because the default behavior is fine and there is nothing special we have to say about them that the *innd* manual page doesn't say well enough. When you've become a bit more familiar with the system, you should read the manual page to see if there is anything that you might want to fine tune.

Three mail messages can possibly be generated from *rc.news* to the news administrator's mailbox. Two are about whether *news.daily* maintenance needs to be run.* A brand new system generates one of these messages ("No .news.daily file") that can be ignored. Otherwise, you should doublecheck to see how the downtime correlates with the time that *news.daily* is normally run from *cron*. If the downtime came before *news.daily* ran or could finish, it should be run manually, in the same way that it would be run from *cron*. Here's an example run using the Bourne shell and Berkeley *Mail* to capture any possible output and mail it to you:

```
% news.daily 2>&1 | Mail -s "news.daily output" $NEWSMASTER
```

See Section 9.5.6 for more on *news.daily*.

The other possible mail message from *rc.news* is "System shut down during expire." This can happen if you are using the `delayrm` option to *news.daily* and the system goes down before an expiration run finishes processing the list of articles to remove. *rc.news* can't tell whether the expiration was interrupted before or after the *history* file rewrite happened, so it forks *expirerm* to remove the articles listed in *expire.rm*.

Some of the functions of *rc.news* make it unsuitable to use to restart *innd* on a running system. When restarting *innd*, you basically want just the *inndstart* part of it along with a check to see whether the server shut down its last run abnormally. INN does not come with such a script, but you can easily craft it from *rc.news* and call it something like *innd.restart*. Example 9-1 shows the script.

Example 9-1: The innd.restart Script

```
#! /bin/sh
##   =()<. @<_PATH_SHELLVARS>@>()=
. /var/news/innshellvars
##   Pick ${INND} or ${INNDSTART}
WHAT=${INNDSTART}
## Set FLAGS as appropriate (and consistent with rc.news).
FLAGS=""
##   RFLAG is set below
RFLAG=""
if [ -f ${SERVERPID} ] ; then
    echo 'INND:  PID file exists -- unclean shutdown!'
    RFLAG="-r"
fi
eval ${WHAT} ${RFLAG} ${FLAGS}
```

---

* The check isn't foolproof; it mainly reports if *news.daily* last finished more than a day before the last reboot. For example, if your *news.daily* normally starts at 3 A.M. and runs to 5 A.M., but your system is down so that it interferes with this but comes up by 5 A.M., the *rc.news* check will probably miss the interruption.

We recommended that WHAT be left as ${INNDSTART}, rather than picking
${INND}. *inndstart* should have the ownership and mode specified in Section
7.4.3 (owner *root*, group *news*, mode 4770). Then INN can be started by anyone in
the *news* group without their having to become the superuser. This script represents the barest essentials of what *rc.news* is trying to do to get *innd* running. The
-r flag is passed if it appears that *innd* didn't go through its normal shutdown
procedure. In this case, it is very possible that the *active* file was not flushed when
the server exited abnormally, so it could be inconsistent with the contents of the
spool directory. Other flags can be defined inside the quotes on the FLAGS= line;
they should be consistent with what you used in *rc.news*.

You might want to create a separate file for the flags you use. Then you can set
FLAGS as follows in both *rc.news* and *innd.restart*:

```
FLAGS="`cat ${NEWSLIB}/innd.flags`"
```

This way you only need to update one file whenever you want to change the way
innd is run.

With the *innd.restart* script, restarting *innd* becomes simply:

```
% innd.restart
```

To restart *innwatch*, use:

```
% innwatch &
```

Both of these commands can be used even if *innd* or *innwatch* is already running, because they both interlock against existing instances of themselves.

9.1.3 Keeping the Server Running

So far, all we've done is get the server process started. We haven't done anything
to guarantee that it is going to keep running. If it is dying from the startup procedure, it will do so rather quickly and usually leave a message via *syslog*'s *news.crit*
facility before it does so. *innd* logs a message before shutdown whenever it can.
About the only thing that can bring it down without a message is an uncaught signal. Here are some of the more common reasons for *innd* death and how to handle them:*

SERVER cant dbminit history No such file or directory
> This is probably the most common first-time problem. It means you don't have
> a complete set of files for the history database in *NEWSCTL*. The three files
> *history*, *history.dir*, and *history.pag* should exist there, as discussed in Sections
> 7.4.2 and 7.4.5.

---

* In versions of INN prior to 1.5, the word SERVER was ME in these messages.

If you have a valid *history* text file, but not *history.dir* and *history.pag*, use the following command to rebuild those files:

```
% makehistory -or
```

If you don't even have a *history* file, or you have one but it is so badly corrupted that you can't get most of it to be useful, use the following command to rebuild all of *history*, *history.dir*, and *history.pag*:

```
% makehistory -o
```

The *news-recovery* manual page has more information on the *makehistory* program and its options. Note that the -s switch to *makehistory* is broken in all versions of INN through 1.5.1.*

SERVER bad_newsfeeds no feeding sites

You must have an entry in the *newsfeeds* file for at least one destination. That is why the sample file in Section 7.4.1 has the TESTING:!*:: line. It's basically a no-op, but keeps *innd*'s internal data structures happy. At some point, you'll want to install a feed back to your news neighbor so postings you make can get out to the rest of the Net; that is covered in Sections 8.2.2.1 and 9.2.4.

SERVER internal no control and/or junk group

control and *junk* are not really Net-wide groups, though they should exist on every news server. These groups are known as pseudogroups. *control* is used for filing control messages (see Section 18.4) and *junk* is used for filing articles for groups that your server does not have in the *active* file (if you've configured WANT_TRASH as DO). These pseudogroups must be in your *active* file, but they should not be posted to directly, so add them (see Section 9.3.3) with the n flag in the fourth field.

SERVER internal no to group

If you have configured MERGE_TO_GROUPS as DO to get all articles posted to groups of the form *to.sitename* filed in the pseudogroup *to*, you have to create that group. As with *control* and *junk*, this group should not be posted to directly, so set the fourth field to n.

SERVER cant GetConfigValue pathhost Error 0

innd needs to know its news name to add to the Path header of each incoming article. It picks this up from the pathhost line in *inn.conf*, so make sure that line is in there. This is one of the things that running *inncheck*, as described at the end of Chapter 7, would have caught.

---

* At one point the code considers the parameter to be the number of lines in the file, and at another it uses it as the number of bytes in the file. Since these two items can easily be two orders of magnitude different, calculations based on treating each as the same value are suspect.

`inndstart cant bind Address already in use`

> The port on which you are trying to run the server, probably the standard NNTP port of 119, is being used by another program. If this is happening with a first-time installation, it is probably because *inetd* is listening on the port. Assuming a standard configuration, find the `nntp` line in the *inetd* configuration file (usually */etc/inetd.conf*) and make sure it is inactive by commenting out or removing the line. Then send a HUP signal to *inetd* to have it reload the file. (Some versions of *inetd* require a restart for the change to take effect.) If you end up seeing this message at some later stage of operation, it is probably because someone tried to start INN when it was already running.

`SERVER cant bind /var/news/run/control Permission denied`

> This is another one of the things that *inncheck* would have complained about had it been run after installation was completed in Chapter 7. The directory that *innd* uses for some private sockets and its *innd.pid* file has the wrong permissions. The pathname given depends on how you set up *config.data*. It should be owned by the news owner and be mode 0770.

This should be sufficient to get *innd* humming along. If you are getting it up to this point but then having problems with it throttling down and refusing news transfers, see Section 9.6 for more help.

9.2 Testing the Installation

Now you've got a high-powered racing machine idling in the garage, but it would be folly to set it loose with the others on the track without first checking its basic integrity. Though INN does not have the regression testing features that C News does, you can do some testing locally, without much hassle to your neighbors.

9.2.1 Receiving Articles

There is only one process ultimately responsible for receiving articles, *innd*. It does all the work of checking an article for syntactic validity, filing the article in the appropriate groups from the *active* file, updating the *active* file article count, registering the message ID in the *history* file, and making the initial determination of what further processing should be done on the article.

9.2.1.1 Receiving via NNTP

Technically, all articles stored by your server are processed by NNTP. This is true even if you are a UUCP-only site in terms of your connectivity. In that case, *rnews* on your end uses NNTP to offer articles to *innd*, even though the articles are actually transferred to your site with a UUCP session.

A very basic NNTP session to send an article looks something like the following:

```
200 uunet InterNetNews server INN 1.5.1 22-Dec-96 ready
IHAVE <test1@kiwi.ora.com>
335
Path: not-for-mail
From: nobody@kiwi.ora.com
Newsgroups: misc.test
Subject: testing new INN installation
Message-ID: <test1@kiwi.ora.com
Date: 14 May 1997 00:00:00 GMT

Short test.
.
235
QUIT
205
```

(Lines that begin with numbers are messages sent from the *innd* server; the other lines are sent to the server.)

First, the sending client offers a message ID to *innd* with the *IHAVE* command.* The server checks its *history* file to see whether it has already heard of the article. If it has, it answers "435 Duplicate." In this example, it hasn't, so it says "335," which to the numerically minded sender means "go ahead and send it."

The client then sends the article, finishing with a final dot (.) on a line by itself. (Any lines that began with a . in the article itself should be preceded with another . by the sending side; e.g., .Pe is sent as ..Pe.) When it is done, *innd* processes the article internally. It verifies the correctness of the headers, notes whether the Date seems reasonable, checks that the article isn't larger than the biggest article the server can accept, and so on. If it likes what it sees, it responds to the client with "235," or effectively, "I got it, thanks!" If it encountered some problem with the article, it says "437" along with some message describing the problem it had with the article.

You can test article reception by manually acting like a normal NNTP transmitter would. First, you have to start up the *innd* server, as described in Section 9.1. Then *telnet* to the NNTP port (usually 119) on the machine on which the server is running. For example, to connect from a shell running on the same machine as the server:

```
% telnet localhost nntp
```

At this point, you should get the "200 ... InterNetNews server" banner, with your news name in place of the "...". You should also see a line in the *news.notice*

---

* Note that *IHAVE* is not the only way to send an article to an INN server. INN also supports the *TAKETHIS* command of the NNTP streaming extension, as described in Section 19.5.3.

file noting the connection. If you cannot make the network link and get a "Connection refused" message from *telnet*, it probably means *innd* is not actually running. Go back to Section 9.1 to try to figure out why not. "Connection timed out" from *telnet* could mean that *innd* is actually running, but it just couldn't service the incoming session because it was doing something like competing with a high machine load or renumbering the *active* file.

If you see "200 ... InterNetNews NNRP server" (note well the "NNRP") or "502 You have no permission to talk. Goodbye.", it indicates that the site from which you are trying to connect is not in the *hosts.nntp* file—add it as discussed in Section 9.3.1 and you should be fine. Both of these messages will cause *nnrpd* to note the connection in the *news.notice* file. If you're connecting to *localhost*, that's the name that the connection appears to come from, so it should be put in *hosts.nntp*.

Once you are successfully connected to the *innd* server, enter an *IHAVE* command like the one in the sample dialogue above. You should use a message ID that the server should not know about, and one that is in your domain. For example, if this is your second time running the test for your server named *kiwi.ora.com*, increase the serial number and offer:

```
IHAVE <test2@kiwi.ora.com>
```

This should garner the 335 response asking for the article to be sent. If you get a 435 response, the server doesn't want the article, and it should tell you why. There are only two reasons it can make that choice at this point: either "Duplicate" because it already has the message ID in its history file or "Bad Message-ID" because the message ID is syntactically illegal. Fix the problem by coming up with a new, valid message ID and try again. If you get a 480 response complaining that your transfer permission is denied, it's because you got the NNRP newsreader daemon, which doesn't support the *IHAVE* peer transfer mechanism. Go back two paragraphs and figure out what went wrong when you connected.

Once *innd* has used the 335 code to tell you to send the article, it sits there patiently waiting for it. Using the prior example as a template, type in your article. The Path and Subject headers can be used as in the example. The From line identifies the author of the article and should be set to your own address. The Message-ID should be what you offered in the *IHAVE* command. Use the most local *test* group you have in your *active* file for the Newsgroups header; it is very bad etiquette to post test messages to groups whose names do not end in *.test*. Finally, the Date line should reflect the current date so that the article is not rejected as too old or too far in the future, so change the day, month, and year to today's date.

After the headers have been entered, press Enter again to leave an empty line after them. It is very important that this line is in fact empty and not just blank—there should be two line endings right in a row. A blank line is interpreted as a continuation of the most recent header, instead of the signal of the start of the body. You don't have to put much in the body, but you must put something. "Short test" is certainly uninspired, but it does have the advantage of brief truth. (Perhaps "I am" would share the same advantages and be more philosophical, but now that I've said so, even that quip loses its poignancy.) Enter whatever you like for a body and then finish the article with a single period (.) on a line all by itself.

The server returns its opinion of the article. It's a pretty objective opinion, where brevity is the highest praise. A simple 235 response means it thinks the article is fine, so it has stored it on the server. There are a score of things that could be wrong with the article; a 437 response provides a reason along with the rejection. Though these reasons are terse, there should be sufficient information in a rejection notice for you to determine what is wrong with the article. Fix it and try again.

The other possible response for your article from the server is 436, indicating that there is a problem that affected storage of the article, and hence, the server wants you to try again later. A "Can't write history" error means that there is some problem with storing the message ID in the *history* database. "No space" is the error given when the server has encountered a full disk partition while writing data somewhere. Both of these problems are covered in Section 9.6.

When you have successfully gotten the server to accept your article, try offering the same one again. This time around the *IHAVE* command should be met with the "435 Duplicate" response, which means the message ID has been correctly added to the *history* file. Finally, enter *QUIT* to end your NNTP session. The server should respond 205 and drop the network connection.

9.2.1.2 Receiving via UUCP

rnews is the program that processes articles transferred to you via UUCP; it takes the UUCP data files, which are presumably bundles of news articles, and offers them to *innd* through a local NNTP session. Strictly speaking, the technique is not limited to UUCP processing. *rnews* has its place even in a solely NNTP environment, where it can be used to inject fully formed articles into the system or process articles that *inews*, the program that originates postings, has spooled because the server was unavailable when the posting was attempted.

Testing *rnews* is easy. If you are doing UUCP, you should run it on the machine that handles your UUCP connections. That machine should be listed in the *hosts.nntp* file on the server. (Be sure that the UUCP machine, if it is not the news server, also has *syslog* entries for the news facility; here, though, it is fine to set the selector to *news.all* and put all *rnews* messages in one file such as */var/log/rnews*.) Simply pass *rnews* a fully formed article, like the one from the NNTP example, on its standard input or as an argument. Be sure that the article has a message ID that isn't in your *history* database and that the Date header is current. If you have such an article saved in the file *test-art*, this command should suffice:

```
% rnews test-art
```

This should cause connection and statistics lines to appear for the session in the news *syslog* files on the server. When *rnews* is run via *uuxqt* by the UUCP system, it also logs the message ID and sending system (as identified by the UU_MACHINE variable that UUCP defines) of each article it offers, and whether the article is accepted or not.

If *rnews* asks you "What server?", it has failed to transfer the article to your server because it didn't know where *innd* was running. This means it couldn't get the server line from *inn.conf* (which should be on the system executing *rnews* in the location specified by _PATH_CONFIG in *config.data*) and NNTPSERVER was not set in the execution environment. Unless you can guarantee that NNTPSERVER will always be set correctly, install *inn.conf* on the UUCP machine with a server line pointing to the *innd* host.

Any unexpected errors with processing the article are logged via *syslog* on the client, and you can also have them sent to the standard error by giving the -v flag to *rnews*. It also tries to save the problem input to the _PATH_BADNEWS directory you configured when you built INN.

One error it can cope with is an unavailable server. If *rnews* cannot make the connection to *innd* to do its *IHAVE* negotiations, it tries to save the input to the spool directory. Try it. First, stop INN from accepting new connections by running this command on the server:

```
% ctlinnd throttle 'testing rnews spooling'
```

Then run your *rnews* test again, with a fresh message ID in the article you have saved in *test.art*. This time you should see a file created in the spool directory, or an error in *syslog* describing why it couldn't spool the article. The only reason for not being able to spool is some problem with the spool directory, which should be clear from the message. If that happens, fix it and try again. You can then allow connections to the server again with:

```
% ctlinnd go 'testing rnews spooling'
```

A final run of *rnews -U*, as you should have specified for *cron* in the installation phase, clears the article from the spool and causes the same logging that your interactive use did.

WARNING   If you are going to receive compressed news batches via UUCP, they must be started with a `#! cunbatch` line for INN's *rnews* to be able to process them. Some C News sites configure their *batchparms* file to use just *compress* to make compressed batches, and this results in a file that starts immediately with the compressed data. Tell them to use *compcun* instead.

9.2.2 Connecting NNTP Newsreaders

Programs that are used to read news can generally access articles using either of two different methods. One method uses the filesystem, either locally or remotely via a networked filesystem like NFS or AFS, while the other gets information with NNTP dialogues. Controlling access for filesystem newsreaders is in the hands of the filesystem; as far as the server is concerned it doesn't even know those newsreaders are there, and you only have to ensure that the directories are available for reading by the users. Making sure that the server's NNTP newsreader services are working takes a little more work.

The collection of NNTP newsreader services is called the "Network News Reader Protocol", or NNRP. INN's implementation of these is in the *nnrpd* program. The *innd* server runs *nnrpd* for an incoming connection that it does not recognize as an NNTP peer (a site from whom you expect to get bulk news transfers). It also spawns the newsreader server if it gets a *MODE READER* command in its NNTP dialogue with a peer. A client cannot get to the *innd* server once it is in the *nnrpd* program.

To test the startup of the *nnrpd* server, *telnet* to the NNTP port of your server as in Section 9.2.1. You should get either "200 (or 201) ... InterNetNews NNRP server" or "502 You have no permission to talk. Goodbye." The 200 message means that the connecting host is allowed to read and post articles, while the 201 message means that the host is only permitted to read articles.

Remember, if you are making a connection from any host that you have listed in *hosts.nntp*, or if you are running *innd* with the `-a` flag to allow peer connections from all hosts, the connection is for an NNTP session directly with *innd*. If you want to allow NNRP news reading from these peer machines, it must be done with newsreader clients that understand the *MODE READER* command. Many older newsreaders do not, so you might need to make some modifications to their startup code to get them to do it. Unfortunately, we can't address the patches needed for each newsreader here.

Since *innd* hands all non-peer connections to *nnrpd* for processing, it is actually *nnrpd* that decides the access rights for potential newsreaders. These are specified in the *nnrp.access* file, which is read every time a new *nnrpd* process starts. The *nnrp.access* file correlates patterns of hostnames with the type of access they should have. The most important thing to remember about the file is that the last matching pattern wins, so in most cases the very first pattern should be one that allows no access, resulting in the "You have no permission to talk" message:

```
*:: -no- : -no- :!*
```

The * glob matches all hosts, while the white space in the third and fourth authentication fields makes it impossible for a host to gain newsreader access. The !* glob at the end is mostly intended to be overly demonstrative of the idea that hosts shouldn't be able to read any groups. Strictly speaking, it isn't necessary since *nnrpd* never reaches that part of the decision-making process.

After the most general line, you can add more specific lines. For example:

```
*.uu.net:Read Post:::*
guest.uu.net:Read:::*,!uunet-local.*
```

These lines allow people on any host in the *.uu.net* domain to to read and post to all groups carried on the server, except for people connecting from *guest.uu.net*, who can read all of the groups except for the *uunet-local* hierarchy. Only R and P are needed in the second permissions field, but Read and Post are clearer and the extra characters are simply ignored.

Since the *nnrp.access* file is only read when *nnrpd* starts up, with no provisions for reloading, any changes made to it while newsreader sessions are in progress do not affect the running sessions. If you make a very important change, you have to terminate the existing NNRP sessions with the *kill* command to force them to reconnect. Don't feel too bad about doing so; the newsreader programs should have provisions for unexpectedly dropped connections.

Here are a couple of quick commands you can try to verify that *nnrpd* is working:

help
: Prints a list of all commands the server knows.

list active
: Prints all groups in your *active* file—not recommended with an *active* file of several thousand lines and a slow terminal session.

group misc.test
: Selects *misc.test* as the current group for further commands and prints how many articles are in the group, along with the minimum and maximum article numbers.

quit
: Ends the NNRP dialogue and drops the network connection.

9.2.3 Posting Articles

Submitting new articles to the network news system with INN is done in one of
two ways: with the *inews* program or with the NNRP *POST* command. These two
methods usually have more user-friendly wrappers that are provided by the newsreader programs, but since they are the most essential links in the posting process,
they should be tested independent of the wrappers. They both require posting
access to the NNRP server. *inews* is really just a front end to a *POST* command that
runs in an *nnrpd* session.*

You don't have as many headers for this posting test as you did for the fully
formed test article in Section 9.2.1; the posting process fills in any required headers that are missing. Thus, it takes care of the problems of generating a proper
date and a unique message ID. *inews* requires only the Newsgroups and Subject
headers, while NNRP's *POST* command also needs the From header because it
does not know the identity of the person submitting the article. As with the example article in Section 9.2.1, a body is also needed, separated from the headers by
an empty line.

To test *inews*, run it with the -h flag, which says that the article has headers starting it, and pass the bare bones article to it on its standard input. You can type it in
directly, finishing with the EOF character (usually Control-D):

```
% inews -h
Newsgroups: misc.test
Subject: testing INN's inews

I am.
^D
```

Just like *rnews*, *inews* asks you "What server?" if it cannot get the `server` line
from *inn.conf* and `NNTPSERVER` is not set in the execution environment. Install
inn.conf on the machine with a `server` line pointing to the *innd* host.

If *inews* cannot connect to the server, it skips its normal check for bogus groups in
the Newsgroups and Followup-To headers, assuming that they're fine, and tries to
spool the article to the spool directory as *rnews* does. If it can't create a file there,
it saves the attempted posting as *dead.article* in the user's home directory. Thus, if
you want spooling to be able to happen on a client machine that can run *inews*,
you need to create the `_PATH_SPOOLNEWS` tree on that machine (with the
`_PATH_SPOOLTMP` and `_PATH_BADNEWS` subdirectories) and be sure that its
cron runs *rnews -U* regularly, perhaps once per hour.

---

* *inews* is smart enough to use the *MODE READER* command if its initial connection to the server gets
innd instead of *nnrpd*.

Most of the errors that are possible at this point are fairly self-explanatory, but there is one that bears further explanation. If you see "441 480 Transfer permission denied," you have to add the server's hostname to its *hosts.nntp* file. You've configured INN to say that you don't have Unix domain sockets and, therefore, the *POST* function of NNRP must create a TCP socket, just like an NNTP peer, to *innd* to transfer the article. If the server isn't in *hosts.nntp*, *nnrpd* just ends up with another *nnrpd* process that can no more do the complete posting job than the first one could. But remember, with the server in *hosts.nntp*, if any NNTP newsreader process gets started from the server, it has to know how to do the *MODE READER* command to get the NNRP server.

If posting via *inews* works, you can deduce that posting with NNRP's *POST* command is working, at least from the machine on which you ran the *inews* test.

9.2.4 Transmitting Articles

In a typical INN system, articles are sent to neighboring NNTP sites using *nntpsend* and to neighboring UUCP sites using *sendbatch*. Both of these programs begin their work the same way, with a list of articles that *innd* generates as it receives them. In this section, you can safely ignore the material on the form of transmission that you won't be using, because the programs are wholly independent.

The *newsfeeds* file provides the initial instructions to INN for further processing of incoming articles. In Section 7.4.1, you either converted your existing B News or C News *sys* file to the *newsfeeds* format or you created this minimal *newsfeeds* file:

```
ME:!*/!local::
TESTING:!*::
```

A thorough discussion of the format of the *newsfeeds* file can be found in Section 8.2.2.1; we'll also be discussing the file in more detail in Section 9.3.1 later in this chapter. For testing purposes, however, you are just going to feed articles back to your own server, rather than bothering your neighbors with possibly faulty transmission attempts. For either NNTP or UUCP transmission, there are two main stages that need to be examined: *innd*'s writing of the article lists, and the ability of *nntpsend* or *sendbatch* to process them.

9.2.4.1 NNTP transmission

This minimal *newsfeeds* file, with your site's name substituted appropriately for **mynewsname**, can be used to test article list creation for NNTP transmission:

```
ME:!*/!local::
mynewsname!:*:Tf,Wnm:
```

The ! in the sitename field of the feed line ensures that no article could possibly have a host in its Path header that matches, and therefore no article can be eliminated from consideration based on that criterion. In other words, every article passes this first matching criterion. The * in the pattern field says to let every good article be matched, no matter what groups are in its Newsgroups header. The third field says what to do for articles that match the first two. For NNTP, we use the Wnm flag to tell *innd* to write the path to the article and its message ID. Because the fourth field is empty, *innd* writes to a file in the spool *out.going* directory that has the same name as the sitename field (e.g., */news/out.going/mynewsname*).

Once the *newsfeeds* file is in place, reload it with *ctlinnd reload newsfeeds "added mynewsname"*. Now you can feed an article to *innd*, either using the technique described in Section 9.2.1 or by posting an article as described in Section 9.2.3. After *innd* has accepted the article, run *ctlinnd flush ''* (flush with an explicit null argument); the flush is necessary because *innd* buffers its writes. Now look at the file in the *out.going* directory.* The file should list the pathname to the newly received article, separated from the message ID by a space.

Stage two of the transmission process is getting the article list processed. The *nntpsend* shell script takes care of all of the housekeeping of shuffling around article lists, making sure that they are flushed, and calling the more elementary programs that really do the NNTP work.

This minimal *nntpsend.ctl* file can be used to test *nntpsend*, when used with the names appropriate for your site:

```
mynewsname!:my.internet.name::-d
```

mynewsname is the name of the test NNTP feed as you have it in the *newsfeeds* file; **my.internet.name** is the full name of your news server for a TCP/IP connection. The third field, empty here, can be filled with a size that is the largest a batchlist will be allowed to grow. It is normally fine to leave this empty unless you have special free space considerations. Normally, the last field can be left empty too, but in this example we pass *innxmit* the **-d** flag to print the NNTP session in the *nntpsend.log*. Since it generates copious output, you definitely don't want to use this for anything but debugging a problematic, and hopefully low volume, feed.

After ensuring that there actually is an article list named *mynewsname!* in *out.going*, simply run *nntpsend* as the news owner. After it finishes, which normally should be very quickly, check out */var/log/news/nntpsend.log*. It should have output much like that described in Section 9.5 later in this chapter, along with a transcript of the NNTP conversation *innxmit* had with *innd*. Since the only article

---

* Remember, if you are using a Unix shell that does history expansion of commands, ! is usually handled as a special character by the shell. You have to quote it with a preceding backslash (e.g., *cat mynewsname\!*) when referring to it in filenames.

that existed in the article list was one that had already been accepted by your server, it should have been rejected as a duplicate. The *innxmit* log line in *news.notice* should confirm that.

After you have tested NNTP transmission, you can set up *newsfeeds, nntpsend.ctl,* and *cron* to do the real work of transmitting articles to your neighbors. This is described in detail in Section 9.3.1.

9.2.4.2 UUCP transmission

If you are going to be using UUCP to send articles, you should either have a test account set up in your UUCP configuration files or be sure that you will not set up a UUCP link with a site during the testing if you are using a real site account.

This minimal *newsfeeds* file, with your site's name substituted appropriately for `testuucpname`, can be used to test article list creation for UUCP transmission:

```
ME:!*/!local::
testuucpname!:*:Tf,Wnb:testuucpname
```

The ! in the sitename field of the feed line ensures that no article could possibly have a host in its Path header that matches, and therefore no article can be eliminated from consideration based on that criterion. In other words, every article passes this first matching criterion. The * in the pattern field says to let every good article be matched, no matter what groups are in its Newsgroups header. The third field says what to do for articles that match the first two. For UUCP, we use the Wnb flag to tell *innd* to write the pathname and size in bytes. Putting the actual UUCP name as the fourth field feed makes an article list that *sendbatch* can actually use.

Once the *newsfeeds* file is in place, reload it with *ctlinnd reload newsfeeds "added tesruucpname"*. Now you can feed an article to *innd*, either using the technique described in Section 9.2.1 or by posting an article as described in Section 9.2.3. After *innd* has accepted the article, run *ctlinnd flush ''*; the flush is necessary because *innd* buffers its writes. Now look at the file in the *out.going* directory.* The file should list the pathname to the newly received article, separated from the byte count by a space.

Stage two of the transmission process is getting the article list processed. The *sendbatch* shell script takes care of all of the housekeeping of shuffling around article lists, making sure that they are flushed, and calling the more elementary programs that really do the UUCP work.

---

* Remember, if you are using a Unix shell that does history expansion of commands, ! is usually handled as a special character by the shell. You have to quote it with a preceding backslash (e.g., *cat mynewsname\!)* when referring to it in filenames.

The *sendbatch* script does not use a configuration file. Unlike most other INN programs and files, it also doesn't have a manual page. Before you run it, you'll have to double check the variables that are set at the head of the script. If any need to be changed, update them according to the general rules in Section 8.1. Then you can run *sendbatch* as follows:

```
% sendbatch -c testuucpname
```

Use the `testuucpname` you have in the *newsfeeds* file without the exclamation point. The `-c` flag tells *sendbatch* to compress the article batches before feeding them to *uux*, thus saving time and money on the UUCP link.

When it's done, *sendbatch* logs some statistics to the *news.notice* file, and *uux* should have queued a batch in the UUCP spool for `testuucpname`. The batch data itself is in a file that starts with the line `#! cunbatch` and is followed by the compressed *rnews* batch. Once you have verified this, the job can be dequeued by removing its three files from the UUCP spool.

The most commonly used switches to *sendbatch* control various aspects of space usage by the batcher. In the list below, an N should be replaced with an integer byte count. Here are the common options:

`-s`N

   The average batch size for a full-sized batch. The default is 50,000.

`-m`N

   Limits this feed to only having the specified number of bytes in the queue at any one time. The default is 1,000,000,000.

`+m` Puts no limit to the number of bytes that can be queued at any time.

`-p`N

   Only batches this many bytes per run, regardless of how much more space might be available in the queue. The default is the `-m` value.

`+p` Puts no limit on the number of bytes that can be batched per run.

After you have tested UUCP transmission, you can set up *newsfeeds* and *cron* to do the real work of transmitting articles to your neighbors. This is described in detail in Section 9.3.1.

9.3 Normal Operation

With INN tested and seemingly working fine, you should be ready to let INN loose on its news processing chores. This section covers the things you will have to do on a recurring basis during normal operation of your server: the updating of feeds, expiration of articles, and the addition and removal of newsgroups. Since the updating feeds section addresses how to open the floodgates with your peers, we'll start with that.

9.3.1 Updating Feeds

When setting up a new NNTP link with a neighbor, there are essentially only three files you need to worry about updating: *hosts.nntp*, *newsfeeds*, and *nntpsend.ctl*. With a UUCP feed, you don't even need to update *hosts.nntp* and *nntpsend.ctl*, but the UUCP links do need to be integrated into your UUCP system.

9.3.1.1 NNTP feeds

The simplest addition is to *hosts.nntp*. You just need to add the full name of the host from which your neighbor initiates NNTP connections. At startup time, INN grabs all of the IP addresses for the machines listed in the file. Whenever the file is reinstalled, or one of your feed sites changes its IP address while keeping the same hostname, the file should be read again:

```
% ctlinnd reload hosts.nntp 'reason for reload'
```

You can establish password-only transfer access to your server by putting a clear text password in the second field of *hosts.nntp*. In this case, the remote site needs to configure its transmitter to send the password. In general, access permissions at the host level without passwords are sufficient to keep unauthorized users in check. You might want to use passwords if the remote end hosts a lot of curious, *telnet*-happy explorers, like a public access machine.

The *newsfeeds* file entry is the most tricky, needing several configuration options to ensure the right articles are being listed for transmission to the upstream site. (If you need help configuring the *newsfeeds* entry for a site, go back to Section 8.2.2.1 for more information.) The important thing for an NNTP feed is that you use the Wnm flag in the third field, to tell *innd* to output the pathname and message ID for each article.

After the new *newsfeeds* file is installed, you can check it with *ctlinnd checkfile*. *ctlinnd* reports an error if any problems were found with the file and reports the details of the problem in the *news.err* log. When the *newsfeeds* file is clean, inform *innd* of the new configuration with:

```
% ctlinnd reload newsfeeds 'added sitename'
```

Finally, for a new outbound NNTP feed, you should add a line to *nntpsend.ctl*. Put the news name of the host (the one you used as the first field in *newsfeeds*) in the first field, its Internet hostname or address in the second field, any upper limit on the size of its batchfiles in the third field, and any special flags (normally none) you might want to use for *innxmit* in the fourth field. Note that you do not need to use *ctlinnd* to tell the server about this change, as it does not use *nntpsend.ctl* at all. *nntpsend* uses it, but it is not a perpetual process, so it loads the new data the next time it runs from *cron.*

9.3.1.2 UUCP feeds

Here we discuss how to configure the news system for a UUCP feed. We do not, however, describe how to actually get the UUCP system configured on your system. (That's the topic of another fine book from the friendly folks at O'Reilly & Associates, *Using and Managing UUCP,* by Ed Ravin, Tim O'Reilly, Dale Dougherty, and Grace Todino.) What we tell you in this book is how to get articles into files that the UUCP system can transfer to neighboring UUCP sites.

The setup of the *newsfeeds* file is almost exactly the same as for an NNTP feed, except that you use the Wnb flag in the third field. This tells *innd* to interpret the fourth field as the name of a file to which to write each article path with its size in bytes. The UUCP batcher uses the byte count to limit batch sizes. If the sitename in the first field is not the site's UUCP name, its UUCP name should be used for the fourth field. This is the name the batcher eventually hands to *uux* for queuing in the proper UUCP spool directory.

To spool article batches for the site, you have to make sure *sendbatch* is called periodically. The easiest way to do this is with a *cron* job that is run only during those hours that your neighbor wants news—for example, during nighttime dialing rates if they are calling long distance. If the site does not want to receive news during the day, be sure that the *sendbatch* execution is started no later than about an hour before the end of the desired batching window. This helps decrease the possibility that news is transferred during higher rate periods, as long as the other site makes a call to clear news batches after your last batching run but before the rates go up. Note that the varying phone rates can be addressed by having the client use a UUCP system that can do graded polling; this allows you to spread the batching load throughout the day, and permits them to select the times when they allow news to be transferred.

9.3.1.3 UUCP ihave/sendme feeds

A discussion of how an *ihave/sendme* feed works is given in Section 19.4.3. It is basically a method that allows one site to offer another the articles it has without the active dialogue used in NNTP sessions. This enables more efficient use of the communications channels to a site that has more than one feed of the same articles coming to it.

WARNING   There is a bit of a security hole here. If a site knows or can guess the message ID of an article, even one that you haven't listed in an *ihave* message, it can request it in a *sendme* message. They could even possibly do so if you haven't set up an *ihave/sendme* feed with the site, if they know how their site is listed in the first field. Though the likelihood of this happening as some sort of meaningful espionage is practically nil, it isn't theoretically nil. To remove the risk, be sure to disallow default *sendme* control messages in *control.ctl* (this is the default as shipped) and only allow them for sites where you use an *ihave/sendme* feed (if any).

The *newsfeeds* entry for an *ihave/sendme* feed looks essentially like this:

```
uucpname!wehave:pattern,pattern...[/distrib,distrib...:\
    Tf,Wm:uucpname.ihave
uucpname:to.uucpname:Tf,Wn:
```

The first line causes a list to be created that has all of the message IDs of articles that match the group and distribution subscription. The second line says to write the pathname of any message posted to the site's special *to* group onto the end of their batchlist.

Periodically, as from *cron*, you should run *send-ihave* with the UUCP name of the site (which is also its batchlist name) as an argument. This writes *ihave* control messages of up to 1000 lines of message IDs each, posting the resulting article to the *to* group for the site, with no Distribution header.

In addition to *send-ihave*, you periodically run *sendbatch* for the site as you normally would for a UUCP feed. This queues any articles pending for the site, including the *ihave* control messages that you are generating. The other articles that *sendbatch* queues get listed in the batchlist for the site by the *sendme* control message script. The *sendme* script is run when an *ihave* control message that you sent to the site was analyzed, and returned a *sendme* control message that listed the message IDs of articles it did not have.

WARNING   We suspect that INN's *ihave/sendme* implementation has never been thoroughly tested. A look at the *sendme* control script suggests at least one possible problem with file interlocking on the batchlist. By simply appending to a batchlist that the script does not have exclusive access to, the script risks corrupting the batchlist, the likely result of which is lost articles, possibly including the *ihave* control messages that help the other site ask for more articles. Proceed with caution.

9.3.2 Expiring Old Articles

In normal operation, *expire* makes its judgments about whether an article should be kept or removed based on criteria you specify in *expire.ctl*, described in Section 8.2.3. The *expire* script is usually run from the *news.daily* job you set up in Section 7.4.5.2. If you ever need to run *expire* manually, you can append to the *expire.log* file in the same way that *news.daily* keeps a record of its run, so that the output appears in the next daily report.

The discussion of the *news.daily* run in Section 9.5.6 talks about the `-q` and `-v1` options to *expire*. There are three other flags for *expire* that you should be aware of. The first option, new as of INN 1.5, is the `-e` switch that aggressively expires crossposted articles. INN's normal expiration behavior is to leave an article around until all of its crossposted groups have passed their expiration dates. This works great when you're trying to keep special groups you really like around for a long time, no matter what other groups the articles were crossposted to. However, when an article is crossposted from less endearing groups (like the very high volume binaries groups) that you have on very short expiration cycles, the `-e` switch makes sure that the article gets zapped at the shortest time you have specified. There is a bit of conflict here if you really want to keep everything in certain groups around for a really long time. At the moment, there is no good way to address that conflict in the expiry program itself.

Another important switch is `-p`, which causes articles to be expired based on the time they were injected into the overall news system, as declared by the Date headers, rather than by when they finally arrived at your site. Normally you want the latter behavior. If it took four days for an article to find its way around the Net to you, and you expire everything at five days, you want more of a chance than just a day to read it. However, imagine that your news server has been down for four days. Rather than your normal feed of perhaps 30 megabytes per day, you end up taking in 120 megabytes in one day. As your poor spool partition is ready to explode, you opt for a manual, emergency run of *expire*. Without `-p`, you end up making no dent in all of the new traffic. With `-p`, you can normalize your space distribution to be more in line with what it would have looked like if everything had been running normally for the preceding days.

The last potentially important flag is `-1`, which you would use if you had your spool space spread across multiple disk partitions. When the spool is on just one partition, a crossposted article is hard linked within the filesystem to each of its group locations. The data remains accessible until all of the hard links are removed. When you use multiple spool partitions, however, symbolic links are made from the other partitions back to the first group in which the article was stored.* If the original file is removed, all of the symbolic links pointing to it are bogus, referencing nothing. The `-l` option says to make sure the original file is around until after all the rest of the links are removed.

One other change you should make if you are using multiple spool partitions is to the `fastrm` line in *expirerm*. You have to remove the `-u` option to *fastrm*, so it does not try to change directories via a relative path. You don't have to remove the `-u` option, however, if your second partition is mounted where it logically belongs in the spool hierarchy (e.g., */news* and */news/alt/binaries*). Make this change as per the editing instructions in Section 8.1.

9.3.3   *Adding and Removing Groups*

Newsgroups need to be added to and removed from your *active* file on a regular basis; there are often a couple of dozen changes per week if you have a full feed. Section 3.3 covers how to make sure that your news system has a view of Usenet that is consistent with what the rest of the world sees. How to decide, in general, whether a group should be on your system or not is discussed in Chapter 16, *Newsgroups and Their Names*. Many of the additions and removals can be handled automatically, but some do require your manual intervention. Automatic group additions and removals are controlled by the *control.ctl* file. This file is described in Section 8.2.4.1.

When INN is automatically adding a group in response to a *newgroup* control message, it looks for a "For your newsgroups file:" line in the body of the message. If it exists, the line that follows is inserted into the *newsgroups* database of one-line group descriptions. If no such line exists in the control message, a description of simply "?" is used instead. Similarly, when INN is automatically removing a group because of an *rmgroup* message, it removes its descriptive line from the *newsgroups* file.

Another form of automatic *active* file maintenance is done with the *actsyncd* program, using *actsync* to find differences between the file on your site and the one on a site you consider authoritative. See Section 8.2.4.2 for a simple script that can be run a few times a day from *cron* to synchronize with the *active* file maintained by the Internet Software Consortium.

Manual updates to the *active* file can be done in two ways: one at a time or in bulk. The one-at-a-time approach involves *ctlinnd* commands like those that are provided in the mail notices for *newgroup* and *rmgroup* messages that are not

---

* If your system doesn't support symbolic links, plan on spending even more money on disks. An article on such a system has to be completely duplicated on each partition where it gets referenced, but INN does not support such copying up through version 1.7.

automatically handled. For example, here are the commands to add *rec.photo.misc* and remove the *rec.photo* group that it superseded:

```
% ctlinnd newgroup rec.photo.misc y group-admin@isc.org
% ctlinnd rmgroup rec.photo
```

Bulk updates normally involve editing the *active* file directly. Both types of manual updates are covered in detail in 3.3.2.

9.4 Ongoing Maintenance

Once it gets going, INN usually needs little in the way of ongoing maintenance and can run handily for weeks and weeks without your intervention. There are, however, a few things you should be aware of in its usual operation. In addition, there are some updates you'll eventually have to make manually. These topics are addressed here.

9.4.1 ctlinnd

The *ctlinnd* program is one of the fundamental programs in the INN suite, though you could conceptually never have to run it as a news administrator. It is used by several shell scripts to control *innd* in various ways, such as flushing files, adding and removing groups, and starting and stopping article reception. You should understand *ctlinnd*'s basic functions, even if you rarely use them. Its manual page documents them in detail, but here's a summary of the highlights:

ctlinnd mode

This command lets you know the basic state that the server is in. A normally running server might have output like this:

```
Server running
Allowing remote connections
Parameters c 14 i 0 (43) l 1000000 o 237 t 300 H 2 T 60 X 0 normal
  specified
Not reserved
Readers separate enabled
```

The first line indicates the basic run state of the server: `running`, `paused`, or `throttled`. Running is the normal state for accepting new articles. Paused indicates a brief interruption in the normal reception of articles and is usually used by *expire* when it is finishing work on the *history* database and by *innwatch* when the load is whatever you configure as "moderate". To be paused means that connections are allowed, but no new articles are accepted. To NNTP clients, the server appears to be running normally—it can even do duplicate rejection and other preacceptance checks. Throttled is the state used when no connections to *innd* at all are desired; no new ones are allowed and existing ones are dropped. (*nnrpd* sessions are unaffected by a throttled server, unless they try to post a new article.) Being throttled indicates a pretty serious problem. *innd* puts itself into this state for a few different errors it encounters, like I/O problems. Both `paused` and `throttled` should be accompanied by a message that describes the reason for being in that state.

You can pause or throttle the server yourself by using the *ctlinnd* command of that name along with a reason. For example, *ctlinnd throttle 'spool disk exploded'** gives an indication to clients trying to connect what problem the server is having. You can return to a run state with *ctlinnd go*, providing either the full text of the reason or a null second argument to *ctlinnd*. Normally the scripts use full reasons to avoid concurrency problems.

The second line, "Allowing remote connections," indicates the state of the *ctlinnd allow* and *reject* commands for permitting new *innd* sessions. Rejecting remote connections can be used to limit the ability of new NNTP peers to connect for article transfers, while allowing existing peers to maintain their sessions. If they are not allowed, a reason should be present here. The fifth line gives essentially the same information, but for new *nnrpd* newsreader sessions; it is controlled by the *ctlinnd readers* command.

The third line indicates the flags that are controlling the server. These can be set with the *ctlinnd param* command and are defined in the *innd* manual page. The particular parameters shown on the third line are always the same, though the values vary from server to server.

In this case, the server is rejecting articles with Date headers older than 14 days. It is allowing an unlimited number of incoming peer transfer sessions and there are currently 43 such sessions. Articles larger than one million bytes are rejected as too large and there are 237 file descriptors available for the *newsfeeds* file entries to use. Every 300 seconds without any activity, the server times out and writes any cached database information. The H, T, and X indicate how the number of connections per minute are being limited. The values here are the defaults. Since X is 0, no checking is done. If X were not 0, a single host could only connect a maximum of H times every X seconds and all connections are limited to T times every X seconds. The server is running as a primary, "normal" server, rather than in "slave" mode. Finally, it is allowing peer transfer connections only from hosts specified in *hosts.nntp*, rather than allowing any host as a peer, which would happen with the `-a` flag to *innd*.

The fourth line is used primarily by *expire* as a form of interlocking against other expiration runs. A reservation means that something (in this case, *expire*)

---

* But *innd* would probably pick up on this error before you had a chance to enter such a command.

is working and that it plans on pausing the server when it needs to interrupt article reception. The *ctlinnd pause* command must give the same reason as the reservation to succeed.

ctlinnd name

This command prints the file descriptors currently in use by the server, for all of its files, processes, and transfer sessions. The *ctlinnd hangup* command can then be used to shut down individual sessions.

ctlinnd shutdown

This command stops the server completely. It takes a reason for doing so as an argument and sends a message to the server asking it to exit. As soon as the server can act on the message, it cleanly flushes and closes its open databases, and then its process disappears. Note that this can potentially take much longer than expected if the server is in its *renumber* operation; it doesn't read the shutdown message until after it completes the *active* file renumbering.

ctlinnd reload

Use this command to update a running *innd*'s configuration as specified in various control files. The server's notion of acceptable peers, the *history* database, the active groups and outgoing feeds, and even the overview database fields to output can all be changed. Remember, *ctlinnd reload* cannot reload the *inn.conf* file for a new `pathhost` value; you must restart *innd* for that.

The *ctlinnd reload* command can take any of the following arguments. The argument must also be followed with a free-text reason for the reload.

all	All reloadable files
active	*active* and *newsfeeds*
newsfeeds	*active* and *newsfeeds*
history	*history*, *history.dir*, and *history.pag*
hosts.nntp	*hosts.nntp*
overview.fmt	*overview.fmt*
filter.tcl	*filter.tcl*
filter.perl	*filter_innd.pl*

ctlinnd newgroup, rmgroup, and *changegroup*

These commands are used to change one group at a time in the *active* file. There is more information about them in Section 3.3.2.2.

ctlinnd begin and *drop*

The *begin* command updates the outgoing feed for a site and *drop* stops it. These commands only affect the named feed in the *newsfeeds* file, instead of reloading the whole thing. This can be faster if you have a really, really large *newsfeeds* file, but we recommend using *ctlinnd reload newsfeeds* for the sake of completeness and as a guarantee that no update is ever missed.

ctlinnd flush

The *flush* command writes any cached data. It is primarily used for getting outgoing feed information fully purged, but it can also be used to get INN's internal idea of the *history* and *active* databases synchronized on disk.

ctlinnd filter

This command takes a y or n argument to turn Tcl filtering on or off, respectively. Perl filtering cannot be similarly controlled; to turn off Perl filtering, you need to install an empty *filter_innd.pl* file and then call *ctlinnd reload filter.perl*.

ctlinnd readers

This command is sort of like a throttle/go command that just controls newsreader clients. It takes a y or n argument to allow or disallow reader access. If the argument is n, it must be followed by a reason to be given to clients that are denied access. If the argument is y, it must be followed by either an empty reason or a reason that matches the one originally given for denying access. Existing *nnrpd* sessions are not affected.

ctlinnd allow and *reject*

These commands can be used to allow or disallow all new incoming peer transfer connections. Existing transfer sessions are not affected, nor are new reader sessions (that don't need to be started as *MODE READER*). This can be useful if you want to stop incoming news but don't want your server paused or throttled.

ctlinnd hangup

The *hangup* command takes a channel number as an argument (see *ctlinnd name*) and closes that channel.

There are several other *ctlinnd* commands, but most administrators never need them. See the *ctlinnd* manual page for a complete rundown.

9.4.2 *innwatch*

The *innwatch* program is a watchdog that guards your system resources. Its main function is to keep track of the disk space being used on partitions that the news system uses, and to control news' contribution to the overall process load of the machine. You defined the major control parameters for it in the *config.data* file when you built INN; they were substituted into the *innwatch.ctl* file that is described in Section 8.2.1.2. See that section if you are having troubles with *innwatch* reporting problems that do not really exist.

Starting *innwatch* should be done in *rc.news*, as described in Section 9.1. Once it starts running, it performs checks every ten minutes to see whether the free space and load average are within the prescribed limits. If they are not, it stops incoming news by sending a *throttle* command to the *innd* server with the reason for the stop. If it pauses or throttles the server because of a moderate to high load average, the next time it checks and finds that the load has returned to acceptable levels it sets the server running again. As distributed, it does not take any action to again allow transfers if *innwatch* throttled *innd* for some non-load related reason.

The *news.daily* maintenance script and *innwatch* are careful about their interactions with each other. If *news.daily* wants to run *expire* and observes that *innwatch* has throttled the server for lack of space, it unthrottles the server when it is done. Aside from manual intervention, this is the only way to get the server going again after *innwatch* has observed a short space condition.

9.5 Log Files

Nearly every error you encounter ends up going to one of INN's log files, rather than confronting you directly. The logs also contain a lot of other useful information about what the system is doing, so you can verify that the system is actually continuing to do work.

9.5.1 Syslogging

As mentioned in Section 9.1.1, the article reception program (*innd*), the article sending program (*innxmit*), and the newsreader serving program (*nnrpd*) all use *syslog* to record statistics and errors.

syslog reports on various aspects of the system, called *facilities*, at different levels of importance, called *priorities*. The system file *syslog.conf*, usually in */etc*, */usr/etc*, or */usr/lib*, controls how messages for various combinations of facilities and priorities are directed; the combination of the two is known as a *selector*. Messages for a particular priority are also directed to every lower priority. That is, a log message sent to *syslog* at the *notice* priority is also checked for matches within its facility at the lower *info* and *debug* priority levels.

INN uses the *news* facility name to log messages. If a major INN program is going to exit abnormally, it logs a message at the *news.crit* selector. You should see these messages very rarely. Once your system is running correctly, the file that collects *news.crit* messages will nearly always be empty.

Significant errors encountered by INN programs appear at the *news.err* selector. These are normally for things like dropped network connections and shouldn't be of much concern.

If you changed the `L_NOTICE` configuration option as suggested in Section 7.2.1.2, informational messages from INN are sent to the *news.notice* selector. If you did not make the change from `LOG_WARNING`, the *news.notice* selector should still catch the messages because the *warning* priority is higher than the *notice* priority.

INN's example *syslog.conf* does not include logging of commands sent from the *ctlinnd* program, used by INN for controlling the *innd* daemon. It also does not include logging of traces of the exchanges going on in NNTP sessions. If you want to see either of these, you have to add *news.info* and *news.debug* selectors, respectively, to *syslog.conf*. It is reasonable to set the selector that writes to the *news.notice* file to be *news.debug* to do this, but we continue to refer to it as the *news.notice* selector in this book.

9.5.2 Articles Received

Each article that *innd* receives is noted in the *news* file in the log directory (e.g., */var/log/news/news*). The basic log line looks something like this:

```
Jun 20 20:17:54.724 + news.stanford.edu <311k8g$dvj@netcom.com>
(alt/fashion/3500) decwrl mcsun naitc-ip! prpa-ip! rutgers!
u01591!
```

The first field is the local time at which the article was received. It claims to be of millisecond resolution, but be aware that the internal time stamp is only updated between passes through all of the active NNTP channels. It is not unusual to see adjacent entries with exactly the same time stamp.

The next field is a single character that indicates the disposition of the article. A + means the article has been accepted and filed in at least one group your server considers valid. A - is used when the article has been rejected because of some problem the server detected with it. A c indicates that this line is registering an article that has been canceled, but for which the server has not yet actually seen the original article. Finally, a j means that it has been accepted, but that it doesn't match any groups in the *active* file, so it has been put in the *junk* pseudogroup.

The sending site is the next piece of information. If you configured `IPADDR_LOG` as `DO`, the Internet hostname or address (depending on how you configured *hosts.nntp* or whether you are running *innd* with the -a flag) of the site that sent it appears, as in the example above. This feature provides more secure auditing. If you do not log by IP address, the name of the first site in the Path header of the article is used instead.

The next field is the message ID of the article, the unique tag by which all sites can identify it. For canceled messages, this is a duplicate line that is used to indicate the article that is being canceled. Thus, one cancel control message, or an article with a Supercedes header, causes two lines to be logged with the same message ID in the fifth field.

If the article has been accepted and you have configured NNTPLINK_LOG as we recommended in Section 7.2.1.6, the location of the first reference to the article in the news spool is listed as the next field.

Articles marked as normal with a + then have the *newsfeed* file entries that they matched listed. This is logged by the first field of each entry for which all of the criteria match.

If the article has been rejected, however, the reason appears next, with the NNTP code for rejection, 437, leading the description. Junked articles list the groups that the server didn't accept as valid, and canceled articles list the message ID of the article being canceled.

9.5.3 Articles Sent

The *nntpsend* program, which is used to control execution of the *innxmit* program that sends articles to your NNTP neighbors, reports its execution in the *nntpsend.log* file. It doesn't actually report what articles were sent to what sites (that's theoretically been done in the *news* log file) or even how many articles were sent (that's done via *news.notice* syslogging). It just keeps track of when it runs, what sites it started transmitters for, and the commands it ran. A typical run looks like this:

```
nntpsend: [11903] start
nntpsend: [11903:11944] begin alterdial.uu.net Mon Jul 22 20:45:12 EDT 1996
nntpsend: [11903:11944] innxmit -a alterdial.uu.net ...
nntpsend: [11903] stop
nntpsend: [11903:11944] end alterdial.uu.net Mon Jul 22 20:48:13 EDT 1996
```

This session indicates that *nntpsend* started as process 11903. It then saw a batchlist to process for *alterdial.uu.net*, so it forked an *innxmit* process with the -a flag (included by default) as process 11944. That process took three minutes to run and then *nntpsend* exited. The last two lines appear out of order because of subshell processing done by */bin/sh*, the interpreter of the *nntpsend* script. *nntpsend* tries to wait for the transmitters it has started, but since it started them from a subshell automatically created by a while loop taking its input from a file, the parent shell is unaware of any of the background jobs. Everything works fine despite this, so you just have to ignore the out of order stop lines in the log.

9.5.4 Articles Removed

Articles that have been expired by the server are indicated in two log files. The first, *expire.log*, is created by *news.daily* to record the *expire* run. It can look like this:

```
expire begin Tue Jul 16 10:33:30 EDT 1996: (-lqv1 -z/var/log/news/expire.rm)
    Article lines processed    763312
    Articles retained          686673
    Entries expired             76639
    Files unlinked              88307
    Old entries dropped         54099
    Old entries retained       228878
    expire end Tue Jul 16 10:54:03 EDT 1996
```

The first line says when *expire* began and what arguments it had. Among other options, this *expire* was told to not actually remove articles, but to list them to the *expire.rm* log. It was also told to output some basic statistics about its run. The last line indicates when *expire* actually finished.*

When it ran, *expire* examined 763,312 lines in the *history* file that represented actual articles on the system. Of those, 686,673 represented articles that were not to be purged. Of the 76,639 that were due to be removed, crossposting meant that there were actually 88,307 references to them in the news spool that needed to be removed. 228,878 message IDs referenced articles no longer on the system; these message IDs were retained in the *history* file to prevent accepting the article again if another incoming feed were to offer it. 54,099 old message IDs were past the normal duration for remembering them.

The *expire.rm* file was created because *news.daily* was invoked with the `delayrm` option, to increase the efficiency of the removal process by taking advantage of things like reduced pathname lookups, disk caches, and directory read ordering. After *expire* finished and this log ended, the *expire.rm* file was sorted and processed by the *expirerm* process, which renamed it to *expire.list* when it finished.

9.5.5 Other Errors

When *innd* starts other programs, it points the standard output streams to the file *errlog*. If you run outgoing UUCP feeds, errors from the batching program are also reported in this file. The *errlog* file should always be empty. When it isn't, the daily report generator includes any messages from it.

---

* It is indented because of a formatting bug in *news.daily*. Rich Salz says the indentation is on purpose, though, "so that you can tell the start of everything by looking for an unindented line." So let's call it a formatting difference of opinion instead.

The last log file that normally appears in the log directory is *unwanted.log*. This file summarizes all the articles that have been rejected by your server because of groups it did not have in the *active* file at the time they were offered. The total number of articles offered and rejected for each named group is listed, with the most frequently rejected groups listed first. A group appearing in this log for a hierarchy you want does not necessarily mean there is a problem with your server.

Chapter 16 contains a lot of information about how groups are created. Section 3.3 talks about how you can responsibly add valid groups to your *active* file. Please do not haphazardly create groups on your server just because they are mentioned in *unwanted.log*, even with a high count.

9.5.6 The Daily Report

The *news.daily* maintenance script that you've set up to run from *cron* generates a report that is normally mailed to the newsmaster. The message covers the real work done by *news.daily*, error messages and all. There is a bit of fluff in there that you'll probably quickly learn to ignore, and some key areas that you'll want to take a more careful look at each time you get the report.

9.5.6.1 innstat

The first thing that *news.daily* does is run the *innstat* program. *innstat* is a conceptually useful program that, in reality, has little use. It provides a snapshot of a lot of different types of information. Generally, you're only looking for one or two pieces of information at any one time, so you'll probably end up just using the appropriate command to find it out.

The output from *innstat* starts with a picture of the server status at the time the report is begun; a glance at whether it is "Server running" is usually sufficient here. Then the disk usage of news-related filesystems is output. It's pretty important to keep an eye on this to see how fast news is eating up your disks. Following that, batch file and log file sizes are listed. While it is possible to spot anomalies here, you'll eventually tune this section out, along with the list of lock files following it. A list of the server connections at the time the maintenance run was started, as provided by *ctlinnd name "* similarly gets ignored, as it is not particularly useful information on a daily basis. So, in effect, the most you'll probably pay regular attention to in the first two screens of the daily report is the disk space usage.*

---

* Want to increase the signal to noise ration? Replace the *innstat* call in *news.daily* with a simple *df* command. If the server is in a state other than `running`, you'll be getting other notification of it anyway.

9.5.6.2   Expiry

Next *news.daily* gets into the meat of the matter—removing the oldest articles that
are eating up your spool space. This is done with *expire*, controlled by the
expire.ctl file (see Section 8.2.3). If you are passing *news.daily* a `flags=-qv1`
argument, as suggested in Section 7.4.5.2, this is when the output described in Section 9.5.4 is generated. The `-v1` option enables the statistics, while the `-q` option
suspends warnings like "Group not matched (removed?) rec.photo — Using
default expiration," which you'll get for *history* entries that reference articles filed
in groups that are no longer in the *active* database. The output of the expiry run
isn't actually inserted into the report until a few more steps are accomplished,
however.

After the expiry run, *news.daily* typically updates the *active* file so that the third
field of each line in it represents the new lowest article number for the group. This
can dramatically help the speed of some newsreader programs by narrowing the
range of articles that they try to look for. The process is facilitated by *ctlinnd
renumber* and usually there is no special indication in the report about it. For this
operation, silence is golden, but if the process doesn't manage to work for a day
(likely only if the server was throttled for some reason), it's not that big of a deal
to wait until the next *news.daily* run to have it happen. Be aware that *ctlinnd
renumber* '' can run for quite a long time if you have several thousand groups,
during which *innd* does no other work—it doesn't accept articles, start new newsreader sessions, or acknowledge other *ctlinnd* commands. If *innd* responsiveness
is very important to you, set the `RENUMBER` variable at the beginning of the
news.daily script to 0, meaning to sleep zero seconds between renumbering individual groups. This causes the entire renumbering procedure to take the least
amount of time it can while still allowing *innd* to give attention to other activities.
If you have no readers on the machine at all, pass *news.daily* the `norenumber`
argument to completely disable the expensive renumbering operation. It is not
useful on feed-only machines.

9.5.6.3   scanlogs starts

The rest of the daily report contains summaries of the log files as provided by the
scanlogs script.* It presents a mix of logged errors, statistical information, generally
interesting notices, and unusual log entries. The most notable errors are printed
right up front, while the other types of messages are all interspersed. It will probably take several days of seeing the report to get a feel for what is normal-looking
output for your system and what is something that bears extra attention. Some sections are left out if *scanlogs* doesn't have anything to say about them, but they'll all

---

* The *scanlogs* script makes use of some very long regular expressions. See the comments about *egrep*
in Section 7.1.1.

be described here. Once *scanlogs* outputs all of its information, it ages ("rolls") the log files into the *OLD* subdirectory of the log directory.

9.5.6.4 Critical syslog messages

The first log that might be printed is the one that holds *syslog* messages at the *critical* level. If there is anything in this log, it is printed in its entirety. There are four basic types of messages you might see here:

- Errors that caused *innd* to throttle itself automatically or exit

- Errors that prevented *inndstart* from bringing up *innd*

- Notices from *innd* that it restarted itself from a *ctlinnd xexec* request

- Complaints from *nnrpd* about failed newsreader authorizations

The first two bear a closer look if they were unexpected. They could well mean that your *innd* is still throttled or not running, and the message should give you a pretty good clue as to why. If you're completely baffled by the message, see Section 9.6.

The third type of message is basically noise of the form "innd: ME execv /news/bin/inndstart." It isn't worth much attention, just as the fourth kind, messages like "nnrpd[26436]: 127.0.0.1 bad_auth," shouldn't cause you much concern. All the latter is saying is that a newsreader client tried to identify itself by username and password, and got something wrong. This is typically because you didn't even have username/password authorization enabled in *nnrp.access*.

9.5.6.5 errlog

Following any critical *syslog* messages, *scanlogs* dumps the entire contents of *errlog* into the report. This log contains the output of programs started by *innd*, errors from the UUCP batcher, and notices of *innd* exiting due to TERM, INT, or DANGER signals. Messages in this log file are often not time stamped and frequently do not indicate very well what was being tried when the error happened. That is, though the rudimentary error is reported, it can be difficult to tell what overall job was being attempted, how the error affected it, and what should be done. Fortunately, there are rarely messages in this file. If you get any, good luck and happy sleuthing.

9.5.6.6 Expiry again

Since *errlog* is usually empty and there shouldn't be any critical *syslog* messages, the output of the *expire* run is usually the first thing that *scanlogs* puts in the daily report. The most notable thing to look for in this section of the report is any error messages mixed in with (or, in the worst case, instead of) the expiration statistics. Unfortunately, the severity of the error isn't usually clear from the possible error messages. Does the message represent something that INN could deal with and move on, or is it something that actually hindered the normal expiry of articles?

To answer that question, run *ctlinnd mode* on the server. If the fourth line indicates that the server is reserved for expiring by a process ID that no longer exists, *expire* had a major problem. It is quite possible that a triad of *history.n** files is also sitting in the *NEWSCTL* directory. If either of these things is true, the consequences are severe. Whatever caused the problem should be fixed, or the history database will grow abnormally, and it might possibly have erroneous pointers from the *history.pag* file to the real data locations in the flat text file *history.* Fixing the history database is described in detail in Section 9.6.2. When the bogus expire reservation can be cleared, use *ctlinnd reserve ' '* to remove it.

9.5.6.7 Bad articles

The next section of the daily report summarizes, by site, the articles that were offered to INN that it didn't like for some reason. This information is all parsed from the *news* log file. First, there is an overall summary of how many bad articles came from each site. Then the information is broken down into broad categories of what was basically wrong with the various bad articles.

The "Top 20 sites sending bad articles" section includes all articles that were rejected after *innd* had already told the sending site to go ahead and transfer it. This includes some duplicates, unapproved articles in moderated groups, groups not in the *active* database, unwanted distributions, and bad headers. Some of the numbers here, and in the category summaries that follow, could represent the same article being counted more than once as it is offered from different sites because *innd* does not enter the message IDs of bad articles in the history database.

If you were offered any articles that were posted only to groups that are not in your *active* database, or that were posted to groups that you have listed in *active* with a j flag, the sites doing so are listed under "Top 20 sites sending junked (unwanted) articles." These articles were received but filed in the *junk* pseudogroup. It could be either that you are missing some groups in your *active* file, or that the sites are sending you things you really didn't want. More on this in a moment.

After the unwanted groups, unwanted distributions are listed in "Top 20 unwanted distributions by number of articles." If you are getting these, you should either add the listed distributions to the distributions subfield of the ME line in your *newsfeeds* file (update it as discussed in Section 8.1 and then do *ctlinnd reload newsfeeds*) or ask the offending feed to send you only the distributions that you request.

Next, there might be a "Top 20 supposedly moderated groups with unmoderated postings" list. If you have any groups listed here, the problem is that someone has the group incorrectly marked as moderated. It might not be your site's problem, but that of your neighbors, or even sites beyond them. The best way to check is to get a comprehensive list of newsgroups (see Section 16.1.4) and look for a "(Moderated)" keyword at the end of the description. If it's there, you're fine. You just threw away an article that wasn't properly approved by the moderator of the group.

"Top 20 unwanted newsgroups" is a very common section to see next. Some of the newsgroups listed might not be valid; if you think that they should reasonably be part of your feed, you should not just create them because they are listed there. Get a list of newsgroups that is authoritative for the hierarchy in question (see Section 16.1.4) and use it to determine whether the group should be created as described in Section 3.3.2. Also be sure to check on the moderation status. If you don't think the group should be in the feed sent by the neighboring site, contact them to have your feed fixed. (Note that telling them about a bogus group could be useless; C News feeds articles it has accepted but filed in *junk* as though the groups in the Newsgroups header were all valid.)

The "Top 20 general message problems" section tallies the rejected articles that had format problems. Possible errors include bodyless articles, illegal message IDs or dates, dates older than the cutoff, missing required headers, and incorrectly counted Lines headers. The last error only appears if you have configured your server for strict checking. Most sites do not configure strict checking, as an incorrect Lines header is a fairly common problem and isn't worth rejecting an article over. The most you will generally ever do with this section is look at it and think to yourself, "My, isn't that interesting." Occasionally, some site will regurgitate a lot of old news to the Net and this will be reflected in many "Too old" errors. If you are getting many of these every day, perhaps your -c flag to *innd* is too small. About 14 days is a good value for it, as long as you keep the /remember/ line of your *expire.ctl* file at least that long and your system can handle the size of the resulting *history* file. Fewer than seven days usually causes the "too old" count to include many articles you never received within those seven days.

After the count of articles with format problems, "Top 20 sites sending news with bad headers" lists the same bad articles totaled by site. Once again, there usually isn't much to do with this information.

9.5.6.8 news.notice

Next comes the "Syslog summary," which condenses the statistics in the *news.notice* file. The actual parsing is done by *innlog.pl*, which first dumps any lines it did not understand verbatim under the heading "Unknown entries from news log file."

If you have configured L_CC_CMD to send messages to the *news.notice* log, a summary of "Control commands to INND," "Newsgroups created," and "Newsgroups removed" is included next. Primarily of passing interest, the summary of groups created and removed can be useful if you are ever in the unfortunate situation of needing to rebuild your *active* file, as discussed in Section 9.6.2.

"Articles received by server" totals the incoming peer connections made to *innd*. The "Took" column counts all normal articles accepted. "Refuse" counts those that were turned down as duplicates at the *IHAVE* or *CHECK* stage of the NNTP dialogue, while "Reject" counts those that had format problems. The "Accpt" [sic] percentage is figured as "Took" / "Offered." The "Elapsed" time is the total time that the connection from that host was active (in hhhh:mm:ss format).

Message IDs that could be identified as syntactically bogus at the *IHAVE* or *CHECK* stage are listed in the section "Bad Message-ID's offered." This information can mostly be ignored except if it appears that the message IDs are being generated at your own site. In that case, you should fix whatever broken program is making them; see Section 18.2.1.3 for the legal message ID syntax. If the message IDs are being originated at a neighbor site, you could be a good Samaritan and inform them of the problem and how it is keeping their articles from being widely propagated.

If your site receives *ihave* or *sendme* control messages (see Section 18.4) for sites that are not in the *newsfeeds* file, these messages are printed next. The thing to do here is to contact the feeding site and have them not send the messages to you, probably by having them block the *to* hierarchy to your site. If they really want to do *ihave/sendme* with you, then you need to fix your *newsfeeds* file as described in Section 9.3.1.

The "Bad commands received" section lists commands that were sent to your server that it did not understand. They are summarized by the number of bad commands per peer feed site. You might want to consider changing *innlog.pl* to instead list the actual bad commands. Having a list of the commands can indicate several things, from benign to possibly malicious. For example, a fairly benign occurrence would be a high number of *XFOO* commands being sent to the server; these are from a program trying to use an experimental extension to the NNTP protocol, and since your server doesn't implement the extension, it just goes about the rest of its business normally. A more notable event is when a misspelled command shows up, or one with embedded terminal control characters. These often indicate that someone was typing at your NNTP port manually, and possibly they were up to no good, such as forging a message.

Every once in a while you might see what appears to be article text as a bad command, and when it does happen you could well see every line of the article listed. This indicates that the two sides of an NNTP dialogue somehow got unsynchronized, and your server was trying to read commands while the sender was trying to send an article. On the innocent side, there is perhaps a programming error that needs to be debugged. Sometimes it is more malicious, and indicates that someone botched a forgery attempt.

Next comes the "Blocked server feeds" section, listing any processes that fell behind while *innd* was trying to write to them. These are for feeds in the *newsfeeds* file. Any time one gets behind, *innd* starts queuing whatever it was trying to write to the process to a file by the name of the feed in the spool's *out.going* directory. Normally they can be fully processed like so:

```
% cd NEWSART/out.going
% mv site site.redo
% ctlinnd flush site
% process-as-in-newsfeeds-file < site.redo
% rm site.redo
```

A script to automatically do this could run several times a day from *cron*.

The "Huge article rejections" section lists, by site, the number of articles that were too big for your site. The "too big" decision is determined by either the value of *innd*'s -1 switch or the value of LOCAL_MAX_ARTSIZE in *config.data* if there is no -1 on the command line.

"INND misc events" summarizes the number of times various log messages occurred:

- "file_number" is equivalent to "cant select Bad file number." This message means that one of the file descriptors passed into INN's select() system call was no longer valid. You should hopefully never see this message, because if you do, it indicates some sort of programming problem.*

- "CCreader" is equivalent to "cant sendto CCreader." These occur when a *ctlinnd* command, or something else using the same communication mechanism that *ctlinnd* does, didn't wait around for a reply to a request that it made. This should be pretty harmless, and usually is the result of a *ctlinnd* command being killed or timing out before the server finished the request. The processing of the request itself was not affected.

- "gethostbyname" is for "cant gethostbyname," which means the server couldn't find any valid namespace record for a host. Unfortunately, this does not list

---

* The known case of having this message show up involves A/UX 3.0 systems, which the INN FAQ says has a kernel bug triggered by *gcc* (so use *cc*).

what name it was trying to look up, so you'll have to go back and *grep* the log for "gethostbyname." Or, you can just double check your *hosts.nntp* entries and your -S command line switch to *innd* specifying a master server, since those are the two places where `gethostbyname()` lookups can cause that error message.

- "free_channel" is equivalent to "free:## internal closing free channel." You should never see this message; if you do, it indicates a programming bug. The message is apparently a safeguard within *innd* to bring attention to any such programming bug as might materialize in the evolution of the program.

If you are using an embedded Perl script to reject some types of incoming messages (see Section 8.3.6), the next section lists the number of articles rejected by the script, broken down by each of the possible reasons that it can give.

If you are using *innfeed*, the beta-test transmitter briefly described in Section 13.2.2, the next thing you'll see is statistics from *innfeed*. The first block of information counts the articles offered to the remote sites and what happened in response; this information is presented just as for *innxmit*, which is discussed in a moment.

Below the table is a list of some miscellaneous *innfeed* log messages. Currently only two can show up here. "hangup" is for "innfeed.*! hangup", which actually comes from *innd*, depends on you having *newsfeeds* entries for *innfeed* that match the regular expression /innfeed.*!/, and assumes you are running *innfeed* as a channel feed from the server. The message is logged by *innd* when the server receives an explicit request to close the *innfeed* subprocess. "write_pending" is for "internal QUIT while write pending." This means *innfeed* needed to disconnect a channel gracefully, but when it got into the code that would send a *QUIT* message to the remote site, it discovered there was other data waiting to be read by the site. This situation either delays the *QUIT* or abruptly disconnects the channel, depending on other state information associated with it. Either way, you shouldn't really have to be concerned about this message.

Statistics from *innxmit* runs come next.* The first block of information counts the articles offered to the remote sites and what happened in response. "Toss" articles are those rejected at the *IHAVE* or *CHECK* stage of the transaction, while "Fail" articles are those that were rejected for some other problem after having been trans-

---

* Actually, in some rare cases, statistics of articles received by *nntpd*, the NNTP Reference Implementation, come next as output from the *innlog.pl* script. This is a very unusual environment to run in and is not covered by this book.

ferred. "Elapsed" time is how long *innxmit* stayed connected to the other end, while "CPU" is the total amount of processor time spent executing the program.*

The block that follows the article transmission statistics reports on the success *innxmit* had in trying to start NNTP dialogues with the remote sites. It tries to report on failures to be authorized for transfer permission ("Auth"), rejected connections due to the remote site having too high a load average ("Load") or being out of space ("Space"), expire locking ("Expire"), network failures like the remote site being down or not running a server on the NNTP port ("Connct" [sic]), and all other problems *innlog.pl* didn't specifically recognize ("Other"). Most connection attempts should succeed; if more than, say, 30% fail, you should investigate, starting by looking at the *news.notice* messages for the site in question.

If you are using *nntplink* to send articles (see Section 13.2.1), information similar to the *innxmit* statistics comes next. The first block of information counts the articles offered to the remote sites and what happened in response; this information is presented just as for *innxmit*.

The connection setup summary for *nntplink* comes next. In these statistics, "EOF" is not necessarily an error; it just means that an *nntplink* that was getting its article list via its standard input channel got an end-of-file condition. This is unusual from an *nntplink* run as a channel from the *newsfeeds* file, but could be otherwise expected. "Sock" errors are from failures to establish the basic network connection (like *innxmit* "Connct" errors), just as "Bpipe" errors represent an unexpected disappearance of the network connection. "Load," "Space," "Exp[ire]," "Auth," and "Other" errors are as with *innxmit*.

The next summary of sent article information is for UUCP batching, if you are using it. It reports on the number of batches created for each site, how many total articles they represent, the total size of the uncompressed articles, and how long the batchers spent in real and CPU time creating the batches. The final percentage represents CPU time as a fraction of real time.

Articles you received from *rnews* jobs running on the server are listed next (although it would make more sense to list them with the other incoming article statistics). These articles are logged for connections made over the local Unix domain socket; *rnews* jobs that come in from the network socket look just like peer NNTP sessions and are included with the "Articles received by server" summary. A count is also given of the number of times a local *rnews* was refused a connection. Bad articles that were offered by these jobs are totaled, then broken down into three categories: unknown newsgroups, unwanted distributions, and

---

* That is, not counting time spent waiting for the disk to respond, etc.

malformed dates. These should be treated the same as they are in the "Top 20 general message problems" section.

The last major section of the report is about *nnrpd* newsreader clients. First comes a tally of the number of normal newsreader sessions from each site, along with how many articles and groups were accessed. The same article or group can be counted multiple times in the total. The new articles that originated at the client host are also counted, along with the number of new articles that the client tried to post but had rejected for some reason. The reasons for rejection are the same as those that would cause an article to be rejected by a peer, except for posting attempts made to moderated groups without approval. Such articles aren't counted here, but mailed to the moderator for posting.

An *nnrpd* session is described as coming from a "curious explorer" when a connection is made from a site that is allowed for newsreader access, but the connection doesn't actually do any newsreader functions—it accesses no article or groups and doesn't try to inject any new articles. These connections are usually either someone manually examining your server or just a newsreader program that started up but exited without reading anything, perhaps because there was no news in the groups the person wanted to read. If you see a connection here from a site you didn't think should be able to access your server, doublecheck your *nnrp.access* file and reload it if necessary.

"NNRP no permission clients" is listed when a site that is not permitted in *nnrp.access* tries to get the newsreader server. If this site is a peer server, it means a *MODE READER* command was attempted and rejected in the peer transfer session to try to get *nnrpd*, the same as if the connection had originally come from a non-peer, non-reader host.

Newsreader processes that sit around idle for too long (the default configured value for `CLIENT_TIMEOUT` is ten minutes) will eventually leave out of sheer boredom.* NNRP timeouts aren't all that interesting, unless you notice them happening a whole lot and your machine is really short on resources. In this case, you might want to remind your users to exit their newsreaders when they are done, to stop sucking up resources on your machine.

Finally, a summary of group accesses is presented by top-level hierarchy and by specific newsgroup. If you need to cut expire times or remove groups entirely from your feed because of space problems, these lists can help you keep what the users want. Note that this information does not get summarized by host or by user because that is generally considered an invasion of privacy.

---

* They'll spew messages from *news.groups* for hours without the same sense of boredom. Go figure.

9.5.6.9 After scanlogs

When the *scanlogs* script is done, *news.daily* does a little housecleaning of stale *ctlinnd* sockets left in _PATH_INNDDIR before plunking the report in the mail to the newsmaster. The date it finished is dropped in *NEWSCTL/.news.daily. rc.news* looks for this file at reboot time to guess whether maintenance might need to be done manually. Finally, an *rnews* unspooling job is run for good measure.

9.6 Troubleshooting Common Problems

Once you have INN up and running, it will probably go for months and months without technical troubles. Eventually, though, you'll be surprised to come into work one day and find the server has throttled itself because it ran out disk space somewhere, or it can't even start because a system crash corrupted one of its databases.

9.6.1 Space Shortages

Every incoming article not only takes up spool space for the storage of the message, but it also adds several dozen bytes in *NEWSCTL* and the log directory by updating the *history* database and news log files. If *innd* ever encounters a full disk partition when trying to write to any of these files, it throttles itself, refusing to accept any new articles. Aside from getting more total disk space or reducing the space consumption of non-news related files, there are a couple of basic strategies you can use to lower the space usage of the news system.

Space usage in the log partition can be decreased either by using *gzip* as the compression program for old logs or by decreasing the total number of old logs that are kept by the news system. Both can be configured in *config.data* as described in Section 7.2. After you've made the desired changes to the _PATH_COMPRESS and _PATH_COMPRESSEXT variables or to LOG_CYCLES, go to the *site* directory and reinstall *scanlogs*. Then go to the *_PATH_MOST_LOGS/OLD* directory and make the existing rolled log files match the new scheme by removing cycles above the new limit, redoing their compression, or both.

The *history* file is the only large, dynamic consumer of disk space in the *NEWSCTL* tree. While it should always have information for the articles actually in your spool space, the message IDs it keeps for expired articles can take up a lot of space. Their primary function is to keep you from asking for articles you have already seen and expired, while still allowing for a propagation delay to your site longer than the default expiration time you use. You can lower the /remember/ value in *expire.ctl* to use less space for these message IDs, but if you do, don't forget to update the -c flag for *innd* in *rc.news* (and our *innd.restart* if you are using it) to be at least as small as the /remember/ value. It is also not recommended, even in this age of hyperfast propagation for most articles, that you reduce it below a week.

An interesting anomaly you might observe on your *NEWSCTL* disk partition is a *du* space usage total that doesn't come close to matching the *df* space usage total. This could be because of open but unlinked files, as when an *nnrpd* newsreader is connected when the new history database is installed by *expire.* On SunOS systems, the following command line prints any open but unlinked files:

```
% pstat -i | awk 'NR==1 || substr($0, 39, 2) == " 0"
  ILOC   IFLAG IDEVICE  INO   MODE NLK UID SIZE/DEV VFLAG CNT SHC EXC TYPE
ff1213e8   R     7, 6 1616 100755  0   0    442368         2   0   0 VREG
```

Then you can use the freely available tool *lsof* to help you identify the processes that have the unlinked file open by correlating the inode, as follows:

```
% lsof | awk 'NR == 1 || $9 == "1616"'
COMMAND   PID   USER   FD   TYPE   DEVICE  SIZE/OFF  INODE NAME
perl     1984   root   txt  VREG   7,  6    442368   1616 /usr (/dev/sd0g)
```

Several BSD systems have *fstat*, which can be used similarly, but a bit more painfully because you have to scan the whole partition. Essentially, you use *fstat* to list all open files on the partition, then use a *find* command, as root, to find all the inodes that *fstat* reported. The inodes you didn't find are the unlinked but open files, and the lines referencing those inodes from the original *fstat* report list which process has them open. A program to do this, *uof,* is in the FTP archive for this book, *ftp://ftp.oreilly.com/pub/examples/nutshell/musenet.*

If you are having a space problem caused by *nnrpd* processes keeping the unlinked history database open, you can ruthlessly kill the transgressing sessions. A newsreader program should be able to gracefully deal with an unexpected end of session.

In the spool partition, getting more space back from a normally operating server is typically a matter of reducing the article retention times in *expire.ctl.* Issues affecting how you set the expiry period are discussed in 3.4. There are other things you can look for that could be contributing to the space problem, if it doesn't appear to be related to the normal, ever-increasing volume of news articles.

First, check for any feeds that are behind and might have unusually large batchlists in the spool directory. It isn't at all unthinkable to have a full volume feed generate a batchlist of several dozen megabytes after only a few days of being down. If a feed's backlog is consuming an obnoxious amount of space on your disks, the most important thing to do is get it out of the way. If you can stash it somewhere and contact the other site about the problem, that would be right neighborly of you. Then again, don't lose much sleep over it if you can't manage to save it somewhere. After all, they didn't let you know they were not going to take any news from you and leave you with resource problems.

Next, look for inconsistencies between your history database and the article spool. This can be done with *makehistory*, which is described in the *news-recover* manual page. *makehistory* has a flaw, in that it does not observe articles spooled for groups no longer in the *active* file. A more complete look at the consistency of the history database with regard to the spool space can be done with this brief script:

```
#! /bin/sh

# source innshellvars
 . /var/news/innshellvars
cd $SPOOL

find `ls | egrep -v '.|lost+found'` -type f ! -name .overview -print |
    sort > SPOOL.LIST
gawk -F'        ' '$3 != "" {print $3}' $HISTORY | tr '. ' '/
' | sort > HIST.LIST
comm -13 HIST.LIST SPOOL.LIST > SPOOL.ONLY
```

There should be no intervening *expire* run between the times that *SPOOL.LIST* and *HIST.LIST* are generated but *innd* can be accepting articles while the script runs. When done, the file *SPOOL.ONLY* should list only regular files that are in the spool space but are not referenced by the *history* file. Examine the list of files for any anomalies. If you want to just remove all of the files listed, you can run the *SPOOL.ONLY* file on the standard input through *fastrm*. INN, unfortunately, does not provide good tools for converting a list of article names into suitable history database entries.

9.6.2 Crash Recovery

File system corruption following a crash can interfere with INN in several ways. Corruption is most likely to occur with files that were active at the time the system crashed, and with an active *innd*, that tends to mean either the spool space, the history database, or the *active* file. A lot of empirical evidence suggests that if any corruption problems are experienced, it will be with the history database and with newly arriving articles. For that reason, it is a good idea to run *makehistory -buv* after a crash. This lets *innd* accept articles while *makehistory* scans the groups listed in the *active* file for articles not in the *history* file. It adds those that have a valid message ID header and removes those that do not, printing out each inconsistency it encounters. The *makehistory* run uses quite a lot of resources if you have a lot of news, so you might want to selectively run it rather that make it automated in *rc.news*.

The *news-recovery* manual page suggests that *newsrequeue* is a program you might want to run after a crash, but in practice that is impractical. To be completely effective, the program essentially requires that you know an interval of time for the message IDs that were lost from the batch file. That interval would have to start at the next message ID after the last one that you know was sent to the remote site, and stop just before the first article you know was listed for the remote site since the system came up. This interval of time will almost certainly be different for every single site you feed, and getting the interval right is crucial for UUCP sites. Even with NNTP feeds, you could be looking at a lot of overhead if you list many articles that they already have. *newsrequeue* is also a resource hog; it opens and scans every article listed in its input.

9.6.3 *active File Recovery*

So you blew away your *active* file because you typed *rm -f *.OLD* instead of *rm -f *.OLD* in the control files directory. When you're done swearing at yourself, shut down *innd*, grab *_PATH_MOST_LOGS/OLD/active.1.Z* and install it, uncompressed, as *NEWSCTL/active*. Bring up *innd* with the -r flag to have it immediately renumber the *active* file. When the logs indicate it has finished with that process, re-apply any *newgroup* and *rmgroup* control messages via *ctlinnd* to reflect group changes that happened since that snapshot of the *active* database was made. You might also try running a known list of valid groups (like ISC's *newsgroups* file, from *ftp://ftp.isc.org/pub/usenet/CONTROL/newsgroups*) through *docheckgroups* to note any anomalies. If you're running *actsync* periodically from *cron*, it should be able to fix up any remaining discrepancies for you.

We don't recommended that you use *makeactive* to generate the *active* file, largely because it doesn't have a good grasp of what's a real group and what's just a hierarchal node, or what the proper moderated status of a group is. If it finds the sub-tree *alt/swedish/chef/bork/bork/bork* in your spool, it generates six *active* group lines for it, even though there is really only one group in that tree. It also leaves the moderated groups like *news.announce.important* marked as unmoderated. This allows users from your site to make postings to the moderated groups that never make it to the moderators. Most likely, these postings will go no further than your own machine. They will be dropped at your neighbor's since they lack the moderator's approval.

9.7 *Wrapping Up*

We hope you now have an operational INN system. Chapters 3, *News Operations*, and 11, *You're a Network Manager Now*, contain a more complete discussion of day-to-day operations of a news system. Good luck!

10

In this chapter:
- *Installing Newsreaders*
- *Operational Issues*
- *Popular Newsreaders*
- *More Information*

Choosing and Installing Newsreaders

This chapter discusses the administrative aspects of newsreaders and includes a very brief look at a few of the more popular newsreaders. Every newsreader is different, but there are some commonalities in the administration of newsreaders, in both installation and operation. To get familiar with a newsreader, you really have to try it out. This chapter should give you a basic idea of what's good and bad about some of the more popular choices. The chapter also discusses where to find more information about newsreaders and where to get the software.

10.1 Installing Newsreaders

Newsreaders can be installed at any time, since they all work from the same stored articles and auxiliary files. It's quite reasonable to give your users a choice of several newsreaders; in particular, novices and power users may prefer different newsreaders.

The installation process usually consists of three steps: making preliminary decisions about parameters that are compiled into the newsreader, compiling the newsreader, and setting up its configuration files (if any). If the newsreader comes as a binary, you can obviously skip the compilation step, but you may have to tinker with the configuration files if the binary was compiled using preliminary decisions that are wrong for your system.

10.1.1 Preliminary Decisions

Non-NNTP newsreaders usually have preconceived ideas about where the article tree and related files live, although for most newsreaders these locations can be overridden by configuration files. More fundamentally, a newsreader has to know where to find its own configuration files. Precisely where you put such configuration files is up to you. If the newsreader is running on the same host as the news database, though, we suggest putting the configuration files in subdirectories of the control-files directory (e.g., */var/news*) so all the news-specific configuration files are together.

If some of a newsreader's ideas about the location of files are wrong, and it's inconvenient or impossible to change them by reconfiguring the newsreader itself, you may be able to work around the problem with symbolic links. For example, old newsreaders sometimes assume that the article tree is in its traditional location, */usr/spool/news*. If you make a symbolic link from there to */news* (or wherever you have put your article tree), that usually clears up this problem without newsreader reconfiguration.

Some newsreaders that access articles via the filesystem assume that the overview files are always in the article tree. Getting around this can be awkward; one workable approach is to have an *.overview* symbolic link in each article directory that points to the real location of the overview file. The latest C News creates such links automatically; INN does not. If your software does not support this feature and you want it done, you need to alter your news software to install such links when new newsgroups are made, so you don't have to maintain the links by hand.

Again, if a newsreader is made up of more than one program, you also have to decide where to put the auxiliary programs. Again, if the newsreader is on the same host as the news database, a subdirectory of */usr/libexec/news* (or wherever you put the relayer software) is a reasonable location.

10.1.2 *Compiling Newsreaders*

Compiling a newsreader can involve all the same portability woes as compiling any other new software on your system. It's difficult to say anything very general about the problems that might arise and how to solve them.

10.1.3 *Configuring Newsreaders*

Once you've got a newsreader built and installed, there are usually some configuration files that need to be adjusted. At the very least, you may want to set some defaults for your users, such as an initial newsgroup subscription list. If the newsreader uses NNTP to access articles, you also need to supply the name of the NNTP server. Most such details can be overridden by individual users, but life is a lot simpler if the defaults produce reasonable behavior.

You should also test the newsreader thoroughly by using its posting, follow-up, and reply-by-mail facilities. Use a local newsgroup, not a worldwide one, for test articles. We strongly recommend that testing be done from a typical user account;

system administrators often extensively customize their own accounts, and this can hide problems and make realistic testing difficult. It can be worth creating a dummy user account solely for the purpose of testing newsreaders.

10.2 Operational Issues

Fortunately, news-reading software rarely causes trouble that requires administrative attention. Nevertheless, there are a couple of ways that newsreaders can cause problems like full disk partitions, lack of memory, or a soaring load.

These problems most often arise when the software does something automatic that doesn't resemble a human actually reading articles. For example, at least one version of the Netscape Navigator NNTP client can clog a server if the user keeps selecting "next article" before the current article has been fully loaded. When this happens, the client drops the current connection and opens a new one to get the next article because it wants to provide fast feedback to users on slow links. Administrators on some systems have seen as many as 80 NNTP newsreader server processes created in less than a minute by this behavior. Along the same lines, some newsreader programs have been observed pre-fetching hundreds of articles that the user doesn't actually read.

Another problem is newsreaders that maintain their own special databases. Not only can the database-generating program sometimes be a resource hog, but the additional space requirements of the database can also lead to filled news filesystems. The good news is that most modern newsreaders have been adapted to work with the "overview" indexing format supported by both C News and INN, so this problem is becoming increasingly rare.

10.3 Popular Newsreaders

This section provides a quick overview of some newsreaders that are either popular or noteworthy for some other reason. For each one, we'll try to give you an idea of what it does for you and what specific problems it has. We've included screen images for most of them, to give you some idea of the flavor of each one, but this isn't terribly satisfying. To find out which newsreaders are best for you, or for your customers, you really need to try them out—no amount of description can substitute for hands-on experience in this area.

Two important features of many modern newsreaders are threading and kill files. Threading refers to the ability of the newsreader to keep track of articles by topic of conversation; each such topic is called a thread. Threading makes it easier for a user to keep track of certain conversations and ignore others. Kill files provide a way to have the newsreader automatically skip over (or "kill") articles that meet certain criteria. For example, a user can specify that all articles with a specific Subject or by a certain author be killed.

Do remember that not all newsreaders are created equal! Decisions about which newsreaders to support should not be based solely on your taste for the various interfaces or on how easy the programs are for you to administer. The look and feel of a newsreader, and, more importantly, how well it can guide novice users to reasonable and responsible behavior, are significant factors in how usable the Net is for people in general and in how your site is perceived in particular.

10.3.1 readnews

The *readnews* newsreader shipped with C News is about as simple as a news-reader can be. It's meant for naive or occasional users, who can just keep hitting Return (or Enter) to move through news (although this may not satisfy today's breed of occasional users, who want to hit buttons with the mouse rather than with their fingers). *readnews* is also useful for testing server software, because it's so simple that very little can go wrong with it.

readnews is too simple for most advanced users; it lacks many useful features and has no support for threading. It does not support NNTP reading at all, so it's only useful on a server host or on a host that has a server's news filesystem mounted via NFS. No real effort has been made to separate it from C News, so installing it on an INN system would require some expertise, and it's not thought that the time and trouble would be worthwhile.

Figure 10-1 shows an example screen from *readnews*, where the user pressed Return at each ? prompt except the last one.

10.3.2 rn

rn is the ultimate ancestor, at least in many concepts, of almost all sophisticated newsreaders. *rn* introduced a wide range of features that are now taken for granted, most notably kill files. *rn* has a full-screen interface (although still text-only), and it incorporates various bits of cleverness that make it usable even over fairly slow connections. NNTP support is available and works well, but must be configured at compile time. There are also extensive (although cryptic) facilities for user customization.

rn itself is basically obsolete, particularly because it provides no thread support; see *trn* below for its most direct modern descendant. *rn*'s command language is complex and not always intuitive, although admittedly an ordinary user doesn't need to know much of it. *rn* inherited its most fundamental flaw from the early days of Usenet: it assumes that you want to read everything in a newsgroup, with occasional exceptions, and makes it quite difficult to be selective.

Figure 10-2 shows an example screen from *rn*.

```
-------------------------
Newsgroup comp.org.usenix
-------------------------

Article 1262 of 1300 (comp.org.usenix) (12 lines) Wed Dec 18 12:16:41 1996
From: Brian Kirouac <bri@mail.his.com>
Subject: DC-SAGE December Meeting
?

   The DC-SAGE December meeting will be Thursday, December 19 1996 at 1900
at the AOL(America Online) facility in Vienna, VA.  The topic for this
meeting will be distributed filesystems with Anne Brink as the speaker.

   For more information and directions see

            http://www.dc-sage.org/meetings/nextmeet.html


?

Article 1263 of 1300 (comp.org.usenix) (693 lines) Wed Dec 18 17:51:53 1996
From: toni@usenix.org (Toni Veglia)
Subject: USENIX 1997 Technical Conference - Hotel Discount Deadline 12/20
?
```

Figure 10-1: readnews screen

```
Article 1290 (10 more) in comp.org.usenix:
From: toni@usenix.org (Toni Veglia)
Subject: Overflow Hotel Info - USENIX 1997 Technical Conference
Date: Fri, 27 Dec 1996 01:05:16 GMT


Since the Anaheim Marriott is now sold out completely, USENIX
has secured additional hotel rooms at the following property:


                 Quality Hotel - Maingate
                 616 Convention Way
                 Anaheim, CA  92802
                 Tel # 714.750.3131
                 Toll free # 800.231.6215
                 Reservation Fax # 714.750.9027


The hotel is located right next door to the Anaheim Marriott.
Please let them know that you are going to be attending the
USENIX Conference.

-The USENIX Association Staff
(Mail) End of article 1290 (of 1300)--what next? [npq]
```

Figure 10-2: rn screen

10.3.3 trn

trn is a descendant of *rn* that has been somewhat modernized and slightly revised to support threading (the name stands for "threaded *rn*"). The virtues of *trn* are similar to those of *rn*. *trn* is often the preferred newsreader of users who got started with *rn*, and remains a useful newsreader for power users in general.

trn also shares some of *rn*'s flaws. The command language is quite intricate, and although it's not needed for simple tasks, it does become necessary when your needs get more complex. *trn* also has a read-almost-everything orientation. Backward compatibility with *rn* is an advantage for old *rn* users and a disadvantage for newcomers.

Do *not* use *trn*'s private auxiliary-database software, as it is an awful resource hog.* Modern versions of *trn* can, and should, use the overview database.

Figure 10–3 shows an example selection screen from *trn*; the reading screen for *trn* looks very much like the one for *rn*.

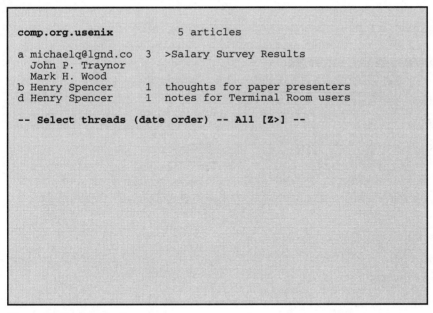

Figure 10–3: trn selection screen

---

* So bad, in fact, that it was the original motivation for Geoff Collyer's creation of the overview database.

10.3.4 tin

tin is another full-screen text-based newsreader. It has an intuitive, easy-to-use interface, which makes it ideal for novice users. *tin* also supports threading and kill files and offers the ability to tag and operate on groups of articles, so it is popular with many power users. *tin* makes it easy to be quite selective about what you read, so it functions well with today's high volume of news traffic.

The one drawback to *tin* is that it redraws the screen quite often. In most settings, this shouldn't be a problem. But if your users are going to be accessing news over slow communications lines, they may find the constant redrawing to be tedious.

Do *not* use *tin*'s private auxiliary-database software. It is somewhat of a resource hog, although it is not as bad as *trn*'s. Modern versions of *tin* can, and should, use the overview database.

Figure 10-4 shows the *tin* newsgroup selection screen.

```
      Group Selection (news.indra.com  18 R)                      h=help
   1   1014   co.jobs
   2     61   co.general
   3      1   comp.risks
   4    206   boulder.general
   5    357   rec.climbing
   6     35   alt.www.hotjava
   7     43   comp.lang.java.api
   8     84   comp.lang.java.misc
   9   1384   comp.lang.java.programmer
  10     75   comp.lang.java.security
  11     17   comp.lang.java.setup
  12     95   comp.lang.java.tech
  13     34   biz.clarinet.webnews.top
  14    447   biz.clarinet.webnews.usa
  15    107   biz.clarinet.webnews.techwire
  16     42   boulder.ads

    <n>=set current to n, TAB=next unread, /=search pattern, c)atchup,
  g)oto, j=line down, k=line up, h)elp, m)ove, q)uit, r=toggle all/unread,
    s)ubscribe, S)ub pattern, u)nsubscribe, U)nsub pattern, y)ank in/out
```

Figure 10-4: tin newsgroup selection screen

10.3.5 Gnus

Gnus is an Emacs subsystem that is distributed with recent versions of GNU Emacs from the Free Software Foundation. Emacs fans tend to love this sort of thing because news handling is integrated into their favorite editor. One of the authors, David Lawrence, uses Gnus as his primary newsreader because it has all of the features you expect in a modern newsreader—threading, kill files, advanced article organization, and more.

On the other hand, GNU Emacs is enormous and starts up very slowly. Invoking it just to run a newsreader is not worth the trouble. If you already have enthusiastic GNU Emacs users, Gnus may be just the thing for them, and you probably already have the Gnus software installed as part of the Emacs distribution. If you or your users prefer a different text editor, Gnus is not so wonderful that it will convert anyone to GNU Emacs.

Figure 10–5 shows the newsgroup selection screen for Gnus, while Figure 10–6 shows a Gnus subject list and a news article.

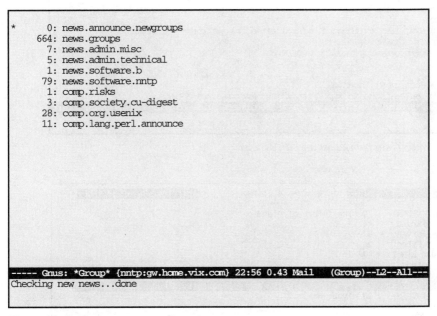

```
*        0: news.announce.newgroups
       664: news.groups
         7: news.admin.misc
         5: news.admin.technical
         1: news.software.b
        79: news.software.nntp
         1: comp.risks
         3: comp.society.cu-digest
        28: comp.org.usenix
        11: comp.lang.perl.announce
```

```
----- Gnus: *Group* {nntp:gw.home.vix.com} 22:56 0.43 Mail   (Group)--L2--All---
Checking new news...done
```

Figure 10–5: Gnus newsgroup list screen

10.3.6 *nn*

The *nn* newsreader offered the first serious competition to *rn*. The elementary philosophy of news reading in *nn* is the polar opposite of *rn*'s. Short for "No News is good news," *nn* encourages the user to read articles selectively, rather than read everything, which is probably appropriate in this day and age.

nn is probably not the newsreader of choice for people who avidly devour everything that happens in their favorite newsgroups. For people who like to skim, though, it may be the best choice.

Do *not* use *nn*'s private auxiliary-database software. It is somewhat of a resource hog, although it is not as bad as *trn*'s. Modern versions of *nn* can, and should, use the overview database. Figure 10–7 shows an article selection screen in *nn*.

```
R  [   15: Heiko W.Rupp         ] Re: Looking for a "Beginners Guide to NNTP"
   [   15: Brett Hawn [NOL STAF] Innfeed
       <  24: Murray S. Kucherawy >
-- Gnus: *Summary news.software.nntp* [30468] {26 more} 23:09 0.13      (Summary)--
From: hwr@pilhuhn.de (Heiko W.Rupp)
Subject: Re: Looking for a "Beginners Guide to NNTP"
Newsgroups: news.software.nntp
Date: 13 Jan 1997 08:30:10 GMT
Organization: The Home Of The Pilhuhn

In <5b6kbo$po7$1@monteverdi.ednet.co.uk>, Joshua Goodall wrote:
: |How about RFCs 977 and 1036?

Else the following paper (as also presented in part1 of the FAQ) will be
of help:
|A good overview for those not familiar with news (from Tom Podnar
<tpodnar@bones.wcupa.edu>):
|    ftp://bones.wcupa.edu/pub/nntp.ps


--
Heiko W.Rupp hwr@pilhuhn.de
INN FAQ can be found in ftp://ftp.xlink.net/pub/news/docs/
-- Gnus: *Article* Re: Looking for a "Beginners Guide to NNTP" 23:09 0.13    (Art
```

Figure 10–6: Gnus subject list and an article

```
Newsgroup: comp.os.plan9                          Articles: 38 of 38/1 NEW

a Steve_Kilbane     70   The future of Plan9?
b Digby Tarvin      46   >
c Digby Tarvin      37   >
d Markus Friedl     26   >
e Brandon Black     64   >
f Eric Dorman       47   -
g Adam Miller       83   >
h S Kotsopoulos    855   Plan 9 from Bell Labs - Frequently Asked Questions [FAQ]
i Digby Tarvin      20   >your mail
j Digby Tarvin      51   >X11
k David Hogan       20   >
l Dan Hildebrand    46   >
m Digby Tarvin      12   ICMP support??
n S Kotsopoulos     31   >
o Brandon Black     43   >
p Scott Schwartz    20   >
q Digby Tarvin      31   >
r edell@alpha2      20   hardware requirements
s Jose Alvarez      28   ABOUT WINDOWS, CURSOR FUNCTIONS AND ED WOOD

-- 16:40 -- SELECT -- help:? -----Top 48%-----
```

Figure 10–7: nn article selection screen

10.3.7 Pine

The "Program for Internet News and Email," or Pine, was originally a derivative of the Elm mailer. It is aimed at novice users, but advanced users may find it suitable, perhaps with a bit of customization. Pine is overwhelmingly popular as a novice-friendly mail reader, so you may already have it serving in that role. As the expansion of the acronym says, it is meant to be a general purpose Internet message handler, so it can also handle news. If your users already use Pine for email, you should consider it for news, to spare your novice users from having to learn a second user interface.

There's not a lot wrong with Pine, if you keep in mind that it was never intended to satisfy all the needs of a demanding expert. One particular problem that does crop up is that it doesn't always distinguish mail messages from news articles sharply enough. Pine users can easily get confused about whether they're dealing with mail or news, and they sometimes post intended-to-be-private mail replies as news because the original mail message had a Newsgroups header.

Figure 10–8 shows the newsgroup selection screen for Pine, while Figure 10–9 shows an example article in Pine.

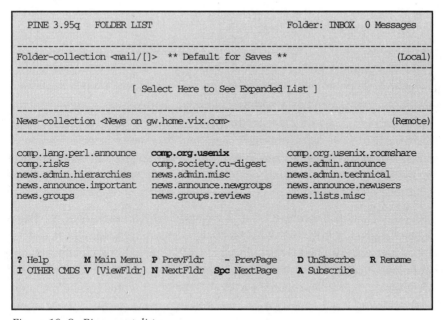

Figure 10–8: Pine group list

```
    PINE 3.95q   MESSAGE TEXT <News on gw.> comp.org.usenix  Msg 9 of 11  9%

   Date: Wed, 12 Feb 1997 01:34:27 GMT
   From: Jackson Dodd <jackson@usenix.org>
   Newsgroups: comp.org.usenix, comp.org.sug, comp.org.uniforum,
       comp.unix.large, comp.unix.admin, comp.infosystems,
       comp.infosystems.gis, comp.infosystems.wais, comp.infosystems.gopher,
       comp.infosystems.interpedia, comp.infosystems.www.misc,
       comp.infosystems.www.authoring.html
   Subject: Workshop on Internet Technologies and Systems (WITS) - Call for Papers



          USENIX Workshop on Internet Technologies and Systems

                  Announcement and Call for Papers
                       December 8-11, 1997
                       Monterey, California
                    http://www.usenix.org/wits97/

   Sponsored by the USENIX Association

   ? Help         M Main Menu  P PrevMsg      - PrevPage    D Delete     R Reply
   O OTHER CMDS V ViewAttch  N NextMsg    Spc NextPage    U Undelete   F Forward
```

Figure 10–9: Pine article

10.3.8 *Netscape Navigator*

Like GNUS with Emacs, if you already have Netscape's Navigator Web browser (or
Netscape's Communicator product), then you already have its newsreader. Unlike
all of the other newsreaders we've covered, this one offers a graphical user interface. We feel obliged to mention it here because it is probably now among the top
three most widely used newsreaders on the planet, if not by now the most widely
used. This newsreader is solely an NNTP client and it is under active commercial
development by Netscape. Some people would say that this means better support
for it, compared to most of the other newsreaders named here, which are primarily labors of love by volunteers.*

As mentioned earlier, some versions of Navigator have been known to cause
administrative headaches because of a poor design decision regarding how to handle a new article request when one is already being retrieved. Also, early versions
of Navigator lacked important features that many Usenet users have long taken for
granted, most notably kill files. Veterans seldom have good words for the program,
generally considering it a step backward, but it is improving and it is quite popular. Even some of the veterans have now diluted their venom toward the program.

---

* We say "some people" because not everyone agrees with this assessment. Enthusiastic volunteers
have been known to provide much better support than large companies.

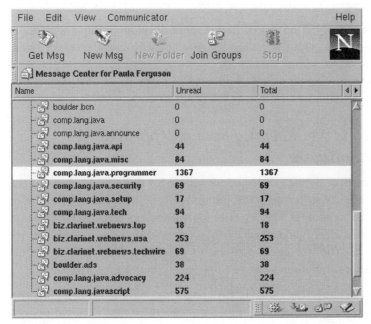

Figure 10–10: Netscape Communicator's newsgroup selection window

Figure 10–11 shows the newsgroup selection window for the latest version of Netscape's newsreader, which is part of the Communicator package.

10.4 More Information

The brief summaries above barely scratch the surface of newsreaders, and many have been left out. There are other clients for the X Window System, Unix text displays, PCs, Macs, and just about any other type of computer someone is using to access the Net. The presence or absence of any newsreader in the preceding section is not an indication of its unsuitability as a newsreader, but rather a shortcoming resulting from the authors' experience with newsreaders. We are both primarily Unix veterans and long ago settled into using the newsreaders we felt suited our needs. By way of an apology for these shortcomings, we have included some pointers to additional information about newsreaders.

10.4.1 Usenet Software: History and Sources

The article "Usenet Software: History and Sources" is posted regularly, with that Subject header, to *news.admin.misc, news.announce.newusers, news.answers, news.software.readers*, and *news.software.b*, by *netannounce@deshaw.com*. As a *news.answers* document, it is available in any *news.answers* archive as *usenet/software/part1*, e.g.:

```
ftp://rtfm.mit.edu/pub/usenet/news.answers/usenet/software/part1
```

In addition to providing a brief history of how Usenet developed, this document is kept reasonably up-to-date with the online locations of various newsreader packages. Brief synopses of numerous newsreaders—those mentioned in this chapter and many more—are provided, as well as pointers to other online documents that describe even more newsreaders, especially PC programs.

10.4.2 The "Good Net-Keeping Seal of Approval" for Usenet Software

In late 1994, Ron Newman penned a document calling for the establishment of the "Good Net-Keeping Seal of Approval." The premise behind this idea is that a lot of blame for the general decline of Usenet is being placed on new users, when in reality, it is the newsreaders being used by these people that are responsible for many of the problems. The document goes on to describe a minimum set of features that a newsreader program must have to be given the "Seal of Approval."

At the time of this writing, the Seal is no longer appearing in *news.answers* archives, but it can be found at *http://www.cybercom.net/˜rnewman/Good-Netkeeping-Seal*.

You should read this document and think about the features it describes when you are deciding what newsreaders to support. Although we might not agree with every last letter in it, it does provide a good overview of many of the features that help make Usenet a better place.

10.4.3 Usenet Groups

The following newsgroups are most relevant to Usenet newsreader programs:

news.software.readers
> Discussion of software used to read network news

comp.os.msdos.mail-news
> Discussion of administering mail and network news systems under MS-DOS

comp.os.os2.mail-news
> Discussion of mail and news applications and utilities under OS/2

These groups discuss particular newsreaders:

news.software.nn
> Discussion about the *nn* newsreader package

comp.mail.pine
> Discussion of the Pine mail user agent and newsreader

gnu.emacs.gnus
> Discussion of news reading under GNU Emacs using Gnus

Finally, these groups sometimes have newsreader discussions:

news.admin.technical
> A moderated group on the technical aspects of maintaining network news

news.software.b
> A discussion about B-news-compatible software

news.software.nntp
> A discussion about the Network News Transfer Protocol

The FAQs for several newsreader programs are crossposted between *news.answers* and *news.software.readers*. You can get the *news.answers* archive index from *ftp://rtfm.mit.edu/pub/usenet/news.answers/index*. Then search for *news.software.readers* to find the appropriate archive name for each FAQ.

10.4.4 FTP Archives

Your favorite Web search engine should be able to turn up a source distribution for whatever newsreader program interests you. To help make things easier, the following site serves as a mirror for every freely available newsreader package mentioned in "Usenet Software: History and Sources":

```
ftp://ftp.uu.net/networking/news/readers
```

11

In this chapter:
- *Network Optimization*
- *Managing People*
- *Your Site and the Law*

You're a Network Manager Now

This chapter discusses the software-independent and somewhat less technical aspects of dealing with an anarchistic network. Like it or not, by joining Usenet, you're signing up to be part of the network management, and you'd better be prepared. The information here should help you run a responsible Usenet fiefdom.

We'll look briefly at optimizing the organization of your news feeds, proceed to a short discussion of dealing with people, and conclude with a look at legal issues and network abuse.

11.1 Network Optimization

As a good network citizen, you should not unduly burden others with the operation of your site. While this clearly applies to such extreme behavior as swamping the Net with many enormous postings all made at once, it also applies to more subtle issues like making the most out of the bandwidth that you have. Optimizing feed topologies is usually overlooked during network capacity planning; thoughtful planning can improve both the regular operation of your news system and its recovery capabilities in the event of an unusual occurrence.

The most important point we can make is that Usenet transport systems do not work best when a single feed uses a single path to deliver all of the articles to your site; it isn't robust or resourceful. Unfortunately, the growing dependence of sites on their Internet service providers (ISPs) has increasingly led to this sort of arrangement. Several major providers have to run multiple servers that do nothing but send news to customer servers, a great many of which are leaf nodes. This arrangement can cause not only a complete loss of incoming news if there is a problem at the provider, but also an increasing backlog of news when everything is operating normally.

Consider the normal NNTP *IHAVE* dialogue, in which it takes a minimum of two times the packet round trip time to exchange an article. This means that your network pipe is sitting idle a lot of the time, waiting for further action on responses that it has sent. Although this problem has been greatly alleviated by the development of the NNTP streaming commands (*CHECK* and *TAKETHIS*—see Section 19.5.3), which are available in INN, the quite common *IHAVE* method of news exchange isn't very good at keeping the network busy. (Of course, if you have other traffic going over that link and it is near capacity, that might be a good thing.)

There are two ways that you can solve this problem. One is to have multiple incoming network links, perhaps two dedicated lines from different ISPs or multiple dial-up connections, so that your feed can send you news over multiple paths. If you have a high-bandwidth TCP/IP line and a lower bandwidth one, you should consider using *nntplink* (see Section 13.2.1) to delay the articles that would be sent over the slower link and thereby reduce the chance that any significant data exchanges happen there.

Another solution is to have multiple incoming news feeds. This redundancy provides for a robust news flow even in the face of a failure on either link. Multiple feeds can also improve resource use, if done properly. Two different sites sending the same feed to your site doubles the NNTP *IHAVE* traffic, but half of those messages should elicit "don't send it" responses. The added data overhead in the *IHAVE/reject* exchanges is relatively small, while the network pipe is kept busy more of the time because the two separate exchanges are not acting in unison. When your server is waiting for a reply to a "go ahead, send it" message in one session, it can also be reading an article in the other session.

If you examine the Path headers of numerous articles, you will see some fascinating and bizarre propagation paths. For example, an article posted to one of the San Francisco Bay Area groups could easily go from a site in that region to an ISP on the East Coast of the U.S., cross the Atlantic to Germany, come back through England to a New England ISP, and then return to the Bay Area.

One reason for this is that very little thought has been given to feed topology in recent years, due to the belief that network bandwidth is far cheaper than it was in the long-distance UUCP days. The feeds for two Bay Area sites may have been arranged with no Bay-Area-only path between them. While it is true that bandwidth is cheaper than it used to be, as more and more high-volume Web traffic is crammed through the network, many sites are discovering that bandwidth is at a premium.

Usenet's flooding algorithm is also contributing to these bizarre routes. Like water rushing down a mountainside, news finds the path of least resistance to get to its destination the soonest. Because major service providers are interconnected by very fast lines, the fastest path between two sites might really involve a trip half way around the world and back, even if it only beats a much shorter route by milliseconds. The network does not necessarily resemble the geographic world for efficiency in its links.

If you can get several sites to participate in a planned news exchange system, you can enhance the robustness and reduce the resource use of all them. Even with several dozen sites, it should not take more than four feeds running on each site to provide improved article propagation times, redundant backups, and even decreased loads on the most heavily loaded sites (such as the service providers). Believe it or not, this kind of volunteer organization does happen, even in this day and age. At least one project like this was done in 1995, involving nearly a hundred sites who had formerly been leaf sites of big Internet service providers.

To get such a system started, you need to collect some data on all of the connections between all of the different sites who want to participate—*ping* and *traceroute* are good tools to use in collecting this information. Be sure to collect data at different times during the day, to eliminate time-based anomalies. Once you have the data, you need to find the paths that have the shortest delays and use the fewest routers. The sites connected by those paths should feed each other. Depending on where the different sites get their Internet service, you'll probably end up with several rings of sites, with each ring connected to the same router. Be sure that you have a couple of connections from each ring to other rings, and don't forget to include a couple of full feeds from major sites outside of your project. (Without the major feeds from outside, your system will only see news that it generates itself.) One of the organizers of the effort in 1995 reportedly had a giant wall map of the U.S.A. on his kitchen wall, so he could use push pins and string to visualize the many routes involved.

11.2 Managing People

Despite the primal wishes of programmers and administrators everywhere, computers don't exist in an environment devoid of users. Without users, Usenet would just be an empty Net (and hardware manufacturers and Internet service providers would have done a lot less business over the past decade).

In order to deal effectively with your users, you should establish policies that are followed consistently at your site. Here are some common issues that you may want to address:

- How users let you know about problems

- How users ask for new software to be installed

- How users request changes in the available newsgroups

- Where users go with questions about their newsreaders

- What is acceptable news reading (i.e., only work-related reading or recreational reading, on company time or off the clock)

- What is acceptable for posted articles

- How you handle transgressions of the policies

Your policy might just be: "See me if you have questions or have observed any problems." Or it might be very detailed on all of these issues. If you work at a big company, you might even have to get the policies approved by people higher up—even if it's not mandatory, this could still be a good idea just in case.

You should strive for a policy that is simple enough to be understood, natural enough to be followed, and liberal enough to let people enjoy Usenet as it was designed. The specific matters of what are widely considered unacceptable articles and the possible legal ramifications of your policies are discussed in the rest of this chapter.

When you are dealing with your users, remember that they can also be useful as volunteer labor. For example, you might need to enlist others to help you with the administration of the system. Although the days when management usually didn't even know their company was a Usenet site seem to be gone, it is still often the case that news is a low-priority item. Folks who volunteer to help you should be highly valued; if you are overworked and underpaid, then let volunteers share as much of your administrator's burden as they can. They can make your life much easier.

Volunteerism can be essential if you or your site becomes responsible for maintaining a periodic informational posting, running a moderated newsgroup, or overseeing the group creation process in some area of the namespace. In these cases, you may be coordinating volunteers from outside of your organization, many of whom you may have never met in person. Sing their praises whenever appropriate and always give them credit when it is due. Competent help can be very hard to find, so use it well, lest you be left all on your own again.

Finally, remember that many of the people you see providing services on the Net are doing so out of no real obligation to you. They generally have real jobs to tend to and a life beyond the confines of the computer screen. Sometimes these services have problems, and your tolerance in dealing with such problems is not only greatly appreciated, but it just might mean the difference between someone continuing a service or abandoning it because of hearing nothing but ingratitude.

11.3 Your Site and the Law

"I'm not a lawyer, and I don't even play one on TV" is a common disclaimer on the Net. It's also the disclaimer for this section. Although we can provide some general advice based on our own consultations with attorneys, our experience, and our view of the prevailing public opinion, none of this matters when you're pulled before the judge in your own case. We also have a decidedly U.S.-centric view of things; sites outside of the jurisdiction of the United States can face vastly different legal issues.

If these issues are important to you—for example, because you're going to be providing news services commercially—it's time to consult an attorney who has expertise in freedom-of-speech issues and computer communications. Even then, be aware that there is not yet a tremendous amount of useful precedent regarding online conduct, so it is not easy to predict how any new legal challenge is likely to go. And there is never a shortage of surprises in verdicts.

The demographics of the Internet changed rapidly in the mid-1990s, from a community heavily populated by scientists, engineers, and students who seemed to lean toward libertarian political ideas, to a community that more closely matches the diversity of the "real world." This change has brought with it an increase in the number of cultural clashes, and with that an increase in the number of threatened lawsuits. Even just growing from a few thousand users back in the early 1980s to a few million users in the early 1990s would cause such pain. The high visibility of the Internet in the mid-to-late 1990s, and the greatly increased money associated with it, has made actual lawsuits an inevitability. Gone are the times when you could just laugh in the face of someone threatening you with his virtual lawyers on the Net. Such groundless threats still occur, but now you need to seriously consider the issues when you're threatened, especially since your organization might represent an attractive "deep pocket" to someone more interested in capitalizing on your punishment than in righting a wrong.

11.3.1 Legal Classifications

A site that gives Usenet service (feeds or newsreaders) to anyone who asks, without making any additional qualifications for the service (other than keeping the bill paid), is classified as an *enhanced service provider* in the United States. This is like a *common carrier*, the classification for businesses like telephone companies and railroad freight firms, but with a bit less governmental regulation than common carriers suffer. By not regulating the content of traffic passing through them, enhanced service providers are believed to be absolved from liability for "illegal" speech (e.g., copyright violations, obscenity, conspiracy, presidential death threats).

There is a sizable grey area here though: if you know that a common use of a particular newsgroup involves illegal speech, what is your liability to keep or remove it? The answer is that no one knows yet. One line of reasoning says that the group is just a repository of messages, so the group itself is not perpetrating illegal speech (except for a few rare names), and that there are probably legal messages in the group in addition to the illegal ones. The opposing argument is that although there might be "massage" parlors that sometimes really do only give massages, it doesn't stop the police from shutting them down for prostitution.

Whether you have reasonable knowledge of the traffic you pass could make all the difference in whether you are held responsible for a problem. You could bill yourself as the "Christian Bookstore of Usenet" and carry only those newsgroups that are supposedly "wholesome." If someone posts pornography to one of those groups, it could be analogous to someone slipping a sexual picture into the middle of a book at the bookstore. Just as the bookstore has no realistic way to expect something like that, your redistribution of the pornographic articles would almost certainly not be an actionable offense. But if you show signs of monitoring the traffic, you're in much more dangerous territory, where a court might find that you should have noticed the pornography.

One particular problem area is brewing. As the number of incidents of network abuse (unwanted advertising, excessively posted articles, and so on) rises, more and more sites want to write clauses into their contracts that allow them to cut off sites that originate widely unpopular articles. While this is arguably good public relations,* it could also be a legal Achilles' heel. If your contract has wording that can be interpreted as making content-based judgments, such as prohibiting hate speech or even just some types of advertising, that's a wide-open invitation to a lawsuit about any content passing through the site. In *Stratton Oakmont, Inc. v. Prodigy Servs. Co.*, for example, Prodigy was found liable for libelous statements made in one of its user forums because it had content-based guidelines for its users and actively attempted to control offensive speech, even though neither of these policies said anything about libel.

The best defense against such liability, if you want to hold customers to a contractual obligation against Net abuse, is to carefully craft the clause to make no content-based decisions. One way to do this is to cut off anyone who is directly or indirectly responsible for a loss of service at your site. For example, if someone's Net abuse results in your site being sent so many complaints that your mail system is rendered unusable, you have a very valid case for abuse of your resources that is completely independent of whatever content caused the vehement reaction.

---

* "Arguably" because, while some people will support this approach, others (the free-speech advocates) will be much more attracted to providers who do not have such cutoff policies.

One view of this liability issue contends that where the user interface runs is a major factor in determining the person or organization that can be held liable. At a store-and-forward only news site, the liability is believed to only extend to messages that actually originate within the organization, and not to messages that are sent to it by its customers. However, providing shell accounts could cause an assumption of liability for any messages originating from any of those accounts.

A related issue concerns the injection point of new messages into the news stream. When you provide access to a newsreader server that accepts new postings, the user interface is not within your organization, but the real injection point into the news stream for customer messages is the server at your site, rather than a server at the customer site. However, *Cubby v. CompuServe* held that CompuServe was *not* liable for defamatory statements in a newsletter published in one of their forums, because they did not exercise any editorial control over the messages uploaded to them. So it would seem that the actual injection point is not considered relevant by the courts.

Don't forget that the current test of obscenity in American courts is the "Community Standards" rule. As a hub site, you could well be held liable in the most prudish jurisdiction that you feed, even if you live in one of the most tolerant parts of the country. This happened in *US v. Thomas*, when a California bulletin board system was found responsible for material that was deemed obscene in Tennessee, which is where investigators accessed it—seemingly just to be able to prosecute in a far more conservative venue.

If this whole area is of concern to you, you might consider signing up for one of the Computers and the Law courses given at conferences like Usenix. These courses provide a lot of information on the current state of legal affairs on the Net and allow you to get some cheap advice from experts in the field.

11.3.2 Problem Articles

There are many different kinds of articles that cause problems for people on the Net: copyrighted material, forgeries, *sendsys* bombs, excessively crossposted articles, excessively multiposted articles, looping gateways, and broken automatic message generators are a few of the annoyances that we've seen. How you handle these problems when your site is involved goes a long way toward establishing what sort of neighbor you are in the Usenet community, and could determine whether you end up in court having to defend your actions.

First, let's look at some of the different types of problem articles and why they are widely considered to be problems. Some are illegal, but most are merely antisocial, violating the more commonly accepted rules of netiquette.

Copyright Violation

This is pretty self-explanatory: the articles contain information that is reproduced in violation of the original author's copyright. As discussed in Section 15.6.8, copyright can become a very ambiguous legal matter, even when you are expert in it, which most people aren't. Some violations are so egregious, however, that there is absolutely no question that copyright has been violated.

Forgery

A forgery is a message that has the real identity of the sender hidden through a deliberate alteration of the From header. The real identity might appear elsewhere, but it's the From header that matters most. A forgery is different from the type of third party posting that is sanctioned in the RFCs, in which the Sender header is supposed to identify the real sender. In a legitimate third party posting, the sender should also remark in the body of the message that it is a third-party post, to allay any undue suspicion. In a forgery, the real sender is trying to hide, so the body of the message is not going to contain any such remark.

Some people consider an article appearing in a moderated group without the moderator's approval to be a forgery, even if the Approved header uses the sender's real identity, not the moderator's, based on the idea that someone else's use of the header is a perversion of the system. (Indeed, some readers of the group will believe that the moderator posted the message, no matter what is in the Approved header.)

Excessive Multiposting

Commonly called "spam," excessive multiposting (EMP) is an increasingly common form of Net abuse. It is the posting of an article to many newsgroups, one at a time. To stereotype them, the articles are very often soliciting money, and are usually not even remotely appropriate to most of the groups to which they are posted. Sometimes the "spammer" makes a token attempt to change the introductory text of the message to be somehow relevant to the groups to which he is posting, but that is rare.

Excessive Crossposting

Less commonly known as "velveeta," excessive crossposting (ECP) is practiced by marginally more responsible Net abusers. It has many of the same characteristics as "spam," but instead of being individually posted many times, the Newsgroups header includes multiple groups. The Breidbart Index (BI) measures the excessiveness (both ECP and EMP) of an article. It is calculated as the sum of the square roots of the group count of each posting of an article. Thus, an article posted seven times to nine groups each would have a BI of 21. Many people consider a BI of 20 or more a clear indication of network abuse.

sendsys Bomb

As discussed in Section 3.2.4, this involves the forging of a *sendsys* control message, so that a victim is bombarded with news feed files automatically mailed from around the world. A similar attack can be launched with *senduuname* or *version* messages, though the reply from each site to those control messages is considerably smaller.

Looping Gateway

When a gateway between mail and news is misconfigured, it can result in the same message appearing over and over and over again, perhaps thousands of times if the people who can stop it aren't aware of the problem for just a few hours. Gatewaying issues are discussed in Chapter 14, *Gatewaying.*

Broken Message Generator

Programs that automatically post messages without human intervention have the potential to become Net abusers. Consider, for example, a process that scans a staging area for articles to post, then removes them when they have been posted (some moderated groups use this general sort of mechanism). When a message shows up in the staging area, but for some reason cannot be removed after it is posted, it becomes the Energizer Bunny of digital communication. Broken message generators are often associated with mail-to-news gateways because of misdirected bounce messages.

Forged messages are the worst offense among problem articles because the person who is ultimately responsible has taken deliberate steps to hide his identity while causing some sort of problem for others. Those "others" could easily include you, if people think that your site had something to do with the forgery. Not surprisingly, a forgery is often part of another type of problem message.

As a news administrator, you have a social responsibility to help people track down the real origin of forged messages that may have involved your site. The easiest way to do this is to keep good records of the origin of every message you receive. The Path header is not enough; you need additional logging information to identify the site that really sent you a message. Fortunately, INN's configuration provides the `IPADDR_LOG` option to enable the logging of every message accepted based on the IP address of the site that sent it to you. Furthermore, if you have received the message via UUCP, INN can log it based on the name of the UUCP site that sent it to you. With C News, unfortunately, the link between the host and its IP address is broken by the separation between C News and NNTP, so the Path header is all you have to go on.

The various news logs have time stamps that allow you to precisely pinpoint when a transfer occurred, so that you can contact the administrator of the sending site to have them research who might have been responsible for creating it there. Of course, if their log just verifies that the Path header is valid from them to you, you can pass on that information to have them trace it further down the line.

You should note that forgery is distinct from anonymous publication, though sometimes it's hard to tell whether someone is trying to be anonymous or whether she is really trying to represent someone else. The Supreme Court of the United States has held that anonymous publication is a constitutionally protected form of speech. Of course, the U.S. Constitution describes what rights the government cannot take from its citizens, not what citizens can do to each other, but that won't stop some people from screaming long and loud about any form of censorship.

Your temperament in dealing with problem articles can go a long way toward achieving a satisfactory and lasting resolution. Keep in mind that *most* problem articles are not sent with malice aforethought; they usually occur because of ignorance. Even the fairly serious information-age crime of copyright violation is often done by well-meaning people who don't realize that they are breaking the law. (It is surprising how widely misunderstood copyright protections still are.) Jumping down the throats of transgressors quite naturally puts them in a combative mood; a calm discussion of the problem may go a lot further toward educating them about the problem and perhaps even eliciting an apology.

Of course, there are still bozos out there who never will understand or who are purposefully trying to get a rise out of people. In the latter case, it's best to treat them just as you would in the schoolyard: don't let them get a rise out of you. If you're not feeling noble enough to do this out of long-suffering patience, do it out of secret malice instead. Nothing annoys these clowns more than watching the intended victim persistently ignore the bait. In our opinion, many of the enduring flame wars on the Net would have much briefer lifetimes if the antagonizers just weren't given the satisfaction of seeing others get agitated.

As far as *sendsys* bombs are concerned, you can help defend against them by not allowing automatically generated replies to *sendsys* requests. With both C News and INN, you can configure your system to mail you any *sendsys* requests, so you can determine which to honor and which to ignore. There probably won't be more than a couple of valid requests per year, if that. Don't just go by what the body of the request says, though: consider the whole article, including its circulation, to determine whether it's someone genuinely mapping a regional hierarchy.

If your site somehow becomes responsible for problem articles, either because you are running a broken gateway or have a user injecting a stream of excessively posted articles, your first task should be to stop the problem. The easiest way to do this is to turn off the program or to block the user who is sending the messages. Then work to make sure the problem doesn't happen again, either by fixing the program or by getting the people responsible for the creation of the articles to knock it off. Easy, right?

Actually, managing the scene in your own backyard can be considerably easier if you are just a private company that isn't providing public access to your services. You can generally establish quite restrictive policies about what is acceptable use of your company's resources without concern for legal retribution: an employee's right to free speech does not extend to being able to say whatever he wants on your letterhead or by using your photocopier. Canceling an unacceptable message that originates from your site is within your rights, as is reprimanding or even firing an employee who just won't behave responsibly. (It should go without saying, however, that doing this capriciously can have a seriously negative impact on employee morale, and possibly even provoke legal challenges.)

To keep up with the ongoing fight against Net abuse, especially excessively posted articles, you can read the newsgroups in the *news.admin.net-abuse* hierarchy:

news.admin.net-abuse.bulletins
> A moderated group that sends bulletins of actions about Net abuse

news.admin.net-abuse.email
> A discussion forum on the abuse of email systems

news.admin.net-abuse.misc
> For discussing network facility abuse, including spamming

news.admin.net-abuse.policy
> A moderated group for the discussion of Net abuse policy

news.admin.net-abuse.sightings
> A moderated group for sightings of Net abuse

news.admin.net-abuse.usenet
> A discussion forum on the abuse of Usenet

The *news.admin.net-abuse.bulletins* group primarily publishes reports about messages that have crossed numeric thresholds for how many groups an article should "reasonably" appear in; that determination is made without any attention to content. The spam fighters don't care whether it was a missing child plea or a Make Money Fast Advertisement. They just combat the egregious abuse of Net resources, and they consider this content-free decision making process to be their key defense against lawsuits.

If you want to monitor for problem articles originating from your own site, consider running a scanning program from your *sys* or *newsfeeds* file. One program that does this, *spamfind*, is available at:

```
http://spam.abuse.net/spam/tools/cancel.txt
```

In this chapter:
- *Plenty of Power*
- *Maintaining the Active File*
- *Dealing with Your Feed*
- *Record Keeping*

12

Leaf Nodes

A leaf node is a site that does not serve as a pathway for articles between other sites. The only articles it sends to its neighbors are locally generated ones. Although leaf nodes can have multiple incoming feeds, they are most commonly fed by only one peer. If this description fits your site, this chapter could help make your job easier.

Leaf nodes might not garner the prestige of the high-volume pumping stations that serve as the main conduits for getting network news around the world, but they do have things a lot easier in many regards. Sitting on the trunk of the tree, the administrators at major nodes have to spend a lot more time and money on the resources necessary to manage the flow of news through their sites. Leaf nodes, on the other hand, have the luxury of being able to set up their news systems to run with little to no administrative intervention for months, or even years, on end.

We believe that this book has more than enough information about network news in it to make you a news guru. However, we also recognize that if you're like ninety percent of the other folks in the world, you're probably not so deeply interested in news that you are digesting every sentence in this book from cover to cover. More than likely, you've read the setup and basic operation chapters for your particular system fairly closely, and now are referring to the sections you think you need as different problems arise. Fair enough, we read manuals that way too.

What we'd like to do now is provide some tips to help keep you from being a permanent novice when it comes to news administration. We'd like to have you progress to the Intermediate Rut, that competent, if not exactly impressive, level of proficiency that's experienced by amateur athletes in countless sports around the world. The result should be a news system that you can ignore most of the time, and deal with expediently when things need to be adjusted or problems arise.

This chapter discusses what to do if you want to run the news system on a leaf node on "autopilot" and not have it bother you. We'll look at how to maintain adequate resources and deal with adding and deleting newsgroups.

12.1 Plenty of Power

If one of your goals is to have minimal human intervention with the news system once you get it running, you're going to have to make sure that you have plenty of system resources to handle the relentless growth of network news. This requires a bit of over-engineering to handle the inevitable fluctuations in volume, but with liberal predictions of growth and conservative specifications of what you want, it can be accomplished.

12.1.1 Disk Space

Perhaps the biggest perpetual problem with news systems is the rate at which they swallow ever-increasing amounts of disk space. While the traffic in certain groups may decrease in volume, these groups are few and far between. Most groups will show a slight increase in traffic over time. The real growth problem is the continual addition of new groups within broader hierarchies. At least as a leaf node, you don't have to worry about outgoing feed lists consuming major chunks of disk space like they do at hubs.

12.1.1.1 Accept only groups with local interest

The best way to ensure a slow growth rate is to be exceptionally specific about the groups that you want to receive. Rather than asking for all of the *comp.graphics* hierarchy, only ask for those groups in the hierarchy that interest the people at your site. This is often done by people who have to pay for the volume of news that they receive, especially UUCP-only sites that have to pay for connection time to their peers.

There is, of course, a downside to this method of specifying every group you want. As the interests of your users migrate, or the groups get reorganized and their usual traffic migrates, your site can end up not carrying the groups that are desired. There are some tools that can help, like the *arbitron* program for measuring group readership, or *dynafeed* for measuring readership and notifying your news feed of any changes. Both of these programs are available in the UUNET archives (*ftp://ftp.uu.net/* in *networking/news/misc/* and *vendor/ClariNet/sources/* respectively). Integrating them seamlessly into your environment for automatic adjustments to your news feed could take quite a bit of effort, though, especially if you have NNTP newsreaders to figure into the equation.

A more realistic approach is to take advantage of the hierarchal nature of Usenet (it was designed that way for a reason), but be very particular about what you take and especially avoid hierarchies that tend to have radical fluctuations in daily volume. Also avoid hierarchies that frequently add new groups, whether they are coming about by means of reorganizations or not. The usual experience in Usenet is that if a group splits into four, it isn't long before you have four times the volume that you originally had, rather than one fourth of the original volume in each new group.

If you need slow growth, you probably want to avoid getting all of the groups in some of the large second-level hierarchies. For example, *soc.culture*, *sci.med*, *rec.sport*, *comp.sys*, and *comp.os* all have numerous proposals for new groups throughout the year. Only take these entire hierarchies if you can handle moderate growth on the order of a doubling in traffic volume every year and a half. If you can handle even more growth than that, you are at your leisure to take all of *alt*, which would be sheer folly if you need more measured growth. The *alt.binaries* hierarchy is notably the worst on Usenet, both for sheer size and wild fluctuations in the daily volume. Many an administrator has cursed that hierarchy when having to deal with filled disks.

12.1.1.2 Get disks much bigger than needed

The easiest and most flexible solution for dealing with the volume of news articles is to buy and use the biggest disks that you can. Your goal should be to start with your disks at less than 25% full, if you don't want to have to deal with full partitions and changing expiration times over the next few years.

Add up how much disk space you'll need for the hierarchies that you want and the amount of time that you want to keep them—the Usenet Calculator at *http://www.netpart.com/free97/usenet.html* should help you with this. Multiply that total by four. This amount of space should get you to the next month without any disk shortages!

But seriously, based on past growth patterns, that amount of space should be sufficient for the next two and a half years (maybe a few months less if you're taking *alt* or a few months more if you're not taking major *alt* subhierarchies). The overall volume of network news was doubling roughly every 15 months from 1984 to 1995, with a very close fit to the curve of actual measurements. Since about mid-1995, overall volume has been doubling in less than a year, sometimes as quickly as nine months. A plateau seems inevitable, but no one knows when that will be and no end is in site.

Make sure that your disks aren't just big; they also need to have reasonable access times for the amount of load you are planning to put on them. If you're getting only a few thousand articles per day and have only a couple of readers, even the

slowest modern disks should be able to support your system. But if you are supporting an entire battalion of readers with hundreds of groups and a hundred
thousand articles per day, the disks should be near the upper end of the reliable,
high-speed scale.

You might also consider spreading out your spool space across multiple drives, if
you want to support high volume nearly effortlessly. In this situation, you could
put the widely variant hierarchies like *alt.binaries* on one partition with a greater
amount of free space reserved above the expected daily volume. Better yet, if your
operating system supports metapartitioning by combining parts of several drives
into one filesystem, that's almost always the best way to go. An additional benefit
is that smaller disks are usually faster than the very high capacity drives. See the
discussion of splitting the news tree in Section 2.7.1.

12.1.1.3 Run expire on a floating schedule

The last disk space matter to consider is that of how to run *expire* to reclaim the
space being used by old articles. If one day your disks are nearly full, all it might
take is a hiccup in the traffic flow to fill them before *expire* runs on the usual fixed
daily schedule.

One way to make your server less sensitive to the volatility in traffic, and to keep
news around the longest, is to run a script once or twice an hour to check how
close you are to filling up. If the amount of free space drops below a certain
threshold, *expire* is run. The threshold that you set should allow sufficient free
space for more news to come in before *expire* actually gets around to removing
articles, since this can take quite a while if your system is heavily loaded or if you
delay article removal by post-processing a list written by *expire*.

C News' *expireiflow* can do this space checking task for you. For INN, we've provided   two   scripts   in   the   O'Reilly   FTP   archive   (available   at
ftp://ftp.oreilly.com/pub/examples/nutshell/musenet) that do essentially the same
thing as C News' *expireiflow* and *doexpire*. They are unimaginatively named
innexpireiflow and *inndoexpire*. You'll need to adjust a couple of pathnames for
your site and ensure that *innexpireiflow* is looking at all of your spool partitions
correctly, but the pair of them should drop into your system pretty easily. Then
you can shorten *news.daily*'s running time (and improve the consistency of its log
reporting interval) with the `noexpire` option, relying on *cron* runs of *innexpireiflow* to manage expiration. Also, if you ever want to run *expire* manually, *inndoexpire is a much easier way of doing it than trying to use news.daily.*

An even better alternative for article space management is *dexpire*, freely available
at *ftp://ftp.ee.lbl.gov/dexpire.tar.Z*. This package, originally designed by Craig Leres
for C News and since ported and improved for INN, has a different, and arguably
more sensible, approach to article expiration policies. Rather than focusing on the

number of days articles should be kept, it instead concentrates on how much disk space news is using. It still allows you to keep some groups longer than others by assigning them a numeric measure of their relative importance to you. People running *dexpire* virtually never encounter a problem with a filled spool disk, even when an enormous burst of news following extended down time completely skews the normal distribution of article ages. *dexpire* is expected to be integrated into the next INN release.

12.1.2 Network Bandwidth

Network bandwidth practically goes hand in hand with disk space matters, and might actually become more of a problem if you have to work with a low bandwidth channel or a long network path to your feed. Occasionally, you need to check just how much time your system spends receiving news, and make sure there's room for growth. If you don't have a sizeable margin to handle increased traffic, you'll have trouble soon. See Section 2.2.2 for a more complete discussion of bandwidth issues.

Once again, the best way to ensure that there's room for growth is overkill. Get a better connection than you need and write yourself a reminder to upgrade it occasionally so you stay ahead of the game.

Do be realistic about how much traffic your link can support, both in terms of news and all of the other traffic it is expected to handle. If you are running an extremely popular Web site at the end of a 28.8K SLIP line, you're just not going to be able to support a large incoming feed. Open the purse for a fatter pipe to the rest of the world, or resign yourself to a greatly reduced feed.

12.1.3 CPU

Unless you have an unusually high number of readers, the CPU power required by a modern news system is a comparatively minor load on a modern machine. It is unusual for a news system to be dominated by CPU time, except for those that do a lot of compressed batching or allow pull-style NNTP feeds such as via the NNTP *newnews* command.

The load of a news system is still greater than zero, however, and it creeps up with each additional, simultaneous NNTP newsreader that the machine supports. If you are getting a small feed to serve only a handful of readers, you can run news on a 386 PC clone or a Sun 3 and still support other services, like general shell access, DNS, or a small FTP archive service. On the other hand, if you want anything approaching a full feed, or have many simultaneous NNTP newsreaders to support, you should plan on dedicating a higher horsepower machine to news. If you want news to be something you can ignore, this machine should have some horsepower for you to grow into, as your organization grows and news traffic increases.

12.1.4 Memory

If you're using C News, you can probably skimp a little on memory. C News was engineered to run as efficiently as possible on small systems. Your memory requirements do increase for each process supporting an NNTP newsreader, though.

INN expects memory to be plentiful on the system, and it wants to keep as much in memory as it can to run as fast as it can. It especially wants to have very fast access to the *history* file, and that file can get big (see Section 2.2.1.1 for some numbers). INN wants to put major parts of this database in memory if possible, and the more that fits in RAM without the additional burden of swapping, the happier your system will be. You should figure that *innd* consumes memory equal to at least 8-10% of the size of the *history* file, and that you also need 2-3% of the size of the *history* file for the rebuilds done by *expire*. Double the size numbers to determine what your requirements will be in 15 months, and set up the machine accordingly.

One tricky problem here is that your system, as normally configured, may not let a single process use as much memory as it wants. Often there are per-process limits on data size. If *innd* cannot fit within the per-process limit, performance will suffer badly. The superuser can raise these limits, but the details of this can be awkward and system-specific, especially since it's common for only some of the shells (command interpreters) on a system to support limit control. It may be necessary to modify *rc.news* to invoke *innd* in a way that permits raising the limit, for example by using the *limit* command that now comes built into many shells.*

12.2 Maintaining the Active File

If you dream of having no administrative involvement with your news system beyond the initial setup, the biggest problem that you face is the responsible maintenance of the list of newsgroups at your site. As discussed in Section 3.3, keeping this list up-to-date is important.

Keeping abreast of the commonly accepted changes to the namespace is not terribly difficult, but it does involve a little time investment. If you try to limit your feed to subhierarchies and groups, instead of taking entire top-level hierarchies, the job may be a little easier.

---

* Some shells call it *ulimit* or another similar name.

Make sure you're actually getting control messages for the groups or subhierarchies you receive. That should help keep your system more or less current. Occasionally, you should go to one of the alternative sources of newsgroup lists and do a *checkgroups*, as discussed in Section 3.3.

12.3 Dealing with Your Feed

Your feed site probably doesn't have a contractual obligation to help you run your news system. If they aren't a paid service provider, they don't have much of an obligation to even give you a news feed. While paid service providers have to be available to make sure that your news is coming through and that your feed is adjusted as often as you want it to be, sites that give feeds away need only maintain them at their convenience.

No matter what your relationship with your upstream feed, you don't want your site to be a problem to them. The best way to ensure that you aren't a problem is to make sure that your site is up and able to receive news as much as possible. You should also make sure that the size of your feed is realistic for how fast you are able to transfer news. The easiest way for you to become a problem is to have an ever increasing backlog of articles filling up your feed's outgoing directory, which forces them to have to deal with space problems on their disks.

If you are the benefactor of a free feed, you should probably minimize your requests to change the groups that you are fed, updating your feed perhaps only a few times per year. The administrator at the other end is probably not a full-time network news administrator; she might be trying to devote only as much time to news as you are at your leaf node. She might be on vacation, consumed with her "real" job, or otherwise unable to update your feed quickly. Allow a liberal amount of time (at least a week or two) for communication. In the unusual event of a real emergency, don't be afraid to take whatever steps you need to, whether denying transfer permission for the site or phoning the upstream site to apprise them of troubles.

If you get your feed from a service provider, it is fair for you to expect to be able to change your feed whenever you like. It might take your provider a day to process your request, along with the requests of their other customers, but it shouldn't take longer than that. Even if you are changing your feed every day, most providers won't even notice the frequency of your requests.

It is likely, though by no means certain, that if your upstream feed is a site that supports many outgoing feeds, the administrator there is more experienced with running network news systems. If you've got a problem, he may well be familiar with it and be able to deal with it quickly, if you supply the necessary information. Before you get on the phone or send email, collect all the information that might be relevant—log entries, dates and times when things happened, any odd things that happened around the same time (even if they don't seem relevant at first glance), details of your system configuration, etc.—and organize it. While you don't want to inundate the person with unneeded information, it's a lot easier and quicker for him to sort through excessive information and find the relevant items than to keep having to ask for things you left out. Besides, it's surprising how often collecting and organizing this information leads you to discover the solution.

12.4 Record Keeping

Record keeping is important for any news system. If you have only infrequent involvement with your news system, however, keeping records of what you do is even more important because you have less intimate familiarity with the system. Administrators around the Net also hope that, when you are no longer the care-taker, the system will not just go on complete autopilot but will be managed by a a responsible successor. That successor will need to know how you've set the system up and why you've done whatever you've done with it. To this end, at least some elementary record keeping is desirable, and a version control system is rec-ommended.

In terms of basic notes, you should keep readily available the versions of various software pieces that you have installed and where you have installed them (both machines and filesystem locations). It is especially important to keep track of any system files you have updated. For example, you probably had to update your system boot procedure to run some startup script for the news system, and may have had to update *inetd.conf* to run an NNTP server. You should also save the news system *crontab* information and any *syslog* configuration you added.

A revision control package is useful in many situations, quite apart from maintain-ing network news. Using SCCS, RCS, or a similar package to track changes to important files in your news system is good insurance against major headaches. You need not put all news configuration files under version control, and you should at least do so for the ones that are most likely to change. Try not to make any changes to the news feed configuration, expiry control, access list, and control message authorization files without checking the revisions into the system.

Finally, it is a good idea to save all correspondence with your feed provider, or indeed any messages you write about the news system. While it is probably true that you'll never look at the majority of the messages again, you might be sur-prised at what useful bits of information end up in otherwise ordinary messages. A quick *grep* over the archived messages could save you hours of trying to find the answer to a question. As Santayana said, "Those who cannot remember the past are condemned to repeat it."

In this chapter:
- *Volume, Volume, Volume*
- *Transmitters*
- *Additional Automation*
- *The Political View*

13

Hub Nodes

Hub nodes are the sites that are responsible for transporting news between all of the various news systems that comprise Usenet. While sites that only pass news between two other neighbors are included in that definition, this chapter is really aimed at major news hubs. Those are sites that feed anywhere from a dozen to several hundred other sites, sending out far more articles than they receive, and that often act as the sole link into Usenet for many leaf nodes. This chapter covers common technical issues as well as the more notable political issues faced by hub sites. We'll use the term "customer" throughout this chapter to refer to the sites that you feed, regardless of whether they're actually paying you for the service.

Before you read this chapter, you should read Chapter 12, *Leaf Nodes.* Most of the issues that affect leaf nodes apply to hubs, simply on a much larger scale. For example, if you need to provide connectivity 24 hours per day, 7 days per week, you want to have your system running without the frequent and unpredictable need for your intervention. Similarly, keeping your *active* file up to date is more important than it is on a leaf node because you set an example for all of the sites you feed.

Both C News and INN are quality software systems. They were programmed under slightly different software engineering paradigms, but nevertheless, they are largely free of glaring bugs and are fairly responsible about thorough error checking with meaningful messages.* Although some MIS types may disdain free software as a disaster waiting to happen because "you get what you pay for," both of these packages can serve as a solid basis for production services. Granted, you will

---

* While C News and INN themselves are pretty solid, some of the auxiliary packages we'll be discussing are not so well done or well shaken down, so they require more careful watching.

probably need to do some tweaking to really get the most out of your environment, but the source code is provided, so this is not difficult.

Dealing with the deluge of news that flows through a hub node is no trivial task. If you feed a few dozen or more active sites and view network news as a significant service, expect news administration to be a full-time job, whether it's handled by one person or spread out among several. The people working on news should be technically savvy, competent at programming, and willing to dig up a lot of answers on their own by combing RFCs and the source code.

13.1 Volume, Volume, Volume

To Usenet old timers, daily traffic of 850,000 messages, totaling nearly 9 gigabytes, seems like fantastic numbers. To have one single machine not only taking that much in, but also redistributing it 15 times or more in a mere 24 hours, was inconceivable on the affordable technology of the 1980s.

A hub site has to deal with the exponentially increasing number of newsgroups, articles, and megabytes involved with network news. In addition, a growing hub site has to deal with an ever swelling number of peers and quite possibly an expanding battery of machines whose only mission is to provide network news services.

13.1.1 Allocating Machine Resources

Chapter 12 gave an overview of how to calculate the resources you need to keep from having to continually upgrade news machines. The two most important resources you want to load up on are disk space and memory. If you're providing a lot of compressed news feeds, you also want a high-horsepower CPU. It goes without saying that you need considerable network bandwidth to run a hub site. You shouldn't even think of being a medium-volume hub unless you have at least a T1 network link; high volume NNTP hubs often have the bandwidth of some combination of T1s, T3s, direct links, FDDI rings, and 10Mbps ATM networks. This chapter also assumes that you are using INN on a machine that has multiple NNTP sources sending it news; C News with the NNTP Reference Implementation is just not a realistic option in this scenario. (However, that doesn't put C News totally out of the equation, as we'll describe shortly.)

The disks you allocate for news should be big enough to hold enough news for the oldest articles that most of your customers want to receive. Tradition seems to peg this number at about two weeks, although one service provider did an unscientific survey about this a few years ago and came up with three days as the most commonly given age. The disks should be quick (with a decent bus, such as Fast SCSI, facilitating the transfers into the system), especially on seeks, because article data is accessed in hundreds of thousands of reads of little files scattered all over the filesystem. Since most large feed systems are disk bound, you want to spread the spool across as many disk controllers as you can. You will probably find utilities like Sun's OnLine: DiskSuite to be helpful here for creating meta-partitions that span multiple drives but appear as one single filesystem, thus avoiding the reduced efficiency of symbolic links. Several other operating systems provide similar metapartitioning tools.

You are going to need gobs of memory to process incoming news, because the server wants to keep the hash table for its very large *history* file in directly accessible memory for fast lookups. In addition, the *active* file and data buffers for each incoming feed eat up some memory, as does the process for outgoing news. A large filesystem cache in fast, random access memory (RAM) is also a tremendous boon for the system. If you are running a large site, we advise that at least 96 megabytes of RAM is the minimum starting point for a server, 128 megabytes is good, and even more is desirable.

The latency of the NNTP *IHAVE* dialogue can be a problem for sites that are trying to take a lot of articles over a relatively small network pipe. Many people believe that the only way to address this with the current NNTP specification is by having concurrent NNTP sessions from the provider to the recipient, thereby keeping the aggregate data channel active more of the time. If you decide to go this route, remember that every site that gets multiple feeds consumes more memory, CPU power, and continuous network bandwidth at the feeding server. Some of the leaf sites you feed are going to be running C News, which performs poorly when NNTP accepts many duplicates, so you probably don't want to just start up dual feeds to those sites if those dual feeds are offering the same articles. Splitting one article list to multiple pipes should work well.

Although not an official part of the NNTP specification, the streaming extension (see Section 19.5.3) that is available in INN and several commercially available news servers tries to address the latency problem by changing the lockstep nature of the transmission protocol. If you can use that streaming extension from your site to the the receiver, you should be able to reap the most out of your bandwidth without using as much increased resource consumption as you would find with multiple parallel processes.

Note that if you use the *innfeed* transmitter, discussed in Section 13.2.2, you will still see increased local resource consumption if you enable multiple parallel connections to the remote sites. If a remote site is using streaming too, these multiple connections are not really helping the remote site any, so it is better for you to disable parallel feeding for streaming recipients. If anything, multiple streaming connections from one site penalize other sites feeding that remote site by unfairly gaining more time for themselves.

On average, the computer resources you need to support your clients should grow in direct proportion to each new feed you add. As a function of the existing capacity, this increased demand on the resources probably won't become evident until you hit the knee in the curve and performance starts obviously degrading. Depending on your hardware and operating system, this degradation could be only a progressive worsening of service or as bad as a precipitous drop.

13.1.2 Mirroring

If you've reached the point where upgrading your existing news machine just can't provide the needed resources, you have to tell all of your customers to go away. If that doesn't sound like a particularly desirable solution, you should consider setting up slave news servers to distribute the load. With a master/slave system, also known as a "mirroring" system, one host, the master, becomes the sequencing host, responsible for giving each article a unique filesystem identity—its filed location—at your site. The master system then redistributes each article to one or more slave systems, which store the articles in each group with exactly the same article numbers.

The alternative to a master/slave system is to have your servers all feed each other as peers. With feeding as peers, the same article will have a different identity on each system. The advantage of the mirroring approach over the feeding as peers approach is that articles have the same identity on all systems. This lets you balance the load of news processing across several servers by allowing you to easily move clients to any news machine within your master/slave system. Being able to move customers at will also makes it easier to recover from system failures.

Mirroring works well with both outbound news feeds and incoming newsreader sessions. Most newsreaders remember articles that have been read based on their filesystem identity, so it is advantageous to have that identity be the same on all systems. By the same token, the pathnames used by the transmitters for outgoing feeds don't need to be recalibrated to determine what articles still need to be sent and what articles were already processed.

INN and C News both provide a mechanism for slave replication, albeit slightly different mechanisms.* With C News, you enable mirroring by having *relaynews* run with the -x option on the master and with the -b option on the slaves. Articles are distributed from the master to the slaves by whatever means you desire. The storage location for the article on the slave system is then determined by parsing the Xref header.

---

* Rich Salz, the author of INN and the *XREPLIC* extension, has been caught saying that he thinks the C News method is better. The next release of INN (version 1.8) will support the C News Xref mechanism.

You do not have to maintain the *active* file on a C News slave system that is only feeding and not providing any newsreader services, because transmitters don't use the *active* file. In fact, C News makes no attempt to update the *active* file even if you do list all of the groups. Thus, if you are providing newsreader services on the slave systems, you have to supplement the system with a periodic copy of the file from the master to the slave.*

INN slave systems, true to their nature, do all final article reception through NNTP. The INN master writes batchlists with the WnR options in the *newsfeeds* file and *innxmit* runs with the -S option to use that batchlist to send *XREPLIC* NNTP commands to the slave. The slave server runs with the -S option to identify the master host. Unlike C News systems, an INN slave's *active* file should have all of the same groups that the master has, as it is updated with each incoming article. In addition, the slave server complains about each article it gets for a group that it doesn't know about but that the master server indicates exists.

There aren't any publicly available packages that help with the task of shifting client services around to balance the load, so you're pretty much stuck with having to roll your own. It isn't that difficult to create some tools to handle this task; it can even be done manually if your load patterns are such that you only need to do it infrequently. Just remember that to ensure complete accuracy, the systems that you are moving feeds between need to be synchronized on their incoming stream of news. If you move a client to a system that is more up-to-date with respect to the master than the one it was previously on, there will be a gap of articles that were never considered for distribution to the feed. Conversely, if you move a feed from a system that was more up to date to one that is less up to date, that will cause articles that have already been queued to be requeued for the site. This second scenario shouldn't be a problem for a properly configured NNTP customer site, but most dial-up UUCP sites won't have a method to keep the duplicates from coming down the wire.

By now, the astute reader will have realized that having only one master server to do article sequencing doesn't scale well in the face of hundreds of NNTP peers who all want to send it articles. Several million *IHAVE* and *CHECK* messages across thousands of NNTP sessions every day can exact quite a toll. You might consider the approach taken by one service provider confronted with this problem. Multiple INN servers, possibly but not necessarily including the master server, all advertise their host addresses as one common name for the set. The non-master incoming servers send the articles that they get to the master for assimilation. This setup

---

* Unless your slave feed is closely in sync with the master, you can end up with windows where the *active* file reflects a maximum article number for a group that corresponds to an article that the slave has not yet processed. This situation dupes newsreader programs into thinking that the article used to exist but has been canceled or expired, and thus should be marked as read.

provides a distribution of the *IHAVE* and *CHECK* load, redundancy in the case of failure by one of the incoming servers, and even continuous incoming services— keeping backlogs from accumulating at sending sites in the event of a failure of the master system.

13.1.3 Hybrid Systems

INN is a clear choice over C News for handling a plethora of simultaneous NNTP peers sending news, but this does not eliminate the possibility of using C News at high-volume sites. In fact, for several years, the most influential site on the Net, in terms of the number of sites that depended on it for their primary news feed, ran a hybrid system. INN accepted incoming articles and C News handled outbound article selection and transmission.

C News' hierarchal newsgroup matching, which it inherited from B News before it, was one of the main reasons for this setup. INN's wildmat newsgroup matching makes it harder to adjust feeds based on group names; in a sense, wildmat pattern matching goes against the grain of the original design intentions of the hierarchal namespace. With C News, it is easier for customer sites that take limited feeds to continue with uninterrupted reception of the areas that interest them, even as those areas reorganize and form subgroups. In our opinion, INN's matching algorithm has not demonstrated any inherent benefits over C News' mechanism.

It can also be argued that continued exposure to both types of news systems helps an administrator to keep informed of how they operate, which makes it easier to help customers who are having difficulty. While this obviously isn't an overwhelming concern, the customer support opportunity should not be overlooked.

The one other major consideration when deciding whether to run C News or INN on the slaves is if you are supporting newsreaders via the slaves. If so, the slaves should probably use INN. For one thing, INN maintains the *active* file on slaves. More importantly, a standard NNTP *IHAVE* feed inherently serializes article processing from reception on the master through filing on the slave, even in the face of common system problems, such as full disks. A C News slave is more likely to receive thousands of articles and push them into a bad batches directory if it has a problem that prevents their filing, while an INN system just flat out refuses to take the articles if it can't file them. When the C News system is fixed, perhaps without human intervention, it just picks up with whatever is still in the *in.coming* directory, possibly skipping dozens of megabytes of otherwise fine articles that it previously punted as bad batches. When the INN slave springs back to life, it just starts accepting articles wherever it left off.

To run a C News system as a slave to an INN server, you need only provide the -x option to have *innd* insert an Xref header in each article, regardless of whether it was crossposted. The C News system should be run as a normal C News slave, interpreting the Xref header of each article for the local storage location.

13.1.4 Tracking Sites

The volume of news isn't the only volume you have to worry about; the growth of your customer base is bound to put additional strain on your personnel resources. For every dozen feeds you start and then never have to deal with again, the Fickle Finger of Fate will push someone your way who needs an extraordinary amount of attention. If they're paying you to give them that attention, they'll expect to hear from you sooner than people who get support for free.

One thing that helps is to have a clear policy statement about your support services. This policy should cover how soon customers should expect a response and just what level of support you are willing to provide (e.g., just news feed maintenance, limited news system consulting, extensive news system consulting). Also include the preferred method of contact. If you have one news administrator who is the sole contact point for all aspects of the system, the telephone should be deprecated in favor of email. You can schedule your day more effectively when you receive email notices than when you have to deal with the constant interruption of phone calls (of course, you probably already know this).

Save all interactions you have with the customers. One of the easiest ways to do this is to have an account name for each, and then save email into an appropriate mail folder named for each account. This makes finding the history of your interaction with a particular customer quick and easy. When you have a telephone conversation with a customer, you can note the highlights in a mail message to yourself and save that too. Finally, if you have to save any important configurations, such as when they have their feed turned off, you can also drop that into a mail message to be saved in the customer's folder.

You might also consider keeping each customer's configuration separate, so that you can assemble it into the necessary system files as needed. This minimizes problems from corrupted or inadvertently removed configurations, and makes it easier to redistribute customers across multiple servers. Additionally, any tools you have to validate the configurations need only be done on small files as customers make changes, rather than on the entire assembled file at the end.

13.1.5 newsxd

newsxd is a software package that can help manage a variety of news transmitters in a central configuration. Although this program is not quite as solidly programmed as C News or INN, it is quite serviceable.

newsxd runs as a daemon. It keeps track of the time, the load, and the number of active transmitters, so that it can control when new transmitters are started. The program is most useful for UUCP batching, where you want to have limits on when the batching is done and the number of batchers that are running concurrently. Furthermore, *newsxd* runs all of the transmitters from one parent process, so it can easily shut them all down or let running ones continue but not start new ones. The status of each transmitter, including when it last ran, its current process ID, or why it isn't running, is readily available through a simple signal interface.

The operation of *newsxd* is controlled by a single configuration file. You define different classes for transmitters and then assign each outgoing feed to a particular class. A `class` specification includes various parameters, such as a limit on the number of simultaneous, active transmitters, an interval for how long the daemon waits before restarting a transmitter for a site after it last ran, and a load limit for running transmitters for that class. The daemon normally only starts a transmitter for a site if it has a batch file indicating that there is work to be done; the `nobatchfile` option causes the program to start a transmitter even if no batch file exists. *newsxd* also tries to rename the batch file to a working name on behalf of the transmitter unless the class option `noworkfile` is specified.

After you define a class, you need to specify the program that is used for that class and any default options that should be passed to the program. The `xmit` line handles the program definition for a class.

The configuration file can also specify some general options, such as the format of batch file and working file names. After you have defined all of the classes and any general options, you specify a `host` line for each feed. The `host` line indicates the class that the feed is in, the times during which the transmitter can be started, and any flags for the transmitter that are peculiar to that host.

Putting all this together, you might have a configuration file that looks something like this:

```
# the transmitter for nntp-fed sites.
# restart after three minutes, run at effectively any load,
# don't need a batchfile to run, and even if there is a
# batchfile don't rename it to a workfile.
# the nntplink program is described in the next section.
class nlink maxxmits=99 interval=180 maxload=150 noworkfile nobatchfile
xmit  nlink /usr/libexec/news/nntplink  nntplink -LU %f %h
# the primary class for uucp-fed sites.
# limit them to five at a time, because they suck up
# a lot of cpu and memory with batching.  they should
# only check for work once per hour, and can't run
# if the load is over 20, which might happen in the middle
# of the night when all batchers are trying to run.
# the xmit line includes a flag to limit each run of the
# batcher to produce only about 2MB worth of batches.
```

```
class   batch   maxxmits=5 interval=3600 maxload=20 noworkfile
xmit    batch   /usr/libexec/news/sendbatch sendbatch -p2000000 -c %f %h
# high volume uucp batchers.  run more frequently, every
# half hour.  can run if the load is under 10, and should
# batch to their queue limit (+p)
class   hvbatch maxxmits=3 interval=1800 maxload=10 noworkfile
xmit    hvbatch /usr/libexec/news/sendbatch sendbatch +p -c %f %h
# low volume uucp batchers.  have very small news feeds, and
# run only twice a day, batching to to their queue limit
class   lvbatch maxxmits=2 interval=43200 maxload=150 noworkfile
xmit    lvbatch /usr/libexec/news/sendbatch sendbatch +p -c %f %h
# unbatched uucp feeds.  rather than running uux from the
# sys file as each article is received, sendunbatch will
# properly keep track of queue limits.  newsxd will rename
# the batch input to a work file for processing.
class   unbatch maxxmits=2 interval=900 maxload=150
xmit    unbatch /usr/libexec/news/sendunbatch sendunbatch %f %h

# new work should be checked for every 20 seconds
queueinterval   20
# the format of a batchfile name
batchfile       /news/out.going/%s
# the format of a workfile name
workfile        /news/out.going/%s.work

# low volume site getting uncompress batches (+c)
# no bigger than roughly 10kb each
host    site            lvbatch Any             flags=+c|-s10000
# regular batcher, for transfers non-peak phone rates
host    andthis         batch   Wk1700-0600|SaSu
# regular batcher, non-peak phone in time zone three hours later
host    another         batch   Wk2000-0900|SaSu
# high volume batchers, runs any time of day
host    bigsite         hvbatch Any
# nntp feeds, with additional flags to transmitter
host    news.foo.com    nlink   Any             flags=-s|foo!
host    news.baz.net    nlink   Any             flags=-s|baz!
```

The source code for *newsxd* is available in the UUNET archives (*ftp://ftp.uu.net/networking/news/misc/*). The distribution comes with a complete manual page that describes the syntax of the *newsxd* configuration file and the signals that the daemon understands. Caveat emptor: *newsxd* is an old package that hasn't had a maintainer in years, but several major sites are known to still be using it for production services.

13.2 Transmitters

You set up a hub node to be in the business of pushing a lot of news. There are currently two freely available tools that are much more up to the task of high volume feeding than *innxmit* running from *nntpsend*: *nntplink* and *innfeed*.

13.2.1 nntplink

The *newsxd* configuration file page used the *nntplink* transmitter for sending articles via NNTP. This program has been used by most hub sites as their primary transmitter because it is highly configurable and normally runs perpetually, forwarding news as soon as it receives it. This program is available at:

```
ftp://ftp.math.ohio-state/pub/nntplink/nntplink.tar.gz/
```

nntplink became the primary tool of the Church of Instantaneous Propagation (see Section 2.3) because it can rapidly take note of new articles and forward them as soon as they arrive. Since this program has enabled such rapid distribution of messages, some of your customers will undoubtedly (and perhaps just a little unreasonably, given the original design and intent of Usenet) expect you to provide such instantaneous retransmission. You might be able to get away with using just *nntpxmit* or *innxmit* for a while, but we expect that you'll eventually need to give *nntplink* a test drive.

Usually, *nntplink* starts up, connects to a site, and offers articles as soon as it knows about them (more on how it finds out what to send in a moment). Whenever a certain number of articles have been offered, or the link has had no transmissions for a specified length of time, the network session is closed. Rather than have the process exit like most other transmitters, *nntplink* waits like a daemon for more articles to appear and then re-establishes the connection to send them. Because it knows how to use the *XREPLIC* command, *nntplink* is also suitable for feeding an INN slave system. However, it does not do streaming with *CHECK/TAKETHIS*.

There are four ways for *nntplink* to discover articles to be fed; any given *nntplink* process can only use one of them. The modes are:

batch file

> This is the traditional batch file method used by *nntpxmit* and *innxmit*. To use it, the *sys* or *newsfeeds* file writes article pathnames and message IDs to a batch file. The file is processed much like the way *tail -f* waits for growth of the file, and *nntplink* is careful to synchronize with the article filing process (*relaynews* or *innd*) to ensure that it doesn't mistakenly interpret a temporary end-of-file condition as the real end of the file, since the process that is writing the list might not yet be done.

log file

> This mode works by having *nntplink* interpret the filed article log. The server should write the article pathname to the log file as well as the message ID (a configurable option with INN, not available in C News as distributed). When the log gets rolled, a signal should be sent to *nntplink* to tell it to start

following a new log file. Before it closes the log file it is reading, *nntplink* reads to the end (if it is not already there) and queues the unsent articles into a batch file that it processes before resuming sending articles from the log file. This process can be repeated across multiple log rollings with no intervening articles able to be sent; no messages should be lost.

funnel

Substantially like batch file mode, all *nntplink*-fed sites use a single file in the batch file directory. INN writes the funnel file by having each site that runs this way use a Tm flag in its *newsfeeds* configuration, pointing the multiple entries to a Tf feed that writes a file with one line for each article pathname, message ID, and sites to receive it. Compared to using log file mode, this increases the amount of writing that *innd* does, but reduces the amount of interpretation each *nntplink* has to do with every line. In the long run, for performance it's probably an even contest, but this is definitely the best method to use for delayed feeds (described at the end of this section). Note that the funnel file has to be rolled just as the log file does, or it will eventually consume all of your free disk space. *nntplink* has an auxiliary command script to handle this task.

stdin

With this mode, *nntplink* works by reading pathnames and message IDs on standard input. This is the favorite method of the Church of Instantaneous Propagation acolytes. The process is forked from *innd* as part of the *newsfeeds* configuration, and the necessary data is fed via a normal interprocess pipe. If the transmitter falls behind in sending the articles coming in on the pipe, *nntplink* can be configured to either queue the backlog into a batch file itself or have *innd* queue it. An auxiliary process then feeds the queued backlog while the *stdin*-reading *nntplink* keeps up with the current news.* Because of reliability issues with the pipe between *innd* and *nntplink*, we recommend either log or funnel mode.

nntplink is relatively easy to configure and build; follow the short *INSTALL* file that comes with it. The general configuration for your operating system is done with an automated script, *configure*, that snoops around your compiler, including files, libraries, and more to determine what desired features your system has and what ones *nntplink* has to do without and improvise around. Pathnames and other site-specific policy parameters are defined in an include file, *include/conf.h*. You should check all of the pathnames, so that they are appropriate for how you have

---

* This method breaks the inherent serializing of NNTP feeds described in Section 13.1.3, but unless you're feeding a slave server this is of little consequence.

built the rest of your news system. Most of the numeric configuration options are fine as they are, but you might want to change a few settings, as described below:

BATCHFILE_REWRITE

> This setting controls how often *nntplink* removes already processed lines from the start of the batch file; it is relevant with all input modes because they all write and use batch files if they fall behind. The intention is to save you space while reducing the inefficiency of having *nntplink* frequently rewriting the batchfile. Given the length of the average batch file line, a value of 16,000 discards roughly 1 megabyte of data from the start of the file every time that many articles have been offered to the remote site.

CLOSE_AFTER

> The value of this parameter can be raised to keep the connection active longer, reducing the overhead of dropping and re-establishing sessions. The drawback to this is that it reduces the time granularity of the statistics on the remote end, which may be of concern to the other administrator. Raising LOG_AFTER has a similar effect on the granularity of reporting in your local logs, but doesn't affect the state of open network sessions.

EXIT_TIMEOUT

> This parameter is practically useless in most modern NNTP environments and can be set to NEVER, because most sessions of anything larger than a trivial feed aren't without pending articles long enough to trigger the timeout. It is especially useless with anything but batch file mode, because there aren't very simple ways to tell when you need to start the transmitter again.

ENTRY_SLEEP

> The value of this setting can be lowered to as little as 1 if you want *nntplink* to notice new articles the instant they are available. This has the unfortunate effect of raising the overall amount of operating system calls made into the kernel for feeds that are usually up to date, but if you're not running anything other than news on the machine, you probably can spare it. Don't set this value low if you're using *stdin* mode, however, as *nntplink* already uses the select() system call to detect data the instant it is available.

FAKESYSLOG

> This parameter is useful even if you have *syslog* because it arguably saves your system a little extra work by not shipping messages through another process, *syslogd*, before dumping them in a file. Of course, you lose some of the configurability of *syslog*, but you might not need it.

SAVE_ART_FAILS

> This setting isn't very useful unless you plan to use the batch lists of failed articles *nntplink* generates when SAVE_ART_FAILS is defined. It usually isn't worth the effort to process them, so you'll just end up with a bunch of annoying files of valueless data cluttering your batch file directory.

Once *nntplink* is operational, the *links* script in its support directory can help manage it by starting site transmitters, shutting them down, and telling them to reopen their input sources. The previously mentioned *newsxd* program is also useful for starting and stopping *nntplink* sessions without having to spend a lot of effort rummaging through the system process table. Even if you choose to use *newsxd*, you should keep *links* around so that you can send signals to all of the *nntplink* transmitters at once, such as to age the log or funnel file or have the transmitters reopen their FAKESYSLOG file.

You should include a *links clear* command in the boot procedure of your system before any process that starts *nntplink* sessions, because *nntplink* notes its running process ID in a file to lock against duplicate invocations. If the system crashes and *nntplink* does not have a chance to shut down gracefully, the ID is not cleared out of the file and could inadvertently block a transmitter from starting after the reboot. This might occur if another process acquires the ID before the new *nntplink* gets a chance to determine that the cached ID is bogus and that it should start anyway.

There is one last nifty feature of *nntplink* that bears mentioning. The -y option enables delayed feeding of articles, inhibiting *nntplink* from feeding an article until a specified amount of time has passed. "Hmm!" you might be thinking. "Why would the acolytes of the Church of Instantaneous Propagation want that?" They don't. It's the deacons of the Church of Conservative Redundancy that want it. If a site is acting as the backup feed for another site, this feature enables them to not have to send any articles in most cases.

For example, say *news.foo.com* wants to get their news primarily from their service provider, but wants the additional reliability of a backup feed from *news.bar.org*. The *nntplink* at *news.bar.org* can run with -y 3600, so it does not offer articles to *news.foo.com* until at least an hour after their arrival. In that time, the article will presumably be offered by the service provider, so the articles offered by *news.bar.org* will mostly be refused as duplicates. In the event that the feed from the service provider is interrupted, however, *news.foo.com* continues to receive news (slightly delayed) via *news.bar.org*. This may even help the service provider catch up on the backlog faster when it recovers, because *news.foo.com* will initially refuse the articles it has already received from the *news.bar.org* backup feed. If you want to use the delayed feed option, funnel mode is the best method.

13.2.2 *innfeed*

There is a new program that is replacing *nntplink* as the dominant high-volume news transmitter on the Net. The *innfeed* program, written by James Brister for the Internet Software Consortium, runs as a single process to handle all outgoing NNTP news feeds. It can open multiple, parallel NNTP channels to a receiving site, as well as use the streaming protocol (see Section 19.5.3) to improve the through-put of each NNTP session.

innfeed is not documented in this book because at the time of its writing the program was still in beta test and not officially released. Its configuration and some major aspects of its operation are still quite subject to change. The current beta version of *innfeed* also has a problem with giving insufficient attention to non-streaming peers that must be resolved.

Despite its beta status, several high-volume sites are very happy using *innfeed* in production services as their primary transmitter. Many of those sites are running patched code that isn't even the most recent official beta release, however, which just illustrates the problem with documenting *innfeed* in this book.

If you want to experiment with *innfeed*, you can get the software from *ftp://ftp.isc.org/isc/inn/innfeed*. Eventually, though, *innfeed* will be integrated into the INN distribution. You should also subscribe to *innfeed-users@vix.com* by sending an email message with a body of only `subscribe` to *innfeed-users-request@vix.com*. Archives of all the previous traffic on that mailing list can be found at *http://www.eerie.fr/~news/innfeed/*.

We do have one suggestion to make regarding the use of *innfeed*. Please don't use streaming with more than two or three parallel feeds for a site. It generally leads to degraded performance on both ends.

13.3 Additional Automation

Running a large hub site can be like a computerized version of the Chinese Water Torture. Each falling drop splashing on your forehead might be trivial in its own right, but the unrelenting sum of them will drive you insane. Operations that only need to be done a couple of times a year at a leaf node are done on a monthly, weekly, or even daily basis at a big installation. Fortunately, the same computer that can increase your workload to frightening proportions can also be made to reduce it to enjoyable levels, leaving you time to hack on interesting new projects.

13.3.1 Monitoring

Monitoring system activity is the first area in which you can improve your news system. Ideally, monitoring tools should take note of real or potential problems and inform the people who can fix them, and more quietly note brief fluctuations and problems for which the system automatically adjusts.

The C News script *newswatch* and INN's *innwatch* are both fair starting points for a monitoring system, but they don't go far enough for a real service provider. Both programs do send email to the news administrator when they detect any anomalies in the items that they check.

newswatch can be instructed to send mail when the number of batches pending in the *in.coming* queue is above a certain threshold, when space is getting a bit too low in some of the news system partitions, or when some locks have been around a bit too long and are likely stale. Some drawbacks of *newswatch* are that it doesn't allow you to specify different free space thresholds on different partitions and it makes no accommodation for consolidating the reports on different directories that share the same disk partition. Another problem revolves around the difficulty of portably determining whether a lock file is stale, which means that *newswatch* has to wait until it's obviously much too old, and that is usually hours after the problem should have been observed and corrected.

innwatch also keeps tabs on the disk space available in different areas, the load average of the machine, and whether *innd* is running. In addition, you can add tasks for *innwatch* to do through the *innwatch.ctl* file. You can add any command you can devise that yields a numeric answer to be compared against a configured constant value. The drawbacks of *innwatch* are the convoluted configuration file and its inability to do much more than some limited control of *innd*.

Of course, these programs are fairly useless if the machine is dutifully blasting warning messages to your mailbox at 4 A.M. when you are home in bed. If you have 24-hour operators monitoring your systems, you can have the email sent to them at the same time as it goes to the news administrators. Just be sure to give them clear procedures for what to do if they get such email, even if it is as simple as calling you. A text pager also comes in handy because you can take the operator right out of the loop (which saves you both extra hassles) and just have the information you initially want automatically delivered by the news system straight to your pager.

So if the C News and INN watchers aren't really complete, what else should you monitor? Here are some more things that can give you a picture of the health of your news system:

- *Incoming news being processed.* Use the log of individual articles received, written by *relaynews* or *innd*. Keep a history of the number of articles processed per minute, so the general performance can be noted and the monitoring tool can observe deterioration.

- *Incoming NNTP performance.* Twice an hour, have a program connect to the NNTP server, offer ten randomly generated articles in a local (unpropagated) test group, offer the same ten articles over again to be rejected as duplicates, and then cancel them. If the program finds any problems—refused articles or duplicates being accepted—have it send immediate notification. Otherwise, keep note of how long it takes for each of those three operations and how long it takes to start a session, to observe the overall performance that people feeding you will encounter. You can then catch it if it starts deteriorating.

- *Outgoing NNTP sessions working.* Use the log written by *nntpxmit, innxmit,* or *nntplink* to check for connections being made and articles being sent. Serious error messages can be immediately reported rather than appearing in the next day's log summary.

- *Outgoing UUCP batching working.* Use the log written by the batcher and report any unknown (non-statistics) lines as probable errors. If no batching is getting done, it should be remedied as soon as possible.

- *Network interfaces working.* Every hour, write *netstat* statistics to a log file. Packet errors reported for the interface should be reported and, depending on their magnitude, either deferred until your regular working hours or looked at immediately if they're very high. A daily summary can report the ratio of output packet collisions to output packets to track when the network is getting congested. More than a 2% collision rate is a bad sign for getting traffic onto your network.

- *System load.* Several times an hour, or even as often as every minute, write the load averages to a log file. If the load goes ballistic, report it. (Make sure your mailer runs under a very high load.) Otherwise, have a weekly report summarize the load averages by day, hour, and minute to help you adjust the execution times of automatically run jobs to reduce the maximum load peaks.

- *Processes out of control.* Once an hour, analyze the whole system process table to spot processes that are using excessive CPU time or that have grown well beyond their normal memory size. You have to determine what's reasonable on a per-process basis, but this can help you identify problems that aren't so egregiously offensive that they obviously grind everything on the system to a halt, but that are making a notable contribution to performance degradation.

You can also write tools that examine the news system logs by having a process run several times per hour to see if the desired service has been performed as expected. If there is an interruption longer than half an hour or so, have the job send notification of the situation. If you're working on the system and expect some aspect of it to behave abnormally, stop the monitoring on it. You should also have another program that keeps tabs on whether all the monitor processes are configured as expected, in case you forget to turn monitoring jobs back on. Speaking from experience, that's a mistake that's easier to make than you might expect. Finally, remember that these log watcher programs need to be designed to work across log rolling.

13.3.2 Trouble Recovery

There are a couple of problems the system can detect in its regular monitoring that it is able to fix on its own. Having the system handle these situations automatically will save you some effort, and hopefully keep emergency calls to a minimum.

C News uses lock files to handle processes that want to modify the same resources. If, for some reason, one of these lock files is left behind when the process holding it disappears—this doesn't normally happen, but on an unstable system anything is possible—programs wanting to use that locked resource will be stalled until the file is removed. C News programs don't make their own determination that the lock is for a dead process, partly because it's difficult to do this reliably and portably. If you have trouble with this, it may be desirable to have a periodic job that examines lock files. This program should get the process ID from each lock file and see if the process is running. If it is not, the program should then check whether the lock file still exists and if it still contains the same process ID. If so, it can delete the lock file.

WARNING   It is dangerous to break a stale lock like this: the resource that it protects may well have been left in an inconsistent state. It's better to investigate such a problem rather than just wiping the lock away and charging ahead. A standard C News running on a stable system does not lose track of locks; any such occurrence is a sign of trouble. On an unstable system or with experimental software, however, automatic lock breaking may be a necessary evil.

Be very careful of the file server issues involved with detecting stale locks via the process ID method described above. If you are having these locks created over a system like NFS (which is a bad idea), the process ID needs to be checked on, whatever machine created the lock. If your organization is such that you can't be sure which machine created the lock, you cannot effectively check for stale locks this way.

In Section 12.1.1.3, we described a technique for running *expire* as available space dictates, rather than on a rigid schedule. More than any other, this simple change to how expiration is done will probably save you the most time and energy.

You can also use a monitoring tool to keep an eye on the log file partition, removing the oldest log files as space gets short. It can remove the oldest rolled log files until enough free space is available. Be careful not to make the program so aggressive that it removes logs as recent as the previous day. If the logs share the partition with other directories, check the other directories to see if they've grown in size abnormally and need to be addressed, rather than just nuking the logs.

A mysteriously full partition that has more space in use than *du* reports has probably fallen victim to a large, unlinked open file. In the *history* file partition, the most likely suspect is an old newsreader process that held the history file open across an *expire* run. A monitoring process trying to get that space back can identify the problem and mercilessly zap newsreader processes that predate the last expiry.

One of the easiest problems to recuperate from is a daemon that has vanished. Make sure all critical system daemons, like *cron*, *innd*, *innwatch*, and *newsxd*, are checked for by a process run frequently by root. (Obviously, you'll have to devise some method to determine if *cron* itself is the absent daemon, perhaps by having another machine *rsh* in to check.) If a daemon doesn't exist, the monitor should restart it and send mail. The monitor can also note if it has been restarted repeatedly in a short time, and request human intervention to fix whatever the problem is that's causing the daemon to exit so quickly.

The *rc.news* script provided with INN really isn't suitable for restarting *innd* if it exits, because it aggressively does things like remove lock files and *innd*'s control socket. A modified form of it, however, is quite useful. See Section 9.1.2 for our *innd.restart* script.

13.3.3 Feed Updates

Changing the subscribed groups for the sites you feed can be the single most labor-intensive job in running a very large news site. The more that you can get the monotonous task of feed updates out of your duties, the happier you'll be. There are several routes to doing so.

Perhaps the easiest way for you to not have to do feed updates is to just not allow them. This is the policy of at least one major Internet service provider (rumored to be at the behest of the corporate lawyers). Everyone getting news from this provider has a full feed configured, and they have to dump what they want at their own end. Of course, this is tremendously wasteful of resources and is not recommended.

Along the same lines, you can also avoid changing your configuration at all by having the feeds all "pull" their news, as with NNTP's *NEWNEWS* or a method that finds news articles by looking at the *active* file, rather than "pushing" it with NNTP's *IHAVE* or *CHECK*. When sites use this method to transfer news, they control the groups that they want to get and can change them at their whim without any involvement for you. Unfortunately, pull-style feeds pummel your news server for even moderate amounts of traffic (with "moderate" being measured relative to "full," not to "sane"). They are generally not used by service providers because of their poor computing resource utilization.

The second easiest way for you to not have to do feed updates is to have somebody else do them. If your organization is large enough to have a customer support or data entry staff, feed updates could be made a part of their normal duties, so you can have time to actually improve the overall system. This is much better for the computing resources at all of the servers involved, but is still a pretty poor use of human resources.

The best solution for news feed maintenance is to automate it as much as possible, ideally so that the customer can change their feed on the fly without having to get a warm body at your end to do something. There are a few tools available for automating subscription updates on your system; two of them are *gup* and *dynafeed*.

The Group Update Program, *gup*, is available in the UUNET archive (*ftp://ftp.uu.net/networking/news/misc/*). It is designed to edit either INN's *news-feeds* file or C News's *sys* file. The customer site updates their subscription list on your system by sending email commands. *gup* does sanity checks of the requests before implementing them, with security handled by giving each site its own password. The results of any changes are mailed back to the registered administrator of the customer site. The package is not refined (the versions out on the Net are labeled "beta" and are a couple of years old), but it can make a good starting point for remote feed configuration.

Brad Templeton of ClariNet Communications Corp. wrote *dynafeed* with the vision of having a much more dynamic web of group propagation. *dynafeed* is available at *ftp://ftp.clari.net/pub/sources/dynafeed.tar.Z*. The essential idea is that to cut down on unnecessary traffic, a leaf site should only take the groups that its users are reading, an intermediate site should take only those groups that either its own users or users at sites fed by it are reading, and so on up the hierarchical chain. The configuration is based on the same *newsrc* format used by newsreader programs to keep track of what a user is subscribed to and has read, but is for sites instead.

Because the system is designed to keep feeds in individual files, you can give each customer site its own limited account on your machine and let it maintain its own subscription file to subscribe and unsubscribe from groups as desired. You can also use one of the program's packages to take email requests for updating the feed. A nice feature for the client is that when a new group is subscribed, some back articles are sent to give users some immediate context for the group.

The *dynafeed* system is several years old now and admittedly has not gotten very widespread use, but don't let that stop you from looking closer to see whether it might be useful in your own corner of the Net. If you do decide to get it, you should also check out *ftp://ftp.uu.net/networking/news/misc/dynafeed.admin.gz*. It provides a different, Perl-based interface to the administration of a *dynafeed* server.

Note that neither *gup* nor *dynafeed* is very secure. It is not difficult for someone to maliciously alter a site's news feed by simply finding the password (which can be retrieved out of an intercepted email message) and then sending a few email commands to delete or overflow the news feed. This might not be the end of the world, but it is something to watch for.

Regardless of the update method you use, if you are maintaining different sub-scription lists and transmitter configurations for many sites, it is a good idea to keep them broken out into their own configurations at a central location, and then merge and distribute them to your servers. This makes the whole operation much less likely to lose the configurations of many sites because of errors while editing only one site. You can also keep each site's configuration under its own revision control system, so that you can readily answer queries about when and how something was changed and easily back out an erroneous or unwanted revision.

13.3.4 *Customer Status Reports*

Sooner or later—more likely sooner—one of your feeds is going to want to know what is going on with their news feed. Even if it is working perfectly, someone will want to know some details about it. The more that you can automate provid-ing answers to their queries, the less time people on your end have to spend answering questions. Most major feed providers admittedly do not yet do enough in this area, but several are trying to improve their services.

The biggest questions in providing this information involve the intended privacy of the data. In other words, if you collect statistics on all of your feeds and then make that information available to all of your customers, are any of those cus-tomers going to scream about their privacy being violated? The more private you want to make the data, the more work you create for yourself. Providing an auto-mated, password-protected system that a customer can use to get information about only their feed involves the highest overhead for initial setup.

In a network that was traditionally so open that sending a *sendsys* control message resulted in nearly every site mailing back their news feed configurations, you could easily take the stance that it isn't much of a concern and that all of the infor-mation you want to return could be returned to any requester. If you feel you must provide tighter access control, you have to carefully analyze the security risks of the intended access method. Alternatively, you can just tell sites that if they don't want their information to be publicly available, they can opt out altogether, which probably requires the rare manual addition of a site to an exemption list.

You also need to determine what methods you are going to use to present the data. Perl programs and shell scripts are probably the easiest ways to gather and analyze the data. Customers can interact with these programs by email, *finger*, or Web requests. Email is the most flexible; even your dialup UUCP feeds can use it. *finger* provides a command-line interface and quicker response time, so it can be more readily integrated into programs at the customers' machines, if they desire. The Web offers the most flexibility in presentation, with CGI scripts that are able to graph historic data on the fly and pages that can reload themselves periodically when used with a compatible browser.

What information should you provide? In general, customers are most interested in the status of their own feed. Beyond that, they are also interested in the status of everyone else's feeds if their own feed seems to be perpetually lagging. If there is an unusual slowdown, they are usually satisfied, relatively speaking, if they can tell that the situation is improving and know how long it will be until things are back to normal.

With all that in mind, the easiest service to implement is one that shows the full configuration of a site's feed, including the host or hosts it is fed from, its subscribed groups and distributions, the transmitter being used, and the configuration of that transmitter. A slightly harder, though not insurmountable, problem is determining what volume of news (number of articles, bytes, and storage size on common filesystem configurations) a feed represents. This can help customers make more realistic choices about just how much news they really want to get.

You can answer the most frequently asked question "How big is my backlog?" with the number of articles the site is behind, the approximate age of articles being sent to the site, and perhaps a rough size estimate on the total volume of the backlogged articles. A command interface here can also help with the inevitable task of clearing a backlog at the customer's request, but don't forget the security issues involved in doing so. Some customers can become very irate if someone truncates their feed when they want to try to handle the backlog.

One problem with providing a backlog size is that some customers have very unreasonable expectations of what Usenet is supposed to be. Usenet is a store and forward network; people used to consider weeklong propagation times the norm. Now some people expect that everything should be delivered instantaneously, and if it is even a couple of hours behind they go ballistic. Without a number to point to, they might not even notice that they are a couple of hours behind the reception time of an article at your site. This does not mean service providers should not take responsibility for getting news to customers in a timely manner, but some education about the fact that news does not need to be instantaneous would do some people good.

In addition to providing information about the feed's backlog status, you can also include the amount of time that your site is able to exchange news with their site, as a percentage of the total time it is trying to, and any errors that your transmitter might have encountered when trying to send news. This latter information is actually useful to let sites know about without them querying, if you are unable to send news for a long time.* The longer that a site goes without taking news, the

---

* Some sites are very poorly administered. Customer support horror story Number One is the customer site administrator who calls demanding to know why his site is not getting news, when his own server is sitting throttled because of a full disk.

harder it will be for them to catch up and the bigger strain it will put on your resources. Having them fix the problem as soon as possible, especially when they would not otherwise be aware of it for days, works in everyone's favor. The easiest way to let them know is to automatically send email at some interval (usually no sooner than two hours after having a problem, and no more frequently than every four hours). Be aware that some administrators find automatic email generated by other sites to be very annoying, so they should be able to opt out of the notification if they don't want it.

Finally, your news server status scripts can provide information about the general health of your own servers to your customers. Measures of how your servers are doing processing incoming news (e.g., the average age of articles received) and sending outbound news (e.g., the average "behindness" of sites and how many are not behind at all) are the most sought-after numbers. Statistics on how much news your site has taken and how much the "behindness" is really your fault are also relevant. Why should you look bad when two dozen PPP customers on 28.8K dialups have requested full feeds? The computation of "fault" is devilishly left as an exercise for the reader.

13.3.5 Identifying Other Tasks for Automation

We have one final tip for helping you determine which others tasks are ripe for automation. If you've told your operations people the same thing so many times that your significant other can do an excellent impersonation of you doing so without having the faintest idea what any of the words actually mean, it is time to automate.*

13.4 The Political View

What a delight it would be if your only concerns as a major news site were technical ones. Technical problems are almost always solvable, no matter how hard it might be to get there. Politics, however, is a much more subjective game, one in which you can come out smelling like either the roses or the fertilizer that feeds them.

13.4.1 Namespace Issues

You might think that namespace issues are technical issues, but they are actually mostly political issues. As a major hub, you are almost certainly going to be feeding numerous leaf sites that have no other news source but you. Thus, your view of the group namespace is essentially their view of the group namespace. Any

---

* David Lawrence thanks his wife, Diane, for helping him realize this rule.

group you don't carry, they won't be able to get articles for, unless they are cross-posted to groups that you do carry.* Similarly, any articles they post to groups that you don't carry usually don't make it out past you to the rest of the Net. You have to balance the desires of some of your customers who want you to carry any group that has ever been heard of with the social responsibility of maintaining a consistent namespace.

Keeping Up with the Joneses

Some sites attach an irrational meaning to how many groups are available from a provider. Total number of groups available at a server is not an especially meaningful measure of how good the server is, especially when most people on the Net are using less than half of the publicly available groups. One service provider once used a bogus *active* file reconstruction method that ended up creating a group at every node in the hierarchy—in the worst case, this meant that seven-level-plus joke *alt* names ended up multiplying into seven or more useless groups. When some people saw that this server had over 15,000 groups (twice the approximate real amount at the time), they began pestering their feeds about how come they weren't being provided that many groups, even though most of the groups in question were spurious.

As discussed in Chapter 16, *Newsgroups and Their Names*, keeping a consistent view of the namespace across sites is one of the most useful things you can do to keep Usenet running smoothly. This doesn't mean that you must keep an exact match of the groups carried by other major hubs, but significant compatibility is desirable. Perhaps the easiest way to attain this is to keep in sync with the Internet Software Consortium's *active* file (*ftp://ftp.isc.org/pub/usenet/CONFIG/active*); numerous sites use this file to define the groups available on their servers. By all means, please do not take the approach of never removing any groups. This irresponsibility would do a disservice to your users by providing a view of the worldwide namespace that is not accurate with regard to most of the rest of the world.

The most significant worldwide problem that is actually exacerbated by hub sites is a namespace problem—two very different hierarchies based at geographically distant locations can collide in a great mess at a hub site if they share the same name. Take the University of Texas and the University of Toronto, for example. In

---

* Even then, maybe they won't, even if the desired group is in their feed. Consider a leaf node that you're feeding only *group.bogus*, a newsgroup that your site doesn't know anything about and hence considers invalid. With C News, any article arriving crossposted to *group.bogus* and to a valid group at your site is forwarded. With INN, no article is ever sent to the site, no matter what valid groups it's crossposted to, because INN considers only valid groups when making such decisions.

the mid-80's, the two sites maintained *ut* hierarchies that were leading happy but distinct lives in their own little sections of the Net. However, as more and more hub sites started taking all of the groups that they could, hierarchies like these started to collide, and it wasn't long before people reading *ut* in Texas were confronted with articles about Toronto.

The eventual progression of news feed topologies has led to sites like UUNET that have to take every regional hierarchy that they can in order to properly service their customers. Customers are increasingly nowhere near the geographic location of their hub, but they still want the local hierarchies for their own area, which makes it inevitable that such top-level names are going to collide. Some sites have worked this out by removing the colliding group names (e.g., not carrying *uw.general* at the University of Washington if there is a *uw.general* at the University of Waterloo), while others have renamed their entire top-level hierarchy to remove all confusion (e.g., the University of Texas renamed their hierarchy to *utexas*).

The last problem with the namespace is quite similar—it's the problem of getting appropriate local distributions to sites outside your geographic area. There are fundamental problems with the design and implementation of the Distribution header, as described in Section 18.2.2.7, but hub sites make those problems much worse. A hub has to deal with two contradictory demands: some customers want appropriate local distributions and others do not want any limitations on the distributions of articles appearing at their site. Some small-area organizations keep their local articles from ever getting to a hub site because they know that once they get there, they are as good as posted all over the world.

One policy that has been reasonably effective is to give every customer, by default, the appropriate distribution subscription for the world, their continent, and their country (e.g., *world,na,usa* for a customer in the United States). Additionally, the top-level name of any hierarchy in which the customer gets any groups is also subscribed, turning a U.S. site's subscription to

```
comp.graphics.misc,talk.environment
```

into

```
comp.graphics.misc,talk.environment/world,na,usa,comp,talk
```

The addition of top-level hierarchies is controversial with distribution namespace purists, who want the distribution namespace to be distinct from the group namespace. This technique, however, acknowledges the real-world fact that many articles are being posted with a Distribution header based on the top-level of the Newsgroups header. Articles with these distributions are clearly intended to be worldwide and there is nothing gained by penalizing the posters when their software generally makes no useful attempt at getting a meaningful distribution.

If you just don't want to bother with specifying distributions at your end, you should remind sites using INN that they can specify just the distributions that they want to receive in the ME line of their *newsfeeds.** This does have the drawback that resources are still used to transfer articles before *innd* can determine that they are unwanted. Because of the resource wastage, it is much better to control the distribution criteria at the feeding end.

13.4.2 *Your Site and the Law*

Potential legal liability for your site was covered in Section 11.3, but it bears reinforcing here. As a major hub site, you have higher visibility in the community, and by serving more clients you naturally have a higher chance of hooking up with someone who will someday want to sue.

A site that has decided to concentrate on just being a major hub for pushing traffic to other sites, rather than an entry point for new traffic of its own, is much more likely to be able to receive the coveted enhanced service provider classification. The important determining factors for it are that you provide access to all comers and do not try to regulate the content of the traffic that you pass. Doing either increases your risk of being found liable in the event that the police come knocking on your door for carrying illegal traffic.

Here's a little story that illustrates what you could be up against. The administrators at a site once sent their service provider a message about the sexual pictures groups. As they reasoned things, since it was known that the groups often trafficked in copyrighted and/or obscene images, their defense in the case of a lawsuit would be that they didn't request the groups, but rather that the provider sent them. If that didn't get them out of trouble, their second approach would be to bring suit against the service provider because the service provider had not exercised due diligence by screening what was sent, and the provider reasonably had to expect that there was some illegal traffic happening in the groups.

In this sort of scapegoating legal climate, where everyone is looking for a way out of trouble, comprehensive advice from a professional is going to be a lot better for your well-being than the information you've gleaned here. Find an attorney, preferably one specializing in communications law.

13.4.3 *Problem Articles*

Several kinds of problem articles, illegal or merely antisocial, were discussed in Section 11.3.2. A major hub site's policies regarding problem articles means much more than a leaf site's to the Net in general, because the policies effectively apply

---

* Unfortunately, there is no corresponding facility in C News—any distributions subfield of the C News ME line is ignored.

to a much larger user base of not only the people using news at the site but also of those at all of the leaf sites that connect to it. The actual policies you establish are best worked out with the help of your legal counsel, but beyond that there is a little more information peculiar to hub sites that we can give you.

As a hub site, we presume that your site has a full feed of most of the newsgroups in the world and also sees most articles within minutes of their being posted practically anywhere in the world. This puts you in an excellent position for noticing problem articles and doing something about them. "Doing something" does not necessarily mean "canceling"; it can simply mean notifying the rest of the community via the *news.admin.net-abuse.sightings* newsgroups and sending a message to the responsible site. You can also help a group moderator to keep an eye on a group by autocanceling or just forwarding any articles that appear to not have really been approved by the moderator. If you want to help identify problem articles coming from or arriving at your site, even if you keep your actions purely local, ask in *news.admin.net-abuse.usenet* for the latest scanning technology.

Remember too that not all problem articles are actually Net abuse; some problem articles might not even be seen at any site except for yours. You may be wondering how that can be, when you propagate all articles, even if they come from one of your leaf sites. The issue here is with invalid articles; these too are problem articles. Say you have a leaf feed that properly sends you only what it generates, but its articles are being rejected due to formatting problems. Those articles are not getting anywhere at all; the people at the leaf site are making an attempt to participate in Usenet but they're talking into a void. If it were you, surely you would want to know that your articles were not getting anywhere. Even if the sending site is not a leaf, if you are running one of the standard news servers, the articles still are not going to make it very far at all.

A nice service to provide, but one that does take some technical development time as well as some thoughtfully planned policy, is to observe problems coming from a particular site and let them know of the problems you are seeing with some or all of their articles. What makes this more than just a trivial task is that you don't want to be flooding administrators with mail or letting them know over and over about a problem that just isn't theirs to fix. However, it still makes sense for you to develop some way to notice the problem and possibly do something about it. For example, one service provider has a daily process that runs through the rejected incoming UUCP batches and observes which ones seem to be batches compressed with *gzip* or *compress* that do not have `#! compcun` headers. The provider then sends email to its own customer support group to have the customer called and told to be sure to use the *compcun* batcher with C News, and not just *compress*, because the latter makes batches that do not work with INN's *rnews*. Customer support is used because every once in a while the site in question is misidentified;

this could be remedied by improving the script so that it could then contact the customer directly.

Messages that have leaked from their intended distribution are also in the problem-but-not-quite-Net-abuse category. These are especially troublesome if the messages are control messages. For example, consider that the escape of a local *newgroup* message for *alt.swedish.chef.bork.bork.bork* is what catalyzed the degradation of the *alt* hierarchy. The escape of a *sendsys* message done on purpose by an administrator to map a local area can result in hundreds or even thousands of pieces of email being crammed into his box. The escape of a *checkgroups* message can confuse many administrators as to just what they should consider the valid groups in a hierarchy.

For years, EUNET took a feed of most of the groups in the original Usenet top-level hierarchies, minus just a few. They periodically posted a *checkgroups* message to *eunet.checkgroups*, to limit distribution to just their European sites, but this message occasionally leaked and confused the rest of the world. A mail gateway running at UUNET took any messages posted to *eunet.checkgroups* and mailed them back to the EUNET administrators so that they could plug any leaks.

David Lawrence sends the following message when he gets a *newgroup* in a hierarchy he has not heard of before (often the result of someone using INN's *makegroup* in an attempt to create a group on their local server):

```
Did you mean to forward this off-site?  If you did, please send me a
list of the groups in the hierarchy with appropriate newsgroups file
descriptions.  I would be happy to carry the hierarchy at the
Internet Software Consortium, which means that many sites who
synchronize from ftp://ftp.isc.org/pub/usenet/CONFIG/active (including
UUNET) will also carry the hierarchy.  If you did not mean for this to
get out, please recheck your configuration and post a message to
news.admin.hierarchies about the accidental leakage of local control
messages.  Thanks.

By the way, if you did not mean for it to go off-site then I strongly
recommend that you never use INN's "makegroup" to create groups.  Use
"ctlinnd newgroup" to make a group on your local server.
```

Recently, another paragraph has been appearing more frequently; it admonishes Netscape's Collabra server for creating groups because it has caused far more leaks then *makegroup* ever did.

14

In this chapter:
- *Known Worldwide Gateways*
- *Posting via Mail*
- *Setting Up a Gateway*
- *Programming a Gateway*

Gatewaying

The similarities of electronic mail messages and network news articles, both in form and intent, make them a natural for being linked together. Many tools that work for one type of message format readily work for the other as well. Individual users also often prefer one environment over the other. As a result, *gateways* exist to facilitate the appearance of email in newsgroups and vice versa.

This chapter begins with a pointer to information on existing gateways. These can save you the hassle of creating a gateway if the mailing list you want to read as news is already available in a worldwide newsgroup. The chapter also addresses how news articles can be posted using email and how a regular link between a mailing list and a newsgroup can be established.* Finally, it discusses some potential pitfalls to watch for should you choose to roll your own software for the task.

14.1 Known Worldwide Gateways

The "Mailing Lists Available in Usenet" article keeps track of the known gateways between public mailing lists and Usenet newsgroups. This article is posted periodically to *news.lists*, *news.groups*, *news.announce.newgroups*, *bit.admin*, and *news.answers* by *newgroups-request@isc.org*, (David Lawrence). The article is also available in any *news.answers* archive as *mail/news-gateways/part1*, e.g.:

```
ftp://rtfm.mit.edu/pub/usenet/news.answers/mail/news-gateways/part1
```

The article lists hundreds of gateways; you should check it to see whether the mailing list you want to see gatewayed is already available as a newsgroup that you can receive.

---

* This chapter does not discuss how to create mailing lists. That is the topic of a forthcoming book, *Managing Mailing Lists* by Alan Schwartz, from O'Reilly & Associates.

If you establish a new worldwide gateway in one of the hierarchies covered by the article, you should have it included. Send email to *gateways-request@isc.org* with the name of the newsgroup, the address of the mailing list, and any special information about the gateway. It is nice if you use the line format that is used in the article, but it is not required.

14.2 Posting via Mail

Most newsgroups do not have public gateways, but that doesn't mean that you can't use email to get an article into a newsgroup. You might want to do this if you want to post to a newsgroup that your site does not carry, if you are traveling and visiting another site that doesn't have any access to news, or if you want to simultaneously post the same message that you are sending as email to a correspondent.*

To post to *group.name* via mail, you can try sending a message to any one of the following addresses:

```
group.name@demon.co.uk
group.name@news.demon.co.uk
group.name@news.cs.indiana.edu
group.name@bull.com
group.name@cass.ma02.bull.com
group.name@undergrad.math.uwaterloo.ca
group.name@magnus.acs.ohio-state.edu
group.name@comlab.ox.ac.uk
group.name@ccs.uwo.ca (Kills headers, generates new Message-ID)
group.name@julian.uwo.ca (Kills headers, generates new Message-ID)
group.name@cs.dal.ca (Limited newsgroups)
group.name@ug.cs.dal.ca (Limited newsgroups)
group.name@paris.ics.uci.edu (Limited newsgroups, kills headers)
group.name.usenet@decwrl.dec.com (Preserves ALL headers)
group.name-news@newsbase.cs.yale.edu
```

Note that these services are not guaranteed to always be available for public access and are subject to change at any time. In fact, don't be surprised if none of them work for general purpose access anymore. You can thank Net abusers for the steady decline of general mail-to-news gateways.

In the headers of the mail message, you should include the headers you would like in the news article. In particular, you need to specify a From header (your mailer will probably provide this automatically) and a descriptive Subject header. Typically only a few other headers, such as Summary and Keywords, can be set.

---

* Conversely, some newsreader posting programs can send email at the same time that they post an article. If your program supports this, it is probably a better route to take because you are more likely to get decent notification of any problems with posting the article. The mail system should be good about returning any errors with either method.

If you want to crosspost an article, send mail to *mail2news@news.demon.co.uk.* The mail message should contain a valid Newsgroups header that has the group names separated by commas (and only commas) as specified in RFC 1036. For example, "Newsgroups: rec.music.misc,rec.video.releases" could be used to crosspost an article requesting information about Hemorrhaging Hamster's latest tantalizing video single. Only one message should be sent regardless of how many newsgroups are specified.

14.3 Setting Up a Gateway

Posting news via the mail services described in the previous section is just fine if you only need to have the occasional mail message injected into news. If you want to establish a complete and automatic gateway between a mail source and a newsgroup, however, it would not be very considerate to simply subscribe one of those sites to the mailing list in question. You should either avail yourself of one of the publicly available gateway services or run the gateway yourself.

14.3.1 Gateway Basics

First we need to discuss some of the higher-level aspects of gateways. If you are using an existing gateway service, you don't have to worry about many of the technical details, but you do need to know a bit about the different types of gateways and the possible consequences of linking the news and mail communities.

Gateways exist in several forms. A given gateway can be fully bidirectional between a mailing list and a newsgroup. Or it can be one way from the list to the group or vice versa. Another possibility is that articles are only partially passed between the group and the list, with a moderator, human or otherwise, selecting articles that are appropriate. Usually a moderator culls messages for the mailing list from the larger pool of articles in the newsgroup, but it isn't inconceivable that the reverse situation could exist.

On either the mailing list side or the newsgroup side, the messages might appear individually or be packaged as digests, with multiple messages collected together into a single meta-message. Mail users often prefer digests because everything can be readily manipulated as one unit in their mailboxes. In addition, they often have digest-bursters that split the mega-message into individual messages, to deal with the matter of reading and deleting some messages while retaining others. News users often prefer individual messages so that newsreaders capable of automatically selecting or eliminating individual messages work better. Also, most newsreaders don't have a decent way of marking only parts of a message as read and keeping those parts from being presented in subsequent sessions.

A gateway can be public, which means that anyone can access the newsgroup that corresponds to a mailing list. Creating a public gateway for a mailing list is only recommended when the overt publicness of a newsgroup is acceptable to the mailing list participants. A public gateway for a newsgroup is also beneficial to people who want to be able to get a newsgroup's traffic in places where there is no news service. A site can also create a private gateway for a mailing list, which means that the corresponding newsgroup is only available as a local newsgroup. Private gateways are usually established so that people can use their newsreader tools on the traffic of a mailing list.

If you are thinking about creating a public gateway, you should poll the readers on both sides of the potential link, after you have apprised them about how the change will be likely to affect the forum as they know it. Traffic on a mailing list with unrestricted incoming traffic from a widely distributed newsgroup is often very different from traffic on a list that exists solely in the mail realm. This is because of differences between the mail and news environments and how they are used by people.

Mail usually has a much more personal feel to it than news. People often give mail a higher priority because their mailboxes include things like job- or school-related material; most people visit their mailboxes more often during the day than they do their news spools. As a result, a mailing list has some advantages over a news-group, such as a generally stronger sense of community among the participants and a better signal-to-noise ratio because people put a slightly higher premium on introducing messages into others' mailboxes.

A mailing list also has the ability to reach more people than a newsgroup because mail is a more widely available service. However, a newsgroup for a particular topic often has more participants because it is easier to find a newsgroup than a mailing list. Newsgroups are all listed in one searchable database; a user can browse the available groups using a newsreader. Although there is a list of "Publicly Accessible Mailing Lists" posted regularly to *news.lists.misc*, the available topics still aren't as "in your face" as they are with newsreaders. Users have to actively seek out mailing lists. Of course, some people would reasonably argue that having to do so is yet one more factor that contributes to the generally higher quality of mailing lists.

Both mailing list members and newsgroup participants should be aware of the differences in how the others perceive the collection of messages that is their combined mail-and-news forum, and try to be sympathetic with the users on the other side. Admittedly, this point is often missed by newsgroup users who don't even realize that their articles are being redistributed via an automatic gateway. Probably more ill will for the idea of news gateways is caused by the indiscriminate people who post off-topic messages to groups that normally have highly relevant traffic. Even conscientious newsgroup users who know about the gateway can't do much about the ignorant people who treat the group as just another group.

Some gateways do try to block random newsgroup users, which can take someone who is sincerely interested in using the group by surprise. Such a gateway sets its mailing list so that it only accepts messages from list members, as identified by their email addresses. This does not preclude being able to post to the group and have the message make it to the list; it only means that a user first has to subscribe to the list. Once subscribed, the user can keep messages from the list out of his mailbox and just follow the newsgroup by setting his subscription to NOMAIL, as described in the introductory message for the mailing list.

It is important that a gateway at least pass some of the newsgroup traffic back to the mailing list, even if it is only a few of the more salient messages. It is very frustrating to the newsgroup community to be participating in what seem to be one-sided conversations that arise because the mailing list users aren't seeing any of the queries and comments posted by the newsgroup users. A list gatewayed to news that doesn't have an easily found return conduit is a service to no one.

Here is a summary of the important issues that you have to resolve before you establish a public gateway:

- You need to decide what type of gateway (i.e., one-way or bidirectional, unrestricted or moderated) you are creating.

- You must get the gateway approved by the mailing list owner and you should be sure that the gateway is acceptable to most of the mailing list readers.

- You should be sure that the gateway is acceptable to most of the newsgroup readers if it is to be linked with an existing newsgroup.

Once those criteria are satisfied, you can go ahead and make the link.

14.3.2 Having Someone Else Run It

The easiest way to link a newsgroup to an existing mailing list is to foist the job off on someone else. This is really only possible for public gateways, since you obviously want the newsgroup to propagate back to your site. (A private gateway should only appear at your site, so you are stuck running the gateway yourself.) If you know a news administrator who runs other gateways, you might be able to get her to gateway the mailing list in which you are interested. In the likely event that you don't know such a person, however, you can probably arrange to have the friendly folks at American University establish the gateway for you.

The procedure for having American University establish a gateway is described in "NetNews/Mailing List Gateway Policy," which is posted regularly to *bit.admin and news.answers* by *jim@american.edu*, Jim McIntosh. The article is available in any *news.answers* archive as *bit/policy*, e.g.:

```
ftp://rtfm.mit.edu/pub/usenet/news.answers/bit/policy
```

You can also retrieve the article by sending the command **send net-gate.policy** as the body of an email message to *listserv@american.edu*.

WARNING   If you maintain a mailing list and are going to have someone else create a public gateway for it, make sure there is only one such site doing so. There are two potential problems with multiple public gateways. First, if two sites are taking articles from the newsgroup and sending them to the list, redundant traffic is sent to the mailing list. Some mailing list software tries to prvent this problem, but some redundant articles still make it through. Second, if the gateways do not generate new message IDs for messages headed to the newsgroup from the mailing list, this causes both technical violations of the news standards and spotty propagation problems for the group.

For example, say that the list *grubs-l@insects.ora.com.* is being gatewayed to both *alt.grubs* and *rec.pets* by separate sites. A list message with ID "<199702182251.RAA89686@larva.ora.com>" is received and processed by each newsgroup, putting two different articles, one with "Newsgroups: alt.grubs" and the other with "Newsgroups: rec.pets" into the news stream. When a site carrying both newsgroups receives the article in one of them, it then later rejects the copy of the article for the other group because of the duplicate message ID. As a result, a reader following only one of the groups will not see all of the traffic. The propagation problem can be avoided by always generating a new message ID for gatewayed mail messages, but that still results in redundant traffic traversing the Net.

The procedure is to first secure the support of the mailing list owner and users, as described in the previous section. After that has been accomplished, post a message with the subject "Gateway for *listname* under discussion" to the newsgroup *bit.admin* to see if there are any other objections. The name of the list, its purpose, and the desired group name, normally *bit.listserv.listname*, should be included. If you want to connect the gateway to an existing newsgroup, crosspost the announcement to that group. Wait a week for any dissenting voices to pipe up. It is unusual for objections to be raised, so in the event that something does come up, cooperate to resolve the conflict. This is one of those political situations on Usenet that can usually be adequately addressed by a combination of rationalization and a little capitulation.

When everything is ready, send email to *news-admin@american.edu* that describes the explicit acquiescence of the list owner, the possibly tacit acquiescence of the list readers, the concurrence of the readers of the existing group if relevant, and any moderation that you plan to use. The folks at American University take care of arranging the mechanics of the actual link, creating the newsgroup if it does not already exist, and updating the "Mailing Lists Available in Usenet" article.

14.3.3 Running It Yourself

If you want to create a private gateway or a gateway to a limited distribution newsgroup, or if you otherwise need to exercise some custom control over the gateway and someone else can't do it for you, you'll have to take responsibility for the gateway at your own news site. In this case, mailing list messages have to be sent to your site to be posted to the group, and articles originating in news have to be delivered from your site to the list.

Gatewaying from mail to news is a more complex job than simply putting in a mail alias to pipe messages to `inews -h -n group.name`. The main problem is that the mail message format standard, RFC 822, is a bit more flexible in what it accepts as legal headers than the news standard. It is rather easy for a mail message's Message-ID header to run afoul of the stricter news article format standard, RFC 1036, and thus be refused by a standards-compliant news system. The problem is not only with the Message-ID header, as Date and other headers can similarly be illegally formatted in a news article. Piping news articles directly to mail is a safer bet, but even then there is the opportunity for a purpose-built program to run interference and provide additional functionality.

14.3.3.1 Getting the software

Rich Salz's *newsgate* program to the rescue!* The *newsgate* package contains a set of programs that were reimplemented from programs originally written by Erik Fair at UC Berkeley. The package includes programs to handle gateways in both directions. It also provides some additional special-purpose filters, including filters to remove "subscribe me" messages and to refile articles into more appropriate groups. The software was posted to *comp.sources.unix* in 1991 and is available through many archives; it was recently turned over to the Internet Software Consortium for maintenance. The *comp.sources.unix* version should be ignored in favor of more recent work. The current version of *newsgate* can be retrieved from

---

* If you happen to have access to a mainframe running Linda Littleton's Netnews news package, you may want to consider using that, as gatewaying is built in. That's how American University's gatewaying services are implemented. The operation of the gateway feature is beyond the scope of this book, but presumably you have access to that server's documentation and can work from there. Try contacting *news-admin@american.edu* if you have problems using Netnews' integrated gateway support.

ftp://ftp.isc.org/isc/inn/contrib/newsgate.tar.Z. Unlike the older version, it incorporates changes that help it work better with INN news servers.

To build the software, follow the instructions in the *README* file. By admission of the original author, the instructions are not very good as a tutorial, so we'll provide some hints here that should help you divine the proper setup for your system.

Start by making backup copies of the *Makefile* and *gate.h* files:

```
% cp Makefile Makefile.dist
% cp gate.h gate.h.dist
```

You'll be editing these files and it is always good to have a pristine version of the original around.

14.3.3.2 Makefile changes

Not surprisingly, the *Makefile* comes with a bias toward INN. If you're using INN, just change DATELIB to point to the *libinn.a* library that should be in your INN source tree. If you deleted the library after installing INN, you can rebuild it with *make install* in INN's *lib* subdirectory. (This does not affect your installed server.) The DATEDEF variable should be defined as -DUSE_PARSEDATE.

If you're running a modern C News system, use its getabsdate() call by uncommenting the DATELIB definition and pointing it at the *libcnews.a* library that you've built. If you've cleaned it up, go to the C News source directory and rebuild it. Define DATEDEF as -DUSE_GETABSDATE.

Finally, change DESTDIR to point to the directory where you want the gateway programs to live. For INN systems, this can be the directory where *innd* lives; for C News, the *relay* subdirectory that contains *relaynews* works just fine. This definition won't work unless you uncomment the cp line for the install target later in the file, so do that too if you want *make install* to do something useful.

You can safely ignore (comment out) the UUCP_INET variable because virtually no one uses hostnames that aren't properly qualified domain names anymore (and the sites that do are honestly too inconsequential to keep track of in a file that converts their names).

14.3.3.3 gate.h changes

If you are using INN, you can let *mail2news* use *inews* for posting. However, we recommend using *rnews* if you want to be able to gateway mail into a newsgroup that you've marked with the n flag (no local posting) in your *active* file. Using *rnews* also bypasses the check for too much quoted material and does not add a signature file if the user that *mail2news* is running as happens to have one. The quoted material check is reasonable for interactive news posting, but a bit improper for a comprehensive gateway that is trying to accurately pass all of the mailing list traffic. Set INEWS to the correct path for INN's *inews* or *rnews* and set ACTIVE to point to your *active*. If you use *rnews*, also change the undef in the NO_H_FLAG line to define.

Make sure that INN's configured directory for _PATH_SPOOLNEWS exists and that *rnews -U* (or a similar wrapper script for unspooling batches) is running on the machine that will be running *mail2news*. This is important regardless of whether you are using *inews* or *rnews* because both spool their input for later processing if the server is unavailable when they first receive messages.

With C News, *mail2news* should use *newsspool*; this program needs to be setuid to the news system owner as per the C News installation. The *newsgate* documentation suggests that *relaynews* is the right program, but this advice is obsolete and should be ignored—*relaynews* is not meant for this task and cannot safely be used for it. With *newsspool*, which is in C News' installed *input* subdirectory, the article is simply spooled for a normal *newsrun* run. If *relaynews* does have a problem while processing it, it saves the message to *in.coming/bad* for later examination.

If *newsspool* encounters an unapproved article for a moderated group, it does not try to submit it to the moderator like *inews* would (which is almost certainly the right thing to do). In addition, *newsspool* avoids things like including a signature file, rejecting an article based on the ratio of included text to new text, and other end-user functions that *inews* performs. The only drawback to *newsspool* is that you cannot use *inews* options with *mail2news*, including the -x flag to change the default Path header that you configure into the program. Set INEWS to the full path to *newsspool* and set ACTIVE to point to your *active* file. Then change the undef in the NO_H_FLAG line to define.

Conversion games with UUCP names are a historic artifact. Comment out the following lines like so:

```
#if 0
#define UUNAME        "/usr/lib/news/.admin/uuname.out"
#define L_SYS         "/usr/lib/uucp/L.sys"
#define UUCP_INET     "/usr/lib/news/.admin/uucp-2-inet"
#endif
```

While you're at it, you should prevent *news2mail* from attempting to use the news Path header as an email address. This is something that most administrators (including, oddly enough, Rich Salz) have been preaching about for years. Find the following line:

```
#define USE_PATH_FOR_FROM
```

Change it to:

```
#undef USE_PATH_FOR_FROM
```

You also define the location of what *newsgate* calls "control files"—runtime configuration files—in *gate.h*. This configuration information can be used to match the text of incoming messages against patterns you define. A successful match can cause actions such as redirecting the message to another group or even dropping it entirely.* If you don't have a real need for this feature, configure it like this:

```
#define IN_ONEPLACE     "/dev/null"
#undef  IN_CMDDIR       "/usr/lib/news/.admin"
```

If you want to experiment with the feature, filesystem performance will be a little better and your spool directory cleaner (which can affect programs such as those that rebuild your *history* file) if you tell the feature to use a separate command directory instead of putting the control files in the group's spool directory. So change the activated define for `IN_CMDDIR` to a directory that suits you. A subdirectory of the general news system's control file directory, such as *NEWSCTL/gateways*, is a good choice.

The `FIXED_PATH` and `GATEWAY_NAME` parameters control how the Path header looks in a mail message injected into news. Ignore `GATEWAY_NAME` as it does not do the right thing—articles may not reach the sender's site or sites beyond it. Instead, define `FIXED_PATH` to be something like:

```
host!not-for-mail
```

host should be a hostname that is fully qualified within your domain but is not the name of your news system. For example, if your news server is *locust.ora.com*, use *gateway.ora.com*, and make sure you at least have a DNS **MX** record for delivery of mail to that name. This guards against collisions with names that other sites might put in a Path header, and it lets you use the site-exclude option of your news feeding configuration to keep messages from looping. Loop prevention is discussed more below.

Change the `undef` for `WHOAMI` to `define` and replace the text between the quotation marks with the name you use for your news system. This is the **pathhost** value from INN's *inn.conf* or the contents of C News' *whoami* file—the name of your site as it appears in the Path header of all the articles you receive.

Comment out the `DO_ADDRESS_CLEANUP` and `DO_GETHOSTBYNAME` parameters with another `#if 0/#endif` pair. Most From headers have become quite reasonable, and the extra work is needless and possibly incorrect when confronted with hosts that use DNS **MX** records.

---

* MAKE.MONEY.FAST and business cards to Make a Wish, be gone!

Pick the mailer system you are using and set the correct path to it. With old versions of *sendmail* (before version 8), only "trusted users" are allowed to set the envelope's sender, which is the address that appears in the initial "From " line of a Unix mail message and is the address to which errors are supposed to be sent. If TRUSTED is defined, *news2mail* tries to setuid to the specified user ID before executing the mailer program. If the setuid fails, the message is dropped, which means that the *news2mail* program either has to be running as root or as the specified user. Modern versions of *sendmail* have discarded the trusted-user notion and anyone can set the envelope sender, so you can safely leave TRUSTED undefined.

If you are using *sendmail*, defining REQUIRE_MESSAGE_ID specifies that *mail2news* should expect all messages it receives to have Message-ID headers. This is a good flag to configure for the internal mailer that is delivering to the program, so be sure a capital M is in the F= definition for the internal mailer, usually Mprog in a reasonably generic *sendmail.cf.*

Similarly, REQUIRE_UNIX_FROM specifies whether the first line that *mail2news* gets is a real header or a Unix "From " envelope. If you're not sure whether to define this value, the best way to test is to define a *sendmail* alias in */etc/aliases* like this:

```
from-test:"| cat >> /tmp/file"
```

Mail something to *from-test* and look at the first line of */tmp/file*. If it is "From ", you have to define REQUIRE_UNIX_FROM.

Several other definitions in *gate.h* are best set based on information in the manual pages for your system. Look up signal() to see what the type of its function argument is (void or int). If your system doesn't have index() and rindex(), you should redefine IDX and RDX as strchr() and strrchr(), respectively. You don't need to worry about the align_t definition. The CHARSTAR_SPRINTF and VOID_EXIT definitions are mostly harmless; if you get them wrong, you should see some fairly obvious compile time errors. Look for */usr/include/sysexits.h* on your system and define HAVE_SYSEXITS if you have it. Look up putenv() and strerror() in the manual pages and then #define what you have and #undef what you don't. Finally, configure a path for *news2mail*'s error log; it's natural to put this log with the rest of your news system's log files. Now you're done editing *gate.h.*

14.3.3.4 Building the software

After you've finished editing *Makefile* and *gate.h*, building the software should be as simple as:

```
% make
```

Contact the The Internet Software Consortium at *inn-bugs@isc.org* if you have any
problems with getting it to compile. Presuming that it's compiled correctly, or that
you can figure out what went wrong and get it to compile correctly, you just need
to install *mail2news* and *news2mail* in their execution directories. You can use
make install if you uncommented the cp line as described when you were editing
the *Makefile*.

You may have noticed two other programs being built: *gag* and *mkmailpost*. These
programs are not really necessary for gatewaying and are mainly intended to aid
very large-scale configuration of gateways. Their use is a bit too specialized to discuss here; consult the manual pages if you think you need to use these programs.

You can also make the *signoff* program as follows:

```
% make signoff
```

This program can be installed in the same directory as the other gateway programs. As described in its manual page, *signoff* is useful for implementing a more
conservative approach to eliding "subscribe me" and "unsubscribe me" messages
than the −F flag of *mail2news*. Using a *signoff* wrapper as described in the manual
page is actually the most responsible way to run a gateway. It allows you to keep
subscription requests from being redistributed to everybody, but because all
rejected messages are sent to the news account, you can catch any messages that
should not have been rejected and inject them properly.

Note that the *signoff* manual page contains a typographic error; it suggests that the
first sample script can be used as a wrapper for *news2mail* when it really should
be *mail2news*. If you choose to use a *signoff* wrapper, install the script from the
manual page (with paths to programs adjusted for your installation) as *mail2news*.
Then install the binary *mail2news* as *mail2news.real*. Be sure to pass the script's
arguments to *mail2news.real* by fixing the call to look like this:

```
/usr/libexec/news/mail2news.real "$@" </tmp/signoff$$
```

(This example assumes that your *NEWSBIN* is */usr/libexec/news*.)

14.3.3.5 Piloting the ship

Now that the software is built and installed, you can configure the actual gateway.
The examples in the next two sections assume that the gateway binaries have
been installed in */usr/libexec/news*. They also assume that your system uses
/usr/lib/sendmail as a mail transport agent, with its aliases and configuration files
located in */etc/aliases* and */etc/sendmail.cf*. Adjust these paths as appropriate for
your own system.

Responsible gateway administration goes beyond simply setting up the programs to do the work. When you are running a gateway, you cannot be asleep at the helm. Errors with the gateway process should never cause mail to go to users who are simply sending messages to the list or posting to the newsgroup. You need to provide an address that allows people to contact the gateway administrator if something about the gateway causes problems. This is especially important if the gateway is causing looping messages. Be sure the addresses you use for error messages and administrative contact are directed somewhere where a real person can address them.

14.3.3.6 Mail into news configuration

To get mail messages into the newsgroup, you have them processed by *mail2news*. The basic process involves subscribing an address to the mailing list you want gatewayed, and then making that address an alias that resolves to a call to *mail2news*.

It's a good convention to use three aliases for each gateway:

```
post-listname
owner-post-listname
post-listname-request
```

post-listname actually does the posting to the newsgroup. Errors that *post-listname* encounters delivering the message should be sent to *owner-post-listname*—newer versions of *sendmail* do this automatically as long as the *owner-post-listname* alias exists. Administrative contact about the gateway can be directed to *post-listname-request*; this is often the same as the errors alias. Let's continue with our *grubs-l* example. Here are aliases suitable for */etc/aliases*:

```
post-grubs-l:           "|/usr/libexec/news/mail2news -n alt.grubs"
owner-post-grubs-l:     postmaster
post-grubs-l-request:   owner-post-grubs-l
```

If your *sendmail* doesn't automatically support error notification to *owner-post-listname*, you can set up error notification with another level of indirection:

```
post-grubs-l: "|/usr/lib/sendmail -oi -fowner-post-grubs-l dist-grubs-l"
dist-grubs-l: "|/usr/libexec/news/mail2news -n alt.grubs"
owner-post-grubs-l:     postmaster
post-grubs-l-request:   owner-post-grubs-l
```

This version of *post-grubs-l* sets the envelope sender of the message to *owner-post-grubs-l* before trying to deliver the message to *mail2news*. The -oi option tells *sendmail* not to take a . on a line by itself as the message terminator because it is possible that the text of the message has a terminator that was already dequoted by the *sendmail* doing the *post-grubs-l* expansion. The second *sendmail* uses EOF to find the end of the message.

Now the *post-grubs-l* alias has to be subscribed to the *grubs-l* list. If the list is at your own site, just put it in as you would any individual user's subscription. Otherwise, contact *grubs-l-request* at the home site for the mailing list and have your *post-grubs-l* alias added. Be sure to specify the hostname for the machine on which the gateway will be run (e.g., "Please subscribe post-grubs-l@ locust.ora.com to grubs-l").

If you manage the mailing list at your own site, one way to cut down on the traffic into the gateway is to set up the mailing list address as an alias that delivers both to the mailing list users and to the gateway. Then you tell the *news2mail* gateway that is forwarding articles for the group to just forward them to the mailing list users, but not to the gateway. A modern *sendmail* side of that configuration would look like this:

```
grubs-l:                 mail-grubs-l, post-grubs-l
owner-grubs-l:           grubman
grubs-l-request:         owner-grubs-l
mail-grubs-l:            :include:/etc/maillists/grubs-l
owner-mail-grubs-l:      owner-grubs-l
post-grubs-l:            "|/usr/libexec/news/mail2news -n alt.grubs"
owner-post-grubs-l:      postmaster
post-grubs-l-request:    owner-post-grubs-l
```

In this configuration, *grubman* is a real user—the manager of the list. He's responsible for adding and removing users. The list users send their messages to *grubs-l@locust.ora.com*. Their messages are sent to the other addresses specified in the file */etc/maillists/grubs-l.* Any errors with the delivery of a message to the mailing list users get reported back to *grubman* so he can deal with them as is warranted, such as by removing invalid addresses. (If your *sendmail* doesn't automatically support the *owner-listname* convention, you'll have to use the indirection shown in the previous example.)

The mail sent to *grubs-l* also gets delivered to *post-grubs-l* for insertion in the newsgroup; errors from that part of the process are reported to *postmaster* instead of *grubman*, so *postmaster* can address whatever technical problems exist. Messages that the news system sends to the list via *news2mail* should be targeted directly at *mail-grubs-l*, bypassing the *grubs-l* alias so that *post-grubs-l* doesn't have to process the message again. This aspect of the configuration is described in the next section.

The above configuration can be split across two sites: one that runs the list and one that runs the gateway (presumably yours), but that requires the cooperation of the list manager and postmaster at the list site. In this case, all of the *post* aliases need to be set up at the gateway site, while the others are created at the list site. It's great if you can get the cooperation of the people at the list site to set this up, but the software is prepared to deal with the matter of duplicates even if you can't.

Unlike news, mail does not require Subject headers in valid messages. Though most messages have them, the above aliases have the potential to keep some messages from being gatewayed to news because they have no Subject headers. This can be remedied either by using the −o option to *mail2news* to specify an Organization header for the message or by using the −x option to specify the gateway name to use in the Path header, even though one is built into *mail2news*. Both options have the implicit effect of adding "Subject: (none)" to a message that doesn't have a Subject header. As distasteful as that is, that's the right thing to do for a full service gateway.

One good aspect of needing to deal with messages without Subject headers is that it encourages the use of an Organization header that clearly reflects the source of the gateway. For example, we can update the *post-grubs-l* alias to both allow messages without Subject headers and to have the following Organization header:

```
Organization: ORA Gateway (problems to post-grubs-l-request@locust.ora.com)
```

Use the following alias to set this up:

```
post-grubs-l: "|/usr/libexec/news/mail2news -n alt.grubs -o
  '.O.R.A .Gateway (problems to post-grubs-l-request@locust..ora..com)'"
```

The . before each uppercase letter in the argument for −o is a guard against *sendmail* configurations that incorrectly convert the text to lowercase. It tells *mail2news* to make sure that each letter following a dot is capitalized. The two dots in a row are replaced with a single dot.

The −o flag does not, for better or for worse, replace an existing Organization header in the message, so there is no way to guarantee that a contact address for the gateway administrator will show up anywhere in the message. The best you can hope for is to trust that people can decipher enough of the header, particularly the Path header, to figure out that a message was gatewayed from your site. Even on the Internet of old, when the relative number of technical users was far greater than it is today, that was a bit much to expect. So, to ensure that your contact address is included and also cut down on the wordiness of the alias, you could choose to not use the −o flag by making a couple of modifications to *mail2news.c*. First, find the following line:

```
    SubjectRequired = TRUE;
```

Change it to:

```
    SubjectRequired = FALSE;
```

Then just add a line right after it to set the default Organization header to something that includes a generic contact address:

```
Strcpy(H.organization,
    "ORA Gateway (problems to postmaster@locust.ora.com)");
```

If you want to still be able to use -o in certain cases, you can let it override the default you just created by deleting the following line from the source code:

```
if (H.organization[0] == ' ')
```

These changes cause any existing Organization header to be replaced. Now you can return to a *post-grubs-l* line that just uses the -n switch to set the name of the group to which to post.

The end result of *mail2news*'s processing is a message with many headers dropped and many other headers massaged. Here is a list of headers that the program changes and inserts:

Path

> *mail2news* adds a custom Path header that points to the gateway; it also includes your news server's name when you see it in news.

From

> This header may be massaged to bring it into standard Internet format.

Newsgroups

> *mail2news* adds a Newsgroups header that lists the target newsgroup of the gateway.

Message-ID

> This header may be tweaked to make it news compliant. If there is no Message-ID, one of two things may happen to the message: If you defined REQUIRE_MESSAGE_ID, *mail2news* reports an error. If you followed our advice and defined INEWS as something other than *inews* or *injnews*, both of which generate a Message-ID when none exists, the news system just refuses the article with a note in its log file about the missing Message-ID header.

Date

> This header is rewritten to be news compliant, but it should still represent the time of the original Date header. If the original date is unparsable, the original value is put in an X-Unparseable-Date header. If the date is unparsable or nonexistent, *mail2news* inserts a Date header that contains the time at which the gateway inserted the message.*

---

* If you think that using the time the gateway injected the article is always the correct behavior (and we might agree with you), you can make this change by putting (void)time(&t) right before the DoDate() call in rfc822write() in *rfc822.c*.

Subject

The Subject header says "(none)" if no subject was provided by the user and you've used the -x or -o flag to tell *mail2news* to provide one.

Organization

If you've configured *mail2news* to use an Organization header, it is added. It may also be added by *inews* or *injnews* if you are using one of those as the insertion tool.

References

This header is constructed from the In-Reply-To header if it exists, with the same message ID tweaking that is done on the Message-ID header. If both References and In-Reply-To exist in the same message, the one that *mail2news* sees last is the one that is used.

Sender

This header is generated from *sendmail*'s envelope "From " header, turning "From grubman@locust.ora.com Sat Jul 6 14:12:34 1996" into "Sender: grubman@locust.ora.com".

Distribution

This header is unaltered. It may also be added if none existed and you specified the -d flag to *mail2news*. Since the Distribution header cannot be overridden if it exists in the message, even with *mail2news -d,* you should not rely on it as part of your protection against duplicates. In fact, since you can't really rely on it to be consistent, you're better off just not using the -d option.

Approved

This header is also unaltered, unless you used the -a flag with *mail2news*, in which case it is added. You need to use the -a option if you are gatewaying into a moderated group; the value should normally reflect the contact address of the gateway administrator, but some moderators might prefer some other address.

The following additional headers are retained from a mail message and left unaltered by *mail2news*:

```
Expires
Control
MIME-Version
Content-Transfer-Encoding
Content-Type
Reply-To
Followup-To
Keywords
Summary
```

No other headers are output by *mail2news*. INN's modernized *inews* might reject the article if Expires does not have a parsable date, but the other alternatives suggested for the configurable INEWS program don't share that problem.

There is some argument over whether Control should be allowed through. It isn't a header that mailers care about, and in a mail message it could just be someone up to no good, especially if the gateway is automatically slapping an Approved header onto news articles it is posting. You should remove the printing of the Control header from rfc822write() in *rfc822.c*, unless you can think of a reasonable need for the functionality at your installation.

14.3.3.7 News into mail configuration

The link for delivering articles from the newsgroup back to the mailing list is controlled by your news system in the same way as are feeds to your neighbors: through INN's *newsfeeds* file or C News's *sys* file. The news system hands messages off to *news2mail* to do the deed.

Here's the C News *sys* entry on *locust.ora.com* to feed *alt.grubs* back to *grubs-l@insects.ora.com*:

```
gate!grubs-l/gateway.ora.com:\
  alt.grubs,!alt.grubs-l.all/all,!local::\
  /usr/libexec/news/news2mail grubs-l grubs-l news@locust.ora.com \
    insects.ora.com
```

The equivalent INN *newsfeeds* entry is:

```
gate!grubs-l/gateway.ora.com:\
  alt.grubs:Tp:\
   /usr/libexec/news/news2mail grubs-l grubs-l news@locust.ora.com \
     insects.ora.com
```

In each entry, the first field is constructed so as to not conflict with any external names someone might ever use in the Path header, but to still provide meaningful logging. The first part of the field, gate!grubs-l, will never match another site in the Path header because the site matching is split on the ! in the header. This first field, up to the first slash or colon, is the name that gets logged into the file where the news system indicates the feed entries that matched for the site, typically */var/news/log* for C News and */var/log/news/news* for INN.

The second part of the first field is the exclusion that prevents looping of messages. It should be the hostname that *mail2news* is putting in the Path header of messages that it sends to the group. This is how the news system identifies messages that have come from the mailing list and therefore should not be sent back to it. If these messages are sent back to the list, it would cause an endless loop unless the mailing list software identifies and suppresses the duplicate messages. Some software does try to do so, but even those packages that do can still miss the occasional message.

The second field describes what groups should be gatewayed back to the list. The goal is to strictly identify just the group that should be gatewayed. With INN, it is simply a matter of specifying the name of the group without wildcards. C News, however, has an implicit hierarchical matching scheme that recurses on every pattern. Even if *alt.grubs* has no subgroups when you establish the gateway, that doesn't prevent someone from coming along and creating subgroups after it's established. The `!alt.grubs.all` part of the pattern keeps any future subgroups from matching. In both cases, control messages for the group match the pattern even though they are filed in the *control* pseudogroup and are not seen by readers of the newsgroup. These messages are elided by *news2mail*, so people on the mailing list don't see cancel messages every time a group user tries to remove an article.

The third field is empty for C News, which tells it to treat the fourth field as a program that should receive the article on standard input. A third field of `Tp` tells INN the same thing.

The fourth field is what controls the program to be executed and its argument. The *news2mail* program is normally called with four arguments: the name of the list as it should appear in the To header, the real address to which the message should be delivered, the gateway administrator's contact address, and the hostname to append to each of the addresses that does not have an `@` sign in it.

In our example, with *grubs-l* hosted at another site, the To header is set to the regular list address and the mail message is really delivered to it. The gateway administrator's address is given as the user *news* on the news server doing the gatewaying; this address is placed in the Sender header and used as the envelope sender by being passed to *sendmail* with the `-f` flag. The address should point to a human who can deal with any errors from the gateway. The *news2mail* sources suggest that the address be sent to the list administrator's contact address (i.e., *grubs-l-request*), but that isn't a very good idea because the list administrator probably won't be able to deal with a problem with the gateway (unless she's also the gateway administrator), so she shouldn't have to deal with error messages from it.

With its arguments in hand, *news2mail* goes to work by reading the article on its standard input. If it sees a Control header or a Subject with the first five characters of "cmsg ", the message is quietly eaten by the program and not sent to the list. The References header is trimmed to just the last three message IDs to conserve header lengths while still providing enough information to build threads.

If you've told *news2mail* to `USE_PATH_FOR_FROM` in *gate.h*, it tries to build a From header for the mail message based on the full name field of the article's From header and some poking around with *uuname* on the values in the article's Path header. The full name is only detected if the header is in "From: user@site (Full Name)" format and the *uuname* groveling is unlikely to turn up many useful conversions. It is much better to keep `USE_PATH_FOR_FROM` undefined, in which case *news2mail* just drops the Path header and leaves the From header unaltered.

The To header is assembled from the first and possibly fourth arguments to *news2mail*; the Sender header is constructed from the third and possibly fourth arguments. A Received header is also built to initiate the mail debugging chain. Its template looks like this:

```
Received: from GATEWAY by host with netnews
        for real-dest (To:-dest)
```

`host` is replaced by `WHOAMI` if you have configured it in *gate.h*, or the return value from a `gethostname()` call if you have not. The mailing list addresses `real-dest` and `To:-dest` are replaced with *news2mail*'s second and first arguments, respectively, possibly appended by the hostname given in the fourth argument. This turns our example into:

```
Received: from GATEWAY by locust.ora.com with netnews
        for grubs-l@insects.ora.com (grubs-l@insects.ora.com)
```

Finally, the following additional headers are retained from a news article and left unaltered by *news2mail*:

```
Subject
Date
Message-ID
Reply-To
Organization
MIME-Version
Content-Type
Content-Transfer-Encoding
```

No other headers are output by *news2mail*.

The complete message is dumped into a temporary file, which gets passed to:

```
sendmail -i -odq -f sender recipient
```

`sender` and `recipient` are as specified on the *news2mail* command line. The `-i` flag is just like the `-oi` flag that tells *sendmail* not to take a `.` on a line by itself as the message terminator because it is possible for a news article to have such a line in its body. The delivery mode is set by `-odq` to have *sendmail* immediately fork and queue the article for delivery the next time the mail queue is processed.

Remember that under this configuration, the only thing keeping the news article from reappearing in the group a second time is the message ID. When *news2mail* delivers the message to the list, the list sends it out to everybody, including the *mail2news* alias. When *mail2news* tries to hand it to news, it's the presence of the message in the *history* database that keeps it from showing up in the group again.

There are two consequences to this: the message ID of the mail message received by *mail2news* must still be the same as the one passed by *news2mail* and the mail message much reach *mail2news* within the message ID retention time that *expire* uses on the *history* file. The latter isn't normally a problem, but if mail delivery is chronically slow or the message ID retention time is quite brief, you need to account for this problem.

The more likely, although still uncommon, problem is that the mailing list is either generating new message IDs for messages it distributes or pathologically stripping message IDs out of all messages. In the case of message IDs being completely removed, the author of the list software should be taken out back and shot. The problem of message IDs being regenerated for messages is also an error on the part of the list software, but could very well be an innocent artifact of how the message is processed.

However, this does not mean that the list cannot be gatewayed to news. It just means that *mail2news* cannot be sent articles that have already appeared in the newsgroup, so the alternate alias configuration of *mail-grubs-l* and *post-grubs-l*, described in the last section, must be used. If both the mailing list and the gateway are hosted on *locust.ora.com*, that makes the *news2mail* line in the news feed entry:

```
/usr/libexec/news/news2mail grubs-l mail-grubs-l news locust.ora.com
```

The corresponding Received header in the mail message looks like:

```
Received: from GATEWAY by locust.ora.com with netnews
        for mail-grubs-l@locust.ora.com (grubs-l@locust.ora.com)
```

This publicly exposes another mail address, *mail-grubs-l*, that might be inadvertently used by someone to mail to the list when they should use *grubs-l*. As such, you might want to remove this line from *news2mail.c*:

```
Fprintf(F, "\tfor %s (%s)\n", ToAddr, buff);
```

The other advantage to having separate mail distribution and posting addresses is that it saves *mail2news* from having to do redundant processing of articles, of which there could be a substantial number in a high-volume group.

There is one last aspect of a news-to-mail gateway that we need to warn you about. If you've been responsible about setting up error reporting to go to you, the gateway administrator, you might discover that the list is not properly configured to have its administrator get bounce messages from attempted mail delivery to its subscribed members. If this is the case, you'll end up seeing error messages for something that you have no way to fix.

If you cannot get the list administrator to properly configure the mailing list, you might be forced to set the third *news2mail* argument to the list maintainer's address (which might be a little antisocial) or even to an alias that sends any errors straight to the bit bucket (`nobody: /dev/null`). Neither of these options are particular palatable because if the list address ever goes away without someone informing you directly, you might never find out about it and the gateway will be pointlessly spinning its wheels. Hopefully, though, if the list administrator approves of the gateway, getting cooperation to fix the list configuration shouldn't be a real problem.

14.4 Programming a Gateway

Maybe you've taken a close look at the *newsgate* package and you've decided that it just doesn't do what you want it to do. If you prefer to start from scratch rather than modify the *newsgate* source to suit your needs, here are some issues about gateways that you should keep in mind during your endeavors.

14.4.1 Error Messages

We can't say much more about error messages that we haven't already said in this chapter. We just want to keep the issue foremost in your thoughts. Problems with gateways have a way of being very large, sometimes as bad as causing an exponential growth of traffic, and usually as bad as causing a large number of people to see the problems in their mailboxes and newsreaders. The gateway administrator is the only person who should get error reports about the gateway, and he should be prepared to deal with the problems immediately.

14.4.2 Header Processing

The primary tenet of header processing is that you should change the contents of as few headers as possible. Even among people who adhere to that principle, there are two schools of thought about how to handle headers: let them all through or only let through a known set.

Rich Salz chose to pass only known headers with *newsgate*. This does an excellent job of cutting down a lot of the cruft that shows up in headers, but does have the drawback that when another header that should be retained shows up, the software has to be updated. This happened when the MIME standard matured, and three new headers had to be recognized by *newsgate*.

The alternative approach tends to add more noise to the headers, but it makes it easier to just leave the gateway software alone after it is installed. In a mail to news gateway, you can safely remove headers that aren't relevant in a newsgroup, such as Received, Status, and To. A news to mail gateway can also eliminate irrelevant headers like Path, Xref, and NNTP-Posting-Host. You can safely remove all X-headers, but if you don't want to swing that broad an axe, at least get rid of the ridiculous X-Mailer and X-Newsreader headers, which are common eyesores.

If a news to mail gateway sees a Control header, it should toss the message, as it is clutter to people on the mailing list. You might have a command-line option that allows such a message to be sent, but it is a bad idea to turn it on for a general-purpose gateway. Sending such messages should be reserved for a very low distribution list that is tracking all of the happenings of a newsgroup, not just the normal messages posted to it.

The Date header of a message being sent from mail to news should reflect the time that the message was actually put into the news stream, which means replacing the contents of whatever was there. This is because the news system uses the Date header to see whether the article is older than the standard amount of message ID history the server keeps, in which case it can't tell whether it already received the article. The news system also rejects messages that claim to have been generated in the future, so if the incoming message has a bogus future Date, as email (especially from personal computer systems) is not unknown to have, the message is dropped. The Date headers of mail messages are often non-compliant with the news header standard, and sometimes even reflect incorrect times. Even if a Date header contains the correct time of the sending of the message, it could be hours or even days old by the time it is propagating in the news stream, which means that its propagation and expiration are influenced accordingly.

The From header and especially the Reply-To header should be left alone. Email addresses on the worldwide Internet have stabilized into a widely followed, consistent address format, much more so than was true at the time *newsgate* was first written. Still, some users have difficulty controlling incorrect generation of the From header on their messages, and use the Reply-To header to compensate. Defer to how they've specified these addresses and let them through unaltered.

The Newsgroups header should, of course, be carefully set to just the destination you want for the message. Some gateways have overlooked explicitly setting the Newsgroups list and inadvertently redistributed the message based on the Newsgroups line that came in as part of the mail message. This may very well not be what was intended: people reply to news articles with mail and the Newsgroups header is often left in by the newsreader's mail interface. If the author, or anyone subsequently responding to the message, includes an address that has a mail-to-news gateway of a list to a site's local group, the email message could end up right back in the group that they were sparing from a posting, rather than in the local gateway's group.

The last header you need to process is the Message-ID header. You have to establish a consistent algorithm for bringing mail message IDs into compliance for the more restrictive news standard. Generating wholly new message IDs for messages is not a good idea. It confuses references to the message, both by machines and by humans, and potentially breaks duplicate detection in a mail-to-news gateway.

14.4.3 Gateways to Multiple Forums

One of the difficult problems to solve with gateways is that of crossposting. Decent newsreaders have the very nice feature of not showing you an article again once you've read it, as long as the article is crossposted. Unfortunately, mail programs have a much harder time detecting multiple copies of the same message.

Here's a scenario that illustrates the crossposting problem Imagine that *grubman* sends a message to both *insects-l* and *grubs-l.* People subscribed to both lists get two copies of the same message, but that's simply an inconvenience. A bigger problem is that the mail-to-news gateway subscribed to each list processes the mail message, so two copies get passed into Usenet. If the gateways are retaining message IDs and the messages go to two different groups, there are now two articles floating around the Net with the same message ID but different Newsgroups headers. Ideally, you'd like these messages to end up crossposted, but in reality, only one of the groups gets the message at each site because the second arrival is rejected as a duplicate.

"Ah!" you say as the light goes on over your head. "The obvious way to fix that is to always generate a new message ID." Go right ahead and implement it that way. But now you have to promise that you will never ever have that mail-to-news gateway attached to an address that gets news-to-mail traffic. Because if you do, you'll create an instant loop.

You still haven't solved the crossposting problem, but at least you've managed to get a better guarantee that the list traffic all appears in your group. This could be important for a local gateway of a mailing list that someone else is gatewaying into a local hierarchy that also reaches you. Deciphered, that sentence means: "Do you have any idea how many people in the world gateway SunFlash?!"

As an example, UUNET gateways many mailing lists into its own internal hierarchy and all of the messages get new message IDs because UUNET receives regional hierarchies from all over the world and some of those hierarchies contain gateways. If one of those gateways manages to get a news article propagated to UUNET before its own gateway inserted the message, the internal UUNET group would never get the message. By generating a new message ID, UUNET isn't directly getting in the way of the propagation of messages in the other groups; however, their propagation is still affected to the extent that they conflict with each other.

On the flip side of this coin, if you have an article crossposted between two groups that each have gateways, the conversation on the mailing list side becomes fractured because each gateway generates a separate message to the individual lists. The recipients of each list won't have any indication that the message also went to other lists, and when their responses head back to Usenet, it won't be crossposted again to the other group.

No one expects you to solve the multiple gateway problem with your gateway program. That best that can be hoped for is addressing it if all of the gateways are under one control. Several workable solutions have been proposed if that limitation is applied to the problem, but no one has distributed software to do it.

In this chapter:
- *Creating a Moderated Group*
- *Getting Postings to the Moderator*
- *Preparing Articles for Distribution*
- *Putting the Articles in the Group*
- *Moderators' Software Tools*
- *The Political Side*

15

Moderating Newsgroups

"In September 1988 my car was repossessed and the bill collectors were hounding me like you wouldn't believe. I was laid off and my unemployment checks had run out. The only escape I had from the pressure of failure was my computer and my modem. I longed to turn my avocation into my vocation. This January 1989 my family and I went on a ten-day cruise to the tropics. I bought a Lincoln Town Car for CASH in February 1989."*

About now you're probably thinking, "Hang on a second, that doesn't belong here!" It doesn't belong in most newsgroups, either. Moderating a newsgroup is one way to control the messages that appear in it; all messages that appear in the group should have the approval of the moderator. This generally means that some human being other than the submitter of the article checks it for its appropriateness for the forum before the general readership sees it.

The only difference between an article in a moderated group and one in an unmoderated group is the presence of an Approved header inserted by the moderator. Most news software doesn't even care what the content of the Approved header is, as long as it exists. While there are other technical aspects of properly creating the group, getting regular user submissions to the moderator, and injecting the article into the regular news distribution channels, in the long run it is really only the Approved header that makes a difference.

Doing a good job of moderating a newsgroup is much more of a political problem than it is a technical problem. So in addition to describing the mechanics of getting articles to the moderator and then into the newsgroup, this chapter tries to provide some advice on practices that make for a successful moderated group.

---

* Copyright 1989 by Dave Rhodes, super-genius.

15.1 Creating a Moderated Group

The first step in making a moderated newsgroup work is to actually create the group. The process of creating a regional or network-wide group is described in Chapter 16, *Newsgroups and Their Names*; this process is the same no matter whether you are creating an unmoderated group or a moderated one. The eventual goal is to have the group exist on the news servers that should be carrying it, properly flagged as a moderated newsgroup.

If you are sending a *newgroup* control message to inform other sites of the creation of the group and to request that they create it too, the **moderated** keyword needs to be appended to the Control header, like this:

```
Control: newgroup comp.os.linux.announce moderated
```

newgroup messages for moderated groups commonly have these two lines in the body:

```
Group submission address:    foo@site.domain
Moderator contact address:   foo-request@site.domain (Moderator's Name)
```

These lines are not processed by any significant software, but do help people reading them know how the group should be configured, in case they need to update any of their databases with the information.

Unless you intend for the group to be widely distributed, please do not send a *newgroup* message for the group. The chances are good that the message will propagate much farther than you expect, causing administrators around the world to receive a mail message about your group or even causing the group to be created at their sites. Be especially wary of using INN's *makegroup* command; control messages for local groups sent via this script regularly escape to the Net. (Thankfully, it is no longer part of the INN distribution.) You have to have very accurate control over your feed configurations to prevent escapes, and even if the control message does go only to the couple of sites that you want it to go to, then they might be the ones who leak it. Be especially careful of feeding control messages either implicitly or explicitly via INN; a feed of the pattern `*,!mylocal.*` still forwards a control message to create *mylocal.group*, unless the Distribution header manages to catch it.

If the group needs to be set up at only a small number of sites, try coordinating it via email to the administrators at those sites. At each site, the administrator can use local commands to create the group only on her server. With C News and INN, the commands are:

```
% cnewsdo addgroup group.name m                        # C News
% ctlinnd newgroup group.name m requester@address      # INN
```

To change the moderation status of a group that already exists in the *active* file, use these commands:

```
% cnewsdo newsflag group.name m                    # C News
% ctlinnd changegroup group.name m                 # INN
```

In each case above, the m flag appears as the fourth field in the *active* group database to indicate to the news transport software that the group is moderated, and that it should not accept articles for the group that lack an Approved header. If someone tries posting to the group without the header, the news system forwards the article to the moderator, as described in the next section. If an article is received from a peer site without the header, it is rejected by the transport agent.

In the *newsgroups* file, a tag of " `(Moderated)`" is used to indicate the moderated status of the newsgroup. This tag is used in *checkgroups* control messages (see Section 3.3.2.1 and Section 18.4.6) for checking for the proper status of the group in the *active* file. The tag is case-sensitive, has a significant leading space, and should be the last thing on the line, with no characters trailing the closing parenthesis.

15.2 Getting Postings to the Moderator

When a posting agent encounters a user's attempt to submit an article to a moderated group, it should mail the article to the submission address for the group. Rather than expect and rely on each of thousands of news servers to maintain up-to-date lists of these submission addresses, a small group of sites maintains aliases for each of them. These sites are called *mailpaths sites*, named after the control file in B News that first implemented the system. A site can then layer forwarding for its local moderated groups on top of the general forwarding database.

15.2.1 Network-Wide Moderated Group Submissions

Each mailpaths site has aliases for widely available moderated groups in the original Usenet hierarchies, *alt*, and many regional and organizational hierarchies. The alias for a group is determined by substituting dashes (-) for dots (.) in the newsgroup name. For example, *news.announce.newgroups* has the alias *news-announce-newgroups* at each mailpaths site.

If you are creating a widely available group that should be known by the mailpaths sites, you need to let *moderators-request@isc.org* know the appropriate information, including the group name, the submission and contact addresses, and the names of the moderators. If your group is being created as part of an official *news.announce.newgroups* proposal, the moderator of *news.announce.newgroups* handles this for you.

The following sites maintain moderated group aliases for use by the rest of the network:

agate.berkeley.edu	*isgate.is*	*funet.fi*
linus.mitre.org	*moderators.univ-lyon1.fr*	*moderators.switch.ch*
nac.no	*ncren.net*	*news.belgium.eu.net*
news.cs.washington.edu	*news.germany.eu.net*	*philabs.research.philips.com*
pipex.co.uk	*relay.eu.net*	*rutgers.edu*
sunic.sunet.se	*ucsd.edu*	*mail.uu.net*

The list of moderated groups on which the mailpaths aliases are based is posted periodically, roughly at the beginning of each month, to *news.lists.misc*, *news.groups*, and *news.answers*. Although you could construct your own aliases based on that list, it is not recommended that you do so because the mailpaths sites receive more timely updates to the list, and in the event that your site ever stops actively maintaining the aliases, they will rapidly become out of date and a problem for your users.

Your site's posting software has to be told how to reach a mailpaths site. INN uses the `moderatormailer` definition from the *inn.conf* file to do this; C News uses the `all` line from the *mailpaths* file.* Both systems take the same type of value, an address specification for getting mail to one of the sites named above, with `%s` being replaced by the dot-to-dash converted name of the group. If you can send mail using normal Internet syntax (*user@host.domain*), these settings will work:

```
moderatormailer: %s@mail.uu.net          # INN's inn.conf
all %s@mail.uu.net                       # C News' mailpaths
```

There is really not much of a science to picking the mailpaths site to use as your default forwarder; each should work equally well. The site *moderators.isc.org* can be used to randomly select the mailpaths host for each message sent to it. This address is just a holder for multiple mail exchanger records in the domain name system. The theory is that such a system is more robust than depending on any one server to always be available, but in practice it has sometimes proven to be a bit problematic for a number of reasons. Our recommendation is that you pick a site and stick with it.

Submissions via the mailpaths sites can be tested by trying to post to the newsgroup *misc.test.moderated*. If your article successfully reaches the moderator of the group, you should receive an automated mail reply confirming the receipt of your message. There is also a regular posting in the group that shows the apparent source of submissions, which may help in diagnosing why your mail was not returned.

---

* INN also has the *moderators* file, as described in Section 8.2.2.5.

15.2.2   Local Moderated Group Submissions

The overall system for getting submissions to moderators is more flexible than just
passing your articles to another site for delivery. The system is capable of supporting groups for which the mailpaths sites do not have aliases, like groups for your
own organization. With C News, this is done in the *mailpaths* control file. INN
uses the *moderators* control file.

The two control files have a lot in common. Both are read until a line matches the
group being sought; your catch-all match should be last. Comment lines can be
included by starting them with a #. In C News' *mailpaths* file, each entry contains
a group pattern like the one used in the *sys* file, followed by white space, followed by an address pattern. With INN, the *moderators* file contains a group pattern like that used in the *newsfeeds* file, followed by a colon, followed by an
address pattern. The address pattern is the same in each file: a mailing address
that has any %s segment replaced by the dot-to-dash converted form of the group
name.

Let's say your company's groups are in the *spacely* hierarchy. You have a couple
of moderated groups there. Because of a new partnership between your company
and another manufacturer, you have also set up a feed to receive their *cogswell*
hierarchy. These groups are only to be distributed between your two companies,
so the mailpaths sites don't have any information on them. Thus, if you are running C News, you need a *mailpaths* file configured like this:

```
spacely          %s@spacely.com
cogswell         %s@cog1.cogs.com
all              %s@moderators.isc.org
```

For INN, the *moderators* file should look like:

```
spacely.*:%s@spacely.com
cogswell.*:%s@cog1.cogs.com
*:%s@moderators.isc.org
```

If a user posts to *spacely.announce*, his message is mailed to the moderator at
spacely-announce@spacely.com. *spacely-announce* is a mail alias in the mailer
configuration for *spacely.com* that points to the real moderator of the group.

It isn't strictly necessary for the address pattern to contain a %s for replacement; a
static address can be used instead. We recommend the group name replacement
method to maintain consistency with the way mailpaths sites handle moderated
groups, to reduce maintenance on your moderator forwarding file, and to conve-
niently put all of your moderation addresses for local groups in your alias file.
Associating a generic submission address with the group, rather than the particular
address of the person who moderates it, helps makes any transition to a new moderator go a little more smoothly.

If INN does not find a match in the *moderators* file, it resorts to the *moderator-mailer* definition from *inn.conf*. If that does not exist, it returns an error. If C News cannot find a matching line, it tries to mail the message to the converted group name locally. This is not a particularly good configuration to rely on with C News; it is best that you include an `all` line as the last line of the file. For historical compatibility, C News treats a group pattern of `backbone` the same as `all`.

15.2.3 Administrative Contact of Moderators

Moderated groups should actually have two addresses associated with them, the submission address and the administrative contact address. Traditionally, these are *foo@site.domain* and *foo-request@site.domain*, respectively. The former address is the one we have been discussing so far. The latter address is used by people to contact the moderator with messages about the group that are not intended to be posted to it. Of course, some people seem to not understand the distinction, or more likely are not aware of it, and use the wrong addresses anyway, but it can still be a useful separation.

15.2.4 Crossposted Articles

When news posting software encounters a moderated group among a list of groups for crossposting, the article should not appear anywhere before it is approved by the moderator of that group. If there is more than one moderated group in the header, the current practice of C News and INN is to mail the article to just one of the groups, usually the first one.

The article is mailed to the moderator of the group with all of the groups of its Newsgroups header still present, so the moderator can do the crossposting. Some users don't expect this behavior, so you might get several submissions from someone who doesn't realize his article has been sent to you and will not appear until it is approved. Handling crossposted articles is described more in the next section.

15.3 Preparing Articles for Distribution

Once an article has arrived in the moderator's mailbox, it should be cleaned up before it is actually posted to the group. The most rigid part of this, as far as the news software is concerned, is arranging a set of headers for the article that make it a legal network news article.

15.3.1 Header Processing

Because C News uses the native mailer to forward articles for moderated groups, it is possible that the news headers appear at the start of the body of the message received by the moderator. This is because mailers have different behaviors regarding what they do when they get a message that starts with legal header lines; some suck the lines up to the first non-header line into the mail header, while others consider the start of the input to be the start of the message body. Some moderators don't care for this inconsistent format at all, as most other news software always seems to put the news headers in the mail message header.

You can check how articles look when sent by your site to a moderator by posting an article to *misc.test.moderated*. The auto-reply message from the group contains the headers of the mail message the moderator received. If it has a Newsgroups header, you're fine. If it doesn't, this means your site is putting the news headers in the body of the message. You can fix this by replacing the *mail* command in *inject/injnews* with the path to a mailer that accepts mail headers in its input. You should change the script rather than changing the path or putting a link named *mail* in *NEWSCTL/bin*, because there are other parts of C News that echo messages starting with lines that look like headers but really aren't.

The issues for individual headers as they pertain to moderated groups are described below. Each subsection about an individual header starts with a general definition of common use of the header and an example. You can also refer to the RFC standards that define the precise syntax of news articles: RFC 822, RFC 1036, and any new one that has succeeded them by the time you're reading this. Chapter 18, *Anatomy of a News Article*, also describes the general syntax of news headers.

There are two general gotchas to be wary of:

- Do not use header lines longer than 250 characters. Very long headers cannot be handled by the default configuration of B News, which, obsolete though it may be, is still around the Net in enough places to have an effect on the propagation of the article. Various other programs might also have a problem with the long headers.

- Wrap long header lines only on the white space within the header. A header line that goes beyond the typical screen width of 80 characters can be broken at white space by inserting a newline right before the space. The continued line must start with a space or tab to be considered a legal header continuation.

15.3.1.1 Approved header

```
Approved: address-of-moderator
Approved: jfurr@acpub.duke.edu
```

This header controls whether the article is actually put into the group or mailed right back to you, the moderator. Its contents should be the administrative contact address for your group in Internet-style format.

Be wary of crossposting. If you are crossposting the article to another moderated group, the presence of the Approved header causes it to be accepted and inserted into the other group too, regardless of whether the approval address for the group is in the article. You should get permission from the moderator of the other group to crosspost the article there, by mailing to the administrative contact address, before you post it. If it is okay with the moderator, you should also include the approval address for the other group in the header, mostly for the benefit of any readers who might notice something out of the ordinary. For example, an article to *news.announce.newgroups* and *rec.food.recipes* would have had this header:

```
Approved: newgroups-request@isc.org, recipes-request@rt66.com
```

You might think that the onus of getting approval from other moderators isn't worth the trouble, and therefore simply forgo crossposting within your group. We don't recommend this approach because it isn't good for the users who read your group. If they also read the other groups in which the message should appear, they will end up seeing it more than once because their newsreader won't be able to tell it is the same article. If there is a group for which you get regular crossposts, you might try to come to an agreement with the other moderator regarding default approval between your groups to save you both time and effort.

15.3.1.2 *Newsgroups header*

```
Newsgroups: list-of-groups-for-posting
Newsgroups: news.announce.newgroups,news.groups
```

This header controls the groups in which the article should appear. Since group names for crossposted groups can be separated only by commas with no intervening white space, it is illegal for this header to be continued on multiple lines.

This header also has a direct effect on the size of the Xref header generated at each site, which could cause the over-250 character problem with B News sites, even though the Newsgroups header is less than that limit. For this reason, it is suggested that the Newsgroups header not exceed roughly 180 characters.

News software varies with regard to how rigorously it checks the validity of groups in the header. You might wish to augment your article preparation with a check for the validity and moderation status of the groups in the header besides your own. This can help guard against surprises like having another moderator ask why you posted to her group without her permission, or having a reader berate you for posting off-topic in an unmoderated group. A couple of programs in the moderator's tools archive (see Section 15.5) can do this for you.

15.3.1.3 From header

```
From: address-of-author (Full Name)
From: root@www.stones.com (Keith Richards)
```

The From header should be in standard Internet format with the address and name of the author of the message. The following format is also legal:*

```
From: Keith Richards <root@www.stones.com>
```

If you are distributing the submissions as a digest, then the From header should be set to the administrative contact address of the group. Digests are an uncommon method of distribution within a network newsgroup, where the readers prefer individual articles, but are preferred by many people who get traffic from a mailing list. The format for digests is described in RFC 934 and RFC 1153.

15.3.1.4 Subject header

```
Subject: title-of-article
Subject: Economists' Resources on the Internet
```

The Subject header is one of the primary headers that readers use to scan news for articles that interest them. The two most important characteristics of good Subject headers are descriptiveness and consistency; you should strive to provide descriptive, consistent headers in your group.

When checking a header for descriptiveness, keep in mind that most newsreaders don't get a full 80-character line into their subject menu display. Try to get the most informative part of the subject within the first 50 characters. It should be a general summary of the main topics of the article. If the article is a follow-up, it should start with the characters "Re: " and be followed by the subject of the article it references,† unless the topic of the new article has departed significantly from the subject. If it has, "Re: " should be omitted and a new, appropriate topic used.

Consistency of subject headers refers to having a standard format that you can use to aid readers in using their automated selection and rejection tools for the group. Using well-defined keywords at the start of a subject can help tremendously; for example, in *rec.arts.ascii* the Subject is supposed to start with one of several phrases that describe whether the content is line art ("Line"), a uuencoded file of moving images ("Animation"), discussion ("Talk"), etc. Using keywords like this accurately is a very valuable service to your readers, and a periodic note about what they can expect with regard to keywords is desirable.

---

* "Acceptable" refers to the basic syntax. The idea that Keith Richards has root access is another topic for discussion, preferably at the local pub.

† Note that there is a blank following the `:`, and that there should be only one occurrence of "Re: ".

Articles larger than about 60 Kbytes should be split and posted in multiple parts. When you do so, include a parenthetical comment at the end of each article's subject that indicates the sequence, like this:

```
Subject: AUDIO: John Cage, 4'33" (Part 1/3)
Subject: AUDIO: John Cage, 4'33" (Part 2/3)
Subject: AUDIO: John Cage, 4'33" (Part 3/3)
```

Enclosing the variable part in parentheses allows newsreaders like Gnus to be able to select or kill the articles as a set, and sort them in their correct order if they do not arrive that way.

15.3.1.5 Followup-To header

```
Followup-To: newsgroups-for-followup-articles
Followup-To: news.groups
```

This header should exist when follow-up postings are not to go to the same groups listed in the Newsgroups header. The syntax of this header is the same as for Newsgroups, but also allows the presence of the sole keyword **poster**. This keyword tells newsreader posting programs that follow-ups should not be sent to any newsgroups, but should instead be mailed to the author of the article.

news.announce.newgroups uses both forms of the header in every article, since it is not a discussion group. Discussion of articles that appear in it is supposed to take place in *news.groups*, so "Followup-To: news.groups" appears in the Request for Discussion articles (keyworded in the Subject with "RFD:") and articles announcing poll outcomes ("RESULT:"). The Call for Votes ("CFV:") articles that actually solicit for the polls all get "Followup-To: poster" to guard against some of the more exceptionally clueless people who post their votes.

15.3.1.6 Reply-To header

```
Reply-To: email-address
Reply-To: mail-server@rtfm.mit.edu
```

Email replies to articles are normally directed to the address in the From header, unless a Reply-To header is present. The usual occasions for needing a Reply-To are that the author wants responses to go to more than one address, or to an address that is not his usual address.

Some people use the Reply-To address to compensate for their broken software, when they don't know how to control the proper From headers. For example, their software might generate "From: tale@beethoven.cs.rpi.edu," when the preferred address is really "From: tale@cs.rpi.edu." If you get a message like this, it is acceptable to replace the contents of From with those of Reply-To, and elide the Reply-To header. You can also remove it whenever it is identical to From. Reducing redundant information is a virtue.

Some articles announce new email services or provide another address to contact for more information. The Reply-To header can be used in these cases to help users get their mail to the right place. For example, in a message announcing the creation of a new mailing list and soliciting new members, the From header can be the author of the article, and the Reply-To header the address that should be contacted to subscribe to the list. This technique probably saves a few misdirected messages from landing in the author's box directly, saving both the sender and the receiver time and trouble.

Similarly, if you are sending a digested compilation of articles to your readers, the Reply-To header should be set to the submission address of the forum. As mentioned above, the From header for a digest should be your administrative contact address.

15.3.1.7 References header

```
References: message-ids-separated-by-spaces
References: <36hgfc$5mv@ucsu.Colorado.EDU> <36q6kq$1pt@news.nevada.edu>
   <AfpYoQvBS2WN4lol06b@mv.com> <36rlr8$10c@pentagon.io.com>
   <36stke$6ds@badger.3do.com>
```

Newsreaders track threads of discussion by using the References header. This mechanism can also be used to group related articles that are posted as a set. Modern newsreader software can then manipulate the articles as a unit. This is one of the more useful headers that a user can take advantage of, so you should try to include it whenever you reasonably can, even if you have to construct an absent one from information provided in the message body.

Message IDs are listed in chronological order, oldest first, in the header. Keep in mind the 250-character limit on headers, as this header grows with each new article added in the chain and can can grow quite lengthy in a long-winded thread. Try to avoid trimming it, but if you really must, leave the oldest message ID and the three most recent ones, to help the newsreaders relate everything.

Articles posted as a set can use just the message ID of the lead article ("Part 1") in each of the other articles. This means, of course, that you need to have the message ID of the first part before you can post the remaining parts. If you normally let the news system generate your message IDs, this could be very inconvenient, so in this case you probably want to generate your own message ID as described in Section 15.3.1.17.

15.3.1.8 See-Also header

```
See-Also: messages-ids-separated-by-spaces
See-Also: <csm-v44i053=toy_os.131819@sparky.sterling.com>
   <csm-v44i054=toy_os.131819@sparky.sterling.com>
   <csm-v44i055=toy_os.131819@sparky.sterling.com>
   <csm-v44i056=toy_os.131819@sparky.sterling.com>
```

The See-Also header was not part of the original standard news article definition, but is a new addition that is supposed to be like using the References header for a set of articles. You should use it in addition to, rather than instead of, the References header by listing the message IDs of each of the other articles in the set in this header, separated by spaces.

15.3.1.9 Organization header

```
Organization: affiliation, location
Organization: Rensselaer Polytechnic Institute, Troy NY, USA
```

This header is normally used to identify the affiliation of the author. Most posting software inserts it automatically if none is present. This could possibly lead to confusion regarding affiliations, if you approve and post another author's article without an Organization header and your own organization is added.

If you get an article without an Organization header, you can form one either from the author's signature in the article or, as a last resort, from his address. For example, if no identification of the author's affiliation can be found, you could turn a From header of "henry@zoo.toronto.edu" into simply, "Organization: toronto.edu". Though you might occasionally see a forum that uses the same Organization header for all of its articles, it provides more information to use a meaningful Organization header whenever you can.

15.3.1.10 Distribution header

```
Distribution: distribution-keyword
Distribution: austin
```

The Distribution header was intended, in the original news standard, to restrict the propagation of an article to a subset of the sites that it would normally reach when posted in a particular group. Unfortunately, as discussed elsewhere, the use of this header has essentially failed in practice due to a variety of factors.

If you are moderating a widely available newsgroup, it is best to forget about trying to use meaningful Distribution headers in your group. The article will probably end up traveling to sites that theoretically shouldn't get it, and will not end up going to some that should.

If your group is organizational or regional, and its availability includes a set of sites that tightly control a particular distribution keyword, this header might be useful for you. Unfortunately, this book cannot help you in identifying the set of keywords for which this is true.

15.3.1.11 Expires header

```
Expires: DD Mmm YYYY HH:MM:SS TZ
Expires: 12 Dec 1996 00:00:00 GMT
```

If there are special considerations affecting the normal lifetime of an article, the Expires header can be used to provide this hint to news system software. It represents the date and the time past which the article should no longer be retained, and might represent either an unusually short lifetime (an article announcing an event can be removed the day after the event) or an unusually long lifetime (your administrative overview of the group should stay available until it is next posted).

While the Expires header can be specified as a relative time in some news systems, like "Expires: 3 weeks," this is not recommended because it can interact very poorly with some systems. Old B News systems, for example, always interpret the time relative to the time that expire is running, and thus never expire the article. It is better to use an explicit date of the form above. Modern news systems tend to simply ignore relative dates entirely.

You can safely use "00:00:00 GMT" as the time and vary only the date. If you want to represent your time zone, do this with a numeric offset, not an abbreviation. See Section 18.2.1.1 for details.

Many news administrators grant a little leeway to moderators to use the Expires header wisely, allowing a longer time for articles in moderated groups before unconditional deletion. Use it responsibly. Also, remember that the header is not a guarantee that the article will be removed at the time you request; the ultimate removal policies are up to individual sites.

15.3.1.12 Supersedes header

```
Supersedes: message-id
Supersedes: <active_775784480@isc.org>
```

The Supersedes header is used to simultaneously cancel a message while providing a new version of it. It lists the message ID of the article to be canceled. This can be very convenient when used in conjunction with the Expires header because you can post a new version of the article before the previous version expires, theoretically leaving the article continuously available.

15.3.1.13 Keywords header

```
Keywords: keywords-separated-by-commas
Keywords: smirk, gross, heard it
```

The Keywords header is supposed to label some of the content of the article. There are no keywords that are in widespread, standard use across newsgroups, though several groups, like *rec.humor.funny* and *comp.os.linux.announce*, try to have meaningful and consistent keywords. Without consistency, keywords in articles are effectively useless and are better left off.

Be wary of keywords chosen by the article's submitter. People are notoriously bad at classifying their own material, and this shows through in spades when the average person tries to come up with the proper keywords for their article.

15.3.1.14 Summary header

```
Summary: summarizing-phrase
Summary: Urban legends supported, challenged, and debunked
```

RFC 1036 encourages use of the Summary header in follow-up articles, presumably to describe how the article content varies from the originally defined Subject header. It is meant only to give a very coarse overview of the article, and should be very terse if it exists. Most readers don't even see it until they select the article for reading. We recommend that if an article warrants an outline of more than 70 characters, the outline should be included at the start of the body of the message.

15.3.1.15 Path header

```
Path: username
Path: bounceback
```

The Path header is a mandatory header used by server news software to track the propagation of an article on its way around the network. When preparing an article for your group, remove the Path header that came with it. Including it could cause the article to not be propagated back to the submitter's site. You should not create your own Path header in your prepared articles, unless either your news software makes a Path that terminates in a real local address on the system (yours or the news server's administrative account), or you inject articles directly into the news system, as via *rnews*. In both of those cases, one like "Path: bounce-back" should be used.

In ancient times (ten whole years ago), some news software used the news path to construct the return address for email replies. This is widely considered to be grossly inappropriate behavior now. Setting the last component of the header to something that should generate a rejection message from your email system combats those few old implementations that are still running out there. We'd also like to believe that it encourages those sites to upgrade to software that is compatible with the rest of the Net, but that's probably overly optimistic.

15.3.1.16 Date header

```
Date: DD Mmm YYYY HH:MM:SS TZ
Date: 12 Dec 1997 16:30:21 GMT
```

The Date header is supposed to indicate the time at which an article is injected into the news system. While conceptually this could be the time at which the author tried to post it to the group and had it mailed to you, you should elide whatever Date is present in the submission and let the news system's posting agent generate it for you.

There are two primary problems with using the date as provided: the mail header standard is more flexible than the news header standard, and news systems try to make some of their decisions about accepting or expiring articles based on the time in the Date header. It's possible that the Date you get in the mail submission isn't legal syntax in a news article. Even if it is, the date might cause the article to be rejected as too old (even with a reasonably accurate date because of feed latency) or too new.

This header is required in the articles propagating around the network, so if you are injecting fully formed messages without the use of a posting agent, you need to make sure it conforms to the legal "DD Mmm YYYY HH:MM:SS TZ" format. (If the time zone you want to use is not GMT, see Section 18.2.1.1 for how it should be specified. Don't just use whatever alphabetic abbreviation is common in your area.)

15.3.1.17 Message-ID header

```
Message-ID: message-id
Message-ID: <879521402.16480@isc.org>
```

The unique identity of an article in the news system is represented in the Message-ID header. You should strike any existing Message-ID line, and, in most cases, allow the news posting system to generate one for you; it is required in the final article. Message IDs are never supposed to be reused, and the system takes care to create one that is theoretically unique, usually based on the time the ID is generated and the process number that created it.

If you must create your own message IDs for some application, such as creating the References headers for a multipart set of articles, be very careful to make sure that it is standards compliant, or the article will not be propagated. In brief, the form of a message ID is:

```
<local-part@host.domain>
```

host.domain is typically the same as in your email address. *local-part* is a unique string made up of alphanumeric characters and those from the set "#$%&'*+-/=?^_`{|}~". Periods (.) can appear, but not as the first or last character, and not adjacent to another period.

Be warned that if your message IDs are predictable, you could theoretically have the messages that you post blocked by an unsavory character who posts messages with those IDs before the real ones reach sites. It is best to use somewhat random message IDs.

15.3.1.18 Sender header

```
Sender: email-address
Sender: newprod-request@zorch.sf-bay.org
```

The Sender header is defined in RFC 1036 to identify the person or program responsible for inserting a message into the news network. The standard occasion for this is when the From header does not represent the account from which the posting was actually made. This is what happens when a moderator approves other authors' articles for the group.

From, Sender, and Originator

The advent of NNTP began a surge in the appearance of the Sender header in articles. This happened because an NNTP client had to define From to identify the author of the article, and when the article was passed to the posting program running on the server, usually via software running as the news owner, a Sender header was automatically added to identify the discrepancy. It replaced whatever Sender was already there.

Unfortunately, this tends to foil the usual attempts by both reader and server software to compare identities in *cancel* messages. The latest generation of the NNTP Reference Implementation uses the non-standard Originator header to identify the user who first posted the article, if different from the From header.

Your main concern with the Sender header is to note whether there is a curious discrepancy between it and the From header. A Sender that indicates a typical administrative account like *usenet* or *news* can be safely ignored. One that seems to point to a user other than the one in the From header could bear further examination, especially if something about the article seems controversial, which might suggest that someone is trying to forge a posting. Handle this as you see fit, perhaps by sending a mail message to each of the From and Sender addresses.

When posting an article, any extant Sender header should be removed. Let your news posting agent do what it does with regard to adding another one, as it may put in either your address or that of the news administration account. Either is acceptable. Alternatively, you can always have it list your group's contact address—this is true to the spirit of RFC 1036 and helps advertise the existence of the address for your readers.

15.3.1.19 System-defined headers

There are other headers that commonly appear in the mail articles that you are turning into news articles. They should normally all be eliminated. Here is a list of some of them and their intended purposes:

To   Used by mailers to identify the recipient of a message.

Apparently-To
>   Used by mailers to identify the recipient of a message.

Cc   Used by mailers to identify the recipient of a message.

In-Reply-To
>   Used by mail user agents to indicate the preceding message in the exchange; can be used to craft a References header.

Received
>   Used by mailers to audit the transfer of a message.

Return-Path
>   Used by mailers to note a definitive route to the message's originator.

Status
>   Used by mail user agents to track what the user has done with a message.

Mime-Version
>   Used by mailers to define messages that make use of the Multipurpose Internet Mail Extensions (MIME).

Content-*
>   Used in MIME messages to describe the message contents.

NNTP-Posting-Host
>   Used to identify the host from which the post was injected.

Originator
>   Used to identify the user that posted the original message.

Lines
>   Used by newsreaders to show the length of an article.

Xref
>   Used by news systems to indicate the storage location of the article on a server.

If an article uses MIME, dealing with it can be a little more tricky than just removing the MIME headers. These headers are described in Section 18.5, but there are two special issues to keep in mind here. One is that you can easily make a Lines header incorrect by removing the headers. The other is that in most groups, many of the readers don't have convenient MIME handling capabilities, so you should probably stick with conventional ASCII messages whenever you can.

15.3.1.20 User-defined headers

Headers not defined in Internet standards should always be prefixed with "X-". Some of the more regularly seen "X headers" include those that announce the mail or the news user agent that the author of the article is using, or those that disclaim the responsibility of the author's organization. As a general rule, these should be removed.

15.3.1.21 Auxiliary headers

Some groups use auxiliary headers to help the process of making archives of articles that appear there. Strictly speaking, these auxiliary headers aren't really headers as far as a news or mail system is concerned. They are in standard header format, but lead the body of the article. Sources and binaries groups, as well as *comp.archives* and *news.answers*, make regular use of these headers.

One widely available package that works with auxiliary headers is the *rkive* suite, available in *comp.sources.misc* archives. It contains several manual pages that describe in detail how auxiliary headers can be used.

15.3.2 Overall Body Formatting

The messages you post should have the same basic body characteristics that messages in unmoderated groups have. Full line lengths, between newline characters, should be between 65 and 75 characters; a right margin of column 70 is recommended for easy reading and citing. Lines over 79 characters long are very annoying to read in some environments, and lines over 512 characters are corrupted by a bug in the NNTP Reference Implementation.

Be careful of characters outside the printing ASCII range (ASCII 32 through ASCII 126, plus tab and newline). While more and more of the transmission network is 8-bit clean, using 8-bit characters still begs the question, "What character set do those 8-bit characters use?" The 7-bit ASCII characters are very well defined and used as-is in a wide variety of character sets internationally, but many of those character sets assign special meaning to characters 128 through 255. To be sure the text is correctly interpreted, the message should have the appropriate MIME headers, particularly Content-Type (see Section 18.5). In the most common 8-bit case, which covers most European character sets, you can use the following header:

```
Content-Type: text/plain; charset=iso-8859-1
```

In certain groups, it is safe to assume that primarily one character set is being used, such as *alt.chinese.text.big5* using BIG 5. Even then, the articles should still include MIME encapsulation, at least to definitively indicate to the newsreader what character set is in use, and possibly also to encode the message in 7-bit ASCII to ensure its safe delivery to all corners of the Net.

As moderator of the group, you can adopt the role of proofreader and editor, fixing small irregularities or even returning submissions for the author to correct. In your formal moderation policy, state how you plan to handle minor and major problems with formatting, spelling, and grammar.

15.3.3 Moderator Comments

Sometimes it is appropriate for you to insert a comment into another author's article before you send it to the group. Such a comment should be enclosed in brackets ([]) and should have a clear identifier that labels it as a comment from you, the moderator. For example, the following format works well in articles cross-posted to groups where people might not even realize a moderator has processed the article:

```
[ group.name's moderator's comment: your comment here. ---
your initials, login name, first name, or the like ]
```

As a general rule, moderator comments should be used very sparingly. Readers, and especially authors, can get very sensitive about interjections placed directly into articles. Usually they should be reserved for providing factual information, like answering a reader's request for a pointer to an archive site. Discussion about something the author has said should be posted in another article, thereby using the same method that other readers of the group use and not abusing the power of being a moderator.

The proper location of a comment depends on the particular comment. If a comment interrupts the flow of an article as the author has written it, try to save the comment for the end of the message or at least the end of the paragraph.

15.3.4 Signatures

The short files that many users automatically attach to the ends of their articles should be preceded by a line of two dashes and a space ("-- "), the conventional indicator of the start of a signature. Many moderators choose not to allow signature files on the messages that they post; others are fairly religious about keeping them under the four-line limit mentioned in the *news.announce.newusers* documentation and enforced by some posting software. Signatures over four lines long are detested by many users, especially when they waste a lot of vertical space or have unnecessary borders and graphics.

One possibly undesired feature to watch out for is the appending of your own signature to articles that you approve for the group. Some moderators intentionally tag each of their group's articles this way to provide omnipresent information about submissions or moderation policy. Most moderators opt to prevent another signature, especially their personal one, from being added.

You can test whether your own signature is appended by preparing an article as you would for insertion into the group, then taking out the Approved header. Try to post it; when it returns to you in mail as another submission, the presence or absence of your own signature should be readily observable. If it's there and you don't want it to be, your basic choices are to rename or remove your *.signature* file, use a special account for the group that doesn't have a *.signature* file, or use a posting agent or posting flag that does not include it.

15.4 *Putting the Articles in the Group*

When you have prepared the headers and body of the article for insertion into the news system, it is then simply a matter of passing it to *inews -h*, a command available with both C News and INN.

We recommend using *inews* over trying to generate a complete set of required headers and then passing that article to *rnews* or the NNTP *IHAVE* command. *inews* creates missing headers for you and usually provides quicker and more helpful error messages in the event of a problem with the article.

Once the article is accepted by the news system, the regular propagation mechanisms used for all articles should take over. If there is a problem here, it probably doesn't have to do with whether the group is moderated. Refer to the sections on testing and running your news transport system to debug the problem.

15.5 *Moderators' Software Tools*

Originally, most moderators were forced to write their submission processing software by themselves, though other experienced moderators would share their sources when asked. Unlike mailers or other types of news software like transport systems and newsreaders, there hasn't been a lot of development in general-purpose, production quality tools for moderators. Nevertheless, the homegrown tools of some moderators have been made available in a public archive.

The moderator's tools archive is available via FTP from *ftp://ftp.landfield.com/ moderators/*. UUNET mirrors the tools directory to *ftp://ftp.uu.net/networking/ news/moderating/*.

The contents of the moderators' tools archive have been generously made available "as is." The archive is a snapshot of existing tools, as they are being used, rather than a formal release of polished software. Many of the sources, scripts, and supporting documentation are not as pretty as their authors might wish, but they work. The tools are being made available so that other moderators can see work-ing examples of how the tasks are handled, and potentially use them as a starting point for their own custom tools. To make the tools most useful, you need to be familiar with the C programming language, the Unix shell, and Perl, in order to adapt them to your own needs.

One other very useful moderator's tool, often used by newer groups with multiple moderators, is Igor Chudov's *STUMP*. It provides many features for supporting shared moderation efforts robustly, all in a nice graphical user interface. See *http://www.algebra.com/~ichudov/usenet/scrm/robomed/robomed.html* for more information.

15.6   *The Political Side*

The following advice is intended to provide one view of what works and what doesn't in the relationship between a moderator and the users of a group. It is based on dozens of collective years of moderation, and is offered as a set of friendly guidelines rather than prescriptive commandments. You should certainly feel free to add your own style to a newsgroup; it is inevitable.

15.6.1   *Why Have a Moderated Group?*

The fundamental reason to have a moderated group is to control the articles that appear in the group. While moderation is occasionally used to support a gateway to a mailing list and automatically let through all submitted articles, the main con-trol desired is that of keeping out undesirable postings, serving the readership by providing a higher signal-to-noise ratio.* There are two main categories of moder-ated groups:

- The postings in the group are intended to be informative only, with no follow-up discussion appearing in the group. The set of people who can post to such a group is relatively small.

- A higher-quality forum is desired by keeping out articles not germane to the topic of the group, redundant articles, or articles that otherwise impede the use of the group by people who want to post there.

The first set of groups is characterized by the many *.announce* and *.info* groups spread through the Usenet namespace. Within the sphere of their topics, these groups are generally meant to have only announcements and periodic informa-tional postings. They are meant to be very low volume compared to their compan-ion unmoderated discussion groups, so that it is easy to find the periodic

---

* This term is borrowed from the radio community. In Usenet, it is used to mean roughly "the number of articles I want to read versus those I shouldn't waste my time on."

information and easy to skim on a regular basis to discover any interesting new events or developments.

The latter set of groups can include discussion groups, groups for which a higher standard is demanded for on-topic articles, and groups that enforce particular constraints on the appearance of articles. For example, a discussion group on a topic that has vocal opponents, like religion or hunting, can be moderated to keep out inflammatory postings. In the "higher standard" class are groups like *comp.risks* and *rec.humor.funny*, which try to not only stay focused but to also provide extra quality control on the submissions. Finally, in those like *comp.mail.maps* or the *comp.sources.** groups, moderators mandate additional formatting of the articles for archiving and file extraction.

There are a few drawbacks to moderated groups. The two major concerns of the Usenet community with regard to moderation are those of censorship and delays. These are discussed in more detail below in Section 15.6.6.

15.6.2 Serving the Readership

The primary ideal to keep in mind with regard to your responsibilities as a moderator is that you are there to serve the users of the group; without them, your role as a moderator is essentially pointless. Try to keep in mind both how people posting to the group and how people reading the articles want to use it. The latter group is invariably larger, and should be given the nod in matters where there are conflicting desires.

One of the best things that you can do is create a moderation policy for your group. This policy should be a readily available, reasonably comprehensive, and mostly static statement that lets everyone know what to expect out of the group. The policy is also useful when questionable situations arise, as it can help you to decide what course to take and defend that decision later if need be. To be readily available, it should both be posted periodically to the group (once a month is fine) and be available via other information servers like FTP and the Web. To be reasonably comprehensive, the policy should include instructions on how articles are submitted, descriptions of special headers you use, a note about any archives of the group, and a statement of the basic guidelines you use for approving articles. Once established, changes to the policy should be infrequent, and you may want to poll your readers about major changes in policy before implementing them. If you do change it, post not only the new version but also a contextual difference listing, as with Unix's *diff -c*, to highlight changes.

It should go without saying that all submissions to the group should be answered. At a minimum, this means having the article appear in the group or sending a rejection notice. Some moderators also have auto-reply programs attached to their moderation address that indicate little more than the receipt of the message, without regard to its final disposition.

If you reject an article that is crossposted to other groups, or do not do the crossposting that is requested, you should inform the poster of that fact so that the article can be directed as desired. If you do not plan to do crossposting, which is discouraged because of its user-unfriendliness but might be appropriate based on the nature of your forum, this should be mentioned in your policy posting.

15.6.3 *Commercial Postings*

The posting of commercial articles is a very sensitive topic on Usenet, especially as more and more people are keying in to what seems to be an extremely low cost way to get advertisements to millions of people. Advertisements, however, run counter to the culture on which Usenet was founded, one of sharing the costs for the benefit of all. Unwanted advertising posted in inappropriate places is effectively a misappropriation of the resources of other people—their disk space, their machine time, and their personal time. Advertising on Usenet is popularly considered to be antisocial and is likely to generate more ill will for a company than any new interest. However, people on Usenet do want information, including information on products they might want to purchase, so this can be a fine line to walk.

First you need to decide whether advertisements are to be allowed at all, either commercial (companies selling things) or classified (individuals selling things). If they are deemed acceptable, you should establish a policy on what form they can take and publish it in your policy statement.

Regarding the frequency of advertisements, most people seem to find repeated advertisements to be undesirable, much the same way they don't want to see repeated articles. Advertisements for a particular product or service should only appear once.

A very fine line exists between advertisements and independent reviews, the latter of which may be desirable to your readers. It is certainly possible for an independent reviewer to offer high praise that sounds a bit like hyped-up advertising from the company. If the reviewer seems to have any personal interest—especially financial—in the success of the product, it's more likely to irritate readers. Practice extra discretion with product and service reviews, looking for any special clues that might reveal the association of the reviewer with the reviewee. The Organization header, posting site, and user's signature file can help here. Don't be hesitant to ask the submitter directly if you have reservations about the review.

Acceptable Advertising?

A good metric for acceptable advertising content has been offered by T. William Wells:

> Having watched the Usenet over the years, I have come up with a simple, easy to remember and apply rule for deciding what is good advertising and what is bad advertising.
>
> Good advertising informs.
>
> Bad advertising persuades.
>
> You can most easily tell persuasion from information by the modifiers. Adjectives and adverbs that make judgments are almost always persuaders ("great") as are those that would appeal to the user based on irrelevant criteria ("new"). Claims that are not backed up by easily available facts, including subjective claims, are persuaders, not information. A claim of benefit to the user, other than those implied by the product itself, is likely a persuader. E.g., "this will do your taxes," of a tax preparation program, is a claim of benefit to the user, implied by the program; that's information. "This will do your taxes better than any other program" is not. It has a judgment ("better") modifier, which is a big clue.

15.6.4 Anonymous Postings

An anonymous posting is one in which the true identity of the poster is not available to the reader. The identity may or may not be known by you, the moderator. Your policy on each form of anonymity is another statement that should go into the periodic posting of the group's guidelines.

Anonymous postings for which you do not know the author are usually seen from anonymous remailers, of which the site *anon.penet.fi* was the most famous until it was closed by its maintainer in the summer of 1996. Many remailers still exist. They don't require any advanced computing skills on the part of the person sending the message, just the ability to send email.

A message submitted through a well-run anonymous remailer is effectively untraceable to its originator, even by contacting the site's administrators. With one-way remailers, you might not even be able to contact the author at all. A "single blind" two-way remailer allows your identity to come through in the headers if you do reply, while a "double blind" remailer keeps the header information anonymous, though you can provide identifying information in the body of your message.

How you choose to act with regard to submissions for which you do not know the originator at all is usually relative to the content of the article and of your group. If posting on the topic could be damaging to the poster, as is often true in support and recovery groups, some leniency for the poster is generally warranted. If posting is potentially damaging to others and can't be substantiated, as with a character assassination, deference to the maligned is probably warranted, lest you find yourself in the middle of ugly accusations of libel with no clear source to hold responsible. Of course, there's a lot of grey area between these two extremes, such as whistle-blowing, where an employee wants to allege wrongdoing in a company but doesn't want to risk termination.

If you do not allow submissions from anonymous remailers, but still want to offer submitters the possibility of remaining anonymous to the readership, you can do the identity stripping yourself. You need to let users know how to submit such postings in the group policy statement. You can do the work yourself, simply by posting under your own identity, or you can create a special mail alias at your site that handles replies as desired. The latter takes just a tad more initial effort, but saves you time in the long run. At the start of an anonymous message, you should include a moderator's comment that indicates you have published the article with the author's name withheld by request.

Of course, it is difficult to ever really know the true identity of someone who has submitted an article because it is fairly easy for someone to be intentionally obscure about their identity while providing something plausible in its place. Sleuthing for every submission is impractical, so you by and large have to trust that what comes in is from who it purports to be from, unless it seems uncommonly controversial, vitriolic, or otherwise potentially damaging to the reputation of the poster. Those postings probably warrant verification by way of a mail exchange before being posted, if the article is otherwise acceptable for the group.

15.6.5 *Handling a Recalcitrant User*

As moderator of a newsgroup, prepare to be flamed by a vocal minority. Assuming you do your job reasonably well, most of the satisfied readers will remain silent. However, whether you deserve it or not, you will receive annoyed criticism from some readers. This is typically of the form:

- Why did you reject my article?

- Who made you God?

- How dare you get sick, go on vacation, and/or neglect the newsgroup for your real life?

It helps to have form letters to deal with some of these questions, notably the first one. Keep the charter of the newsgroup handy, too. It is valuable in helping to quiet a complainer, particularly if the charter was one publicly approved by vote.

Remaining calm in the face of this sort of criticism is the best defense. If there are actual facts under the heated rhetoric, address those calmly and ignore the tone of the criticism. Apart from that, your best defense is probably just to ignore the poster, especially if he seems to be the only one whining. Resist the temptation to have the last word in an argument, even if the argument is in public. Drawn out bickering only serves to undermine respect for you and your role.*

15.6.6 *Addressing Widespread Dissatisfaction*

As mentioned above, there are primarily two reasons that people have a problem with moderation: issues of censorship and time delays before articles appear in the group. Less commonly, readers can become bitter about the moderator's attitude or style.

If there is a lot of grumbling going on about the group, listen carefully to the complaints. Identify their basis and see how they can be addressed without ostracizing other readers. If it can be addressed with a minor change in your policies or a non-controversial revision of the charter, simply implement it. In questionable areas or those that would significantly change the charter or your policies, it is wise to take a public survey of what the readers want. The benefits of a survey are that they not only help you decide what to do, but they also document what the readers want and let your readers know that you are responsive to their interests.

15.6.6.1 *Censorship*

The censorship issue comes up because people fear they won't be able to get their messages out to the general public if the moderator doesn't approve. This concern can be alleviated by pointing out the many unmoderated groups that exist. You never have to tell someone that their article should not be in Usenet if it isn't appropriate for your group; you can point them to a suitable unmoderated group. With regard to First Amendment arguments, remember that not all of the Net is in the United States of America.† Even if it were, freedom of speech is a protection against government encroachment on the exchange of ideas; editing what appears in controlled forums like newspapers has been happening on American soil since at least the time of Benjamin Franklin. A moderator is more akin to an editor than to a state censor.

---

* If you're still tempted to strike back, remember that nothing annoys such people more than being ignored.

† Indeed, maybe even you're not. Take a look out your window to try to ascertain this.

If you moderate a discussion group, you should probably let almost everything that is on topic through, unless your group is characterized as having an unusually high discourse standard. You risk running into antagonism from users if you develop a reputation as a tyrant.

15.6.6.2 Time delays

With modern news transport systems, an article posted to an unmoderated newsgroup usually reaches most of the machines that it should reach within a few hours of posting. On NNTP-connected hosts, it can often be on thousands of servers in mere minutes. In very unusual cases, going through the moderator might be faster than getting a message out via an unmoderated group, but by and large the moderator adds a delay that doesn't otherwise exist. Even if it does take some time for the news on the poster's site to get out to other sites, the sheer fact that the message has to go through your site and be propagated back to the poster's server, rather than appearing instantaneously in the group on the poster's server, creates a delay that some posters might not understand. This is usually the source of multiple submissions of the same article to your group.

Time delays of a few days are not usually a problem for groups that are not oriented toward discussion, but they can be deadly for a lively conversation. Turnaround time of less than a day is widely expected for discussion groups. Announcement groups also expect timely announcements on the order of within a day of submission. Most users are understanding of weekend breaks for moderators.

There are a few things you can do to keep delays down in the groups where it really matters. One is to make it as easy as possible on yourself to post a message. Ideally, you want to be able to pipe an approved mail message into a script that injects it into news at the press of a keystroke. The moderator's software archive, described in Section 15.5, has some help to offer here. Similarly, form letters help speed up rejections. Having multiple or backup moderators for the group, as described in Section 15.6.9, can also spread the load to keep the group running even if you have some interference for a little while. Finally, some moderators run software that allows for automatic approval of submissions to groups for a defined set of regular posters and other contributors have their submissions directed to a human moderator, who can then handle the article the usual way.

The expected turnaround time for articles should be stated in your moderation policy. Don't be too idealistic; give yourself an attainable standard. If you will not be able to perform your duties for an unusual length of time, you should post an administrative note to the group to inform the readership of the variance from the norm.

15.6.6.3 Attitude

How you treat your readers, both during conversation in the group and in administrative contact, is important and can end up being a real problem if your readers don't like your attitude. You need to decide whether you are going to be in the shadows of the operation of the group, nearly indistinguishable from an automatic filter, or if you are going to be more visible and proactive with regard to stimulating submissions for the group.

Though it has happened rarely, a moderator who ignores a lot of mail, insults users, sets himself on a pedestal, or otherwise alienates the readership is going to have a group that is much worse off for it. Being antagonistic with contributors to the group is the worst offense; it results in the loss of the source of the articles for the group. In addition, try not to be too protective of a group from the influences of people who want to help make it better for everyone.

If they sense an attitude problem, users won't be shy about pointing it out. Take into account the possibility that your messages have been misinterpreted, but if it happens frequently, consider how you can make your sentiments more clear. Be willing to publicly apologize if someone was slighted in a message that could have been misinterpreted by more people than just an overly sensitive reader.

15.6.6.4 Style

The form in which postings appear can readily become a sore spot with posters. Reformatting of articles to fit a consistent standard will probably be met without comment, but gratuitous changes to them will at least get noticed by the poster. Fixing minor typographic errors is usually acceptable, but rewrites are something best left to the original author. Authors can be very protective about the appearance of their *.signature* files; have a stated policy on how you handle them.

Be wary of moderator's comments in postings. As we discussed earlier, these have been known to be the source of some complaints, especially if they are abused. Don't use moderator's comments to interject commentary that is best done in a separate article under the moderator's name, putting the moderator on the same level as other participants in the group. Don't let this completely scare you away from them, however. As noted before, they can be useful to answer direct questions that have short, factual answers, saving everyone the time and effort of further messages about it.

15.6.7 Forged Approvals

If someone is very upset with you for rejecting an article, the poster might try to forge the approval of the article. While canceling other people's postings on Usenet is a bad thing, one of the widely agreed upon situations for its applicability is by moderators canceling articles that they did not approve in their groups. You are the arbiter of what appears in the group; if something is there that you do not think should be, it is within your domain to cancel it. There is a program called *cancel.pl* in the moderator's archive (see Section 15.5) that takes an article to be canceled on its standard input and generates a fully formed *cancel* message and sends it to *rnews*.

WARNING   When you cancel a message for your group, you also cancel that message in every group to which it was crossposted, regardless of whether the Newsgroups header of your *cancel* message names those other groups.

Do not rush to the conclusion that an article appearing in your group without your prior approval has been put there with malice. It might well have been an innocent error, especially from a fellow moderator. News software is notoriously bad about handling multiple moderated groups in the Newsgroups header. It doesn't especially care whether the approval has come from all of the moderators of all of the groups. If you would have approved the article anyway, there is nothing to be gained by canceling it.

If you find an article in your group that you did not approve, try to determine where it came from based on the header clues. Contact the originator and find out why it happened. Don't be unnecessarily confrontational; you're more likely to keep the problem from recurring if you don't berate the perpetrator. If you are in unresolved

opposition, you can try contacting the administration at the offender's site by working through the standard contact addresses of *newsmaster, news, usenet, postmaster,* and *root* until you get a hold of someone in authority. In the unfortunate event that they don't care to deal with the problem, you might have to try to contact their news feeds. The Path header of the original article should indicate at least one of them.

One other unapproved posting you might want to just let be is an April Fool's prank, posted close to the 1st of April. Most such pranks are crafted with humorous intent. As long as it is not malicious, leaving the posting can entertain readers and demonstrate that even the ornery moderator has a sense of humor.

15.6.8 Copyright

There are several issues involving copyright that you should be aware of as a moderator. They involve the inherent copyright of original submissions, the copyright of republished works, the copyright of your own creations, and compilation copyrights on what appears in the group. The summary we've provided here is, to the best of our knowledge, accurate; it is, however, not strict legal advice. There is also a very informative FAQ on copyright law posted near the middle of each month to *misc.legal, misc.legal.computing, misc.int-property, comp.patents,* and the related **.answers* groups. It is a high-quality document that is recommended reading for moderators. If you have a particular legal question that could affect your actions, you should consult a qualified lawyer.

Copyright provides legal protection for the expression of ideas. It allows particular exclusive rights to an original creator for actions such as publication, translation, adaptation, and performance. It does not protect the ideas themselves, whether factual, philosophical, or algorithmic; only their representation is covered. Original, in this context, has a very liberal standard that refers primarily to the method of germination of the idea and not its temporal relation to other expressions of the same idea, even if identical.

Under the terms of the international Berne Convention for the Protection of Literary and Artistic Works, the current revision of which has been signed by most countries, copyright for a work exists as soon as it is created. There is no requirement for notice or registration, though a notice might be useful to alert others, obviating claims of innocent infringement.

Works that are not copyrighted are in the public domain. They may be used by anyone without any restrictions. Since copyright now widely applies to the vast majority of created works by default, new public domain works are much rarer. It usually takes an explicit statement of the abandonment of copyright by the holder to put a work in the public domain.

"Fair use" is the doctrine that allows for limited use of a copyrighted work for any of several reasons, traditionally for purposes such as reporting, teaching, commentary, or research. Whether use by a non-holder is protected by this doctrine is fairly subjective and not easily determinable by some rigid standard; there is no specific requirement for maximum length or percentage of the total work. When in doubt, it is best to secure permission from the holder. At the very least, it's respectfully polite to ask, even if there wouldn't have been a violation.

15.6.8.1 Submitter copyrights

As noted above, any submission you receive for the group almost certainly has some form of copyright on it, unless the submitter has explicitly given notice of copyright abandonment. The act of submitting something to the computer network cannot be seen as an abandonment of copyright; in fact, the reason for copyright is to protect a creator after a work has been made publicly available. However, receiving a submission for your moderated group is reasonably a request for you to distribute on the copyright holder's behalf, even if that request is not expressly stated. This is the way that Usenet has operated since moderated newsgroups began and is akin to sending letters to the editor of a newspaper.

Note that there is a possible area of confusion if you get what appears to be a submission to the group at your administrative contact address, or an administrative request at the submission address. Publishing private mail is a violation of the Berne Convention, so if there is any question regarding whether a message was really intended for publication, it is both polite and probably legally required to obtain permission for posting it.

How you choose to handle copyrights with apparently unrealistic terms is another matter; it probably doesn't warrant a statement in your group's guidelines but might involve you in a debate or two with group participants. There are some people who put copyright statements in their articles to attempt to retain some aspect of distribution rights, such as lack of propagation to commercial news sites, which is unrealistic to expect in the network news environment. You have very little control over where an article goes when it is published, but you might know that your group is propagated somewhere the submitter doesn't want the article to go to. Returning the submission is probably the safest course of action, so you can't be blamed for causing an infringement that you reasonably expected.

15.6.8.2 Republished works

Keep an eye out for excerpts of works that didn't originate in the Usenet community, like newspaper or magazine articles, book citations, source code, pictures, or audio recordings. These require permission from the copyright holder to be posted. To accept a submission that claims "Reprinted without permission" reflects badly on your responsibility as a moderator.

It is unclear where responsibility would really lie for an infringement in someone else's article posted by you. If the submitter presented it as an original work, you would probably be held blameless. If it was clearly someone else's work without clear permission, however, you could be held liable. If the submitter reported that the material was used with permission but it really wasn't, it seems reasonable that the liability would be with the submitter. Courts aren't always reasonable, though.

The traditional style of discourse in Usenet is to cite the previous writer's work in a thread and then add commentary in reply. This practice is probably covered by the "fair use" doctrine and accepted as a community standard. It is not necessary for the follow-up author to secure permission even if the entire previous article was quoted verbatim.

Articles forwarded from other public forums can be a bit of a grey area. Republication from another widely available newsgroup is generally accepted as permissible. Forwarding from a mailing list that doesn't have publicly available archives is a bit more of a touchy subject with people, and it is best to treat it as private mail, not because of law but rather because of etiquette.

15.6.8.3 Periodic post copyrights

The periodic postings that appear in your group should probably carry an explicit statement that either asserts copyright or abandons it. In most cases, you should assert copyright with liberal distribution terms, as the intent of most network news groups is to distribute information widely. Once you post an article, you have little knowledge of where it goes from there. Archives might save it automatically, other archives might mirror those archives, people might forward it to other interested readers, some sites might never expire it, and so on. In a worldwide newsgroup, it has probably also gone to a couple of countries where copyright protection is minimal or nonexistent. Fretting over specific distribution methods is pretty meaningless, and you probably don't have much of a claim for damages in a lawsuit anyway.

This topic has received a lot of debate on the Net due to the surge of publications, from news stories to books to CD-ROMs, about the Internet and its resources. Many companies who would otherwise know better have violated Usenet author copyrights by not securing permission for republication beyond the scope expected by publication within a network newsgroup. Not everyone just blithely appropriates others' work, though, so be prepared with an answer if someone asks to use your periodic postings. It is at your discretion whether to allow it or not. Here is one form answer to such requests:

```
Yes, you may use it and any of the other informational postings I make.

You must cite the original authors and editors of the articles, given
in the auxiliary headers of each article.  You should also note that the
documents have minor changes on a regular basis, so any version you use
will be out of date in the amount of time it takes to get your
manuscript through final draft to the publisher.  The article may be
reformatted to suit your media, but the content should be used
verbatim.

Finally, I would like a complimentary copy of the finished work sent to
the address below.  Thank you very much.

Name
Address
```

15.6.8.4 *Compilation copyrights*

A compilation copyright is the copyright asserted by arranging the works of others into a new expression of those ideas. For example, it is the copyright asserted by a professional journal over the volumes of papers that it publishes. The telephone book is copyrighted even though it is simply a list of factual information. In a more unusual case, West Publishing has claimed copyright on the numbering of pages in its legal references, as the decisions themselves cannot be copyrighted.

Popular opinion seems to be that compilation copyright for a newsgroup should not be done. A compilation copyright is largely meaningless in the context of a newsgroup and could be seen as an affront to all of the people who make the group work, especially the contributing authors. Unless you are actively arranging articles for a very high quality forum, rather than simply approving the appearance of articles, a compilation copyright doesn't signify much in the way of a new expression of the ideas that the participants could have just put in an unmoderated group.

A compilation copyright on the newsgroup, if any, should probably be liberal, as with those on periodic postings. In any event, a compilation copyright cannot supplant the rights of the original author without explicit assignment.

15.6.9 *Enlisting Help*

Moderating a group for 52 weeks of the year can prove to be an onerous task. Eventually, you'll probably want to take a vacation, or maybe you'll become ill, or perhaps little gremlins will snark your computer, making it unavailable for days. Perhaps you have a very high-volume group that requires a few dozen hours per week to moderate, or maybe there are proactive changes you'd like to make regarding the group but don't have enough time to work toward them. If your group is about a controversial topic, you might want some checks and balances on your approvals and rejections.

All of these issues warrant having other people closely involved in the operation of the group. There are a few different typical roles these people can take, each serving one or more of the needs of the group.

You can choose these people in any of several ways. Soliciting volunteers from the readership by way of a public request is one popular method. Appointing people who you already know to be suitable is also common. Whatever the method, when you have recruited help, their roles should be documented in the group's policy posting.

15.6.9.1 Backup moderators

The simplest insurance for group continuity is a backup moderator. It is strongly recommended that every group have someone who can take over the moderation of the group in a pinch. Usually the need for a backup moderator is for temporary service, but it could possibly be longer. When you decide to retire from moderating the group, the backup moderator is the most likely candidate for your replacement.

You should exchange telephone numbers with your backup moderator, so you have off-the-Net contact information in the event that you cannot contact each other via email. You should make sure that the backup moderator knows how to process submissions for the group. A trial run or two could be good to impart a feel for the process and fine-tune any details. Make sure the two of you understand under what circumstances she is expected to assume duties, including the unlikely but possible event that you simply disappear without a trace.

The backup moderator should probably be on the submissions mail alias, getting articles when you do. This will make a transition relatively seamless. You could also put her on the administrative contact alias, to show how you run the group, including why you reject various articles. In this case, the backup moderator is essentially a shadow of you.

15.6.9.2 Advisory councils

An advisory council can be very useful for consulting on topics of concern without having to go to the whole readership to ask. Discussing the issues with a smaller group of interested parties helps keep the group running smoothly on topic. Similarly, an advisory council can be beneficial with matters you don't proactively question; if you do something with a submission that doesn't seem quite right, someone other than the submitter can discuss it with you.

An advisory council might be by invitation or open to all, depending on what effect you are looking for. If you want a small group of confidants that you feel you can trust to reasonably tell you when you've overstepped your bounds but not nitpick every single thing you do, handpicking is the way to go. Open discussion on the meta-issues of the group's moderation, however, could call for a council open to anyone.

The council might receive all submissions for a group, or perhaps only those that are rejected. Along these lines, the group *sci.med.aids* has a novel approach toward handling its possibly contentious rejections. This group uses an open mailing list that receives all rejected submissions, along with the reason for their rejection. The moderators have found it to be very educational and it also allows interested parties to argue the meta-issues together, but off of the group itself.

You might also find a strong, sympathetic supporter in an advisory council if there are any complaints about how you have been handling the job. If the council sees the sort of work you do behind the scenes on a regular basis, they should have a much better understanding of it all than those who witness your work just by what appears in the group.

15.6.9.3 Multiple moderators

Using more than one active moderator is one of the most complicated ways to run a newsgroup. While it can be very robust for handling some circumstances, such as spreading the workload or coping with the loss of a moderator, it can also be tricky to manage. Having more than one person making the decision of what appears in the group and what doesn't is politically advantageous, and brings more diversity to the group, a quality that could benefit even technical groups. Very high-volume groups are especially well-suited for multiple moderators, as it is practically required to keep the group functioning. Groups have been known to have as many as ten co-moderators working as a team.

The technical issue with having multiple moderators is in coordinating the processing of messages. There is some software in the moderator's archive (see Section 15.5) to help with this task. Submissions have to be distributed to the moderators, and their eventual disposition has to be communicated to the other moderators.

There are three main methods for distributing messages: systematic, random, and comprehensive. Systematic distribution hits each moderator in turn; the first submission goes to the first moderator, the second submission to the second moderator, and so on. Random distribution sends a submission to a moderator pseudorandomly selected from a list of them all. Comprehensive distribution sends each submission to every moderator. The submission alias should point to a program that implements the desired method.

The drawback to submissions only going to one moderator is the increased possibility that they'll be lost in a black hole. If that one moderator is negligent in performing his expected duties, the messages he receives will languish in his queue, with possibly none of the other moderators knowing for some time.

A comprehensive distribution scheme suffers from giving everyone close to the same workload as if each were the only moderator, but it does diminish the average time delay for postings and greatly reduces the chance that any particular posting will be overlooked. A similar effect could be attained with one queue that each of the moderators can access. A message stays in the queue until someone accepts it or rejects it, possibly acquiring comments for other moderators to review before deciding its final acceptance or rejection.

No matter the incoming scheme, rejections should be distributed among all moderators so that other moderators can honor them in the event that a poster simply attempts to resubmit an article. A rejection should be open to possible reversal by majority assent, but the authority of a co-moderator should not be undermined by individual action. One method of determining what to do with a submission is that used by *sci.med.aids*. All moderators see each submission, and two yes votes accept it or two no votes reject it; it is resolved as soon as one of these criteria is met.

Cooperation problems among co-moderators are rare, but they can occur and can end up being extremely ugly when they do, especially if they are bad enough to affect what group participants notice. A policy for how to handle conflicts, from minor to major, should be documented in the periodic posting. The writing of the policy should not be put off until the first problem arises. It should be be done when the group is created, and each moderator joining the team should agree to it. Normally this involves some form of voting among the moderators first, then among the readership at large if that proves to not resolve the problem.

In the worst case, with a readership taking sides and warring with each other, the moderators with the problems should probably pass the group on to entirely new people. It might be best not to do this by appointment, but instead by opening the process of selecting a moderator to the readership, such as by vote. This is an extremely murky and unpleasant area of Usenet policy; strive for the resolution that leaves the least virtual carnage.

If possible, it is good to have an independent facilitator for the moderators of the group. This person should have no special interest in the group, but can host the mail aliases, maintain the distribution mechanism, control the archive, and provide other support for the operation of the group. The facilitator does not have responsibilities for receiving, reviewing, posting, or rejecting articles, but should be able to post a note to the group in the event that some aspect of support needs to be communicated to the readers.

15.6.10 Getting Out of the Moderator Business

Eventually, it will come time for you to stop moderating the group. Perhaps you're moving on, or you don't feel you can give the group the attention it needs, or maybe it's just a defunct group.

If the group still has an interested readership, you should make the transition to a new moderator as painless as possible for both the new moderator and the users. Selecting a new moderator can be done by simply appointing your successor from among people with whom you already have a rapport, such as your backup moderator, or by polling the readership for qualified volunteers. If the backup moderator takes the position, a new backup needs to be found, warranting a poll of the group anyway.

Keep the users informed of what's happening. Describe the qualifications of the new moderator if he is not already a public figure in the group. Let them know if the submission and contact addresses are changing. Since you have done the proper introduction of the new moderator, she should only have to post a "Hi, I'm here!" type of message when her tenure starts.

If the address for your group is known by the mailpaths sites, you should contact *moderators-request@isc.org* regarding any changes to the status or address of the group. For a group that is continuing as moderated, the information needed to process the change is the name of the group, the submission and contact addresses, and the names of the moderators. If your group is not known by mailpaths sites, be sure to update local references to the group's addresses.

Removing a defunct group should be done according to the procedures appropriate for the hierarchy in which it is located. Contact *newgroups-request@isc.org* for advice on how to remove a group in the original Usenet hierarchies. If the group is in the *alt* hierarchy, simply send a proper *rmgroup* for it and be sure to identify yourself as the moderator. See Section 16.3 for more details.

It might be the case that the group is still desired, just not as a moderated group. Like removing a group, changing its status should be done according to its hierarchical location.

16

In this chapter:
- *A Brief Survey*
- *Namespace Theory*
- *Changing the Namespace*

Newsgroups and Their Names

The collective set of names of Usenet groups is called its *namespace*. The process of developing that namespace is a very divisive issue within network news administration. This chapter discusses the current hierarchies of Usenet newsgroups and describes the procedures for creating new newsgroups. This is mostly background material, though you may find the survey of newsgroup hierarchies useful when deciding which newsgroups to get. If you are considering creating a new newsgroup, you'll need to read the material on changing the Usenet namespace.

16.1 A Brief Survey

With many thousands of newsgroups now in existence, it's obviously impossible to discuss all of them. That would take a whole book—indeed, such books already exist. We'll just look briefly at the major top-level hierarchies, to give you a general impression of what's out there.

16.1.1 The Big Eight

The eight top-level hierarchies that comprise "mainstream" Usenet probably have the best propagation of any hierarchies. The Great Renaming (see Section 17.3.2) created seven top-level hierarchies; the eighth, *humanities*, was somewhat of an afterthought and came about much more recently. The eight mainstream hierarchies are:

comp—computers
> A very large hierarchy, with hundreds of newsgroups—and more being added every month—that discuss everything even vaguely related to computers. Since Usenet got started in the computer science community, this strong presence is not really a surprise.

humanities—literature and fine arts

A late addition to the top-level hierarchies, partly because it is arguably somewhat redundant with the *rec.arts* sub-hierarchy, but well established now. This hierarchy is intended for more serious and philosophical discussion of these topics than that typically found in *rec*.

misc—other stuff

The organizers of the Great Renaming tried hard to avoid having a "miscellaneous" hierarchy, but couldn't in the end. This hierarchy contains a variety of topics that just don't quite fit elsewhere, like home maintenance, consumer issues, and classified ads.

news—Usenet itself and Netnews software

A relatively small hierarchy, devoted to the underlying business and technology of Usenet itself. Includes a few oddballs like *news.announce.conferences*.

rec—recreational activities

Another very large hierarchy that contains groups for almost everything that human beings do for fun: music, sports, hobbies, etc.

sci—science and technology

The organizers of the Great Renaming couldn't think of a better short name for this hierarchy; it is intended to cover almost everything scientific and technological, not just pure science. For example, the *sci.space.** newsgroups are home to the spaceflight enthusiasts.

soc—social and cultural topics

A midsized hierarchy with many of its groups located under *soc.culture*, the sub-hierarchy that contains newsgroups about specific ethnic and national groups. This hierarchy also contains newsgroups for general social topics like college life, feminism, and women's issues.

talk—debates

This small but noisy hierarchy was created as a place to put groups that host raging, perpetual debates. The idea is that it is better to have them in a separate hierarchy that choosy news administrators can exclude and uninterested people can ignore. For example, *talk.politics.guns* is about gun control and such, while non-controversial aspects of firearms sports and hunting are in various *rec* newsgroups.

The procedure for creating a newsgroup in one of the mainstream Usenet hierarchies is quite formal. Chapter 17, *A Brief History of Usenet*, discusses the history of this procedure; we'll examine the current details later in this chapter. The current procedure is important, partly because of the importance of the mainstream hierarchies and partly because some of the other major hierarchies have copied parts of the procedure for their own use.

16.1.2 Other Major Hierarchies

A number of other major, worldwide, top-level hierarchies have come to exist over the years, for a variety of reasons. In some cases, the originators apparently just wanted their own little empire, generally because they wanted to make their own rules about such things as newsgroup creation.* In others, there was an intention that distribution be different from, or more limited than, the traditional Usenet newsgroups. Here's a list of some of the other major hierarchies:

alt—serious and silly subjects randomly mixed

This hierarchy originated as an attempt to set up an alternative distribution network for newsgroups that the then-influential Usenet backbone sites disliked (see Section 17.3.4). Its abhorrence of any systematic process for controlling newsgroup creation in *alt* eventually caused it to degenerate into near-chaos, although there are still occasional "serious" newsgroups to be found here. The lack of a formal procedure also means that *alt* can respond very quickly to fast-breaking news by creating special newsgroups as needed.

bionet—professional biology

This tightly organized hierarchy is the result of a systematic and fairly successful attempt to create high-quality newsgroups for communication among serious biologists.

bit—Bitnet mailing lists

This is one of the hierarchies originally dedicated to Netnews redistribution of Bitnet mailing lists. Many of the mailing lists have survived the demise of Bitnet itself, and so the hierarchy continues to exist today, hosting gateways for numerous Internet mailing lists.

biz—business-oriented traffic

This was intended as a more openly commercial hierarchy, where the vague and informal constraints against advertising and other commercial posts in the mainstream Usenet hierarchies would not apply. It was never as successful as its organizers hoped, but it still carries some traffic.

clari—ClariNet

A hierarchy of newsgroups that contain news from various commercial news services. Distribution is limited to paying subscribers.

gnu—the GNU project of the Free Software Foundation

The first hierarchy devoted to the activities of a particular organization, in this case one that works toward the publication and distribution of freely available software.

---

* In a number of cases (hierarchies we have not described here), it is widely felt that less rational motives, perhaps including sheer ego, were also a factor. Many of the newer top-level hierarchies have very limited distribution and don't seem to fulfill their ostensible purposes very well.

Newsgroup creation procedures in these hierarchies vary widely. In *alt* it's almost total chaos, while hierarchies like *gnu* and *clari* are centrally administered and create new newsgroups when their administrators think it's indicated.

16.1.3 Regional and Organizational Hierarchies

Almost every distinct region with significant Usenet activity has at least a few regional newsgroups. "Region" here can mean almost anything: a country, an ethnic or linguistic area, a state or province, a metropolitan area or a city. Usually these newsgroups are mostly for regional issues and news, plus inherently local things like for-sale notices. Sometimes, especially when the region speaks a language other than English (which is the de facto language of the worldwide newsgroups), quite general topics can appear in regional hierarchies.

Organizations with significant Usenet activity also tend to have their own organizational newsgroups, and these can even be found on several levels in large organizations. For example, large universities typically have both university-wide and department-specific newsgroups, sometimes organized into an overall hierarchy and sometimes not.

Although it might appear sensible to organize such hierarchies within an overall geographical structure, so that a Toronto local-events newsgroup might be something like *can.ont.tor.events*, in practice it's almost always done at the top level: the Toronto local-events newsgroup is just *tor.events*. This is usually done because sites who want a wide region often don't want smaller areas with it—wanting the Canada-wide groups is not a good indicator for also wanting the local Toronto groups. There are potential problems here due to name collisions, but so far such problems have been rare enough that ad hoc solutions have sufficed. For example, perennial headaches arising from both the University of Toronto and the University of Texas having *ut.** newsgroups were eventually resolved when the University of Texas switched to *utexas.**.

Regional hierarchies usually have informal, consensus-driven group creation procedures. This isn't the case, however, with some of the largest hierarchies, like the Japanese (*fj*), German (*de*), and French (*fr*) hierarchies. Organizational hierarchies are usually under the direct control of the news administrator(s) for the given organization, though in cases like universities, there may be enough different people under that heading that again, one sees informal consensus-driven procedures.

16.1.4 Getting More Information

The closest thing to an authoritative list of the mainstream Usenet newsgroups is the ISC *newsgroups* file maintained by David Lawrence, available from the ISC archive at *ftp://ftp.isc.org/pub/usenet/CONFIG/newsgroups*.

The "Alternative Newsgroup Hierarchies" articles are a series of postings to *news.answers* that list all of the newsgroups in a number of the other major hierarchies. These postings contain one view of the current *alt* newsgroups, as well as *bionet, bit, biz, clari, gnu, k12, vmsnet,* and several other hierarchies. The articles are available in any *news.answers* archive as *alt-hierarchies/part[1-5],* e.g.:

```
ftp://rtfm.mit.edu/pub/usenet/news.answers/alt-hierarchies/part[1-5]
```

Lists of the newsgroups in various other hierarchies can often be found in various postings in *news.admin.hierarchies.*

16.2 Namespace Theory

As with most real-world systems, the theory of the Usenet namespace does not always match up with practice. This is due to both inherent limitations in the system and the sociopolitical issues involved in trying to get thousands of autonomous news administrators to agree on what particular newsgroups should be called. The structure of the newsgroup namespace has two primary goals: to help people find forums where they can read and submit articles about their interests, and to make it easier for news administrators to manage their sites. The main vehicle for trying to address both of these sometimes conflicting goals is a topically based, hierarchically formed taxonomy. Not every ideal for a newsgroup name can be satisfied, so tradeoffs are inevitably made. Both the topical and hierarchical aspects should be considered when naming a group.

The topical aspect of the naming system is an outgrowth of viewing Usenet as an information system. Topical organization is intrinsically more useful and extensible for a worldwide information system than a social model that tries to group messages based on the people who sent them rather than on their content. However, Usenet is not only an information system, it is also an entertainment system. While a social model can be more useful in entertainment systems, its extensibility is rather poor in the face of a contributor base of tens of thousands of authors, and the topical model is also still quite useful for entertainment purposes. Thus, the topical model has the greatest utility for both information and entertainment uses and is the standard to follow when deciding on the name of a new group.

The hierarchical aspect of the naming system tends to group closely related topics. This helps people find other topics in which they are likely to be interested. For example, a user interested in computer graphics software can see several such packages grouped together in a sorted list. The hierarchical scheme can also help administrators apply broad policy decisions for sets of groups. Thus, a system administrator might want to get a feed of groups ostensibly about science or more quickly expire groups that have very high daily volume. Note that the last use of grouping isn't particularly topically oriented, but rather it addresses a general aspect of the form of traffic. Very high volume just happens to be one of the criteria that a news administrator might find useful to handle with a broad policy decision. Collecting all the groups that match that criteria into one hierarchy helps in implementing the policy.

16.2.1 Creating Syntactically Valid Names

A newsgroup name is composed of lowercase letters, digits, and the characters plus (+), hyphen (-), underscore (_), and dot (.). Name elements, also called *components* or *levels*, are separated by dots; each element is limited to 14 characters in length.* Each element of a newsgroup name must start with a letter or digit and contain at least one alphabetic character. It is strongly suggested that names do not start with a digit, and that hyphens be used in preference to underscores where needed.

16.2.2 Choosing Good Names

Being able to create a syntactically valid name is easy; coming up with one that is useful to both users and administrators is quite a bit harder. There are a lot of different factors that go into choosing a good name, some of which are very important, some of which should not be focused on, and some of which get more attention than they deserve.

Clarity is important, both to the people interested in the group and to the people who are not interested in the group. Most users are presented daily with a list of anywhere from a few to a few dozen new groups that their newsreader is offering to subscribe them to; these decisions often have to be made based on the group name in the absence of any additional description for the group. Some people make the suggestion that users should subscribe and read a few messages to find out what a group is about, but that is not practical. A sufficiently descriptive name for the group not only helps keep people from wasting their time with the group, but also keeps them from wasting the time of the other readers of the group with off-topic messages. On the other hand, people who are genuinely interested in a group might have a harder time finding it, or never find it at all, if the name isn't quite obvious.

Consistency is another important quality in a large classification system: groups of a related purpose should have similar name elements. This manifests itself in

---

* This is not only a throwback to a less enlightened age of Unix filesystem design, but a concession to the less enlightened restrictions of the NBS/NIST FIPS-151 interpretation of ISO POSIX.1. It requires the system to choke on an object name that is longer than 14 characters. News started on Unix and had names up to 14 characters very early in its development, so software written for platforms with more restrictive name lengths has already had to deal with the length problem and is not considered relevant to the length limit.

conventions such as *.announce* groups used as moderated forums for announcements related to a particular topic and *.misc* groups used as the general group in a
hierarchy when a more specific group does not apply. Consistency also applies to
less commonly used name elements, like naming groups for off-road enthusiasts as
rec.autos.off-road and *rec.bicycles.off-road*, or both without the hyphens, rather
than one with the hyphen and one without.

Precedent is how consistency starts. A previously accepted name has strong
weight when a similar proposal for a new group comes down the line. Breaking
new ground, by creating a new hierarchy under which several groups are eventually expected, should be fully examined with regard to any existing groups that
make sense in the new scheme. This might warrant renaming the old groups or
not pushing for the new hierarchy. The proposal should also be examined with
regard to the expected growth of the proposed area. Deviating from established
practice only makes sense when there are notable benefits that outweigh any
drawbacks and when the deviation makes sense in the overall view of how the
Net works.

Each successive element in a newsgroup name more specifically defines the topic
of the group. A dot (.) should not be used just as a word separator or as if it were
a comma. For a group about photographic film and commercial photo finishing,
rec.photo.film+lab is strongly preferred to either *rec.photo.film.labs* or especially
rec.photo.film.and.labs.

The overall length of a newsgroup name is not the important issue that many people make it out to be. Most group names are never typed in full by the majority of
the users of the group, who often select a newsgroup by picking it from a menu,
clicking on its name, or just running into it as the next item in their newsreader.
To those who would complain about needing to type the group name into articles,
note that even the shortest group names are commonly abbreviated even further
by group participants when referring to the group in writing. The general admonishment regarding name length is "Don't Abbreviate!"* What you consider an obvious abbreviation might be indecipherable to most people, or even worse, it could
be interpreted as something completely different from what was intended. The
clarity of a name is much more important than saving a few characters.

Duplicate groups have no place in a topically oriented classification system. They
separate substantially similar traffic and divide the user community unnecessarily.
Overall traffic is increased by people posting redundant traffic to each forum
because they are unaware of the other forum, and personal resources are wasted
by people aware of both forums. This is sometimes a problem when a single
group should exist logically in more than one place on the Net; should a group on

---

* Often seen as "Dnt Abrv8!"

Unix security issues be *comp.security.unix* or *comp.unix.security*? Still, only one name can be used because multiple names for the same forum are not implemented adequately in widely available news software.

One metric for the expected breadth of a hierarchy can be found in the human factors guide of having roughly seven items in a list for selection, give or take two. While not entirely appropriate for news, it is somewhat relevant to news browsers that present the hierarchical tree as recursive menus and it could help some news administrators in the face of very large trees of groups. For example, rather than having every make of automobile in the *rec.autos* hierarchy with other non-make-specific groups, *rec.autos.makers.** is only for groups focused on particular makes of automobiles.

Group names should be value-neutral, neither praising nor condemning the relative worth of the topic of the group, but simply advertising the topic that is supposed to be discussed within. Along the same lines, many people think getting a particular newsgroup name is some sort of badge of validation—that the name itself advocates or encourages a particular point of view—but that is a fallacy. For example, having a group named *comp.fish* does not mystically advance the theory that fish should be seen and discussed primarily with regard to their relationship to computers. Drawing from a real-life example, the existence of the *rec.drugs* hierarchy is not a statement that the majority of Usenet believes that pharmaceuticals should be used recreationally.

In addition, the position of a group in the namespace hierarchy is not a statement of relative worth. The group that everyone on the Net is expected to read, *news.announce.important*, is a third-level group. Some group advocates believe that not putting their group at the second level is an insult, but that's simply not true. A group should be put at the level that makes sense based on its relationship to other groups already in the hierarchy—there's no value judgment involved in this decision.

Of course, having value-neutral group names does not preclude that people will doubtless attach some value to the traffic inside them. This is human nature, and can't be avoided. It is a feature of the system that not only do hierarchical group names enable administrators to get whole realms of topics that are appropriate for their site, but they also enable administrators to exclude whole realms. A value judgment—whether on the grounds of resources, business worth, readership, or whatever—is inherent in deciding what to carry and what not to carry at a site.

Thus, it is not justified to keep a huge pictures group in the *alt* hierarchy out of *alt.binaries.pictures.** because some people do not like the association with the erotica groups there or because many administrators exclude *alt.binaries.pictures.** because of its volume. Administrators have chosen to corral all huge pictures groups in *alt* under that hierarchy; circumventing the policy that some administrators have applied to that hierarchy is antagonistic to the very sites that the groups' advocates want to carry the group.

In group name elements, more widely understood words are definitely favored over less familiar ones. *rec.self-abuse.egregious* is less desirable as a name than *rec.self-abuse.very-bad*, even though the term "egregious" is arguably more descriptive and a lot more fun to say.

Similarly, the name of a group should be in a language consistent with the major hierarchy in which it is located, because that language is the primary basis for determining how familiar a term is. This does not mean that various languages should not be used in relevant groups. A group for discussing Spanish culture could quite reasonably contain some postings in the Spanish language. However, a group for Spanish ham radio operators to converse in Spanish does not belong in a worldwide English-oriented hierarchy like *rec.radio.amateur*. Many regions have created their own topically oriented, top-level hierarchies in which they can use the language of their choice and expect to find a significantly more appropriate audience.

Group names are primarily inclusive, not exclusive. The hierarchical classification of a group is generally not intended to restrict postings on a related topic if no group for that related topic exists, even if the name implies otherwise. Thus *comp.home.automation* can be used to discuss home automation devices that do not actually include what are typically thought of as computers. Strict interpretation of names with regard to acceptable articles is too restrictive for real-world applications of hierarchical classification.

A group should not be named in terms of what it is not because it makes future division of the group illogical. If the groups for job postings were created as *misc.jobs.offered.computer* and *misc.jobs.offered.non-computer* and then science groups gained enough of a share of the non-computer traffic to warrant their own group, the name *misc.jobs.offered.non-computer* would look peculiar alongside *misc.jobs.offered.computer* and *misc.jobs.offered.science*. *misc.jobs.offered.non-computer* would very likely still attract some science job postings, and such a naming scheme doesn't otherwise appreciably help people who have to scientific job interests or non-computer and non-scientific job interests.

Mailing-list names are considered mostly irrelevant when naming newsgroups. In the early days of the Net, *net.sunspots* was used to publish a digest for Sun computer users; it had nothing to do with solar astronomy. The name was novel as a title for a mailing list, but it wasn't very helpful as a newsgroup name. The Usenet namespace exists apart from the mailing list namespace and is used very differently. If the list name happens to be a good group component too, that's great, but whether it is a good group component is considered completely apart from whether the mailing list is using it.

A newsgroup should not double as a branching node in the hierarchy. In other words, there shouldn't be both a *comp.protocols.iso* group and a *comp.protocols.iso* sub-hierarchy. While all known major software can certainly handle this, and there are numerous examples of it in the worldwide hierarchies, there are both administrative and namespace consistency reasons for keeping the two uses of a name component distinct. It simplifies news system administration for sites interested in specifically taking or excluding the topic area, because strictly correct matching patterns can be more succinctly specified. Rather than saying `comp.protocols.iso,comp.protocols.iso.*` in an INN *newsfeeds* file, a site can just use *comp.protocols.iso.** if the general ISO group is included as another branch in the hierarchy.*

In the case of group reorganizations, renaming the base group to a *.misc* group also emphasizes to some sites that a change has been made. This can be very important to the way feeds are configured, especially with the advent of INN and its break from the C News hierarchical feeding structure. While C News automatically sends new *soc.foo.bar.** groups to a site with a subscription pattern of *soc.foo.bar*, INN does not. Having traffic in the reorganized group dry up makes it especially clear to people that the reorganization has happened and that feeds, *active* files, and newsreaders should be adjusted as necessary. News server filesystem performance is also better when the kernel routine that looks up pathnames doesn't have to search a directory full of articles to find the subdirectory for an article posted to a subgroup.

Experience has also shown that having subgroups without a real group at each of their hierarchical nodes reduces misposting and crossposting by encouraging people to find the most appropriate group for their message, rather than just shooting it to a group at the top of the tree with the expectation that all interested readers will find it there. Not having antecedent groups also addresses the perception by some people that their topic is somehow being relegated to a less worthy stature by being named as a subgroup to some other group. Finally, not having groups also serve the function of being hierarchical nodes for subgroups makes various visualizations of the namespace, particularly those presented by graphical newsreaders, much more useful.

Dividing the namespace too precisely, so that there are many very narrowly focused groups within a subhierarchy, becomes a game of losing percentages. Usenet is uncommon in that it is probably the most major database that allows contributors to categorize their own material. People not skilled in library

---

* Lazy INN patterns such as `comp.protocols.iso*` are not recommended because they don't match the name on a name boundary. Consider using INN to get all of the *comp.arch* hierarchy but not getting any of the *comp.archives* hierarchy. Yes, patterns can be written to avoid these cases when you're aware of them, but they require greater care and might break with future new groups.

science—who constitute the vast majority of the population—are notoriously bad at classifying their own work. When a topic gets divided into many narrowly focused groups, it tends to lead to an increase in misdirected messages, and this rapidly diminishes the overall value of the system.

Another aspects of the problem of self-classification is that users who want a new group for an unaddressed topic tend to place a lot of significance on the name given to the group. They often consider the unaddressed topic more worthy and more important that any of the existing groups that might cover it because the topic is their particular passion. Special interest tends to obscure a vision of the bigger picture of how a topic fits in the namespace. Many emotional buttons are easily pushed with regard to things that really shouldn't be a problem, such as the group's level in the hierarchy. The ultimate truth is that when all is said and done, the people interested in the topic are going to use the group as long as it has any remotely identifiable name, regardless of its position in the overall hierarchy. The initial battles over the name will largely be irrelevant to the people using the group, unless the final name happens to be truly terrible.

In principle, Usenet is a cooperative anarchy, so it doesn't really have formally "official" and "bogus" newsgroups that are enforceable anywhere other than at each individual site. However, keeping a coherent picture of what most administrators think the Usenet namespace looks like helps everyone to use network news more effectively. To this end, it is not a service to users to carry groups that are not widely considered valid. People posting to such groups will find propagation of their postings to be poor, and thus potential responses to be limited.

16.2.3 Naming Controversies

Impassioned arguments about group names, generally with little hard science backing them up, are still the single biggest points of division over new group proposals. Even when the arguments do have rational backing, naming remains largely a sociopolitical skill that is filled with compromises between what might seem ultimately true and what is now desirable. In most cases, the latter has a very strong mitigating effect on the former.

Take, for example, that on an essential level, biology is significantly chemistry which would not really exist except for the physics of atoms. However, *sci.physics.chemistry.biology.entomology*, a group for those who study insects, doesn't adequately reflect the way most people, notably the scientists who would be using the group, tend to think of the world.* This name wouldn't help people find the group and it also wouldn't help the vast majority of news administrators apply policies to it. In order to find an acceptable name, a balance must be struck between how closely related the topics are on a working basis, the existing classifications outside of Usenet, the existing classifications within Usenet, and, lastly and leastly, the overall length of the name.

The *sci* hierarchy is an especially interesting area to review because of the tendency of scientists to view group names as having stature, often as a result of budgetary battles they have to endure for research funding.† Proponents often point to the interdisciplinary nature of their field and therefore insist that it "deserves" a second-level group. *sci.geo.oceanography* is a good example of this problem. It is so named because oceanography is an earth science and other aspects of it can reasonably be discussed in the group so named. However, oceanographers consider the science to be multidisciplinary in that it includes aspects of biology, chemistry, and physics, so like many scientific groups, their desire was to have a *sci.oceanography* group that transcended all of *sci.bio.**, *sci.chem.**, *sci.geo.**, *sci.physics.**, and others.

It is not very useful to make every science group that has multidisciplinary aspects a second-level group, however, because so many disciplines fit this bill that the second-level namespace of *sci* would become overly broad, making it harder to group significantly related topics and reducing the administrative utility of the namespace. This does, of course, lead to another problem. If the biological aspects of oceanography eventually warrant being split out of the group, should the new group be *sci.bio.marine* (to go to the sites that have indicated a special interest in marine biology) or should it be *sci.geo.oceanography.biology* (to go to the sites that have indicated a special interest in oceanography)? In the long run, either is acceptable enough for interested people to find the group.

Now let's look at a group that has a cryptic name, *rec.music.gaffa*. This group name is interesting because it is occasionally cited by people who want to use their own cryptic name for a new group. Many people who enjoy Kate Bush's music probably would not be able to identify *rec.music.gaffa* as the place to read about that performer. The name comes from "Suspended in Gaffa," a Kate Bush song that alludes to being stuck in gaffer's tape. When the group was created in the late 1980s as a gateway for the LoveHounds digest, the name *rec.music.gaffa* was preferred over *rec.music.kate-bush* by the group's activists, to indicate that discussion topics could go beyond the direct scope of Kate Bush's works and

---

* Henry Spencer once dubbed this the "Dewey Decimal Disease": the urge to classify things in miniscule nitpicking detail, beyond all reason or utility.

† None of this commentary is meant to be derogatory—it is just meant as an observation of the evolution of several newsgroup proposals for *sci* groups.

include artists with a similar musical bent. That the casual reader, especially one who might primarily follow the other artists, would understand this from *rec.music.gaffa* is a bit of a stretch for even the most fanatical Kate Bush fan to sincerely believe.

The group *soc.genealogy.french* illustrates the principle that a more widely understood term is better than an esoteric one. The scope of the group is all people who have ancestors who spoke French, had French names, or lived in places inhabited by French speakers or where records were kept in French. The newsgroup name was chosen specifically not to limit the group to the country of France. In the discussion phase of the group, *.francophone* was advanced by the proponents of embracing the concept that it wasn't about the country of France. These people were eventually convinced that *.french* really enjoys the same broad scope but is more readily understood by the average person.

Another large naming argument that dealt with the use of a less widely recognized term occurred with *rec.arts.manga*. In the proposal, manga was defined as Japanese comics. Thus, the *news.groups* and *rec.arts.comics* crowd thought the group should clearly be named *rec.arts.comics.japanese*. The proponents of the group were positively aghast at that notion, and firmly dug in their heels with a stalwart determination to never even begin to compromise on the name, not even as *rec.arts.comics.manga*. The resulting debate eventually saw the proponents try to avoid describing manga in the charter as Japanese comics, even though that's still the first thing most manga fans tell someone who asks what manga is. It was a rather transparent move, but nevertheless the hordes of fans, who primarily just wanted a group to use, managed to get a passing vote of 513 people in favor of the group to the unusually large opposition tally of 226 people who mostly voted against the proposal on the basis of its name.

As previously mentioned, even though there is no limit to the length of a newsgroup name, each group name element can only contain 14 characters. This can cause problems with elements that really need to be longer than 14 characters. Groups like *sci.techniques.crystallography*, *soc.culture.bosnia-herzegovina*, and *comp.parallel.connection-machine* all have to make concessions to shortened group names that might or might not be as identifiable as the full version, but still are probably more informative than ones that use acronyms. It has been suggested that instead of names like *soc.culture.bosna-herzgovna* and *comp.parallel.connect-machine*, it would be acceptable to make the occasional exception for a non-expandable node. Thus, *soc.culture.bosnia.herzegovina* would probably never see another group under *soc.culture.bosnia*, but at least the real-world name of the region would not be corrupted.*

Here's one last look at a naming controversy before we move on to the actual group creation process. A group for the religion practiced by the followers of Hazrat Mirza Ghulam Ahmad of Qadian was proposed. The controversy revolved around the relationship of this religion to the Islamic religion. The followers call the religion Ahmadiyya Islam and themselves Ahmadi Muslims. To them, the name of the group would have quite reasonably been *soc.religion.islam.ahmadiyya*. Traditional Muslims were major opponents of the group, as they considered that it was heretical to call this religion a form of Islam. A name that seemed to lend validity to that idea was completely unacceptable to them. A major war erupted over this point.

From a namespace perspective, the whole issue of who was more "right" could be sidestepped by just naming the group *soc.religion.ahmadiyya*, inside of which Ahmadi Muslims could call themselves Islamic as much as they liked. This group would not have been tied to the extant *soc.religion.islam* group, which did want to be associated with the Ahmadi group. Both groups could be reasonably appeased, at least from an administrative vantage point—the warring over whether Ahmadiyya was Islam would doubtless continue no matter what the involvement of Usenet. The proponents, however, wanted no part of that compromise. They seemed more interested in getting the political prize of having the token "islam" in the name.

Their pursuit of this eventually proved to be their undoing, although in fairness it must be noted that it really isn't known how the tide of debate would have turned if they had capitulated on the hierarchical location of the group. It is possible that the traditional Muslims would have found some other point for opposing the basic existence of the group, but they would probably have been on more shaky ground in the eyes of independent news administrators. In the end, extremely questionable vote taking for the proposal was the final reason for invalidating the entire poll for the group. This also led to the use of independent third-party vote takers for all future mainstream Usenet group polls.

These controversies are just a few of the many that have occurred in Usenet's history. Lest you be discouraged about trying to create a new group, you should know that the large majority of proposals can make it from idea conception to group creation without any real quarrels about names.

---

* Ignoring, for this discussion, the highly volatile political situation in that part of the world.

16.3 Changing the Namespace

Now that you understand naming issues, we can go on to discuss how to change the namespace. There are two fundamental stages in changing the namespace: building consensus about what should be done and then actually getting it done at all of the relevant sites. In terms of possible changes, you can add groups, remove groups, and change the moderation status of groups. We'll mostly look at adding groups, which is by far the most common change. The process for effecting either of the two other changes is very similar.

The degree of difficulty in changing the namespace is proportional to how widely distributed you want the new group to be (or how widely distributed the existing group is). If the change only applies on your own server, the process is trivial. If you want a worldwide change, expect a bit more work.

16.3.1 Local Changes

If you only want to change a group within your own organization, and especially if the group is only on one or more servers that you control, the consensus-building process is nonexistent. All you have to do is find the time to make the necessary changes. As discussed in Section 3.3.2.2, you use the *cnewsdo* command with C News or the *ctlinnd* command with INN to make individual changes. Be sure to make the necessary changes on all of the news servers in your organization (if you have more than one).

Most news server administrators do not operate their servers for a community of just one. At some point, a user, whether it be someone above or below you in the political hierarchy of your organization, will come to you with a desire to create a new newsgroup. For these occasions, it is good to have a policy in place. This policy can be as simple as, "if you ask for it, you get it." Keep in mind, however, that not every request is completely realistic or within the bounds of acceptable use of the server as defined by the people who own the machine. You may want to discuss the idea with the user and then decide whether or not to create the group. It is probably in your own best interest to be open-minded about any ideas for new groups, though, as it will help keep your users happy.

16.3.2 Wider Areas

Creating a group on servers beyond those that you control requires the cooperation of the administrators of those other servers. Technically, you need to have them agree to establish the group on their machines and you also need two-way propagation paths for the articles posted to the group.

Some regional hierarchies are ideally distributed to only a small number of sites that are physically within the region. These are the only sites that really care what groups are in the hierarchy. Such a regional hierarchy tends to have an informal group creation process along the lines of "run it up the flagpole and see who salutes." Running an idea by the other administrators can involve contacting them by email, posting to an appropriate administrative group, or doing both. The administrative group is generally named *foo.config*, *foo.news*, or something similar for a hierarchy named *foo*. Use the *foo.general* group if there is no administrative group.

When soliciting the other administrators, you should present a rationale for why you think the group should be created, a charter for what traffic is appropriate in the group, and a declaration of any moderators or gateways that the group is expected to have. The rationale is usually based on a sustained volume of messages being posted in another group where they are either inappropriate or are contributing to general crowding in the group. Sometimes it is based on a new service that you want to provide, like weather forecasts or social-event announcements. The charter for the group is usually a simple definition of what is supposed to appear in the group, and perhaps a statement of what is not appropriate if there is the possibility for confusion.

After you have presented your idea, wait for feedback. You may not get much feedback, but remember that silence is not assent. If no one says anything, try again. If you can't get anyone to reply, it is quite likely there just isn't enough interest in the group (or maybe no one is seeing your messages—make sure that they are actually getting out). If people make negative comments about the idea, they generally do so with some constructive criticism, though it might be a little hard to see. Try to work any such feedback into the proposal to make it better; this isn't always possible, but a serious consideration of the matter is exactly what the consensus-building process is about.

When there seems to be general agreement on the soundness of your proposal, you can begin the actual creation of the group, as discussed in Section 16.3.4. If you are trying to create a new organizational or regional hierarchy and want it widely distributed, send an email request to *usenet-lists@isc.org* with a list of the groups, in the style of the *newsgroups* file (described in detail in Section 3.3.2.2).

The *alt* hierarchy is a worldwide hierarchy that many people think should work on essentially the same consensus-building process. In truth, however, the *alt.config* group is frequently bypassed and there are some seriously conflicting opinions about what should be considered a valid group in the *alt* hierarchy. Despite this fact, putting up with a bit of a struggle in *alt.config* will probably help you in the long run, either by getting a better name for the group or maybe even by encouraging you to try for a better distributed group in one of the mainstream

Usenet hierarchies. At the very least, it will give you an up close and personal view of an interesting social system.

Most other large hierarchies, both regional and worldwide, have some person or group of people who are generally considered to be the authorities concerning what groups are valid. They might or might not have a formalized group creation method in place. For example, it is pretty much directly up to the whim of the Free Software Foundation whether a group is considered valid in the *gnu* hierarchy. Many hierarchies have a system that starts with a discussion phase and then moves into a polling phase that measures support for the proposal. The results of the poll determine whether the coordinator for the hierarchy declares the group valid. If the hierarchy you are interested in has such a policy, it should be readily apparent in the administrative group for the hierarchy. For example, look for a group like *de.admin.news.announce* (for the German hierarchy) or *fj.news.announce* (for the Japanese hierarchy) where the formal stages of new group proposals are conducted.

16.3.3 *Mainstream Usenet Changes*

The article "How to Create a New Usenet Newsgroup" is posted periodically to *news.announce.newusers*, *news.answers*, *news.groups*, *news.admin.misc*, and *news.announce.newgroups*. This article outlines the process for group creation in the mainstream Usenet hierarchies: *comp, humanities, misc, news, rec, sci, soc,* and *talk*. The article is available in any *news.answers* archive as *usenet/creating-newsgroups/part1*, e.g.:

```
ftp://rtfm.mit.edu/pub/usenet/news.answers/usenet/creating-newsgroups/part1
```

In late 1992, a group of mentors was established to help people with mainstream group creation. Contacting them through *group-mentors@acpub.duke.edu* with the basic idea you have for a group should lead to an experienced volunteer working with you to form a solid proposal.

16.3.3.1 *A formal proposal*

The first step in creating a new group is developing a formal proposal. The proposal should include a charter for the group, the rationale for creating it, a statement of moderation policy if the group is moderated, and a statement of any intent to hook it to a mailing list. Things like the history of the topic, an extensive definition of what the topic is, or a FAQ article for the topic do not belong in the proposal. However, these items can be made into a separate posting for *news.groups* during the discussion phase.

The charter describes what sort of articles are appropriate for the group. It may also describe a few notable examples of inappropriate articles, especially if they could be easily construed as otherwise being appropriate. For example, the pro-grammers in the PC clone drivers group wanted to discuss the process of program-ming hardware device drivers, but didn't want random requests from people who simply wanted to get particular drivers. The charter made it clear that driver requests were unwelcome. A charter should not include subjective statements about how worthy the topic is or why the group should be created. The charter, taken in full, should be able to stand alone and be read with accurate tense and external references a decade after the creation of the group. Since the mainstream Usenet hierarchies are worldwide hierarchies, the charter should clearly be rele-vant to people throughout the world.

It is the rationale that attempts to persuade people that the group should be cre-ated. Salesmanship on how worthy the topic is on some sort of moral relativism scale, whether compared to other Usenet groups or to the world at large, should be kept to a minimum. What you should provide is some sort of acknowledgment of any other electronic forums that currently discuss the topic and a description of how they are inadequate in continuing to serve those who are interested in fol-lowing it. It is important that you be nice in this assessment and avoid denigrating the users of other forums. It is especially compelling to be able to point to an active mailing list that directly deals with the topic, if it does not have a good approximate group in network news.* In this case, you should describe the num-ber of subscribers to the list and the approximate number of messages that appear on it daily. A list that gets a couple of dozen articles per day and has hundreds of subscribers is a good candidate for a new newsgroup.

If the group is to be moderated, the moderation statement describes who the pro-posed moderator or team of moderators is, their qualifications for the position, and any special policies there might be with regard to the moderator, such as a term limit or a mandate to maintain an archive for the group. The basic duty of modera-tors is to uphold the charters of groups by rejecting articles that do not conform to them.

Finally, if there is a relevant mailing list supporting the rationale, it should be noted whether there is an intent to gateway the mailing list to the group, and if so whether it would be a one-way or bidirectional gateway and if any special policies would apply to the gateway. For example, a gateway from an unmoderated news-group to a moderated mailing list might involve the moderator of the mailing list culling only the appropriate articles for the list from the group.

---

* This is why it is commonly suggested that a mailing list be the first step toward creating a news-group, to demonstrate interest.

16.3.3.2 The discussion

Once the proposal is formalized, it should be submitted to *news.announce.newgroups* as a Request for Discussion (RFD). The best way to ensure that the right thing happens with getting your proposal to *news.announce.newgroups* is to mail it to *newgroups@isc.org*. At the start of the body of the message, list the most relevant groups to which the RFD should be sent, up to a total of 200 characters. You need to include "Newsgroups: news.announce.newgroups,news.groups", so you only have 153 more characters. This limit is due to a propagation problem with articles that have excessively long header lines.

Be sure to check whether any of the groups you list are moderated (other than *news.announce.newgroups* and *news.groups*). If you contact the moderators of those groups and secure prior approval for crossposting official stages of the proposal to the group, it helps speed the process and makes life a little easier for the moderator of *news.announce.newgroups*. Otherwise, it is possible that any moderated groups will be eliminated when the article is processed for posting. Here is a sample start of a *news.announce.newgroups* submission:

```
Please post to:

Newsgroups: news.announce.newgroups,news.groups,comp.ai,comp.ai.edu,\
comp.ai.genetic,conp.ai.neural-nets,comp.ai.vision

comp.ai.vision is moderated.  The moderator has approved crossposting
using his tag "moderator@vislist.com".
```

If a group does not exist in Internet Software Consortium's *active* file (*ftp://ftp.isc.org/pub/usenet/CONFIG/active*), it is not included in the crossposting. This is especially relevant to very low-volume *alt* groups.

A message intended for *news.announce.newgroups* should not publicly appear anywhere—not in *news.groups* or in any other Usenet group and not on any mailing lists—before it is published in *news.announce.newgroups*. The time of publication of an article in *news.announce.newgroups* is the official time by which the beginning of each stage of the group creation process is measured. The admonishment against submitting the message elsewhere is to combat confusion that can be caused by it, especially if some discussion with *group-advice@isc.org*, which helps maintain a consistent picture of the overall Usenet namespace, leads to a change in the proposal after the initial submission.

After an article has appeared in *news.announce.newgroups*, if you wish for it to have additional distribution beyond the original Newsgroups line, you should take the message as it appears in *news.announce.newgroups*, rather than the copy that you mailed, and forward it without additional comment to the other forums in which you want it to appear. The reason for using the copy from *news.announce.newgroups* is that it contains any appropriate formatting corrections, date corrections, and perhaps minor corrections to things like the list of crossposted newsgroups, and it has the quasi-official blessing of the *news.announce.newgroups* moderator. The admonishment to refrain from making additional comments attached to forwarded copies is intended to put the proposal on the same even ground on which it originally appeared.

After the proposal has appeared in *news.announce.newgroups*, a public discussion period of no less than three weeks is used to refine the proposal. As with the consensus-building process mentioned for smaller hierarchies, this is the time when you take the criticisms of others into account and build the final proposal that will be voted on. This process could lead to a different name for the group, a change in moderation status, or perhaps significant alteration of the charter.

If there is a notable change in the proposal, such as any change of name or moderation status or a substantial change to the charter, it should be resubmitted to *news.announce.newgroups* in the same manner as the first version. The changes to the proposal should be clearly summarized at the start of the new proposal, so people who saw the first version can be keyed into how it has been revised. If the proposal does not notably change during the discussion period, the proposal should not be resubmitted to *news.announce.newgroups*, but you can tell people of the changes in the other relevant groups. Repeated modifications of the RFD should not be sent to *news.announce.newgroups* less than a week apart. Note that the clock for the three-week discussion period does not restart each time a new RFD is posted, but a Call for Votes (CFV) must be at least a week from the last posting of the RFD.

16.3.3.3 The vote

About two weeks after your proposal is posted, you should receive a questionnaire from the coordinator of the Usenet Volunteer Votetaker, currently Bill Aten. If you have not received such a questionnaire after 15 days or so, write to *uvv-contact@uvv.com* to request one. The questionnaire helps a votetaker prepare the poll for your proposal. The votetaker handles the mechanics of preparing and submitting the actual Call for Votes article.

As discussed in Section 17.3.3, there is an unusual dichotomy regarding what "yes" and "no" votes are supposed to measure. "Yes" votes are supposed to measure the number of people interested in the group. Effectively, they are supposed to be an affirmative answer to the question, "Would you use this group if it were created?" "No" votes are not supposed to have anything to do with whether the respondent would use the group if it existed; they are intended only to gauge significant faults with the proposal, like whether its name or moderation policy would negatively affect Usenet by setting a bad precedent. In practice, this policy is not particularly good for handling administrative concerns about proposals, which probably shouldn't be left to a popular vote of an ad hoc body of people who are more interested in getting a group than they are with the finer points of information systems management. However, the process is biased in favor of approving proposals rather than denying them, which appears to match the popular opinion among users and administrators alike.

It is also worth noting that the poll is purposefully supposed to be a largely self-selecting interest poll. While in a real democracy it is the duty of every citizen to become informed about and vote on every matter, in a Usenet group creation poll it is your duty to vote only on proposals for groups that you intend to use or with which you have significant problems. To register sympathy support for a group that you do not intend to read distorts the measure of interest that the poll is primarily trying to identify.

Furthermore, any attempt to stuff the ballot box is frowned upon, with possible damaging consequences that could include cancellation of an active poll or invalidation of the results. Campaigning for the group is at the comparatively innocuous end of the scale, but direct email campaigns (rather than broadcasts to lists or groups) are more invasive and also possibly more damaging to the results because of spite voting. Automatic scripts, such as in the login sequence of a system's users, are a quick route to vote cancellation. You are better off just using the normal CFV distribution channels of the newsgroups and mailing lists that are stated in the CFV itself, without additional campaigning. Any other ideas for CFV distribution should be discussed with your votetaker.

The polling period lasts for three weeks, after which the votetaker sends the final tally in a "RESULT" article to *news.announce.newgroups*. For verification purposes, it includes a list of every person who responded to the poll and how they all voted. Results are not available to anyone except the votetaker and the *news.announce.newgroups* moderator before they are posted. A group must get at least 100 more "yes" than "no" votes and it must have at least twice as many "yes" votes as "no" votes to pass. Thus, a vote of 97/13 fails due to lack of sufficient interest, a vote of 503/312 fails due to massive objection to the proposal, and a vote of 120/16 passes.

16.3.3.4 The aftermath

A waiting period of at least five days is initiated following the announcement of the results, during which time people can bring any problems with the polling procedure or the final poll list to the attention of the *news.announce.newgroups* moderator via *newgroups-request@isc.org*. If there are no serious objections that could invalidate the vote, the *news.announce.newgroups* moderator handles the creation of the group, as described in Section 16.3.4. If the poll is invalidated, the reasons for it are posted by the moderator, and the CFV can be redone after a week of delay for the arguments about it to settle down.

A poll that fails either the 100-vote or two-thirds margin criteria causes a six-month block on proposals of essentially the same topic. Changing the moderation status or name, if those were points of contention, is not a sufficient change in the proposal to get around the six-month wait.

If the poll passes, proposals for groups on topics that are embraced by the charter of the new group are similarly blocked, but only for three months. This gives the new group a chance to establish its traffic patterns, so that the initial burst effect of a new group is diminished and users can get a more realistic view of the regular traffic for the group. If the proposal was a reorganization of an existing group or groups (as discussed below), this three-month prohibition also applies to proposals to change any of the groups directly involved in the reorganization.

16.3.3.5 Reorganization

A proposal can recommend the creation of several new groups at once. In this case, the groups are voted on in parallel, with each group passing or failing on its own. You cannot have a single mainstream vote to create more than one group, such as you might think would make sense when trying to create a new hierarchy. Only groups that are very closely related should be bundled in a parallel vote proposal because of the tendency for voters to vote the whole ticket. This leads to an increase in vote participation in each individual group's poll. Crossover voting by people in favor of groups that they have no opposition to, rather than just abstaining, distorts the interest measurement.

16.3.3.6 Group removals

Removing a group from the mainstream Usenet hierarchies is generally accomplished through a vote to rename it, which follows the same basic procedure as simply adding a new group. This is usually done as part of reorganization, such as renaming the parent group that splits into a hierarchy of groups. This means that the measure of support for the replacement group can be measured in basically the same manner, and a transition can be effected by creating the group and giving it some time to get established before removing the old one.*

You may have observed a small problem with this procedure. It means that a defunct group that does not have enough interest to pass a renaming vote cannot effectively be removed, just shuffled around some. This is not really true, however,

---

* The delay before removing the old group is two months for an unmoderated group. It is only a week for a moderated group, because the only person injecting traffic directly into the group is the moderator, who simply switches to using the new group.

because the group can be renamed to a group that already exists, with the proviso that if the vote fails, then both groups remain unchanged, rather than having the one group that would have united the two removed.

Another option is to have a straight vote to remove the group. This tends not to work in a proposal whose only item is the group removal, due to lack of sufficient interest in the group. Even the namespace purists can't seem to get agitated enough about removing the group to get the 100-vote minimum. However, in a reorganization of a hierarchy, where groups are being created in addition to the one being removed, it's already been noted that the number of people interested in individual items of the entire proposal raises the overall level of participation in the group removal item. The question is phrased so that people voting a pretty straight ballot support the removal if they support the creation of the new groups and oppose the removal if they oppose the new groups. Admittedly, this skews the vote the same way that the overall parallel vote on unrelated groups does. Since that is precisely the point of doing it this way, it would be disingenuous to claim that there isn't a little bit of a double standard here. It is just another bias built into the system to get what seems to be widely considered the most desirable result.

One untested method of group removal is to have a vote of confidence, or reau-thorization vote, for the group. It would essentially be like an initial vote to create the group, but if it failed, the group would be removed. Since group removal is inherently a hostile act to anyone who might be a serious user of the group, this might warrant locking out opposition votes and simply conducting it as a straight interest poll. If the supposedly defunct group can muster at least 100 people that want to keep it, it should remain.

Keep in mind that all of these methods suffer from inherent hostility. This is usu-ally most evident in reorganizations where there is an active user community and someone is trying to cause a change that makes reasonable administrative sense but that would nevertheless be disruptive to the established users of the group.

16.3.3.7 Converting moderation status

Problems with a group can sometimes be solved by making it moderated, or con-versely by unmoderating a moderated group. For example, *comp.lang.visual* is a newsgroup for discussing visual programming languages—languages in which programs are written using graphic symbols rather than text. The group had a big problem with people who kept using it to post about Microsoft's Visual Basic and Visual C++, which are textual languages with support for easier GUI design. To get their group back on topic, the *comp.lang.visual* users elected to moderate their group, so a moderator could point the people with off-topic posts to the right forums. The system that they used to do this was the same as creating a new group: discussion, vote, 100-vote margin and two-thirds majority for a passing vote. It would work exactly the same way to unmoderate a group.

16.3.3.8 Abuse

It is not difficult to imagine ways of abusing the group-changing procedures. When this happens, it is treated on a case-by-case basis. On the rare occasions when it has happened in the past, despite all the verbal shrapnel flying around, the Net marched on. Everyone adjusted, and it was back to business as usual.

16.3.4 newgroup and rmgroup Messages

As discussed in Section 3.2.1, the control messages that advise other sites of someone's desire to have them add or remove a newsgroup are called *newgroup* and *rmgroup* respectively. Modern C News and INN implementations allow you to cede some of your authority for *active* file modifications to other people via the *controlperm* and *control.ctl* files, as described in Section 5.1.2.2 and Section 8.2.4.1. This is the mechanism by which *group-admin@isc.org*, the *news.announce.newgroups* moderator, creates and removes groups on your machine.

The only technically necessary requirements for a *newgroup* or *rmgroup* message are a Control header that defines the requested change and an Approved header that is a token indication of who is asking for the change. The system really uses the Sender header, or the From header if Sender is absent, to determine who is requesting the change, so the Approved header requirement is just insurance against clueless people trying to do something they shouldn't.

Since the spring of 1996, cryptographically signed control messages have been available to help with rigorous authentication of the sender of a control message. This allows sites to enable automated *newgroup* and *rmgroup* messages with extremely few fears about the possibility of someone forging the identity of a well-known control message issuer. If you will regularly be issuing maintenance control messages for a hierarchy, you will probably find the *signcontrol* script at *ftp://ftp.isc.org/pub/pgpcontrol/signcontrol* to be quite useful. You should also let *tale@isc.org* (David Lawrence) know what hierarchy you will be maintaining and provide the information requested in *ftp://ftp.isc.org/pub/pgpcontrol/README.html*.

Control messages often spread farther than you expect. Unless you have very firm control on what the propagation of your control message will be—and this means not only being absolutely sure of your own feeds to neighbor sites, but of their feeds to their neighbors, and so on—it's a bad idea to use control messages for group changes meant for a very limited set of machines. Such changes are best done by asking the appropriate news administrators to do them manually (using the procedures described in Section 3.3.2.2).

WARNING   Just as C News' first implementation of *inews -C* (long since
              changed) once caused a lot of *newgroup* messages to leak and get
              distributed much farther than people intended, INN's *makegroup*
              caused similar problems. Even if *makegroup* is used carefully for its
              intended purpose, it still doesn't lend itself to an adequately descrip-
              tive body of why the change is being requested, so please don't use
              makegroup to send control messages.

If you are going to send a control message, it is a good idea to include some information in the body of the message regarding what you are trying to accomplish.
Templates for a new unmoderated newsgroup, a new moderated newsgroup, and
a newsgroup removal finish this chapter. They are similar to what the
news.announce.newgroups moderator uses to generate his control messages.

The one-line group description (and only that line) in a *newgroup* message is
automatically captured and installed by widely deployed news server software; the
software keys off of the line that says exactly "For your newsgroups file:". The
line immediately after that line should list precisely the name of the group being
created, followed by spaces or tabs and then the description. Please use the *newsgroups* line format described in Section 3.3.2.2. The other text in the control message is provided as immediate information for the news administrators who are
asked to make the change and as long-term archival information available to
everyone.

For a moderated newsgroup, you can't count on the mailpaths sites picking up the
moderator's address from the body of the message, so if it should be in the *mailpaths* database, send the information to *moderators-request@isc.org*, as described
in Section 15.2.1. Note that if the group is being created as part of an official
news.announce.newgroups proposal, the moderator of *news.announce.newgroups*
handles this for you.

The text in italics in the following templates should be replaced with the relevant
information for your group. After you have filled in the template, run the message
through *inews -b* to have it posted. If you're using INN, you can preview the final
posted article—to see whether an unwanted Sender header or other modifications
are creeping in—by giving the −D option to *inews*. Note that INN's *inews* does not
let you post a *newgroup* or *rmgroup* control message unless you are the news
user or in the news system's group.

Here is the template for creating an unmoderated newsgroup:

```
From: you@site.domain (your name)
Newsgroups: group.name
Subject: newgroup group.name
```

```
Control: newgroup group.name
Approved: you@site.domain

group.name is an unmoderated newsgroup that is being created per
[discussion? vote? where? when?]

For your newsgroups file:
group.name               description.

The charter:

THE CHARTER (DESCRIPTION OF APPROPRIATE TRAFFIC) FOR THE GROUP.
```

Here is the template for the creation of a moderated newsgroup:

```
From: you@site.domain (your name)
Newsgroups: group.name
Subject: newgroup group.name moderated
Control: newgroup group.name moderated
Approved: you@site.domaiOR

group.name is a moderated newsgroup that is being created per
[discussion? vote? where? when?]

Group submission address:   submit@site.domain
Moderator contact address:  submit-request@site.domain (name of moderator)

For your newsgroups file:
group.name               description. (Moderated)submit@site.domain

The charter:

THE CHARTER (DESCRIPTION OF APPROPRIATE TRAFFIC) FOR THE GROUP.
```

And finally, here's the template for deleting a newsgroup:

```
From: you@site.domain (your name)
Newsgroups: group.name
Subject: rmgroup group.name
Control: rmgroup group.name
Approved: you@site.domain

Please remove group.name. [why? superseded? defunct? unapproved?]
```

A Brief History of Usenet

This chapter provides a brief discussion of Usenet's history and development. The information here is mostly background material; you may find it of interest in understanding the current policies and politics of Usenet.

17.1 Origins

Usenet's philosophical origin lies in the mailing lists started in the 1970s on the ARPAnet. Its actual beginning, however, was in North Carolina in 1979, over a UUCP-based network. From there, Usenet grew explosively, finding its way back onto the ARPAnet (since renamed the Internet), and growing through several generations of progressively improving software.

17.1.1 Beginnings

Most modern computer networking originated with the ARPAnet project, started in the mid-1960s by the Advanced Research Projects Agency (ARPA) of the United States Department of Defense. At the time, ARPA was a major source of funding for advanced computing research, with a broad outlook that did not demand immediate relevance to military applications. Having just funded a number of major computing facilities at universities and other research institutions, ARPA began to explore the notion of connecting them together to share resources and data, and the ARPAnet was born.

One major surprise in the early history of the ARPAnet was the importance of electronic mail. When the early planners of the network considered potential applications, email was barely even thought about. Certainly, no one expected that email would be the single biggest use of the network within a few years, but that was exactly what happened.

Then, as now, much email was straightforward person-to-person correspondence. However, the notion of the mailing list—a special mail address that would resend any incoming mail to a list of other addresses—appeared very early. Specialized mailing lists for small groups appeared first, as an obvious extension of being able to address an email message to more than one destination. These lists were followed by larger mailing lists, often with relatively open membership, that existed to broadcast messages to anyone interested in discussing a particular topic. At the time, it was not widely realized that this was a rather different style of communication, and there was little thought given to using a different approach for it.

The discussion-oriented mailing lists, unlike their more specialized predecessors, quickly began to have problems with the sheer volume of traffic. As membership in the busier discussion lists soared into the hundreds, not only were there many messages, but mailing one copy to each participant put severe loads on the host where the mailing list was located. These problems were addressed by various stopgap solutions, such as digests (grouping multiple messages into a single large one) and remailers (enlisting other hosts as assistants to the central mailing host).

In retrospect, it's fairly clear that this was the time to step back and consider whether person-to-person mail was really the right way to handle this new form of communication, but at the time that wasn't so obvious. Bulletin-board systems did not exist then, at least not in any widely recognized form, although their predecessors were found within individual computing communities. In any case, the inertia of the already-substantial ARPAnet community made it difficult for a competing approach to the problem to get started; even today, Netnews has not fully replaced discussion-group mailing lists in some corners of the old ARPAnet.*

17.1.2 The Disenfranchised Strike Back

The biggest problem of the ARPAnet, from the viewpoint of the computing community at large, was its limited membership. Joining the ARPAnet involved a significant investment in facilities and communications equipment, and its origin as a research network produced a confused series of policy changes on who was eligible to join. The ARPAnet eventually evolved into today's Internet, but for a while it was a relatively exclusive club that was open only to the fortunate.

As the ARPAnet's electronic community became better known, many organizations that were interested in joining found that they couldn't. (In some cases, an organization did join, but only specific people or groups within the organization were given ARPAnet access.) This sparked various projects to establish alternatives.

---

* Mailing lists remain useful for groups with restricted memberships and for gatewaying onto primitive networks that don't provide for broadcast communication, but they make no sense for open-membership discussion groups on modern networks. Mailing lists just don't scale well.

Some of the alternatives, like Bitnet, became exclusive clubs in their own right, with the same problems of expensive and restricted access.

In 1979, a few enthusiastic programmers at Duke University and the University of North Carolina (UNC) started exploring the potentials of the newly released Version 7 of Unix. Unix then ran on minicomputers that were often controlled by individual university departments or groups within them, so there was little organizational inertia to overcome when experimenting. Among the novel features of Version 7 was a software package dubbed UUCP (Unix to Unix CoPy), which did inter-host file transfer and remote command execution. Unix had long supported electronic mail on individual machines, but one little-advertised feature of Version 7 was that the mail system could use UUCP's communications facilities to send mail to users on other hosts, using file transfer to ship the mail message and remote execution to make the receiving host process it. The documentation on this was sketchy and obscure.

The most interesting aspect of UUCP, from the viewpoint of a handful of student programmers with no money, was that it could use ordinary telephone modems to connect hosts. This seems obvious today, but at the time it wasn't. Modems of the time were very slow, typically 300 bits per second, and the ability for the modem to dial the phone itself was a rare and expensive extra. Modems were normally used to connect a user's terminal to a computer system, with the dialing done by hand using an attached telephone. Doing inter-host communication this way basically hadn't occurred to anyone; compared to the permanently connected high-speed data lines of the ARPAnet, it looked impossibly slow and clumsy. But UUCP had facilities for using phone lines, including the ability to store outgoing traffic until a phone connection was available.

The Duke/UNC group—primarily Steve Bellovin, Stephen Daniel, Jim Ellis, and Tom Truscott—thought that even slow and clumsy networking was better than nothing. They proceeded to figure out UUCP and get it running, first within their own facility and then across the phone lines, aided by an improvised autodialer addition to a modem. It wasn't as good as the ARPAnet: with connections made intermittently and at low speed, it wasn't practical to do remote login or other highly interactive forms of connection. But one could transfer files and send mail, and even with limited speed and unpredictable delays, that was much better than nothing.

The Duke/UNC group didn't stop there, however. The programmers had a key insight that largely eluded the ARPAnet community: mail is not a good way to do broadcast communication. They proceeded to build what we would now call a distributed bulletin-board system, and Netnews was born. After some false starts and experimentation, the software package that became known as A News emerged. This software was still relatively crude, and it was not designed for heavy traffic (since its authors expected only a few articles a day). The Duke/UNC group paid relatively little attention to the problem of organizing the traffic, although it did occur to them that local and network-wide discussions should be separated and that discussions needed names. The user interface was primitive, and the article format was not readily extended. Nevertheless, A News made it possible to put an electronic community together with only the most minimal investment in equipment.

17.1.3 Usenet Is Born

Many university computer science departments had Unix systems by this time, and all of them envied the lucky few with ARPAnet access. At the winter 1980 Usenix conference* in Boulder, Colorado, Jim Ellis gave a talk about the UUCP-based network and the Netnews software.

Shortly thereafter, the emerging network was dubbed "Usenet," in a conscious play on "Usenix," as the Duke/UNC group was hoping to get the Usenix Association involved in organizing and running the network. That never actually happened, but the name stuck.

Usenet started small, initially in a "star" configuration centered on one host at Duke. In the beginning, the Duke host did most of the phone calling because most other sites had receive-only modems that couldn't dial the phone. That arrangement didn't last, however, as traffic grew and the Duke people discovered that trying to bill other sites for long-distance charges was too difficult.

And traffic certainly did grow, as Usenet expanded and as people discovered it as both a technical resource and a recreational forum. Table 17–1 shows Usenet growth, in terms of sites and number of articles per day, for the first ten years.

Table 17–1: Usenet Growth, First Ten Years

Year	Sites (approx.)	Articles/Day (approx.)
1979	3	2
1980	15	10
1981	150	20
1982	400	50
1983	600	120
1984	900	225
1985	1,300	375

---

* The Unix Users' Group, then-recently renamed the Usenix Association to avoid trademark problems, held technical conferences twice a year.

Table 17-1: Usenet Growth, First Ten Years (continued)

1986	2,500	500
1987	5,000	1000
1988	11,000	1800

As the numbers in Table 17-1 suggest, an enormous number of people were interested in joining an electronic community, if it could be done cheaply and without
political problems. Inexpensive (well, relatively inexpensive) autodialing modems
were starting to appear, and many organizations were buying them for other reasons, so startup costs were often zero. And the (dis)organization of Usenet, with
no central authority and no formal "acceptable use" policy, meant that anyone
could join. So almost everyone in the Unix computing community did.

17.2 Growing Pains

For most of its first ten years, Usenet was carried mostly by UUCP over phone
lines. Fortunately, modem technology was improving rapidly. In 1980, most of the
modems involved ran at 300 bits per second. By 1988, however, many were
Telebit Trailblazers running at 18,000 bits per second. Through much of this
period, there was an informal set of hosts known as the "Usenet backbone" that
did much of the long-distance calling to connect different areas. Since long-
distance calls cost money, it made sense to centralize the long-haul transmission to
avoid sending the same articles over the same route more than once. The administrators of the backbone hosts had a considerable influence on Usenet's development, as we will see later.

17.2.1 B News and C News

The software also improved greatly in the same period. A News' limitations
became serious fairly quickly. Starting around 1981, Matt Glickman and Mark Horton at the University of California at Berkeley rewrote A News extensively for better performance and improved organization. (They also took the opportunity to
change the article format to a more extensible one, more or less harmonized with
the format used for ARPAnet mail.) The result was dubbed B News, and it fairly
quickly replaced A News.

By 1985, even B News was starting to show its age. Various incremental improvements had kept it ahead of the traffic growth for a while, but performance was still
relatively poor and limits were being reached. Geoff Collyer and Henry Spencer at
the University of Toronto began experimenting with rewriting various parts of the

software to deal with performance problems and other limitations, and the result eventually became C News.* C News has been steadily improved and updated since, and is still handling the load adequately. Later news software development has gone off in other directions, which we'll describe shortly.

One other development that C News accelerated was the separation of transport software from newsreader software. A News bundled everything together: not only was it all together in one package, it was all together in one program. B News separated the various functions into different programs, but it still came with its own newsreader program (and later with two newsreader programs). Independently written newsreader software eventually began to appear, and C News encouraged this trend by not including any substantial newsreader software.†

17.2.2 From Anarchy to Order (Almost)

In the beginning, there was little systematic organization within Usenet. Procedures for naming and creating new newsgroups were informal. This didn't last, though, as participation grew and disputes arose.

For much of the 1980s, Usenet decision making was dominated by the system administrators of the vaguely defined Usenet backbone. The central role of the backbone sites in news transmission gave their administrators considerable influence over what got transmitted and what didn't, and it was natural enough for them to get together when decisions needed to be made. This group was eventually dubbed the "Backbone Cabal"; we'll discuss it at greater length later in the chapter.

The Backbone Cabal's most visible achievement was the so-called "Great Renaming," in which the rather haphazard newsgroup naming scheme was rationalized into the seven original Usenet hierarchies in 1986–1987. The Cabal's influence gradually declined after that, as alternative networking technologies reduced the importance of long-distance phone calls in connecting Usenet sites, and as continued growth started to make the Cabal itself too large for effective decision-making. For routine matters like newsgroup creation, the Cabal was replaced by a voting scheme whose evolution we'll describe later. For more drastic actions, like the Great Renaming, there simply isn't any group that wields the necessary influence any more.

---

* Geoff Collyer & Henry Spencer, "News Need Not Be Slow," Proceedings of the Winter 1987 Usenix Technical Conference, Usenix Association, 1987.

† This was originally done for strictly pragmatic reasons: the source for the best newsreader software of the time, *rn*, was almost as big as the rest of C News, and Collyer and Spencer didn't want to double the size of their distribution.

17.2.3 Pumping Bits

Although Usenet originally evolved in isolation from the ARPAnet, connections between the two appeared fairly early. First some newsgroups were gatewayed from the more prominent ARPAnet mailing lists. Bidirectional mail gateways led stormy political lives, due to problems with "access to the ARPAnet" policies, but generally persisted simply because the gateways were useful. And eventually a new trend appeared: using the Internet (as the ARPAnet was then becoming) as a transmission route for Netnews.

The ARPAnet's permanent high-speed connections had always been attractive to Usenet administrators troubled by growing long-distance phone bills. As political restrictions on access to the ARPAnet/Internet eased, interest in Netnews transmission across it grew. Furthermore, some of the more farsighted Internet administrators realized that Netnews—despite its humble origins—was technically superior to mailing lists for broadcast transmission, and could solve some of the problems the Internet was having with unmanageably huge mailing lists.

The outcome of this was the development of the Network News Transfer Protocol (NNTP) and the first implementation of it in early 1986. This implementation is often confusingly referred to as NNTP as well; it is more aptly called the NNTP Reference Implementation (NRI) instead. This work was done largely by Brian Kantor and Phil Lapsley at the University of California, both at San Diego and Berkeley, with contributions by Erik Fair, Steven Grady, and Mike Meyer, among others. Although NNTP had its defects, notably performance problems and built-in confusion over whether it is a transport protocol or a remote-reading protocol, it got Netnews onto the Internet.

The endless growth of traffic, fundamental technical limits on the capabilities of modems, and the obvious economic issues quickly pushed most of the long-haul Usenet transmission links off telephones and onto the Internet. NNTP more slowly took over local distribution as well, as volume grew to the point that transmission of a full news feed by modem simply became impractical.* Eventually, Rich Salz developed a new news transport software package, InterNetNews (INN), to increase the efficiency of NNTP transmission. UUCP over dialup lines continues to survive around the edges of Usenet, carrying low-volume partial feeds to leaf nodes.

---

* Ironically, where NNTP once replaced UUCP, UUCP is now sometimes replacing NNTP. NNTP, although well-designed in some respects, incurs significant overhead per article. When there is no doubt about which articles need to be transmitted, bundling them into a single file and compressing it before transmission exploits costly or slow connections much more effectively. The usual Internet file-transfer software is designed for interactive use rather than background store-and-forward operation, and is awkward for this purpose in other ways as well, so UUCP is being used—with connections made over the Internet rather than by dialing the phone—to fill the gap.

17.3 *Namespace History*

Now let's take another look at Usenet history, this time with specific regard to the network newsgroup namespace. The most enduring scars of particular wars over group creation have been inflicted in battles over what to name newsgroups.

17.3.1 *Beginnings*

Steve Bellovin reports that when Usenet was in its infancy, the original design estimate was for a maximum traffic volume of two articles per day. At this expected level of traffic, the namespace could grow rather chaotically. In fact, there wasn't much of a concern about a namespace of thousands of newsgroups.

In the early days of network news, local newsgroups generally had just one component, like so:

dept   Information about the department

general   Articles of general interest to local readers

system   Important system announcements

The few network-wide groups that were exchanged between machines were originally placed under the top-level name *NET.* Mark Horton and Matt Glickman came on the scene from Berkeley in 1981 with the first version of B News and promptly demonstrated their distaste for capital letters by changing *NET* to *net.* The *net* groups were the primary unmoderated worldwide Usenet groups for the next half decade. Some additional hierarchical depth began to emerge over the next couple of years, as sport groups went to *net.sport.*, groups about Usenet itself appeared as *net.news.*, micro computer groups grew below *net.micro.*, and so on.

When the site *ucbvax* at Berkeley joined the Net, the *fa* groups were introduced to a wider audience. *fa* stood for "From ARPAnet"; it contained messages gatewayed from Internet mailing lists. At the time, the Internet was not carrying any appreciable amount of network news traffic.

By Usenet's fourth birthday at the end of 1983, Usenet traffic had swelled to a whopping 200 articles per day, and there were nearly that many worldwide groups in the *net* and *fa* hierarchies. Many groups received no traffic in a day; there were very few high-volume groups, even for the slower communications facilities of the time. Regional hierarchies had already made their appearance, and some, like *can* (Canada) and *ont* (Ontario), still exist, predating the current worldwide hierarchies.

About this time, some organization of the chaos started to shape up. The group *net.news.group* appeared, with the intended purpose of discussing the creation of new newsgroups. In addition, the "List of Active Newsgroups" began being posted periodically, to give a consistent view of the newsgroups that were widely available around the Net.

The Backbone Cabal came into existence in the early 1980s to help the flow of news around the network. The term was originally intended as a lighthearted appellation for the group. The Cabal were the administrators of a group of sites who agreed to use whatever resources were necessary (within reason) to carry all of the Usenet traffic and to retransmit it around the clock, rather than waiting for night telephone rates. Because members of the Cabal were willing to foot the major part of the bill for getting Usenet to work, they had policy-making powers about what groups they would carry and hence what groups would realistically be available to the rest of the network.

The *mod* hierarchy for moderated groups was born when Brian Redman created the newsgroup *mod.ber* ("ber" was his login name) in 1983. With the advent of B News version 2.10.2 in 1984, the *mod* hierarchy was cemented into place with more widespread software support. The moderation mechanism was derived from the way that several Internet mailing lists and bulletin board systems worked.

An interesting name came out of this time. The group *net.motss* was created to discuss homosexual issues, with the cryptic acronym standing for "Members Of The Same Sex." The name was intentionally obfuscated, though not to slip by the news system administrators. At the time, a relatively small group of administrators had a pretty firm grasp on newsgroup naming. The not-unrealistic fear was that sites might have to pull the plug on all of Usenet because of some higher powers-that-be, not savvy in the Net, overreacting to public, off-the-Net controversy if the group was observed by morally opposed people. It was hoped that the name would completely slip by them. To what degree this worked is not certain. There never was a significant outcry about such a group on Usenet, but whether that was because the expected opposition was there and clueless or because they were just not there, is impossible to know.

17.3.2 The Great Renaming

By early 1985, the Net had grown considerably from its humble origins. Nearly a thousand sites were exchanging news, and traffic volume was reaching the astounding threshold of a megabyte per day. As traffic continued to rise, members of the Backbone Cabal recognized the need for a better newsgroup naming system. In early 1986 they began planning for the Great Renaming of *mod*, *net*, and *fa* to the "Big Seven" hierarchies: *comp*, *misc*, *news*, *rec*, *sci*, *soc*, and *talk*. Much of the work was accomplished through email discussion, and some of the final details were worked out at the Atlanta Usenix conference in the summer of 1986. The renaming was to be done by creating the newsgroups, using B News' alias mechanism to internally alias the old groups to the new ones at each server, and then finally sending *rmgroup* messages for the obsolete names.

There was a technological hurdle in the way of renaming all of the groups, however. B News 2.10, the server software run by nearly all of the Net, could not adequately handle unmoderated groups and moderated groups mingled in the same hierarchy. Rick Adams, B News' maintainer, added that functionality to make B News version 2.11, which was released in late 1986. In the meantime, the Great Renaming of the unmoderated groups occurred in the summer of 1986.

By February of 1987, Rick observed (using the *version* control message) that over 50 percent of the sites on Usenet were running B News 2.11. People were also growing more and more confused over the mix of old and new naming schemes, so it was now or never. The Great Renaming was completed in March with the final move of the moderated groups into the Big Seven namespace. No cosmic catastrophes are recorded as coincident with the final move.

17.3.3 Newsgroup Creation

As part of the Great Renaming, the Backbone Cabal instituted a process to measure interest in new groups. The process was designed to help determine which topics had enough supporters around the network to warrant the use of resources, both human and machine, for newsgroups. A polling procedure was used to measure the interest in a proposed newsgroup.

The basic group creation process at the time was:

1. Someone interested in a topic proposed that a group be created to discuss the topic.

2. The Backbone Cabal discussed the potential of the new group and defined a name for it.

3. The general body of news administrators were polled regarding interest in the group.

4. If enough news administrators thought it was a good idea, the Cabal created the group.

Usenet users who were not administrators rather quickly found problems with this scheme, in that they did not think the interests of all of the readers of the Net could be adequately represented by the smaller body of administrators. Comparisons to representative democracy were shot full of holes, as administrators were not elected by the users of the sites they managed, and it was thought to be highly unlikely that administrators would regularly poll their own users to find out which proposed groups they wanted.

As a result, the group creation process was transformed into a discussion-and-vote system that was open to everyone—this was an early form of the current group creation process discussed in 16.3.3. The Backbone Cabal ceded all aspects of group proposals, including naming, to the group proponents. The discussion was to take place in *news.groups* (the new name of *net.news.group*). The vote was a "yes" or "no" vote, with the requirement that a group needed 100 more "yes" votes than "no" votes to pass.*

The main purpose of the poll was an interest vote. The "yes" versus "no" nature of the polling was partly intended to obfuscate the interest poll under the guise of a democratic vote and partly intended to give administrators the ability to refuse a group en masse if they found sufficient problems with the proposal, like with the name of the group. "Yes" votes were supposed to measure interest in the group— a raw count of how many people would use the group if it were created. However, "no" votes were not supposed to measure the reciprocal: how many people would not use it. The "no" votes were supposed to indicate how many people had problems with the creation of the group as it was proposed (mostly on semi-technical grounds, and independent of whether they might even use the group if it were created despite their objection).

One problem with the older consensus method was that people who didn't get a consensus were constantly whining that it was only a couple of obstinate opponents who were ruining it for the multitudes that wanted their group. The hope was that even though the new system was rather thin on real aspects of democracy, people who didn't muster enough support in the interest poll would just drop the issue after they lost their vote because Americans (the vast bulk of the Net at the time) were supposedly socialized that way. Administrators were still ultimately the rulers of their machines and could carry groups or not as they desired.

The procedure for the wide-open polling scheme was written by Greg Woods and called the "Guidelines for Usenet Group Creation," or the "Guidelines" for short, to further emphasize that administrators were free to ignore them at will. Adherence to The Guidelines was very sketchy at first. Several groups were created that did not pass a vote as specified in the Guidelines, including one of the most popular groups, *rec.humor.funny*. It failed to get its 100-vote margin with a final tally of 64 "yes" to one "no." The proponent and proposed moderator, Brad Templeton, nevertheless succeeded in getting enough sites to carry the group to make it viable.

A back door of sorts was installed for some of the Cabal administrators in the form of a set of groups called the "INET distribution." Erik Fair linked Internet mailing lists with demonstrable traffic into groups in the Big Seven namespace. However, to allow those sites with less bandwidth to be able to opt out (as well as those

---

* The two-thirds majority rule didn't come about until later.

sites who just flat out opposed skipping the vote), he put a "Distribution: inet" header in all of the messages, so that the *sys* file (this was pre-INN) could be used to only send the groups to the sites that wanted them. This was a shortcut for the Cabal to use when it just wanted to create a group without the fuss of two months of public discussion and voting.

In early 1986, a proposal for *rec.music.rock-n-roll* was shot down by the Backbone Cabal. Shortly thereafter, *rec.drugs* was also shot down when the Cabal refused to carry the group after it supposedly passed its poll. Then Richard Sexton made a proposal for *rec.fucking*, which he later said was a joke that was never really meant to go to *news.groups*. Sex is an extremely popular topic, though, and the proposal took off on its course, mutating into *rec.sex* and then finally *soc.sex*, as most sex-related discussions were already taking place in *soc.singles*. It went to vote and passed; the Cabal did its best to simply deny that the proposal ever even existed, again refusing to carry the group.

The reason the Cabal* wanted to prevent groups like *rec.drugs* and *soc.sex* was that they had justifiable concerns about waking up one day to headlines about immorality on their computers, and then having management pull the plugs on Usenet. They were not interested in attracting external scrutiny, and they felt that group names clearly proclaiming topics that conservatives objected to were unnecessary attractors to such scrutiny. The network itself was very different in those days. Organizations usually did not have computers devoted specifically to news, and often the higher-ups in the company didn't even know news existed. An awkward flinch by a panicking middle manager would have been enough to get a site shut down.

17.3.4 Complications Appear

In response to the problems getting *rec.drugs* created, John Gilmore started the *alt* ("alternative") hierarchy. The intention was that these groups would use distribution paths outside the Backbone, and hence would not be subject to the policies of the Backbone Cabal. Initially, *alt* was a separate network with its own UUCP connections. The advent of NNTP made alternative distribution paths even more feasible, as the protocol used TCP/IP to route news across the dedicated lines of the Internet. With NNTP, the central role of the Backbone disappeared, and it was much easier to set up an alternative distribution network.

Only a couple of groups were originally created in *alt*, and the hierarchy was of little note until the Cabal's rejection of *soc.sex*. The creation of *alt.sex* was a

---

* It should be noted that typical descriptions of the Backbone Cabal tend to convey the impression that they were a closely knit group who always acted in concert. That facade was generally presented to the world, but in truth, there was not nearly as much unity as the image suggested.

defining moment for news, and almost instantly led to people working on increased propagation of the *alt* hierarchy. The influence of the Backbone Cabal dropped markedly as many sites ignored their decision on *soc.sex* and set up propagation paths that did not use the backbone.

The next major upheaval in the mainstream group creation procedure didn't materialize for nearly two years. After 1987 sailed by without notable incident, Bob Webber proposed *comp.protocols.tcp-ip.eniac* in early 1988. His intent was to demonstrate that the vote tabulation criteria was a farce, and that any proposal, no matter how stupid an idea and clearly a joke, could pass a Guidelines vote. He succeeded in demonstrating that, and news administrators succeeded in demonstrating that simply passing through the process did not mean that they would carry the group. Gene Spafford refused to list the group in his "List of Active Newsgroups" and the group never did achieve meaningful distribution.

Later that year came a much more serious proposal. It was on a topic that no one opposed, yet the proposal ran into serious opposition. At the heart of the issue was how widely propagated each hierarchy tended to be by default, and hence how widely distributed a new newsgroup in one of those hierarchies was likely to be. The proponents wanted *comp.women*, a group to discuss women's roles and problems in the field of computing, insisting that it be in *comp* to receive the broadest distribution instead of in the less widely propagated *SDC* hierarchy. The resulting fight about this placement was an epic even among the often highly inflammatory debates on the Net.

The problem, as administrators saw it, was that the group polluted the namespace. The issue was not that the topic wasn't worthy of discussion, but that the *comp* hierarchy was a technically oriented hierarchy yet the proposed group was socially focused. To namespace purists, it was nearly unimaginable that the group wouldn't go in *soc*. The debate was especially unusual in that the Backbone Cabal's messages about the matter, which were normally just kept to the private backbone mailing list, became public and really heated up the fight. Discourse quickly left the level platform of reason and ballooned into an enormous fracas of personal attacks and largely emotional stances.

Eventually the proponent, Patricia O'Tauma, said *comp.society.women*, one of the alternatives proposed as a compromise to at least keep the socially oriented traffic well-demarcated within *comp*, would be acceptable to her. Karl Kleinpaste, a Cabalista, was tired of the ongoing rage and decide to settle it. He informed the Cabal of his intent to create *comp.society.women* at the end of the day if no one objected. By close of business, his mailbox had been silent. He sent the *newgroup* message that Friday night and promptly left for the San Francisco Usenix conference that weekend. His mailbox had never seen such a firestorm as he was greeted with when he finally read email on Tuesday. He reports getting hate mail about the issue for two months afterward. The backbone mailing list fell silent, presumably because everyone decided to use Kleinpaste for their screeds instead.

17.3.5 Anarchy and Organization

A couple of months later, in late 1988, Gene Spafford officially shut down the backbone list. The glory days of the Cabal had long since passed; the height of their power was 1985 to 1986, when they succeeded in the Great Renaming. The power of the group to unitedly accomplish Usenet administrative development had waned to the point where people had become tired of the effort they were putting in for what little they felt was really accomplished. It is generally agreed that *comp.society.women* was just the final straw on a camel whose knees were already weary and buckling from the long desert walk. Spafford was left as the authority with his List of Active Newsgroups and the Guidelines were the primary vehicle for convincing him to update it.

Over the next couple of months, it became clear to administrators that without the centralized decision making of the Cabal, it was too difficult to follow *news.groups* to discover emerging new group proposals. *news.announce.newgroups* was created in early 1989 as a filter for group proposals, allowing for the formal stages of proposals to be tracked apart from the voluminous discussion surrounding them. Greg Woods, a former Cabal member and original author of the Guidelines, was drafted to be the first moderator for the group.

Perhaps the most notable inroad made during Woods's term was the creation of *rec.arts.erotica*, a moderated newsgroup rather clearly labeled as being about sex but still fairly widely accepted by news administrators. Some sites still refused to carry the group, but most found no problem with it, or at least found that having a moderator to hold accountable for the traffic made it acceptable.

Another memorable group creation battle that is still recounted by old-timers on the Net happened during the Woods tenure. This one bore remarkable similarity to the *comp.women* row—a proposal to increase the propagation of a forum for aquarium enthusiasts, who at the time were using a group named *alt.aquaria*. They wanted *sci.aquaria*, and nothing else would do. *rec.pets.fish* and even a pained compromise offering of *sci.bio.aquaria* were all flatly refused and the debate in *news.groups* raged. In the end, Richard Sexton ended up scoring a most remarkable coup, by getting acceptable propagation for not just one Big Seven aquarium group, the originally sought *sci.aquaria*, but a second one, *rec.aquaria*. Though the distribution of these groups was hurt by the fights, it was probably still at least as good as *alt.aquaria* at the time and eventually became much better.

By late in that year, Woods had already grown justifiably weary of the job, particularly because the aquaria debates had so emotionally involved him. As the sole person filling an authoritative role that used to be shared by several members of the Cabal, the *news.announce.newgroups* moderator was a magnet for much more personal criticism. The political stress and constant attention was much greater than most Net users have to deal with, and there was little chance for a break from it. Despite that, Woods took a respite from the responsibility in December, temporarily entrusting the group to Eliot Lear. When Woods returned, he realized that he had enjoyed the holiday far too much to cast himself in that role again, so he retired as moderator of the group and left the job to Lear.

Within a year, Lear already had to deal with a couple of large flame wars about different groups. The one that seemed to lead to his eventual passing of the moderatorship was the *comp.unix* reorganization, which proposed, among many other things, the removal of *comp.unix.wizards* by renaming it to *comp.unix.internals*. The group had grown nearly useless to real "Unix Wizards" because of the elementary user questions being asked there and the posturing of wannabe wizards. The debate about this item during the discussion phase was comparatively light; the eruption by several stalwart readers of the group, after the renaming was announced as having passed, was much more pyrotechnic.

Though largely based on emotional attachment to the group's old name, despite the problems it had, chief among the rational arguments was that respected authorities like Doug Gwyn couldn't use the replacement group because they were prohibited under the terms of non-disclosure agreements from discussing "Unix internals." *comp.unix.internals* was created in accord with the proposal result, and, after much gnashing, *comp.unix.wizards* was also restored to its original status, with little change in the problems it had before the *comp.unix* reorganization.*

After 13 months in the hot seat, Lear turned the title of moderator of *news.announce.newgroups* over to David Lawrence, then the news administrator for Rensselaer Polytechnic Institute, a major university news site. That brings the situation in mainstream Usenet to roughly the current day, as David Lawrence still moderates *news.announce.newgroups* as of this writing. While several notable developments in mainstream group creation have happened during his term as moderator, including more formalized and consistently identifiable proposals, regular control messages from a single source to implement poll results, and the use of third-party poll takers instead of the proponents of the group, the situation in *news.groups* remains much the way it was on the backbone list before it. Current newsgroup-creation procedures are described in Section 16.3.3.

---

* Eventually the problems led to another attempted solution, the moderation of the group in 1993.

17.3.6 The Rot Sets in on alt

Meanwhile, *alt* continued to grow in a much more free-spirited way. Without a clear authority figure, advocates of new groups often bypassed even the nominal consensus method of group approval expected by the *alt.config* regulars. Anarchy with a capital A was the order of the day in *alt* and it eventually led to a namespace that is considered the morass of the worldwide hierarchies.

It wasn't always that way in *alt*. In fact, though the naming of groups was a little freer in the early stages of the hierarchy, it was still generally oriented around topics people really wanted to talk about. Although it had an overly broad second-level namespace, *alt* was still reasonably good at following the hierarchical naming forms of the mainstream groups.

The beginning of the end (well, one sort of end) of *alt* can be traced back to a leaked *newgroup* message for *alt.swedish.chef.bork.bork.bork*. Intended for local distribution at Harvey Mudd College, it was sent far and wide because an increasing number of C News installations weren't configured to pay attention to the "Distribution: local" header that would have stopped the newgroup at B News sites.* The humor value of the name, even among curmudgeonly administrators, was enough to get it pretty well established around the network. Everyone had a good laugh and tried to get back to business as usual.

But business in *alt* was never to be the same. Over the next several months there was an explosion of joke *alt* groups that were meant primarily to be funny in name, if not especially interesting in topic. The situation got worse as more and more people used group names either to assail the character of others or to parade themselves and their pet interests.

Some people tried to slow the flood of poorly thought-out groups by sending *rmgroup* control messages to remove those that appeared to be jokes, had no previous discussion, duplicated existing groups, or were "bad" for some other reason. Other particularly determined administrators decided that there was no such thing as a bogus group in *alt* and that *newgroup* messages were the exercise of free speech, but that *rmgroup* messages were not. At least one even went so far as to take *rmgroup* messages and recraft them as *newgroup* messages purporting to be from the person who was trying to remove the group, a practice which continues to this day. It is this behavior that led to the resignation by namespace purists around the world that *alt* groups just will not die except by the exodus of any perceptible audience for the group—the empty shell of the group, however, will live on at far more sites than should be warranted.

---

* Some blamed this on C News—which required explicit attention to such configuration issues, and sometimes didn't get it—but the C News authors consider it the fault of careless administrators and of ill-advised reliance on undocumented B News features.

This is not to say there are no good groups in *alt*; many good groups have been created there, either because the proponents were unaware of the group creation process for the better propagated mainstream hierarchies or because they found the process too onerous. (That the group creation process is more onerous contributes to the better reputation, and hence to the better propagation, of the mainstream groups.) Some of the most popular groups, and most of the highest volume ones, are found in *alt*—for example, the sex groups that the Cabal originally wouldn't let into the mainstream hierarchies.

The *alt* hierarchy is home to the massive volume of postings in *alt.binaries*, which has done a very respectable job of corralling the postings of large files of images and sounds in one area that administrators can treat with special policies because of their size. Many varied sexual interests have found outlets under *alt.sex* and numerous groups for fans of particular sports teams can be read in *alt.sports*. You will have to wade through a lot of poor names to find the pockets of consistency, but they do exist.

When David Lawrence inherited the regular "Alternative Newsgroup Hierarchies" postings from Gene Spafford, it came with a request that the tradition of whimsical *alt* group descriptions continue. David Lawrence complied with this and continues to do so. Typically, the groups that get such descriptions are ones that did not have a properly formed newsgroups line in the control message that created the group. The list only attempts to catalog seemingly active newsgroups and is cleansed of moribund ones just before it is posted. It is only one view of the *alt* hierarchy, and is not intended to be definitive. Bruce Becker posts another view regularly, which includes every *alt* group for which he has seen a *newgroup* message, regardless of whether the group has gone dormant. This posting, called "Another listing of newsgroups in the "alt" hierarchy" is posted to *alt.answers*.

17.3.7 Digressions

People who were not happy with either the mainstream group creation procedure or that of *alt* went off and created their own hierarchies with varying group creation procedures. A few of these hierarchies are listed in Section 16.1.2. The creation of these top-level hierarchies is less common than might otherwise be expected, mostly because it takes a lot of work to get a new one widely propagated, especially if it is of narrow focus. Even the poorly propagated *alt* groups get better average propagation than most other hierarchies.

Hundreds of other regional or organizational hierarchies also exist. Regional hierarchies tend to have informal consensus-driven group creation, except in the largest hierarchies like the Japanese (*fj*), German (*de*), and French (*fr*) hierarchies. Organizational hierarchies tend to be under the direct control of the news administrator(s) for the organization in question.

Worldwide propagation to the majority of the Net is not the intent with such hierarchies, so they don't get it. This does lead to one other problem that has affected
the Net since the earliest days. Two organizations can end up creating what seems
to be natural top-level names for themselves and find that they end up getting articles from each other. For example, *ut* was used by both the University of Texas
and the University of Toronto, and crosspostings to the *ut.general* group of one
usually showed up in the *ut.general* group of the other. This problem can usually
be avoided by more descriptive top-level names, such as *utexas*.

18

In this chapter:
- *Basic Layout and Character Codes*
- *Headers*
- *Body*
- *Control Messages*
- *MIME*

Anatomy of a News Article

This chapter goes into detail about what an individual news article looks like, as stored on disk or exchanged between hosts. This is primarily background information, but you may find it useful for troubleshooting purposes.

As discussed briefly in Chapter 1, *Introduction*, there have been several documents that defined the standard news article format. The first document, now obsolete, was RFC 850. Later, small revisions produced RFC 1036, which is getting rather dated, but is still the current Netnews standard. Work on a major revision got as far as a preliminary draft and then stalled; efforts are now underway to get this going again.* The basics have not changed; the new revision mostly just defines details more precisely, and documents places where common practice differs from RFC 1036. This chapter follows the new revision, with occasional notes on the differences between it and RFC 1036. Some of the material in this chapter is, in fact, taken from the new revision.†

Software authors should be aware that this chapter is neither complete enough nor precise enough to be a substitute for the RFCs. The intent here is to give a general idea of what's going on, not to dot all the i's and cross all the t's. If you need to know the exact rules—which you do, if you're trying to write software that uses them—there is no substitute for reading the RFCs themselves.

This chapter begins with a look at the overall organization of a news article. Headers are then discussed in detail, while some rules for the body are covered only briefly. The chapter concludes with a look at a couple of special topics: control

---

* The preliminary draft can be found at *pub/news.txt.Z* or *pub/news.ps.Z* or *ftp.zoo.toronto.edu*. Information about the revived effort can be found at *http://www.landfield.com/usefor/*.

† That material is Copyright 1993, 1994 Henry Spencer. All rights reserved. Used by permission.

messages and the Multipurpose Internet Mail Extensions (MIME) conventions for mail/news message bodies.

18.1 Basic Layout and Character Codes

The format of news articles is a specialized and mutated version of the format used for Internet mail messages. The mail format is defined in RFC 822, as amended by RFC 1123. (A number of further extensions have been added by later RFCs, but most of those are irrelevant here.) If you are already familiar with Internet mail-message format, be cautious in carrying that experience over to news. The news format is intended to be compatible with the mail format, so that any valid news article is also a valid mail message, but the news format has many restrictions to make news articles easier to process.

18.1.1 Overall Format

A news article consists of some *headers** followed by an empty line followed by a *body*. The empty line marks the end of the headers and separates them from the body. The headers are precisely specified and must follow detailed rules, while the body must observe only a few restrictions. Both headers and body are lines of ASCII text.

18.1.2 End-Of-Line

Precisely how the end-of-line is marked depends on context: the type of host the article is being stored on and the protocol being used to transmit it. On Unix hosts, each line ends with a newline character, which is the ASCII linefeed (LF, decimal character code 10). The same convention is used in articles sent via UUCP. However, the Internet protocols, including NNTP, normally mark the end-of-line with a carriage return, linefeed combination: an ASCII carriage return (CR, code 13) followed by a linefeed (LF, code 10).

There are other conventions in use on some odd systems. The only restriction is that character codes other than CR (13) and LF (10) must not be used as end-of-line markers. Transmitting or receiving an article often requires converting between end-of-line conventions. The problems that result from omitted or botched conversions can be very mysterious if you aren't on the lookout for them.

---

* The Internet mail community tends to speak of the whole thing on the front as the header and of the individual items within it as *header fields*, but this usage has never caught on consistently in the news community.

18.1.3 Characters

Technically, a line can contain any ASCII* character (any code in the decimal range 0-127) except NUL (0), LF (10), and CR (13), but in practice it is unwise to use *control characters* (codes 0-31 and 127) other than backspace (8), tab (9), and formfeed (12), which have commonly accepted meanings (see the sidebar).

Backspace, Tab, and Formfeed

Backspace should be used only for underlining. Underlining is done by using a sequence of underscores (code 95) followed by an equal number of backspaces followed by the characters to be underlined.† (This order causes devices that show only the most recent of several overstruck characters, rather than an overstruck combination, to show the underlined character rather than the underline itself.) Newsreading software should recognize underlining and translate it to the appropriate commands for devices that support it.

The tab character stands for enough horizontal whitespace to reach the next of a set of fixed positions. There is no standard set of positions, so tabs should be avoided if precise spacing is essential. One common convention is that tab positions are 8 columns apart, at columns 9, 17, 25, etc., where the first column is number 1.

Formfeed, which is Control-L, marks a point at which newsreading software should pause and await human interaction before displaying further text.

18.1.4 Cooperating Subnets and Language Issues

Many of the rules in this chapter can be broken, or at least bent, in a *cooperating subnet*, which is a set of news-exchanging hosts that agree to do things differently among themselves. The word subnet is used to emphasize that a cooperating subnet is typically not an isolated universe; traffic leaving the subnet must comply with the rules of the outside world.‡

---

* ASCII refers to the character set defined by the ANSI X3.4 standard. It defines meanings for character codes 0-127 only. There are many character sets that also define meanings for codes 128-255 and they are sometimes incorrectly referred to as ASCII if their codes 0-127 are the same as those of ASCII. There are also some related character sets that define a few of the codes 0-127 differently, to provide symbols needed in non-English languages, and these too are sometimes incorrectly referred to as ASCII. When we say ASCII in this chapter, we mean real ASCII, ANSI X3.4.

† How you actually enter a backspace character is specific to the news posting software you are using.

‡ The word subnet is used with several different meanings in networking. Don't confuse the use here with other uses, such as in TCP/IP addressing and routing. A cooperating subnet is just a set of hosts that exchange news and have agreed to their own rules; they don't need to be on the same physical network, let alone the same TCP/IP subnet.

In particular, in non-English-speaking countries it's fairly common for cooperating subnets to exchange news using non-ASCII character codes, so that non-ASCII symbols needed for the local language can be used in news articles. Conventions for this vary widely, but articles with non-ASCII contents should use MIME conventions (see Section 18.5). Using MIME, it is possible to transmit any character set and any form of binary data using only ASCII characters. Equally important, such articles are self-describing, so the newsreader software can tell which code-to-symbol mapping is intended.

Another issue with regard to non-English languages is that various constant strings used in headers, such as the month names in the Date header, are derived from English words. These strings don't change from country to country; the English-derived forms are always used in the articles themselves. Software can (and should) translate as necessary when presenting such strings to humans or receiving them from humans.

18.2 Headers

Every news article starts with a set of headers that describes the article and contains control information for use by news software. The first empty line ends the headers, separating them from the body of the article. The order of the headers is not significant.

Each header begins at the start of a line, and most headers can be continued onto subsequent lines by beginning the continuation line(s) with whitespace. A continued header is processed as if the line breaks within it did not exist, but the whitespace is retained. So a line break within a header can appear before any whitespace and nowhere else. Each header starts with a *header name*, followed by a colon (:) and some whitespace,* followed by the *header contents*. The header name identifies the header and indicates the format of its contents. Header names shouldn't contain anything except letters, digits, and possibly hyphens separating words. More general forms are legal in mail, but some news software gets upset about them. Header names are case-insensitive, so, for example, the following header names are all equivalent:

```
Message-ID
message-id
Message-Id
MeSsAgE-iD
```

There is a preferred case convention that is used when writing about standard headers—each word in the header name has its first letter capitalized and the rest

---

* This whitespace is not required in mail, but it is mandatory in news. RFC 1036 was (probably unintentionally) worded to require it, and some news software insists on it.

lowercased, with minor exceptions—and headers in articles usually follow this convention, but it's not mandatory.

News software is required to ignore any headers that it doesn't recognize (except to pass them on to other software, as appropriate). This makes it possible to extend the news format without causing problems for older software. By putting the extensions in new headers, the old software doesn't see them. Header names starting with "X-" are, by convention, reserved for non-standard extensions that have meaning only to specific senders and recipients.

Headers with no content (i.e., nothing following the header name, colon, and whitespace) are called *empty headers* and are defined to have no effect. There's really no point in including empty headers in an article, but some software packages do generate them. Even in an empty header, the whitespace following the color is mandatory.

Whitespace in headers theoretically can be either ASCII spaces (32) or tabs (9). In practice, using tabs is unwise: news software doesn't consistently treat tabs as equivalent to spaces.

The mail-message format permits comments, enclosed in parentheses, to appear anywhere that whitespace can appear in a header. The news format, however, only allows comments in a few precisely specified places. We'll mention these places as they come up.

18.2.1 *Mandatory Headers*

An article must have one, and only one, of each of the following headers: Date, From, Message-ID, Subject, Newsgroups, and Path.

18.2.1.1 *Date*

The Date header contains the date and time when the article was posted, in a tightly specified standard format. For example:

```
Date: Mon, 15 Apr 1996 22:10:13 -0400 (EDT)
```

The day of the week (with its following comma), the seconds (with their preceding colon), and the time zone name (with its enclosing parentheses), are optional. Everything else is required and must be in the order shown. The time zone name is actually a comment, and is the only comment allowed; it must come after the numeric specification of the time zone.

Day-of-the-week and month names are always exactly three letters and are case-insensitive. The day can be one or two digits. The year can be two or four digits, but two-digit years are very strongly discouraged and are always interpreted as beginning with "19" (to firmly discourage their use, since they will be ambiguous within a few years).

The -0400 specifies a time zone, in this case one that is four hours west of GMT; the name that follows is a comment for human readers. Alternatively, the time zone can be given as "UT" or "GMT" (which are synonyms) without the comment. These are the only valid forms. In particular, time zone names other than "UT" or "GMT" must never appear except in the comment. There are simply too many different time zone names, and too many names that are used for more than one time zone, for a standard set of names to be useful. For example, there are different time zones named "EST" in North America, Eastern Europe, Brazil, Australia, and Easter Island, so this name is hopelessly ambiguous.

18.2.1.2 From

The From header contains the electronic address, and possibly the full name, of the article's author. The address may come first, followed by the full name in parentheses, or the full name may come first, followed by the address in angle brackets. The second form is preferred. In either case, the full name can be left out altogether. Here are some examples:

```
From: eggman@kiwi.ora.com (R.I. Red)
From: "R.I. Red" <eggman@kiwi.ora.com>
From: eggman@kiwi.ora.com
From: <eggman@kiwi.ora.com>
From: Rhode Island Red <eggman@kiwi.ora.com>
```

If a full name appears first in the address, it may have to be enclosed in quotes, depending on exactly what characters it contains; the rules are complicated, but most software packages get them right. In fact, "the rules are complicated" is a good way of summing up the From header.

The address should be a valid and complete Internet domain address that can be reached by an Internet host (possibly via a DNS **MX** record and a forwarder). Other forms are still sometimes seen, but they are discouraged.

You may sometimes see addresses like *eggman%rooster@kiwi.ora.com*, possibly even with more than one % in the first part. This form is used when, for example, the host *rooster* isn't known to the world at large, but *kiwi.ora.com* knows how to reach it. The % is a sort of secondary @, so the address means "send it to *kiwi.ora.com* and tell them to send it to *eggman@rooster* because they know who *rooster* is and you don't."

You may still occasionally see addresses like *rooster!eggman@kiwi.ora.com*, but they are strongly discouraged because they are ambiguous. This one could mean *eggman%rooster@kiwi.ora.com* or *eggman%kiwi.ora.com@rooster*, although the former is rather more likely nowadays.

18.2.1.3 Message-ID

The Message-ID header contains the article's message ID, which is a unique identifier that distinguishes the article from every other news article. For example:

```
Message-ID: <642@kiwi.ora.com>
```

The < and > are parts of the message ID, not peculiarities of the Message-ID header.

Message IDs are kept unique, network-wide, by having them contain the name of the host where the article was posted and by requiring that host to generate its message IDs in some way that guarantees no duplicates (ever). Old posting software generally just numbered articles in sequence on each host; newer posting software typically bases its message IDs on date and time, sometimes encoded for compactness. Here are some examples:

```
<55458@kiwi.ora.com>
<9404061937.aa03201@kiwi.ora.com>
<eggman.765649274@kiwi.ora.com>
<1996Apr6.172705.7066@kiwi.ora.com>
<CnutAK.3vD@kiwi.ora.com>
```

The crucial use of message IDs is for telling articles apart. Hosts with multiple news feeds can easily get the same article several times and must have a way to detect the duplicates. Articles with the same message ID are treated as identical copies of the same article even if they are not in fact identical.

18.2.1.4 Subject

The content of the Subject header (the "subject" of the article) is a short phrase that describes the topic of the article. The subject is otherwise pretty much up to the author. For example:

```
Subject: my CDROM reader doesn't work
```

If the article is a follow-up to an earlier article, the subject normally begins with "Re: ", like this:

```
Subject: Re: my CDROM reader doesn't work
```

You'll occasionally see this repeated, like so:

```
Subject: Re: Re: Re: my CDROM reader doesn't work
```

This style is not really correct; posting software should insert the "Re: " only if there isn't one there already.

A subject change is often flagged by making the new subject of the form:

```
Subject: new topic (was: old topic)
```

This convention isn't a standard, but it's very widely used.

18.2.1.5 Newsgroups

The Newsgroups header specifies which newsgroup (or groups) the article is posted to. The header contains a comma-separated list of newsgroup names, *without* whitespace after the commas. For example:

```
Newsgroups: news.software.b,news.admin.technical
```

Newsgroup names may be listed in any order. Because this syntax doesn't allow whitespace within the header's contents, it's impossible to continue a Newsgroups header across several lines. Eventually, the syntax will probably be changed to permit whitespace after the commas, but be aware that this isn't allowed now. Some news software doesn't allow the space at all; other software misbehaves on seeing it.

Naming several newsgroups in the Newsgroups header (crossposting the article) is far superior to posting separate identical articles to each newsgroup. News-reading software can detect crossposted articles and show them to the user only once. However, crossposting an article to a large number of newsgroups is seldom appropriate and is discouraged.

It is legitimate to crosspost to newsgroups that do not exist on the author's host, provided that at least one of the newsgroups does exist there. This comes about because not all hosts get all newsgroups, but it is nevertheless desirable for a follow-up to go to the same newsgroups as the original article.

18.2.1.6 Path

The Path header indicates the relayers that an article has already visited, so that redundant transmission can be avoided. It contains a list of news names, separated by path delimiters (!). The name after the final delimiter is the local part of a mailing address; this name is normally the portion of the author's mailing address that comes before the @. Consider the following example:

```
Path: fee!fie!foe!fum
```

This header contains three news names: *fee*, *fie*, and *foe*. The *fum* is the mailing-address part. This syntax has the disadvantage of containing no whitespace, making it impossible to continue a Path header across several lines. Eventually, the syntax will probably be changed to allow whitespace after the delimiters, but bear in mind that this is not valid now.

A relayer must prepend its news name and a delimiter to the Path content in all articles it processes. A relayer must not pass an article to a neighboring relayer whose news name is already mentioned in an article's Path header. For example, the host *fee* knows not to relay this article to *fie* or *foe*, since they have already seen it.

An article won't be sent to a relayer already mentioned in its Path header, so the Path header must not contain news names other than those of relayers the article has passed through as news. The moderators of moderated newsgroups, and the implementers and maintainers of gateways, need to be careful to supply appropriate Path headers. For example, a posting to a moderated newsgroup isn't a news article until the moderator has approved it and posted it—before that point, it's just a mail message—so when it leaves the moderator's host, that host's name should be the only one in the Path header.

A host and its neighbors need to agree on what news names they use in their Path headers, and any name changes have to be negotiated carefully. A news name for a host needs to be unique among all the relayers that will ever see articles processed by the host. A news name is normally either an "official" name for the host the relayer runs on or some other "official" name controlled by the same organization. Except in cooperating subnets that agree to some other convention (and don't let articles using their private conventions escape beyond the subnet), a news name must be either a UUCP name registered in the UUCP maps (without any domain suffix such as *.UUCP*) or a complete Internet domain name.

The use of Internet domain names in the Path header presents a minor problem: domain names are case-insensitive, but the Path content is case-sensitive. Relayers using domain names as their news names must pick a standard form for the name, and use that form consistently to the exclusion of all others. The preferred form for this purpose is the all-lowercase form.

The contents of the Path header somewhat resemble an old UUCP-style mailing address, using manual routing and the ! address syntax. Some old software tried to use it as a reply address. This never worked perfectly, especially when moderators or gateways were involved, and it no longer works well at all, so don't do it.

18.2.2 Optional Headers

Many other headers are potentially useful in articles. Many mail headers are relevant, but they aren't discussed here unless they are particularly relevant to news. The following optional headers are either specific to news or of particular note in news articles. Note that this list is not complete.

An article might contain some of these headers or all of them. A few of the headers become mandatory in some circumstances; these situations are explained under the individual headers. If an article contains any one of these optional headers, it must contain only one instance of that header.

18.2.2.1 Expires

The Expires header specifies when the article is no longer useful and should be removed (i.e., expired). Its syntax is the same as that of the Date header. For example:

```
Expires: Mon, 22 Apr 1996 21:15:00 GMT
```

In the absence of an Expires header, the expiry date of an article is decided by the administrators at each host the article reaches. The administrators can also restrict the extent to which the Expires header is honored.

The Expires header has two main applications:

- Removing articles that aren't useful after a specific date, such as event announcements, which can be removed once the day of the event is past

- Preserving articles expected to be of prolonged usefulness, such as information aimed at new readers of a newsgroup

This header is sometimes abused by people who specify very long expiry dates on ordinary articles. Individual hosts have their own policies for expiration of news and these shouldn't be overridden without good reason. Most modern expiry software permits site administrators to set limits on expiry times. Very few sites will keep an article around for more than a few months, regardless of what its Expires header says.

When preparing an Expires header for an article whose utility ends on a specific day, beware of software that defaults the time of day to 00:00. A meeting on July 7th remains of interest on the 7th, so either specify a time of day after the meeting ends or specify expiry on the 8th.

18.2.2.2 Reply-To

Normally, email replies to an article go to the address in the From header. The Reply-To header overrides this behavior by specifying a different reply address. The syntax is the same as that of the From header. For example:

```
From: Rhode Island Red <eggman%rooster%hen%capon@kiwi.ora.com>
Reply-To: Rhode Island Red <eggman@kiwi.ora.com>
```

The Reply-To header is mainly useful when the author knows that the From address is incorrect, either because the software is broken or because the author's preferred mailing address isn't on the news host. Using a Reply-To header is better than including a similar request in the article body, because reply-preparation routines in newsreader software can take account of Reply-To automatically.

18.2.2.3 Followup-To

The Followup-To header specifies which newsgroup(s) should receive follow-up articles. The syntax is like the Newsgroups header, except that the magic word `poster` means that follow-ups should be mailed to the article's reply address rather than posted. In the absence of Followup-To, follow-up articles should go to the newsgroups listed in the Newsgroups header. Here's an example of the Followup-To header:

```
Newsgroups: sci.space.science,sci.space.tech
Followup-To: sci.space.tech
```

The Followup-To header never contains an email address. To direct follow-ups to an email address that is not the address in the From header, say *eggman@kiwi.ora.com*, use the following combination:

```
Followup-To: poster
Reply-To: eggman@kiwi.ora.com
```

18.2.2.4 Sender

The Sender header identifies the poster, in the event that this differs from the author identified in the From header. The syntax is the same as for From. For example:

```
From: Rhode Island Red <eggman@kiwi.ora.com>
Sender: <joe.moderator@kiwi.ora.com>
```

In the absence of Sender, the poster is assumed to be the author. The idea is that articles are sometimes posted on behalf of other people—moderators do this constantly—but there needs to be a header that identifies the poster, for use in tracing problems and abuses.

18.2.2.5 References

The References header lists message IDs, separated by whitespace, of previous articles to which this one is a follow-up. For example:

```
References: <642@kiwi.ora.com> <23443.97@chickadee.ora.com>
```

Follow-up articles are required to have a References header. In practice, the References header is often misused as a "see also" header, to cite articles which are related in some other way than by follow-up.

RFC 1036 allowed follow-up-preparation routines in newsreader software to shorten the References header by deleting some message IDs. This is a thoroughly bad idea; shortening should be avoided. Unfortunately, some news software now does it systematically. If it is absolutely necessary to shorten the header, never delete the first message ID, any of the last three message IDs,* or any message ID mentioned in the body of the follow-up.

18.2.2.6 Control

The Control header marks the article as a control message, requesting an action other than the usual filing and relaying of the article. The header content specifies the desired action(s). Control messages are discussed in more detail in 18.4.

18.2.2.7 Distribution

The Distribution header specifies geographic or organizational limits on an article's propagation. For example, an article intended to propagate only within O'Reailly & Associates might have a header like:

```
Distribution: ora
```

In principle, the Distribution header could contain a list of distributions, like the list of newsgroups in the Newsgroups header (and using the same syntax, in fact), but this is rarely done. If there is no Distribution header, the default distribution is *world.*

A relayer must not pass an article to another relayer unless both of the following are true:

- The relayer is configured to transmit at least one of the article's newsgroups.
- The relayer is configured to transmit at least one of the article's distributions.

In effect, the only role of distributions is to limit propagation, by preventing transmission of articles that would have been transmitted had the decision been based solely on newsgroups.

Despite the syntactic similarity and some historical confusion, distributions are not newsgroup names. The whole point of putting a distribution on an article is that it is different from the newsgroup. A meaningful distribution corresponds to some sort of region of propagation: a geographical area, an organization, or a cooperating subnet.

Distributions have suffered from the completely uncontrolled nature of their namespace, the lack of feedback to authors on incomplete propagation resulting from use of random trash in Distribution headers, and confusion with top-level hierarchy names (arising partly because many regions and organizations do have internal newsgroups with names that resemble their internal distributions). These problems have resulted in much garbage in Distribution headers. Many sites have

---

* This is to give some hope of being able to reconstruct the complete thread despite an occasional missing article.

opted to maximize propagation of such ill-formed articles by essentially ignoring distributions. Unfortunately, this practice interferes with legitimate uses. The situation is bad enough that distributions are largely useless, except within cooperating subnets that make an organized effort to limit propagation of their internal distributions.

The distributions *world* and *local* have no standard magic meaning (except that *world* is implied if none is given).

18.2.2.8 Keywords

The Keywords header contains one or more phrases that describe some aspect of the content of the article. Keywords are separated by commas. The following Keywords header contains only one keyword (a rather unlikely and improbable one):

```
Keywords: Thompson Ritchie Multics Linux
```

The header should probably have been written:

```
Keywords: Thompson, Ritchie, Multics, Linux
```

This particular error is unfortunately rather widespread.

Bear in mind that user-chosen keywords are notoriously poor for indexing purposes unless the keywords are picked from a predefined set. When keywords are not chosen from a predefined set, the Keywords header is really pretty useless.

18.2.2.9 Summary

Like Subject, Summary contains a user-supplied phrase which has no special meaning to news software. It's intended to summarize the article's content. Some newsreader software displays the Summary header, if any, as an aid to the reader.

18.2.2.10 Approved

The contents of the Approved header give the mailing addresses, and possibly the full names, of the people approving the article for posting. The syntax is the same as From; if more than one approver is named, commas (possibly followed by whitespace) separate them. All articles in moderated newsgroups must have an Approved header, indicating that the moderator has approved the article. The moderator normally adds this header when posting the article. The presence or absence of this header allows posting software to distinguish between approved postings (which are real articles) and unapproved contributions (which, until they are approved, are really only email messages to the moderator). An Approved header is also required in certain control messages, to reduce the probability of accidents.

There has been work on cryptographic methods for authenticating Approved headers to ensure that the claimed approval really was bestowed. Unfortunately, this functionality is not yet universally implemented.

RFC 1036 restricted the Approved header to a single address or name. However, multiple moderation is no longer rare, and multi-moderator Approved headers are already in use.

18.2.2.11 Lines

The Lines header indicates the number of lines in the body of the article, as a decimal integer. With increasing use of MIME encodings (see Section 18.5), this is no longer very useful because it indicates the length of the encoded body rather than the real content.

18.2.2.12 Xref

The Xref header indicates where an article was filed by the last relayer to process it. Like the Path header, the Xref header changes as the article travels, although in a different way. Normally, Xref is regenerated completely by each relayer. It contains the relayer's news name, followed by one or more locations, separated by whitespace. Each location is a newsgroup name, a colon (:), and the article number. For example:

```
Xref: kiwi.ora.com news.software.b:3557 news.admin.tech:7502
```

The relayer's news name is included so that software can determine whether the header is current or not. If the news name doesn't match the one at the start of the Path header, the Xref header is out of date and should be ignored. A relayer must use the same name in Xref headers as it uses in Path headers.

News-reading software can exploit the location information to avoid presenting the same article to a reader several times. The information is sometimes available in system databases, but having it in the article is convenient. Relayers traditionally generate an Xref header only if the article is crossposted, but this limitation is not mandatory. There is at least one new application, *mirroring*, or keeping news databases on two hosts identical (see Section 13.1.2), where the header is useful in all articles.

A relayer that is inserting an Xref header into an article must delete any previous Xref header. A relayer that is not inserting its own Xref header should still delete any previous Xref header. A relayer might delete the Xref header when passing an article on to another relayer. (RFC 1036 specified that the Xref header was always deleted when an article was passed on, but the major news implementations have never obeyed this rule, and applications like mirroring depend on this disobedience.)

18.2.2.13 Organization

The Organization header contains a short phrase that identifies the author's organization. The header should mention geographical location (e.g., city and country) when it is not obvious from the organization's name. For example:

```
Organization: O'Reilly & Associates, Sebastopol, CA, USA
```

The motive here is that the organization is often difficult to guess from the mailing address, is not always supplied in a signature, and can help identify the author to the reader.

18.2.2.14 Supersedes

The contents of the Supersedes header specifies article(s) to be canceled on arrival of this one, as a list of message IDs separated by whitespace. See the discussion of *cancel* in Section 18.4. Supersedes is normally used where the article is an updated version of the one being canceled.

The ability to use multiple message IDs in Supersedes is relatively new; some news software doesn't handle such Supersedes headers correctly.

18.2.2.15 Also-Control

The Also-Control header identifies an article as a control message as well as a normal news article and specifies the desired actions. An article with an Also-Control header is filed and passed on normally, but the content of the Also-Control header is processed as if it were found in a Control header. See Section 18.4.

18.2.2.16 See-Also

The See-Also header lists message IDs of articles that are related to this one but are not its precursors, using the same syntax as References. This header provides a way to group related articles, such as the parts of a single document that have to be split across multiple articles due to its size, or to give cross-references between parallel threads of discussion.

This is a relatively new header, so most news software doesn't implement it yet and its future is uncertain. The References header is often misused for this purpose.

18.3 Body

Although the article body is unstructured for the purposes of news administration, structure may be imposed on it by other means, notably MIME headers (see Section 18.5). Theoretically, an article can have no body, but some old software reacts badly to this, so it's best for all messages—including control messages—to have something in the body. Some posting software automatically supplies a body like "This article was probably generated by a buggy newsreader" if the author doesn't provide one.

18.3.1 *The Line Eater*

Some very old relayer software discards part of the body when the first non-empty line of the body begins with whitespace. This bug, the "line eater," is probably still found in backward parts of Usenet, so it's best not to provoke it by having the first non-empty line start with whitespace. (Hosts in quiet backwaters of Usenet can be amazingly slow about updating their software; there are still a fair number of hosts running B News, which has been obsolete and unmaintained for years.)

18.3.2 *Quoting*

When responding to a previous article, it is unwise to assume that all readers understand the exact context. The order in which articles arrive at a particular host depends somewhat on transmission paths. In addition, articles are occasionally lost for various reasons. Therefore, readers may see a follow-up article without seeing the original. To give a reader some context, it is common to quote some of the previous article. This is properly done by prefacing each quoted line with the character > (and no other). This results in multiple levels of > when quoted context itself contains quoted context.

Quoted context should be edited to trim it down to the minimum necessary. However, software authors should avoid trying to enforce this by simplistic means, such as a limit on the number of quoted lines. Such ill-conceived limits are easily evaded with nonstandard quoting conventions, which make the resulting articles harder to understand (for both software and humans).

18.3.3 *Signatures*

Early difficulties in inferring return addresses from article headers led to signatures. A *signature* is a short piece of closing text that is automatically added to the end of articles by posting software, identifying the author and supplying information such as email and postal addresses. A signature is separated from the body by a delimiter line containing two hyphens (ASCII code 45) followed by one blank (code 32). The choice of delimiter is somewhat unfortunate, since it relies on preservation of trailing whitespace, but it is too well-established to change. There is work underway to define a more sophisticated signature scheme as part of MIME, and this will presumably supersede the current convention in due time.

18.3.4 Size Limits

In principle, there should be no limits on article size or line length. In practice, it's best to keep lines down to 70-75 characters and articles within a limit of about 60 Kbytes. Ultra-long lines cause trouble for a lot of newsreader software and can be mangled by badly written transport software (like the current implementation of the NRI). News originated in environments where line breaks in plain text files were supplied by the user, not the software. Be this good or bad, a lot of reading and posting software assumes that articles follow this convention, and it's often inconvenient to read or respond to articles that violate it.

The 60 Kbytes limit on articles is annoying when posting very large messages, like sources to large programs. Many cooperating subnets can use larger limits, but some news software often doesn't cope well with really huge articles (say, a megabyte long). The occasional huge articles that appear (by accident or through ignorance) typically leave trails of failing software, system problems, and irate administrators in their wake.

Therefore, it's best to observe the 60 Kbytes limit by splitting longer messages into a sequence of shorter pieces. When doing so, the Subject of each article should show the total number of parts, plus the position of this part in the whole sequence. The convention (as described for moderated postings in Section 15.3.1.4) is to end the Subject with a part indicator like "(Part 2/3)." If there are many parts, it's a good idea to use leading zeros as necessary so that every sequence number in the set has the same number of digits, to simplify sorting. MIME `message/partial` conventions can be used to facilitate automatic reassembly of a large document split into smaller pieces for posting. Some newsreader software also offers automated help based on Subject headers that indicate multi-part articles.

18.4 Control Messages

A *control message* is an article that contains control information.* When a relayer receives a control message, it takes action beyond just filing and passing on the article.

The execution of the action requested by a control message is subject to local administrative restrictions, which might cause the relayer to deny a request or refer it to an administrator for approval. (The details depend on the software.) We've refrained from putting "if the local administrator permits it" on the end of every sentence that describes a control message, to keep the wording simple, but it's

---

* "Control article" would be more consistent terminology, but "control message" is too well-established to change.

implicitly there throughout this section. Even where the wording says that a control message is ignored, "ignoring" it might involve reporting it to an administrator.

The presence of a Control, Also-Control, or Supersedes header signifies that an article is a control message. An article that contains an Also-Control or Supersedes header is also an ordinary article, while an article that contains a Control header is just a control message, nothing else. A Control or Also-Control header contains a verb that specifies the action to be taken, possibly followed by some parameters, separated by whitespace, that indicate the details. A Supersedes header is equivalent to an Also-Control header with an implicit *cancel* verb.

Thus, the following three headers are equivalent in effect, except that the first one marks the article as only a control message, while the others piggyback that function on top of a normal article:

```
Control: cancel <9404061937.aa03201@kiwi.ora.com>
Also-Control: cancel <9404061937.aa03201@kiwi.ora.com>
Supersedes: <9404061937.aa03201@kiwi.ora.com>
```

Control messages are typically handled and filed specially, so that a reader doesn't see them in the newsgroups they claim to belong to unless they are also ordinary articles. The special handling usually involves filing them in a pseudogroup named *control.*

18.4.1 cancel

A *cancel* message requests that one or more previous articles, called the *target* articles, be canceled, or removed from the host as thoroughly as possible. The articles are identified by message IDs that are given as parameters. A *cancel* message is normally posted to the same newsgroups, with the same distribution, as the article it is meant to cancel. The body of a *cancel* message is a comment that news software must ignore; it should contain an indication of why the cancellation was requested.

RFC 1036 permitted only a single message ID in a *cancel* message. Support for canceling multiple articles is highly desirable for some unusual applications, but it isn't universal yet.

If a target article has already arrived and hasn't yet expired, the relayer checks the *cancel* message for validity by comparing the addresses in the From headers in the target article and the control message. (Be warned that there is historically some confusion as to which headers should be checked when both From and Sender headers are present. Checking the From headers is correct.) This check is more accident prevention than authentication, as it is fairly trivial to forge articles. Moreover, authorities other than the author sometimes have legitimate reason to cancel articles, so there are situations that require such forging. (For example, the author may be unavailable, uncooperative, or malicious.) Effective authentication of *cancel* messages is still an unsolved problem.

If a target article has not arrived yet, a problem arises. It's not practical to hang on to the *cancel* message until the target article arrives, especially since it may never arrive. The relayer's usual response is to just assume that the addresses would match, and to make a *history* entry for the target article as if it had arrived. Then, when the canceled message arrives, it is rejected as a duplicate.

18.4.2 ihave, sendme

The *ihave* and *sendme* control messages implement a crude, batched predecessor of NNTP. They are largely obsolete on the Internet, but they still see use in the UUCP environment, especially for backup feeds that are normally active only when a primary feed path has failed. Note that the *ihave* and *sendme* messages discussed here have absolutely nothing to do with NNTP, despite some similarities of terminology. See Section 5.1.3.7 for information about setting up the C News *sys* file to handle *ihave/sendme* messages. The *control.ctl* file, discussed in Sections 8.2.4.1 and 9.3.1.3, handles these messages for INN.

The *ihave* and *sendme* messages share the same syntax; each is followed by a single parameter that lists a news name. The body of an *ihave* or *sendme* message is a list of message IDs, one per line. The news name identifies the host sending the message. The *ihave* message says that the sender has articles with the specified message IDs, which may be of interest to the recipient. The *sendme* message asks the recipient to relay the articles with the specified message IDs to the sender.

These control messages are normally point-to-point messages, sent from exactly one relayer to precisely one other relayer. This is normally done by using newsgroups that go only to the destination relayer. By convention, such newsgroups have names of the form *to.relayer*. A relayer advertises its new arrivals to another using *ihave* messages, and the recipient uses *sendme* messages to request the articles it lacks.

These point-to-point control messages should arguably flow by some other protocol, such as mail. There's no reason to use a broadcast transmission system like news for them; it adds complexity that is often confusing. However, early Unix mail systems did not lend themselves to this—in particular, they were often incapable of feeding incoming mail into a program rather than into a mailbox file—and the designers of *ihave/sendme* decided that it was better to have the news system do the whole job.

18.4.3 *newgroup*

A *newgroup* control message requests that a new newsgroup be created. The parameters are the newsgroup name and an optional keyword, `moderated` or `unmoderated`. If there is no second argument, the default is `unmoderated`. A *newgroup* message must have an Approved header. The *controlperm* file (see Section 5.1.2.2) specifies how C News handles *newgroup* messages, while the *control.ctl* file (see Section 8.2.4.1) performs this function for INN.

The body of a *newgroup* message is a comment, which news software must ignore, except if the body contains a descriptor of the following form:

```
For your newsgroups file:
rec.arts.comics      Comic books, animation, visual story telling.
```

A descriptor contains two lines. The first line must be exactly as shown, while the second line is a description of the group being created. If the body contains a descriptor, the relayer takes care of adding the description to the *newsgroups* file. A description line for a moderated group must end with " (Moderated)" (the space before the open parenthesis is required). The description line cannot be continued onto later lines, but is not limited to any particular length.

The remainder of the body should explain the purpose of the newsgroup and the decision to create it. Administrators often look for such information when deciding whether to comply with creation requests.

While it might seem harmless to create a newsgroup, in practice there is a fair number of erroneous or frivolous newgroup messages, especially for newsgroups in the *alt* hierarchy. Some administrative control should be exercised.

If a *newgroup* message names a newsgroup that already exists, the effect is that the message requests a change in the newsgroup's moderation status or description line. The same rules apply.

18.4.4 *rmgroup*

A *rmgroup* message requests that a newsgroup be deleted. The newsgroup is named as a single argument. A *rmgroup* message must have an Approved header. The body of the message is a comment, which news software must ignore. The body should explain why the group is being deleted. Administrators often look for such information when deciding whether to comply with deletion requests. The *controlperm* file (see Section 5.1.2.2) specifies how C News handles *rmgroup* messages, while the *control.ctl* file (see Section 8.2.4.1) performs this function for INN.

Unexpected deletion of a newsgroup is disruptive, so news software typically refers *rmgroup* messages to an administrator rather than executing them automatically. Hosts within a well-controlled organization might want to automatically execute *rmgroup* messages from within the organization, but care is still indicated, as abuses have occurred. Sites using the *pgpverify* script from *ftp://ftp.isc.org/pub/ pgpcontrol/pgpverify* can use cryptographic authentication to enable safe automatic processing of control messages.

18.4.5 sendsys, version

These messages, both of which require an Approved header, are used to find out about other hosts' news feeds and news software. A *sendsys* message requests that a description of the relayer's news feeds be mailed to the article's reply address. If an argument is given, only the relayer that it named should respond. A *version* message requests that the name and version of the relayer software be mailed to the reply address. This message does not have any arguments. For both types of messages, the body is a comment.

There has been considerable malicious misuse of these control messages, since they can be used to ask thousands of hosts to send mail to a particular address, flooding the victim with unwanted mail. They still have a legitimate role in regional network mapping, but some precautions are in order. Modern news software typically waits 24 hours before responding, giving administrators time to cancel inappropriate requests. It also ignores a request if the reply address isn't of the form `newsmap@host`, thus making it impossible to victimize normal users. News administrators should arrange for mail to *newsmap* on their systems to be discarded (without reply) unless legitimate mapping is in progress.

Different networks set different rules for the legitimacy of these messages, given that they may reveal details of an organization's network topology that are sometimes considered proprietary. On Usenet, willingness to respond to these messages has been held to be a condition of network membership: the topology of Usenet is public information. If an organization wants to belong to such a network while keeping its internal topology confidential, it should organize its internal news software so that all articles reaching outsiders appear to be from a single "gatekeeper" system, with the details of internal topology hidden behind that system.

18.4.6 checkgroups

A *checkgroups* control message contains a supposedly authoritative list of the valid newsgroups within some subset of the newsgroup namespace. There are no arguments to this control message. Each line in the body contains a description line for a newsgroup, as described previously for the *newgroup* message. (Some other, ill-defined forms of the *checkgroups* message body were formerly used.) The *controlperm* file (see Section 5.1.2.2) specifies how C News handles *checkgroups* messages, while the *control.ctl* file (see Section 8.2.4.1) performs this function for INN.

A *checkgroups* message applies to all hierarchies containing any of the newsgroups listed in the body. The *checkgroups* message asserts that the newsgroups it lists are the only newsgroups in those hierarchies.

When a relayer processes a *checkgroups* message, it should compare the local list of newsgroups (and their moderation status) in the specified hierarchies against the newsgroups listed in the message. The results of such a check might be used for automatic corrective actions, or they might be reported to the news administrator in some way. Automatically updating descriptions of existing newsgroups is relatively safe, so these are often handled directly. However, most current news software reports requests for additions or deletions to an administrator rather than handling them automatically.

There is a minor problem with the *checkgroups* concept: not all newsgroups in a hierarchy necessarily propagate to the same set of machines. Therefore, the advice of a *checkgroups* message should always be taken with a grain of salt and should never be followed blindly.

18.4.7 senduuname

There once was a *senduuname* control message, but it is now obsolete. *senduuname* resembled *sendsys*, but it requested transmission of the list of hosts that the receiving host had UUCP connections to. Although well-intentioned, this was never really very useful and modern news software does not implement it.

18.5 MIME

MIME (Multipurpose Internet Mail Extensions) is an upward-compatible set of extensions to RFC 822, currently documented in RFCs 2045-2049, for describing and structuring message bodies. MIME is meant for mail, but is quite relevant to news as well. We'll just hit the high points of MIME here; see the MIME RFCs themselves for more information, as they are very readable.

18.5.1 MIME Headers

MIME defines some new headers:

MIME-Version

> States which version of MIME a message uses (and thereby confirms that it does use MIME).

Content-Type

> Specifies the type of data the body of the message contains, including provisions for multipart bodies where each part has its own type. Auxiliary information can also be included, for situations where a particular content type exists in different variants.

Content-Transfer-Encoding

> Specifies how the body (or body part) has been encoded, so that data that cannot be sent "raw" can be automatically encoded and decoded as necessary.

Content-ID

> Assigns unique identifiers to body parts, so that they can be referred to by other body parts.

Content-Description

> Analogous to a Subject header, but describes a specific body part.

MIME headers are mail headers, and like most mail headers, the syntax of MIME headers is complex, with parenthesized comments allowed almost anywhere.

18.5.2 Content Types

There are a wide variety of MIME content types, and more appear every month. A content type is specified as a type and a subtype, separated by a slash (/) in the Content-Type header. Subtype-specific auxiliary information may follow. For example:

```
Content-Type: text/plain; charset=ISO-8859-1
```

This says that the body (part) is text, and specifically that it is plain text in a particular character set (ISO8859-1).

The intent of the type/subtype system is that the type specifies the general nature of the data, while the subtype pins down the details. The set of types is small, so that software can understand the complete set and have some idea of how to deal with data whose subtype it does not recognize. The types are:

text

> Textual information, in a specified character set and possibly in some sort of formatted description language. Major subtypes are:

> plain

> > Ordinary text, in a specified character set (default is ASCII). `text/plain` is the default content type.

> enriched

> > Text that uses a simple description language that supports alignment control and character attributes like underlining. See RFC 1896 for details.

> html

> > Text that is tagged using a subset of HTML (see RFC 1866 for details, although the official rules are often ignored) for display by software such as Web browsers.

multipart

> Several body parts, possibly of different types, related in some specific way. Major subtypes are:

> **mixed**
>
> > Independent parts bundled in a specific order, details otherwise unspecified.
>
> **alternative**
>
> > The parts are different ways of expressing the same content, ordered from poorest to best, so that readers with different capabilities can use the best version their equipment supports.
>
> **digest**
>
> > Like **mixed** but more compact, specialized for mail-message-like body parts.
>
> **parallel**
>
> > Independent parts in no special order, intended to be presented simultaneously.

message

> A mail message (or news article). Major subtypes are:

> **rfc822**
>
> > A mail message, possibly itself using MIME.
>
> **partial**
>
> > A fragment of a larger message, with identification and other details to permit automatic reassembly.
>
> **external-body**
>
> > A reference to a body that can be obtained by some other means, such as FTP, with details specified.
>
> **news**
>
> > A news article, conforming to RFC 1036 or its successor, intended for reading by the human recipient.

image

> A graphic image.

audio

> Sound, such as voice or music.

video

> Moving images, possibly including supplementary audio.

application

Data that doesn't fit any of the other types, especially data that is comprehensible only to specific software. A few subtypes are:

octet-stream

Binary data of unspecified nature.

postscript

A PostScript program. Typically the program would cause a document to be printed.

news-transmission

A news article or batch of same, defined by RFC 1036 or its successor, intended to be processed by a relayer at the destination.

Subtypes whose names begin with **X-** are non-standard subtypes with meanings specific to the sender and the receiver. One common usage is **application/X-***program*, where it is expected that the recipient has the *program* referred to.

18.5.3 Content Transfer Encodings

Many of the MIME content types require the ability to transport arbitrary binary data, which isn't possible with mail or news without some sort of encoding. Thus, the Content-Transfer-Encoding header specifies how the content has been encoded. The MIME encodings are:

7bit

No encoding. The content is lines of ASCII text, each shorter than 1000 characters. This is the default encoding.

8bit

No encoding. The content is lines of text, each shorter than 1000 characters, possibly containing codes with the 8th bit set.

binary

No encoding. The content is arbitrary sequences of bytes. Neither mail nor news can transmit this reliably; it's included to document the situation.

quoted-printable

Data that is mostly ASCII text but contains some non-ASCII characters or some ultra-long lines. The sequence =*XX*, where *XX* is a hexadecimal value, encodes a (possibly) non-ASCII character. An = followed by an end-of-line indicates an end-of-line not present in the original data, inserted to limit line length.

`base64`

> Any sequences of bytes, encoded by representing every group of 3 bytes as 4 characters from the alphabet A - Z, a - z, 0 - 9, +, and / (chosen to pass unscathed through all known mail systems). Ends of lines in the encoded form are not significant.

When the `base64` and `quoted-printable` encodings are applied to text, the text is in Internet canonical form, meaning that any end-of-line encoded as anything but end-of-line must be an Internet canonical end-of-line: CR followed by LF.

18.5.4 Non-ASCII Characters in Headers

MIME also addresses the problem of non-ASCII characters in headers. This problem can come up when someone whose full name contains non-ASCII characters wants to include it in a From header. Non-ASCII character codes are absolutely, completely forbidden in headers. MIME provides an encoding mechanism for encoding non-ASCII symbols using ASCII codes. An example of a header using this mechanism is:

```
From: =?ISO-8859-1?Q?Andr=E9?= Pirard <PIRARD@vm1.ulg.ac.be>
```

The goal is to put an "e" with an acute accent on the end of the user's first name. The mysterious-looking stuff between the =? and the ?= is in three parts, separated by ?: a character set, an encoding, and the text. The character set comes from a standard list of names. The encoding is Q (resembling `quoted-printable`) or B (resembling `base64`).

Such encodings are allowed in certain specific headers, subject to a long list of restrictions. They can't be used just anywhere.

18.5.5 Checksums

The MIME effort has also produced RFC 1864, defining a Content-MD5 header to carry an MD5-based checksum of the contents of an article or a body part. This process detects most accidental modifications to the contents.

19

Flow and Processing of Traffic

In this chapter:
- *News Propagation*
- *Article Storage and Indexing*
- *Batching for Transmission*
- *Transmission by UUCP*
- *Transmission by NNTP*
- *Last-Resort Transmission Methods*

This chapter covers how news is moved around, both between hosts and within a host. It begins by outlining how news propagates among hosts, ignoring details of exactly how the articles are transported from one host to the next. It also describes how news is stored and indexed on each host.

The chapter then goes on to talk about ways of getting news from host to host. We cannot cover every detail of the various transport software packages, but we do provide a short outline of the news-related issues. The emphasis here is not on how to make your news software talk to the transport package, but rather on the possibilities that exist, how the packages work (which is relevant to news troubleshooting), and why you should choose one package over the other.

The information here is all background material. You may find it helpful for troubleshooting or writing new software. It's necessarily somewhat of a grab bag of vaguely related topics.

19.1 News Propagation

News articles are sent from one host to another by a wide variety of means, but there are a number of common issues that are independent of the details. We'll talk about the actual transport of articles later in this chapter. For the moment, just assume that there's a way to send an article from one host to the next. Now the question is, which articles should be sent?

19.1.1   The Flooding Algorithm

On the most basic level, decisions on which articles to send to which hosts are made by what's called a *flooding algorithm*. In other words, send each article to all other hosts known to the sending host, flooding the network with copies of the article.

The flooding algorithm does guarantee that the article goes pretty well everywhere, but by itself it's not enough. For one thing, unless the article was posted locally, "all other hosts" includes the host the article came in from. Clearly, it's undesirable to have each article going back and forth between each pair of hosts forever. Indeed, given the flow volume of Usenet, it's undesirable to have any large number of articles retracing their steps even once.

This problem is prevented by the Path header. Before passing an article on to other hosts, the sending host puts its own name into the article's Path header. The flooding algorithm is then modified so that it never sends an article to a host whose name is already in the Path header. This ensures that a particular copy of an article never reaches the same host twice.*

In some ways, though, this has only delayed the problem. What happens if another copy of the article reaches the host by a different route? For reliability in the presence of unreliable links and unreliable hosts, news networks are often redundant, with deliberate cross-connections so that articles do reach hosts by multiple routes.

The final barrier to multiple copies of an article is the presence in each article of a unique identifier—the message ID (see the discussion of the Message-ID header in Section 18.2.1.3)—and a date. Each host keeps a history of all the articles it has received recently, listing them by their message IDs. If an incoming article has a message ID that is already in the host's history, the incoming article is discarded. So onward transmission of a copy of the article finally stops when it reaches a host that has already seen a copy.

What happens if one route through the network simply is a lot slower than another, so that a second copy of an article reaches a host long after the first? Remember that only recent articles are remembered in the history: it's not practical to retain history for long enough to be absolutely confident that no more copies of an article will ever appear.† An incoming article that is stale—too old to be in the history any more, assuming that an earlier copy reached this host the instant the

---

* Provided that the host doing the sending knows the other host by the name that the other host is putting into the Path header. When incoming articles are trying to loop back to the host that sent them, the usual reason is confusion over names.

† You might think that a few days would suffice, but on Usenet, you'd be wrong. Before the date check was added, it wasn't unknown to have articles reappear a month or more after their first arrival.

article was posted—is also discarded, as is any article with no date or an incomprehensible date.

The history and staleness checks are not a complete substitute for the Path check because these checks have to be done by the receiving host. If the transmission link is fast and cheap and interactive, it may be possible to ask the receiving host to do the checks before the whole article is sent, but otherwise they can't be done until after transmission. So the Path check is still useful to prevent unnecessary transmission in the first place.

Because the flooding algorithm relies on the Message-ID and Date headers to prevent duplicates, it's quite important that news software never damage or rewrite these headers. Once in a while there is a burst of apparently duplicated articles on Usenet. This is usually because defective software somewhere is giving those articles new message IDs or new dates. This makes them new articles as far as the flooding algorithm is concerned, even if their content exactly duplicates that of older articles.

The flooding algorithm and the informal way in which news feeds are often arranged makes it quite difficult to limit propagation of newsgroups. The flooding algorithm is very good at delivering news despite failures and problems. The negative side of this is that it's also very good at finding leaks in barriers and at exploiting truly obscure routes that nobody ever thought of. Controlling propagation requires determined effort and careful planning.

Even in the absence of deliberate attempts to limit it, news propagation is a very disorderly process and the routes news follows are often surprising. Simplistic models in which news usually follows predictable paths are wrong often enough that they should not be used as a basis for configuration planning or software design.

19.1.2 Newsgroups and Distributions

In practice, not all news is of interest to all hosts, and, in some cases, an organization's internal news shouldn't go outside the organization even if people outside would be interested. So the flooding algorithm is modified further, to limit where articles go.

Each article belongs to one or more newsgroups, indicating (in theory) the general topic of the article. Hosts can limit which newsgroups are sent to which other hosts. Each article also belongs to one or more distributions, indicating (in theory) geographic or organizational limits on where the article should go. Hosts can also limit which distributions are sent to other hosts. The precise rule is that an article should be sent to another host only if at least one of its newsgroups and at least one of its distributions should be sent to that host.

Limiting transmission by newsgroup is straightforward and works well. Distributions have been less satisfactory, however. The idea behind distributions was reasonable: rather than having a local counterpart for each worldwide newsgroup, allow posters to produce articles that would circulate in the worldwide newsgroup, but only within a limited region. Unfortunately, there have been some snags in the implementation of the concept.

The big problem with distributions is that they've always been somewhat vaguely defined, with no good way for users to find out which distributions are legitimate in their area. Specifying a nonexistent newsgroup in a posting often causes the article to be rejected, or poorly propagated, and even the latter supplies some degree of feedback about the error. Unfortunately, propagation of distributions has always been more forgiving.

In particular, in the early days of the concept, sending a host the *sci* newsgroups usually meant you also sent them the (nonexistent) *sci* distribution, due to software limitations. By the time it became possible to control newsgroups and distributions independently, there was already a lot of trash in Distribution headers and many hosts opted to continue being forgiving. As a result, articles with nonsense distributions often propagated a long way, far enough that it was hard for the poster to tell that there was anything wrong.

The combination of permissive hosts and sloppy posters (and posting software) created a vicious circle, to the point where distributions are almost meaningless today. Specifying a distribution isn't likely to do a lot of good unless a real effort has been made to control the propagation of that particular distribution (e.g., a company making an effort to keep an internal distribution truly internal). In practice, propagation control is almost entirely based on newsgroups.

One further complication that arises with some software packages should be mentioned. In general, the set of newsgroups that is sent to a host is determined by control files at the neighboring hosts, the ones that send the host articles. However, there is also a notion of what newsgroups a host subscribes to—that is, the ones it accepts. If a host receives newsgroups that are not in its subscription list, it quietly discards those articles. This system was originally devised for controlling newsgroup-creation requests (since a request to create a newsgroup could be contained in an article posted to a different newsgroup, which might reach hosts with no interest in the new newsgroup). However, if the transmission links are fast and cheap, a host might wish to have its neighbors send it a fairly broad set of newsgroups, and fine-tune which ones it actually accepts using its subscription list. This saves having to bother administrators at neighboring sites every time a small change needs to be made.

19.2 Article Storage and Indexing

When an article arrives at a host, the host's relayer must first determine whether it is valid, new, and interesting—that is, whether it follows the article format rules, is neither stale nor a duplicate, and is in at least one newsgroup that the host subscribes to. If it doesn't pass all three of these checks, the article is discarded. If it does pass, however, the relayer accepts the article, and files it in the host's news database for local reading.

In principle, a host's news database can be organized in any convenient way. It could even employ a general-purpose database software package, although most of them are ill-suited to the job. In practice, however, most news databases use a semi-standard organization dating back to the days of B News, and most newsreader software expects this organization.

19.2.1 Newsgroups and Pseudogroups

When filing an article, the first decision a relayer must make is what newsgroups to file it under. They aren't necessarily the same as the ones listed in the article's Newsgroups header, for several reasons.

First, if the article is a control message (see Section 18.4) and is not also a normal article—that is, if it contains a Control header—it is filed in the pseudogroup *control* and nowhere else.* If it's both a control message and a normal article, it's filed only as a normal article.

Second, the article is filed only under newsgroups that are already known to the relayer. New newsgroups are not created automatically just because an article lists them in its Newsgroups header. If none of the article's newsgroups are known, but at least one of them does fit within the host's subscription list, the article is filed in the pseudogroup *junk*.

Third, a host may want to rename newsgroups locally or to file two or more network-wide newsgroups under the same newsgroup locally. This shouldn't be done routinely because it causes problems if local users try posting to those newsgroups, but in unusual situations it can be helpful. Most relayer software provides a way to specify that articles in a particular newsgroup should really be filed under a different newsgroup.

All of these decisions affect only where the article is filed on the host. The Newsgroups header of the article is not rewritten or modified in any way. Depending on the relayer software, decisions on whether to send the article to other hosts

---

* INN offers the option of a more complex scheme, in which it is filed in one of several subgroups of a *control* pseudo-hierarchy.

may be based either on the Newsgroups header or on where the article is filed locally. In particular, articles in the *junk* pseudogroup may still be eligible to be sent to other hosts. Historically, this is in fact why *junk* exists. If, for some reason, a host doesn't know about a newsgroup, but has a subscription list that permits it, articles in that newsgroup end up in *junk* and still flow through that host properly.

19.2.2 *The Article Tree*

Once the relayer knows the newsgroup(s) in which an article is to be filed, it does the filing in the article tree. The article tree is a directory tree, with a directory for each part of a newsgroup's name and a file for each article. For example, articles in *comp.lang.pascal* are filed in the directory *comp/lang/pascal*. It's possible to have files and subdirectories mixed in a directory. For example, before a recent reorganization, the *sci/space* directory contained both the articles of the *sci.space* newsgroup and subdirectories for the *sci.space.shuttle* and *sci.space.news* newsgroups.*

As discussed in Chapter 2, *Getting Ready*, exactly where the article tree is located in the file system is slightly system-dependent, although */usr/spool/news* was the original location (and some newsreaders still expect to find it there). On more modern systems, */news* is a sensible location.

Within the directory for each newsgroup, there is a file for each article in the newsgroup. The filenames are just numbers in sequence, so the 59th[†] article in *comp.lang.pascal* is *comp/lang/pascal/59* and the next article in that newsgroup is then *comp/lang/pascal/60*. When an article is crossposted, the file for it appears once in each of its newsgroup directories, typically by having each of the entries for it be a link to the same file.

For example, if articles A and B are posted to *comp.lang.pascal* only, article C is crossposted to *comp.lang.pascal* and *comp.lang.lisp*, and article D is posted to *comp.lang.lisp* only, the article tree might look like what is shown in Figure 19–1. Here A and B are articles 57 and 58 in *comp.lang.pascal*, C is both article 59 in *comp.lang.pascal* and article 1195 in *comp.lang.lisp*, and D is article 1196 in *comp.lang.lisp*.

The article tree can be split across multiple filesystems, by having one or more of its directories be either symbolic links or mount points for filesystems. If the article

---

* A few working directories for the news software are often also located at the top level of the article tree. They are easily distinguished because they have names containing dot (.), such as *out.going*. Since a dot in a newsgroup name becomes slash (/) in an article-tree filename, a directory name containing a dot cannot correspond to a newsgroup name.

† Note that on a different host, it might be the 58th or the 61st or the 1062nd; these numbers are host-specific.

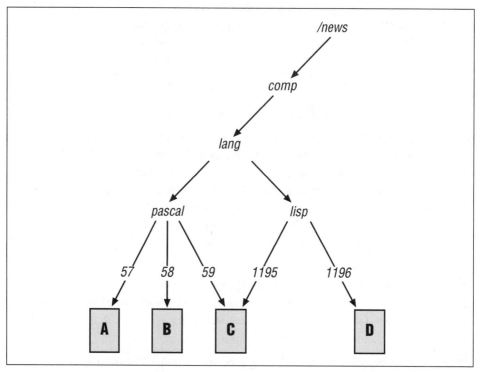

Figure 19–1:   Sample article tree

tree is split, crosspostings may have to be implemented using symbolic links or even multiple copies of the article. Most relayers try to use normal links, but resort to symbolic links or copies as necessary.

19.2.3 The History File

To reject duplicate articles, a host must keep a history of recently received articles. To expire filed articles, or to remove them after a suitable length of time, a host must keep a list of currently filed articles. These two bookkeeping jobs have been combined into a single file, the *history* file, and an auxiliary index into it. These files are logically part of the news database, but for historical reasons normally reside in the directory used for control files, originally */usr/lib/news*. In the modern order of things, */etc/news* would make more sense as a location, but the presence of the large and constantly changing *history* file and its auxiliaries interferes with this and makes */var/news* better.

The *history* file itself is an ASCII text file that contains one line per article. Each line is split into fields, separated by tabs. A line for an article that is not in the database (e.g., because the article has expired) contains two fields (and only a single tab, separating the two). A line for an article that is in the database contains three fields. For example:

```
<55458@kiwi.ora.com>    765649274~-
<55502@kiwi.ora.com>    765649278~765845200     comp.lang.pascal/57
<677@ora.com>  765649279~-    comp.lang.c/92 comp.answers/22
```

The three fields contain the following information:

- The message ID of the article.

- Two or more subfields, separated by tildes (~). The first subfield is the date (and time) when the article was filed, encoded as a decimal integer giving the number of seconds since some epoch (for Unix, the epoch is midnight, January 1, 1970 GMT). The second subfield is either the article's expiry date (expressed as either the ASCII contents of its Expires header or as a decimal integer encoding that date), or -, which indicates that there is no explicit expiry date. Third and later subfields, if present, are relayer-specific.

- If the third field is present, it is the pathname of the article in the article tree, relative to the top of the tree. If the article is filed in more than one place in the tree, all the pathnames are listed, separated by blanks. The pathnames are given in a slightly curious form: every slash (/) except the last one is replaced by a dot (.), so each pathname is the newsgroup the article was filed under, followed by a slash, followed by the article number.

Technically, handling of a *cancel* control message (see Section 18.4) requires rewriting its *history* entry to indicate that the article is no longer present. In reality, this typically is not done. Programs using the *history* file have to be prepared for the possibility that an article may be listed as present in the database when in fact it has been removed. (The reverse situation, where an article is still present but is not listed, is not supposed to happen.) This also makes it possible to simply remove articles in an emergency, without worrying about updating the *history* file.

The *history* file is reasonably well-suited to one of its purposes, tracking articles for expiry. Expiry decisions are typically based on the article's filing date, its explicit expiry date if any, and the newsgroup(s) it is filed under. Since all of these things are found in the *history* file,* the decision can be made without having to examine the article itself. Updating individual *history* entries would be difficult, but since the expiry program makes a sequential sweep through the entire file anyway, it simply builds a new copy as it goes and then installs the new one as the *history* file at the end of the process.

---

* As of the arrival of C News, that is. The complex structure of the second field was developed as a way to add more information—specifically, the expiry date—without breaking existing programs that only used the first and third fields.

However, these is a problem when it comes to the *history* file's other purpose, duplicate-article rejection. Determining whether a message ID is in the *history* file requires a search of the entire file, which can be very time-consuming if the file consumes many megabytes, which it usually does on a modern news system. This problem is dealt with by maintaining an index into the file, which can be used to look up a line by message ID.

The original *history* index used the Unix *dbm* library, which records key/value pairs in two complex binary files (in this case, *history.dir* and *history.pag*) that could be searched very quickly. For the *history* index, the key was the message ID and the value was the offset of the relevant line in the *history* file. This worked reasonably well with small *history* files, but as news volume grew and the *history* file expanded, the limitations of *dbm* became increasingly problematic. The *dbm* files became very large themselves and lookups slowed down. Problems also appeared in heterogeneous networks because the *dbm* file format depended on the byte order of the host creating it. Finally, when news started spreading to hosts running non-Unix operating systems, the proprietary nature of *dbm* required a replacement, but the lack of documentation on its algorithms and file formats hampered providing one.

Most relayers now use a different indexing package, *dbz*, originally invented by Jon Zeeff and later extensively reworked by Henry Spencer for use in C News. *dbz* provides a more or less *dbm*-compatible interface and uses the same filenames (*history.dir* and *history.pag*), but internally it is completely different. It stores only offsets into the *history* file, using the *history* file itself to store the keys. The index files are much smaller and lookups much quicker. The byte order used is recorded in the files and reordering is done as necessary. Finally, the *dbz* source is freely redistributable and highly portable.

The *history* index is updated by the relayer as it files articles and is rebuilt by the expiry program as it removes them. In an emergency, it can be rebuilt from the *history* file using a utility program supplied with the relayer.

19.2.4 The Active File

The news database clearly needs a central list of known newsgroups, with some associated control information. Most of this information is found in the *active* file, again located with the control files (originally in */usr/lib/news*) although it is logically (mostly) part of the database. The format of this information has evolved more or less by historical accident.

The *active* file is an ASCII text file that contains one line per known newsgroup. Each line contains four fields, separated by blanks:

- The newsgroup name

- The number of the latest article filed

- In theory, the number of the earliest article still in the database, although in practice this number often lags somewhat behind actual article expiries

- A control code that indicates the nature of the newsgroup

The second and third fields may have leading zeros; the second field should have some, because some relayers update it in place and cannot add another digit when one is needed. (Also, for historical reasons, both fields should be a minimum of five digits long, although with any luck there's no software left that insists on this.)

The fourth field is a somewhat confused control code that can have one of the following values:

y   An ordinary newsgroup.

n   An ordinary newsgroup except that local users are not allowed to post to it.

m   A moderated newsgroup.

x   A group that is not subscribed to by this host (even if it is allowed by more general subscription lists elsewhere).

=*othernewsgroup*
  Articles arriving in this newsgroup should be filed in *othernewsgroup* instead.

The order of lines in the *active* file was once the order in which newsgroups were presented to the user by newsreader software. Nowadays that is under the user's control and the order of lines in the file is of no significance. Thus, new entries normally are just appended to the end of the file.

After the format of the *active* file was established, it became apparent that there is a need for one more item of information about each newsgroup: when it was created. This is important because newsreader software needs to have an easy way of determining whether a newsgroup is new, so it can decide whether to ask the user if he wants to read it. Older newsreaders used slow and rather fallible heuristics for this. Newer ones consult the *active.times* file, which resides in the same directory as *active*.

The *active.times* file is an ASCII text file, with one line per newsgroup, where each line contains three fields separated by blanks:

- The name of the newsgroup

- The date of its creation, as seconds since an epoch (for Unix, the epoch is midnight, January 1, 1970 GMT)

- The mail address of the group's creator, although little or no software uses this

The *active.times* file must be kept sorted by creation date, which is normally trivial since new entries are simply appended to the end.

19.2.5 The Overview Database

Long ago, newsreader software simply presented articles in the order of their arrival. This quickly became unsatisfactory and new newsreader software presented one newsgroup at a time, with the articles within the newsgroup shown in order of arrival. Eventually, this too began to present difficulties, as news volume grew and discussions proliferated. Newer newsreader software began to use the References headers in the articles to connect articles into threads of discussion, so that a user could read one thread at a time. This made it possible to follow individual discussions even within a busy newsgroup, a capability that had long been wanted.

However, the threading newsreaders presented their own problem: the information they needed to organize the presentation of articles was spread widely through the news database and was expensive to gather. Such newsreaders could not start up quickly unless this information was collected in a central file for each newsgroup. So a threading newsreader typically added an auxiliary-database file for each newsgroup, maintained by an extra program. Unfortunately, each threading newsreader had its own private format for the auxiliary database files. Worse yet, some of the database files were very expensive to update.

Early in 1993, Geoff Collyer (with funding from UUNET Communications Services, later to become UUNET Technologies) defined a unified database format, the *news overview* database (or "overview files"). This new format was meant to be well documented and easy to update. Collyer also supplied sample library routines to access it. Because Collyer was one of the C News co-authors, C News naturally supported the new format first, but INN and then the NNTP Reference Implementation also picked it up. All major relayers, and most newsreader packages, now support overview files, and the private auxiliary databases are quietly dying out.

The overview database consists of a single extra file, *.overview*, in each newsgroup's directory. An alternative organization, now often used, puts the overview files in another directory tree, independent of, but with the same structure as, the article tree for quicker access to the files. (Some relayers maintain symbolic links from the article tree to the overview tree to make this change transparent to news-readers.)

An overview file for a newsgroup is an ASCII text file that contains one line per article (the lines can become very long). Each line contains several fields, sepa-rated by tabs. Any tabs or newlines in the original data are translated to blanks. The first eight fields are mandatory and their order is fixed:

- Article number (i.e., the filename)

- Topic (contents of the Subject header)

- Author (contents of the From header)

- Date (contents of the Date header)

- Message ID (contents of the Message-ID header)

- Precursors (contents of the References header); may be empty if there is no such header

- Article size in bytes

- Alleged article size in lines (contents of the Lines header); may be empty if there is no such header

An overview file is sorted in numerical order based on the value of the first field.

There may be more fields, each consisting of an entire header (including header name and colon), not just the contents as with the mandatory fields. The choice of headers to be included in this way depends on the implementation, although one very common and useful inclusion is the Xref header.

19.3 *Batching for Transmission*

For efficient bulk transmission and processing of news articles, it is often desirable to transmit a number of articles as a single block of data, or *batch*. A batch is a sequence of articles, each preceded by a header line that specifies its size. A header line consists of #!, followed by a single space and **rnews**, followed by another single space and the size of the article as a byte count in decimal notation, followed by the end of the line.* Whatever convention is used to signify end-of-line, each end-of-line in the article counts as exactly one byte for purposes of computing the size. Here's the outline of an example batch:

---

* Beware that some software inserts non-standard trash after the size.

```
#! rnews 627
Newsgroups: sci.space
...rest of article, 605 bytes...
#! rnews 1235
article totaling 1235 bytes
#! rnews 802
article totaling 802 bytes
```

Note that "Newsgroups: sci.space" with the line end characters, is exactly 22 characters, hence the 605 byte length for the rest of the first article.

When transmitting news over communications links that are slow or that are billed by the bit, it is often desirable to apply data compression to news batches. The receiving host then has to know which compression method was used. The preferred way to convey this information is by "out-of-band" communication, separate from the data of the batch. This cleanly separates the two and makes processing easier.

However, if there is no way to send out-of-band information along with a batch and it's not practical for the administrators of the hosts to simply agree on a compression method, there is a convention that can be used to bundle the information with the batch. The batch is compressed, and then a header is prepended to it. This header starts with #! and is followed by a single space and a compression keyword. The only truly widespread compression keyword is cunbatch, which indicates that compression was done with the widely used *compress* program.

Note that the format of a batch resembles the executable-script format found in many versions of Unix. However, it is extremely unwise to just feed incoming batches to a command interpreter without first checking to see exactly which commands are specified in the #! lines.

19.4 Transmission by UUCP

In the beginning, all news transmission went via UUCP, the "Unix to Unix CoPy" package. Significant amounts of news transmission still do, particularly out on the fringes of Usenet where leaf nodes often have only dial-up modems as links to the outside world.

19.4.1 Basic UUCP

As its name might suggest, UUCP started out as a file-transfer facility and its network protocol still basically does nothing else. The only thing the UUCP protocol can do is transfer a data file from one host to another; remote command execution is done with a stylized filename convention allowing a command to be sent as one file with its input data as another. Inter-host electronic mail was added, crudely, by defining a command (*rmail*) whose purpose was to accept a mail message (transferred as another file) and send it onward. The Duke/UNC inventors of Usenet (see Chapter 17, *A Brief History of Usenet*) added an *rnews* command, analogous to *rmail*, for accepting and forwarding news.

Any sophisticated interaction between the two hosts must be built on top of this relatively crude foundation. In particular, no real-time interaction between higher-level software packages is possible. This limitation is strengthened by the traditional use of UUCP with auto-dialing modems, with connections made intermittently and possibly only at times of low phone rates. A further complication is that the UUCP protocol imposes significant startup and shutdown delays for transmission of each file, so there is strong incentive to bundle several small transmissions into a single large file and to use data compression to reduce the size of the resulting files.*

All of this contributed heavily to the original model of news transport. Host X figures out which articles should be sent to host Y (without actually consulting host Y), packages them up into one or more large batches, compresses the batches, and sends them. Host Y receives the batches, perhaps some substantial time later, and must then deal with them without consulting host X. See Section 19.3 for the exact format of batches and some notes on their processing.

There is really only one way to send news via UUCP: take an article, or a batch of articles, and transfer it as a file, with a request that the receiving host run the *rnews* command on it. This generally is done by invoking UUCP's *uux* command, typically with an incantation along the lines of:

```
uux - -r -gd host!rnews
```

The article or batch is used as *uux*'s standard input. Details vary slightly between different versions of UUCP. In particular, it may be necessary to supply *uux* with a -z or -n option to avoid having the other host send you mail reporting the results of the *rnews* command. You may also need to alter the value given in the -g option, which specifies the grade (priority) of news transmission relative to other kinds of traffic; d is the traditional grade for news, but it may not be right for all hosts.

When the batch arrives at the other host, its UUCP software tries to run *rnews*. UUCP typically isn't allowed to run just any command; the *rnews* command is allowed only if *rnews* is in the list of permitted remote commands, which is usually found in a UUCP control file.† Assuming execution of *rnews* is permitted and the UUCP software can actually find a command by that name (which means that

---

* In the early 1980s, when all this got started, modems were relatively unintelligent devices that did not do any form of data compression themselves.

† Some very old UUCP implementations had the permitted-commands list compiled into the binaries.

the command must be placed where UUCP looks for it), the *rnews* command sees the incoming news on its standard input, and makes arrangements to pass it on to the news software.

19.4.2 UUCP Over TCP

Although UUCP got started in an environment of modems and phone lines, it can run over most any communications link. In particular, many modern UUCP implementations support running the UUCP protocol over a TCP/IP connection. This may seem a little strange: why not use NNTP instead? While NNTP has its advantages, UUCP's compressed batches are still a much more efficient way to ship news articles in bulk. This can be important if the TCP/IP connection is slow or expensive to use.

Once a connection is made, UUCP has provisions for negotiating which low-level protocol it uses to transfer each file. UUCP protocols are known by single letters. The traditional UUCP protocol, the g protocol, copes well with noisy phone lines, but is inefficient for communications links like TCP/IP connections, which handle their own error correction and flow control. There are several less-standardized UUCP protocols meant for use over error-free flow-controlled connections; consult the documentation for your UUCP software to see what you've got.

19.4.3 ihave/sendme

The noninteractive nature of news transmission by UUCP is troublesome in one situation: where a host is getting more than one feed for redundancy, but one of the feeds is particularly fast or cheap, so that the others are best used only as backups. In such a case, it's desirable for the backup feeds to ask the destination "Did you get article <3x6z@kiwi.ora.com>?" and send it only if the answer is "No."

While this can't be done interactively with UUCP, it can be done, if a bit slowly and clumsily, using the *ihave* and *sendme* control messages described in Section 18.4.* The feed site sends the destination *ihave* messages indicating which news articles are available, and the destination replies with *sendme* messages indicating which ones are desired.

This *ihave/sendme* protocol is a bit slow and not entirely reliable (if a control message gets lost, nobody ever finds out about it). Sending the control messages as news articles is also somewhat inelegant.

---

* Note that the *ihave* and *sendme* messages discussed here have absolutely nothing to do with NNTP, despite some similarities of terminology.

19.5 Transmission by NNTP

UUCP's major competitor for transporting news is NNTP, the Network News Transfer Protocol, defined in RFC 977. NNTP is one of the Internet family of protocols and is normally used over a TCP/IP connection (although it could, in principle, be used over any error-free flow-controlled transmission path). RFC 977 is rather old; would-be implementers are warned that some ill-documented extensions to it are in common use.

NNTP is actually two protocols rolled into one. It can be used to transport news from one host to another, but it can also be used by newsreader software to access the news database on a server host. This confusion of purposes is somewhat regrettable, and some server implementations in fact split the two functions, switching to a different mode or even to a different server program if the client begins using "reader" protocol requests.*

19.5.1 News via NNTP

NNTP software is rather more diverse than UUCP software because the protocol is much more powerful and flexible. A number of different approaches have been employed, including using the newsreader side of the protocol as a transport interface by which the destination host can "pull" interesting news across the link rather than having it "pushed" by the sender in the traditional UUCP manner. In practice, however, the most widely used approach to NNTP transport closely resembles that used for UUCP transport.

In orthodox NNTP news transport, the sending host creates a connection to an NNTP server on the destination host. (The means for doing this are not specified by the protocol, although in a TCP/IP environment, any incoming connection request on port 119 wants to talk to an NNTP server.) For each article on the to-be-sent list, the sending host sends an NNTP *IHAVE* command with the message ID of an article. For example:

```
IHAVE <23426896@kiwi.ora.com>
```

If the destination host does not yet have that article, it replies with a "send it" acknowledgment code, the sending host sends it, and the destination host acknowledges successful transmission. (This last acknowledgment is present so the

---

* An early attempt at a revision of NNTP decided that new newsreader-oriented functionality should be separated into a distinct protocol (tentatively dubbed "NNRP"). However, that effort lost momentum and died, so this decision cannot be considered final.

sender knows that it may remove the article from the to-be-sent list.) If the destination host already has the article, the acknowledgment code indicates this and the sender doesn't attempt to send it.*

As a news transport mechanism, NNTP has both advantages and disadvantages compared to UUCP. Its one huge advantage is that a host receiving multiple news feeds generally receives only one copy of each article. Set against this are some disadvantages: no provision for data compression, a lockstep protocol, no official provisions for 8-bit text (although many implementations simply fail to enforce RFC 977's restriction to 7 bits), and some rather sloppy early implementations.† Some of NNTP's shortcomings have been addressed by ad hoc extensions, but they are as yet poorly documented and unstandardized.‡

19.5.2 Implementations

There are three NNTP implementations of interest as transports: the Reference Implementation, SNNTP, and INN.

The Reference Implementation is old and creaky, and has received little maintenance effort in recent years. It works satisfactorily with C News, although there are various mismatches of style and configuration that betray its separate origins. At the moment, it's the only "full service" NNTP implementation, providing newsreader as well as transport functionality, for use with C News.

SNNTP is a new transport-only NNTP implementation, written by Mark Moraes and Geoff Collyer, which is supplied as "contributed software" with the current C News distribution. It is small and efficient, and somewhat better integrated with C News. Its major limitation is that it does not provide the newsreader side of NNTP at all, although it has provisions for passing control to a customer-supplied program if the client makes a newsreader-side request.§

Both the Reference Implementation and SNNTP run into a problem if a site gets multiple feeds via NNTP: there can be a significant delay between NNTP's delivery of an article and C News' processing of it. During this period, an NNTP server can't determine whether an article has already arrived just by looking for it in the news database. This is particularly awkward because multiple NNTP feeds often offer the same article in fairly rapid succession. The solution to this—not beautiful,

---

* The NNTP *IHAVE* message and related machinery discussed here have absolutely nothing to do with the *ihave/sendme* control messages, despite some similarities of terminology.

† Most notably, RFC 977 limits NNTP protocol request/acknowledgment lines to 512 characters, but places no limit on the length of lines within articles. Some NNTP software, notably the Reference Implementation, limits all lines to 512 characters and misbehaves if an article contains longer lines.

‡ Efforts toward producing a revised NNTP specification have recently been revived; see *http://www.academ.com/academ/nntp/ietf.html* for details.

§ Future C News releases may include such a newsreader-server program.

but workable—is Paul Vixie's Message-ID Daemon, *msgidd,* also shipped with current C News distributions. It is a small daemon that NNTP servers can consult to determine whether an article has arrived recently or not.

INN has NNTP support integrated into its relayer daemon, eliminating any need for separate software (and also, incidentally, eliminating the *msgidd* problem). Like SNNTP, it too passes control to a separate program when presented with news-reader-side requests; unlike SNNTP, INN also supplies the program.

19.5.3 Streaming NNTP

In the summer of 1994, Jef Poskanzer, Van Jacobson, and Craig Leres did the initial work of developing an extension to the standard NNTP protocol that allowed for *streaming* news transfers—transfers that do not involve network-induced delays caused by waiting for responses in a lockstep protocol. We describe it, and subsequent developments, here in some detail because it has not been documented well elsewhere.

The 1994 proposal allowed a sending site to use the existing *STAT* command to see whether an article's message ID was known by the receiving server. The sender did not have to wait for a reply but could go on sending more commands. When the response to a *STAT* came back that said the indicated message ID was not known by the server, the sender could use the *TAKETHIS* command to send the entire article followed by the conventional terminator of a period on a line by itself. It did not have to wait for a reply; the other side could take as long as it needed to say whether the article was accepted. The result was that *STAT* and *TAKETHIS* commands could be intermingled, to make the best use of network bandwidth by always keeping traffic going as much as possible in both directions simultaneously. This largely avoided the penalties incurred by needing to wait for a response to each command.

This proposal is close to what was eventually adopted in production NNTP servers. (Streaming still isn't included in a formally approved specification, though it is in the draft generated by the NNTP Version 2 effort.) As implemented in NNTP servers today, the role of the *STAT* command for streaming has been superseded by the *CHECK* command. The *TAKETHIS* command still has the same name as in the initial proposal.

The responses to *CHECK* can be any of the following:

```
238 <message-id> please send
431 <message-id> try again later
438 <message-id> got it, don't send
438 <message-id> bad id, don't send
```

The message ID must be included with the leading numeric value, but as with most NNTP commands, the explanatory text is free-form and completely optional. Note that there is no numeric distinction between a bad message ID and one the server already has.

The responses to *TAKETHIS* can be either of the following:

```
239 <message-id> received, thanks
439 <message-id> rejected
```

The message ID must be included with the leading numeric value, but as usual, the explanatory text is free-form and completely optional. Note that there is no numeric distinction made between a permanent rejection of the article and a transient failure where retransmission would be desired later. Perhaps the best way to indicate a transient failure is to just not acknowledge the article.

One additional optimization possible with streaming occurs when the sending site observes that the receiving site is accepting nearly all of the articles it is getting *CHECK* messages for. There is no requirement that a message ID be previously checked with *CHECK* before being used in *TAKETHIS*, so in this case the sender can just stop issuing *CHECK* commands and send a constant stream of articles, led by the appropriate *TAKETHIS* commands. This optimization not only saves a few dozen bytes per article on the wire, but also halves the number of history-database lookups a receiving site needs to do for each message ID being offered.

The sender does need to be careful to keep track of the responses to the *TAKETHIS* commands, too. If the receiver starts rejecting a high number of articles, any savings from not issuing *CHECK* commands is lost to the resources consumed by sending entire articles that are then rejected. A suggested threshold for stopping *CHECK* commands is 95% of articles being accepted; a reasonable threshold for starting them again is 10% rejections.

19.6 Last-Resort Transmission Methods

While UUCP and NNTP are generally the best ways to transport news, almost any technique that can get bits from one place to another can be used. There are some unusual methods that deserve mention as last resorts for the desperate.

19.6.1 News via Email

The communication technique of last resort is generally electronic mail, particularly in old networks, strange networks, or networks set up by ignorant people. You can often get email from point X to point Y when nothing else will get through. For such situations, it is possible to send news via email.

In general, it is not wise to simply send news articles as mail messages, despite the similarity of format. Mail-handling software often feels free to manipulate various headers in undesirable ways. (In some cases, such as with Sender, such manipulation is actually mandatory.) The mail-handling software also often feels free to report things like transmission problems to the article's author rather than to the local administrators. In general, news sent as mail should be encapsulated, to separate the mail headers and the news headers. If the intended recipient is a human, any convenient form of encapsulation may be used. When mail is being used as a transport path between two relayers, however, a standard method is desirable.

The old standard method was to mail the news to *rnews* on the destination host, with whatever mail headers were necessary for successful transmission. The news article (including its headers) was sent as the body of the mail message, with an N prepended to each line. The N reduced the probability of an innocent line in a news article being taken as a magic command to mail software, and made it easy for receiving software to strip off any lines added by mail software (e.g., the trailing empty line added by some UUCP mail software).

This method has its weaknesses. In particular, it assumes that the mail transmission channel can transmit nearly arbitrary body text undamaged. When mail is being used as a transmission path of last resort, however, the mail system often has inconvenient preconceived notions about the format of message bodies. Various ad hoc encoding schemes have been used to avoid such problems.

The modern method is to send a news article or batch to *rnews* as the body of a MIME mail message, using content type `application/news-transmission` and MIME's `base64` encoding (which is specifically designed to survive all known major mail systems). The MIME Content-MD5 header defined in RFC 1864 can also be used as a checksum to detect accidental damage to the contents.

19.6.2 *News via Physical Mail*

If there is no way of getting bits from one host to the other over wires at all, there is still the possibility of using slower forms of transportation. For a while, the news feed from North America to Australia was done via air-freighted magnetic tapes. This approach obviously can lead to rather long propagation delays, particularly if people on the other end respond to posted articles. It also requires manpower at both ends. However, it is not fundamentally difficult.

In a somewhat similar vein, at various times several companies have sold CD-ROM news feeds. Once a week (or however often was needed), you got a CD-ROM with the latest Usenet news. The inability to post was a limitation, but apparently it met some organizations' needs. The combination of growing news volume and increasing availability of direct Internet connections seems to have made this unprofitable; as of mid-1997, we don't know of anyone who's still providing this service.

Index

Symbols

* (asterisk)
    designating comment lines, 144
    designating specificity, 113
    in pattern field, 228–229
    as wildcard, 184
@ (at sign)
    in email addresses, 90, 336
    leading group pattern, 184
    style of negation, 185
 (backslash) continuing long line, 92, 183
[ ] (brackets) for moderator comments, 361
: (colon)
    separating fields, 92, 101, 183, 197
    for site not requiring password, 188
, (comma) in Newsgroups header, 431
- (dash) in newsgroup names, 345
! (exclamation point)
    beginning exclusive tokens, 186
    designating shell command, 64
    leading group pattern, 184
    as path delimiter, 431
    in sitename field, 227, 229
    style of negation, 185
> (greater than) prefacing quoted lines, 439
% (percent sign) in email addresses, 90, 429
. (period) in host names, 180, 385
+ (plus) marking normal articles, 242
# (pound sign) for comments, 89, 101, 347

/ (slash)
    beginning filenames, 103
    separating MIME type from subtype, 446
    separating subfields, 101–102, 183
~ (tilde) separating subfields, 457

Numbers

386 compilers, 72
486 compilers, 72
7-bit ASCII characters, 182, 360
7bit, 8bit encoding, 448

A

A News, 3, 408
abbreviations, avoiding, 386
absolute bounds on expiry times (see
        expiry, dates, explicit)
access (see news, servers)
ACT_STYLE parameter, 148
active file, 8, 92, 111, 120, 122, 131,
        458–460
    control command, 43
    control flag, 51
    creating, 174
    keeping on INN server, 155
    maintaining, 288
    modifying, 49
    recovering after crash, 257
    setting up properly, 132

active file (cont'd)
  synchronizing with remote file, 196
  warning concerning, 125
active.times file, 44, 111, 459
actsync program, 155, 257
actsync.cfg file, 195–196
actsyncd program, 155, 235
Adams, Rick, 415
addgroup utility, 46, 120
addmissing program, 134
addngs utility, 46, 124
address spoofing, reducing, 150
administering news (see news, administer-
    ing)
administration
  contact alias, 376
  feed hosts administrators, 35, 37, 59, 289
    contacting, 37, 371
  managing people, 274–275
  responding to forging, 280
  scheduling, 297
  soliciting administrators, 395
  user restrictions, 58
Advanced Research Projects Agency
    (ARPA), 406
advertisements, 365
advisory councils, 376
AIX, installing INN on, 156
aliases, 51, 146
  newscrisis, 115, 123, 125, 131, 135
  newsdaily, 135
  newsmaster, 115, 123, 125, 135, 146, 175
  newsuser, 146, 175
  owner-post-listname alias, 330
  post-listname alias, 330
  post-listname-request alias, 330
  for reporting trouble, 115
  for urgent addresses, 68
all line, 98, 346
Also-Control header, 438
alt hierarchy, 92, 94, 382, 417
  alt.binaries hierarchy, 285
  alt.config group, 395
  "Alternative Newsgroup Hierarchies"
      articles, 384, 422
  rot setting in on, 421–422
alternative content subtype (MIME), 447
.announce groups, 363

anonymous
  postings, 366–367
  publications, 281
  remailers, 366
ANSI C compiler, 70
apologizing to users, 370
application content type (MIME), 448
application/news-transmission content type,
    469
Approved header, 343, 349, 436
  authenticating, 437
arbitron program, 284
archiving, 8–9, 42, 54–55, 74
  increasing numbers of sites, 55
  newsgroups, 43
  selectivity in, 54
ARPA (Advanced Research Projects
    Agency), 406
  ARPAnet, 3, 406
ARTICLE command (NNTP), 58
article tree, 8, 55, 83, 100, 151, 455–456
  splitting across filesystems, 455
articles
  all going to junk, 132
  anonymous, 366–367
  archiving old, 8–9
  average length of, 13
  backlogged (see backlogged articles)
  bad, 247–248
  batching (see batches, article)
  broadcasting, 407
  commercial, 365
  composing, 5
  crossposted (see crossposting articles)
  defined, 1, 424–440
    basic layout, 425–427
    body of, 6, 360, 438–440
    (see also headers)
  enormous, 36, 440
  expiring old, 74, 131, 234–235, 246–247
    policy concerning, 52–54, 169
    problems with, 134
    program for, 16
    shortening, 36
    (see also expire)
  fetching, 5
  flow of, 127–132
  followup, 5

articles (cont'd)
    identifying true author of, 367
        (see also forging)
    incoming, looping back, 22, 133
    indexing, 14, 454–461
        package for, 69
        software for, 259
    log of individual, 305
    matching, 185
    message IDs, 353, 358
    meta-messages, 320
    multi-part, 353, 440
    multiple, 320
    not files to newsgroups, 132
    packages as digests, 320, 351, 353, 407
    passing, 10
    posting, 226–227
    preparing for moderated newsgroups,
        348–362
        header processing, 348–360
    problematic, 278–282, 315–317
    processing is not done, 132
    processing with newsrun, 129–130
    reading selectively, 265
    receiving, 219–224, 241–242
        via UUCP, 222–224
    rejecting, 378
    removing, 243
    returning to submitter, 373
    sent, 242
    sequencing, 295
    size limits on, 440
    slow, 54
    splitting, 352
    storing, 454–461
    style of, 370
    submitting to newsgroups, 345–348
        copyright, 372
        crossposting and, 348, 350
        groups not listed in file, 180
        local groups, 347
        moderated, 362
        network-wide groups, 345
    target, 441–442
    transforming, 9
    transmitting, 227–230
        (see also transmitters)
ASCII text files, 6, 425

asterisk (*)
    as wildcard, 184
    designating comment lines, 144
    designating specificity, 113
    in pattern field, 228–229
asymmetric feeds, 106
asynchronous filesystem operation, 30
at sign (@)
    in email addresses, 90, 336
    leading group pattern, 184
    style of negation, 185
Aten, Bill, 399
audio content type (MIME), 447
authentication
    of Approved header, 437
    of cancel messages, 442
    PGP, 194–195
AUTHINFO PASS command, 188, 190
AUTHINFO USER command, 190
auxiliary headers, 360
awk utility, 139, 153

B

B News, 4, 203, 410
    hosts still running, 439
    newsreaders compatible with, 271
backbone (see networks)
Backbone Cabal, 414–417
backends subdirectory, 142
backlogged articles, 16, 311
    outgoing, 37
    queued, 301
backslash (/) continuing long line, 92, 183
backspace character, 426
backup moderators, 376
backups (see archiving)
bad articles, 247–248
bad-expiry utility, 54
bad subdirectory, 130, 326
bandwidth, 18–19, 22, 36, 287
    nntplink transmitter and, 273
    paying by, 12
    reducing requirements for, 19
    required for hub site, 292
bang (!) (see exclamation point)
base64 encoding, 449, 469
batch file mode, 130, 300
batcher program, 106, 108, 142

batches, article, 129–130
  checking, 306
  defined, 461
  for transmission, 461–462
batchlists, 171, 295
batchparms file/line, 105, 107–110, 125,
        130, 133, 224
  /default/ line, 108
batchsplit program, 130
Bellovin, Steve, 413
Berkeley networking, 139
Berne Convention (copyright), 372
BI (Breidbart Index), 279
bidirectional gateways, 320, 397
"big eight" hierarchies, 380
/bin directory, 66
binaries hierarchy, 185
binary encoding, 448
bionet hierarchy, 382
bit hierarchy, 382
Bitnet, 408
biz hierarchy, 382
blocks, 13–14
BNU Permissions file, 175
body, article, 6, 360, 438–440
"Bogus Usenet Groups" article, 43
boolean values in parameters, 144
boot-time startup (installing INN with), 174
bounce-back path, 356
bounced messages, misdirected, 280
/bounds/ line, 98
brackets ([ ]) for moderator comments, 361
branching nodes, 389
Breidbart Index (BI), 279
Brister, James, 303
broadcasting, 407
broken message generator, 280
BSD-derived filesystems, 14, 156–158
bug, "line eater", 439
BUILD script, 167
bulk transmission, 103
bulletin-board systems, 1, 407

C

C News, 2, 4, 411
  advantages of, 296
  building, 64–77
  checking/testing, 78, 119–126
  cleaning up, 117–118

Cleanup Release, 63, 65, 119
    patches to, 63
  configuring, 89–118
  installing, 62, 78–80
    verifying, 114
  NNTP support in, 63
  running, 119–137
  troubleshooting, 132–134
  user interface files, 111–112
C programming language
  compiler, 72
  development environment, 139
  library, 146–147
Cabal, Backbone, 414–417
Call for Votes (CFV) articles, 42, 352, 399
cancel messages, 9, 39–40, 95, 149,
        441–442, 457
  authenticating, 442
  hard-coded, 194
  ignoring, 40
  Sender header and, 358
cancel.pl program, 371
CD-ROMs, 10, 469
censorship, 368
CFLAGS, modifying, 85
CFV articles, 42, 352, 399
CGI scripts, 310
characters, acceptable, 426
CHECK command, 186, 467
CHECK_INCLUDED_TEXT variable, 148
checkactive program, 125
checkgroups control message, 39, 43, 95,
        345, 444–445
checkgroups utility, 39, 43–45, 50, 94, 205,
        289
checknews version (C News), 75, 79
checksum_article procedure, 210
    (see also MD5-based checksum)
checksums, MIME, 449
chgrp command, 173
chown command, 173
clari hierarchy, 95, 382
ClariNet newsgroups, 95, 382
class specification, 298
classification
    codes for, 137
    done by author, 390
    system, large, 385
cleaning up C News, 117–118

Cleanup Release (see C News)
CLIENT_TIMEOUT parameter, 253
CLX_STYLE parameter, 147
cnewsdo command, 79, 120, 394
Collabra, 3"
collision rate, 306
Collyer, Geoff, 4, 36, 410, 460, 466
colon (:)
    for site not requiring password, 188
    separating fields, 92, 101, 183, 197
comma (,) in Newsgroups header, 431
commercial articles, 365
communications links, 10
    (see also bandwidth)
community, electronic, 1
comp hierarchy, 380
compcun program, 108, 316
compilation copyright, 375
compilers, 70
compiling newsreaders, 259
compress program, 108
compression (see data compression)
CompuServe, 278
conf.h file, 80–85
conf.h.dist file, 80
config program, 143
config.data file, 168, 254
configdata.h, editing, 165
config.dist master file, 143
configuring
    C News, 89–118
    feed hosts, 301
    INN (InterNetNews), 177–212
        control files, 179–198
        scripts, 198–212
        updating files, 177–179
    innwatch program, 152
    mail2news, 330–335
    mailing lists, 339
    news systems, 36
    newsgate program, 329
    newsreaders, 259
    NNTP daemon, 56
conf/makeinc file, 71
conf/maker file, 72
consistency
    in naming, 385
    Subject headers, 351
consultants, hiring, 60

Content-Description header, 446
Content-ID header, 446
Content-MD5 header, 449, 469
Content-Transfer-Encoding header, 182,
        446, 448–449
Content-Type header, 182, 445
control.ctl file, 403
contracts, 277
control files, 28
    in C News, 89–112
    in INN, 179–198
        control messages, 193–196
        expiry, 192–193
        general operation, 179–183
        news flow, 183–192
        newsreaders, 196–198
    in NRI, 112–114
    small, backing up, 29
Control header, 335, 435
    Also-Control header, 438
    gateways and, 340
control messages, 9, 37–41, 440–445
    Approved headers in, 436
    checking for active scripts, 50
    claimed author of, 93
    forging, 280
    via INN, 344
    INN scripts for, 203–208
    for newsgroups changes, 41–42
    types in controlperm, listed, 93
    ways to handle, listed, 93
control pseudogroup, 185, 218, 336, 454
control.ctl file, 194–195, 442
control-files directory, 259
control.log file, 208
controlperm file, 93–95, 403, 443
cooperating subnets, 426, 432
copyright issues, 279, 281, 372–375
correspondence, saving all, 290
costs, 2, 10, 36
    paying by bandwidth/byte, 12
CPU processing power requirements,
        19–20, 287
crashes
    preparing for, 30, 55, 116
    recovery from, 256
cron file, 131
cron utility, 175

crontab file, 99, 115
    per user, 175
crontab utility, 122, 129, 131
crossposting articles, 5, 8, 94, 100
    aggressively expiring, 234
    detecting, 431
    discouraging, 365
    excessive (ECP), 279
    gateways and, 341
    limiting, 58
    linking to, 215
    (see also articles)
ctime program, 131
ctl directory, 129
ctlinnd program, 236–239
    checkfile command, 231
    flush command, 228, 239
    mode command, 200, 236
    newgroup command, 50, 204, 207
    reload command, 178, 238
        reload newsfeeds command, 228, 247
    renumber command, 204, 245
    rmgroup command, 50
cunbatch command/line, 75, 79, 224, 462
customers (see users)
Cyclone, 2
cylinder groups, 15

D

D News, 3
daemons, vanished, 308
daily report, 244–254
dash (-) in newsgroup names, 345
data compression, 18, 20, 129
    agreeing on method for, 462
Date header, 357, 428
    gateways and, 340
dbm indexing package, 69, 458
dbz indexing package, 28, 69, 81, 458
    library, 145
    patch for, 166
dead newsgroups, 39
dead.article file, 226
decompression, 129
dedicated lines, 18
dedicated news servers, 32
default script, 207
#define, 81
delayrm option, 216

delays (see propagation)
delngs utility, 48
denial-of-service attacks, 57
dexpire program, 286
df command, 15, 73, 153, 182
    space usage total, 255
Diablo, 3
digest content subtype (MIME), 447
digest-burners, 320
digests, 320, 351, 407
    From header for, 353
Digital Unix 4.0 (installing INN on), 158
disk space (see storage space)
DiskSuite utility, 293
distrib.pats file, 190–192
distribution, 6
    list, 102
    terms, liberal, 374
Distribution header, 183, 354, 435, 452–453
    forget about using, 191, 436, 453
    magic meanings assigned to, 436
    problems with, 314
distribution subfield, 185
DNS MX record, 429
docheckgroups script, 39, 205, 257
documentation (see record keeping; online
        documentation; system, manuals)
doexpire script, 131, 134
doexplode script, 129
DOINNWATCH parameter, 201
doit action, 194
domain addresses, 429
domain parameter, 180
domkov script, 130
dospace auxiliary program, 131
dot (see period)
drives, spooling across multiple, 286
    (see also filesystems; spooling)
du command, 100, 255
duplicate newsgroups, 386
dynafeed program, 284, 309

E

ECP (excessive crossposting), 279
    (see also crossposting articles)
ed editor, 121
efs filesystems, 160
egrep program, 139, 165
8bit encoding, 448

Ellis, Jim, 409
email, 10, 406
    addresses, 90
    piping news as, 324
    posting via, 319
    transmitting news via, 468
    UCB Mail program, security and, 56–57
email messages
    directing, 175
    handling incoming, 75
    Internet format, 425
    piping news articles as, 324
    posting articles via, 319
    (see also posting)
EMP (excessive multiposting), 279
empty headers, 428
empty lines, ignoring, 144
enhanced service providers, 276
enriched content subtype (MIME), 446
EOL (end-of-line) character, 425
errlog file, 122, 136, 243, 246
error messages, 77, 87
    "Bad Message-ID" message, 221, 249
    "NNRP no permission clients", 253
    "System shut down during expire" mes-
        sage, 216
    "undefined symbols" error message, 77,
        87
    "Unknown control message" notice, 207
    "unresolved references" error message,
        77, 87
/etc/rc boot-up command file, 116
excessive crossposting (ECP), 279
    (see also crossposting articles)
excessive multiposting (EMP), 279
    (see also multiposting)
exclamation point (!)
    beginning exclusive tokens, 186
    designating shell command, 64
    leading group pattern, 184
    as path delimiter, 431
    in sitename field, 227, 229
    style of negation, 185
exclude subfield, 184
expire program
    bogus reservation, 247
    memory requirements, 288
    running on floating schedule, 286
    (see also bad-expiry utility; expiry)

expire subdirectory, 142
expirebot program, 17, 53, 98–100
expire.ctl file, 169, 192, 215, 245
    space problems and, 255
expireiflow program, 286
expire.log file, 243
expireover.fmt file, 198
expire.rm script, 201, 203, 235, 243
Expires header, 355, 433
expiry
    control file, default, 52
    dates, 457
        explicit, 53–54, 96, 134
        long, 433
        never, 97, 192
    INN scripts for, 203
    not happening, 134
    (see also articles, expiring old)
explist file, 95–98, 131, 134
    all line at end, 98
    detailing, 98
    matching expiry policy, 96
    override entries, 100
explode program, 129
exploder files, 129
expov script, 131
expovguts program, 131
external-body content subtype (MIME), 447

F

-f flag, 178, 336
f flag (UUCP), 103
F flag (UUCP), 105
fa groups, 413
facilities, logging, 240
Fair, Erik, 4, 416
fair use doctrine, 372
FAKESYSLOG symbol, 83
FAQs (Frequently Asked Questions lists),
        60, 156
Fast SCSI bus, 292
fastrm command, 203, 235
feed hosts, 206, 315
    administration of (see administration)
    asymmetric feeds, 106
    configuring, 301
    dealings with, 289
    defined, 1
    delaying, 303

feed hosts (cont'd)
    entry, 202
    filling outgoing directory, 289
    limiting to subhierarchies, 288
    names of, 22, 90
    newsfeeds file (see newsfeeds file)
    obtaining, 11–12
    outbound, 37, 55
    quantity of, 12
    testing, 124–126
    topologies of, 314, 444
    updating, 231–234, 308–310
fgetline( ), 69
file headers, 130
file modes (in INN), 146
file permissions (see permissions)
files, large unlinked open, 307
filesystems
    accessing news through, 26
    backing up, 29
    integrity of, 30
    layout of, 27–31
        big files, 27–29
        filesystems and disk drives, 29–30
    operating asynchronously, 30
filter_art script, 211
filter_innd.pl file, 211
filter_mode function, 212
filter_news procedure, 210
filter_nnrpd.pl file, 212
filter_post function, 212
filtering news traffic, 154–155, 239
filtering readers traffic, 239
filter.tcl file, 210
firewalls, 58
FIXED_PATH parameter, 327
flames, 367
flooding algorithm, 57, 273, 451–452
flow (see traffic)
followups (see articles)
Followup-To header, 226, 352, 434
forging, 279
    article approval, 370–371
    control messages, 280
    messages, 249–250, 280–281
    moderator approval, 370–371
    situations requiring, 441
formfeed character, 426
486 compilers, 72

fqdn field, 171
Free Software Foundation, 140, 382
free space, leaving substantial, 35
FreeBSD 2.0 (installing INN on), 158
Frequently Asked Questions (FAQ) lists, 60,
        156
From header, 351, 429
    altering, 279
    for digests, 353
    gateways and, 340
    not changing, 326
fromhost parameter, 180
frontends subdirectory, 142, 171
FSF (see Free Software Foundation)
fstat utility, 255
full feed, 12, 126
full keyword, 171
functions, missing, 77
funnel mode (nntplink), 301

G

gag program, 329
gate.h, newsgate program and, 325–328
gatekeeper hosts, 25
gateways, 58, 184, 318–342
    bidirectional vs. one-way, 320, 397
    getting approval for, 322
    handling crossposting, 341
    header processing, 339–341
    looping, 280, 335
    multiple, 342
    "NetNews/Mailing List Gateway Policy"
        article, 322
    programming error messages, 339
    public, 321
    setting up, 320–339
    software for, 9
    worldwide, 318
    (see also mail)
gcc compiler, 72
generator, message, 280
getabsdate program, 131, 325
gethostname( ), 337
Gilmore, John, 417
Glickman, Matt, 4, 410, 413
GNU C compiler, 72
gnu hierarchy, 382
GNU versions, 140, 158
Gnus newsreader, 264, 271

granularity, 302
graphical user interface, 268
Great Renaming, 380, 414–415
greater than (>) prefacing quoted lines, 439
grephistory command, 206
group file, 146
group subscription patterns, 185, 188
Group Update Program, 309
GROUPDIR MODE, 146
groups (see newsgroups)
GUI, newsreader with, 268
gup utility, 309
Gwyn, Doug, 420
gzip utility, 140, 151

H

hate speech, 277
HAVE_SETSID parameter, 159
HAVE_UNIX_DOMAIN option, 147
HAVE_UUSTAT variable, 150
hdb version, queuelen, 73
header files, 70
headers, 6–7, 427–438
    auxiliary, 360
    empty, 428
    length constraints, 349
    MIME (see MIME)
    order of, 427
    processing, 339–341, 348–360
    rules for, 6
    system-defined, 359–360
    user-defined, 360
    (see also under individual header
        names)
HELP command, 180
help, getting, 59–61
hierarchies
    history of, 413–423
    organizational, 422
    presenting as recursive menus, 387
    regional, 281, 395, 422
    second-level, 285
    taxonomies of, 384
    worldwide, 397
    (see also subhierarchies; under individ-
        ual hierarchy names)
high-speed networks, 23, 25

history files, 8, 14, 28, 54, 69, 122, 134, 217,
        254, 456–458
    creating, 174
    fast access to, 288
    large, 96, 293
    rebuilding, 131
history.dir file, 217
history.pag file, 217
Horton, Mark, 4, 410, 413
hostname command, 74
hosts (see feed hosts; gatekeeper hosts)
hosts.nntp file, 170, 187–188, 231
HP-UX 10.20 (installing INN on), 159
html content subtype (MIME), 446
hub nodes, 291–317
    defined, 291
    political issues of, 312–317
huge articles (see articles, enormous)
humanities hierarchy, 381
HUP signal, 219
hyphen (-) in newsgroup names, 345

I

ICD_SYNC_COUNT parameter, 149
ihave script, 206
IHAVE/REJECT, 293
    exchanges, 273
    negotiations, 223
    NNTP feeds and, 186
ihave/sendme protocol, 105–106, 202
    control messages, 109, 194, 233, 249,
        442, 464
    information leaks and, 58
    UUCP feeds, 232
illegal speech, 276
image content type (MIME), 447
IN_CMDDIR parameter, 327
include command, 71
include directory, 85
    config.make file, 76
incoming
    articles, 22, 127–129, 133
    news, 91–100
in.coming subdirectory, 84, 116, 121, 125,
        127, 130
    bad directory, 122, 130, 326
index( ), rindex( ), 328
index files, 28

indexing (see articles; dbm indexing package; dbz indexing package)
INET Distribution groups, 416
inetd daemon, 115, 219
inews command, 75, 79, 180, 325
    -h option, 362, 404
INEWS_PATH variable, 148
inews program, 127, 226
    command, 142, 151, 202
.info groups, 363
information, making available, 2
injnews program, 127
inn directory, 142
INN (InterNetNews), 2, 138–176
    boot-time startup for, 174
    building, 167–169
        building the programs, 168
        checking build/configuration, 167, 169
        preparations for, 143–167
    configuring, 177–212
        control files, 179–198
        scripts, 198–212
        updating files, 177–179
    daemons, 150
    history of, 412
    installing, 169–176
        configuring site data files, 169–171
        replacing old news system, 171–172
        with root access, 172–173
        without root access, 173
    manual
        locating pages, 145
        making, 141
    running, 213–257
        keeping it running, 217–219
        normal operation, 230–236
        outgoing maintenance, 236–240
        starting INN, 213–219
        starting news system, 214–217
    scripts in, 198–212
        for control messages, 203–208
        embedded scripting languages, 209–212
        for expiry, 203
        for general operation, 199–201
        for log file processing, 208–209
        for news flow, 201–203
    setting options, 145–165

sources, 138–143
    retrieving, 140–141
    roadmap to, 142–143
    unpacking, 141
    system requirements for, 138–140
    testing installation, 219–230
    troubleshooting, 254–257
inncheck program, 176, 199, 219
inn.conf file, 170, 179–182, 346
    installing, 223
INND_DBZINCORE parameter, 149
innd program, 47, 51, 178, 180, 208
    death, common reasons for, 217
    failing to run, 188
    memory required for, 288
    subdirectory, 142
innd utility, 44
inn.daily, 203
inndoexpire script, 286
innd.pid file, 219
innd.restart script, 216
inndstart program, 173
innexpireiflow script, 286
innfeed program, 251, 303
innfeed transmitter, 293
innlog.pl script, 208, 248
innshellvars file, 152
innstat script, 200, 244
INNWATCH_DF parameter, 159
INNWATCH_HILOAD parameter, 200
INNWATCH_LIBSPACE parameter, 153
INNWATCH_LOLOAD parameter, 200
innwatch program, 200, 305, 239–240
    configuring, 152
INNWATCH_SPOOLSPACE parameter, 153
innwatch.ctl file, 182–183
innxmit program, 142, 202, 208, 242, 306
    manual page for, 189
    runs, 295
inodes
    consumption of, 15–16
    shortage of, 82
inshellvars file, 199
installing
    C News, 119–126
    INN (InterNetNews), 169–176, 219–230
    InterNetNews, article about, 141
    newsreaders, 258–260
installit.sh, editing, 173

internal newsgroups, 54
Internet, 4
    daemon, 115
    demographics of, 276
    domain addresses, 429
    domain names, 90
    message handler, 267
    service providers (ISPs), 272
Internet Software Consortium (see ISC)
InterNetNews (see INN)
IPADDR_LOG option, 150, 241, 280
IRIX 5.2, installing INN on, 160
ISC (Internet Software Consortium), 138,
        303, 324, 329
    active file of, 313, 398
ISO C compiler, 70
ISPs (Internet service providers), 272

J

junk pseudogroup, 51, 92, 97, 185, 218,
        247, 454–455
    all articles going to, 132

K

Kantor, Brian, 4, 412
Keller, Robert, 160
kernel routines, 389
Keywords header, 355, 436
kill command, 225
kill files, 260

L

L_CC_CMD parameter, 249
L flag (UUCP), 105
L_NOTICE option, 241
language issues, 427
Lapsley, Phil, 4, 412
latency problem, 293
Lawrence, David, 38, 42, 94, 264, 317–318,
        383, 420, 422
L.cmds file, 175
ld step, 72
leaf nodes, 272, 283–290
leakage, 57–58
Lear, Eliot, 420
legal issues, 276–282, 315
    copyright (see copyright issues)

letter bombs, 59
libcnews.a library, 71
libel accusations, 367
libraries
    C News, 71
    functions of, 68
    system-specific, 73
    (see also C Programming language; dbm
        indexing package; dbz indexing
        package; Standard I/O; tape)
LIKE_PULLERS option, 149
limit command, 288
"line eater" bug, 439
Lines header, 437
links script, 303
lint utility, 164, 167
LINUX 2.0.18 (installing INN on), 161
load (see traffic)
*LOAD parameters, 152
local/regional
    articles, restricting to, 105
    configuration, 154
    hierarchies, 281, 395, 422
    namespace changes, 394
    newsgroups, 6, 23, 125, 133, 259, 347,
        383
        forwarding to, 133
        for testing, 120
    postings, not being forwarded, 133
LOCAL_MAX_ARTSIZE parameter, 150, 250
lock files, 44, 151, 307
LOCK_STYLE parameter, 146
lockstep protocol, 19
log file mode (nntplink), 300
log line, 126
LOG_NEWS facility, 146
logger program, 213
logging and log files, 28, 83, 122, 136, 194,
        240–254
    individual articles, 305
    levels (in INN), 146
    processing scripts, 208–209
    syslog (see syslog program)
logical network, 2
looping (see articles; gateways)
ls command, 82
lsof tool, 255
lumps, traffic, 36–37

M

magnetic tape (see tape)
mail (see email; email messages)
mail2news program, 325
    configuring, 330–335
    gateways for, 280
    headers, 333
    removing headers, 340
mailing lists, 3
    addresses, 331, 388
        not completing, 91
    advantages of, 321
    configuring properly, 339
    forwarding from, 374
    "Mailing Lists Available in Usenet" arti-
        cle, 318, 323
    "NetNews/Mailing List Gateway Policy"
        article, 322
    origins of, 407
    owner of, 322
    "Publicly Available Mailing Lists" article,
        321
mailname file, 90–91, 114
mailpaths file, 110–111, 346–347
mailpaths sites, 181, 190, 345, 379
make program, 71
    make check, 114
    make clean, 117, 178
    make cmp, 114
    make config parameters (in INN), 145
    make diff, 179
    make diff-installed, 179
    make install, 177–178, 329
    make logger, 213
    make setup, 89
    make signoff, 329
    make spotless, 118
    make sterile, 118
    make tidy, 117
    make veryclean, 117
makeactive program, 257
makedirs.sh script, 172
makefile command, 76
Makefile file, 72, 85–86, 178
    newsgate program, 325
makegroup script, 45, 207, 344
    misused, 317
    warning concerning, 404
makehistory program, 218, 256

man subdirectory, 117
MANIFEST file, 142
manuals (see system, manuals)
mapping networks, 40, 115
master server (see news, servers)
master/slave system, 294
matching
    articles, 185
    expiry policy, 96
    newsgroups, 110, 296
    pattern matching, 184
McIntosh, Jim, 322
MD5-based checksum, 449, 469
ME (special name), 92, 101, 124, 187, 315
mean time between failures (MTBF), 36
memory
    C News requirements, 288
    continuous, 139
    hub site requirements, 293
    minimizing use of, 68
    requirements, 20, 32
    segmented, 139
MERGE_TO_GROUPS parameter, 218
message content type (MIME), 447
message IDs
    chronological listing of, 353
    random, 358
Message-ID daemon (see msgidd)
Message-ID header, 6, 121, 333, 357, 430,
    451
    "Bad Message-ID" message, 221, 249
    gateways and, 341
messages
    broken generator of, 280
    mail (see mail messages)
    news (see articles)
Microsoft Exchange Server, 3
MIME (Multipurpose Internet Mail Exten-
    sions), 445–449
    content transfer encodings, 448–449
    content types, 446–448
    headers, 182, 359, 445–446
mime-contenttype parameter, 182
mime-encoding parameter, 182
MIME-Version header, 445
mime-version parameter, 182
MINFILES symbol, 83
minfree parameter, 14
MINFREE symbol, 82

minimum free space configuration parameter, 14
mirroring, 25, 294–296, 437
misc hierarchy, 381
    misc.test.moderated group, 346, 349
MISSING_OBJ parameter, 147, 156, 166
MISSING_SRC parameter, 147, 156, 166
mixed content subtype (MIME), 447
mkmailpost program, 329
mkov program, 130
mmap( ), 145, 148
    cautions with FreeBSD, 159
mod hierarchy, 414
MODE READER command, 170, 188, 224, 227, 253
modems, 18, 408, 412
moderated keyword, 344
moderated newsgroups, 7, 44, 53, 97, 110, 180, 343–379
    aliases available, 345
    bringing diversity to, 377
    comments by moderator, 361
    contacting moderators, 348
    control file, 347
    converting newsgroups to, 402
    creating, 344–345, 405
    declaration of moderator, 395
    distributing articles among moderators, 377
    electing to have, 402
    flag controlling, 96
    forged moderator approval, 370–371
    form letters from moderator, 368–369
    help for moderators, 375–378
    moderation policy statement, 364, 397
    moderator's attitude, 370
    moderator's signature, 361
    policy for, 364
    politics and, 363–379
    quitting as moderator, 378
    signature of moderator, 361
    software for, 362, 369
    soliciting administrators, 395
    (see also articles, submitting to newsgroups)
moderatormailer expression, 180, 346
moderators file, 190, 347
moderators.isc.org site, 346
monitoring activity, 277, 304–306

Moraes, Mark, 466
mount points, 455
ms macro package, 142
MS-DOS operating system, 270
msgidd daemon, 82, 86, 116, 466
MTBF (mean time between failures), 36
multi-part
    articles (see articles)
    multipart content type (MIME), 447
    names, 5
multiposting (see crossposting; EMP)
Multipurpose Internet Mail Extensions (see MIME)
MUNGE_GECOS parameter, 148
MX records, 429

N
n flag (UUCP), 105
names
    good, 385–390
    multi-part, 5
    organization-specific, 23
    special (see ME)
    valid, 385
namespace issues, 312–315, 380–405
    controversy, 390–393
    history of, 413–423
    making changes in, 394–405
    theory of, 384–393
net groups, 413–414
NetNews
    defined, 1
    history of, 3–5, 408
    Redistribution of, 382
    workings of, 5–10
Netscape Collabra Server, 3
Netscape Navigator, 268
Network News Reader Protocol (see NNRP)
Network News Transfer Protocol (see NNTP)
networks
    filesystem (see filesystems)
    high-speed, 23, 25
    managing, 272–282
    mapping, 40, 115
    news (see news, systems)
    optimizing, 272–274
    (see also bandwidth)
never (expiry time), 97

NEWBIN/nntp subdirectory, 86
newfs program, 15
newgroup control message, 38, 41–42, 93,
	344, 403, 443
	legitimate, 94
newgroup script, 204
newgroup.log file, 208
Newman, Ron, 270
news
	administering, 34–61
		centrally, 57
		getting help, 59–61
		time requirements for, 20–21
	articles (see articles)
	database, 7
		overview, 460
		standard organization of, 8
	via email, 468
	feeds (see feed hosts)
	groups (see newsgroups)
	how long to keep it, 16–17
	how much to get, 12–21
	incoming, 91–100
	INN scripts for, 201–203
	name, 22, 90
	neighbors, 59
	outbound, 100–106
	owners of, 30–31, 56, 65
	via physical mail, 469
	readers (see newsreaders)
	servers
		access to, 25–27, 315
		commercial, 2
		dedicated, 32
		keeping running, 217–219
		master versus slave, 25, 142
		official, 24
		organizing, 25
		paused, 236
		reasonable access times for, 285
		running, 236
		strict checking of, 248
		throttled, 236
		upgrading no longer possible,
			294–296
	as source of help, 60
	systems
		configuring, 36
		hybrid, 296

	inheriting, 34
	internal, 23–27
	replacing old, 171–172
	starting, 214–217
	time-sensitivity of, 21
	transports, 4
/news directory, 27, 455
news content subtype (MIME), 447
news hierarchy, 125, 381
	news.admin hierarchy, 384
		news.admin.net-abuse hierarchy, 282
		news.admin.net-abuse.sightings, 316
	news.all, 222
	news.announce hierarchy
		news.announce.important, 387
		news.announce.newsgroups, 42–43,
			345, 352, 398, 404, 419
	news.answers, 60, 384
	news.groups, 352, 416
	news.lists.misc, 321
	news.software hierarchy
		news.software.b, 60, 63
		news.software.news, 60
		news.software.nntp, 156
		news.software.readers, 60
news news owner, 30
news2mail program, 328
	configuring, 335–339
	removing headers, 340
NEWSARTS directory, 83, 151
	in.coming (see in.coming subdirectory)
	out.going (see out.going subdirectory)
NEWSBIN directory, 78, 85, 99, 150
	ctl directory, 129
	nntp subdirectory, 88
	out.master directory, 129
newsboot command, 116
newscrisis alias, 115, 123, 125, 131, 135
news.crit selector, 200, 240
NEWSCTL directory, 79, 84, 99, 122, 151
newsdaily alias, 135
news.daily script, 203, 208, 216, 244–254
	innwatch and, 240
newsdaily script, 134
news.err selector, 231, 241
newsfeed-style group subscription pattern,
	188

newsfeeds file, 170–171, 183–187, 218, 227, 229, 247, 295
  file entry, 231
newsgate program, 324
  building, 328
  configuring, 329
  Makefile changes, 325
newsgroups, 2, 452–453
  adding and deleting, 38–39, 235–236, 379, 405
    formal proposal for, 396–397
  archive of, 43
  articles not filed to, 132
  charter for, 368, 395
  choosing, by local interest, 284
  control files, 111
  "Current Status of Usenet Newsgroups Proposals" article, 43
  dead, 39
  disadvantages of, 321
  discarding on arrival, 55
  down time, 35
  duplicate, 386
  "Guidelines for Usenet Group Creation", 416
  hierarchies of, 2, 5, 38
  "How to Create a New Usenet News-group" article, 396
  independent facilitator for, 378
  internal, 54
  keeping different lengths of time, 17
  lists of, 102, 413
  local (see local/regional)
  matching, 110, 296
  moderated (see moderated newsgroups)
  names, 345
  "New Usenet Groups" article, 43
  not on feed, 41
  organizational, 383
  policy statements for, 364
  posting to, 101
  rationale for, 363, 395, 397
  reading, 36
  regional (see local/regional)
  support and recovery groups, 367
  unknown, 136
  unmoderated, 44, 404
  unwanted, 55–56
  (see also hierarchies)

newsgroups file, 44, 46
  making changes in, 41–52
    bulk updates, 48–51
    hearing about, 41–43
    single updates, 45–47
  neighbor's, copying, 124
Newsgroups header, 6, 226, 350, 431
  gateways and, 340
newshist command, 137
newsmap, 95, 115
newsmaster alias, 115, 123, 125, 135, 146, 175
news.notice file, 208, 241, 248–253
NEWSOV directory, 83, 152
newsreaders, 258–271
  compiling, 259
  configuring, 259
  connecting NNTP, 224–225
  FTP archives on, 271
  "Good Net-Keeping Seal of Approval", 270
  installing, 258–260
  letter bombs, 59
  list of popular, 260–269
  old, 259
  operating, 260
  software, 5, 31, 426
    newsgroups relevant to, 270
    old or badly written, 66
    supporting via slaves, 296
news-recovery manual page, 256
newsrequeue program, 256
newsrun program, 84, 122, 125
  not running properly, 132
  processing articles with, 129–130
NEWSSITE variable, 107
NEWSSITEDIR variable, 107
newsspool program, 80, 326
news-transmission content subtype (MIME), 448
newsuser alias, 146, 175
newswatch script, 103, 134, 305
newsxd program, 203, 297–299, 303
NFS, avoiding, 31
nn newsreader, 265, 270
nnmaster, upgrading with, 164
NNRP (Network News Reader Protocol), 224

nnrp.access group, 170, 197
nnrpad subdirectory, 143
nnrpd newsreader, 180, 208, 224
    available space and, 255
    clients, 253
    testing, 169
nntp_access file, 113–114
    values for, 113
NNTP (Network News Transfer Protocol),
        4, 465–468
    batching, 105
    benefits of, 12
    C News support, 63
    daemon
        accessing news through, 26
        configuring, 56
        for C News feeds (see msgidd)
    dual function of, 5, 113, 465
    feeds, updating, 231
    history of, 412
    information leak, 58
    multiple incoming feeds from, 19, 33,
        86, 116, 303, 466
        not handled well, 82
    news via, 465–466
    newsgroup on, 269, 271
    receiving articles via, 219–222
    streaming, 467–468
    transmitting articles via, 227–229
NNTP Reference Implementation (see NRI)
nntp subdirectory, 86
NNTPLINK_LOG parameter, 149, 242
nntplink transmitter, 252, 273, 300–303, 306
nntpsend script, 202, 242
nntpsend.ctl file, 171, 189, 231
nntpsend.log file, 228
NNTPSERVER parameter, 181
nntpxmit program, 109, 306
nobatchfile option, 298
nodes (see branching nodes; hub nodes;
        leaf nodes)
noexpire option, 286
non-ASCII character codes, 427
    in headers, 449
non-root operation, 165
non-urgent reports, 68, 135
noworkfile option, 298

NRI (NNTP Reference Implementation), 4,
        63, 412, 466
    building, 80–87
    control files, 112–114
    daemon, 81–85
    installing, 88
    logs, maintaining, 83
    Originator header, 358
    unpacking, 63
nroff, formatting in, 142
ntohs, conflicting types, 157

O

obscenity, 278
octet content subtype (MIME), 448
OnLine: DiskSuite utility, 293
online documentation, 64, 117
    (see also record keeping)
optimization, 72, 99, 272–274
organization file, 91
Organization header, 170, 332, 354, 438
organization parameter, 181
organizational hierarchies, 383, 422
Originator header, 358
OS/2 operating system, 270
outages, 14, 35
outbound feed hosts, 37
outbound news, 100–106
    batching, 103–104
    local articles only, 105
    transmission, 107–111
out.going subdirectory, 103, 125, 130, 189,
        250
out.master directory, 129
out-of-band information, 462
overchan program, 142, 170
over-engineering, 284
overview database, 460–461
overview directory, 152
.overview file, 123
overview files, 8, 14, 28, 83, 460
overview.fmt file, 112, 171, 198
ovsplit program, 130
owner-post-listname alias, 330
ownership
    in INN, 146
    mailing lists, 322
    news, 30–31, 56, 65

P

packet errors, 306
parallel content subtype (MIME), 447
parsecontrol script, 152, 204, 209
partial content subtype (MIME), 447
partial feed, 12
partitioning, 27, 234
passwd file, 146
passwd.nntp file, 171, 189
password, requiring, 188
patch program, 139
patches, 178
_PATH_BADNEWS directory, 223
_PATH_COMPRESS variable, 254
_PATH_COMPRESSEXT variable, 254
Path header, 6, 104, 133, 356, 431, 451
    second subfield in, 104
_PATH_INNDDIR variable, 254
_PATH_NEWSHOME parameter, 154
pathhost parameter, 170, 178–179
pathnames, looking up, 389
paths to common programs (in INN),
        150–152
pattern field, 184
pattern matching, 184
paused server, 236
peak traffic, 14
peer
    feed sites, 188, 296
    transfer mechanism, 221, 239
people, managing, 274–275
percent sign (%) in email addresses, 90, 429
performance degradation, 306
period (.) in hostnames, 180, 385
periodic posting, 374
Perl programming language, 139
    configuration, 155
    scripts, embedding, 153
permissions, 373
    customizing, 80
    deception regarding, 373
    defining, 67
    mask (umask), 199
    no need for exact, 30
PGP authentication, 194–195
pgpverify script, 204
philosophical discussion, 381
Pine newsreader, 267, 270

ping utility, 274
piping news articles to mail, 324
plain content subtype (MIME), 446
plus (+) marking normal articles, 242
pnews program, 127
policy issues, 275
policy statement
    local namespace changes, 394
    about support services, 297
political issues
    hub nodes, 312–317
    moderated newsgroups, 363–379
polls, 393, 402
POST command, 226
POSTBUFFER symbol, 82
postdefltdist file, 112
postdefltgroup file, 112
poster keyword, 352, 434
posting, 5
    agents for, 6
    defined, 1
    local, not being forwarded, 133
    via mail, 319
    tests, 120–124
    periodic, 374
    third-party, 279
    (see also articles)
post-listname alias, 330
post-listname-request alias, 330
postnews utility, 75, 79, 120
postscript content subtype (MIME), 448
pound sign (#) for comments, 89, 101, 347
precedent in naming, 386
pre-compression, 18
priority, 127, 463
    logging, 240
privacy issues, 310
problem articles, 315–317
problems (see trouble)
processor power (see CPU processing
        power requirements)
Prodigy Servs. Co., 277
propagation, 21, 450–453
    delays, end-to-end, 19, 21
    instantaneous, 21, 300
    moderation and, 369
pseudogroups (see control pseudogroup;
        junk pseudogroup)
public domain, 372

public gateways, 321
putenv( ), 328

Q

queue of news batches, 73, 203
queuelen script, 132
queue-length limit, 107
QUIT command, 222
quiz program, 64–76
    defaults in, 115
    deleting answers from, 118
quoted-printable encoding, 448
quoting previous article, 439

R

random message IDs, 358
rc.news script, 174, 201, 214, 308
    starting innwatch in, 240
Re: line, 430
readers, human (see users)
reading newsgroups, 36
readnews newsreader, 75, 79, 123, 261
readnews.ctl file, 112
rebuild process, 14
rec hierarchy, 381
record keeping, 290, 375
recovering from crashes, 256
Redman, Brian, 414
redundancy, massive, 21, 303
References header, 353, 434
regional (see local/regional)
regression tests, 78, 119
REJECT (see IHAVE/REJECT)
relayers, 4
    configuring to ignore distributions, 6
    names of, 90, 431
    software for, 7–10, 29, 454
        choosing, 32–33
relaynews utility, 44, 129, 136
    enabling mirroring with, 294
REM_STYLE parameter, 148
remailers, 366, 407
REMEMBER_TRASH parameter, 211
/remember/ value, 215, 248
    lowering, 254
Reply-To header, 352–353, 433
    gateways and, 340
report script, 132

reports, 68, 93
republished works, 373
Request for Discussion (RFD) articles, 42,
        352, 398
requests for information, 2
REQUIRE_MESSAGE_ID parameter, 328
REQUIRE_UNIX_FROM parameter, 328
reviews, independent, 365
revision control package, 290, 310
rfc822 content subtype (MIME), 447
RFD articles, 42, 352, 398
rindex( ), 328
rkive suite, 360
rmail command, 75, 462
rmgroup control message, 38, 41–42, 93,
        403, 443
rmgroup script, 195, 205
rmgroup.log file, 208
rn newsreader, 139, 261
rnews program, 75, 79, 142, 152, 222, 356,
        463
    for gatewaying, 325
RNEWS_LOG_DUPS parameter, 148
RNEWS_SAVE_BAD parameter, 148
rnews script, 127
rolling over files, 29, 300, 306
root, running as, 30, 84, 139
running server, 236
rwx permissions bits, 67

S

Salz, Rich, 4, 138, 324, 412
samples subdirectory, 143, 177
scanlogs script, 208, 245, 254
scheduling, for administrator, 297
sci hierarchy, 381
search path, 66–67
security concerns, 26, 56–59
    copyright (see copyright)
    forging (see forging)
    passwords, 188–189
    permissions (see permissions)
    privacy, 310
    problem articles, 278–282
    volunteers and, 275
    UCB Mail program and, 56–57
    UUCP ihave/sendme feeds, 233
    (see also legal issues)
sed editor, 141, 158

See-Also header, 354, 438
select( ), 139, 302
selector, logging, 240
sendbatch program, 229, 232
    common switches for, 230
sendbatches script, 107, 130, 133, 203
Sender header, 358, 434
send-ihave script, 202
sendme protocol (see ihave/sendme protocol)
sendme script, 206
send-nntp script, 171, 202
sendsys control message, 40–41, 94, 115, 206, 310, 444
    ignoring, 95
    sendsys bomb, 280–281
send-uucp script, 171, 203
senduuname control message, 207, 280, 445
sequencing articles, 295
server parameter, 181
server/Makefile file, 87
server/msgid.h file, 87
servers (see news, servers)
setngs utility, 48
set-UID, 31
7bit encoding, 448
7-bit ASCII characters, 182, 360
shell accounts, 278
shell commands, 64
shell files, 67
shell scripts, 143, 151, 198–212
    difficulties with, 78
    embedding, 209–212
shrinkfile manual page, 189
signal( ), 328
signature files, 361, 439
    policy regarding, 370
signoff program, 329
site files, 178
site subdirectory, 143, 169, 177, 254
sitename field, 183
size, article, 440
slash (/)
    beginning filenames, 103
    separating MIME type from subtype, 446
    separating subfields, 101–102, 183
slave replication, 294
slave server, 25

slow connections, 261
SNNTP, 466
soc hierarchy, 381
socket( ), 139, 147
sockets
    filesystem, 151
    opening Internet, 170
    stale, cleaning out, 254
software
    authors of, 424, 450
    choosing, 31–33
    documentation, importance of, 59
    emailing authors of, 61
    packages available, 2
    (see also gateways; moderators; relayers)
Solaris, installing INN on, 161–162
space (see storage space)
spacefor script, 74, 131
Spafford, Gene, 418, 422
spam, 279
spamfind program, 282
Spencer, Henry, 4, 410, 458
splitting articles, 352
spooling, across multiple drives, 286
SPOOL.LIST file, 256
SPOOL.ONLY file, 256
staff, data entry, 308
stale lock, breaking, 307
stale sockets, cleaning out, 254
Standard I/O library (stdio), 70
    speedups, 76
startup_innd.pl script, 210
startup.tcl script, 210
STAT command, 467
status reports, 68
statvfs version, df command, 74
stdin mode (nntplink), 301
stdio, 70, 76
stdio package (Sun), 163
stlinnd command, 394
storage space, 13–18, 35, 74, 284–287
    available, 13–15, 153, 182
    checking for, 126
    required for hub site, 292
    rule-of-thumb guidelines for, 17–18
    shortages of, 131, 135, 254–256
store and forward network, 278, 311
Stratton Oakmont, Inc., 277

strcgr( ), 70
strchr( ), 328
streaming
    commands, 273
    INN extension for, 293
    news transfers, 467–468
    protocol, 303
strerror( ), 328
striping, 27
strrchr( ), 328
su command, 201
subhierarchies
    blocking, 55
    checking, 205
    limiting feed hosts to, 288
    (see also hierarchies)
Subject header, 332, 351–352, 430
submissions, mail alias for, 376
    (see also articles)
subroutines, 68
subst program, 76, 118, 167
Summary header, 356, 436
SunOS 4.1 (installing INN on), 162
Supersedes header, 355, 438
superuser access, 120, 135, 139, 172, 178
    unavailable, 165
surges, traffic, 14, 35–36
symbolic links, 27, 66, 83, 152, 259, 455
sync( ), 69
sys file, 91–92, 100–111, 125
    /all in second field, 102
    outbound news, 100–106
        batching, 103–104
        local articles only, 105
        transmission, 107–111
sys2nf utility, 142, 170–171
syslog directory, 175
syslog program, 83, 166, 240–241
    confusion between priorities, 146
    critical messages from, 246
    verifying, 213–214
system
    administrator (see administration)
    calls, 68, 77
    headers defined by, 359–360
    identifying, 90–91
    manuals, 64, 68, 115, 121
        UUCP, 75
    monitoring activity on, 304–306

news (see news systems)
perspective of, 5
System V Release 4 (installing INN on), 164

T

tab character, 426, 428
TAKETHIS command, 467
talk hierarchy, 381
tally.control script, 208
tally.unwanted script, 209
tape, 10, 469
target articles, 441–442
Tcl configuration of INN, 153
TCP/IP networks, 10, 464–465
telephone lines, noisy, 464
Templeton, Brad, 309, 416
terse reporting, 93
text content type (MIME), 446
Tf feed, 301
third-party posting, 279
threading, 260, 353
386 compilers, 72
threshold, minimum free space, 14
throttled server, 236
tilde (~) separating subfields, 457
time zones, 428
timeout, resetting, 83
tin newsreader, 264
Tm flag, 301
to pseudogroup, 92, 218, 233
to-go file, 103, 129
tokens, 185–186
touch command, 178
traceroute utility, 274
tracking sites, 297
traffic, 2, 14
    average, 81, 306
    growth rate of, 285, 292–299
    heavy, 26, 81
    lumps, 36–37
    managing, 34–37, 450–470
    peaks, 14
    regulating content of, 315
    splitting, 29
    surges, 14, 35–36
    uneven, 35
transmission
    bulk, 103
    last-resort methods, 468–470

transmission (cont'd)
  name, 22
  by NNTP, 465–468
  overhead, per-batch, 108
  size, limiting, 37
  by UUCP, 462–464
  (see also bandwidth; network)
transmitters, 299–304
transmitting articles, 227–230
transport, 4, 10, 116
trash, throwing away quickly, 97
trees (see article tree; hierarchy trees)
trn newsreader, 171, 263
troff
  handling, 117
  formatting in, 142
Trojan horse attacks, 59
trouble
  C News, 132–134
  INN, 254–257
  innd death, reasons for, 217
  problem articles, 278–282
  recovery from, 306–308
trouble reports, 68, 115, 135–136

U

UCB Mail program, security and, 56–57
ulimit command, 288
Ultrix 4.3 (installing INN on), 164
umask, 67, 79, 88
UMASK symbol, 83
#undef, 81
underlining, 426
Unix
  running, 139
  systems, 2, 15
    filesystem semantics of, 31, 69
  utility programs, 66
Unix to Unix Copy (see UUCP)
unmoderated newsgroups, 44
  creating, 404
  (see also moderated newsgroups)
unwanted.log file, 209, 244
upact shell script, 131
updating feed hosts, 231–234, 308–310
urgent reports, 68, 135
USE_PATH_FOR_FROM, 337
Usenet, 2, 406–423
  aliases, 146

attacks on, 57
average article length, 13
as cooperative anarchy, 390
as entertainment system, 384
expectations regarding, 311
hierarchies, 92
history of, 409–412
namespace (see namespace)
"Usenet Software: History and Sources"
    article, 269
volume, rapid growth in, 14
worldwide defaults, 182
Usenet Calculator, 285
Usenix Association, 409
Usenix conference, 278
usenntpxmit command, 109
user interface, C News, 111–112
user name, 65
users
  access, 239
  alienating, 370
  apologizing to, 370
  dealing effectively with, 274
  educating, 58
  feedback from, 395
  handling dissatisfied, 368–370, 377
  headers defined by, 360
  local groups of, 59
  measuring, 284
  moderators to serve, 364
  perspective of, 1, 5–7
  polling, 364
  providing status reports to, 310–312
  reading mail more than news, 321
/usr directory
  /usr/bin, 66, 75
  /usr/contrib/bin, 66
  /usr/include, 70
  /usr/lib/news, 8, 84, 456
  /usr/libexec, 29
  /usr/libexec/news, 259
  /usr/local/bin, 75
  /usr/news/bin, 150
  /usr/spool/news, 8, 27, 85, 259, 455
  /usr/spool/overviews, 83
  /usr/ucb, 66
UUCP (Unix to Unix Copy), 175, 408
  benefits of, 12
  compressed-batch feeds from, 19

UUCP (Unix to Unix Copy) (cont'd)
  feeds, updating, 232
  Mapping Project, registering with, 170
  multiple incoming feeds from, 148
  neighbors, 53
  receiving articles via, 222–224
  transmission, 103
  transmitting articles via, 229–230
UUCPnet, 2
uuname command, 207, 337
UUNET Technologies, 12, 341, 460
uustat, 150
uux program, 108, 230, 232, 463
  interface, 131
uuxqt program, 223

V

/var directory
  /var/log/news, 151
  /var/log/news/news, 335
  /var/log/news/nntpsend.log file, 228
  /var/news directory, 456
    /var/news/active, 43
    /var/news/etc, 151
    /var/news/locks, 151
    /var/news/log, 335
    /var/news/run, 151
    /var/news/run/control, 219
    /var/news/spool, 151
variation, cyclic, 14
velveeta, 279
verbose reporting, 93
VERIFY_CANCELS option, 149
verifying C News installation, 114
version control message, 40, 94, 115, 280,
    444
  ignoring, 95
version control system, 290
version script, 206
vfork( ), 82
viauux program, 108, 131
video content type (MIME), 447
Vixie, Paul, 466

volume (see traffic)
volunteers, 275, 375
voting, 378
  parallel vote proposals, 401
  Usenet Volunteer Votetaker coordinator,
    399
  (see also CFV articles; polls)

W

Wall, Larry, 139
warez group, 185
Webber, Bob, 418
Wells, T. William, 365
whitespace, not ignoring, 92, 101, 170, 183,
    431
  (see also empty lines, ignoring)
whoami file, 90, 114
WHOAMI parameter, 327, 337
wildcards, 184
wildmat-style patterns, 184, 193
Wnb flag, 229, 232
Wnm flag, 186, 228
WnR options, 295
Woods, Greg, 416, 419
worst-case measurements, 35
wrapper script for editing newsgroups, 47
wrapping long header lines, 349
writelog program, 209
writev( ), 166

X

X- headers, 360
xargs rm line, 203
xfs filesystems, 160
xmit line (newsxd), 298
X-PGP-Sig header, 204
Xref header, 296
XREPLIC command, 300
XREPLIC NNTP command, 295

Z

Zeef, Jon, 458

About the Authors

Henry Spencer got his BSc at the University of Saskatchewan and his MSc at the University of Toronto. He worked as a Unix systems programmer at the University of Toronto for a number of years before becoming an independent consultant and author.

Henry ran the first Usenet site in Canada (and the first outside the U.S.), which was part of the Usenet "backbone" in its early days. He and Geoff Collyer wrote C News, one of the two major software packages for network news transport and storage. Henry worked on a first draft of the replacement for RFC 1036, which defines the format and protocols of network news. He was involved in the early definition of CANet (the Canadian national research network) and was primary speaker at the Workshop On NetNews of the RNP (Brazil's National Research Network) in Rio de Janeiro in August 1992, as a United Nations technical consultant.

Henry is also a founding member and past board member of the Canadian Space Society, a Fellow of the British Interplanetary Society, and an occasional consultant to the Canadian Space Agency. He was head of mission planning for the now-dormant Canadian Solar Sail Project.

David Lawrence has been the moderator of *news.announce.newgroups*, the clearinghouse for the creation of new mainstream newsgroups, since February 1991. He first gained access to Usenet and the Internet in 1986, and by 1988 he was the administrator of Rensselaer Polytechnic Institute's news server, an influential hub for dozens of Usenet sites. In 1992, he moved to northern Virginia to become the news system administrator for UUNET Technologies for five years, and has recently taken a position with the Internet Software Consortium, where he can concentrate on programming freely available software for the Internet community. His administrative duties for Usenet include maintenance of the mainstream newsgroup namespace and management of the worldwide database of newsgroup moderators.

Outside of work, David's passions include motorcycling (he has chosen not to own a car for the past eight years), inline skating, volleyball, alpine skiing, and hiking. He particularly likes endurance activities, such as commuting 12 miles each way on Rollerblades, skiing the entire time the slopes are open, and being entered in the 1997 Iron Butt Rally, a motorcycling challenge of 11,000 miles in 11 days. David wed Diane Horan in May 1997, and they now live in the forested mountains of the northeastern United States, settling down to start their family in northern Vermont.

Colophon

The animals featured on the cover of *Managing Usenet* are domestic fowl. Chickens have been domesticated for at least 4000 years. Nearly all of the ancient civilizations kept domestic fowl. There are currently approximately 150 breeds of domestic fowl. Selective breeding has led to the development of fowl with a variety of body types, colors, skull features, feather density, and tail feather length. Today chickens are raised primarily for egg and meat production. Wild fowl live in small flocks in which a "pecking order" becomes established among both hens and roosters. Rank fights begin when chicks are only a few weeks old. Until relatively recently most domestic fowl lived in these small flocks, also. However, economics have now prevailed, and on most modern chicken farms the birds live in small, windowless, temperature-controlled coops.

Edie Freedman designed the cover of this book, using a 19th-century engraving from the Dover Pictorial Archive. The cover layout was produced with Quark XPress 3.3 using the ITC Garamond font.

The inside layout was designed by Nancy Priest and implemented in gtroff by Lenny Muellner. The text and heading fonts are ITC Garamond Light and Garamond Book. The illustrations that appear in the book were created in Macromedia Freehand 7.0 and Adobe Photoshop 4.0 by Robert Romano. This colophon was written by Clairemarie Fisher O'Leary, with assistance from Kevin O'Leary.

Whenever possible, our books use RepKover™, a durable and flexible lay-flat binding. If the page count exceeds RepKover's limit, perfect binding is used.

 *More Titles from O'Reilly*

System Administration

Essential System Administration

By Æleen Frisch
2nd Edition September 1995
788 pages, ISBN 1-56592-127-5

Thoroughly revised and updated for all
major versions of UNIX, this second edition of *Essential System Administration*
provides a compact, manageable introduction to the tasks faced by everyone responsible for a UNIX system. Whether you use a
stand-alone UNIX system, routinely provide administrative support for a larger shared system, or just want an understanding of
basic administrative functions, this book is for you. Offers
expanded sections on networking, electronic mail, security, and
kernel configuration.

System Performance Tuning

By Mike Loukides
1st Edition November 1990
336 pages, ISBN 0-937175-60-9

System Performance Tuning answers the fundamental question: How can I get my UNIX-
based computer to do more work without
buying more hardware? Some performance
problems do require you to buy a bigger or
faster computer, but many can be solved sim-
ply by making better use of the resources you already have.

Using & Managing UUCP

By Ed Ravin, Tim O'Reilly, Dale Dougherty &
Grace Todino
1st Edition September 1996
424 pages, ISBN 1-56592-153-4

Using & Managing UUCP describes, in one
volume, this popular communications and file
transfer program. UUCP is very attractive to
computer users with limited resources, a
small machine, and a dial-up connection. This
book covers Taylor UUCP, the latest versions of HoneyDanBer
UUCP, and the specific implementation details of UUCP versions
shipped by major UNIX vendors.

termcap & terminfo

By John Strang, Linda Mui & Tim O'Reilly
3rd Edition April 1988
270 pages, ISBN 0-937175-22-6

For UNIX system administrators and programmers. This handbook provides information on writing and debugging terminal
descriptions, as well as terminal initialization,
for the two UNIX terminal databases.

Managing NFS and NIS

By Hal Stern
1st Edition June 1991
436 pages, ISBN 0-937175-75-7

Managing NFS and NIS is for system administrators who need to set up or manage a
network filesystem installation. NFS
(Network Filesystem) is probably running at
any site that has two or more UNIX systems.
NIS (Network Information System) is a distributed database used to manage a network of computers. The
only practical book devoted entirely to these subjects, this guide
is a "must-have" for anyone interested in UNIX networking.

Volume 8: X Window System Administrator's Guide

By Linda Mui & Eric Pearce
1st Edition October 1992
372 pages, ISBN 0-937175-83-8

This book focuses on issues of system
administration for X and X-based networks—not just for UNIX system administrators, but for anyone faced with the job
of administering X (including those running X on stand-alone workstations).

O'REILLY™

TO ORDER: **800-998-9938** • **order@oreilly.com** • **http://www.oreilly.com/**
OUR PRODUCTS ARE AVAILABLE AT A BOOKSTORE OR SOFTWARE STORE NEAR YOU.
FOR INFORMATION: **800-998-9938** • **707-829-0515** • **info@oreilly.com**

Web Server Administration

Network Administration

Using & Managing PPP

By Andrew Sun
1st Edition March 1998 (est.)
400 pages (est.), ISBN 1-56592-321-9

Covers all aspects of PPP, including setting up dial-in servers, debugging, and PPP options. Also contains overviews of related areas, like serial communications, DNS setup, and routing.

Managing IP Networks with Cisco Routers

By Scott M. Ballew
1st Edition October 1997
352 pages, ISBN 1-56592-320-0

Managing IP Networks with Cisco Routers is a practical guide to setting up and maintaining a production network. It discusses how to select routing protocols and how to configure protcols to handle most common situations. It also discusses less esoteric but equally important issues like how to evaluate network equipment and vendors and how to set up a help desk. Although the book focuses on Cisco routers, and gives examples using Cisco's IOS, the principles discussed are common to all IP networks, regardless of the vendor you choose.

Topics covered include:

- Designing an IP network
- Evaluating equipment and vendors
- Selecting routing protocols
- Configuring common interior protocols (RIP, OSPF, EIGRP)
- Connecting to external networks, and configuring exterior protocols (BGP)
- Ongoing network management: troubleshooting and maintenance
- Security and privacy issues

sendmail, 2nd Edition

By Bryan Costales & Eric Allman
2nd Edition January 1997
1050 pages, ISBN 1-56592-222-0

This new edition of *sendmail* covers sendmail Version 8.8 from Berkeley and the standard versions available on most systems. It is far and away the most comprehensive book ever written on sendmail, the program that acts like a traffic cop in routing and delivering mail on UNIX-based networks. Although sendmail is used on almost every UNIX system, it's one of the last great uncharted territories—and most difficult utilities to learn—in UNIX system administration.

This book provides a complete sendmail tutorial, plus extensive reference material on every aspect of the program. Part One is a tutorial on understanding sendmail; Part Two covers the building, installation, and m4 configuration of sendmail; Part Three covers practical issues in sendmail administration; Part Four is a comprehensive reference section; and Part Five consists of appendices and a bibliography.

In this second edition an expanded tutorial demonstrates hub's *cf* file and *nullclient.mc*. Other new topics include the #error delivery agent, sendmail's exit values, MIME headers, and how to set up and use the user database, *mailertable*, and *smrsh*. Solution-oriented examples throughout the book help you solve your own sendmail problems. This new edition is cross-referenced with section numbers.

sendmail Desktop Reference

By Bryan Costales & Eric Allman
1st Edition March 1997
74 pages, ISBN 1-56592-278-6

This quick-reference guide provides a complete overview of the latest version of sendmail (V8.8), from command-line switches to configuration commands, from options declarations to macro definitions, and from m4 features to debugging switches—all packed into a convenient, carry-around booklet co-authored by the creator of sendmail. Includes extensive cross-references to *sendmail*, second edition.

Network Administration *(continued)*

How to stay in touch with O'Reilly

1. Visit Our Award-Winning Web Site

http://www.oreilly.com/

★ "Top 100 Sites on the Web" —*PC Magazine*
★ "Top 5% Web sites" —*Point Communications*
★ "3-Star site" —*The McKinley Group*

Our web site contains a library of comprehensiveproduct information (including book excerpts and tables of contents), downloadable software, background articles, interviews with technology leaders, links to relevant sites, book cover art, and more. File us in your Bookmarks or Hotlist!

2. Join Our Email Mailing Lists

New Product Releases

To receive automatic email with brief descriptions of all new O'Reilly products as they are released, send email to:
listmanager@list.ora.com
Put the following information in the first line of your message (*not* in the Subject field):
subscribe oreilly-news

O'Reilly Events

If you'd also like us to send information about trade show events, special promotions, and other O'Reilly events, send email to:
listmanager@list.ora.com
Put the following information in the first line of your message (*not* in the Subject field):
subscribe oreilly-events

3. Get Examples from Our Books via FTP

There are two ways to access an archive of example files from our books:

Regular FTP

- ftp to:
  ftp.oreilly.com
  (login: anonymous
  password: your email address)
- Point your web browser to:
  ftp://ftp.oreilly.com/

FTPMAIL

- Send an email message to:
  ftpmail@online.oreilly.com
  (Write "help" in the message body)

4. Contact Us via Email

order@oreilly.com
To place a book or software order online. Good for North American and international customers.

subscriptions@oreilly.com
To place an order for any of our newsletters or periodicals.

books@oreilly.com
General questions about any of our books.

software@oreilly.com
For general questions and product information about our software. Check out O'Reilly Software Online at **http://software.oreilly.com/** for software and technical support information. Registered O'Reilly software users send your questions to: **website-support@oreilly.com**

cs@oreilly.com
For answers to problems regarding your order or our products.

booktech@oreilly.com
For book content technical questions or corrections.

proposals@oreilly.com
To submit new book or software proposals to our editors and product managers.

international@oreilly.com
For information about our international distributors or translation queries. For a list of our distributors outside of North America check out:
http://www.oreilly.com/www/order/country.html

O'Reilly & Associates, Inc.
101 Morris Street, Sebastopol, CA 95472 USA
TEL   707-829-0515 or 800-998-9938
           (6am to 5pm PST)
FAX   707-829-0104

Titles from O'Reilly

Please note that upcoming titles are displayed in italic.

WEB PROGRAMMING

Apache: The Definitive Guide
Building Your Own Web
  Conferences
Building Your Own Website
CGI Programming for the World
  Wide Web
Designing for the Web
HTML: The Definitive Guide,
  2nd Ed.
JavaScript: The Definitive Guide,
  2nd Ed.
Learning Perl
Programming Perl, 2nd Ed.
Mastering Regular Expressions
WebMaster in a Nutshell
Web Security & Commerce
Web Client Programming with
  Perl
World Wide Web Journal

USING THE INTERNET

Smileys
The Future Does Not Compute
The Whole Internet User's Guide
  & Catalog
The Whole Internet for Win 95
Using Email Effectively
Bandits on the Information
  Superhighway

JAVA SERIES

Exploring Java
Java AWT Reference
Java Fundamental Classes
  Reference
Java in a Nutshell
Java Language Reference, 2nd
  Edition
Java Network Programming
Java Threads
Java Virtual Machine

SOFTWARE

WebSite™ 1.1
WebSite Professional™
Building Your Own Web
  Conferences
WebBoard™
PolyForm™
Statisphere™

SONGLINE GUIDES

NetActivism   NetResearch
Net Law   NetSuccess
NetLearning   NetTravel
Net Lessons

SYSTEM ADMINISTRATION

Building Internet Firewalls
Computer Crime: A
  Crimefighter's Handbook
Computer Security Basics
DNS and BIND, 2nd Ed.
Essential System Administration,
  2nd Ed.
Getting Connected: The Internet
  at 56K and Up
Linux Network Administrator's
  Guide
Managing Internet Information
  Services
Managing NFS and NIS
Networking Personal Computers
  with TCP/IP
Practical UNIX & Internet
  Security, 2nd Ed.
PGP: Pretty Good Privacy
sendmail, 2nd Ed.
sendmail Desktop Reference
System Performance Tuning
TCP/IP Network Administration
termcap & terminfo
Using & Managing UUCP
Volume 8: X Window System
  Administrator's Guide
Web Security & Commerce

UNIX

Exploring Expect
Learning VBScript
Learning GNU Emacs, 2nd Ed.
Learning the bash Shell
Learning the Korn Shell
Learning the UNIX Operating
  System
Learning the vi Editor
Linux in a Nutshell
Making TeX Work
Linux Multimedia Guide
Running Linux, 2nd Ed.
SCO UNIX in a Nutshell
sed & awk, 2nd Edition
Tcl/Tk Tools
UNIX in a Nutshell: System V
  Edition
UNIX Power Tools
Using csh & tsch
When You Can't Find Your UNIX
  System Administrator
Writing GNU Emacs Extensions

WEB REVIEW STUDIO SERIES

Gif Animation Studio
Shockwave Studio

WINDOWS

Dictionary of PC Hardware and
  Data Communications Terms
Inside the Windows 95 Registry
Inside the Windows 95 File
  System
Windows Annoyances
Windows NT File System
  Internals
Windows NT in a Nutshell

PROGRAMMING

Advanced Oracle PL/SQL
  Programming
Applying RCS and SCCS
C++: The Core Language
Checking C Programs with lint
DCE Security Programming
Distributing Applications Across
  DCE & Windows NT
Encyclopedia of Graphics File
  Formats, 2nd Ed.
Guide to Writing DCE
  Applications
lex & yacc
Managing Projects with make
Mastering Oracle Power Objects
Oracle Design: The Definitive
  Guide
Oracle Performance Tuning, 2nd
  Ed.
Oracle PL/SQL Programming
Porting UNIX Software
POSIX Programmer's Guide
POSIX.4: Programming for the
  Real World
Power Programming with RPC
Practical C Programming
Practical C++ Programming
Programming Python
Programming with curses
Programming with GNU Software
Pthreads Programming
Software Portability with imake,
  2nd Ed.
Understanding DCE
Understanding Japanese
  Information Processing
UNIX Systems Programming for
  SVR4

BERKELEY 4.4 SOFTWARE DISTRIBUTION

4.4BSD System Manager's
  Manual
4.4BSD User's Reference Manual
4.4BSD User's Supplementary
  Documents
4.4BSD Programmer's Reference
  Manual
4.4BSD Programmer's
  Supplementary Documents
X Programming
Vol. 0: X Protocol Reference
  Manual
Vol. 1: Xlib Programming Manual
Vol. 2: Xlib Reference Manual
Vol. 3M: X Window System User's
  Guide, Motif Edition
Vol. 4M: X Toolkit Intrinsics
  Programming Manual, Motif
  Edition
Vol. 5: X Toolkit Intrinsics
  Reference Manual
Vol. 6A: Motif Programming
  Manual
Vol. 6B: Motif Reference Manual
Vol. 6C: Motif Tools
Vol. 8 : X Window System
  Administrator's Guide
Programmer's Supplement for
  Release 6
X User Tools
The X Window System in a
  Nutshell

CAREER & BUSINESS

Building a Successful Software
  Business
The Computer User's Survival
  Guide
Love Your Job!
Electronic Publishing on CD-
  ROM

TRAVEL

Travelers' Tales: Brazil
Travelers' Tales: Food
Travelers' Tales: France
Travelers' Tales: Gutsy Women
Travelers' Tales: India
Travelers' Tales: Mexico
Travelers' Tales: Paris
Travelers' Tales: San Francisco
Travelers' Tales: Spain
Travelers' Tales: Thailand
Travelers' Tales: A Woman's
  World

International Distributors

UK, Europe, Middle East and Northern Africa (except France, Germany, Switzerland, & Austria)

INQUIRIES
International Thomson Publishing Europe
Berkshire House
168-173 High Holborn
London WC1V 7AA, United Kingdom
Telephone: 44-171-497-1422
Fax: 44-171-497-1426
Email: itpint@itps.co.uk

ORDERS
International Thomson Publishing Services, Ltd.
Cheriton House, North Way
Andover, Hampshire SP10 5BE, United Kingdom
Telephone: 44-264-342-832
(UK orders)
Telephone: 44-264-342-806
(outside UK)
Fax: 44-264-364418 (UK orders)
Fax: 44-264-342761 (outside UK)
UK & Eire orders: itpuk@itps.co.uk
International orders: itpint@itps.co.uk

France

Editions Eyrolles
61 bd Saint-Germain
75240 Paris Cedex 05
France
Fax: 33-01-44-41-11-44

FRENCH LANGUAGE BOOKS
All countries except Canada
Phone: 33-01-44-41-46-16
Email: geodif@eyrolles.com

ENGLISH LANGUAGE BOOKS
Phone: 33-01-44-41-11-87
Email: distribution@eyrolles.com

Australia

WoodsLane Pty. Ltd.
7/5 Vuko Place, Warriewood NSW 2102
P.O. Box 935, Mona Vale NSW 2103
Australia
Telephone: 61-2-9970-5111
Fax: 61-2-9970-5002
Email: info@woodslane.com.au

Germany, Switzerland, and Austria

INQUIRIES
O'Reilly Verlag
Balthasarstr. 81
D-50670 Köln
Germany
Telephone: 49-221-97-31-60-0
Fax: 49-221-97-31-60-8
Email: anfragen@oreilly.de

ORDERS
International Thomson Publishing
Königswinterer Straße 418
53227 Bonn, Germany
Telephone: 49-228-97024 0
Fax: 49-228-441342
Email: order@oreilly.de

Asia (except Japan & India)

INQUIRIES
International Thomson Publishing Asia
60 Albert Street #15-01
Albert Complex
Singapore 189969
Telephone: 65-336-6411
Fax: 65-336-7411

ORDERS
Telephone: 65-336-6411
Fax: 65-334-1617
thomson@signet.com.sg

New Zealand

WoodsLane New Zealand Ltd.
21 Cooks Street (P.O. Box 575)
Wanganui, New Zealand
Telephone: 64-6-347-6543
Fax: 64-6-345-4840
Email: info@woodslane.com.au

Japan

O'Reilly Japan, Inc.
Kiyoshige Building 2F
12-Banchi, Sanei-cho
Shinjuku-ku
Tokyo 160 Japan
Telephone: 81-3-3356-5227
Fax: 81-3-3356-5261
Email: kenji@oreilly.com

India

Computer Bookshop (India) PVT. LTD.
190 Dr. D.N. Road, Fort
Bombay 400 001
India
Telephone: 91-22-207-0989
Fax: 91-22-262-3551
Email: cbsbom@giasbm01.vsnl.net.in

The Americas

O'Reilly & Associates, Inc.
101 Morris Street
Sebastopol, CA 95472 U.S.A.
Telephone: 707-829-0515
Telephone: 800-998-9938 (U.S. & Canada)
Fax: 707-829-0104
Email: order@oreilly.com

Southern Africa

International Thomson Publishing Southern Africa
Building 18, Constantia Park
138 Sixteenth Road
P.O. Box 2459
Halfway House, 1685 South Africa
Telephone: 27-11-805-4819
Fax: 27-11-805-3648

O'REILLY™

O'Reilly & Associates, Inc.
101 Morris Street
Sebastopol, CA 95472-9902
1-800-998-9938

Visit us online at:
http://www.ora.com/
orders@ora.com

O'REILLY WOULD LIKE TO HEAR FROM YOU

Nineteenth century wood engraving
of a bear from the O'Reilly &
Associates Nutshell Handbook®
Using & Managing UUCP.

BUSINESS REPLY MAIL
FIRST CLASS MAIL   PERMIT NO. 80   SEBASTOPOL, CA

Postage will be paid by addressee

O'Reilly & Associates, Inc.
101 Morris Street
Sebastopol, CA 95472-9902